"This volume is edited by two leading figures in research on occupational health and wellbeing and contains contributions from major scholars in this field. The coverage of topics is comprehensive and well organized. The volume will be a major asset to researchers and practitioners in psychology and management."

–**Michael O'Driscoll**, *Emeritus Professor of Psychology,*
University of Waikato, New Zealand

"Cooper and Leiter lead outstanding teams of international scholars on the cutting edge of wellbeing at work. This five section volume delivers powerful content addressing the positive sides of the individual, the workplace, and the mechanisms for enhancing wellbeing."

–**James Campbell Quick**, *Endowed Chair, Goolsby Leadership Academy,*
The University of Texas at Arlington, USA

"Cooper and Leiter's Companion provides a timely insight into the broad spectrum of research on physical and mental wellbeing at work. This is a unique and much-needed publication for scholars, students, and practitioners interested in ensuring employee health and fulfilment."

–**Krystal Wilkinson**, *Senior Lecturer, Business School,*
Manchester Metropolitan University, UK

"Work can cause, contribute to, or trigger disease, and very often does so (pathogenesis). But it can also be a powerful promoter of health and wellbeing (salutogenesis). Much of the outcome depends on our working and living conditions. Two eminent scientists in this field, Cary L. Cooper and Michael Leiter, focus on both of these two aspects in this new, highly knowledgeable and extremely relevant volume."

–**Lennart Levi**, *Emeritus Professor of Psychosocial Medicine,*
Karolinska Institutet, Sweden

"This Companion provides an informative and up-to-date collection of articles by highly regarded scholars and practitioners regarding the nature, causes, and consequences of workplace wellbeing (and ill-being). Importantly, a range of practical interventions at the employee and organizational level are provided, making it a valuable resource for students, practitioners, and scholars."

–**Ashlea Troth**, *Associate Professor, Griffith Business School,*
Griffith University, Australia

The Routledge Companion to Wellbeing at Work

Over recent years, many companies have developed an awareness of the importance of an active, rather than passive, approach to wellbeing at work. Whilst the value of this approach is widely accepted, turning theory into effective practice is still a challenge for many companies.

The Routledge Companion to Wellbeing at Work is a comprehensive reference volume addressing every aspect of the topic. Split into five parts, it explores different models of wellbeing; personal qualities contributing to wellbeing; job insecurity and organizational wellbeing; workplace supports for wellbeing; and initiatives to enhance wellbeing. The international team of contributors provide a solid foundation to research and practice, including contemporary topics such as architecture, coaching, and fitness in the workplace.

Edited by two of the world's leading scholars on the subject, this text is a valuable tool for researchers, students, and practitioners in HRM and organizational psychology.

Sir Cary L. Cooper, CBE, is the 50th Anniversary Professor of Organizational Psychology and Health at the University of Manchester, UK. He is President of the CIPD, President of the British Academy of Management, and President of RELATE. In 2015 he was number one on *HR Magazine's* "Most Influential HR Thinkers" list, and he received a Knighthood from the Queen in 2014 for his contributions to the social sciences.

Michael P. Leiter is Professor of Organizational Psychology at the School of Psychology, Deakin University, Geelong, Australia. He has published widely in all the leading journals in the field, and is a global scholar on job burnout, speaking throughout the world on this topic and on organizational health and wellbeing more generally.

Routledge Companions in Business, Management, and Accounting

Routledge Companions in Business, Management, and Accounting are prestige reference works providing an overview of a whole subject area or subdiscipline. These books survey the state of the discipline including emerging and cutting edge areas. Providing comprehensive, up-to-date, definitive works of reference, Routledge Companions can be cited as authoritative sources on the subject.

A key aspect of these Routledge Companions is their international scope and relevance. Edited by an array of highly regarded scholars, these volumes also benefit from teams of contributors that reflect an international range of perspectives.

Individually, Routledge Companions in Business, Management, and Accounting provide an impactful one-stop-shop resource for each theme covered. Collectively, they represent a comprehensive learning and research resource for researchers, postgraduate students and practitioners.

Published titles in this series include:

The Routledge Companion to Strategic Risk Management
Edited by Torben J. Andersen

The Routledge Companion to Philanthropy
Edited by Tobias Jung, Susan Phillips, and Jenny Harrow

The Routledge Companion to Marketing History
Edited by D. G. Brian Jones, and Mark Tadajewski

The Routledge Companion to Reinventing Management Education
Edited by Chris Steyaert, Timon Beyes, and Martin Parker

The Routledge Companion to the Professions and Professionalism
Edited by Mike Dent, Ivy Bourgeault, Jean-Louis Denis, and Ellen Kuhlmann

The Routledge Companion to Contemporary Brand Management
Edited by Francesca Dall'Olmo Riley, Jaywant Singh, and Charles Blankson

The Routledge Companion to Banking Regulation and Reform
Edited by Ismail Ertürk and Daniela Gabor

The Routledge Companion to the Makers of Modern Entrepreneurship
Edited by David B. Audretsch and Erik E. Lehmann

The Routledge Companion to Business History
Edited by Abe de Jong, Steven Toms, John Wilson, and Emily Buchnea

The Routledge Companion to Qualitative Accounting Research
Edited by Zahirul Hoque, Lee D. Parker, Mark A. Covaleski, and Kathryn Haynes

The Routledge Companion to Accounting and Risk
Edited by Margaret Woods and Philip Linsley

The Routledge Companion to Wellbeing at Work
Edited by Sir Cary L. Cooper and Michael P. Leiter

The Routledge Companion to Wellbeing at Work

Edited by Sir Cary L. Cooper and Michael P. Leiter

LONDON AND NEW YORK

First published 2017
by Routledge
4 Park Square, Milton Park, Abingdon, Oxon OX14 4RN

and by Routledge
605 Third Avenue, New York, NY 10017

First issued in paperback 2022

Routledge is an imprint of the Taylor & Francis Group, an informa business

British Library Cataloguing-in-Publication Data
A catalogue record for this book is available from the British Library

Library of Congress Cataloging-in-Publication Data
A catalog record for this book has been requested

ISBN 13: 978-1-03-247681-0 (pbk)
ISBN 13: 978-1-138-95594-3 (hbk)

DOI: 10.4324/9781315665979

Typeset in Bembo
by Apex CoVantage, LLC

Contents

Figures

Tables

Contributors

Tim Anstiss: Tim is a medical doctor with qualifications in occupational, sports, and exercise medicine. He has guided, coached, and supported hundreds of troubled staff and managers; delivered numerous workshops on wellbeing, resilience, self-compassion, confidence, and personal effectiveness; and trained thousands of health care professionals in motivational interviewing, shared decision making, and behavior change coaching.

Peter Bacevice: Pete is Director of Research for HLW International – a global architecture and design practice – where he oversees a variety of projects related to workplace assessment, benchmarking, and analytics. His project work has included real estate portfolio studies and guidelines for workplace design, planning, and user engagement. He is also a researcher with the University of Michigan's Ross School of Business, where he is affiliated with the Center for Positive Organizational Scholarship. Pete divides his time professionally between New York and Ann Arbor, Michigan. He holds a Ph.D. in Education from the University of Michigan.

David W. Ballard: David holds a Psy.D. and an MBA, and is Assistant Executive Director for Organizational Excellence at the American Psychological Association (APA). In that capacity, he is responsible for leadership, direction, evaluation, and management of all activities related to the APA's Center for Organizational Excellence, which includes the association's Psychologically Healthy Workplace program. David has provided research, consultation, and training to government agencies, corporations, medical schools, and universities in the areas of workplace health and productivity, public health, prevention, and health care finance.

Cristina G. Banks: Cristina is Director of the Interdisciplinary Center for Healthy Workplaces and a Senior Lecturer at the Haas School of Business, University of California, Berkeley, where she has taught graduate and undergraduate courses in leadership and management for 32 years. As a Managing Director for the Berkeley Research Group, a global expert firm, she consults to Fortune 500 companies. She has 38 years of experience, founding and leading two consulting firms, Terranova Consulting Group and Lamorinda Consulting. She is a Fellow of the Society for Industrial-Organizational Psychology and the APA. She was awarded the APA Presidential Citation for Innovative Practice.

Larissa K. Barber: Larissa earned her Ph.D. from Saint Louis University. She is currently an Assistant Professor in the Social/Industrial-Organizational Psychology program at Northern Illinois University. Her research focuses on the topics of sleep, employee stress and health, personality, and counterproductive work behavior. Her research has been published in a variety of outlets, including the *Journal of Occupational Health Psychology, Stress & Health, Applied Psychology: Health and Wellbeing, Organizational Research Methods,* and the *Journal of Organizational Behavior.*

Christopher T. Boyko: Christopher is a 50th Anniversary Lecturer in Design at Lancaster University. He currently is examining the relationship between wellbeing and the built environment as part of the UK EPSRC-funded Liveable Cities project. This research builds on previous research about urban density within the planning process and mapping sustainable urban design decision-making processes for the EPSRC-funded Urban Futures and VivaCity2020 projects, respectively. Christopher's general research interests include urban design, sustainability, use of digital technology in cities, and wellbeing in urban environments.

Helen Elizabeth Brown: Helen is a Postdoctoral Research Associate working in Behavioral Epidemiology at the University of Cambridge. Helen's Ph.D. thesis examined the relationship between presenteeism and physical activity, reviewing methods of assessing presenteeism, examining cross-sectional associations between presenteeism and physical activity, and identifying potential avenues for intervention.

Christopher J. Budnick: Christopher is a Ph.D. candidate in the Social/Industrial-Organizational Psychology program at Northern Illinois University. His research focuses on interpretive biases during social interactions, evaluative situations, self-regulation, and job search processes. His research has been published in *Anxiety, Stress, & Coping, the Journal of Organizational Behavior,* and the *Journal of Employment Counseling.*

Janelle H. Cheung: Janelle is a postdoctoral researcher at Oregon Health and Science University. Her research focuses on occupational health psychology with a specific emphasis on economic stress and employee wellbeing, and the promotion of employee safety, health, and wellbeing in the workplace.

Chun-Yi Chou: Chun-Yi Chou, M.Sc., is currently a doctorial student in the Department of Business Administration, National Taiwan University, Taiwan (ROC). Her major research interests are work engagement and wellbeing, motivation, and other organizational behaviors. She has published several papers in referred journals.

Alexandra C. Chris: Alexandra is a Ph.D. candidate in Industrial/Organizational Psychology at the University of Guelph. She works under the supervision of Dr. M. Gloria González-Morales in the Occupational Health and Positive Psychology Lab. Alexandra's research interests include workplace incivility, organizational commitment, and the application of positive psychology principles for promoting mental health. Alexandra has consulted with private and public organizations in Canada on matters related to change management, training and leadership development, and employee health and wellbeing.

Cathleen Clerkin: Cathleen is Senior Research Faculty member at the Center for Creative Leadership. Her areas of expertise include neuroscience and holistic leadership development, women's leadership and social identity management, and creativity and innovation. Cathleen's research has been published in numerous academic and popular press outlets, and she has received recognition for her work from the National Science Foundation. Cathleen graduated Phi Beta Kappa from the University of California, Berkeley, and earned her Master of Science and doctorate degrees in psychology from the University of Michigan, Ann Arbor. She completed a postdoctoral fellowship at the Center for Creative Leadership before joining as a faculty member in 2015.

David Collinson: David is Distinguished Professor of Leadership and Organization in the Department of Leadership and Management, Lancaster University. He has previously held positions at the universities of Warwick, South Florida, Saint Andrews, and Manchester. David is the founding Co-Editor of the journal *Leadership* and founding Co-Organizer of the International Studying Leadership Conference. David's primary research interests focus on leadership and followership dialectics, power and identities, conformity and resistance, gender and masculinity, and safety and dangerous work.

Rachel Cooper, OBE: Rachel is Professor of Design Management and Co-Director of ImaginationLancaster at Lancaster University as well as Chair of the Lancaster Institute for the Contemporary Arts. She has authored several books in the design field, including *The Design Agenda* (Wiley 1995), *The Design Experience* (Ashgate 2003), and *Designing Sustainable Cities* (Wiley 2009). Rachel's research interests cover design management, design policy, design in the built environment, and design against crime.

Alex Davda: Alex is a Business Psychologist and Client Director at Ashridge Executive Education at Hult International Business School based in the Middle East. Alex has broad experience in the United Kingdom, Europe, and the Middle East, supporting clients in the application of a range of innovative and often large-scale assessment and development approaches. His specific research interests are in the area of positive psychology, resilience, and wellbeing at work. He has published a number of research articles and a book chapter in this area and is a weekly columnist for the *National Newspaper,* an English-language newspaper published in the United Arab Emirates. Before joining Ashridge, Alex worked as an assistant psychologist in the UK Prison Service, delivering cognitive behavioral programs to offenders. He holds a First Class Honours degree in Psychology and a Master's degree in Occupational Psychology.

Arla Day: Arla is a Professor in Industrial/Organizational Psychology at Saint Mary's University, specializing in Occupational Health Psychology, and she is the Director of the CN Centre for Occupational Health and Safety. She is a Fellow of the Canadian Psychological Association, and she was a Canada Research Chair at Saint Mary's University in Industrial/Organizational Psychology for 10 years. She has authored articles, chapters, and books pertaining to healthy workers and workplaces, respect and civility in the workplace, leadership, occupational stress, employee wellbeing, and work-life balance; and she has focused her research on developing and implementing effective organizational and individual initiatives and training programs.

Jennifer J. Deal: Jennifer is a Senior Research Scientist at the Center for Creative Leadership (CCL©) in San Diego, California, an Affiliated Research Scientist at the Center for Effective Organizations at the University of Southern California, and a contributor to *The Wall Street Journal*'s "Experts" panel on leadership. She has written a number of books, articles, and book chapters on a variety of subjects including generational issues, the Always On work environment, cultural adaptability, global management, and women in management. Her most recent book, *What Millennials Want From Work* (McGraw-Hill Publishers) was published in 2016. She holds a B.A. from Haverford College and an M.A. and Ph.D. in Industrial/Organizational Psychology with a specialty in Political Psychology from Ohio State University.

Evangelia Demerouti: Eva is Professor at Eindhoven University of Technology, the Netherlands, and distinguished professor at the University of Johannesburg, South Africa. Her research interests include topics from the field of work and health, including Positive Organizational Behavior, job (re)design, work-family interface, crossover of strain, and job performance. She has published several national and international papers and book chapters on these topics in journals such as *Journal of Applied Psychology, Journal of Occupational Health Psychology,* and *Journal of Vocational Behavior.* She is also a reviewer for various national and international scientific journals and Associate Editor of *Journal of Occupational Health Psychology* and *European Journal of Work and Organizational Psychology.*

Norman Dolan: Norman is an Adjunct Professor in the School of Public Administration at the University of Victoria. He was awarded a Doctoral Fellowship from the Social Sciences and Humanities Research Council and received his doctorate in Public Administration from the University of Victoria. His research interests include program and policy design and evaluation, organizational learning, and conflict resolution.

Norman has more than 30 years of experience as a senior manager, including over 10 years as a therapist and Director of Child and Family Services at the YM/YWCA. He is recently retired from the Department of National Defence and Canadian Forces as Senior Investigator with the Ombudsman. He has published in the areas of child and youth care practice, organizational effectiveness, and governance in the public and not-for-profit sectors, and conducted numerous evaluations of public and private sector programs and organizations.

As President of Beaubear Management Ltd., Norman continues to teach university-level courses and present professional development seminars in research methods, program evaluation, performance measurement, and conflict resolution as well as provide consulting services to organizations and companies in the public service, education, and private sectors.

Lonneke Dubbelt: Lonneke is a guest researcher affiliated with Eindhoven University of Technology. Her research focuses on conditions that help employees thrive. Furthermore, she is interested in the behavior of employees that helps them create those conditions – specifically, proactive behavior that allows employees to create their own optimal work conditions. She has a special interest in the conditions and behaviors that help women thrive at work.

Kaitlyn R. Erb: Kaitlin holds a Master of Science and is a doctoral student of Industrial/Organizational Psychology at Saint Louis University. She has spent most of her graduate career conducting research in areas related to the psychologically healthy workplace, with an emphasis on employee wellbeing. She also currently serves as an associate consultant with a consulting agency, working with clients to utilize quality research to inform organizational practice.

Jill Flint-Taylor: Jill is a Professor of Organizational Psychology at Ashridge Executive Education at Hult International Business School, where her role is Adjunct Faculty and Research Fellow. A registered practitioner psychologist, she has provided consultancy support to a wide range of organizations over the past 25 years. She also develops psychometrics and online tools for use in selection, appraisal, development, and wellbeing. Resilience, leadership, and management have always been at the center of her work, and in recent years she has made a study of the impact that leaders and managers have on levels of engagement and wellbeing in their teams. Jill has a Ph.D. in Psychology from the Institute of Psychiatry at King's College, University of London. Her publications include the book *Building Resilience for Success* (Palgrave Macmillan 2013), co-authored with Professor Sir Cary Cooper and Dr. Michael Pearn.

Lyndon Garrett: Lyndon is a doctoral candidate of Management and Organizations at the Stephen M. Ross School of Business, University of Michigan. His research interests revolve around examining relational processes of interpersonal and group bonding, high-quality connections, thriving, and meaningful work. His work is primarily qualitative, with a focus on unpacking the relational work that occurs in moments of interaction and day-to-day practices. His dissertation is qualitatively looking at how high-quality connections form through play in sports teams and theater casts.

Caroline Gatrell: Caroline is Professor of Organisation Studies at University of Liverpool Management School. Caroline's research centers on family, work, and health. From a sociocultural perspective, Caroline examines how working parents (both fathers and mothers) manage boundaries between paid work and their everyday lives. In so doing she explores interconnections between gender, bodies, and employment, including development of the "Maternal Body Work" concept.

Her work is published in leading journals, including *Human Relations; British Journal of Management; Gender, Work and Organization; Social Science and Medicine; International Journal of Management Reviews;* and *International Journal of Human Resource Management.*

She is Co-Editor-in-Chief of the *International Journal of Management Reviews.*

Debra Gilin Oore: Debra is an Industrial/Organizational Psychologist and Professor in the Psychology Department at Saint Mary's University in Canada. She is also the Principal Investigator for the Partnership for Productive Organizational Conflict, a research-to-practice collaboration of Canadian experts on workplace conflict resolution interventions funded by the Social Sciences and Humanities Research Council of Canada.

Debra's research focuses on the implications of conflict for work stress and wellbeing, how personality and thinking styles influence conflict handling, and organizational conflict interventions. Her teaching at the undergraduate and graduate levels focuses on Industrial/Organizational Psychology, organizational development, research methods, and multivariate statistics.

Daniel Goering: Daniel is a Fulbright Graduate Research Fellow at the University of Tokyo's Graduate School of Medicine. He conducts research on stress and wellbeing in the workplace, entrepreneurial wellbeing, and leadership, and he investigates best practices to help organizations implement evidence-based management. He is passionate about bridging the academic-practitioner gap and is engaged in many efforts to help translate research into practice and policy.

M. Gloria González-Morales: Gloria is an Associate Professor of Psychology at the University of Guelph. Gloria's research involves the disciplines of Occupational Health Psychology and Positive Organizational Psychology. She studies issues such as work stress and eustress, respect and incivility in the workplace, gender and sexual diversity, work-life relationships, and mental health promotion programs based on emotion regulation and mindfulness. Her work is published in leading academic journals, including *The Journal of Applied Psychology, Journal of Organizational Behavior, Journal of Occupational Health Psychology,* and *Work & Stress.* Her work has been supported by funding from the Social Sciences and Humanities Research Council.

Heather J. Gordon: Heather is a behavior change consultant and a visiting researcher in work and organizational psychology at Eindhoven's University of Technology IE&IS: HPM Group in the Netherlands. Her interests include exploring the innovative strategies that employees use on the job to help them enjoy their work while also performing well. In addition, she has expertise in designing behavior change interventions and insights-based research.

Matthew J. Grawitch: Matt is a Professor within Saint Louis University's School for Professional Studies, the academic unit responsible for providing education to working professionals. He currently serves as the Associate Dean of Graduate and Professional Education, guiding the direction of graduate education within the school. He conducts most of his research in the areas of stress and the psychologically healthy workplace, and he currently serves as the primary research consultant to the APA's Psychologically Healthy Workplace Program. He is a frequent writer and presenter on psychological health in the workplace.

Henna Hasson: Henna is an Associate Professor and coleader of the Procome research group at Medical Management Centre, Karolinska Institutet. She is also head of the Unit for Implementation at the Stockholm County Council. Her focus is on researching implementation and effects of organizational interventions.

Peter Hosie: Peter is a management academic with Central Queensland University, Australia. His distinguished academic and research track record has yielded more than 100 refereed publications. His research focusses on the impact of determinants of happiness on managers' job performance, employee mental health, and the effects of organizational diversity and change in the workplace. He is published in the *Personnel Review, Asia Pacific Journal of Human Resources, Adelaide Law Review Journal, The International Journal of Human Resource Management, International Journal of Workplace Health Management, European Business Review, Journal of Travel,* and *Tourism Marketing.*

Maria Karanika-Murray: Maria is an Associate Professor in Occupational Health Psychology at Nottingham Trent University, United Kingdom. Her research focuses on how workplaces that enable healthy and productive work can be developed, workplace climate, older workers, organisational interventions, intervention evaluation, and presenteeism. She has published widely for both academic and practitioner audiences and her work has been funded by the European Agency for Safety & Health at Work, the UK Health & Safety Executive, the UK Economic & Social Research Council, Heart Research UK, and the European Commission.

E. Kevin Kelloway: Kevin is the Canada Research Chair in Occupational Health Psychology and Professor of Psychology at Saint Mary's University in Halifax Nova Scotia, Canada. A prolific researcher, he is a Fellow of the Association for Psychological Science, the Canadian Psychological Association, the International Association of Applied Psychology, and the Society for Industrial/Organizational Psychology. He is a recipient of the Distinguished Contribution award from the Canadian SIOP and of the Distinguished Psychologist in Management Award from the Society of Psychologists in Management. He is Associate Editor of the *Journal of Occupational Health Psychology, the Journal of Organizational Effectiveness: People and Performance,* and of *Work & Stress.*

Russel PJ Kingshott: Russel is a Senior Lecturer in Marketing at Curtin University, Australia, and serves on the editorial review board for the *Journal of Business Research.* His research on relationship marketing, business-to-business marketing, service employee wellness, psychological contracts, marketing strategy, and services marketing appears in the *Journal of Marketing Management, Journal of Service Management, European Journal of Marketing, Industrial Marketing Management,* and the *Journal of Services Marketing.*

Dorothy Klotz: Dorothy is a professor in Management Systems in the Gabelli School of Business, Fordham University. She holds a Ph.D. in Management Science from the Smeal College of Business, Pennsylvania State University. Professor Klotz's research includes incentive design mechanisms, character-based leadership, employee wellbeing, and curriculum design. Her publications have appeared in *Management Science,* the *Rand Journal of Economics,* and the *Journal of Innovative Education.* Several of her participatory learning exercises are widely used by educators and corporate trainers.

Heather Spence Laschinger: For 25 years, Heather investigated the impact of nursing work environments on nurses' empowerment for professional practice, their health and wellbeing, and the role of leadership in creating empowering working conditions. A major focus of her research was examining the link between nursing work environments and nurse and client outcomes. The results of this research have been translated into several policy documents, including the Magnet Hospital Accreditation Program in the United States. Research findings have also been used to inform workplace practices in health care work settings worldwide. In 2009, she was awarded the Arthur Labatt Family Nursing Research Chair in Health Human Resources Optimization to lead a broad research agenda examining issues related to the planning and management of nursing and health services to ensure high-quality care across health care sectors. She has received several prestigious national and international awards for her work in academic and professional communities, including the Distinguished University Professor Award and Hellmuth Prize at Western University and fellowships in the Canadian Academy of Health Sciences and the American Academy of Nursing. She was also been appointed by the Ontario Minister of Health as Healthy Work Environment Champion for the province. Heather passed away in late 2016.

Luo Lu: Luo Lu, D.Phil, University of Oxford, UK, is the Distinguished Professor in Department of Business Administration, National Taiwan University, Taiwan (ROC). Her major research interests are culture and self, subjective wellbeing, stress and adjustment, work stress and organizational health, and other personality/social/IO psychological topics. She has been awarded the Distinguished Research Award by the Ministry of Science and Technology, ROC. She has published more than 180 papers in referred journals and is the series editor, author, or coauthor of more than 20 books and book chapters. She is currently the Editor-in-Chief of *Research in Applied Psychology* (Taiwan). She has served on several editorial boards of international psychological and managerial journals.

Christina Maslach: Christina is a Professor of Psychology (Emerita) at the University of California, Berkeley. She is widely recognized as one of the pioneering researchers on job burnout. She is the author of the Maslach Burnout Inventory and has written numerous articles and books, including *The Truth About Burnout* (Jossey-Bass 1997). Several of her articles have received awards for their significance and high impact, and she recently received a lifetime career achievement award for her work on burnout. Currently, she is the founding Co-Editor of the e-journal *Burnout Research.* Her record of both outstanding teaching and research led to her receiving a national award as Professor of the Year.

Jonathan Passmore: Jonathan is a chartered psychologist and holds five degrees. He holds a professorship at the University of Evora, Portugal, and is also managing director for Embrion (a psychology consulting company). He has published widely, with more than 100 scientific papers and book chapters, and 30 books. His most recent work is an eight-volume series on Industrial and Organizational Psychology. He has won several awards, including the 2015 Association for Business Psychology Chairmans Award for Excellence.

Ashlyn M. Patterson: Ashlyn is a Ph.D. candidate in Industrial-Organizational Psychology at the University of Guelph working under the supervision of Dr. M. Gloria González-Morales. Ashlyn's research interests include workplace incivility and civility, mentoring at work, and emotion regulation. She has presented her research at conferences in Canada, the United States, and Europe. She previously completed her M.A. in Industrial-Organizational Psychology at the University of Guelph and her Honors B.A. in Psychology at Acadia University. Ashlyn actively consults with organizations in Canada in areas such as competency modeling, selection interviews, change management, and leadership development.

Samantha A. Penney: Samantha is a doctoral candidate in Industrial/Organizational Psychology at Saint Mary's University. Her research focuses on promoting psychologically healthy workplaces and employees through training and individualized interventions. She has presented this work at national and international conferences. Samantha has acted as an internal leadership and organizational development consultant for a large national organization. She is a member of the Nova Scotia Psychologically Healthy Workplace committee and the CN Centre for Occupational Health and Safety. Prior to her doctoral studies, Samantha received a Master of Science from Saint Mary's University in Industrial/Organizational Psychology and a Bachelor of Arts (Hon.) in Psychology from Lakehead University.

Tahira M. Probst: Tahira is an Edward R. Meyer Distinguished Professor of Psychology at Washington State University Vancouver. Her research focuses on economic stress and job insecurity with a particular emphasis on understanding multilevel characteristics of these phenomena. She is currently Co-Editor of Stress and Health and sits on the editorial boards of the *Journal of Occupational Health Psychology, Occupational Health Science, Military Psychology,* and the *Journal of Business and Psychology.*

Laura Radcliffe: Laura is Lecturer in Organizational Behavior and Director of the Masters of Research Program at the University of Liverpool Management School. Her research focuses on how people manage their various roles and identities, with a particular interest in the relationship between work and other life domains, including a consideration of the impact of organizational policies and gender diversity. To explore these issues she draws on methodological approaches that have the ability to capture in-depth understanding of people's lived, daily experiences. Her research has been published in journals such as *Human Relations* and the *Journal of Occupational and Organizational Psychology.*

Emily Read: Emily is an Assistant Professor in the Faculty of Nursing at the University of New Brunswick. She is a CSEP-certified personal trainer and a geriatric rehabilitation nurse, and she worked at the Parkwood Institute in London, Ontario, before moving to Fredericton. Her research interests include health care leadership and management, social capital and healthy workplace relationships, workplace health and wellbeing, new graduate nurses' transitions to the workplace, and healthy aging and technology.

She completed her Ph.D. at the University of Western Ontario in 2016, specializing in nursing leadership and health services research. Her dissertation work involved development and validation of a new questionnaire to assess social capital in the workplace and examine its role in nurses' work life. She has been involved with several provincial and national studies examining new graduate nurses' experiences during their transition to practice and nurses' aspirations to take on leadership roles. In 2008–2010, she was involved in the DaTA Study, a self-monitoring technology and physical activity intervention for older adults with metabolic syndrome in rural Ontario. She is currently a New Brunswick colead for a CIHR-funded study to examine the effectiveness of passive in-home monitoring technology for keeping older adults safely in their homes longer.

Anne Richter: Anne has a Ph.D. in psychology and works as a researcher at Medical Management Centre, Karolinska Institutet, Stockholm, Sweden. In her research she investigates leadership development to foster implementation in the health care sector. Moreover, she investigates how work environment factors affect the implementation process. In addition to her work as a researcher she is employed at the Unit for Implementation at the Center for Epidemiology and Community Medicine, Sweden, and is responsible for a project on an implementation leadership training for line managers in health care.

Marian N. Ruderman: Marian is Director of the Research Horizons Group at the Center for Creative Leadership and has more than 30 years of experience in the field of leadership development. She has been involved in different aspects of leadership development including research, product development, and management. Her current research focuses on bringing the latest advances from neuroscience into leadership development. She has written numerous books, articles, and book chapters for scholars, HR professionals, and practicing managers. Marian is a Fellow of both the APA and the Society for Industrial/Organizational Psychology. She received her Bachelor of Arts degree from Cornell University and her Ph.D. in Psychology from the University of Michigan.

Gemma Ryde: Gemma is a Postdoctoral Research Fellow at the University of Stirling in physical activity, sedentary behavior, and health. Gemma's research interests are broadly in the area of physical activity and sedentary behavior in the workplace setting, and her Ph.D. is in this topic area. Her work to date has focused on the measurement, prevalence, and influences (correlates) of physical activity and sedentary lifestyles, and the development and delivery of interventions to modify these behaviors.

Ben J. Searle: Ben is a Senior Lecturer in Organizational Psychology at Macquarie University. His program of research encompasses wellbeing (including stress, engagement, emotions, attitudes, and behaviors) as well as the mechanisms that connect wellbeing with individual and workplace characteristics. He has received awards for his research as well as for teaching excellence. His professional expertise includes assessing employee wellbeing (assisting in the development, evaluation, and interpretation of workplace surveys) and helping organizations to manage wellbeing, and as well as designing and providing workplace training and development. Ben communicates to the public about the field of organizational psychology at mindonthejob.com.

Piyush Sharma: Piyush is a Professor of Marketing at Curtin University, Australia. He serves as an Associate Editor for the *Journal of Business Research* and *Journal of Services Marketing,* and a member of the editorial review boards of the *Journal of the Academy of Marketing Science, European Journal of Marketing, Journal of Service Theory and Practice,* and *International Journal of Emerging Markets.* His research on cross-cultural consumer behavior, branding and marketing strategy, and services and international marketing appears in the *Journal of International Business Studies, Journal of the Academy of Marketing Science, Journal of Service Research, Journal of Service Management, Journal* *of Business Research, European Journal of Marketing, Journal of Advertising, Journal of Marketing Management,* and *Journal of Services Marketing.*

Akihito Shimazu: Akihito is Professor of Human and Social Sciences, the Kitasato University, Japan. His research interests include job stress and coping, stress management in the workplace, work engagement, workaholism, work-home interface, and the application of IT for workplace intervention. He has published on a wide array of topics in journals such as *Cross-Cultural Research; Journal of Behavioral Medicine; International Archives of Occupational and Environmental Health, Social Science & Medicine;* and *Work & Stress.*

Robert R. Sinclair: Bob is a Professor of Industrial-Organizational Psychology at Clemson University. He is a founding member and Past President of the Society for Occupational Heath Psychology, Associate Editor of the *Journal of Business and Psychology,* and Editor-in-Chief of *Occupational Health Science.* His research focuses on health-related aspects of organizational climate, economic stress, and the employment relationship.

Oi Ling Siu: Oi Ling is Professor and Head of the Department of Applied Psychology at Lingnan University in Hong Kong. Her research interests are in Occupational Health Psychology, specifically occupational stress, psychology of safety, and work-life balance. Oi Ling is the Editor of the *International Journal of Stress Management,* and the Associate Editor of the *Journal of Occupational Health Psychology.* Oi Ling has published more than 75 refereed journal articles and many book chapters.

Gretchen Spreitzer: Gretchen is the Keith E. and Valerie J. Alessi Professor of Business Administration at the Ross School of Business at the University of Michigan. Her research focuses on employee empowerment and leadership development, particularly within a context of organizational change and decline. Her most recent research examines how organizations can enable thriving, especially in contexts dealing with the new world of work such as coworking spaces. This is part of a new movement in the field of organizational behavior known as Positive Organizational Scholarship.

Clare Stovell: Clare is a Ph.D. candidate at Lancaster University Management School. Her research focuses on work-family balance and the process by which couples divide earning and caring responsibilities. With regards to this topic, she is particularly interested in the perspective of fathers and the role played by preferences. Prior to her doctoral studies, Clare was a graduate student in Sociology at the University of Oxford. Her Master's thesis looked at the contrast between fathers' attitudes and behavior in the sharing of child care.

Michelle R. Tuckey: Michelle is an Associate Professor of Psychology at the University of South Australia. Her program of research on wellbeing at work focuses on understanding the mechanisms involved in workplace bullying and occupational stress, and advancing the risk management of psychosocial hazards at work. Michelle has published more than 75 journal articles, edited books, book chapters, and research reports on these topics. She currently serves on the editorial boards of the *Journal of Occupational Health Psychology* and *International Journal of Stress Management,* and on the Management Committee of Crisis Intervention and Management Australasia. Michelle's research has also been translated into policies and practices that protect the psychological health and safety of workers within a range of organizations, and informed two national surveillance systems of psychosocial risks.

Machteld Van den Heuvel: Machteld is an Assistant Professor in Work and Organizational Psychology at University of Amsterdam, the Netherlands. Her research focuses on building a happy and healthy workforce, and developing interventions to boost work engagement, health and wellbeing, and adaptivity. Areas of interest are mindfulness, meaning, and job crafting. She applies insights from academic work in the field as a trainer/coach. She is a member of the European Association of Work & Organizational Psychologists and serves as a reviewer for various international scientific journals.

Ulrica Von Thiele Schwarz: Ulrica is a psychologist and an Associate Professor in Psychology at Mälardalen University, Sweden. She coleads the Procome research group at Medical Management Centre, Karolinska Institutet. Her research is focused on uncovering how to design, conduct, and evaluate innovative improvement initiatives in organizations, and its effects on organizational as well as employee outcomes.

Thomas A. Wright: Tom is the Felix E. Larkin Distinguished Professor in Management at Fordham University and holds a Ph.D. from the University of California, Berkeley. Similar to the Claude Rains character from the classic movie, *Casablanca,* he has published in many of the "usual suspects." In recognition of his career accomplishments, he has been awarded Fellow status in the Association for Psychological Science, the APA, the Western Psychological Association, and the Society of Industrial and Organizational Psychology. He enjoys spending time with his wife (Kay), family, and friends; hiking in the mountains; walking on a quiet beach; prayerful meditation; and competitively lifting weights.

Despoina Xanthopoulou: Despoina is Assistant Professor of Organizational Psychology at the School of Psychology, Aristotle University of Thessaloniki, Greece, and Visiting Fellow at the Newcastle University Business School, UK. Her main research interests include job (re)design, employee wellbeing, recovery, crossover and spillover processes, and diary studies. Her research has been published in peer-reviewed journals such as the *Journal of Applied Psychology, Human Relations,* and the *Journal of Occupational Health Psychology.* She is Associate Editor of the *Journal of Personnel Psychology* and the *European Journal of Work & Organizational Psychology.* She is co-coordinator (elected) of the Division of Organizational Psychology of the Hellenic Psychological Society.

The state of the art of workplace wellbeing

Michael P. Leiter and Cary L. Cooper

It is no longer sufficient for employers to prevent injuries on the job; we expect employers to make a deliberate and constructive contribution to sustaining employees' physical and mental wellbeing. It is not good enough to do no harm; responsible employers design work to enhance employees' health and fulfillment at work. Despite evidence of this ideal gaining traction globally, it is a long way from becoming a reality.

Healthy work life remains more of a dream than a reality for most people for two main reasons: First, not every individual, business, or government has actively embraced improving employee wellbeing as a core business responsibility. Second, as becomes evident reading the state-of-the-art chapters in this volume, much remains to be discovered, designed, and shared about workplace wellbeing initiatives. Although research has clearly established advantages of employee wellbeing for organizational productivity and employee satisfaction (Robertson & Cooper, 2011), research has been slower to critically evaluate methods for enhancing employee wellbeing (Chen & Cooper, 2014). Moving research discoveries into practical, cost-effective practices remains a major challenge.

At the heart of the matter lie five core issues:

1 Defining workplace wellbeing
2 Identifying accountability for workplace wellbeing
3 Articulating a strategic, holistic approach to workplace wellbeing
4 Identifying initiatives that contribute to enhancing wellbeing
5 Identifying leadership perspectives and capacities supportive of workplace wellbeing

Defining workplace wellbeing

Defining *wellbeing* presents something of a challenge. The research community – including the authors in this volume – have not even agreed upon the word's spelling. Have we or have we not progressed beyond the hyphen? The editorial staff at Routledge will assure consistent spelling in the final proofs but their work will smooth over rifts. The starting point for defining the term accepts its multi-faceted nature (Dodge, Daly, Huyton, & Sanders, 2012). Workplace wellbeing encompasses physical health and comfort, mental health, a preponderance of positive over negative affect, and positive attitudes towards work. Dodge et al. (2012) moved away from well-being as a stable subjective state to emphasize its relational quality as an equilibrium of resources with challenges. Wellbeing from this perspective goes beyond how people feel at a moment to encompass how they make sense of their context, the expectations of others, and their confidence in their capacity to meet the challenges they encounter or anticipate encountering.

The broad, multi-faceted nature of wellbeing results in a rich, diverse research field, but one that presents challenges for incremental progress. For example, a study may assess physical wellbeing with the single-item Global Health Status measure (DeSalvo, Bloser, Reynolds, He, & Muntner, 2006) and mental wellbeing with the five-item Mental Health Index (Ware & Sherbourne, 1992) without explicitly addressing the question of equilibrium or respondents' evolution of their work context. Developing shared perspectives on core conceptual dimensions of wellbeing will facilitate the development of widely accepted, theory-based measures. As demonstrated in this volume, the state of the art has developed to include credible measures with foundations in health psychology, psychologically healthy workplace models, and positive psychology.

Accountability

Article 7 (b) of the United Nation's *International Covenant on Economic, Social and Cultural Rights* states that citizens of member countries have the right to safe and healthy working conditions (United Nations, 1966). But as Albuquerque and Evans (2012) pointed out, these rights remain ideals without mechanisms to enforce their application. Substantive rights lack substance without procedural rights to assure their implementation, evaluation, and maintenance. The lack of explicit enforcement means that much of the progress in workplace health initiatives has occurred voluntarily. The nonmandatory pursuit of workplace health initiatives has reflected (1) convincing research demonstrating the cost-effectiveness of workplace health programs (e.g., Rongen, Robroek, van Lenthe, & Burdorf, 2013), (2) their contribution to attracting and retaining talent (Montague, Burgess, & Connell, 2015), and (3) the desire to maintain a positive corporate image (Arena et al., 2013). From all three perspectives, the physical and mental wellbeing of employees benefits businesses as well as the employees.

However, all is not entirely well with workplace wellbeing. For example, in the United States, 4,679 fatal workplace injuries occurred in 2014, up 2% from the number in 2013 (Bureau of Labor Statistics, 2015). At the very least, employees hope to return home alive at the end of the workday. Regarding physical health, many workers contend with equipment and workstations that fall well short of ergonomic ideals. The increased awareness of the negative consequences of excessive sitting has highlighted the shortcomings of many work settings for assuring that employees at minimum maintain their health rather than deteriorating as a consequence of their work.

The range of perspectives in this volume also convey the message that responsibility for workplace wellbeing does not rest solely on employers: Employees have a role to play as well. As with occupational safety, employees exercise some degree of discretion in the thoroughness with which they make use of workplace resources that support wellbeing. Making the most of workplace resources requires employees to develop the skills, attitudes, and inclinations to make wellbeing a core personal value as well as a corporate value. The power of employee attitude for safety and wellbeing was highlighted by Alberta Premier Rachel Notley, who credited the thorough occupational safety culture of the Canadian oil exploration employees with the evacuation without injury of 90,000 residents of Fort McMurray in the face of a monstrous forest fire (Enright, 2016). A community without a deep perspective on safety and wellbeing would be unlikely to take the correct actions on that scale in emergency situations.

A strategic, holistic approach to workplace wellbeing

A strategic, holistic approach to workplace wellbeing goes beyond measuring engagement versus burnout or reducing sickness absence. A holistic model includes primary (wellbeing audits), secondary (e.g., training and development on safety, physical health, and workplace diversity), and tertiary (e.g., employee assistance program [EAP]) perspectives (Giga, Cooper, & Faragher, 2003). A holistic model has both a long-term perspective (considering employees' productivity and thriving over their lifetime) and a broad perspective (considering the physical, emotional, cognitive, social, and spiritual dimensions of life).

Primary

Wellbeing audits provide an essential quality of infrastructure for a psychologically and physically healthy workplace. They make a definitive statement of organizational values by assessing the employees' perspectives on the qualities that define a constructive and fulfilling workplace. Although such audits include indicators of problems or shortcomings, their principal focus is on the positive qualities that the organization hopes to sustain and develop. In assessing these qualities organizations imply a commitment to enhancing them.

Wellbeing audits take a long-term perspective in that they occur as a regular part of organizational life. Rather than responding to obvious problems reactively, their focus remains on actions that organizations can take to build on their strengths. Providing reports summarizing audit responses to operating units within participating organizations, for example, provides a benchmark for assessing progress, evaluating leadership, and defining needs for further training for leaders and others within the units.

Secondary

Training for wellbeing includes skills as well as attitudes and perspectives that organizations hope to encourage to support workplace wellbeing. In parallel with core training on workplace safety, secondary initiatives on wellbeing provide information and inspiration to employees regarding practices and opportunities for enhancing their physical and mental wellbeing in the course of carrying out their responsibilities. These initiatives may be as simple as encouraging employees to adopt workstations with a standing as well as sitting option or establishing routines for moving around more often during the course of their workdays. To complement primary initiatives, such as providing healthier food options at work, training initiatives can provide opportunities to explore new foods that may not have previously been part of some employees' repertoires. Similarly, training and fun events encourage employees to make good use of exercise facilities. Often, building awareness does not suffice; training and marketing complete the training cycle, ensuring a good return on an organizational investment in wellbeing.

In the global economy of the 21st century, workforces have become increasingly diverse on multiple dimensions – gender, age, national origin, family structure, religion, and profession, among others. Leaders cannot reasonably assume that everyone entering their workforce shares values about work, assumptions about workplace roles, or the degree of formality that is appropriate for workplace communications. While this diversity of backgrounds brings strengths and perspectives to workplaces, it requires active dialogue among employees to establish a coherent workplace culture. To begin the process, a facilitated conversation within workgroups about their expectations and assumptions helps to clarify how people interpret signs of civility and respect.

Subsequently, explicit discussion of workplace culture would be included as part of the process of integrating new employees into the workgroup.

Tertiary

Broad-based EAPs build wellbeing in the course of alleviating acute problems. Such programs may take a prospective approach to facilitating employees' recovery from a physical injury through physiotherapy or occupational therapy. The aim includes both recovery from the injury as well as insuring that employees establish a new level of physical wellbeing. Similarly, treatment in the wake of emotional disturbances contributes to employees' resilience when encountering potentially distressing incidents at work. Ideally, EAPs would link to active lifestyle coaching for employees to assure that they establish routines for exercise, mindfulness, or other practices that help to maintain their capacity to thrive through their work and in their personal lives. In that way the treatment options responding to injuries or disruptive events include both recovery as well as enhancing employees' capacity to address future challenges.

Practical, effective, validated intervention

Although meaningful progress has occurred in designing, implementing, and evaluating organizational interventions to enhance wellbeing, much work remains to be done. Intervention research presents serious challenges regarding costs, timescales, and the complexity of the research/organization relationship.

Nielsen (2013) described a challenge in organizational intervention research arising from that complex relationship inherent in applied research. Sound ethical methods call upon a participatory approach to the design and implementation of interventions. Informed consent works directly in opposition to the double-blind randomized control trial that is the gold standard for evaluating the effectiveness of interventions. When participants have full knowledge of the research questions, it is difficult to disguise a control group activity as the actual intervention unless it shares so many features with the intervention that has a similar impact on participants. The process inherently underestimates the potential for human qualities beyond the research design to influence implementation and evaluation. For example, a manager's enthusiasm for a healthy workplace initiative may influence the thoroughness of its implementation, the extent of employees' participation, and the response set that participants bring to evaluation surveys. A meaningful proportion of a work unit's benefit from a program may arise from that enthusiasm rather than the program design. Nielsen (2013) points out that the theoretical framework for intervention research rarely encompasses the full scope of human and design factors that can play a role in determining the outcome.

These concerns emphasize the argument for going beyond one-off initiatives to improve some dimension of workplace wellbeing to refining a comprehensive perspective on the nature of wellbeing. An essential principle along these lines is emphasizing that wellbeing does not reside solely within individuals but is a quality of social relationships, workgroups, organizational units, and entire organizations. The process of designing, implementing, and evaluating intervention needs to appreciate the essential role of context for any intervention process.

The need for well-designed interventions is underscored by the intervention conundrum (Leiter & Maslach, 2015; Leiter, Peck, & Gumuchian, 2015). Problems with wellbeing – however defined – arise effortlessly. Neglect and inaction undermine wellbeing. However, actions to improve wellbeing require careful planning, dedicated commitment, money, and coordinated action. Progress requires a concerted effort sustained over a considerable time. It also requires organizations to be ready for change in order to implement new policies and practices in a meaningful and enduring fashion, upsetting the status quo (Holt, Armenakis, Harris, & Feild, 2007).

Another dimension of the researcher/organizational relationship concerns access to institutional data. Intervention studies require organizational records to supplement information available through surveys, interviews, and observation. A simple willingness to share such information with researchers constitutes one step towards such access, but it is not sufficient in itself. Rarely is organizational data readily available in a manner that aligns perfectly with the time frame and the organizational structure associated with the intervention. That sort of alignment requires dedicating the time and talents of people with the technical expertise to seek out the relevant information in the organizational databases, structure that information as needed to address research questions, and make the information available to the interested parties. Usually people with these capabilities are entirely too busy already, requiring a genuine commitment from leadership to provide information on absences, indicators of presenteeism, or productivity measures.

Leadership and skills where they are needed

For the most part, supervisors receive training on managing schedules and budgets – but most challenges arise from managing people. Providing meaningful and enduring support for employees' wellbeing requires leaders at every level of an organization to have a long-term perspective on people that includes their fulfillment and thriving as well as their contribution to productivity and their role in the logistics of getting the work done.

To address the contributions to wellbeing of positive social encounters at work, supervisors need skills and perspectives allowing them to operate effectively on three levels: one-on-one conversations, mediating strained relationships between employees, and maintaining a respectful workgroup climate. The first level concerns supervisors' capacity to conduct one-on-one conversations with employees on difficult issues. When employee performance falls short of expectations, the immediate point of contact rests with first-line managers (FLMs). Without confidence in their capacity to conduct these conversations, FLMs will shy away from what they anticipate to be a confrontation. That outcome would leave performance problems neglected until they reach crisis proportions. Without a refined degree of empathy, FLMs will fail to conduct the conversation in a way that employees perceive as fair and respectful. Many employees report feeling unjustly treated at work. The process of performance evaluation – as an annual ritual or a incident-based response – challenges employees' sense of mastery in their work. Conveying focused and meaningful criticism of performance while conveying respect and fair-handedness presents significant challenges. However, doing so makes a meaningful contribution to employee wellbeing.

A second level of social sophistication for FLMs occurs when they intervene in strained working relationships among people on their units. Mediation is a sophisticated skill as it involves clarifying opposing positions, searching for a resolution, and encouraging people to move towards a shared solution. The perception of justice plays an important role in mediation and conflict resolution because people have concerns about their FLM taking the other party's side against them. This kind of intervention contributes seriously to workplace wellbeing because social mistreatment at work serves as a major contributor to distress (Day & Leiter, 2014; Hershcovis, 2011). Unresolved incivility between colleagues has the potential to spiral into more intense mistreatment involving a larger circle of individuals in the workplace. Strained relationships in this way may contribute to workplaces becoming socially dysfunctional over time.

The third level of social sophistication concerns the overall social climate of the workgroup. Although everyone on a unit contributes to defining its social ambiance to some degree, FLMs play an outside role. With training, support, and encouragement, FLMs can set a tone for employees that enhances the level of civility in their social encounters with one another. Simple acts of acknowledging one another or expressing appreciation for colleagues' contributions to shared tasks contribute to defining a workplace culture (Leiter, 2012). The leaders' behavior regarding these qualities conveys to employees that these are legitimate and important ways to interact with one another.

On another level, the actions and attitudes of senior leadership convey the true organizational value for respect and wellbeing to leaders throughout the organizational structure. The salience of these values depends on more than the good intentions of executives or the occasional inspiring words from the CEO. These values become embedded through repeated conversation, ongoing organizational communications, and expert coaching to help individual leaders build a wellbeing perspective into their day-to-day work.

It was back in 1968 that Bobby Kennedy, the best president the United States never had, gave a powerful speech at the University of Kansas when on the election trail for the Democratic nomination of president, when he argued that Gross National Product was not a measure of a society's success, rather it was Gross National Wellbeing:

> Too much and for too long, we seemed to have surrendered personal excellence and community values in the mere accumulation of material things. Our Gross National Product now is over $800 billion a year, but that GNP – if we judge the United States by that – that GNP counts air pollution and cigarette advertising, and ambulances to clear our highways of carnage. It counts special locks for our doors and the jails for the people who break them. It counts the destruction of the redwood and the loss of our natural wonder in chaotic sprawl. It counts napalm and counts nuclear warheads and armored cars for the police to fight the riots in our cities. . . . Yet the GNPs does not allow for the health of our children, the quality of their education or the joy of their play. It does not include the beauty of our poetry or the strength of our marriages, the intelligence of our public debate or the integrity of our public officials. It measures neither our wit nor our courage, neither our wisdom nor our learning, neither our compassion nor our devotion to our country, it measures everything in short, except that which makes life worthwhile.

The structure of this book

We have organized the book into five sections: models of wellbeing, personal qualities contributing to wellbeing, job insecurity and organizational wellbeing, workplace supports for wellbeing, and initiatives to enhance wellbeing.

Models of wellbeing

The first section presents a variety of models of wellbeing to demonstrate the range of concepts that people have brought to bear on this complex, multi-faceted issue.

In Chapter 2, Jill Flint-Taylor and Alex Davda develop the concept of individual resilience. They reflect upon the ways in which resilience develops and changes over the life span to identify principles relevant to interventions to enhance resilience. They review efforts to apply the resilience construct to teams or organizations, noting the insights drawn from this work and the challenges for future research on this level of construct. The chapter notes the importance of diversity of team composition for resilience.

In Chapter 3, Ben J. Searle and Michelle R. Tuckey explore the value of differentiating challenge, hindrance, and threat in the stress process with its implication for wellbeing. Essentially, they note ways in which distinct qualities of workplace demand have strikingly different implications for developing or inhibiting wellbeing at work.

In Chapter 4, Christina Maslach and Cristina G. Banks consider the range of psychological connections with work. They present their ideas as part of a thorough historical perspective on psychological health within work psychology. Their primary message for intervention design concerns the importance of giving a central role to employees' personal motives and aspirations in order to create viable and enduring workplace designs.

In Chapter 5, Peter Hosie, Russel PJ Kingshott, and Piyush Sharma review research and theory on the determinants of mental health at work. They provide an integrative framework to understand and evaluate current initiatives on the policy level to improve workplace wellbeing as well as a framework for subsequent research on policy developments.

In Chapter 6, E. Kevin Kelloway provides an overview of research methods and measures for assessing wellbeing at work. He points out the paucity of rigorous research that evaluates the impact of interventions in a credible fashion. He also makes recommendations for developing a rigorous but practical approach to intervention research regarding workplace wellbeing.

Personal qualities contributing to wellbeing

Models of wellbeing have pointed towards both personal and organizational factors contributing to wellbeing. This section of the book considers enduring personality characteristics as well as an enduring personal activity: sleep.

In Chapter 7, Thomas A. Wright and Dorothy Klotz write on character, personality and wellbeing. They consider the cardinal qualities of character – valor, industry, integrity, critical thinking (wisdom), and self-regulation – as well as the Big Five personality traits – extraversion, agreeableness, conscientiousness, openness, and stability. They review existing research and reflect on future research initiatives focusing on character and personality in wellbeing research.

In Chapter 8, Christopher J. Budnick and Larissa K. Barber consider sleep as an essential process in supporting wellbeing at work and beyond. They consider the relationship of wellbeing and sleep as reciprocal, with each enhancing or constraining the other in an amplifying dynamics. They identify gaps in existing research on these questions, proposing directions for future research.

Job insecurity and organizational wellbeing

Workplace wellbeing initiatives do not always operate against a neutral background. Often they function in direct opposition to forces that weaken or actively undermine employees' wellbeing.

In Chapter 9, Tahira M. Probst, Robert R. Sinclair, and Janelle H. Cheung provide an overview of research on the impact of economic stressors on employees, specifically unemployment, underemployment, and job insecurity. They note personal, organizational, and broader social factors that shape individual vulnerability to these stressors. They also provide suggestions for future research and action to counter economics stressors at work.

In Chapter 10, Luo Lu and Chun-Yi Chou provide an overview of long working hours and presenteeism in Asia. They draw upon social cognitive theory (SCT) to consider the distinct implications of working long hours in Confucian-influenced societies. Central to their perspective is the role of self-efficacy within the SCT framework of environment, individual, and behavior.

In Chapter 11, Ashlyn M. Patterson, Alexandra C. Chris, and M. Gloria Gonzalez-Morales consider the deleterious implications for wellbeing of workplace incivility. They reflect upon the subjective nature of incivility, the role of culture in interpreting uncivil behavior, and the measurement of incivility. They contrast incivility with its opposite, civility, to propose future research directions.

Workplace supports for wellbeing

The design and management processes of workplaces have implications for wellbeing. Structural qualities and policies have enduring implications as they remain constant for extended periods.

In Chapter 12, Chris Boyko and Rachel Cooper consider the physical design of offices and other workplaces for employees' wellbeing. They note four central qualities for workplace quality: noise and air quality; light and lighting; windows, views and nature; and privacy. They consider the implications for contemporary alternative workplace designs such as group settings versus individual offices. They note the importance of personal control in the experience of office space.

In Chapter 13, Heather Spence Laschinger and Emily Read consider the implications of policies that support workplace empowerment for employee wellbeing. The implications of a sense of mastery or agency in one's work relates to fundamental psychological motives. They call upon Kanter's theory of structural empowerment in their evaluation of research in this area.

In Chapter 14, Gretchen Spreitzer, Peter Bacevice, and Lyndon Garrett consider coworking policies and their implications for wellbeing at work. They consider the delicate balance of autonomy versus community as a primary issue in employees' thriving at work, and they discuss the potential of coworking policies as part of workplace wellbeing initiatives.

In Chapter 15, Marian N. Ruderman, Cathleen Clerkin, and Jennifer J. Deal draw upon the Job Demands–Resources (JD-R) model to consider the deleterious effects of long work hours on wellbeing. The chapter considers five approaches for alleviating the impact of long work hours: sleep, mindfulness, physical movement, social connection, and positivity.

In Chapter 16, Clare Stovell, David Collinson, Caroline Gatrell, and Laura Radcliffe consider workplace policies with implications for work-life balance with an emphasis on working fathers. They emphasize the issue of matches and mismatches of workplace policies with the aspirations and values of employees. In reviewing potential interventions or policy developments, they acknowledge the potential conflict between improving balance with gender roles regarding work and career.

Initiatives to enhance wellbeing

An essential test of any theory or research model rests in its capacity to produce positive change in employees' sense of wellbeing. This section considers a variety of initiatives for enhancing wellbeing. The range of approaches considered here demonstrate the wealth of ideas being considered.

In Chapter 17, Tim Anstiss and Jonathan Passmore consider the role of coaching in improving workplace wellbeing. Coaching focuses primarily on the factors that are within individuals' scope of control within work life with emphasis on pacing throughout the workday and recovery activities when away from work.

In Chapter 18, Matthew J. Grawitch, David W. Ballard, and Kaitlyn R. Erb consider the contribution of the American Psychological Association's Psychologically Healthy Workplace program. They consider four psychological connections with work – engagement, workaholism, exhaustion, and satisfaction – within a model of workplace wellbeing. They note the contribution of material support, emotional support, and need fulfillment as sustaining wellbeing.

In Chapter 19, Evangelia Demerouti, Despoina Xanthopoulou, Machteld Van den Heuvel, Lonneke Dubbelt, and Heather J. Gordon outline the myriad ways in which job resources contribute to wellbeing at work. In this chapter, they provide a valuable overview of the perspective of the JD-R model to the challenge of assessing, supporting, and enhancing wellbeing at work. They focus on the role of leaders in facilitating employees' access to resources.

In Chapter 20, Oi Ling Siu provides an overview of the most prominent techniques for stress management in the workplace, including cognitive behavior therapy, meditation, relaxation, mindfulness, and exercise. In this chapter she reflects on the research support for the efficacy of these various techniques. She also considers strategies for combining various approaches to achieve a comprehensive workplace wellbeing initiative.

In Chapter 21, Gemma Ryde provides an in-depth consideration of the potential for physical exercise to contribute to workplace wellbeing. In addition to reflecting on contemporary initiatives, she provides a historical perspective on the evolution of physical activity programs in workplaces over recent decades.

In Chapter 22, Arla Day and Samantha A. Penney present a three-component framework of wellbeing initiatives in terms of an initiative's (1) content and focus, (2) context, and (3) program development and implementation processes. They emphasize the importance of relationship factors of trust, caring, and respect in developing, implementing, and sustaining workplace wellbeing initiatives.

In Chapter 23, Maria Karanika-Murray, Henna Hasson, Ulrica von Thiele Schwarz, and Anne Richter consider in-depth initiatives to improve workplace wellbeing through enhancing organizational leadership. They present a leadership development program that is practical, actionable, and aligned to the organizational goals for workplace wellbeing. They also identify important directions for subsequent research to assess the contribution of such initiatives.

In Chapter 24, Akihito Shimazu and Daniel Goering review a participatory approach towards enhancing workplace wellbeing in Japan. They consider complementary actions to both reduce the negative impact of stressful conditions while proactively building resources to support wellbeing. They reflect on participatory approaches to developing wellbeing and their distinct role in Japanese culture.

In Chapter 25, Debra Gilin Oore and Norman Dolan consider conflict resolution initiatives as having far-reaching implications for workplace wellbeing. They note that social relationships at work have broad implications for wellbeing versus distress. The chapter considers the range of approaches to conflict management and resolution in contemporary workplaces.

References

Albuquerque, A., & Evans, D. P. (2012). Right to health in Brazil: A study of the treaty-reporting system. *Sur International Journal on Human Rights*, 9(17), 115–137.

Arena, R., Guazzi, M., Briggs, P. D., Cahalin, L. P., Myers, J., Kaminsky, L. A., . . . & Lavie, C. J. (2013). Promoting health and wellness in the workplace: A unique opportunity to establish primary and extended secondary cardiovascular risk reduction programs. *Mayo Clinic Proceedings* (Elsevier), 88(6), 605–617.

Bureau of Labor Statistics. (2015). *Census of Fatal Occupational Injuries Summary, 2014*. Available at: www.bls.gov/news.release/cfoi.nr0.htm (accessed 12 June 2016).

Chen, P., & Cooper, C. L. (2014). *Work and Wellbeing*. Oxford and New York: Wiley-Blackwell.

Day, A., & Leiter, M. P. (2014). The good and bad of working relationships: Implications for burnout. In: M. P. Leiter, A. B. Bakker, & C. Maslach (eds.), *Burnout at Work: A Psychological Perspective*. Hove Sussex: Psychology Press, 56–79.

DeSalvo, K. B., Bloser, N., Reynolds, K., He, J., & Muntner, P. (2006). Mortality prediction with a single general self-rated health question. *Journal of General Internal Medicine*, 21(3), 267–275.

Dodge, R., Daly, A. P., Huyton, J., & Sanders, L. D. (2012). The challenge of defining wellbeing. *International Journal of Wellbeing*, 2(3), 222–235.

Enright, M. (June 12, 2016). Rachel Notley's terrible, horrible, no good, very bad year. *The Sunday Edition*. CBC Radio. Available at: www.cbc.ca/radio/thesundayedition/losing-gordie-howe-and-muhammad-ali-rachel-notley-broken-escalator-phenomenon-james-joyce-1.3622438/rachel-notley-s-terrible-horrible-no-good-very-bad-year-1.3622455 (accessed 12 June 2016).

Giga, S., Cooper, C. L., & Faragher, B. (2003). The development of a framework for a comprehensive approach to stress management interventions at work. *International Journal of Stress Management*, 10, 280–296.

Hershcovis, M. S. (2011). "Incivility, social undermining, bullying . . . oh my!": A call to reconcile constructs within workplace aggression research. *Journal of Organizational Behavior*, 32, 499–519.

Holt, D. T., Armenakis, A. A., Harris, S. G., & Feild, H. S. (2007). Toward a comprehensive definition of readiness for change: A review of research and instrumentation. *Research in Organizational Change and Development*, 16, 289–336.

Kennedy, R. F. (1968). Remarks at the University of Kansas, March 18, 1968. John F. Kennedy Presidential Library and Museum. Available at: www.jfklibrary.org/Research/Research-Aids/Ready-Reference/RFK-Speeches/Remarks-of-Robert-F-Kennedy-at-the-University-of-Kansas-March-18-1968.aspx

Leiter, M. P. (2012). *Analyzing and Theorizing the Dynamics of the Workplace Incivility Crisis*. Amsterdam: Springer.

Leiter, M. P., & Maslach, C. (2015). Conquering burnout. *Scientific American Mind*, 26, 32–37.

Leiter, M. P., Peck, E., & Gumuchian, S. (2015). Workplace incivility and its implications for well-being. In: P. Perrewe, C. C. Rosen, & J. R. B. Halbesleben (eds.), *Research in Occupational Stress and Well-Being: Mistreatment in Organizations* (Vol. 17). Oxford, UK: Emerald/Elsevier, 107–135.

Montague, A., Burgess, J., & Connell, J. (2015). Attracting and retaining Australia's aged care workers: Developing policy and organisational responses. *Labour & Industry: A Journal of the Social and Economic Relations of Work*, 25(4), 293–305.

Nielsen, K. (2013). Review article: How can we make organizational interventions work? Employees and line managers as actively crafting interventions. *Human Relations, 66,* 1029–1050.

Robertson, I., & Cooper, C. L. (2011). *Wellbeing: Productivity and Happiness at Work*. London: Palgrave Macmillan.

Rongen, A., Robroek, S. J., van Lenthe, F. J., & Burdorf, A. (2013). Workplace health promotion: A meta-analysis of effectiveness. *American Journal of Preventive Medicine*, 44(4), 406–415.

United Nations. (1966). *International Covenant on Economic, Social and Cultural Rights*. Available at: www.ohchr.org/EN/ProfessionalInterest/Pages/CESCR.aspx (accessed 12 June 2016).

Ware Jr., J. E., & Sherbourne, C. D. (1992). The MOS 36-item short-form health survey (SF-36): I. Conceptual framework and item selection. *Medical Care*, 30(6), 473–483.

Part I
Models of wellbeing

2

The resilient person and organization

Jill Flint-Taylor and Alex Davda

Overview

The concept of resilience is attracting considerable interest in today's climate of uncertainty and change. It is not a new topic, however, even in the work context. For many years there has been a well-established stream of research and practice relating to the development of individual resilience, with the cognitive behavioral approach (Neenan, 2009) being particularly well documented in the popular press and academic literature. Recently, the growing influence of the positive psychology movement (Snyder & Lopez, 2009) has led to an expansion of the range of approaches and interventions seen to be relevant to strengthening resilience in individuals and organizations. Further insights and practical guidance are also emerging from the neurobiological approach to treating mood and anxiety disorders (Southwick & Charney, 2012).

Resilience and pressure

In this chapter we review some of the main trends in resilience research and discuss implications for building resilience in the organizational context. It is important to emphasize at the outset that the nature and determinants of resilience are very different at individual, team, and organizational levels. At every level, however, resilience is defined and distinguished from related concepts (such as performance) by its relationship to pressure: the management of pressure is integral to both the *process* and the *outcomes* of building resilience. At the individual level, pressure plays a central role in the development of resilience, which in turn delivers better outcomes in coping with future pressures. That is, under the right conditions, a high level of "stretch" pressure can be instrumental in building resilience, while staying in one's comfort zone over the long term can have a detrimental effect. Similarly, exposure to negative experiences that are difficult but mild enough not to inflict lasting damage can have an inoculating effect (Khoshaba & Maddi, 1999), and may even positively influence the underlying neuro-biological mechanisms of resilience (Haglund, Nestadt, Cooper, Southwick, & Charney, 2007).

The processes and outcomes of managing pressure are also integral to understanding and defining resilience at the team and organizational levels. When leaders improve the way workplace pressures are managed for the group as a whole, this is reflected in positive employee survey results, especially in relation to high levels of wellbeing, job satisfaction, and employee engagement. When negative (hindrance) pressure is allowed to get the upper hand, this leads to undesirable outcomes such as higher levels of employee stress, increased intentions to quit, lower job satisfaction, and lower commitment (Podsakoff, LePine, & LePine, 2007). These outcomes in turn have implications for employee retention, customer satisfaction, productivity, and other measures of organizational performance (Robertson & Cooper, 2011). Therefore, the capacity of individuals and teams to manage pressure is central to an organization's ability to take advantage of stretching opportunities, manage risk, and generally deal with environmental and industry change, competition, and tough economic conditions in a resilient way.

As indicated earlier, increasing the resilience of a group (team or organization) is not simply a matter of strengthening the personal resilience of individual employees. Similarly, resilient teams form just one element of organizational resilience. Many studies of organizational resilience relate to systems, processes, technology, and other factors outside the scope of this chapter. Here we focus on the resilience of people at both the individual and group level.

The resilient person

In general conversation, describing someone as "resilient" would not typically lead to being challenged to explain what you mean. The everyday use of the term is widely understood, particularly in relation to the behavior and outcomes that might be expected when someone comes under pressure. However, scratching the surface of this shared understanding reveals a very different picture. For example, many people view resilience as a fixed trait, while others see it more as a resource that develops through experience. Similarly, within the academic arena a number of diverse perspectives on the nature of resilience have emerged over the years, although a certain level of consensus now appears to be developing on some of the most fundamental principles.

The terms *individual, personal, emotional,* and *psychological resilience* are largely interchangeable. Together they encompass many "broad and multidimensional construals of resilience, which conflate stress, coping skills, emotions, cognitions, and environmental characteristics" (Lightsey, 2006, pp. 101–102). One of the most important and unifying trends in recent years has been the growing recognition of resilience as complex and dynamic.

There is a long-established tradition of studying resilience in the context of deprivation and other serious life challenges during childhood (Masten & Narayan, 2012; Rutter, 2007). However, there is growing support for the view that "resilience does not come from rare and special qualities, but from the everyday magic of ordinary, normative human resources in the minds, brains and bodies of children, in their families and relationships and in their communities" (Masten, 2001, p. 235).

Studies of personal resilience over the lifespan have identified the following factors that make a positive contribution to strengthening resilience (summarized by Masten & Wright, 2010):

- Learning to manage your attention, emotional reactions and behavior effectively (self-regulation)
- Building strong relationships and drawing on them for support (relationships and social support)
- Having the intellectual ability to analyze a situation and come up with a good response (although the relationship between intellect and personal resilience is not a linear one)
- Enjoying the challenge of overcoming obstacles and mastering new skills
- Getting in touch with what really matters to you (sense of meaning, purpose or "coherence")

- Being part of a community with shared beliefs, practices, and traditions (especially in the context of how to view loss and adversity in general)

From this perspective, individual resilience can be viewed in terms of capability, process, and outcome, since it develops and plays out through the complex interaction between person and situation. An early argument for this view was put forward by Masten, Best, and Garmezy (1990). As an alternative to a strict trait approach, they proposed a more open-process model of resilience in which adaptation to stress is conceived of as a dynamic process involving both internal capabilities and external resources. This view has gained ground over the years; it is now well-evidenced and widely subscribed to among those researching resilience from diverse perspectives and traditions (Reich, Zautra, & Hall, 2010).

Some of these researchers use the term *resiliency* to differentiate the personal characteristics element from the overall process of resilience. This can be a useful distinction, but we have observed that in organizational practice use of the term *resiliency* risks perpetuating an overemphasis on fixed traits at the expense of a more nuanced understanding. In particular, it can lead to an underappreciation of the role played by attitudes, emotions and other "state-like" constructs. This in turn results in underestimating the importance of context, an issue that we address specifically at a later point. Overall, therefore, we support the use of *resilience* as a single, umbrella term (Peterson & Seligman, 2004) that reflects the complex and multidimensional nature of personal resilience rather than seeking to reduce it to a unitary or a dichotomous construct.

The resilient person – a workplace perspective

An individual's capacity to manage everyday pressure is clearly important across his or her life, but for many people the workplace is where this capacity is most frequently tested. Some studies have focused on the need for resilience in particularly challenging jobs such as social work (e.g., Howard, 2008). Others have taken the view that many work contexts are subject to increasing levels of challenge and change, making resilience widely relevant to individual wellbeing and organizational performance.

The latter view is discussed by Cooper, Flint-Taylor, and Pearn (2013), in the context of exploring what managers and organizations can do to support the strengthening of personal resilience. Based on a review of the literature, the authors propose four clusters of "personal resilience resources" relating to (1) self-confidence, (2) sense of purpose, (3) personal adaptability, and (4) social support. The aim is to provide a framework that captures the complex nature of resilience while making it easier for individuals to take stock, identify specific strengths and risks, and work out what approaches would be most useful in sustaining and building on their current resilience capability. Once the complexity of resilience is appreciated, it becomes evident that there are many different approaches that can be used to strengthen it. These approaches are drawn from various fields of theory and practice, including cognitive therapy and positive psychology.

The work of the positive psychology movement has had a significant impact on the study of resilience in organizations. For example, the construct of psychological capital (PsyCap) has been linked to work performance, satisfaction, and organizational commitment (Luthans, Norman, Avolio, & Avey, 2008). PsyCap represents a trait-state continuum spanning across pure positive traits (intelligence), trait-like constructs (conscientiousness), state-like psychological resources (including resilience), and positive states (moods and emotions).

Another approach with particular relevance for the work context is centered on the construct of "hardiness," conceptualized as encompassing three components: control (influencing events), commitment (engagement/purpose), and challenge (seeing problems as challenges, not threats).

Hardiness is said to act as a resistance resource that can mitigate the adverse effect of stressful life events (Kobasa, Maddi, & Khan, 1982). Evidence has shown that hardy people perform better and stay healthier in the face of stress. Hardiness has been associated with fewer physical and mental health symptoms in Gulf War soldiers (Bartone, 1999) and lower levels of somatic and psychological distress in university students (Beasley, Thompson, & Davidson, 2003). Hardiness has also been shown to increase the use of planned coping mechanisms and the influence of positive affect in people who have experienced job loss (Crowley, Hayslip, & Hobdy, 2003). Leader performance has been predicted by hardiness (Bartone, Eid, Johnson, Laberg, & Snook, 2009).

Later discussions of hardiness present the "3Cs" as "resilient attitudes" rather than dispositions (Maddi & Khoshaba, 2005, p. 13) and add "two vital skills of transformational coping and social support" (p. 19) which are described as complementing the resilient attitudes (p. 5). As a result of these revisions, the hardiness approach now aligns well with some of the most important research trends and findings summarized in the previous section. In terms of categorizing the personal characteristics associated with resilient outcomes, the hardiness attitudes and skills also reflect many elements of the core themes that emerged from the literature review mentioned earlier (Cooper et al., 2013).

Based on their research in the field of sport, Clough, Earle, and Sewell (2002) developed a model of "mental toughness," extending the hardiness model to include the notion of confidence (an individual's confidence in his or her own abilities and interpersonal confidence). In a broader work context, mental toughness ratings were found to be higher for people in senior positions, with mental toughness generally increasing with age, suggesting that it can be developed (Marchant et al., 2008). More work needs to be done to establish the generalizability of the "mental toughness" construct outside the domain of sport (Crust, 2008). Nevertheless, together the constructs of mental toughness and hardiness help to demonstrate the relevance of a dynamic, interactive, and developmental view of resilience in the context of organizational performance and developmental interventions.

The resilient person – personality and individual differences

These days, rather than looking for a specific resilience trait (or set of traits), researchers are interested in understanding the complex relationships between many different personality traits and the capacity, process, and outcomes of resilience. The main framework used in these studies has been the influential and widely researched Five-Factor Model (FFM) of personality (Costa & McCrae, 1992), which describes personality in terms of five broad clusters of traits.[1] For example, hardiness has been found to be positively related to the FFM constructs of Extraversion and Openness to Experience, and negatively related to Neuroticism (Parkes & Rendall, 1988; Maddi, 2002).

More broadly, a review of the literature on personality and coping with adversity concluded that personality influences the frequency of exposure to stressors, the type of stressors experienced, and appraisals of stressors (Carver & Connor-Smith, 2010). Reported findings included the following: Neuroticism is associated with perceiving events as highly threatening and coping resources as low; Conscientiousness predicts low stress exposure; Agreeableness is associated with low levels of interpersonal conflict and social stress; Extraversion, Conscientiousness, and Openness to Experience are associated with perceiving events as challenges rather than threats, and with a positive assessment of coping resources.

Interestingly, it appears that an individual's response to stress is not simply a matter of the presence of specific traits, but also of the interaction between traits. For example, someone who scores high on Neuroticism and low on Conscientiousness is more likely than average to experience stress and see events as threatening, while those with low Neuroticism and high Extraversion scores typically respond in a more resilient way (Grant & Langan-Fox, 2006; Vollrath & Torgersen, 2000).

The complex relationships between personality traits and resilience highlight the need to take context into account, as discussed later in this chapter. For example, being well-organized and conscientious can be helpful for managers, as their need for order can be useful in preempting problems and coping with more predictable stressors. However, a manager who favors an unstructured approach and is more open to experience may be more able to respond in a flexible way and generate creative solutions during times of uncertainty and ambiguity (Flint-Taylor, Davda, & Cooper, 2014).

Some studies have included additional psychological constructs alongside FFM personality traits in their investigation of personal resilience. Looking at the way resilient people appeared actively to generate positive emotions when faced with potentially stressful circumstances, Tugade and Fredrickson (2004) suggested that people use a variety of strategies, relating to humor, relaxation, and optimism. Studying reactions to the September 11, 2001, attacks, they found that low levels of Neuroticism, high levels of Extraversion and high levels of Openness to Experience were all associated with resilient outcomes. Self-confidence or self-efficacy has also been identified as core to resilience, negatively correlated with Neuroticism, and positively correlated with Extraversion (Skodol, 2010). Competence (a facet within Conscientiousness) has been shown to be closely associated with self-esteem and internal locus of control (Costa, McCrae, & Dye, 1991).

The characteristic of optimism has also been identified as central to resilience. A resilient person is optimistic and hopeful about the outcome of even difficult situations such as physical illness or the loss of a significant other (Peterson, 2000). Although optimism and pessimism are clearly related, the underlying personality characteristics associated with optimistic and pessimistic thinking are not direct, polar opposites. Introverts who are emotionally stable (low on Neuroticism) may be rather serious and "downbeat" in style, without believing that things will generally turn out badly. Conversely, a "neurotic extravert" may be full of anxiety and become discouraged quite easily, but then bounce back again quickly in response to a positive turn of events.

In summary, it is difficult to overemphasize the extent to which personal resilience is complex and multidimensional, even at the level of personality. As we now know that past experiences, current psychological state, and context are integral to an individual's resilience, it is not surprising that it can be difficult to design a resilience training program to suit everyone.

The resilient person – developmental interventions in an organizational context

The starting point for personal resilience development clearly varies widely from one individual to another, not simply in terms of each person's overall capacity but also in terms of which elements are stronger and which are weaker. So, for example, one person may be particularly good at drawing on social support but inclined to take a pessimistic view when things go wrong, while one of their colleagues neglects their support network when under pressure at work but makes time for exercise however busy they are.

Such individual differences are easily accommodated within a one-to-one coaching approach, which is well suited to helping someone evaluate and increase his or her current resilience capacity. For example, coaching based on a cognitive-behavioral solution-focused approach has been shown to enhance goal attainment, increase resilience and workplace wellbeing, and reduce depression and stress (Grant, Curtayne, & Burton, 2009).

Another proven approach involves a program of workshop sessions and self-managed individual activities, contextualized to a particular work environment, spread over a number of weeks, and using a variety of developmental techniques. These techniques are typically drawn from the treatment of anxiety and depression, and increasingly also from research findings in the field of positive psychology (Proudfoot, Corr, Guest, & Dunn, 2009; Seligman & Fowler, 2011; Waite, 2004). Good results have also been achieved by using an integrated approach to strengthening resilience through selection and development, for example in a call center context (Callaghan & Thompson, 2002). These studies include performance outcomes such as improved sales and retention, in addition to improved wellbeing and personal resilience.

However, few organizations have an appetite for implementing tailored programs that extend over a period of time; the most common format is that of a resilience workshop lasting one day or less. A systematic review of work-based resilience training interventions in the period 2003–2014 found a lack of coherence in design and implementation, and only tentative evidence for an impact on performance and other outcomes beyond individual resilience (Robertson, Cooper, Sarkar, & Curran, 2015). This does not detract from the performance-related outcomes reported in the individual studies cited earlier, but it does emphasize the importance of being prepared to invest in a well-validated design when introducing a resilience development intervention for an organization.

Today, techniques from cognitive-behavioral and positive psychology form the core of most well-validated resilience development interventions. These techniques include disputing pessimistic assumptions, reframing problems, merit finding, avoiding thinking traps, applying strengths-based development, learning new skills, and practicing mindfulness (Cooper et al., 2013). Additional insights and support for such approaches come from the study of behavioral, biological, and situational factors associated with a resilient response to adversity or trauma (Yehuda, Flory, Southwick, & Charney, 2006). The latter approach is particularly helpful in emphasizing the resilience benefits of looking after one's physical condition, facing fears, finding a resilient role model, and developing a robust set of core beliefs and values.

In addition to using one of the two broad approaches described earlier (individual coaching or an extended program of contextualized activities), there are a number of other factors to consider when introducing resilience-building programs. In particular, organizations are often surprised by the negative impact of failing to establish individual and organizational readiness, conditions already proven to be critical for the effective introduction of leadership development programs (Robertson, 2004).

The resilient organization

When it comes to resilience in organizations and communities, the term is used quite specifically by a number of disciplines, including change management, technology, disaster recovery, economics, and sociology, as well as psychology. We have observed that this frequently causes confusion, and is often what lies behind being challenged to explain what one means in referring to resilience in a work context. For our purpose here we focus on the emerging construct of team resilience, which we regard as being absolutely fundamental to building a resilient organization in any context.

As our introductory discussion on resilience and pressure makes clear, to understand what equips a team to respond in a resilient way we need to go beyond the personal resilience of individual team members to study the team as a unit. Research on this is still in its early days, but there is growing interest in extrapolating definitions of resilience from the study of individuals to the study of teams (West, Patera, & Carsten, 2009). The question of team resilience has been explored from various angles, including a systems approach (Edson, 2012), positive psychology (West et al., 2009), and the management of posttraumatic stress (Paton, 2003).

One approach has been to adapt individual resilience measures to suit the team context. For example, one study adapted the PsyCap questionnaire (Luthans, Avolio, Avey, & Norman, 2007) to investigate the predictive relationship between team-level positive psychological capacities (team optimism, team resilience, and team efficacy) on the one hand, and team outcomes including cohesion, cooperation, coordination, conflict, and team satisfaction on the other hand (West et al., 2009). Another study adapted items from various sources to produce a team resilience survey, which was then used to investigate the view that good relationships and constructive interactions among team members are central to team resilience.

Some of the main findings to date include: the value of collective positive emotions for team resilience and performance (Meneghel, Salanova, & Martínez, 2014), four main resilient characteristics of elite sport teams (Morgan, Fletcher, & Sarkar, 2013), and increased team effectiveness in a crisis situation when team members have a similarly positive disposition (Kaplan, LaPort, & Waller, 2013). It is worth noting that the latter finding is quite specific, and that there are also ways in which diversity is likely to benefit team resilience, although these require further investigation. One of the most recent and comprehensive accounts of team resilience to date (Alliger, Cerasoli, Tannenbaum, & Vessey, 2015) describes the three behavioral strategies (minimize, manage, and mend) that resilient teams use to deal with pressures, stressors, and difficult circumstances, and describes four sets of actions that leaders can take to improve team resilience.

Flint-Taylor and Cooper (2017) propose a framework for building team resilience that draws on their research on workplace pressure, personal resilience, and leaders' impact, together with related research in areas such as positive psychology and team effectiveness. Their focus is on what leaders and managers can do to build team resilience, a discussion that complements their detailed review of what can be done to support the development of personal resilience in the organizational context (Cooper et al., 2013). It is our firm belief that, working together, organizations and those who work in them can do much to strengthen resilience at the individual, team, and organizational levels.

Looking ahead

The broad area of team resilience is one that is likely to attract more attention in future, both from researchers and from organizational practitioners. More specifically it is worth highlighting the need for further research on the relationship between team diversity and team resilience. Other topics of increasing interest and importance include the neurobiological approach, the design and validation of resilience assessments, and approaches that do more to factor in the role that context plays in the processes and outcomes of resilience.

Team diversity

Related findings from the wider literature on diversity and team effectiveness suggest a complex relationship between team diversity and team resilience. For example, while culturally homogenous teams may benefit from stronger social integration and good communication, culturally diverse teams often gain an advantage through enhanced creativity and general satisfaction (Stahl, Maznevski, Voigt, & Jonsen, 2010). A diversity of knowledge and skills has a particularly strong effect on a team's ability to innovate (West, Hirst, & Richter, 2004), but it is also generally accepted that diversity of any kind helps to reduce the risk of unhealthy consensus or "group think." Further research designed to look specifically at diversity and team resilience would be very worthwhile.

A neurobiological approach

At the same time as general interest in resilience has increased among academics and practitioners in various fields, there has also been rapid progress in developments within the science of neurobiology. From this has emerged a steadily growing stream of research on the neurobiology and psychobiology of individual resilience (Feder, Nestler, Westphal, & Charney, 2010; Russo, Murrough, Han, Charney, & Nestler, 2012). The focus of much of this research is based on the recognition that there are many ways of strengthening the factors that protect individuals from the negative effects of stress, and that it is useful to study this from multiple perspectives including that of genetic influences on biological processes. This approach is, therefore, consistent with the idea that research and practice should address the need for a greater understanding of the complexity and multidimensional nature of the forces at play in building and sustaining resilience.

Assessing resilience

Unsurprisingly, there appear to be as many different measures of individual resilience as there are theoretical frameworks for describing and researching the topic. Cooper et al. (2013) summarize and discuss the range of measures available, together with conclusions from published reviews of the field (e.g., Windle, Bennett, & Noyes, 2011). Some of these measures are considerably more robust and well-validated than others, and as is not uncommonly the case with psychometric tools there is often a weak relationship between validity and popularity with organizational practitioners. In addition to continued efforts to improve and evaluate existing measures, it is to be hoped that the advances in knowledge described in this chapter will be applied to help develop a new generation of resilience assessments that take proper account of the interaction between a person and their situation, and of the multiple perspectives on resilience as capability, process, and outcome.

When it comes to developing assessments of team resilience, it is very early days, with most approaches to date drawing on existing person or situation measures and extrapolating these to the construct of team resilience. While these methods have their value they also have their limitations, and there is an argument to be made for a more integrated approach that looks at team resilience from different perspectives (Flint-Taylor & Cooper, in press).

Importance of context

As our review of the individual resilience literature makes clear, in looking at what contributes to a resilient person, much time is spent seeking to understand the person and focusing on assessment and development strategies designed to target the individual. The trend is influenced by popular research focused on personality and other individual constructs like hardiness (Kobasa et al., 1982), ego depletion (Baumeister, Bratslavsky, Muraven, & Tice, 1998), mental toughness (Clough et al., 2002), and emotional intelligence (Goleman, 1998).

This approach clearly has its merits and attractions, as such characteristics prove beneficial across a range of situations and personal resilience is rapidly coming to be seen as today's popular life skill. Yet the focus appears somewhat skewed towards the individual end of the person–situation interaction. Less time is spent understanding the person's context and the multitude of factors that contribute to this, thereby affecting the process and outcome aspects of resilience. Unfortunately, this can have negative consequences for individuals and organizations. It is still all too common for both an individual's career and general wellbeing to be undermined by ill-informed assumptions about resilience because the person has been labelled in a particular way without proper acknowledgement of situational influences (Flint-Taylor & Davda, 2015). Someone may, for example, be overlooked for promotion because a brief but difficult episode in their home life has led their boss to label them "lacking in resilience." As trained practitioners, we are not void of blame, since the classic resilience-building technique of encouraging clients to focus on changing how they think about and respond to the situation may unintentionally detract from exploring contextual factors and the extent to which these lie within the client's control.

Context can be explored and understood through a number of lenses: an individual's life as a whole; his or her organization, workplace, team, friendships, and personal relationships. All of this rich information helps to contextualize the assessment and development of resilience to an individual's situation. There are some strands of research that help us to understand the role of context in resilience processes and outcomes. For example, studies of workplace stress have identified the situational or hygiene factors that contribute to creating a stressful work environment (HSE, 2001). Research by Karademas (2006) has looked at the role of social support in self-efficacy and optimism (factors known to contribute to personal resilience), highlighting a productive network of relationships and ultimately a supportive environment as beneficial. Other studies have explored the stress and wellbeing implications of the "fit" between a person and their work environment (Edwards & Rothbard, 1999).

However, just as personal resilience research is too much about the person, the study of environmental factors often appears too far removed from the individual. For example, organizational stress and wellbeing audits are rarely designed to factor in individual differences among employees, although it is quite common to find group-level differences in personality traits known to be associated with effective stress management, wellbeing, and resilience. In other words, these audits and associated research studies risk entirely attributing certain findings to situational factors (workplace stressors), when in fact the results should be explained in terms of a common trend in the interaction between individuals and their situation. Therefore, it is fundamental we focus on the process of interaction between individuals and their work and life situation.

Through consulting with a range of organizations and by conducting specific research with the National Society for the Prevention of Cruelty to Children (NSPCC) in the charity sector (Davda, 2012), we realized that simply taking into account the environment as a whole was not enough to truly contextualize the nature and complexity of resilience in different situations. Contextualizing resilience is similar to calls for Situational Leadership (Graeff, 1997; Hersey, Blanchard, & Natemeyer, 1979). The core concept is that different types of resilience are required in different situations and, therefore, context becomes "king." The implication is that your approach to a challenging situation should be tailored by factoring a deep understanding of that situation in your interventions and approaches.

For example, there are times when confidence and purpose are fundamental to resilience and there are times where overconfidence and a dogmatic, rigid purpose can actually create further stress in you and in others. Equally, there are work situations that require particular behaviors to be magnified or toned up/toned down. We all come to situations with our personality, ability, and other characteristics that underpin our capacity to respond in a resilient way, but then there is an interaction between us and our context. This makes both the building and exercising of resilience very much a process and an outcome rather than an isolated set of characteristics.

Application and conclusion

The authors of this chapter recently conducted an applied research project that incorporated several of the core principles and emerging agenda themes discussed here. Our study involved the design and validation of an integrated resilience assessment and development intervention, taking account of both sides of the person–situation interaction as well as addressing individual and team resilience. The context chosen for the research was that of working for an international development organization and being posted away from one's home country to lead a team working in a conflict-affected region or a similarly difficult environment. An initial inquiry stage was carried out to inform the development of the resilience assessment and development materials and procedures, with a focus on evaluating and improving participants' capacity to respond in a resilient way as well as their ability to strengthen team resilience. Participants undertook a set of online assessments prior to engaging in a blended learning program with a strong emphasis on self-managed learning and peer engagement. The results of this study support the value of the approach for improving resilience at the individual and team levels, and the benefit of extending the approach to other organizational contexts in future.

This is an exciting and productive time for research on resilience in individuals and organizations, with a steady stream of findings emerging to inform the work of practitioners and the resilience-building activities of leaders and managers. To benefit from this, it is essential to establish a clear, shared understanding of what is meant by resilience, and of the many different ways in which it can be strengthened at individual, team and organizational levels.

Note

1 The five factors, or broad clusters of personality traits, are Openness to Experience, Conscientiousness, Extraversion, Agreeableness, and Neuroticism.

References

Alliger, G. M., Cerasoli, C. P., Tannenbaum, S. I., & Vessey, W. B. (2015). Team resilience: How teams flourish under pressure. *Organizational Dynamics*, 44, 176–184.

Bartone, P. T. (1999). Hardiness protects against war-related stress in Army reserve forces. *Consulting Psychology Journal*, 51, 72–82.

Bartone, P. T., Eid, J., Johnson, B. H., Laberg, J. C., & Snook, S. A. (2009). Big five personality factors, hardiness, and social judgment as predictors of leader performance. *Leadership and Organization Development Journal*, 30, 498–521.

Baumeister, R. F., Bratslavsky, E., Muraven, M., & Tice, D. M. (1998). Ego depletion: Is the active self a limited resource? *Journal of Personality and Social Psychology*, 74(5), 1252–1265.

Beasley, M., Thompson, T., & Davidson, J. (2003). Resilience in responses to life stress: The effects of coping style and cognitive hardiness. *Personality and Individual Differences*, 34(1), 77–95.

Callaghan, G., & Thompson, P. (2002). We recruit attitude: The selection and shaping of routine call centre labour. *Journal of Management Studies*, 39(2), 233–254.

Carver, C. S., & Connor-Smith, J. (2010). Personality and coping. *Annual Review of Psychology*, 61, 679–704.

Clough, P., Earle, K., & Sewell, D. (2002). Mental toughness: The concept and its measurement. In: I. Cockerill (ed.), *Solutions in Sport Psychology*. London: Thomson, 32–45.

Cooper, C. L., Flint-Taylor, J., & Pearn, M. (2013). *Building Resilience for Success: A Resource for Managers and Organizations*. Basingstoke: Palgrave Macmillan.

Costa, P. T., & McCrae, R. R. (1992). *Revised NEO Personality Inventory and NEO Five-Factor Inventory Professional Manual*. Odessa: Psychological Assessment Resources.

Costa, P. T., McCrae, R. R., & Dye, D. A. (1991). Facet scales for agreeableness and conscientiousness: A revision of the NEO personality inventory. *Personality and Individual Differences*, 12(9), 887–898.

Crowley, B. J., Hayslip, B., & Hobdy, J. (2003). Psychological hardiness and adjustment to life events in adulthood. *Journal of Adult Development*, 10(4), 237–248.

Crust, L. (2008). A review and conceptual re-examination of mental toughness: Implications for future researchers. *Personality and Individual Differences*, 45(7), 576–583.

Davda, A. (2012). *Moving towards a Resilient Process: A Positive Approach to Understanding and Developing Resilience in the NSPCC*. Berkhamsted: Ashridge Business School.

Edson, M. C. (2012). A complex adaptive systems view of resilience in a project team. *Systems Research and Behavioral Science*, 29, 499–516.

Edwards, J. R., & Rothbard, N. P. (1999). Work and family stress and well-being: An examination of person-environment fit in the work and family domains. *Organizational Behavior and Human Decision Processes*, 77(2), 85–129.

Feder, A., Nestler, E. J., Westphal, M., & Charney, D. S. (2010). Psychobiological mechanisms of resilience to stress. In: J. W. Reich, A. J. Zautra, & J. S. Hall (eds.), *Handbook of Adult Resilience*. New York: The Guilford Press, 35–54.

Flint-Taylor, J., & Cooper, C. L. (2017). Team resilience: Shaping up for the challenges ahead. In: M. F. Crane (ed.), *Managing for Resilience: A Practical Guide to Employee Wellbeing and Organizational Performance*. London: Routledge, 129–149.

Flint-Taylor, J., & Davda, A. (2015). Understanding and developing personal resilience. In: R. J. Burke, K. M. Page, & C. L. Cooper (eds.), *Flourishing in Life, Work and Careers*. Cheltenham: Edward Elgar, 67–82.

Flint-Taylor, J., Davda, A., & Cooper, C. L. (2014). Stable personal attributes and a resilient approach to work and career. *SA Journal of Industrial Psychology*, 40(1), 1137–1147.

Goleman, D. (1998). *Working with Emotional Intelligence*. Bloomsbury: London.

Graeff, C. L. (1997). Evolution of situational leadership theory: A critical review. *The Leadership Quarterly*, 8(2), 153–170.

Grant, A. M., Curtayne, L., & Burton, G. (2009). Executive coaching enhances goal attainment, resilience and workplace well-being: A randomised controlled study. *Journal of Positive Psychology*, 4(5), 396–407.

Grant, S., & Langan-Fox, J. (2006). Occupational stress, coping and strain: The combined/interactive effect of the Big Five traits. *Personality and Individual Differences*, 41, 719–732.

Haglund, M. E. M., Nestadt, P. S., Cooper, N. S., Southwick, S. M., & Charney, D. S. (2007). Psychobiological mechanisms of resilience: Relevance to prevention and treatment of stress-related psychopathology. *Development and Psychopathology*, 19, 889–920.

Hersey, P., Blanchard, K. H., & Natemeyer, W. E. (1979). Situational leadership, perception, and the impact of power. *Group & Organization Management*, 4(4), 418–428.

Howard, F. (2008). Managing stress or enhancing wellbeing? Positive psychology's contributions to clinical supervision. *Australian Psychologist*, 43, 105–113.

HSE. (2001). *Tackling Work-Related Stress: A Managers' Guide to Improving and Maintaining Employee Health and Well-Being*. Sudbury: HSE Books.

Kaplan, S., LaPort, K., & Waller, M. J. (2013). The role of positive affectivity in team effectiveness during crises. *Journal of Organizational Behavior*, 34, 473–491.

Karademas, E. C. (2006). Self-efficacy, social support and well-being: The mediating role of optimism. *Personality and Individual Differences*, 40(6), 1281–1290.

Kobasa, S. C., Maddi, S. R., & Khan, S. (1982). Hardiness and health: A prospective study. *Journal of Personality and Social Psychology*, 42, 168–177.

Khoshaba, D. M., & Maddi, S. R. (1999). Early experiences in hardiness development. *Consulting Psychology: Practice and Research*, 51, 106–116.

Lightsey, O. R. (2006). Resilience, meaning, and well-being. *The Counseling Psychologist*, 34, 96.

Luthans, F., Avolio, B. J., Avey, J. B., & Norman, S. M. (2007). Positive psychological capital: Measurement and relationship with performance and satisfaction. *Personnel Psychology*, 60, 541–572.

Luthans, F., Norman, S. M., Avolio, B. J., & Avey, J. B. (2008). Supportive climate and organizational success: The mediating role of psychological capital. *Journal of Organizational Behavior*, 29, 219–238.

Maddi, S. R. (2002). The story of hardiness: Twenty years of theorizing, research and practice. *Consulting Psychology Journal; Research and Practice*, 54, 175–185.

Maddi, S. R., & Khoshaba, D. M. (2005). *Resilience at Work: How to Succeed No Matter What Life Throws at You*. New York: AMACOM.

Marchant, D. C., Polman, R. C. J., Clough, P., Jackson, J. G., Levy, A. R., & Nicholls, A. R. (2008). Mental toughness: Managerial and age differences. *Journal of Managerial Psychology*, 24, 428–437.

Masten, A. S. (2001). Ordinary magic: Resilience processes in development. *American Psychologist*, 56, 227–238.

Masten, A., Best, K., & Garmezy, N. (1990). Resilience and development: Contributions from the study of children who overcome adversity. *Development and Psychopathology*, 2, 425–444.

Masten, A. S., & Narayan, A. J. (2012). Child development in the context of disaster, war and terrorism: Pathways of risk and resilience. *Annual Review of Psychology*, 63, 227–257.

Masten, A. S., & Wright, M. O. (2010). Resilience over the lifespan: Developmental perspectives on resistance, recovery, and transformation. In: J. W. Reich, A. J. Zautra, & J. S. Hall (eds.), *Handbook of Adult Resilience*. New York: The Guilford Press, 213–237.

Meneghel, I., Salanova, M., & Martínez, I. M. (2014). Feeling good makes us stronger: How team resilience mediates the effect of positive emotions on team performance. *Journal of Happiness Studies*, 17(1), 239–255.

Morgan, P.B.C., Fletcher, D., & Sarkar, M. (2013). Defining and characterizing team resilience in elite sport. *Psychology of Sport and Exercise*, 14(4), 549–559.

Neenan, M. (2009). *Developing Resilience: A Cognitive-Behavioural Approach*. Hove: Routledge.

Parkes, K., & Rendall, D. (1988). The hardy personality and its relationship to extraversion and neuroticism. *Personality and Individual Differences*, 9, 785–790.

Paton, D. (2003). Stress in disaster response: A risk management approach. *Disaster Prevention and Management: An International Journal*, 12, 203–209.

Peterson, C. (2000). The future of optimism. *American Psychologist*, 55(1), 44–55.

Peterson, C., & Seligman, M. E. P. (2004). *Character Strengths and Virtues*. New York: Oxford University Press.

Podsakoff, N. P., LePine, J. P., & LePine, M. A. (2007). Differential challenge stressor–hindrance stressor relationships with job attitudes, turnover intentions, turnover, and withdrawal behavior: A meta-analysis. *Journal of Applied Psychology*, 92, 438–454.

Proudfoot, J. G., Corr, P. J., Guest, D. E., & Dunn, G. (2009). Cognitive-behavioural training to change attributional style improves employee well-being, job satisfaction, productivity, and turnover. *Personality and Individual Differences*, 46, 147–153.

Reich, J. W., Zautra, A. J., & Hall, J. S. (eds.). (2010). *Handbook of Adult Resilience*. New York: The Guildford Press.

Robertson, I. T. (2004). *World-Class Leadership Development – A Survey of Practices in Leading Organizations*. London: Cabinet Office.

Robertson, I., & Cooper, C. (2011). *Well-Being at Work*. London: Palgrave Macmillan.

Robertson, I. T., Cooper, C. L., Sarkar, M., & Curran, T. (2015). Resilience training in the workplace from 2003 to 2014: A systematic review. *Journal of Occupational and Organisational Psychology*, 88, 533–562.

Russo, S. J., Murrough, J. W., Han, M., Charney, D. S., & Nestler, E. J. (2012). Neurobiology of resilience. *Nature Neuroscience*, 15, 1475–1484.

Rutter, M. (2007). Resilience, competence and coping. *Child Abuse and Neglect*, 31, 205–209.

Seligman, M. E. P., & Fowler, R. D. (2011). Comprehensive soldier fitness and the future of psychology. *American Psychologist*, 66(1), 82–86.

Skodol, A. E. (2010). The resilient personality. In: J. W. Reich, A. J. Zautra, & J. S. Hall (eds.), *Handbook of Adult Resilience*. New York: The Guildford Press, 112–125.

Snyder, C. R., & Lopez, S. J. (eds.). (2009). *Oxford Handbook of Positive Psychology*. Oxford: Oxford University Press.

Southwick, S. M., & Charney, D. S. (2012). *Resilience: The Science of Mastering Life's Greatest Challenges*. Cambridge: Cambridge University Press.

Stahl, G., Maznevski, M., Voigt, A., & Jonsen, K. (2010). Unraveling the effects of cultural diversity in teams: A meta-analysis of research on multicultural work groups. *Journal of International Business Studies*, 41(4), 690–709.

Tugade, M. M., & Fredrickson, B. L. (2004). Resilient individuals use positive emotions to bounce back from negative emotional experiences. *Journal of Personality and Social Psychology*, 86(2), 320–333.

Vollrath, M., & Torgersen, S. (2000). Personality types and coping. *Personality and Individual Differences*, 29(2), 367–378.

Waite, P. J. (2004). Determining the efficacy of resilience training in the work site. *Journal of Allied Health*, 33, 178–183.

West, B. J., Patera, J. L., & Carsten, M. K. (2009). *Team Level Positivity: Investigating Positive Psychological Capacities and Team Level Outcomes*. Management Department Faculty Publications (Paper 21). Lincoln: University of Nebraska.

West, M. A., Hirst, G., & Richter, A. (2004). Twelve steps to heaven: Successfully managing change through developing innovative teams. *European Journal of Work and Organizational Psychology*, 13(2), 269–299.

Windle, G., Bennett, K. M., & Noyes, J. (2011). A methodological review of resilience measurement scales. *Health and Quality of Life Outcomes*, 9(1), 1.

Yehuda, R., Flory, J. D., Southwick, S., & Charney, D. S. (2006). Developing an agenda for translational studies of resilience and vulnerability following trauma exposure. *Annals of the N.Y. Academy of Science*, 1071, 379–396.

Differentiating challenge, hindrance, and threat in the stress process

Ben J. Searle and Michelle R. Tuckey

Introduction

Chris, Harper, and Taylor are all sales staff at a software company. They all work long hours in order to reach their monthly sales targets. Today, their new boss, Sam, announces that they need to prepare for a formal performance review. This announcement has a big impact on all three salespeople, but each one is affected in a different way.

Taylor's reaction is to worry. The company has been struggling recently due to a new competitor in their market, and there's some risk that staff will be laid off to improve financial performance. As Sam is new to the company, Taylor is concerned that past employee achievements may be ignored. Having recently lost a big client, Taylor fears this may become the focus of the review. As a result, Taylor finds it more and more difficult to concentrate as the day of the review approaches, making it harder and harder to perform well.

Chris's reaction is very different. The company's recent difficulties have contributed to some staff departures, which have in turn created some new opportunities for promotion. Chris sees this performance review as an opportunity to highlight personal strengths that can help the company achieve its goals, and to then discuss how to achieve a promotion. Reflecting on recent sales performance, Chris focuses on successes and this contributes to a sense of confidence that the performance review will go well. This confidence motivates Chis to perform well in the days leading up to the review.

Chris's and Taylor's different reactions to the same situation reflect two sides to the stress process. Taylor's reaction is characterized by an interpretation (or "appraisal") of the situation as a *threat*, the perceived risk of personal harm and loss. Threat appraisals influence Taylor's emotion (largely negative), cognition (preoccupation with risks, negative events and potential negative outcomes) and behavior. Chris's reaction, by contrast, is characterized by *challenge* appraisal, the perception of opportunities for personal gain or personal growth. This focus on the situation's opportunities has implications for Chris's emotion (largely positive), cognition (focus on positive events and outcomes), and behavior.

Although threat and challenge are two important ways that the situation can be appraised, they are not the only ways that people can interpret a high-stakes situation. Harper's response to news of the performance review is different again: frustration. "What a stupid waste of time!" thinks

Harper, "A performance review, right when we're trying to maximize our sales to keep this company in business. This is such a nuisance." Harper delays preparation for the review until the last minute, and goes into the review feeling annoyed.

Harper has interpreted the situation in a qualitatively different way from the responses of Chris or Taylor. Unlike Taylor, Harper is not concerned about the personal risks of being reviewed, although these employees are alike in that their perception of the event (the review) is quite negative. Unlike Chris, Harper does not consider personal opportunities presented by the performance review, although Chris and Harper are both concerned with supporting the company's goals. Harper has appraised the review as a *hindrance*, perceiving it to be an obstruction to the accomplishment of personally relevant goals.

In this chapter, we outline the conceptual basis for differentiating the stress process into the three components of challenge, hindrance, and threat. We identify the distinguishing characteristics of these three components, identify typical job demands associated with each, and present research that identifies different consequences of challenges, hindrances, and threats.

Multidimensional models of work stressors

The key proposition underpinning job characteristics models of occupational stress is that two core aspects of the job – known as job demands and job resources – are the primary determinants of employee psychological (i.e., cognitive and emotional) health and wellbeing. Broadly speaking, job demands are aspects of the work and work environment that require sustained effort, while job resources help workers to reduce job demands, attain goals, and/or promote learning and skill development (see de Jonge & Dormann, 2003).

The most well-known model of this type is Karasek's (1979) Job Strain model, also known as the Job Demands–Control (JD-C) model, which outlines the main and additive effects of two psychosocial job attributes: psychological job demands (i.e., aspects of the work that present potential sources of psychological stress) and job decision latitude (i.e., autonomy to make decisions and discretion to utilize skills in order to manage job demands). Working in a job where psychological demands are high but decision latitude is low is considered to be "high strain" because there is limited possibility for workers to take decisive actions and/or utilize their skills to manage the stressors they face. Jobs that are high on both dimensions are classified as "active," considered to be challenging and motivating and support employees to learn new behavior patterns, whereas those that are low on both are classified as "passive" as they lack stimulation and possibilities for control. Finally, "low strain" jobs are those low on psychological demands in combination with high decision latitude. Later, lack of social support was included as an additional risk factor, exacerbating the negative effects of high strain jobs (Karasek, Triantis, & Chaudhry, 1982).

Another influential theory has been Siegrist's Effort–Reward Imbalance (ERI) model (Siegrist, 1996, 1998). Rather than the task profile, this model considers the reciprocity between work-related efforts and rewards. According to the theory, the degree to which the efforts injected into work are rewarded by valued, socially defined rewards (such as money, esteem, job security, and career prospects) influences health and wellbeing. Jobs wherein workers experience a lack of reciprocity between costs (i.e., efforts) and gains (i.e., rewards) create strain, which is exacerbated for "overcommitted" employees (i.e., those who feel excessive work-related commitment together with a high need for approval).

Both of these theories have proved valuable, being easy to understand while also highlighting key working conditions that influence work-related health and wellbeing, with clear implications for workplace interventions. However, simplifying job characteristics into either demands or effort on the one hand, and either control or rewards on the other hand, fails to capture the complexity of occupational stress or the variety of potential stress prevention and intervention points. For many years, in the absence of an explicit theoretical model, research into other types of job demands and job resources was somewhat neglected. The more recent Job Demands–Resources (JD-R) model (Bakker & Demerouti, 2007; Demerouti, Bakker, Nachreiner, & Schaufeli, 2001) builds on the JDC and ERI models to address this concern.

The JD-R model predicts that in terms of employee wellbeing, job demands are harmful and job resources are helpful. By highlighting job demands and job resources as core factors in the stress process, and by encompassing generic processes linking demand and resources to health and wellbeing, the JD-R model recognizes that occupations have unique risk and protective factors representing the two broader categories (Bakker & Demerouti, 2007). According to the model, in a process of *health impairment*, energy is depleted over time in response to excessive or prolonged demands, leading to a range of psychological and physiological costs (Bakker, Demerouti, & Schaufeli, 2003). By contrast, job resources are the core ingredients of the *motivational* process that fosters work engagement, wherein resources stimulate personal growth, learning, and development both intrinsically, by meeting basic psychological needs (e.g., autonomy, relatedness, and competence; see Ryan & Deci, 2000), and extrinsically, by enabling the completion of work goals (Bakker, Demerouti, Taris, Schaufeli, & Schreurs, 2003; Demerouti et al., 2001).

Importantly, the JD-R model elaborated on former job design models by incorporating a much wider variety of potentially motivating work resources (Bakker & Demerouti, 2007): in addition to autonomy, skill utilization, and rewards, the model also embraced such job characteristics as social support and coworker support (which were later additions to the JDC model; Karasek et al., 1982) as well as performance feedback, task identity, and task significance (which were part of the Job Characteristics model, a theory of task-based motivation by Hackman & Oldham, 1975). It should also be recognized that compared to earlier models, it also incorporated a wider range of job demands (Bakker & Demerouti, 2007), as shown in Figure 3.1. These extended from the earlier focus on workload (Karasek, 1979) to a concept of demands that also included broader conceptualizations of task demands (e.g., task complexity and change), as well as social and emotional demands (e.g., bullying/harassment), and even organizational and environmental factors (e.g., noise and other distractions).

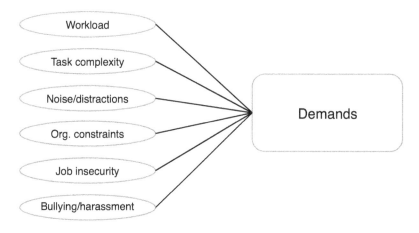

Figure 3.1   Three models categorizing job demands: the JD-R model

Different types of job demands: challenges and hindrances

Although distinctive risk and resilience factors are recognized with the JD-R model, the original model did not distinguish among qualitatively different types of job demands. Rather, all demands were considered potentially harmful, with the potential to deplete energy and incur psychological costs with ongoing exposure (Demerouti et al., 2001). Yet job demands can have positive effects, for instance when they allow workers to utilize and develop their abilities (de Jonge & Dormann, 2003). Recognizing the idea that not all job demands have the same types of effects, Cavanaugh, Boswell, Roehling, and Boudreau (2000) identified two distinct types of stress in organizational settings: challenge stress and hindrance stress. Challenge stress involves "work-related demands or circumstances that, although potentially stressful, have associated potential gains for individuals," whereas hindrance stress arises from "work-related demands or circumstances that tend to constrain or interfere with an individual's work achievement" (Cavanaugh et al., 2000, p. 68). Cavanaugh and colleagues used this approach to categorize job demands as either challenges or hindrances, as shown in Figure 3.2.

While Cavanaugh's initial approach considered the stress caused by challenging demands compared to the stress caused by hindrance demands (Cavanaugh et al., 2000), the Challenge-Hindrance framework quickly became a popular way to aggregate measures of perceived job demands into two clusters. Meta-analytic evidence supports this approach. While challenge job demands are positively associated with exhaustion, they are also positively related to job satisfaction, organizational commitment (Podsakoff, LePine, & LePine, 2007), and performance (LePine, Podsakoff, & LePine, 2005), and negatively related to turnover intentions and behavior (Podsakoff et al., 2007). The meta-analyses show the opposite pattern of relationships for hindrance demands, except that hindrances have a greater negative effect on exhaustion than do challenges.

Recognizing the inconsistent results concerning the relationship between job demands and work engagement, Crawford, LePine, and Rich (2010) integrated the Challenge-Hindrance distinction to advance the JD-R model. They proposed that hindrance demands would be negatively related to engagement, because the frustration experienced when trying to overcome blockages should lead to withdrawal of energy and active coping efforts. Conversely, they expected challenge demands to have a positive relationship with work engagement because the associated positive emotions and active coping behaviors should stimulate greater investment of

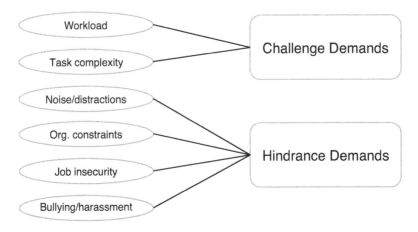

Figure 3.2 Three models categorizing job demands: the Challenge-Hindrance framework

the self and increased job-related effort in response to such demands. The results of their meta-analysis supported these predictions, showing in addition that both types of demands had a positive relationship with burnout. Challenge job demands had a net positive effect, however, when their positive influence on work engagement was considered. On the whole, the meta-analysis showed that differentiating between challenge demands and hindrance demands improved the overall model fit and consistency of the model, compared to the simpler differentiation of job characteristics into demands versus resources. This finding supported the notion that even if demands and resources influence different psychological systems (as indicated by the JD-R model), different types of demands may also have their impacts via different systems.

Yet if lots of job characteristics can collectively be described as demands because they require sustained effort (Demerouti et al., 2001), and if these job demands typically lead to exhaustion, then why should we see differences in their effects? To answer this question, we need to look at the stress process more closely, and consider the role of appraisal.

Appraisal and the stress process

The evolutionary advantages of the stress process were best popularized by Selye (1950). His model, the General Adaptation Syndrome, describes stress in terms of a system whereby an animal facing a threat is more likely to survive if the threat stimulus triggers an adaptive response: adrenaline released into the bloodstream causing the reallocation of physiological resources to facilitate survival behaviors (commonly known as the "fight or flight response"). Selye commented on how this process survives in modern humans, and is experienced in the presence of stimuli that are not actually life threatening, precisely because the process provides an animal with a better chance of survival if it can be initiated in response to a broad range of possible threats.

For many years, Selye's central message was on the downside of the stress response in humans (Szabo, Tache, & Somogyi, 2012). Much of Selye's research preceding and following the description of the General Adaptation Syndrome model demonstrated that long-term exposure to threats, provoking repeated or continuous activation of (what became known as) the sympathetic nervous system, can cause significant harm. However, many years after his seminal works on stress and its negative consequences, Selye was influenced by emerging work by other scholars such as Levi (1971) who had identified that even though the experience of stress is often negative, it was also true in some cases that the experience of stress is positive. This led Selye (1974) to differentiate the physiological stress response into two subjective experiences: "distress" (negative) versus "eustress" (positive).

But what determines whether a situation will provoke eustress or distress? This was not something that could be explained with Selye's original model, which focused on physiological phenomena; more psychological explanations were required. The most influential of these was Lazarus and Folkman's (1984) Transactional model. According to this model, we constantly process stimuli in our environment, with particular attention to how situations and events are likely to affect us personally. If the personal stakes seem high, there is a great deal of difference between expecting the situation to result in harm or loss (threat appraisal), and expecting it to result in growth or gain (challenge appraisal). This initial judgment of whether the situation contains something bad (or good), known as primary appraisal, can happen so fast it can be considered preconscious (e.g., Bradley, Mogg, & Lee, 1997) and can defy conscious awareness. Even though the appraisal process can be quick, it can have profound implications.

As predicted by Lazarus and Folkman (1984), and as demonstrated in empirical studies, whether a situation is appraised positively or negatively can influence emotions, cognitions, and behaviors, especially those cognitions and behaviors associated with coping (e.g., Folkman & Lazarus, 1985;

McCrae, 1984; Searle & Auton, 2015). Lazarus and Folkman (1984) argued that different appraisals stimulated different emotional states, whereas Lazarus (1991) argued that appraisals affected the goals of coping efforts (e.g., making the most of an opportunity versus minimizing risk of harm). This means that two people exposed to the same situation can both experience an intense stress response, but their feelings, thoughts, and actions may differ substantially if they have appraised the situation differently.

The Challenge-Hindrance-Threat model

Despite challenge and threat being the two core types of primary stress appraisal in Lazarus and Folkman's (1984) Transactional model, theory, and methods within the field of occupational stress research have not captured threat when differentiating job demands, instead applying the categories of challenge and hindrance (Cavanaugh et al., 2000). Some researchers have mapped these two categories onto the primary appraisals from the Transactional model, explicitly equating hindrance with threat (e.g., Lepine et al., 2005, pp. 765, 767; van den Broeck, de Cuyper, de Witte, & Vansteenkiste, 2010, pp. 738, 741; Webster, Beehr, & Love, 2011, p. 506). However, although the notion of hindrances captures some of the "negative" aspects of work-related demands, there is a strong case for treating threats as a distinct from hindrances.

To begin with, threat and hindrance are defined differently. Threats are defined in terms of anticipated personal harm or loss (i.e., expecting something bad to happen; Lazarus & Folkman, 1984). Hindrances are defined in terms of obstacles to achievement (i.e., expecting something good *not* to happen, or at least to be delayed or made more difficult to obtain; Cavanaugh et al., 2000). We do not believe that these concepts are equivalent.

Although hindrances were not mentioned in the original work on the Transactional model, Lazarus later reconsidered this position, stating "Frustration is often treated as an emotion, but like challenge and threat, I regard it as an appraisal" (1991, p. 827). Reflecting on this view of frustration as a third form of primary appraisal (distinct from challenge or threat), and considering how frustration (defined in the Oxford Dictionaries as "the prevention of the progress, success, or fulfilment of something,") has long been linked to obstacles to self-relevant goals (e.g., Dollard, Doob, Miller, Mowrer, & Sears, 1939), we came to equate frustration with hindrance appraisal (Tuckey, Searle, Boyd, Winefield, & Winefield, 2015).

This distinction can be applied within models that categorize job demands. We have argued that the existing construct of *hindrance demands*, those that are commonly appraised as interfering with the achievement of personal or professional goals (Cavanaugh et al., 2000), can be differentiated from *threat demands,* "work-related demands or circumstances that tend to be directly associated with personal harm or loss" (Tuckey et al., 2015, p. 133), as shown in Figure 3.3. Threat demands, such as workplace bullying or job insecurity, can involve undermining basic psychological needs or thwarting professional self-identity. Threat demands may have more serious consequences than hindrance demands, because anticipated negative personal impact is more closely aligned with the evolutionary bases for stress than is anticipated delays to goal accomplishment.

To capture the potential for anticipated harm or loss to the self (threats) that can arise from certain types of job demands, as distinct from obstacles to (hindrance) and opportunities for (challenges) goal attainment, we recently proposed the Challenge-Hindrance-Threat model of occupational stress (Tuckey et al., 2015). Our conceptual framing and empirical work demonstrated that threat job demands and threat appraisal can be distinguished from challenge and hindrance job demands and appraisals, and that each type of demand and appraisal plays a unique role in predicting employee psychological health and wellbeing.

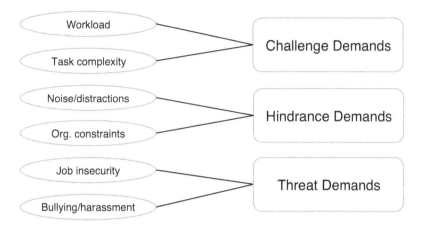

Figure 3.3 Three models categorizing job demands: the Challenge-Hindrance-Threat model

A study of stressors

The first study we conducted (Tuckey et al., 2015, Study 1) explored job demands in the retail industry considered threatening, hindering, or challenging by way of their commonly held meanings. We hypothesized that threat job demands would be positively associated with psychological distress given the inherent negative expectations for future outcomes, the associated spectrum of negative emotions (see Lazarus & Folkman, 1984), and the threat to maintaining a positive self-image and feeling positively regarded by others (see Semmer, McGrath, & Beehr, 2005). Exhaustion should also arise, as workers invest more and more energy to avoid the initial threat and manage the negative emotions that follow (i.e., a positive relationship between threat demands and exhaustion). Finally, we expected threat job demands to lead to disengagement from work, evidenced by a negative association with dedication to work, as workers attempt to manage the negative emotions and consequences rather than the demand itself. Based on findings and reasoning similar to that discussed earlier, we expected hindrance job demands to be associated with greater levels of exhaustion and distress, and lower levels of work dedication. Finally, we anticipated challenge job demands to be negatively related to psychological distress, positively related to exhaustion, and positively related to work dedication.

We tested the hypotheses using a two-wave survey design, with data from 609 retail workers, 220 of whom responded six months later. Drawing on pilot interview data, we operationalized threat job demands as extreme customer-related social stressors, emotional demands, and role conflict; hindrance job demands as role ambiguity; and challenge job demands in terms of task complexity and pressure. A confirmatory factor analysis provided support for the proposed three-dimensional Challenge-Hindrance-Threat representation of job demands, as compared with a series of alternative models (e.g., where the covariance of hindrances and threats was constrained to equal 1). Results of the structural equation modelling were consistent with our hypotheses, which predicted threat job demands to be both distressing and exhausting, as well as having the potential to undermine dedication to work. We also found that even though challenge demands are mildly exhausting, when considered simultaneously with threats and hindrances they may have the potential to reduce distress and are associated with increased dedication. There were mixed results regarding hindrances, indicating that they may not be associated with exhaustion and distress when the effect of threat job demands is accounted for. This does not mean that hindrance demands are without negative consequences; rather, it shows that for the outcomes we examined, such consequences were negligible relative to the powerful effects of threat stressors. Overall, this study indicates that threat job demands are conceptually and empirically distinct from challenges and hindrances, and suggests that they have a unique influence on employee health and wellbeing outcomes.

A study of appraisals

Another study we conducted (Tuckey et al., 2015, Study 2) explored threats, hindrances, and challenges by way of individual appraisals of daily work experiences. This approach differed from the stressor study described in the last section by addressing a number of problems with stressor-categorization research, including:

1   Placing demands into categories (i.e., challenges, hindrances, or threats), even if done following consultation with representatives of an identifiable occupational group, assumes that everyone within that group appraises a given demand in the same way. Yet a key feature of the Transactional model is that different people can and do appraise the same situation differently. By measuring appraisals directly, we allow for a demand to be associated with different appraisals by different people.
2   Placing demands into categories, while intuitive, assumes that each demand can fit into only one category. Yet following Lazarus and Folkman's (1984) approach to appraisal, it would be possible for an event or situation to be appraised simultaneously as both challenging and threatening. By measuring appraisals directly, we allow for a demand to be associated with multiple appraisals (or none).
3   Placing demands into categories, and then looking at the effects of demand categories on wellbeing, assumes that differential effects on wellbeing are due to the appraisals underlying each category. Yet there may be other factors driving effects of stressor categories on wellbeing, such as physical impacts or associated resource availability, that do not have their effects via an appraisal mechanism. By measuring appraisals directly, we can determine the extent to which effects of demands on wellbeing are mediated by appraisals.

Some demands, such as workload or time pressure, can be appraised in a variety of ways: as challenging, as hindering, or as both challenging and hindering (e.g., Searle & Auton, 2015; Webster et al., 2011). Searle and Auton (2015) showed that time pressure (typically considered a prototypical challenge demand; Widmer, Semmer, Kaelin, Jacobshagen, & Meier, 2012) influences mood and coping behavior differently depending on whether it is appraised as a challenge (which led to enthusiasm and problem-focused coping) or a hindrance (which led to anger and venting). This pattern indicates that stress appraisal plays a critical role where there is scope for multiple interpretations of a demand's potential impact.

However, other demands are predominantly appraised in only one way (e.g., responsibility as a challenge, not a hindrance; Webster et al., 2011). Does this mean that in such situations, individual appraisals are less important? Possibly not, since there is still room for individuals to vary in the extent to which they see the demand as challenging, hindering or threatening.

In Study 2 reported by Tuckey et al. (2015), we chose to investigate employees' appraisals of some prototypical challenge, hindrance, and threat demands, to determine the role of appraisal in the effects of those demands on wellbeing states. We hypothesized that skill demands would be primarily appraised as a challenge, since the pressure to apply multiple skills at work not only helps to maintain those skills, it can also enhance them, leading to a sense of achievement and growth. We expected organizational constraints (e.g., bureaucratic requirements or procedural barriers; Peters & O'Connor, 1980) to be primarily appraised as a hindrance, since they are typically expressed as obstacles to tasks and goals. We also expected role conflict (e.g., managing different expectations from different stakeholders) to be primarily appraised as a threat, since it can impact one's sense of personal identity, it can involve higher levels of personal evaluation and criticism, and it is commonly associated with high levels of anxiety (Hamner & Tosi, 1974).

Regarding appraisals, we sought to demonstrate that appraisals of hindrance and threat, as well as challenge, could be differentiated empirically. We also expected that challenge appraisals would be associated with more positive wellbeing states, whereas hindrance and threat appraisals would be associated with more negative wellbeing states.

We tested the hypotheses using an experiential survey, also known as a diary study, a multilevel approach that allowed us to examine the changeable aspects of work demands, stress appraisals, and wellbeing states within-participants rather than just between-participants. This involved 207 student-sourced employees (of 268 who completed the first survey) completing an online survey daily for three days. Instead of assessing how each stressor was appraised (although we have done that in other research, e.g., Searle & Auton, 2015), this study simply asked participants to evaluate each day's overall experiences in terms of challenge, hindrance, and threat. In this way, we could see how day-to-day levels of perceived demands were associated with day-to-day levels of each appraisal type. Appraisals were measured using the scales of challenge and hindrance appraisal developed by Searle and Auton (2015), while threat appraisals were measured using a scale described by Feldman, Cohen, Hamrick, and Lepore (2004).

Multilevel confirmatory factor analysis not only demonstrated that appraisals of challenge, hindrance, and threat could be differentiated from one another, but also showed that this three-factor model of appraisal measurement was superior to a two-factor model that combined hindrances with threats. This showed that our appraisal measure was capable of differentiating between seeing one's daily work experiences as threatening and seeing those experiences as hindering one's achievements.

Analyzing the multilevel data via structural equation modeling revealed that although there was variation both between- and within-participants, each of the three demands studied was associated with only one form of stress appraisal: skill demands with challenge appraisal, organizational constraints with hindrance appraisal, and role conflict with threat appraisal, just as predicted. This pattern suggests that some demands are consistently associated with a particular form of stress appraisal, but nevertheless there are some differences in how demands impact on appraisal of the day's work experiences, both between people and within people from one day to the next.

Moving on, our results showed that our participants experienced different wellbeing states depending on how they appraised the day's work experiences. Those with greater challenge appraisal reported higher levels of activated positive affect (high-intensity positive moods such as enthusiasm and excitement). Those with greater hindrance appraisal reported higher levels of fatigue. Those with greater threat appraisal reported higher levels of anger and anxiety. In this way, the results showed that wellbeing outcomes can also be differentiated on the basis of daily stress appraisals.

Finally, results showed that the effect of skill demands on activated positive affect was largely mediated by challenge appraisal, and that the effect of role conflict on anger was partially mediated by threat appraisal. These results highlight why stress appraisals are a sound basis for categorizing demands, but they also demonstrate that categorization alone may be insufficient to capture the mechanisms underlying effects of demands on wellbeing. Much seems to depend on the way that individuals appraise their situations. However, there are many practical advantages of relatively simple models of job design; in the absence of evidence on individual appraisals, we believe that there is great merit in differentiating work demands into challenges, hindrances, and threats.

Practical implications

It is clear from the body of work on challenges, hindrances, and more recently threats, that differentiating types of job demands can have important implications for our collective understanding of the occupational stress process in terms of why, how, and which stressors and appraisals contribute to positive and negative health and wellbeing outcomes. In practice, understanding the nature and effects of different types of job demands and stress appraisals is crucial to ensure that organizational prevention efforts are grounded in evidence and focused in the right direction, and to reveal intervention strategies wherein employees can be active agents in maintaining their wellbeing.

Clearly, not all demands are equal. Challenge demands appear to have a positive impact on employees, and it is tempting to approach morale problems by increasing challenges through stretch goals and challenging assignments. However, there are some suggestions that the benefits of challenge demands may be limited at very high levels of challenge, or when experienced alongside high levels of hindrance demands. This means that managers need to be careful, as it cannot be assumed that increasing challenge demands will automatically improve employee wellbeing.

Rather, based on our research, we recommend that threats should be the focal point for managing risks associated occupational health and wellbeing. In saying this, we do not mean to suggest that hindrances should be ignored. In an ideal world, managers should seek to eliminate, substantially reduce, or otherwise find ways to mitigate both threat demands and hindrance demands, to provide employees with the best environment for tackling challenges. However, our evidence to date suggests that of the three types of demands, threats may be the most serious in terms of their effects, and should therefore be considered the highest priority for investigation and action.

There are many ways that action could be taken towards management of threat demands. The provision of adequate staffing and appropriate training could go a long way towards minimizing customer-related social stressors and emotional demands, for example. Training would also be useful to prevent or minimize role conflict, as would the implantation of effective work systems and team structures to support the clear and smooth flow of information. Recognition should be given to the costs of "flexible" approaches to workforce planning, as these can involve lower levels of job security.

Not all of the steps towards effective stress management need to be top-down. Employees could also be empowered to become active agents in the management of their threats, hindrances, and challenges. Job crafting is increasingly recognized as a powerful technique that employees can and do use to change the way their work is performed (Wrzesniewski & Dutton, 2001). It involves employees enacting their job role in unique ways, modifying which tasks they perform, which relationships they maintain, and which interpretation they place on their purpose, to achieve a more satisfying, and meaningful experience at work. Attention has recently been given to differentiating job crafting activities that increase challenges from those that reduce hindrances (e.g., Tims, Bakker, & Derks, 2012). It may also be possible for employees to adapt their jobs, or themselves, to reduce anticipated threats, as may be the case where employees in more precarious roles take on additional responsibilities that affect the long-term sustainability of their organization.

However, another reason for organizations to be particularly proactive in managing threat demands is that threats tend to provoke avoidance behaviors (e.g., King & Gardner, 2006). This means that employees may be less willing or able to craft their own roles in the face of threats. Besides, many of the threat demands we have identified (e.g., job insecurity or workplace bullying) may involve forces outside an employee's control. We believe that organizations have a responsibility (in many countries, this is actually a *legal* responsibility) to anticipate threats to employees' physical or psychological wellbeing, and to take appropriate action to eliminate or otherwise manage those threats.

Conclusion

We have emphasized the key differences between hindrances and threats, in terms of their defining qualities, the types of demands that would typically yield threat appraisals as distinct from demands that would typically yield hindrance appraisals, and the more powerful wellbeing consequences of threats as opposed to hindrances. However, we recognize that some demands may be seen as both threats and hindrances (and even as challenges too!), and that many of our recommendations around threats and hindrances would be similar. This does not, in our view, render the distinction meaningless, just as the similarities between anxiety and anger (both intense states of negative affect) do not mean that these are functionally equivalent emotions. Research on the distinction between hindrances and threats is at a very early stage, but is already showing intriguing insights in terms of wellbeing, motivation, and behavior. We encourage researchers and practitioners to give due consideration to this as they investigate and take action in the field of occupational stress.

References

Bakker, A. B., & Demerouti, E. (2007). The Job Demands–Resources model: State of the art. *Journal of Managerial Psychology*, 22, 309–328.

Bakker, A. B., Demerouti, E., & Schaufeli, W. B. (2003). Dual processes at work in a call centre: An application of the Job Demands–Resources model. *European Journal of Work and Organizational Psychology*, 12, 393–417.

Bakker, A. B., Demerouti, E., Taris, T. W., Schaufeli, W. B., & Schreurs, P. J. G. (2003). A multigroup analysis of the Job Demands–Resources model in four home care organizations. *International Journal of Stress Management*, 10, 16–38.

Bradley, B. P., Mogg, K., & Lee, S. C. (1997). Attentional biases for negative information in induced and naturally occurring dysphoria. *Behaviour Research and Therapy*, 35, 911–927.

Cavanaugh, M. A., Boswell, W. R., Roehling, M. V., & Boudreau, J. W. (2000). An empirical examination of self-reported work stress among U.S. managers. *Journal of Applied Psychology*, 85, 65–74.

Crawford, E. R., LePine, J. A., & Rich, B. L. (2010). Linking job demands and resources to employee engagement and burnout: A theoretical extension and meta-analytic test. *Journal of Applied Psychology*, 95, 834–848.

de Jonge, J., & Dormann, C. (2003). The DISC model: Demand-induced strain compensation mechanisms on job stress. In: M. Dollard, A. H. Winefield, & H. R. Winefield (eds.), *Occupational Stress in the Service Professions*. New York: Taylor & Francis, 43–74.

Demerouti, E., Bakker, A. B., Nachreiner, F., & Schaufeli, W. B. (2001). The Job Demands–Resources model of burnout. *Journal of Applied Psychology*, 86, 499–512.

Dollard, J., Doob, L. W., Miller, N. E., Mowrer, O. H., & Sears, R. R. (1939). *Frustration and aggression.* New Haven, CT: Yale University Press.

Feldman, P. J., Cohen, S., Hamrick, N., & Lepore, S. J. (2004). Psychological stress, appraisal, emotion and cardiovascular response in a public speaking task. *Psychology & Health,* 19, 353–368.

Folkman, S., & Lazarus, R. S. (1985). If it changes it must be a process: Study of emotion and coping during three stages of a college examination. *Journal of Personality and Social Psychology*, 48, 150–170.

Hackman, J. R., & Oldham, G. R. (1975). Development of the Job Diagnostic Survey. *Journal of Applied Psychology*, 60, 159–170.

Hamner, W. C., & Tosi, H. L. (1974). Relationship of role conflict and role ambiguity to job involvement measures. *Journal of Applied Psychology,* 59, 497–499.

Karasek, R. A. (1979). Job demands, job decision latitude, and mental strain: Implications for job design. *Administrative Science Quarterly*, 24, 285–308.

Karasek, R. A., Triantis, K. P., & Chaudhry, S. S. (1982). Coworker and supervisor support as moderators of associations between task characteristics and mental strain. *Journal of Organizational Behavior*, 3, 181–200.

King, M., & Gardner, D. (2006). Emotional intelligence and occupational stress among professional staff in New Zealand. *International Journal of Organizational Analysis*, 14, 186–203.

Lazarus, R. S. (1991). Progress on a cognitive-motivational-relational theory of emotion. *American Psychologist,* 46, 819–834.

Lazarus, R. S., & Folkman, S. (1984). *Stress, Appraisal, and Coping.* New York: Springer.

Lepine, J. A., Podsakoff, N. P., & Lepine, M. A. (2005). A meta-analytic test of the challenge stressor-hindrance stressor framework: An explanation for inconsistent relationships among stressors and performance. *Academy of Management Journal*, 48, 764–775.

Levi, L. (1971). *The Psychosocial Environment and Psychosomatic Disease.* London: Oxford University Press.

McCrae, R. R. (1984). Situational determinants of coping responses: Loss, threat, and challenge. *Journal of Personality and Social Psychology*, 46, 919–928.

Oxford Dictionaries. (n.d.). Frustration [Def. 2]. Retrieved 12 November 2013 from www.oxforddictionaries.com/definition/english/frustration.

Peters, L. H., & O'Connor, E. J. (1980). Situational constraints and work outcomes: The influences of a frequently overlooked construct. *Academy of Management Review,* 5, 391–397.

Podsakoff, N. P., LePine, J. A., & LePine, M. A. (2007). Differential challenge stressor-hindrance stressor relationships with job attitudes, turnover intentions, turnover, and withdrawal behavior: A meta-analysis. *Journal of Applied Psychology*, 92, 438–454.

Ryan, R. M., & Deci, E. L. (2000). Self-determination theory and the facilitation of intrinsic motivation, social development, and well-being. *American Psychologist*, 55, 68–78.

Searle, B. J., & Auton, J. C. (2015). The merits of measuring challenge and hindrance appraisals. *Anxiety, Stress and Coping*, 28, 121–143.

Selye, H. (1950). *The Physiology and Pathology of Exposure to Stress: A Treatise Based on the Concepts of the General-Adaptation Syndrome and the Diseases of Adaptation.* Montreal: ACTA Medical Publishers.

Selye, H. (1974). *Stress without Distress.* Philadelphia, PA: J.B. Lippincott Co.

Semmer, N. K., McGrath, J. E., & Beehr, T. A. (2005). Conceptual issues in research on stress and health. In: C. L. Cooper (ed.), *Handbook of Stress Medicine and Health* (2nd ed.). New York: CRC Press, 1–43.

Siegrist, J. (1996). Adverse health effects of high-effort/low-reward conditions. *Journal of Occupational Health Psychology*, 1, 27–41.

Siegrist, J. (1998). Adverse health effects of Effort-Reward imbalance at work. In: C. Cooper (ed.), *Theories of Organizational Stress* (pp. 190–204). Oxford: Oxford University Press.

Szabo, S., Tache, Y., & Somogyi, A. (2012). The legacy of Hans Selye and the origins of stress research: A retrospective 75 years after his landmark brief "letter" to the editor of Nature. *Stress*, 15, 472–478.

Tims, M., Bakker, A. B., & Derks, D. (2012). Development and validation of the job crafting scale. *Journal of Vocational Behavior*, 80, 173–186.

Tuckey, M. R., Searle, B. J., Boyd, C. M., Winefield, A. H., & Winefield, H. R. (2015). Hindrances are not threats: Advancing the multi-dimensionality of work stress. *Journal of Occupational Health Psychology*, 20, 131–147.

Van den Broeck, A., De Cuyper, N., De Witte, H., & Vansteenkiste, M. (2010). Not all job demands are equal: Differentiating job hindrances and job challenges in the Job Demands–Resources model. *European Journal of Work and Organizational Psychology*, 19, 735–759.

Webster, J. R., Beehr, T. A., & Love, K. (2011). Extending the challenge-hindrance model of occupational stress: The role of appraisal. *Journal of Vocational Behavior*, 79, 505–516.

Widmer, P. S., Semmer, N. K., Kaelin, W., Jacobshagen, N., & Meier, L. L. (2012). The ambivalence of challenge stressors: Time pressure is associated with both negative and positive well-being. *Journal of Vocational Behavior,* 80, 422–433.

Wrzesniewski, A., & Dutton, J. E. (2001). Crafting a job: Revisioning employees as active crafters of their work. *Academy of Management Rreview*, 26, 179–201.

4

Psychological connections with work

Christina Maslach and Cristina G. Banks

The relationship between the worker and the job

With the advent of the Industrial Revolution, some fundamental changes took place with regard to how we thought about people as "workers" and about their work environment as the "job." Particularly notable is what happened in the United States in the 20th century, with the use of scientific ideas and methods to improve the world of work.

Fitting the person to the job

Prior to 1900, workers were usually skilled craftsmen, and the work was individualized, specialized, slow, inefficient, and of variable quality (Heminger, 2014). At the turn of the century, the American economy was sluggish and in need of overhaul. In an effort to eliminate wastes of human effort, and to reduce errors and accidents arising from poor execution of work, President Theodore Roosevelt called for a remedy to the lack of "national efficiency" and supported strategies that promised to dramatically improve economic output and prosperity. Frederic W. Taylor, an engineer and management consultant, answered that call with a book entitled *Principles of Scientific Management* (1911). Taylor described improvements in productivity, quality, efficiency, accuracy, and task cycle times that could be obtained by applying scientific principles to each element of a person's work and then scientifically selecting, training, and developing workers to maximize productivity and efficiency. By "science," Taylor meant an empirical assessment of the physical movements and context of the job through *time studies* to determine how the work elements could be reconfigured, streamlined, and paced in a way that would eliminate slack and inefficiencies and would maximize physical stamina by minimizing exertion. The shift to the industrialization of work brought in new concepts of engineering and scientific evidence to reform production work and jobs in general.

Taylor's colleague Frank Gilbreth introduced engineering concepts into the design of work by devising a procedure for analyzing jobs under laboratory conditions to eliminate wasted motion (*motion studies*) and to provide equipment to permit maximum efficiency (Gilbreth, 1911). Together with his wife, Lillian Gilbreth, who was the first industrial psychologist, Gilbreth also introduced the notion of "worker-oriented" job analysis where operations, equipment and training could be rearranged for workers with different characteristics (e.g., left-handed, amputee) to gain the most productivity. Lillian Gilbreth specialized in designing work for handicapped employees and served as a consultant to the Institute of Rehabilitation Medicine, which was dedicated to helping veterans who lost limbs in World War I. Whereas Taylor focused on the development of the most efficient job and matching people with specific characteristics and training to maximize productivity, the Gilbreths focused on how work could be designed and adapted to a wider spectrum of individuals who, with the right equipment and training, could work (Primoff & Fine, 1988).

Hugo Munsterberg also contributed to Roosevelt's call for greater economic efficiency, by introducing the concept of scientific selection of workers into jobs (Munsterberg, 1913). Munsterberg's validation studies enabled American employers to select job candidates who had the knowledge, skills, and abilities to succeed in the jobs that had been redesigned to be highly productive and efficient. Extending these principles of scientific selection, Walter Van Dyke Bingham and Walter Dill Scott devised a general classification system for jobs and set qualifications required for performing work within each classification. Bingham and Scott played a pivotal role in the classification and placement of millions of men joining military service in World War I. Matching soldier traits and abilities to job requirements through a systematic array of screening tools, such as the Army Alpha, significantly improved soldier performance and the effectiveness of the military force (Mitchell, 1988). In recent decades, increasingly sophisticated selection and performance measurement systems, tailored to specific interests of the employer (such as customer satisfaction, employee retention, and product innovation), have been developed to provide direct feedback to company decision-makers for making adjustments to the operation, resources, and people, in order to maximize gains (Cascio, 2006).

In 1917, scientific management broadened into the general field of "industrial engineering," which is defined as the engineering of work processes and the application of engineering methods, practices, and knowledge to production and service enterprises in order to increase and improve production and service activities (Badiru, 2014). Most retail, service, and production entities today utilize industrial engineering principles and/or tools to help manage their customer-facing and general business activities. Industrial engineering is applied to the design of jobs (i.e., the most economic way to perform work); the establishment of performance standards and benchmarks for quality, quantity, and cost; and the design and installation of facilities. For example, industrial-engineered work scheduling programs in many of today's restaurants determine how many workers are assigned per shift and how many hours any particular worker is assigned work, based on historical sales data. Such programs minimize labor costs and maximize productivity by controlling the number of labor hours "spent" per hour and by assigning employees who have the lowest cost.

Thus, modern-day job design and employee selection were born, and few deviations from this approach have emerged since. The significance of all of these events cannot be overstated, as they have contributed to the highly engineered work, no-slack labor budgets, bare-bones headcount, and on-demand workers that characterize many of today's modern workplaces. These early and ever-present engineering approaches to job design and selection focused on human *capabilities* (knowledge, skills, and abilities) to the neglect of human *motivation* to do such work and of the physical and psychological consequences of highly engineered work. Thus, fitting the person to the job was an insufficient strategy. It is no surprise that workers across hierarchical levels and occupations have experienced higher levels of job stress and negative consequences as a function of how work, work environments, and working conditions have been structured and executed for decades.

Fitting the job to the person

The recurring theme in these early time-and-motion approaches to job design was to determine how to best fit the person to the job by maximizing the person's *ability* to perform these new models of efficient work processes. But gradually there began to be an acknowledgement that some unique human characteristics needed to be taken into account, which led to some initial efforts to fit the job to the person.

This shift became evident by the mid-1950s when there was a growing recognition that workers needed safe and hazard-free environments in which to do their job. The focus was on identifying risk factors and occupational hazards, and developing procedures to prevent the occurrence of accidents, injuries, disease, and death. This often meant that the workplace had to adjust to the innate "limitations," "shortcomings," or "flaws" of human beings. In general, the implicit guiding framework was how to make the workplace "less bad" for people (as opposed to making it better). The impact of these health and safety interventions was often judged by organizational outcomes, such as reductions in lost productivity and health care costs.

Much of this health and safety research was conducted by professionals in the fields of human factors engineering and ergonomics. Human factors and ergonomics (HFE) is defined as the scientific discipline concerned with the understanding of the interactions among humans and other elements of a system (the "human-machine" interface), and the application of theory principles, data, and methods to work design, in order to optimize human wellbeing and overall system performance (Chapanis, 1995). HFE professionals study human capacities and limitations such as physical and cognitive abilities, knowledge, personality, and physiology in relation to the physical and psychological environment in which people work. They design equipment or other elements of a work environment that is optimally compatible with the capacities and limitations of workers in a specific application. For example, HFE professionals study airline cockpit displays and pilot performance using those displays. Based on a scientific analysis of pilot performance, the display is modified and/or the pilot is trained to eliminate performance problems caused by these limitations (e.g., Mosier, Sethi, McCauley, Khoo, & Orasanu, 2007). The introduction of computers into modern work processes has made the human-machine interface much more complex and multifaceted, making optimization of the interface more challenging and the problems arising from human limitations and information overload more difficult to solve (Eppler & Mengis, 2004).

HFE implicitly acknowledges that an engineering approach to job design and selection of qualified candidates alone does not produce the best results for workers or employers. By taking a *systems* view of the worker in interaction with all the factors within the work process system, HFE provides a fuller picture of the multiple determinants of worker productivity and wellbeing. It evaluates components of the total system, which includes the environment (the organization, tasks performed, ambient features), the operator (capabilities, training, psychological responses), and the "machine" (equipment features, controls, tools, information) to achieve the greatest fit between humans and systems to generate outcomes such as safety, comfort, productivity, usability, or affective needs such as job satisfaction or life happiness (Karwowski, 2012).

Goodness of fit

In all of these prior efforts to improve the work environment and its effectiveness, the central framework has been one of the fit between the worker and the workplace. Which aspects of the person and the job are investigated and/or changed may vary widely, but the core underlying assumption that a "good fit" will yield positive outcomes continues to be an enduring one, not only in practice but in research. A consistent theme throughout the relevant research has been the problematic relationship between the individual and the situation, which has also been described in terms of misfit, mismatch, imbalance, or misalignment: for example, the demands of the job exceed the capacity of the individual to cope effectively, or the person's efforts are not reciprocated with equitable rewards. Some of the earliest models of organizational stress focused on the positive goal of "person-job fit," which was assumed to predict less strain and better adjustment (French, Caplan, & Harrison, 1982; French & Kahn, 1962).

In the 1990s, the emergence of the field of occupational health psychology had an important impact on notions of "fit" in the workplace. It made a distinction between the work environment, the individual, and the work-family interface. A lack of "goodness of fit" or incompatibility across these three dimensions was proposed as the mechanism through which workplace factors lead to employee distress and ill health. Occupational health psychology also reframed the approach to worker wellbeing around *healthy* work environments. These environments are characterized by high productivity, high employee satisfaction, good safety records, low frequencies of disability claims and union grievances, low absenteeism, low turnover, and absence of violence (Quick, 1999).

Other theorizing has continued to highlight the importance of both individual and contextual factors, and their interrelationship, but has developed more complex definitions of "fit." For example, fit has been defined by Kristof (1996) in terms of both *similarity* between the person and the job (e.g., both have the same values), and *complementarity* (e.g., one provides what the other needs or wants). "Fit" has also been extended to multiple aspects of the job, such as person-organization, person-group, and person-supervisor fit (Kristof-Brown, Zimmerman, & Johnson, 2005).

Models of person-job fit have potentially important implications for interventions to improve wellbeing in the workplace. For example, the notion of "fit" is implicit in the job characteristics model, which advocates redesigning jobs to enhance intrinsic motivation (Hackman & Oldham, 1980). Newer examples of person-job fit are the areas of work life model that identifies six key areas in which fit or misfit can take place: workload, control, reward, community, fairness, and values (Leiter & Maslach, 2004). Imbalances in resources and demands are central to the conservation of resources theory (Hobfoll, 1989) and Job Demands–Resources theory (Demerouti, Bakker, Nachreiner, & Schaufeli, 2001). In other theories, the concept of a fit between the person and the job is not explicitly mentioned, but is evident in such concepts as "autonomy support" – which refers to how managers (the job environment) can behave towards workers (the person) to encourage and help them become more self-reliant (Deci, Connell, & Ryan, 1989).

Psychological factors at work

What aspects of individuals might be most relevant to the "goodness of fit" between themselves and their job? As noted earlier, the primary focus for many years was on the physical characteristics of workers and their human capabilities. But people's psychological characteristics, such as their motives and emotions, were often neglected or not deemed as important. However, a more comprehensive effort to understand the worker's *psychological* experience at work got under way in the 1930s, and now there is an extensive research literature on this central component of human beings.

Motivations and needs

The pioneering psychological work on human motivation took place more than half a century ago, with the proposal that what motivates people to take action are several core needs. Some of these needs were postulated to be inborn, but others were thought to be learned. The earliest theories proposed the following needs: achievement, affiliation, and power (Atkinson, 1964; Murray, 1938); self-actualization and social recognition (Maslow, 1943); and competence (White, 1959). A basic assumption was that there would be individual differences in need *strength*, which would predict variations in people's responses.

Although these original motivation theories were meant to explain human behavior in general, several subsequent theories were designed to focus on motivation in the workplace. Some of these theories dealt with factors that underlie extrinsic (hedonic) motivation, such as reinforcement theory (Ferster & Skinner, 1957), expectancy theory (Vroom, 1964), and goal-setting (Locke & Latham, 1990). Although extrinsic motivators have been shown to increase productivity and satisfaction, their effects are believed to be short-lived and conditional on the presence of additional rewards or incentives. Other theories focused more on intrinsic (eudemonic) motivators, which provide *meaning* to the worker though the act of performing the work (e.g., Herzberg, 1966; Maslow, 1943). Subsequent theories brought together both intrinsic and extrinsic motivation, proposing that both were critical for good job performance and satisfaction, but varying in their hypotheses about how the two motivational processes affected each other (Deci, 1971; Porter & Lawler, 1968).

More recently, attention has shifted from need *strength* to need *satisfaction*, which is now assumed to be the primary driver of motivation and action. The basic assumption is that satisfaction of core needs will promote psychological health and wellbeing. Currently, the most robust model of need satisfaction is Self-Determination Theory (SDT), which proposes a self-determination continuum ranging from amotivation (a lack of self-determination) to intrinsic motivation (fully self-determined), with several types of extrinsic motivation in between these two endpoints (Deci & Ryan, 2000). A further distinction is made between *autonomous* motivation (which is intrinsic and freely chosen) and *controlled* motivation (which is extrinsic and driven by external constraints). SDT posits that intrinsic motivation is based on the satisfaction of three basic psychological needs: autonomy, belongingness, and competence. The satisfaction of these three needs is considered crucial to people's ability to thrive in all parts of their lives, including the places where they work. Much research has been done using the theoretical framework of SDT, so it has clearly become one of the major theories of work motivation (Gagné & Deci, 2005; Van den Broeck, Ferris, Chang, & Rosen, 2016).

The psychosocial aspects of stress

Another major contributor to the understanding of individual wellbeing in the workplace came with the modern recognition of the age-old phenomenon of stress. The seminal work of Hans Selye (1956, 1967) showed that environmental factors (stressors) could cause stress-related illness via a three-stage process of alarm, resistance, and exhaustion. Subsequent research on stress and coping found increasing evidence of the importance of a person's internal experience of strain, which plays a mediating role between causal stressors and various outcomes (including both physical and mental health). The work of Richard Lazarus and his colleagues identified the critical psychological construct of the *cognitive appraisal* of stressors as either threats or challenges (Lazarus & Folkman, 1984). This personal appraisal, or psychological perception, of something in either negative or positive terms, had major effects on subsequent coping strategies and behaviors. The role of psychosocial factors in stress has continued to grow in importance, within both the medical and social sciences.

More recently, there has been a greater interest in *job stress*, and recognition that it can be a significant occupational hazard. Stress impairs job performance by reducing people's capacity for complex physical skills and by impairing cognitive functioning. Stress compromises the immune system, increasing the risk of viral and bacterial infections, and thus leading to higher rates of absenteeism and sick leave. The chronic tension associated with stress increases vulnerability to musculoskeletal problems. Empirical evidence has been found for the negative effects of job stress on physical health (especially cardiovascular problems), as well as on psychological wellbeing (e.g., job dissatisfaction, negative affect, burnout). Job stress is also predictive of various behavioral responses, such as lowered job performance, problems with family relationships, and self-damaging behaviors (see Kahn & Byosiere, 1992; Sauter & Murphy, 1995). Without a doubt, the worker's psychological experience of the workplace is a crucial part of the fit between the person and the job.

Positive psychology

Positive psychology is the study of the conditions and processes that lead to the optimal functioning of people, groups, and institutions (Gable & Haidt, 2005; Seligman & Csikszentmihalyi, 2000). By expanding the research focus to positive factors, and not simply negative ones, this approach led to the reframing of many psychological concepts. For example, rather than just studying illness or antisocial behaviors, researchers have shifted to studying health or prosocial behaviors. In particular, positive psychology introduced the role of positive emotions as a critical element of wellbeing (Fredrickson, 2001). Positive emotions (such as joy, gratitude, inspiration, and pride) are more than feelings – they are embodied states that come with action tendencies and their own urges, cognitive appraisals, and physiological reactions. When experienced, they signal to us that we are safe and not at risk, and thus they broaden our attention in the present, open us to new experiences, and help us to explore, build, collaborate, and share with others.

This positive psychology approach has been applied to the workplace, setting in motion a greater emphasis on the promotion of worker wellbeing (Turner, Barling, & Zacharatos, 2002). The fields of Positive Organizational Scholarship (POS) and Positive Organizational Behavior (POB) have emerged as a way to examine these concepts in the context of the workplace, in order to promote employee health and positive organizational outcomes. The general focus has been on the ways in which employees and organizations flourish and display strength, resilience, and vitality (see Bakker & Schaufeli, 2008; Cameron, Dutton, & Quinn, 2003; Luthans, 2002). In spite of its recent popularity in organizational research, however, support for the positive organizational research agenda is not without controversy (see Fineman, 2006), and there is acknowledgement of the need for more work on both theory and methodological challenges. Nonetheless, recent reviews of workplace wellness programs rooted in this positive psychology paradigm have shown some improved outcomes for individuals and organizations (Cameron, Mora, Leutscher, & Calarco, 2011; Meyers, van Woerkom, & Bakker, 2013).

Psychological needs and wellbeing at work

What are the key lessons to be drawn from this prior research? First, there are important psychological qualities that a person brings to the workplace and experiences there. Second, the fit between the person and the job is of critical significance. A possible conclusion that could be drawn is that these psychological qualities might be the basis for a better person–job fit, and thus for better personal and job outcomes. The best candidate for the key psychological factor seems to be *need satisfaction* – and there is growing support for the idea that need satisfaction is critical for linking the fit between job characteristics and personal wellbeing at work (see Greguras & Diefendorff, 2009; Van den Broeck, Vansteenkiste, De Witte, & Lens, 2008).

The following sections provide summary reviews of the empirical research on the connection between various psychological needs and wellbeing outcomes. They include the three core needs postulated by SDT (autonomy, belongingness, and competence) but also several other psychological needs, or states, that have emerged as important psychological factors for workers.

Autonomy

The need for autonomy has been defined in SDT as people's desire to experience ownership of their behavior and to act with a sense of volition (Deci & Ryan, 2000). This sense of volition can be achieved through having the opportunity to make personal choices, but also through the full endorsement of an externally induced request. However, prior research in work and organizational psychology had defined autonomy in different terms, such as personal freedom, discretion, or independence (e.g., Hackman & Oldham, 1976), or personal control (e.g., the Demand-Control model, Karasek & Theorell, 1990).

Consistent with the SDT conceptualization of autonomy, numerous cross-sectional studies have identified positive associations between employee task discretion and control over work pace with overall job satisfaction, performance, and employee mental health (Andreassen, Hetland, & Pallesen, 2010; Hall et al., 2006; Kalleberg, Nesheim, & Olsen, 2009; Park & Searcy, 2012; Thompson & Prottas, 2006). Some have argued that satisfaction of the need for autonomy is the most important need contributing to overall job satisfaction and intent to stay among paid employees (Boezeman & Ellemers, 2009).

However, empirical evidence linking schedule flexibility and variability in working hours with employee mental health and job satisfaction is mixed (Costa, Sartori, & Åkerstedt, 2006; Nijp, Beckers, Geurts, Tucker, & Kompier, 2012). For example, a systematic review of work-time control and employee outcomes found consistent evidence for improved job-related outcomes (e.g., job performance, turnover) but limited effects on employee health and wellbeing as measured by self-reported fatigue, overall health, and sickness absence (Nijp et al., 2012). Fewer studies have examined this relationship experimentally. Among autonomy intervention studies, such as job crafting or job redesign, there is mixed evidence for a causal relationship between workplace autonomy and improved psychological wellbeing (Bambra, Egan, Thomas, Petticrew, & Whitehead, 2007; Holman & Axtell, 2015; Holman, Axtell, Sprigg, Totterdell, & Wall, 2009); positive employee health behaviors (Moen, Kelly, Tranby, & Huang, 2011); or job-related outcomes such as job motivation, satisfaction, and performance (Nijp et al., 2012).

Belongingness

The need for belongingness or relatedness has been defined as the human striving for close and intimate relationships and the desire to achieve a sense of communion and belongingness (Baumeister & Leary, 1995). This basic concept has also been studied under other terms, such as social connection, affiliation, and recognition.

Evidence from cross-sectional and observational studies in the workplace suggests that positive coworker relationships and perceived social climate have significant positive effects on employee wellbeing and job-related outcomes (Lindberg & Vingård, 2011; Lohela, Björklund, Vingard, Hagberg, & Jensen, 2009; Luchman & Gonazález-Morales, 2013). Coworker support has also been found to be a protective factor against employee exhaustion and turnover intent (Ducharme, Knudsen, & Roman, 2007). Consistent with the model of need satisfaction described earlier, there is also evidence that employees' need to belong moderates the positive relationship between spirit of camaraderie and affective wellbeing (Rego & Souto, 2009). Social connections at work also have direct physical health implications. For example, positive social interactions at work were found to be associated with improved cardiovascular health and strengthening of the immune and neuroendocrine systems (Heaphy & Dutton, 2008).

There are fewer intervention studies examining the causal impact of social connectedness or teamwork on employee psychological wellbeing and organizational outcomes, and evidence from these experimental studies has been inconclusive (Bambra et al., 2007; Buller & Bell, 1986; Kaplan et al., 2014). However, a longitudinal intervention program focused on improving civility among nurses has been found to be effective in enhancing these collegial work relationships, and also in reducing absenteeism and burnout (Leiter, Day, Gilin Oore, & Laschinger, 2012; Leiter, Laschinger, Day, & Gilin Oore, 2011).

Competence

The need for competence represents individuals' desire to feel capable of mastering the environment, to bring about desired outcomes, and to manage various challenges (White, 1959). The SDT version of competence also emphasizes mastery of the environment, but includes the development of new skills. For competence in the workplace, the need has been described in terms of using one's energy efficiently to be effective at work and take care of one's work tasks. Similar constructs have been labeled as achievement or accomplishment.

Satisfaction of this need for competence in the workplace was assessed among 600 cross-occupational employees in Norway, and it was found to be significantly associated with work enjoyment (Andreassen et al., 2010). Another study found that satisfaction of the need for competence was strongly and negatively correlated with self-reported depression and anxiety (Baard, Deci, & Ryan, 2004). In a study of 121 nurses and pharmacists, satisfaction of the need for competence was more important than either autonomy and belongingness, and accounted for the most variation in mindfulness and vitality, two outcome measures of general and exercise-related wellbeing (Bernard, Martin, & Kulik, 2014). However, in a reversal of this pattern, competence did not predict intrinsic motivation in two cross-sectional studies of Norwegian employees, although both autonomy and belongingness were significant predictors (Dysvik, Kuvaas, & Gagné, 2013).

Positive emotions

A large body of evidence has highlighted the relationship between employees' negative emotional experiences and adverse health and organizational outcomes (Kirkham et al., 2015). However, as mentioned earlier, there are now some theoretical models that link positive emotions and employer practices to employee wellbeing and positive organizational outcomes. Recent work in positive organizational psychology and Positive Organizational Behavior has begun to substantiate these models with empirical evidence from cross-sectional, longitudinal, and experimental studies (Bowling, Eschleman, & Wang, 2010; Cameron et al., 2011; Rajaratnam, Sears, Shi, Coberley, & Pope, 2014; Sears, Shi, Coberley, & Pope, 2013). For example, in an application of the happy-productive worker and broaden-and-build theses, a study found that job satisfaction predicted supervisor-reported job performance, and high levels of psychological wellbeing moderated this relationship (Wright, Cropanzano, & Bonett, 2007).

The aggregate construct of "psychological capital," defined by positive feelings of hope, optimism, efficacy, and resiliency, has also been examined in the context of the workplace. Several cross-sectional and longitudinal studies have identified positive associations between measures of psychological capital and job-related affective wellbeing (Avey, Luthans, Smith, & Palmer, 2010; Culbertson, Fullagar, & Mills, 2010; Luthans, Norman, Avolio, & Avey, 2008). A meta-analysis of

51 studies also found strong evidence of a positive association between employee psychological capital and job-related attitudes, such as job satisfaction and organizational commitment, and positive behaviors including employee citizenship (Avey, Reichard, Luthans, & Mhatre, 2011). Positive employee behaviors such as commitment, citizenship, and helping behaviors have also been associated with employees' positive affect (Fisher, 2002; Ilies, Scott, & Judge, 2006).

Psychological safety

Given the earlier focus on how to protect workers from physical safety hazards, it is not surprising that there has been growing attention paid to workers' personal sense of feeling safe on the job. One approach was to conceptualize workplace safety climate as a higher-order construct, comprised of first-order factors including management values, safety practices, safety communication, safety training, and other factors. It presumes that safety climate is an antecedent for safety performance in organizations, which results in behaviors that directly promote safe work practices (Griffin & Neal, 2000).

A distinct, but conceptually related approach focused on psychological safety among team members (Edmondson, 1999). This concept was introduced as a model of team learning, in which reported psychological safety (which is characterized by interpersonal trust, respect, and caring within work teams) is positively related to team performance. In other words, do team members feel that the team is a safe place for interpersonal risk taking? This construct has been tested empirically in literature examining optimal team functioning. For example, one study found that psychological safety and task conflict act synergistically to improve overall team performance (Bradley, Postlethwaite, Klotz, Hamdani, & Brown, 2012). However, less research has examined how team psychological safety has affected individual employee wellbeing.

Recently, psychosocial safety has assumed a more prominent role in this conceptualization of workplace safety climate (Bronkhorst, 2015). Psychosocial safety climate (PSC) refers to employees' shared perception of management policies and practices that protect them from psychological and social risk or harm such as bullying, violence, aggression, and work stress (Dollard & Bakker, 2010). In other words, PSC can be thought of as a distinct organizational-level climate factor that buffers employees against psychosocial stress or harm (Idris, Dollard, Coward, & Dormann, 2012). Studies have shown that PSC moderates the relationship between emotional demands and emotional exhaustion, while predicting a change in work engagement through skill discretion (Dollard & Bakker, 2010). Another study, using cross-sectional data from a randomly selected sample of Australian households, drew similar conclusions regarding PSC as a determinant of employee psychological health and engagement, and as a moderator of psychosocial hazards such as bullying and harassment (Law, Dollard, Tuckey, & Dormann, 2011). A cross-national study, using data from 31 European countries, found that PSC, along with job redesign and positive psychosocial work conditions, is positively associated with worker health (Dollard & Neser, 2013).

Fairness

Fairness is the extent to which decisions at work are perceived as being just, and people are being treated with respect. Although there has not been any theoretical construct of a psychological *need* for fairness, it could be argued that such a need is indeed important to people, and that the satisfaction of that need would lead to positive work and health outcomes. There has, in fact, been a lot of empirical evidence about how perceived unfairness at work is a significant source of job stress (see the review by Robbins, Ford, & Tetrick, 2012).

Fairness has also been implicated in other constructs such as inequity (e.g., as seen in the effort-reward imbalance model of Siegrist, 1996), and procedural justice, in which the fairness of the process is more important to people then the favorableness of the outcome (Lawler, 1968; Tyler, 1990). Recent research has shown that procedural justice is a factor in predicting need satisfaction and positive work outcomes (Gillet, Colombat, Michinov, Pronost, & Fouquereau, 2013). Organizational justice is another construct that includes the core notion of fairness, and is hypothesized to be an important component of employees' healthy psychological states. There is emerging evidence linking justice and fairness to positive employee outcomes, including job satisfaction, high performance, and low turnover intention (Harris, Andrews, & Kacmar, 2007; Janssen, Lam, & Huang, 2010).

Meaning

Research is finding that, in general, the experience of meaning in one's life is associated with many aspects of positive functioning (King, Heintzelman, & Ward, 2016). If people are doing something that they value, and that gives a sense of purpose to their life, it can be an important source of work motivation as well. Although this has not been labeled as a psychological *need* for meaning or values, it clearly has relevant antecedents in concepts of self-actualization and personal growth. Factors that predict, mediate, or hinder employees' sense of meaning or purpose in their work has been one research focus of scholars in Positive Organizational Behavior (Grant, 2007; Rosso, Dekas, & Wrzesniewski, 2010).

Empirical evidence is emerging to support the theoretical frameworks linking employees' perceptions of meaningful work, employee wellbeing, and positive job-related outcomes (Arnold, Turner, Barling, Kelloway, & McKee, 2007; Steger, Dik, & Duffy, 2012). For example, one study found that employee meaningfulness is negatively associated with absenteeism, and that this relationship is mediated by work engagement and employee wellbeing (Soane et al., 2013). Job crafting is also being used as a tool to enhance job-person fit and augment employee meaningfulness (Tims, Derks, & Bakker, 2016; Wrzesniewski, LoBuglio, Dutton, & Berg, 2013). In particular, it has been hypothesized that job-crafting efforts guided by employees' strengths and passions have the potential to foster meaningfulness for employees, thereby improving employee job satisfaction and organizational outcomes (Berg, Dutton, & Wrzesniewski, 2013). A study of 253 adults found that job crafting predicted employee subjective and psychological wellbeing through satisfaction of the intrinsic needs consistent with SDT (Slemp & Vella-Brodrick, 2014).

Prescription for building healthy workplaces

Recent sets of studies provide clear evidence that certain features of work and the workplace pose a danger to employee health. These alarming statistics have spurred renewed efforts to address worker health and wellbeing more comprehensively, and in ways that improve organizational practices, as well as how people work. One study examined 10 workplace stressors (unemployment, lack of health insurance, exposure to shift work, long working hours, job insecurity, work-family conflict, low job control, high job demands, low social support at work, and low organizational justice), and found that these caused more than 120,000 unnecessary deaths per year and an excess annual health care cost of 5%–8% of the total spend on health care (Goh, Pfeffer, & Zenios, 2016). Another study examined the impact of five working conditions (physically demanding job, high time pressure, low job control, low rewards, and a lack of physical activity) on "working life expectancy" (at what age one is likely to leave employment because of illness or injury) and "working years lost" (due to premature exits from the labor force). There were significant negative effects on both of these outcomes, contributing collectively to almost four years difference (Burdorf, 2015).

Such evidence has spurred various interventions and programs to improve employee health and wellbeing, both by mitigating and eliminating bad effects, and by promoting good effects. However, scientific reviews of the effectiveness of such programs have revealed somewhat disappointing outcomes. In the United States, studies have found relatively low rates of participation by employees in various wellness programs (Agency for Health Care Research and Quality, 2016; Mattke et al., 2013). For example, in one report less than 20% of those employees identified for health intervention actually participated in a targeted program. In general, there was only weak evidence for the impact of programs for smoking cessation, consumption of fruits and vegetables, and physical activity. These results suggest that wellness programs, as currently conceived and implemented, do not have motivating properties, and thus they may be missing a key driver of behavior change. Without having a strong motivational component to encourage employee participation, these programs are unlikely to be perceived as fulfilling an important need, thus depriving employees from benefitting from improved health and ultimately greater wellbeing.

New strategies

The literature reviewed in this chapter makes a strong case that core human needs are the key to psychological wellbeing, and that satisfaction of these needs can lead to multiple desirable outcomes, both personal and organizational. Sustained and long-lasting work motivation emanates from intrinsic needs that have personal meaning and significance to the individual worker. Satisfaction of these needs, through performance of the work itself and/or the significance of this work, can result in productivity that is highly satisfying and that promotes psychological wellbeing. A reasonable next step toward achieving wellbeing at work is to determine how need satisfaction can become an integral part of a worker's job and work environment. For organizations, the central questions are: Which are the most important needs for organizations to address? How can organizations best ensure the satisfaction of these needs?

Need satisfaction as the core of interventions and programs

Based on the prior literature review, a case can be made that seven needs have the potential for providing the "engine" for sustained and long-lasting work motivation and psychological wellbeing: autonomy, belongingness, competence, psychosocial safety, positive emotions, fairness, and meaning All of these needs have been empirically linked to intrinsic work motivation and wellbeing. Thus, these seven needs have a solid basis as candidates for integration into interventions and programs that will promote wellbeing.

Knowing how this integration can be accomplished is the challenging part. Following the job characteristics model (Hackman & Oldham, 1980), several aspects of job and task design can be modified to increase the probability of need satisfaction through performance of the work itself. What is important is how the worker *perceives* the qualities inherent in this work: Does the work stimulate feelings of competence and mastery? Is there autonomy in some aspects of how the work is accomplished? Does the worker feel safe and treated fairly when tasks are performed? Are there opportunities for building a sense of belonging within the organizational community and for experiencing positive feelings and meaningful pride in the work?

Parallel questions need to focus on the many ways in which the work environment, in all its many dimensions, can provide opportunities for need satisfaction. For example, does the organizational culture promote intrinsically important values that are consistent with those of workers?

Do organizational policies enable workers to have sufficient autonomy and control over their work lives, in order to accommodate personal and family-related issues? Is the workstation and workspace design such that it supports work accomplishment, promotes social connections, and enables privacy and control over disruptions? Is the built environment (walls, indoor environmental quality, interior design, outdoor environment) such that workers are free from toxic materials and safety hazards, and that they derive pleasure from being in these spaces? Are leadership and management helpful and supportive of workers' performance and accomplishments, and do they recognize their achievements?

Wellness programs can be treated similarly: in what ways should these programs be designed, implemented, and managed such that workers are motivated to participate through satisfaction of important needs? Seen through the lens of need satisfaction, all aspects of the job and workplace environment can be modified or designed in a manner that will reinforce these seven needs, and remove barriers to need satisfaction.

Participant involvement

An important conclusion of the research literature on procedural justice is that participation in a change effort results in greater understanding of the problem to be solved and lasting commitment to its solution (Kim & Mauborgne, 1997). Also, participation in decision making has been shown to result in better decisions and acceptance of decisions (Vroom, 2004). Given the value that comes with participation, it is reasonable to suggest that any effort to design or modify the job or the work environment will be most successful if recipients of those changes were involved in the process – *particularly with respect to what will lead to their need satisfaction*. Often decisions about program design, interventions, and other organizational changes are made without user/consumer/receiver input. Instead, a common step in new building design is to gain occupant reactions *after* the changes have been made, by conducting postoccupancy surveys. This can result in some very difficult and costly situations that could have been avoided if the occupants had been engaged in the change process in advance. To maximize employees' motivation to accept and internalize change, it is critical to determine just what will maximize this motivation from a psychological perspective. The more behavior change or change acceptance is motivated by these core intrinsic factors, the more likely that change will occur – and occur *willingly* – because of the impact of need satisfaction.

A classic example will illustrate this point. Prior to World War II, Welsh coal miners worked in small groups, sharing and exchanging tasks, enabling social interaction and working at their own pace. After the war, coal-cutting machines were introduced to increase efficiency and lower costs. The job was changed to include larger groups of workers, each man working independently on a small set of repetitive tasks with little or no interaction among the men. Work carried over from shift to shift, and problems on any shift had to be solved on subsequent shifts. Productivity plummeted, dissatisfaction rose, absenteeism increased dramatically, grievances were filed, and the company experienced frequent work process breakdowns. To correct the problems, the work was changed to bring back the aspects of the job that met the miners' core needs: self-selected work teams, decreased interdependence between shifts, and increased task variety. Productivity and efficiency increased beyond the company's expectations, and job satisfaction returned (Hendrick, 2006).

Work with organizational and interdisciplinary partners

Psychological wellbeing is a multi-faceted and complex construct, and it is affected by everything that humans interact with – physically and psychologically. In the workplace, this means that psychological wellbeing can be affected by a multitude of factors, including the job, the work environment, coworkers, management, organizational policies, work demands, work-life issues, physical health, and so on. To achieve the goal of psychological wellbeing in the workplace, it will be important to address all relevant factors in an integrated, comprehensive manner.

Thus, there is a clear need for psychologists to work with interdisciplinary partners who know about factors that promote worker health and wellbeing in disciplines outside of psychology. These fields include public health, occupational health, nutrition, business, industrial hygiene, architecture, interior design, human factors/ergonomics, computer science, human resources, and sociology. Each discipline has approached the topic of health and wellbeing from its own perspective, but is often relatively ignorant of the relevant contributions of the other fields. An important future goal would be to develop a method for combining these perspectives in a way that would lead to (1) a comprehensive and integrated view of a healthy workplace, and (2) an effective process for how to build and maintain it. The Interdisciplinary Center for Healthy Workplaces was designed to accomplish this integration of knowledge across disciplines, with the purpose of identifying the key factors that can be integrated into a comprehensive approach to worker health and wellbeing.[1] Need satisfaction is the common element across these literatures, and will be the driver of recommendations for change in this comprehensive approach.

Conclusion

The knowledge exists to begin building healthy workplaces in a robust, compelling way. Psychologists can contribute significantly to the design of healthy workplaces, along with their academic and practitioner partners. This is because psychology is deeply rooted in its understanding of human needs and how people's satisfaction directly affects their work motivation, quality of life, and their physical and psychological wellbeing.

Note

1 Healthy Workplaces website: healthyworkplaces.berkeley.edu.

References

Agency for Healthcare Research and Quality. (2016). *Comparative Effectiveness Review: Total Worker Health.* AHRQ Publication No. 16-EHC016-EF.

Andreassen, C. S., Hetland, J., & Pallesen, S. (2010). The relationship between "workaholism," basic needs satisfaction at work and personality. *European Journal of Personality*, 24(1), 3–17.

Arnold, K. A., Turner, N., Barling, J., Kelloway, E. K., & McKee, M. C. (2007). Transformational leadership and psychological well-being: The mediating role of meaningful work. *Journal of Occupational Health Psychology*, 12(3), 193–203.

Atkinson, J. (1964). *An Introduction to Motivation.* New York: D. Van Nostrand.

Avey, J. B., Luthans, F., Smith, R. M., & Palmer, N. F. (2010). Impact of positive psychological capital on employee well-being over time. *Journal of Occupational Health Psychology*, 15(1), 17–28.

Avey, J. B., Reichard, R. J., Luthans, F., & Mhatre, K. H. (2011). Meta-analysis of the impact of positive psychological capital on employee attitudes, behaviors, and performance. *Human Resource Development Quarterly*, 22(2), 127–152.

Baard, P. P., Deci, E. L., & Ryan, R. M. (2004). Intrinsic need satisfaction: A motivational basis of performance and well-being in two work settings. *Journal of Applied Social Psychology*, 34(10), 2045–2068.

Badiru, A. B. (2014). General introduction. In: A. B. Badiru (ed.), *Handbook of Industrial and Systems Engineering.* Boca Raton FL: CRC Press/Taylor and Francis, 3–44.

Bakker, A. B., & Schaufeli, W. B. (2008). Positive organizational behavior: Engaged employees in flourishing organizations. *Journal of Organizational Behavior*, 29, 147–154.

Bambra, C., Egan, M., Thomas, S., Petticrew, M., & Whitehead, M. (2007). Review: The psychosocial and health effects of workplace reorganisation 2: A systematic review of task restructuring interventions. *Journal of Epidemiology and Community Health*, 61(12), 1028–1037.

Baumeister, R. F., & Leary, M. R. (1995). The need to belong: Desire for interpersonal attachments as a fundamental human motivation. *Psychological Bulletin*, 117, 497–529.

Berg, J. M., Dutton, J. E., & Wrzesniewski, A. (2013). Job crafting and meaningful work. In: B. J. Dik, Z. S. Byrne, & M. F. Steger (eds.), *Purpose and Meaning in the Workplace*. Washington, DC: American Psychological Association, 81–104.

Bernard, D., Martin, J. J., & Kulik, N. (2014). Self-determination theory and well-being in the health care profession. *Journal of Applied Biobehavioral Research*, 19(3), 157–170.

Boezeman, E. J., & Ellemers, N. (2009). Intrinsic need satisfaction and the job attitudes of volunteers versus employees working in a charitable volunteer organization. *Journal of Occupational and Organizational Psychology*, 82(4), 897–914.

Bowling, N. A., Eschleman, K. J., & Wang, Q. (2010). A meta-analytic examination of the relationship between job satisfaction and subjective well-being. *Journal of Occupational and Organizational Psychology*, 83(4), 915–934.

Bradley, B. H., Postlethwaite, B. E., Klotz, A. C., Hamdani, M. R., & Brown, K. G. (2012). Reaping the benefits of task conflict in teams: The critical role of team psychological safety climate. *Journal of Applied Psychology*, 97(1), 151–158.

Bronkhorst, B. (2015). Behaving safely under pressure: The effects of job demands, resources, and safety climate on employee physical and psychosocial safety behavior. *Journal of Safety Research*, 55, 63–72.

Buller, P. F., & Bell, C. H. (1986). Effects of team building and goal setting on productivity: A field experiment. *Academy of Management Journal*, 29(2), 305–328.

Burdorf, A. (December 9, 2015). *Assessment of the Impact of Workplace Health Programs on Health and Working Life*. Pathways to Prevention: Total Worker Health® – What's Work Got to Do with It? NIH Conference, Bethesda, MD.

Cameron, K. S., Dutton, J. E., & Quinn, R. E. (2003). Developing a discipline of Positive Organizational Scholarship. In: K. S. Cameron, J. E. Dutton, & R. E. Quinn (eds.), *Positive Organizational Scholarship: Foundations of a New Discipline*. San Francisco, CA: Berrett-Koehler, 361–370.

Cameron, K., Mora, C., Leutscher, T., & Calarco, M. (2011). Effects of positive practices on organizational effectiveness. *The Journal of Applied Behavioral Science*, 47(3), 266–308.

Cascio, W. F. (2006). *Managing Human Resources: Productivity, Quality of Work Life, Profits*. Boston: McGraw Hill/Irwin.

Chapanis, A. (1995). *Human Factors in System Engineering*. New York: Wiley.

Costa, G., Sartori, S., & Åkerstedt, T. (2006). Influence of flexibility and variability of working hours on health and well-being. *Chronobiology International*, 23(6), 1125–1137.

Culbertson, S. S., Fullagar, C. J., & Mills, M. J. (2010). Feeling good and doing great: The relationship between psychological capital and well-being. *Journal of Occupational Health Psychology*, 15(4), 421.

Deci, E. L. (1971). Effects of externally mediated rewards on intrinsic motivation. *Journal of Personality and Social Psychology*, 18, 105–115.

Deci, E. L., Connell, J. P., & Ryan, R. M. (1989). Self-determination in a work organization. *Journal of Applied Psychology*, 74, 580–590.

Deci, E. L., & Ryan, R. M. (2000). The 'what' and 'why' of goal pursuits: Human needs and the self-determination of behavior. *Psychological Inquiry*, 11, 227–268.

Demerouti, E., Bakker, A. B., Nachreiner, F., & Schaufeli, W. B. (2001). The Job Demands–Resources model of burnout. *Journal of Applied Psychology*, 86, 499–512.

Dollard, M. F., & Bakker, A. B. (2010). Psychosocial safety climate as a precursor to conducive work environments, psychological health problems, and employee engagement. *Journal of Occupational and Organizational Psychology*, 83(3), 579–599.

Dollard, M. F., & Neser, D. Y. (2013). Worker health is good for the economy: Union density and psychosocial safety climate as determinants of country differences in worker health and productivity in 31 European countries. *Social Science & Medicine*, 92, 114–123.

Ducharme, L. J., Knudsen, H. K., & Roman, P. M. (2007). Emotional exhaustion and turnover intention in human service occupations: The protective role of coworker support. *Sociological Spectrum*, 28(1), 81–104.

Dysvik, A., Kuvaas, B., & Gagné, M. (2013). An investigation of the unique, synergistic and balanced relationships between basic psychological needs and intrinsic motivation. *Journal of Applied Social Psychology*, 43(5), 1050–1064.

Edmondson, A. (1999). Psychological safety and learning behavior in work teams. *Administrative Science Quarterly*, 44(2), 350–383.

Eppler, M. J., & Mengis, J. (2004). The concept of information overload: A review of literature from organization science, accounting, marketing, MIS, and related disciplines. *The Information Society*, 20, 325–344.

Ferster, G. B., & Skinner, B. F. (1957). *Schedules of Reinforcement*. New York: Appleton-Century-Crofts.

Fineman, S. (2006). On being positive: Concerns and counterpoints. *The Academy of Management Review*, 31, 270–291.

Fisher, C. D. (2002). Antecedents and consequences of real-time affective reactions at work. *Motivation and Emotion*, 26(1), 3–30.

Fredrickson, B. L. (2001). The role of positive emotions in positive psychology: The broaden-and-build theory of positive emotions. *American Psychologist*, 56, 218–226.

French, J. R. P. Jr., Caplan, R. D., & Harrison, R. V. (1982). *The Mechanisms of Job Stress and Strain*. London: Wiley.

French, J. R. P., Jr., & Kahn, R. L. (1962). A programmatic approach to studying the industrial environment and mental health. *Journal of Social Issues*, 18, 1–48.

Gable, S. L., & Haidt, J. (2005). What (and why) is positive psychology? *Review of General Psychology*, 9, 103–110.

Gagné, M., & Deci, E. L. (2005). Self-determination theory and work motivation. *Journal of Organizational Behavior*, 26, 331–362.

Gilbreth, F. B. (1911). *Motion Study*. New York: Van Nostrand.

Gillet, N., Colombat, P., Michinov, E., Pronost, A., & Fouquereau, E. (2013). Procedural justice, supervisor autonomy support, work satisfaction, organizational identification and job performance: The mediating role of need satisfaction and perceived organizational support. *Journal of Advanced Nursing*, 69, 2560–2571.

Goh, J., Pfeffer, J., & Zenios, S. A. (2016). The relationship between workplace stressors and mortality and health costs in the United States. *Management Science*, 62, 608–628.

Grant, A. M. (2007). Relational job design and the motivation to make a prosocial difference. *Academy of Management Review*, 32(2), 393–417.

Greguras, G. J., & Diefendorff, J. M. (2009). Different fits satisfy different needs: Linking person-environment fit to employee commitment and performance using Self-Determination Theory. *Journal of Applied Psychology*, 94(2), 465–477.

Griffin, M. A., & Neal, A. (2000). Perceptions of safety at work: A framework for linking safety climate to safety performance, knowledge, and motivation. *Journal of Occupational Health Psychology*, 5(3), 347–358.

Hackman, J., & Oldham, G. (1976). Motivation through the design of work: Test of a theory. *Organizational Behavior and Human Performance*, 16, 250–279.

Hackman, J. R., & Oldham, G. R. (1980). *Work Redesign*. Reading, MA: Addison-Wesley.

Hall, A. T., Royle, M. T., Brymer, R. A., Perrewé, P. L., Ferris, G. R., & Hochwarter, W. A. (2006). Relationships between felt accountability as a stressor and strain reactions: The neutralizing role of autonomy across two studies. *Journal of Occupational Health Psychology*, 11(1), 87–99.

Harris, K. J., Andrews, M. C., & Kacmar, K. M. (2007). The moderating effects of justice on the relationship between organizational politics and workplace attitudes. *Journal of Business and Psychology*, 22(2), 135–144.

Heaphy, E. D., & Dutton, J. E. (2008). Positive social interactions and the human body at work: Linking organizations and physiology. *Academy of Management Review*, 33(1), 137–162.

Heminger, A. R. (2014). Industrial revolution, customers, and process improvement. In: A. B. Badiru (ed.), *Handbook of Industrial and Systems Engineering*. Boca Raton, FL: CRC Press/Taylor and Francis, 45–49.

Hendrick, H. (2006). Sociotechnical systems theory: The sociotechnical systems model of work systems. In: W. Karwowski (ed.), *International Encyclopedia of Ergonomics and Human Factors*. Boca Raton, FL: CRC Press/Taylor and Francis, 2966–2968.

Herzberg, F. (1966). *Work and the Nature of Man*. Cleveland: World Publishing.

Hobfoll, S. E. (1989). Conservation of resources: A new attempt at conceptualizing stress. *American Psychologist*, 44, 513–524.

Holman, D., & Axtell, C. (2015). Can job redesign interventions influence a broad range of employee outcomes by changing multiple job characteristics? A quasi-experimental study. *Journal of Occupational Health Psychology*, 21(3), 284–295.

Holman, D., Axtell, C. M., Sprigg, C. A., Totterdell, P., & Wall, T. D. (2009). The mediating role of job characteristics in job redesign interventions: A serendipitous quasi-experiment. *Journal of Organizational Behavior*, 31, 84–105.

Idris, M. A., Dollard, M. F., Coward, J., & Dormann, C. (2012). Psychosocial safety climate: Conceptual distinctiveness and effect on job demands and worker psychological health. *Safety Science*, 50, 19–28.

Ilies, R., Scott, B. A., & Judge, T. A. (2006). The interactive effects of personal traits and experienced states on intraindividual patterns of citizenship behavior. *The Academy of Management Journal*, 49(3), 561–575.

Janssen, O., Lam, C. K., & Huang, X. (2010). Emotional exhaustion and job performance: The moderating roles of distributive justice and positive affect. *Journal of Organizational Behavior*, 31(6), 787–809.

Kahn, R. L., & Byosiere, P. (1992). Stress in organizations. In: M. D. Dunnette & L. M. Hough (eds.), *Handbook of Industrial and Organizational Psychology* (Vol. 3). Palo Alto, CA: Consulting Psychologists Press, 571–650.

Kalleberg, A. L., Nesheim, T., & Olsen, K. M. (2009). Is participation good or bad for workers? Effects of autonomy, consultation and teamwork on stress among workers in Norway. *Acta Sociologica*, 52(2), 99–116.

Kaplan, S., Bradley-Geist, J. C., Ahmad, A., Anderson, A., Hargrove, A. K., & Lindsey, A. (2014). A test of two positive psychology interventions to increase employee well-being. *Journal of Business and Psychology*, 29(3), 367–380.

Karasek, R., & Theorell, T. (1990). *Stress, Productivity, and the Reconstruction of Working Life*. New York: Basic Books.

Karwowski, W. (2012). The discipline of human factors and ergonomics. In: G. Salvendy (ed.), *Handbook of Human Factors and Ergonomics*. Hoboken, NJ: Wiley, 3–37.

Kim, W. C., & Mauborgne, R. (1997). Fair process: Managing in the knowledge economy. *Harvard Business Review*, 75, 65–75.

King, L. A., Heintzelman, S. J., & Ward, S. J. (2016). Beyond the search for meaning: A contemporary science of the experience of meaning in life. *Current Directions in Psychological Science*, 25, 211–216.

Kirkham, H. S., Clark, B. L., Bolas, C. A., Lewis, G. H., Jackson, A. S., Fisher, D., & Duncan, I. (2015). Which modifiable health risks are associated with changes in productivity costs? *Population Health Management*, 18(1), 30–38.

Kristof, A. L. (1996). Person-organization fit: An integrative review of its conceptualizations, measurement, and implications. *Personnel Psychology*, 49, 1–49.

Kristof-Brown, A. L., Zimmerman, R. D., & Johnson, E. C. (2005). Consequences of individuals' fit at work: A meta-analysis of person-job, person-organization, person-group, and person-supervisor fit. *Personnel Psychology*, 58, 281–342.

Law, R., Dollard, M. F., Tuckey, M. R., & Dormann, C. (2011). Psychosocial safety climate as a lead indicator of workplace bullying and harassment, job resources, psychological health and employee engagement. *Accident Analysis & Prevention*, 43(5), 1782–1793.

Lawler III, E. E. (1968). Equity theory as a predictor of productivity and work quality. *Psychological Bulletin*, 70, 596–610.

Lazarus, R. S., & Folkman, S. (1984). *Stress, Appraisal, and Coping*. New York: Springer.

Leiter, M. P., Day, A., Gilin Oore, D., & Laschinger, H. K. S. (2012). Getting better and staying better: Assessing civility, incivility, distress and job attitudes one year after a civility intervention. *Journal of Occupational Health Psychology*, 17, 425–434.

Leiter, M. P., Laschinger, H. K. S., Day, A., & Gilin Oore, D. (2011). The impact of civility interventions on employee social behavior, distress, and attitudes. *Journal of Applied Psychology*, 96, 1258–1274.

Leiter, M. P., & Maslach, C. (2004). Areas of worklife: A structured approach to organizational predictors of job burnout. In: P. Perrewé & D. C. Ganster (eds.), *Research in Occupational Stress and Well Being* (Vol. 3). Oxford, UK: Elsevier, 91–134.

Lindberg, P., & Vingård, E. (2011). Indicators of healthy work environments – A systematic review. *Work*, 41, 3032–3038.

Locke, E. A., & Latham, G. P. (1990). *A Theory of Goal Setting and Task Performance*. Englewood Cliffs, NJ: Prentice Hall.

Lohela, M., Björklund, C., Vingard, E., Hagberg, J., & Jensen, I. (2009). Does a change in psychosocial work factors lead to a change in employee health? *Journal of Occupational and Environmental Medicine*, 51(2), 195–203.

Luchman, J. N., & González-Morales, M. G. (2013). Demands, control, and support: A meta-analytic review of work characteristics interrelationships. *Journal of Occupational Health Psychology*, 18(1), 37.

Luthans, F. (2002). The need for and meaning of Positive Organizational Behavior. *Journal of Organizational Behavior*, 23, 695–706.

Luthans, F., Norman, S. M., Avolio, B. J., & Avey, J. B. (2008). The mediating role of psychological capital in the supportive organizational climate – employee performance relationship. *Journal of Organizational Behavior*, 29(2), 219–238.

Maslow, A. H. (1943). A theory of motivation. *Psychology Review*, 50, 370–396.

Mattke, S., Hangsheng, L., Caloyeras, J. P., Huang, C. Y., Van Busum, K. R., Khodyakov, D., & Shier, V. (2013). *Workplace Wellness Programs Study: Final Report*. Santa Monica, CA: RAND Corporation.

Meyers, M. C., van Woerkom, M., & Bakker, A. B. (2013). The added value of the positive: A literature review of positive psychology interventions in organizations. *European Journal of Work and Organizational Psychology*, 22, 618–632.

Mitchell, J. L. (1988). History of job analysis in military organizations. In: S. Gael (ed.), *The Job Analysis Handbook for Business, Industry, and Government*. New York: Wiley, 30–47.

Moen, P., Kelly, E. L., Tranby, E., & Huang, Q. (2011). Changing work, changing health: Can real work-time flexibility promote health behaviors and well-being? *Journal of Health and Social Behavior*, 52(4), 404–429.

Mosier, K. L., Sethi, N., McCauley, S., Khoo, L., & Orasanu, J. M. (2007). What you don't know can hurt you: Factors impacting diagnosis in the automated cockpit. *Human Factors*, 49(2), 300–310.

Munsterberg, H. (1913). *Psychology and Industrial Efficiency*. Boston: Houghton Mifflin.

Murray, H. A. (1938). *Explorations in Personality*. New York: Oxford University Press.

Nijp, H. H., Beckers, D. G., Geurts, S. A., Tucker, P., & Kompier, M. A. (2012). Systematic review on the association between employee worktime control and work-non-work balance, health and well-being, and job-related outcomes. *Scandinavian Journal of Work, Environment & Health*, 38(4), 299–313.

Park, R., & Searcy, D. (2012). Job autonomy as a predictor of mental well-being: The moderating role of quality-competitive environment. *Journal of Business and Psychology*, 27(3), 305–316.

Porter, L. W., & Lawler, E. E. III. (1968). *Managerial Attitudes and Performance*. Homewood, IL: Irwin-Dorsey.

Primoff, E. S., & Fine, S. A. (1988). A history of job analysis. In: S. Gael (ed.), *The Job Analysis Handbook for Business, Industry, and Government*. New York: Wiley, 14–29.

Quick, J. C. (1999). Occupational health psychology: The convergence of health and clinical psychology with public health and preventive medicine in an organizational context. *Professional Psychology: Research and Practice*, 30, 123–128.

Rajaratnam, A. S., Sears, L. E., Shi, Y., Coberley, C. R., & Pope, J. E. (2014). Well-being, health, and productivity improvement after an employee well-being intervention in large retail distribution centers. *Journal of Occupational and Environmental Medicine*, 56(12), 1291–1296.

Rego, A., & Souto, S. (2009). Does the need to belong moderate the relationship between perceptions of spirit of camaraderie and employees' happiness? *Journal of Occupational Health Psychology*, 14(2), 148.

Robbins, J. M., Ford, M. T., & Tetrick, L. E. (2012). Perceived unfairness and employee health: A meta-analytic integration. *Journal of Applied Psychology*, 97, 235–272.

Rosso, B. D., Dekas, K. H., & Wrzesniewski, A. (2010). On the meaning of work: A theoretical integration and review. *Research in Organizational Behavior*, 30, 91–127.

Sauter, S. L., & Murphy, L. R. (eds.). (1995). *Organizational Risk Factors for Job Stress*. Washington, DC: American Psychological Association.

Sears, L. E., Shi, Y., Coberley, C. R., & Pope, J. E. (2013). Overall well-being as a predictor of health care, productivity, and retention outcomes in a large employer. *Population Health Management*, 16(6), 397–405.

Seligman, M. E. P., & Csikszentmihalyi, M. (2000). Positive psychology. *American Psychologist*, 55, 5–14.

Selye, H. (1956). *The Stress of Life*. New York: McGraw-Hill.

Selye, H. (1967). *Stress in Health and Disease*. Boston: Butterworth.

Siegrist, J. (1996). Adverse health effects of high-effort/low-reward conditions. *Journal of Occupational Health Psychology*, 1, 27–41.

Slemp, G., & Vella-Brodrick, D. (2014). Optimising employee mental health: The relationship between intrinsic need satisfaction, job crafting, and employee well-being. *Journal of Happiness Studies*, 15(4), 957–977.

Soane, E., Shantz, A., Alfes, K., Truss, C., Rees, C., & Gatenby, M. (2013). The association of meaningfulness, well-being, and engagement with absenteeism: A moderated mediation model. *Human Resource Management*, 52(3), 441–456.

Steger, M. F., Dik, B. J., & Duffy, R. D. (2012). Measuring meaningful work: The work and meaning inventory (WAMI). *Journal of Career Assessment*, 20, 322–337.

Taylor, F. W. (1911). *Principles of Scientific Management*. New York: Harper Bros. Publishing.

Thompson, C. A., & Prottas, D. J. (2006). Relationships among organizational family support, job autonomy, perceived control, and employee well-being. *Journal of Occupational Health Psychology*, 11(1), 100–118.

Tims, M., Derks, D., & Bakker, A. B. (2016). Job crafting and its relationships with person–job fit and meaningfulness: A three-wave study. *Journal of Vocational Behavior*, 92, 44–53.

Turner, N., Barling, J., & Zacharatos, A. (2002). Positive psychology at work. In: C. Snyder & S. J. Lopez (eds.), *Handbook of Positive Psychology*. New York: Oxford University Press, 715–728.

Tyler, T. R. (1990). *Why People Obey the Law*. New Haven, CT: Yale University Press.

Van den Broeck, A., Ferris, D. L., Chang, C. H., & Rosen, C. C. (2016). Review of research on Self-Determination Theory's basic psychological needs at work. *Journal of Management*, 20, 1–35.

Van den Broeck, A., Vansteenkiste, M., De Witte, H., & Lens, W. (2008). Examining the relationships between job characteristics, burnout, and engagement: The role of basic psychological need satisfaction. *Work & Stress*, 22, 277–294.

Vroom, V. H. (1964). *Work and Motivation*. New York: Wiley.

Vroom, V. H. (2004). Decision making: The Vroom-Yetton-Jago models. In: G. R. Goethals, G. J. Sorenson, & J. M. Burns (eds.), *Encyclopedia of Leadership*. Thousand Oaks, CA: Sage Publications, 322–325.

White, R. W. (1959). Motivation reconsidered: The concept of competence. *Psychological Review*, 66, 297–333.

Wright, T. A., Cropanzano, R., & Bonett, D. G. (2007). The moderating role of employee positive well being on the relation between job satisfaction and job performance. *Journal of Occupational Health Psychology*, 12(2), 93–104.

Wrzesniewski, A., LoBuglio, N., Dutton, J. E., & Berg, J. M. (2013). Job crafting and cultivating positive meaning and identity in work. *Advances in Positive Organizational Psychology*, 1(1), 281–302.

5

Determinants of mental health in the workplace

Peter Hosie, Russel PJ Kingshott, and Piyush Sharma

Introduction

[M]ental health in the mainstream of public policy have demonstrated, mental health policy is no longer limited to a segregated enclave under the direction of a specialized bureaucracy. It has moved into the mainstream across a wide range of public policy dimensions.

(Goldman, Sherry, & Alegria, 2009, p. 1215)

Declining mental health is an endemic global phenomenon. The magnitude and nature of this affliction has societal, organizational, and individual implications, given that mental health has no geographic, cultural, or organizational boundaries. According to the World Health Organization (2013), at least 450 million people suffer from mental health problems in both developed and underdeveloped countries. The United Nations estimates that 25% of world's population experience a mental health episode during their lifetime, which is both a cause and a consequence of major socioeconomic problems such as poverty, compromised education, gender inequality, ill health, and violence, among others (United Nations, 2010). Globally, some 3%–4% of the Gross National Product is estimated to be spent on problems related to mental health within the workplace (World Health Organization, 2003). Eventually, the hidden cost of mental health in the workplace is likely to be far greater in terms of lost individual performance and organizational productivity. Clearly, urgent attention and action are essential to help curb this problem.

Dealing with poor mental health in society should be viewed equally as a policy and workplace problem. Typically, one in 10 employees are estimated to suffer from depression, anxiety, stress, or burnout in the European Union, United States, Canada, and Australia during their working lives (Gabriel & Liimatainen, 2000). Accumulated evidence suggests that work environments contribute to a range of mental ailments across a wide spectrum of employment settings (e.g., Lim, Kim, Kim, Yang, & Lee, 2010; Love, Edwards, & Irani, 2010; Pasca & Wagner, 2012; Puig et al., 2012; Travers & Cooper, 1993). Hence, a major responsibility of finding solutions to mental health afflictions inevitably rests with organizations where these arise. The real issue facing organizational decision-makers is not whether they have to deal with mental health issues but rather *how* they can best tackle this growing problem in the context of limited resources.

Whilst there is considerable literature indicating the problems are inherent within organizations, one promising avenue of research in explaining how to address mental health issues relates to how positive actions can yield both desirable individual wellbeing and effective organizational outcomes (e.g., Cameron, Mora, Leutscher, & Calarco, 2011; Gabriel & Liimatainen, 2000). Affirmative action in wider societal settings is known to help improve the mental health of individuals in the workplace (e.g., Hickie, 2004; Pirkis et al., 2005), suggesting similar organizational initiatives and interventions can help contribute to the wellbeing of those suffering mental health symptoms and disorders. Initiatives by organizations to improve the mental health of their workforce will have correspondingly positive societal ramifications. Healthy workforces signal a healthy society. Hence policy and managerial decision-makers both stand to gain through collective action designed to improve individual mental health in the workplace.

In this respect, policy and organizational initiatives are akin to two sides of the same coin. Accordingly, both policy and organizational stakeholders need to be cognizant of the impact mental health potentially has within and on each person's sphere of influence, in developing and implementing effective strategies directed at improving the situation. With that notion specifically in mind, the main aim of this chapter is to synthesize the literature to help contextualize the impact of mental health on and within organizations in light of policy decisions and/or actions pertaining to mental health. As mental health has no physical boundaries (Kitchener & Jorm, 2004), the variety of mental health afflictions will also permeate many facets of people's lives such as the workplace, societal institutions, and broader society. We develop a conceptual framework (Figure 5.1) that unravels the link between these and the four elements of mental health, namely personal wellbeing, coping, symptoms, and disorders. Based on our review of extant literature, we posit these four elements influence and are strongly influenced by aspects of organizations, governments, and wider society. To the best of our knowledge this is the first time such an approach has been adopted in the extant literature. Through this framework we are able

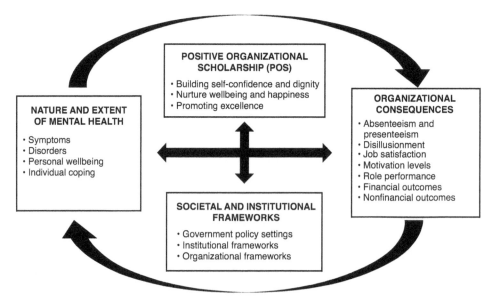

Figure 5.1 Interaction of Nature and Extent of Mental Health, Organizational Consequences, Positive Organizational Scholarship, and Societal and Institutional Frameworks

to infer how mental health problems in society have a range of consequences for organizations. Similarly, mental health problems in organizations impact on society. Within the framework, the potential links between these domains are suitable for testing. In all, the conceptual framework helps to provide a better understanding of the potential role that government, societal entities, and organizations can play in helping to deal with issues concerning mental health.

Our framework synthesizes the various strands of research and thinking about mental health in the workplace and identifies areas for testing constructs and their inter-relationships. Central to our argument is that the domains of Nature and Extent of Mental Health, Positive Organizational Scholarship (POS), Societal and Institutional Frameworks, and Organizational Consequences are intertwined. An understanding of the interactive effects of these domains will place decision-makers in an optimal position to find solutions to these growing workforce and societal mental health problems. In the sections that follow, we explore the magnitude and cost of mental health problems within society and the workplace; links between POS and mental health; the "happier-and-smarter" and "sadder-but-wiser" hypotheses; societal and institutional frameworks that impact on mental health; and finally the contribution, implications, and future research directions of mental health.

We used a simple methodology to identify the relevant extant literature suitable for analysis. Google® and Google Scholar® were scrutinized using the following keywords: mental health, public policy, conceptual, framework, organization, wellbeing, consequences, Positive Organizational Scholarship, workplace, world health organization. A substantial number of high-quality reports into mental health were identified from countries in Europe, the United Kingdom, the United States, Australia, and Canada. The websites of other credible international organizations concerned with mental health were also closely examined, including the International Labour Organization, World Health Organization, and the US Department of Health and Human Services. We now turn our attention to defining mental health before reviewing the relevant literature on mental health in society and the workplace.

Theoretical background

Defining mental health

From a macro perspective, "mental health" refers to the state of successful performance of mental function, resulting in productive activities, fulfilling relationships with other people, and an ability to adapt to change and to cope with adversity (US Department of Health and Human Services, 1999). This comprises four elements that reflect both positive (*personal wellbeing* and *coping*) and negative (*symptoms* and *disorders*) dimensions – influenced by individual factors, social interactions, societal structures and resources, and cultural values (Korkeila et al., 2003). Disorders are those health conditions characterized by alterations in thinking, mood, or behavior (or some combination thereof) associated with distress and/or impaired functioning (US Department of Health and Human Services, 1999).

Warr's Vitamin model (1986, 1987, 1994, 2007) provides a more focused description of mental health in relation to work. This model synthesizes prior research and theories about job-related mental health to develop an evidence-based integrated model of mental health in the workplace context. More recently, Warr (2007, p. 132) introduced 12 features of jobs and environmental categories that underlie job-related affective wellbeing: opportunity for control, opportunity for skill use, externally generated goals, variety, environmental clarity, contact with others, availability of money, physical security, and valued social position; and supportive supervision, career outlook, and equity. In this context, *stress* and *burnout* are used predominantly to describe afflictions linked to work outcomes, whereas mental health and depression are context-free (see Hosie & Sevastos, 2010). In fact, *stress* is not generally regarded as a medical condition, whereas depression and anxiety are (Cooper, 2005). This illustrates that the mental health problem is quite complex to define and conceptualize, let alone address. We do not, however, propose to articulate the various forms of mental illness but rather to provide an overview of the nexus between the various afflictions, society, and the work environment. Therefore, our purpose is to provide a framework that encapsulates these aspects so employers and policy-makers can better contemplate their role in helping to reduce mental health problems in the workplace. In doing so, we aim to provide a suitable platform for future empirical research into this growing problem and subsequently provide potential solutions.

Cost of workplace mental health

Mental health problems in the workplace are not a new phenomenon. It is worth noting that hidden, or indirect, costs of mental health place additional burdens on the consequential public monies in areas of social care, education, housing, criminal justice, and social security systems (Knaap, 2003). Whether this is attributed to real increases in the incidence of such problems or simply improved reporting and documentation methods will always be a point for debate. What is not in dispute is that the direct as well as indirect costs of mental health have been on the rise for decades. In this regard, there is an unequivocal body of evidence that the global financial cost from negative aspects of mental health is debilitating for both industry and society. The estimated cumulative global economic output lost to mental disorders will amount to US$16.3 trillion between 2011 and 2030 (Bloom et al., 2011). This cost has increased significantly over the last few decades and is predicted to substantially increase into the future, and is not bound by geography.

For example, more than a decade ago, the cost of stress at work, and related mental health problems in the European Union alone was estimated to average between 3% to 4% of Gross National Product, amounting to a €265 billion cost annually (Levi, 2002). During 2000, a survey of the then-15 EU member states found over half of their total 160 million workers reported having a very high incidence of sick leave, citing stress and mental strain as the principal reason (World Health Organization, 2005). In United Kingdom, stress, depression, or anxiety was the largest contributor to the overall estimated annual days lost due to work-related illness (Tasho, Jordan, & Robertson, 2005). The British economy lost approximately 3.5% of Gross National Product per annum, equating to £40 billion per year on stress-related illness (Toohey, 1995). In the same period, work-related stress alone cost businesses and governments across the European Union about €20 billion in absenteeism and related health costs. These estimates do not even include the costs of lower productivity, higher staff turnover, and reduced ability to innovate (Konkolewsky, 2004).

Typically, in the United Kingdom time off work for stress related illnesses has increased by 500% since the 1950s. In 2003, more than half a million Britons believed they experienced work-related stress that made them ill (Jones, Huxtable, Hodgson, & Price, 2003). At least 5% of all British workers found their job either very or extremely stressful. These stress levels translated into an estimated average of 28.5 working days lost in each year per affected worker, making this type of ailment very costly for the British economy. More recent UK data indicates a growing problem in terms of both the overall economy and public costs. Typically, around 42% of people claiming work related benefits are diagnosed with mental health conditions, up from 28% since 1997 (Hay, 2010). The UK Royal College of Psychiatrists estimated that up to 30% of British employees experience mental health problems. The question of cause and effect on mental health in the workplace still remains largely unresolved. Despite this, about one in every 20 working-aged

Britons experience major depression at any given point in time (Gabriel & Liimatainen, 2000) and this evidently impacts on public funds and industry.

In an Australian context, mental health disorders are the third largest contributor to the overall cost burden of disease (Begg et al., 2007). Depression alone is very widespread, whereby 20% of Australians are estimated to suffer from the affliction (Beyondblue, 2008; Rosenberg & Hickie, 2013). In an earlier study, Goldie (2004) notes that time off work for mental illness–related compensation claims averaged 96.1 days of lost productivity, compared to 28.9 days for other health claims. Brammall (1999) reported work-related stress claims for compensation in Australia rose from 1.7% in 1985–1986, to 5.1% in 1997–1998. During the time of this study, work-related stress claims were estimated to double in the period 1992–1997, costing the economy in excess of AUD$200 million annually. An estimated $5.9 billion is attributable to workplace distress in Australia, with to cost of depression costing in the order of $12.6 billion (Fels, 2016).

Current expenditure was almost AUD$6.9 billion (or $309 per person) for the 2010–2011 period, an increase from $238 per person since 2006–2007 (Australian Institute of Health and Welfare, 2013). Recently, an estimated 1.9 million Australians (9% of the population) received mental health services during 2010–2011, including 15 million mental health related general practitioner visits in 2011–2012 (Australian Institute of Health and Welfare, 2013). Similar patterns are observed in the United Kingdom, United States, and Canada.

In North America during 2009–2010, Oliffe and Han (2014) report that approximately 78% of short-term and 67% of long-term disability claims were mental health related. Clinical depression is one of the most common illnesses in the United States, with costs estimated to range between US$30 billion and $44 billion per annum to treat (Gabriel & Liimatainen, 2000). These authors also report that one in 10 working-age US adults became affected with the ailment each year, resulting in a loss of approximately 200 million working days. The overall cost from depression to US businesses amounts to around US$25 billion a year in absenteeism and low productivity, and a further $15 billion for treatment (Moskowitz, 1998).

Clearly, attitudes towards the problem need to change: a failure to take responsibility for employee wellbeing will have both a wider long-term as well as a more immediate range of negative consequences for organizations. In fact, employers have a duty to take care of their employees in the workplace to protect them from injuries derived through physical and/ or psychological wellbeing (Cooper & Cartwright, 1994). In this respect, it is largely immaterial whether poor mental health and associated costs were: (1) directly caused by the work environment, (2) brought into the work environment from preexisting conditions, or (3) a combination of both. Irrespective of the attribution, when viewed through the employer lens, reduced mental health levels within the workforce lead to losses in employee productivity and performance. From a productivity vantage, let alone a legal and moral stance, it makes perfect sense for organizations to play a greater role in helping find solutions to these seemingly intractable problems. Given the nature of the mental health challenge, it is evident that the best approach for them to take would be to ensure organizational policy and procedures concurrently serve the best interests of both organizations and their employees.

POS and mental health

Based on the previous discussion, we argue that shifting focus to explore the positive view of the mind (Cameron & Caza, 2004; Snyder & Lopez, 2002) has potential to contribute to explaining how organizations can respond to many mental health challenges. This approach should also help inform managerial actions designed to simultaneously serve organizational and employee interests. Our argument extends the POS domain, which helps explain and predict the occurrence, causes, and consequences of issues concerning individual, group, organizational, and mental health. We reinforce the main thrust of POS in relation to mental health as it underpins the logic inherent in this chapter.

POS is the study of dealing with positive "outcomes, processes and attributes of organizations and their members" (Cameron, Dutton, & Quinn, 2003, p. 4). While not grounded in any particular theory, POS draws on theories, models, and constructs that help explain how human excellence within organizations can be encouraged. POS can help explain the positive actions that employers can take to improve the mental health of their employees. Typical examples of POS studies include recognizing the impact of positive affect, organizational citizenship behaviors, psychological capital, and prosocial behavior within organizations (Avey, Nimnich, & Pigeon, 2010; Baruch, O'Creevy, Hind, & Vigoda-Gabot, 2004; Castro, Douglas, Hochwarter, Ferris, & Frink, 2003; Mayfield & Taber, 2010; Sun, Aryee, & Law, 2007).

POS attempts to explore how individuals' quality of life can be enhanced, particularly those who work within and are affected by organizations (Roberts, 2006). POS is conceptualized in terms of caring, compassionate support, forgiveness, inspiration, fostering respect, integrity, and gratitude, as well as the creation of meaningful work (Cameron et al., 2011). It can help explain how organizational decision-makers can assist in the rehabilitation of individuals suffering from poor mental health, because the elements in POS identified by Cameron et al. (2011) cut across many of the areas in the literature depicted to help improve mental health and individual wellbeing. For example, the well-established positive association between workforce participation and elevated psychological wellbeing (Dooley, Fielding, & Levi, 1996; Mathers & Schofield, 1998) indicates the merit of adopting a POS approach to improving individual mental wellbeing.

Such practice and scholarly endeavors in relation to POS focus on understanding those dynamics associated with and leading to developing human strength that produces resilience, restoration, and vitality. Through this activity, employers can cultivate extraordinary individuals, units, and organizations. POS helps focus our attention on understanding how decision-makers can increase the *positive* rather than reducing all problem solutions to examining the *negative* within organizations (Caza & Caza, 2008). Based on studies and evidence cited, it is apparent that organizations are not only central to help finding societal mental health solutions but in doing so will also need to take a more proactive approach. This necessitates organizations take positive affirmative action. Whilst we do acknowledge the critics of POS (e.g., Fineman, 2006; Held, 2004), as research in this domain potentially yields individual and organizational benefits associated with managerial POS action, this body of knowledge simply cannot be ignored.

Work by Cameron et al. (2011) reveals that POS practices help enhance organizational performance levels, which they attribute directly to amplifying (creation of positive emotions), buffering (enhancing resilience, solidarity and efficacy) and heliotropic (attraction towards positive energy) effects of such managerial action. Psychological capital, defined as "an individual's positive psychological state of development," has a positive effect on an employee's role performance and job satisfaction levels, both of which are strongly associated with mental wellbeing, and this provides a further indication of the role of positivity within organizations (Luthans, Avolio, Avey, & Norman, 2007, p. 542). On a similar trajectory, earlier work by Bagnall (2004) observed that although unhappiness (which is intrinsically negative) may be a much more interesting phenomena to research, happy people do better in almost every sphere of life. For example, Lyubomirsky, King, and Diener (2005) found that happy people tend to acquire more favorable life circumstances that engender success – a condition that holds across multiple life domains, such as marriage, friendship, health, and job performance.

Clearly, there is merit in building programs within the work setting designed to stimulate and foster happiness and positivity among employees. The potential organizational benefits of cultivating these are well documented (Pressman & Cohen, 2005; Seligman & Csikszentmihalyi, 2000), indicating that organizations should help to propagate happiness, wellbeing, courage, citizenship, healthy work, and healthy working relationships. We conceptualize such positive action within the workplace in terms of actions designed to enhance self-confidence and dignity, nurturing wellbeing and happiness, and to promote employee excellence. Collectively, these comprise elements of the POS domain within our framework (Figure 5.1). The literature strongly indicates that the key to unlocking an individual's full potential and subsequent mental wellbeing is through such forms of constructive managerial actions.

Critics argue that the POS approach is merely self-centered on the part of decision-makers (e.g., Fineman, 2006; Roberts, 2006), but we advocate this positive method has merit for a number of reasons. Any effort to help reduce individual suffering can, and should, be a prime organizational concern. Put more directly, it is time all the bad news about diminished mental health and consequences in the workplace is countervailed by good news stories. Such a viewpoint clearly falls under the auspices of POS. Initiatives such as beyondblue and Mental Health First Aid (MHFA), in Australia, are excellent examples of positive action taken within the wider community context. These efforts consistently show that increased mental health knowledge and decreased stigma contribute to individual empowerment to help others within the community (Hickie, 2004; Menhenhall & Jackson, 2013).

Indeed research in occupational psychology centers on incorporating happiness, wellbeing, courage, citizenship, and satisfaction with healthy work and healthy relationships (Cameron et al., 2003; Keyes & Haidt, 2003). There is growing resistance in psychology to be obsessing over the dark side of human existence – in favor of effort being directed towards a more positive view of the mind (Cameron & Caza, 2004; Snyder & Lopez, 2002). Such intense enthusiasm for POS is naturally balanced with the countervailing experience of emotional darkness (Jung, 1933), simply because nurturing a positive environment does not mean an absence or the total elimination from suffering. Both belong to the human narrative. Seligman (cited in Hosie and ElRakhawy, 2014, 122) tempers the case for POS by recognizing this potential duality: "By working on mental illness we forgot about making the lives of relatively untroubled people happier, more productive and more fulfilling. We didn't develop interventions to make people happier; we developed interventions to make people less miserable." Such conceptualization suggests that addressing mental health can be approached from either the "positive" or "negative" vantage as either is simply attempting to provide a remedy for either side of the same coin.

"Happier-and-smarter" and "sadder-but-wiser"

Herein it is posited that interest in "happier-and-smarter" ("enthusiasm-naivety") and the "sadder-but-wiser" ("depressive-realism") hypotheses (Staw & Barsade, 1993) is synonymous within the broader context of research efforts directed towards POS. In this regard, Staw and Barsade's (1993) "happier-and-smarter" and the "sadder-but-wiser" hypotheses are considered integral to any discussion pertaining to POS. These authors found a positive relationship between dispositional affect and employee performance. However, Weiss and Cropanzano (1996) contend these positive emotional responses are inclined to produce decrements in performance. These authors reason that activities resulting from a negative state are more extensive and constantly disruptive than those stemming from a positive emotional state. A "depression-realism" effect indicates depressed people may sometimes make more accurate judgments compared to their less-depressed counterparts. In this conceptualization, emotional behaviors have the potential to facilitate, to interfere, or simply to be unrelated with behaviors in the job domain (Weiss & Cropanzano, 1996). Indeed, reactions to negative events produce stronger reactions than the reactions to positive experiences (Taylor, 1991).

Individuals experiencing positive moods are more likely to engage in simplified heuristic processing when making judgments and decisions (Sinclair & Mark, 1992). In contrast, those individuals experiencing a negative mood are likely to be more prone to utilizing systematic information-processing strategies. Individuals reporting negative affect tend to focus attention on improving the quality of decisions made (Forgas, 2002; Schwarz & Bless, 1991). Perhaps this is because people with negative affect are more sensitive to organizational reality, where "depressive realism" effects depressive tendencies that avoid a range of biases, such as optimism (Lichtenstein, Fischoff, & Phillips, 1982; Martin & Stang, 1978) and the illusion of control (Langer, 1975). As such, individuals who are less positive exercise more accurate information processing (Weiss & Cropanzano, 1996). For example, a person with depressive tendencies is less likely to overestimate his or her capacity to deal with ambiguous task circumstances (Tabachnik, Crocker, & Alloy, 1983). Such a counterintuitive position regarding the possible decrements in performance resulting from the emotion-performance relationship is likely to be contentious. The pursuit of microconcerns of positive and negative affect in the workplace needs to be connected with the macroconcerns and initiatives of society.

Overall, a common theme has emerged from the experience of dealing with mental health policy, namely the critical importance of engaging a wide array of stakeholders in the development and success of national policy and frameworks. In Australia, for example, all three tiers of government have usually been responsible for mental health policy, program, and services. Moreover, there is considerable overlap between service provision between the government, private, and not-for-profit sectors. These services are delivered either directly or by outsourcing to private agencies capable of providing enduring holistic solutions (Rosenberg & Hickie, 2013). Evidence to date suggests that the most effective solutions are provided by community organizations, not government. Rosenberg and Hickie (2013) made the case for the emergence of collaborative and coordinated care in response to this challenging public policy issue. As with any consumer-based system, they argued that collaborative care needs to provide integrated options capable of providing effective delivery systems. In this scenario, new models of "joined-up services" delivery needs to informed by existing and emerging evidence of what is effective for consumers of mental health solutions. Mental health needs to overcome the existing "policy silos" to overcome a complex system that is "characterised by fragmentation and inconsistency" (Rosenberg & Hickie, 2013, p. 16).

Societal and institutional frameworks that impact mental health

There are personal and environmental determinants of poor mental health that include an individual's attributes and interactions; sociocultural, economic, political, and environmental factors, such as national policies, social protection, living standards, working conditions; and community support mechanisms (World Health Organisation, 2013). With these in mind, the World Health Organization developed the Mental Health Action Plan 2013–2020 to promote global mental wellbeing, provide care, enhance recovery, promote human rights, and reduce mortality, morbidity, and disability for persons with mental disorders (World Health Organisation, 2013). This plan is based on a number of recommended universal principles that can be tailored to member states to ensure consistency with their national priorities and specific circumstances. There is no universal grand plan to solve global mental health problems, as countries are at different stages in developing and implementing policy responses for this growing problem. For example, between 76% and 85% of people received no treatment for their mental disorder in low-income and middle-income countries, whereas this ranged between 35% and 50% for high-income countries (World Health Organisation, 2013).

Some governments have already taken steps through programs designed to promote the mental wellbeing of their citizens. For example, the Australian National Mental Health Commission Strategies and Action Plan 2012–2015 has been developed to monitor and report on the state of mental health in Australia. Although still in its infancy, the plan comprises a national reporting card, benchmark of performance, identification of key priorities and data gaps, and an evaluation mechanism to chart progress against a 10-year roadmap promoting improved mental health. One of the successful spin-offs of the strategy was the formation of the independent, not-for-profit public entity beyondblue, with key priorities that include: (1) increasing awareness of depression and anxiety; (2) reducing stigma and discrimination; (3) improving help seeking; (4) prevention and early intervention; (5) reducing impact, disability, and mortality; and (6) facilitating learning, collaboration, and research (beyondblue, 2013). At inception this national collaborative model was initially funded by the Federal and Victorian Governments, with $17.5 million each year over five years. Beyondblue now attracts funding from other state governments in partnership with a range of businesses, educational, and community organizations.

Another Australian initiative is the Mental Health First Aid (MHFA), which developed courses in 2000 that are offered by the Centre for Mental Health Research, Australian National University. The main reason for the program was to help those many suffers in workplaces who wait far too long before seeking help. MHFA aims to increase public recognition of the early warning signs and symptoms pertaining to anxiety, depression, psychotic disorders, and substance abuse disorders (see www.mhfa.com.au). It is a direct type of affirmative action and specifically targets sufferers. The course has been so successful that it is now replicated worldwide (Menhenhall & Jackson, 2013; Terry, 2010; Zilnyk, 2010). MHFA has also been shown to be quite versatile in terms of its adaptability to cater to a range of settings that include different countries and targeted employment initiatives (Jorm & Kitchener, 2011). MHFA has the capacity to be tailored to align with the various national and state level priorities and capabilities in each jurisdiction. Major MHFA outcomes include increased mental health knowledge, decreased stigma, and increased confidence in helping persons with a mental health crisis (Menhenhall & Jackson, 2013). By increasing mental health literacy through the course, members of the public (and work colleagues) can provide initial help in acute mental health crisis situations, as well as emotional support, for those experiencing mental illness before professional help can be sought.

Experiences of the role of national frameworks and platforms in the prevention of mental health such as beyondblue and MHFA are not unique to Australia. For example, during 2003–2004, Canadian health care experts and economic policy leaders declared their first-ever Business Year for Addiction and Mental Health forum. Through this forum a charter was developed that was aimed at mobilizing key stakeholders (namely trade unions and employers in the private and public sectors) through national and international efforts, and was aimed at preventing the debilitating effects of workplace depression, anxiety, and addiction. The Mental Health Commission of Canada has subsequently developed a national standard to provide a systematic approach to developing and sustaining a psychologically healthier workplace (Mental Health Commission of Canada, 2013). The Canadian plan comprises three strategic pillars – namely prevention, promotion, and resolution – designed to reduce the incidence of 13 workplace factors known to contribute to poor mental health. Similar to the Australian frameworks, this particular initiative also casts the net wide in terms of engaging stakeholders in the debate by including unions, employer groups, and employers, among others. Involvement from leaders of such entities are crucial to ensure the psychological wellbeing of the work force (Gilbert & Blisker, 2012). Inputs and support from these stakeholders are tantamount for such programs to gain traction.

Conceptual framework and contributions

Drawing upon existing frameworks described in previous sections, we posit that organizational actions, depicted through POS and various national policy frameworks and initiatives, and encapsulated by the Societal and Institutional Frameworks, are highly interdependent. The effects of these domains on one another and their moderating powers in the recursive relationship between mental health and organizational consequences are reflected in our conceptual framework. Through this we offer an overarching perspective on how to juxtapose mental health within organizations and wider society. Specifically, the escalating incidence of poor mental health in society permeates many facets of people's lives, creating numerous challenges. The individual's mental wellbeing has become analogous to the workplace and society. In an effort to help understand the problem, we have synthesized the literature and articulated a framework that contextualizes the nature and extent of poor mental health in the context of these domains. The main scholarly contribution of this approach is fivefold.

First, it offers a unique insight into mental health problems. Adopting this perspective has made it possible to juxtapose the institutional influencers of mental health. These were modelled in terms of domains comprising Nature and Extent of Mental Health, POS, Societal & Institutional Frameworks, and Organizational Consequences.

Second, the framework reveals the critical importance of understanding how the interactive effect of policy settings and managerial action plays a critical role in finding solutions to this problem. By inference, a joint government-organizational action has the potential for a greater impact on poor mental health than unilateral and/or independent efforts of either party. Such interaction is also envisaged to potentially comprise other stakeholders, such as employees, employer groups, industry bodies, and unions. We do not specifically discuss these stakeholder contributions in detail in this chapter, but the evidence shows how valuable their inputs are with respect to the many known mental health challenges (Hickie, 2004; Mental Health Commission of Canada, 2013).

Third, in line with calls from the International Labor Organization and the World Health Authority and other entities, the framework indicates that an organizations response (or lack of) to the mental health challenge is central to finding solutions to this conundrum. Since organizations are seen to be both the *source* and proposed *solution* to the mental health problem, they need to shoulder more of the burden for finding solutions. In that regard, their actions can have positive or negative consequences for both the firm and wider society. Thus, the moderating effects of POS and Societal and Institutional Frameworks potentially enhance (dampen) the positive (negative) outcomes. Our synthesis of the literature reveals that a healthy workforce usually equated to a healthy society, and vis-à-vis, so affirmative action by organizations under the auspices of POS is depicted herein to have widespread benefits.

Fourth, available studies in this domain are largely descriptive in nature, thus developing and testing appropriate cause-effect models with pertinent constructs would be most beneficial. This is because research findings would potentially help policy and organizational decision-makers decide on *how* and *where* they can direct their limited resources to achieve maximum effect.

Fifth, there appears to be no systematic examination in the extant literature as to what types of workplaces (and role types) lead to the recursive relationship between mental wellbeing and organizational consequences. Since this nexus may vary across work settings, the blanket view taken in the literature to designate the link between poor mental health and the workplace is not ideal. Clearly, a typology comprising various professions and the mental health consequences of each work setting is worth exploring in more detail. This would help employers become more vigilant in ensuring its decision-makers are cognizant of mental health problems, their likely consequences for the individual and organizations, and perhaps more importantly, what they can do about these problems. However, lessons still need to be learned on how to prepare organizations to deal with growing cases of aliments such as stress, depression, and anxiety in the workplace.

Ultimately, the framework developed in this chapter could be used to help decision-makers determine which job roles are more susceptible to mental health problems. This would enable them to identify high-risk employees and determine precisely what remedial action needs to be taken. Potentially this would minimize the wasteful use of limited resources in trying to develop programs for nonexistent problems.

Sixth, the framework indicates how affirmative action, under the semblance of POS, can help improve the mental wellbeing of employees. Various forms of "positive" action are cited in the literature but none appear to be specific to the context of mental health. Thus, identifying and testing an effective compendium of positive action specific to this setting that could help improve mental health within the workplace research-praxis priorities. The success of MHFA program shows the value in proactive action on mental health outcomes (Menhenhall & Jackson, 2013; Terry, 2010; Zilnyk, 2010) but since research may uncover a much wider range of policy and practice options in the repertoire of the framework for dealing with this line of inquiry merits further investigation.

On a final note, whilst the principal aim of this research was to provide a framework to help articulate mental health problems in the workplace, we have also uncovered a range of managerial implications. In the first instance, managers should recognize that the sheer scale and scope of poor mental health within society means that it will inevitably afflict their work environment. This means organizational decision-makers also need to play a role in formulating viable solutions to the problem. Executives and managers need to realize that they are in a unique position to influence key stakeholders because their actions can contribute towards and potentially help reduce mental health problems. On the basis of our synthesis of the literature, the most effective approach would be to take a proactive stance and develop positive action in conjunction with government and other stakeholders. Failure to do this would inevitably result in a further increase in the incidence of mental health in the workplace and this would ultimately put more pressure on the public funds. In order to take corrective action, policy-setters are then likely to take legislative measures that would have the effect of transferring the cost burden and responsibility of ameliorating mental health back onto the employer. Therefore, it is in organizations' best interests to take the leadership in breaking the vicious cycle between poor mental health, the workplace, and society.

Directions for future research

In addition to its scholarly contributions, our framework can serve as a platform for guiding future research. Potential trajectories include at least four avenues: First, the framework points to a recursive relationship between the incidence of mental health in society and consequences of this on organizations. These two domains are moderated by the interactive effects of actions stemming from policy and organizational decisions. Such links need to be empirically explored across a wide range of settings and jurisdictions. Second, the central role of organizations in contributing to solutions to the problem needs to be examined in more detail than in available studies. Third, our framework highlights the positive possibilities of various organizational actions for improving mental health, but empirically generalizable studies in this area are scant. As Sutton, Hocking, and Smythe (2012) noted, despite the view in the literature that "occupation is beneficial for mental wellbeing, there is limited research exploring the experience and meaning of occupation in the context of the recovery process" (p. 143). Fourth, and finally, the direction and strength of the link between affirmative organizational action and its association with positive mental health outcomes needs to be empirically established across settings.

Acknowledgement

The authors wish to acknowledge the generous feedback on the paper provided by Therese Jefferson, Ph.D., Curtin Graduate School of Business and three anonymous British Academy of Management 2015 reviewers.

References

Australian Institute of Health and Welfare. (2013). *Mental Health Services in Brief 2013*. Canberra, Australia: Australian Institute of Health and Welfare.

Avey, J. B., Nimnich, L., & Pigeon, N. G. (2010). Two field studies examining the association between positive psychological capital and employee performance. *Leadership and Organization Development Journal*, 31(5), 384–401.

Bagnall, D. (2004). Science of happiness: The secret of happiness is the holy grail of the new millennium. *The Bulletin*, December 15, A6.

Baruch, Y., O'Creevy, M. F., Hind, P., & Vigoda-Gabot, E. (2004). Pro-social behaviour and job performance: Does the need for control and the need for achievement make a difference? *Social Behavior and Personality*, 32(4), 399–412.

Begg, S., Vos, T., Barker, B., Stevenson, C., Stanley, L., & Lopez, A. D. (2007). *The Burden of Disease and Injury in Australia 2003*. PHE 82. Australian Institute of Health Welfare, Canberra.

beyondblue. (2008). *The National Depression Initiative, Research: Target Research in Depression, Anxiety and Related Disorders 2001–2007*. Melbourne, Australia: beyondblue.

beyondblue. (2013). *Annual Report 2012–13*. Melbourne: beyondblue.

Bloom, D. E., Cafiero, E. T., Jané-Llopis, E., Abrahams-Gessel, S., Bloom, L. R., Fathima, S., . . . & Weinstein, C. (2011). *The Global Economic Burden of Noncommunicable Diseases*. Geneva: World Economic Forum.

Brammall, B. (1999). Ambition a big stress. *Herald Sun*, March 17th, 11.

Cameron, K. S., & Caza, A. (2004). Contributions to the discipline of positive organisational scholarship. *American Behavioral Scientist*, 47(6), 731–739.

Cameron, K. S., Dutton, J. E., & Quinn, R. E. (eds.). (2003). *Positive Organizational Scholarship: Foundations of a New Discipline*. San Francisco, CA: Berrett-Koehler Publishers Inc.

Cameron, K., Mora, C., Leutscher, T., & Calarco, M. (2011). Effects of positive practices on organizational effectiveness. *The Journal of Applied Behavioural Science*, 47(3), 266–308.

Castro, S. L., Douglas, C., Hochwarter, W. A., Ferris, G. R., & Frink, D. W. (2003). The effects of positive affect and gender on the influence tactics – Job performance relationship," *Journal of Leadership and Organizational Studies*, 10(1), 1–18.

Caza, B. B., & Caza, A. (2008). Positive organizational scholarship: A critical theory perspective. *Journal of Management Inquiry*, 17(1), 21–33.

Cooper, C. L. (2005). *Handbook of Stress Medicine and Stress* (2nd ed.). Boca Raton, FL: CRC Press.

Cooper, C. L., & Cartwright, S. (1994). Healthy mind, healthy organization: A proactive approach to occupational stress. *Human Relations*, 47(4), 455–471.

Dooley, D., Fielding, J., & Levi, L. (1996). Health and unemployment, *Annual Review of Public Health*, 17, 449–465.

Fels, A. (2016). *Leading, Collaborating, Advising, Reporting*. Canberra: Australin Government, National Mental Health Commission.

Fineman, S. (2006). On being positive: Concerns and counterpoints. *Academy of Management Review*, 31, 270–291.

Forgas, J. P. (2002). Towards understanding the role of affect in social thinking and behavior. *Psychological Inquiry*, 13(1), 90–102.

Gabriel, P., & Liimatainen, M. R. (2000). *Mental Health in the Workplace: Introduction*. Available at: www.ilo. org/public/english/bureau/inf/pr/2000/37.html (accessed 12 February, 2014).

Gilbert, M., & Blisker, D. (2012). *Psychological Health and Safety: An Action Guide for Employers*. Centre for Applied Research in Mental Health and Addiction, Mental Health Commission of Canada, Vancouver.

Goldie, S. (2004). *Mental Illness Education Australia*. Translated by Sydney, New South Wales.

Goldman, H. H., Sherry, A. G., & Alegria, M. (2009). Conclusion: Mental health in the mainstream of public policy, 166(1), 1215–1216.

Hay, L. (2010). In practice. *Perspectives in Public Health*, 130, 57.

Held, B. (2004). The negative side of positive psychology. *Journal of Humanistic Psychology*, 44, 9–46.

Hickie, I. (2004). Can we reduce the burden of depression? The Australian experience with beyondblue: The national depression initiative. *Australasian Psychiatry*, 12(Supplement 3), S38–S46.

Hosie, P., & ElRakhawy, N. (2014). The happy worker: revisiting the "happy-productive" worker thesis. In: P. Chen & C. Cooper (eds.), *Wellbeing: A Complete Reference Guide, Volume III, Work and Wellbeing*. Wiley-Blackwell, Oxford, 122.

Hosie, P., & Sevastos, P. (2010). A framework for conceiving of job-related affective wellbeing. *Management Revue: The International Review of Management Studies*, 21(4), 406–436.

Jones, J. R., Huxtable, C. S., Hodgson, J. T., & Price, M. J. (2003). *Self-Reported Work-Related Illness in 2001: Results from a Household Survey*. Sudbury, UK: HSE Books.

Jorm, A. F., & Kitchener, B. A. (2011). Noting a landmark achievement: Mental first aid training reaches 1% of Australian adults. *Australian and New Zealand Journal of Psychiatry*, 45(10), 808–813.

Jung, C. G. (1933). *Modern Man in Search of a Soul*. London, UK: Routledge & Kegan.

Keyes, C. L. M., & Haidt, J. (eds.). (2003). *Flourishing: Positive Psychology and the Life Well-Lived* (1st ed.). Washington, DC: American Psychological Association.

Kitchener, B. A., & Jorm, A. F. (2004). Mental health first aid training in a workplace setting: A randomized controlled trial. *Biomed Central Psychiatry*, 4, 23.

Knaap, M. (2003). Hidden costs of mental illness. *The British Journal of Psychiatry*, 183, 477–478.

Konkolewsky, H. H. (2004). Stress speech: European week for safety and health. In: S. Iavicoli (ed.), *Stress at Work in Enlarging Europe*. Rome, Italy: National Institute for Occupational Safety and Prevention, 29–43.

Korkeila, J., Lehtinen, V., Bijl, R., Dalgard, O. S., Kovess, V., Morgan, S., & Salize, H. J. (2003). Establishing a set of mental indicators for Europe. *Scandinavian Journal of Public Health*, 31, 451–459.

Langer, E. (1975). The illusion of control. *Journal of Personality and Social Psychology*, 32(2), 311–328.

Levi, L. (2002). More jobs, better jobs, and health. In: M. F. Dollard, A. H. Winefield, & H. R. Winefield (eds.), *Occupational Stress in the Service Professions*. London, UK: Taylor & Francis, ix–xii.

Lichtenstein, S., Fischoff, B., & Phillips, L. D. (1982). Calibration of probabilities: The state of the art in 1980. In: D. Kahneman, P. Slovic, & A. Tversky (eds.), *Judgment under Uncertainty: Heuristics and Biases*. New York: Cambridge University Press, 306–334.

Lim, N., Kim, E. K., Kim, H., Yang, E., & Lee, S. M. (2010). Individual and work related factors influencing burnout of mental health professionals: A meta-analysis. *Journal of Employment Counseling*, 47(2), 86–96.

Love, P. E. D., Edwards, D. J., & Irani, Z. (2010). Work, stress, support and mental health in construction. *Journal of Construction Engineering and Management*, 136(6), 650–658.

Luthans, F., Avolio, B. J., Avey, J. B., & Norman, S. M. (2007). Positive psychological capital: Measurement and relationship with performance and satisfaction. *Personnel Psychology*, 60(3), 541–572.

Lyubomirsky, S., King, L., & Diener, E. (2005). The benefits of frequent positive affect: Does happiness lead to success? *Psychological Bulletin*, 131(6), 803–855.

Martin, M., & Stang, D. (1978). *The Pollyanna Principle*. Cambridge, MA: Schenkman.

Mathers, C. D., & Schofield, D. J. (1998). The health consequences of unemployment: The evidence. *The Medical Journal of Australia*, 168(4), 178–182.

Mayfield, C. O., & Taber, T. H. (2010). A pro-social self-concept approach to understanding organizational citizenship behaviour. *Journal of Managerial Psychology*, 25(7), 741–763.

Menhenhall, A. N., & Jackson, S. C. (2013). Instructor insights into delivery of mental health first aid USA: A case study of mental health promotion across one state. *International Journal of Mental Health Promotion*, 15(5), 275–287.

Mental Health Commission of Canada. (2013). *Psychological Health and Safety in the Workplace: Prevention, Promotion and Guidance to Staged Implementation*. Québec: Bureau de Normalisation and Canadaian Standards Association.

Moskowitz, D. B. (1998). Marshalling forces to battle depression. *Business & Health*, 16(9), 71–72.

Oliffe, J. L., & Han, C. S. E. (2014). Beyond workers' compensation: Men's mental health in and out of work. *American Journal of Men's Health*, 8(1), 45–53.

Pasca, R., & Wagner, S. L. (2012). Occupational stress, mental health and satisfaction in the Canadian multicultural workplace. *Social Indicators Research*, 109(3), 377–393.

Pirkis, J., Hickie, I., Young, L., Burns, J., Highet, N., & Davenport, T. (2005). An evaluation of beyondblue, Australia's national depression initiative. *International Journal of Mental Health Promotion*, 7(2), 35–53.

Pressman, S. D., & Cohen, S. (2005). Does positive affect influence health? *Psychological Bulletin*, 131(6), 925–971.

Puig, A., Baggs, A., Mixon, K., Park, Y. M., Kim, B. Y., & Lee, S. M. (2012). Relationship between job burnout and personal wellness in mental health professionals. *Journal of Employment Counseling*, 49(3), 98–109.

Roberts, L. M. (2006). Shifting the lens on organizational life: The added value of positive scholarship. *Academy of Management Review*, 31(2), 292–305.

Rosenberg, S., & Hickie, I. (2013). Managing madness: Mental health and complexity in public policy. *Evidence Base*, 3, 1–19.

Schwarz, N., & Bless, H. (1991). Happy and mindless, but sad and smart? The impact of effective states on analytic reasoning. In: J. P. Forgas (ed.), *Emotion and Social Judgement*. Oxford, UK: Pergamon Press, 55–71.

Seligman, M. E. P., & Csikszentmihalyi, M. (2000). Positive psychology: An introduction. *American Psychologist*, 55(1), 5–14.

Sinclair, R. C., & Mark, M. M. (1992). The influence of mood state on judgement and actions: Effects on persuasion, categorization, social justice, person perception and judgemental accuracy. In: L. L. Martin & A. Tesser (eds.), *The Construction of Social Judgements*. Hillsdale, NJ: Lawrence Erbaum, 1165–1193.

Snyder, C. R., & Lopez, S. J. (eds.). (2002). *Handbook of Positive Psychology*. New York: Oxford University Press.

Staw, B. M., & Barsade, S. G. (1993). Affect and managerial performance: A test of the sadder-but-wiser vs. happier-and-smarter hypotheses. *Administrative Science Quarterly*, 38(2), 304–331.

Sun, L. Y., Aryee, S., & Law, K. S. (2007). High performance human resources practices, citizenship behavior and organizational performance: A relational perspective. *Academy of Management Journal*, 50(3), 558–577.

Sutton, D. J., Hocking, C. S., & Smythe, L. A. (2012). A phenomenological study of occupational engagement in recovery from mental illness. *Canadian Journal of Occupational Therapy*, 79(3), 142–150.

Tabachnik, N., Crocker, J., & Alloy, L. B. (1983). Depression, social comparison and the false consensus effect. *Journal of Personality and Social Psychology*, 45(3), 688–699.

Tasho, W., Jordan, J., & Robertson, I. (2005). *Case Study: Establishing the Business Case for Investing in Stress Prevention Activities and Evaluating Their Impact on Sickness Absence Levels, HSE Books, 2005. (RR295)*. Manchester: Health & Safety Executive.

Taylor, S. E. (1991). The asymmetrical impact of positive and negative events: The mobilization-minimization hypothesis. *Psychological Bulletin*, 110(1), 67–85.

Terry, J. (2010). Experiences of instructors delivering the mental health first aid training programme: A descriptive qualitative study. *Journal of Psychiatric and Mental Health Nursing*, 17, 594–602.

Toohey, J. (1995). Managing the stress phenomenon at work. In: P. Cotton (ed.), *Psychological Health in the Workplace: Understanding and Managing Occupational Stress*. Brisbane: The Australian Psychological Society, 51–71.

Travers, C. J., & Cooper, C. L. (1993). Mental health, job satisfaction and occupational stress among UK teachers. *Work and Stress: An International Journal of Work, Health and Organizations*, 7(3), 203–219.

United Nations. (2010). *Mental Health and Development: Integrating Mental Health into All Developments Efforts Including MDGs*. New York: World Health Organization.

US Department of Health and Human Services. (1999). *Mental Health: A Report of the Surgeon General*. Rockville, MD: U.S. Department of Health and Human Services, Substance Abuse and Mental Health Services Administration, Center for Mental Health Services, National Institutes of Health.

Warr, P. B. (1986). A vitamin model of jobs and mental health. In: G. Debus & H. W. Schroiff (eds.), *The Psychology of Work and Organisation: Current Trends and Issues*. Amsterdam, Holland: Elsevier Science, 157–164.

Warr, P. B. (1987). *Work, Unemployment and Mental Health*. Oxford, UK: Clarendon Press.

Warr, P. B. (1994). Age and work. In: P. Collett & A. Furnham (eds.), *Social Psychology at Work*. London: Routledge, 236–253.

Warr, P. B. (2007). *Work, Happiness, and Unhappiness*. Mahwah, NJ: Lawrence Erlbaum Associates.

Weiss, H. M., & Cropanzano, R. (1996). Affective events theory: A theoretical discussion of the structure, causes and consequences of affective experiences at work. In: B. M. Staw & L. L. Cummings (eds.), *Research in Organizational Behavior: An Annual Series of Analytical Essays and Critical Reviews*. Greenwich, CT: JAI Press, Inc., 1–74.

World Health Organization. (2003). *Investing in Mental Health*. World Health Organization.

World Health Organization. (2005). *Mental Health and Working Life: Impact, Issues and Good Practices*. WHO European Ministerial Conference on Mental Health: Facing the Challenges, Building Solutions. Available at: www.euro.who.int/document/mnh/ebrief06.pdf (accessed 14 February 2014).

World Health Organization. (2013). *Mental Health Action Plan 2013–2020*. World Health Organization.

Zilnyk, A. (2010). Mental health first aid: A life skill we should all have? *Perspectives in Public Health*, 130, 61–62.

6

Toward evidence-based practice in organizational wellbeing

Methods and measures

E. Kevin Kelloway

Introduction

Many organizations have now implemented, or are considering implementing, programs and policies to improve the health and wellbeing of employees (Goetzel & Ozminkowski, 2008; Goetzel, Roemer, Liss-Levinson, & Samoly, 2008). Such efforts may stem from the recognition that the health of employees has consequences for productivity and other organizational outcomes (e.g., absenteeism, presenteeism, turnover), or it may arise from the belief that organizations are responsible for their employees' wellbeing. Whatever the rationale, there has been burgeoning interest in creating a healthy workplace (Day, Kelloway, & Hurrell, 2014) – one in which organizational goals of profitability and productivity are integrated with employee wellbeing. (Sauter, Lim, & Murphy, 1996).

A concern for employee wellbeing extends beyond issues of physical health. Indeed, the World Health Organization (WHO) defines health as state of physical, psychological, and social wellbeing that goes beyond the absence of illness or infirmity (World Health Organization, 1948). Employee mental health problems and illnesses are increasingly recognized as being among the most costly issues facing employers in the developed world (Dimoff & Kelloway, 2013). In Canada, mental health problems are the leading cause of workplace disability, accounting for 70% of disability costs (Mental Health Commission of Canada [MHCC], 2012), and are estimated to cost the Canadian economy upwards of $50 billion annually (MHCC, 2012). In the United States, US$150 to $300 billion is lost each year due to stress-related illnesses and health, and productivity losses (American Institute of Stress, 2005; Sauter, Murphy, & Hurrell, 1990), with much of this attributable to depression and lost work days due to poor mental health (Center for Disease Control, 2014). Similarly, in the European Union, depression is estimated to account for more than €135 million each year – just under 5% of the GDP (McDaid, 2011).

These substantial costs have resulted in a burgeoning healthy workplace movement in which organizations institute programs and benefits aimed at improving employee wellbeing (Day et al., 2014). An extensive literature has emerged assessing the effectiveness of health-related programming in organizations (Dimoff, Kelloway, & MacLellan, 2014). Dimoff et al. (2014) concluded that this literature is

> characterized by methodological inadequacies including poor research design (e.g., the lack of control groups and reliance on questionable outcome measures), poorly articulated logic

(i.e., inadequate articulation of how a given outcome translates into organizational performance) and narrow focus (e.g., focusing on single conditions, outcomes, or types or organizations.

(p. 317)

In addition to questions about whether programs result in a financial return to the organization, a more fundamental question is whether the programs achieve their stated aims of improving health. There are at least three reasons why health-related programming in organizations might be ineffective: First, the program or benefit may be inappropriately targeted, being used by individuals who may not benefit from the intervention. Thus, organizations that offer gym memberships in an effort to make it easier for employees to be physically active frequently find that they are "preaching to the choir" – the benefit is utilized by those employees who would have gone to the gym anyway, and the program, although well-intended, does not improve the physical health of a broader group of employees.

Second, the resources provided by organizations may be underutilized (Linnan, et al., 2008; Reynolds & Lehman, 2003). As noted by Linnan et al. (2008), the key challenge for employers is getting employees to use resources when they need them. This is especially true given that the people who could often benefit the most from these resources are also the least likely to use them (Hunt & Eisenberg, 2010; Linnan et al., 2008). In formulating their resource utilization model, Dimoff and Kelloway (in press) suggested that individuals (1) may not recognize that they require a program, service, or resource; (2) may not be aware of what resources are available; or (3) may not use available resources because of other concerns (e.g., stigma). As a result, potentially useful programs such as employee assistance programs remain typically underutilized by employees (Able Minded Solutions, 2010; Canadian Medical Association, 2013).

Third, the resource or program provided by the organization may not be effective. The rigorous assessment of programs and interventions designed to improve employee wellbeing is still more noted by its absence than its presence. As a result, programs are implemented and maintained in organizations without careful consideration of whether or not they are achieving the intended results. In this context, Dimoff et al. (2014) suggested that evaluators of health programs often end up as advocates for the programs – offering friendly interpretations of the data and overly optimistic projections of the gains to be achieved.

In this chapter, I want to suggest that the credibility of organizationally based health initiatives is largely based on our ability to adopt an evidence-based perspective. That is, we as researchers will contribute most to employee health through our critical appraisal of wellness initiatives – focusing on what works and how it works in order to offer the most efficient and effective programs to organizations and their employees.

Towards evidence-based practice in employee wellbeing

The concept of evidence-based practice first emerged in the field of medicine, where concern surrounding the lack of empirical evidence for many common treatments and practices arose (Smith, 1991). As a result, medical interventions or therapies could be overused (i.e., applied to cases not likely to benefit from the treatment), underused (i.e., not used in cases that meet the criteria for a specific treatment), or misused (i.e., therapies applied when the evidence of effectiveness is questionable; Walshe & Rundall, 2001).

These concerns have found resonance in a variety of disciplines (Gray, Elhai, & Schmidt, 2007; Hemsley-Brown, & Oplatka, 2005; Kelly, Deane, & Lovett, 2012; Lilienfeld, Ritschel, Lynn, Cautin, & Latzman, 2013), including management, with many scholars noting parallel concerns in organizational research and practice (e.g., Pfeffer & Sutton, 2006; Rynes et al., 2002). Advocates of evidence-based management point to problems in organizational decision-making and suggest that organizational decisions and practices should be based on systematic research (Rousseau, 2006). Sackett, Strauss, Richardson, Rosenberg, and Haynes (2000) have suggested that evidence-based practice is a two-step process. In the first step, the necessary evidence must be generated; in the second, the evidence must be used to make informed decisions. Baba and HakemZadeh (2012) have provided a comprehensive discussion of how evidence gets used in organizations. In this chapter, I focus more particularly on the generation of evidence regarding employee health and wellbeing.

Fundamentals: what to measure

To show that a program had an effect on employee wellbeing, one must show that (1) employee wellbeing has changed and (2) the change in employee wellbeing can be attributed to the intervention or program that was implemented. Before addressing either concern, one must first define what constitutes "wellbeing" for any given program. Offering a comprehensive definition of health is a daunting task that goes beyond the scope of this chapter. However, I take as a starting point based on the observation that wellbeing goes beyond the absence of illness or disorder. Pragmatically, Kelloway and Day (2005) described four types of outcomes that are often measured to assess workplace initiatives (psychological, physiological, behavioral, and organizational) that provide a useful categorization for our discussion.

Psychological measures

Psychological indices of wellbeing typically focus on either affect (e.g., mood) or cognition (e.g., concentration), with the former predominating in studies of workplace wellbeing and the latter frequently referenced in the research on occupational health and safety (see for example, Wong & Kelloway, 2015). Measures of depression, anxiety, burnout, and impaired mood (e.g., Baba, Jamal, & Tourigny, 1998) reflect disturbances of affect. The extent of these reactions ranges from the domain of mental-health problems (e.g., Harvey, Kelloway, & Duncan-Leiper, 2003), to more severe mental disorders, such as clinical depression (Wang & Patten, 2001).

Although measures of affect have been largely based on a pleasure–displeasure dimension, Warr (1987) suggested that affective wellbeing could be characterized along two dimensions (pleasure and arousal) derived from Russell's (1979, 1980) circumplex model. Both Warr (1987) and VanKatwyk, Fox, Spector, and Kelloway (2000) provided measures that operationalize this view.

Warr (1987) also introduced a useful distinction between context-specific (i.e., job related) and context-free (i.e., general wellbeing) mental health. One would expect that measures of context-specific wellbeing would be more sensitive to changes in the workplace or in working conditions. Programs and interventions aimed at the individual, such as meditation or stress management, might be more likely to have their primary effect on measures on context-free wellbeing.

Cognitive measures of wellbeing may include the ability to make decisions, or stay focused on a given task. Safety researchers, for example, have suggested that the most common types of human errors (e.g., accidents) are skill-based slips and lapses due to inattention (Baysari, Caponecchia, McIntosh, & Wilson, 2009; Hobbs, Williamson, & Van Dongen, 2010; Salminen & Tallberg, 1996). Again, measures of cognitive attention have included both context-free (e.g., Broadbent, Cooper, Fitzgerald, & Park, 1982) and context-specific (Wallace & Chen, 2005) failures.

One persistent problem with psychological measures of wellbeing is that they almost uniformly rely on self-report and this gives rise to concerns that (a) responses may be distorted by individuals "faking good" or "faking bad," (b) that relationships among these measures may be inflated or distorted by the influence of individual characteristics (e.g., personality traits) or common method variance, or that (c) measures of psychological wellbeing may be confounded with self-reports of the conditions thought to predict wellbeing. For example, the perception of being in control is frequently identified as a predictor of disturbances in affect, such as depressive symptomatology. However, a perceived lack of control is also commonly recognized as a symptom of depression, and it is possible that perceived lack of control is an outcome, rather than a predictor, of depression (for an empirical example, see Kelloway & Barling, 1994).

Physical wellbeing

Measures of physical wellbeing can subsume a wide range, from diagnosed conditions to specific physiological measures. Diagnostic measures may be relatively insensitive to changes in the organizational environment as such conditions (e.g., cardiovascular disease) may take years to develop or remediate. Measures of minor psychosomatic symptoms such as sleep disturbances, upper respiratory infections, and digestive problems (e.g., Schat & Kelloway, 2000) may be more sensitive to environmental influence, but may also suffer from the same issues with self-report as do psychological indices of wellbeing. Thus, organizational studies of wellbeing frequently turn to physiological measures such as heart rate, blood pressure, cortisol production, and galvanic skin response, which are less prone to self-report bias and can be observed in situ (see for example Wong & Kelloway, 2016).

The logic for such measures is rooted in the well-known "fight or flight" response to stress (Cannon, 1915). The response comprises activation of the sympathetic nervous system, which then releases epinephrine and norepinephrine, thus increasing blood pressure and heart rate to prepare the body for evolutionary-adaptive actions (Sapolsky, 1994). The allostatic load model of stress physiology posits three stages in the progression of stress (McEwen & Stellar, 1993; for a review, see Ganster & Rosen, 2013). The initial adaptations to stress are primary processes consisting of psychological, physiological, and psychosomatic changes in the central nervous system including increased heart rate, blood pressure, and cortisol production. Continuous activation of these lead to secondary processes, which are adjustments in the immune, cardiovascular, and metabolic systems as reactions to the excess or deficit in primary allostatic load mediators. Finally, at the tertiary stage, eventual disease diagnosis, psychological disorders, and even mortality may result. Physiological measures may, therefore, be useful in assessing instantaneous changes as a result of environmental conditions and may even be useful in detecting a secondary process (see for example Wong & Kelloway, 2016).

Behavioral indices

The vast majority of healthy workplace programs have been devoted to improving the physical health of employees, with the most common foci of healthy workplace programs being weight loss, improved cardiovascular fitness, and smoking cessation (Baicker, Cutler, & Song, 2010). Such interventions frequently focus on lifestyle factors, such as nutrition, exercise, and sleep. Measures of these may be useful indicators of the success of such programs. Such measures are frequently standardized (e.g., the use of food diaries or use of the metabolic equivalent of tasks [MET] to assess physical activity) and administered in such a way to minimize self-report bias. Alternatively, the increased use of wearable technology permits more objective assessment of sleep and physical activity.

Organizational indices

Advocates of healthy workplaces frequently advance an argument based on the return on investment (ROI) of such programs (e.g., Baicker et al., 2010; Goetzel, Ozminkowski, Sederer, & Mark, 2002), suggesting that increasing the health of the workplace will generate an economic return to the organization. Despite numerous problems with efforts to assess the ROI of such programs (Dimoff et al., 2014), researchers have focused on changing organizational indices as indices of program effectiveness. Some of the most common organizational metrics used to evaluate the cost-effectiveness of healthy workplace programs include increased performance; decreased absenteeism, accidents and injury rates; and reduced employee turnover (Goetzel et al., 2002; Henke, Goetzel, McHugh, & Isaac, 2011; Jex, 1998; Kessler et al., 1999; Mills, Kessler, Cooper, & Sullivan, 2007).

Organizational indices such as these are notoriously difficult to change (Johns, 1991) and there has been considerable effort in organizations already to minimize negative and maximize positive outcomes. Moreover, the links between the focus of the intervention and an organizational outcome may be extremely tenuous. For example, a "psychologically healthy work program" may be implemented with the express goal of minimizing absenteeism. Certainly there is evidence linking stress to absence (Hardy, Woods, & Wall, 2003); however, meta-analytic evidence suggests that these effects are very small (Darr & Johns, 2008). In turn, this suggests that one must have an extremely effective program that has a huge effect on employee stress in order to reduce absenteeism. As Dimoff et al. (2014) suggest, researchers must be careful not to become advocates by overselling the putative benefits of a given program.

Methods

Although research on workplace wellbeing has flourished in recent years, it is still reasonable to conclude that we know very little about the dynamics of wellbeing and the relationship of workplace conditions to individual wellbeing. Our lack of knowledge, or our ambiguous understanding, stems from a pervasive reliance on cross-sectional studies in organizational research (Austin, Scherbaum, & Mahlman, 2002; Stone-Romero, 2011; Zapf, Dorman, & Frese, 1996). Numerous reviewers have called for more longitudinal and intervention research that would allow a clearer specification of the nature of the constructs of interest (e.g., Kelloway & Francis, 2012).

Kelloway and Francis (2012) suggested that research in occupational health psychology could be considerably advanced by developing theories around the notion of change in constructs, such as wellbeing (e.g., Garst, Frese, & Molenaar, 2000). This would mean that researchers need to understand the nature (or form) of the change, the duration and timing of the change, and potential causes of the change (Ployhart & Vandenberg, 2010). Similarly, Pitariu and Ployhart (2010) suggested that such a theory should consider the time (when a specific relationship should occur), duration (how long a relationship should exist), and shape (the form of the relationship over time) of a relationship.

In making this suggestion, Kelloway and Francis (2012) also noted a need for longitudinal descriptive research in occupational health psychology. Perhaps nowhere is this need more obvious than in studies of employee wellbeing. I would suggest that despite a wealth of research on constructs such as satisfaction, engagement, or burnout at work, we know comparatively little about how these indices of wellbeing develop over time. Ployhart and Vandenberg (2010) defined "descriptive longitudinal research" as research that examines how a particular phenomenon or construct changes over time. Such research would typically involve repeated measurement among a group of employees over time (e.g., Rosel & Plewis, 2008). The questions of interest in such research are focused on understanding the nature of change over time: Does such change occur? When does it occur? How often does change occur?

Kelloway and Francis (2012) noted the irony that we have few theories about wellbeing that specify the nature of change – yet it is common for reviewers to suggest that theory is the best guide to answering such critical questions as the timing of measures (Ployhart & Vandenberg, 2010). Sherlock Holmes taught us: "'It is a capital mistake to theorize before one has data. Insensibly one begins to twist facts to suit theories, instead of theories to suit facts" (Doyle, 1892). Without descriptive longitudinal research there are few grounds on which to base theories of wellbeing that incorporate the notion of change.

Examining change in wellbeing over time assumes that we can identify "true" change as opposed to a variety of methodological artifacts. Chan (1998) observed that our observation of change can reflect "true" changes in the construct of interest, changes in the calibration of our measurement instruments, or changes in the conceptualization of the constructs we are studying. Golembiewski, Billingsley, and Yeager (1976) labeled these alpha (i.e., true change), beta (i.e., changes in calibration), and gamma (i.e., changes in conceptualization) change. Although researchers typically begin by establishing that measurement invariance (i.e., the absence of beta and gamma change; Chan, 1998) over time, it is likely that even beta or gamma change can tell us something interesting about the nature of wellbeing overtime.

Predictive longitudinal research (Ployhart & Vandenberg, 2010) extends the study of change by focusing on variables that predict change over time. Theoretically, identification of the predictors of change in wellbeing is important, as it allows us to identify the organizational conditions associated with enhanced or impaired wellbeing. More pragmatically, such research allows us to identify the potential for intervention research in organizations – systematic variation of the predictors in order to improve employee wellbeing.

Intervention research – particularly interventions that incorporate a control group and randomization – has long been considered the gold standard for evidence in many fields of inquiry. When randomization is not possible, quasi-experimental methods (e.g., Cook & Campbell, 1979) may be used to offset the potential confounds and limitations that result. The absence of a control group, however, poses a serious limitation to many studies evaluating workplace interventions designed to improve wellbeing (Dimoff et al., 2014).

Interventions in organizations, including those targeting employee wellbeing, are also notoriously difficult to conduct (see Karinika-Murray & Biron, 2015). Numerous logistic and organizational problems can arise that result in interventions not having the intended effect, having unintended effects, or having consequences that make it impossible to disentangle the effects of the intervention from other organizational practices. Although these pragmatic concerns pose a challenge to the researcher, they are also reflective of organizational life. Despite the desired purity of our research designs, rarely do organizational practices emerge in isolation or in a way that is devoid of organizational politics (Hakel, 1983).

Despite these challenges, intervention research remains the single greatest source of knowledge about the conditions that affect wellbeing in organizations. If we can show that an organizational practice results in a change in wellbeing that cannot be attributed to other causes, then we have learned a great deal about workplace practices and policies that influence individual wellbeing.

Evidence-based practice requires practice-based evidence

With the growing popularity of evidence-based practice in a variety of disciplines has come the recognition of the gap between "science" and "practice" in organizations. (e.g., Briner, Denyer, & Rousseau, 2009; Briner & Rousseau, 2011; Rousseau & Barends, 2011). Authors have largely attributed this gap to a lack of knowledge on the part of human resources practitioners (Charlier, Brown, & Rynes, 2011; Furnham, 2008; Rynes, Colbert, & Brown, 2002; Rynes, Giluk, & Brown, 2007), noting that both practitioner journals (Rynes et al., 2007) and MBA programs provide inadequate coverage of evidence-based practices (Charlier et al., 2011).

Although advocates of evidence-based practice have focused on organizational decision-makers' ignorance of the evidence, I propose an alternate view. Essentially I argue that evidence-based practice requires practice-based evidence and that the research methods commonly employed to study employee wellbeing do not provide clear evidence or guidance for practice.

Consider, for example, the well-researched links between work hours and wellbeing. Concerns that working hours are increasing, at least for some groups of employees, have led to researchers examining the impact of work hours on a variety of individual outcomes. For the most part, researchers have considered only the possibility of negative outcomes on working long hours. These have included the potential for working long hours to be associated with outcomes such as employee stress (e.g., Park, Kim, Chung, & Hisanaga, 2001), accidents (Trimpop, Kirkcaldy, Athanasou, & Cooper, 2000), lifestyle behaviors (Sparks, Cooper, Fried, & Shirom, 1997), and work–family functioning (Ng & Feldman, 2008). This focus is consistent with a widespread belief among workers that working longer hours is detrimental to physical and psychological wellbeing (e.g., Ettner & Grzywacz, 2001).

Meta-analytic evidence suggests small to moderate correlations between hours of work and various indices of wellbeing (e.g., Ng & Feldman, 2008; Sparks et al., 1997). On the face of it, this evidence would suggest that reducing hours of work would result in improved wellbeing for individuals. However, the evidence in actuality provides a wide range of interpretations and does not provide clear guidelines for practice.

Even setting aside all of the common methodological caveats regarding common method variance (Podsakoff, MacKenzie, Lee, & Podsakoff, 2003) and causal inference (Kelloway, 2014), there is a more fundamental concern. A correlation coefficient indicates the degree of linear association between two variables but conveys almost no information when applied to individual prediction (Gardner & Neufeld, 2013). Thus, even when we know that there is a moderate relationship between hours of work and work–family conflict, we are not able to predict what would happen to an individual's level of work–family conflict if we were able to reduce role overload.

Moreover, although correlations assess linear associations in the data, they may not be sensitive to a variety of nonlinear relationships that have important implications for practice. For example, Warr's (1987) "vitamin" model of mental health suggests that some environmental features have nonlinear relationships with wellbeing. Warr (1987) specifies two types of relationships: constant effect (CE) and additional decrement (AD) relationships. In CE relationships, increases in an environmental feature are associated with wellbeing up to a certain point, after which there is no further effect. AD relationships suggest that an environmental feature is positively associated with wellbeing up to a point, after which further increases adversely affect wellbeing. Given a reasonably large sample, both forms of relationship may contain sufficient linearity to result in a statistically significant correlation – however, the existence of a correlation does not necessarily mean that increases in the predictor are always associated with increases in wellbeing. Moreover, the correlation provides no information as to the point of inflection (i.e., the point at which the nature of the relationship changes).

The point at which hours of work become deleterious to wellbeing is obscured by the data. Almost universally, researchers who have assessed work hours have asked simply, "On average, how many hours per week do you work?" As Sparks et al. (1997) note with respect to the studies in their meta-analysis,

> across the samples used in the meta-analysis, individuals' weekly working hours varied greatly. Some individuals worked only a minimum number of hours per week (e.g., 3–4 hours). Across all samples, the actual working hours reported ranged from 0.5 to 110 hours per week.
>
> *(p. 401)*

Thus, although researchers express concern with "long" work hours (e.g., Ng & Feldman, 2008), their actual data includes a wide range of work hours, and the studies results are not reported in a way that would suggest a critical point (e.g., 37.5 hours/week) beyond which negative effects would accrue. It is clear that most researchers do not hypothesize that the relationship between work hours and individual wellbeing is linear. Rather, most seem to suggest that work hours become deleterious only to individual wellbeing when they reach some critical point.

For example, some studies have suggested that physical health problems manifest when individuals work in excess of 48 hours per week (e.g., Barton & Folkard, 1993). Spurgeon, Harrington, and Cooper (1997) note that determining an exact cutoff was not justified by the data, but also suggest that weekly hours exceeding 50 could lead to occupational stress. Based on their study of fatigue among Japanese workers, Nagashima et al. (2007) suggested that work hours should be limited to less than 260 hours/month (i.e., 65 hours/week) to prevent excessive fatigue. Other studies of fatigue have resulted in similar conclusions. For example, Park et al. (2001) suggested that working 60 hours a week was a useful cutoff point for assessing cumulative fatigue in their sample. Similarly, Konz (1998) suggested prolonged overtime of over 12 hours per day should be avoided. Although it may not be possible to determine the precise cutoff that leads to adverse consequences, it does seem clear that the relationship between work hours and outcomes such as fatigue is nonlinear, with negative effects being observed only after a significant number of overtime or excess hours have accrued.

Other researchers have found that negative outcomes, such as work–family conflict, were experienced less often by part-time than by full-time workers (e.g., Kelloway & Gottlieb, 1998). That is, rather than suggesting that excessive work hours (i.e., exceeding 40 hours/week) result in negative outcomes, these authors suggested working fewer hours was associated with less stress and work–family conflict than was working full-time hours. In either case (i.e., only extensive work hours are deleterious or anything more than 20 hours/week results in negative outcomes), a nonlinear relationship exists and the resulting bivariate correlation would be expected to be low (e.g., Sparks et al., 1997).

Ng and Feldman (2008) found evidence for four such relationships between work hours and specified constructs. Although their report does not identify the breaking points of the curves, they suggest that "the slopes of the relationships of work hours with work-to-family conflict and with family to-work conflict became more positive as work hours increased" and "the slopes of the relationships of work hours with mental strain and with physical health problems became less positive as average work hours increased" (p. 871). These findings suggest that work–family conflict or family–work conflict increases disproportionately with extra hours worked. Conversely, after reaching a certain level, mental strain and physical health were not further impaired by working longer hours. Thus the empirical data suggest that the effect of work hours on individual wellbeing depends on the number of hours worked each week. However, the data do not permit the identification of a single critical value or cut point beyond which working more hours is harmful. I would suggest that this is the single most important piece of information for organizations concerned about their employees' wellbeing and we should be concerned that the evidence does not provide guidance for organizational practice.

In a related vein, organizational researchers have almost uniformly assumed that wellbeing can be measured along a continuum. In contrast, medical researchers have distinguished "diagnosable" conditions based on clinical criteria or level of dysfunction (e.g., clinical depression vs. depressed affect) or on the basis of large-scale epidemiological studies (e.g., high blood pressure being defined as blood pressure greater than 120/80). Organizational researchers look askance at this practice, based on the known problems of dichotomizing continuous variables (e.g., MacCallum, Zhang, Preacher, & Rucker, 2002). However, the existence of diagnostic "problem states" allows one to determine the level of predictors.

Again, we know that work hours are associated with impaired wellbeing. The practical question for organizational decision-makers is, "How many hours per week can someone work without impairing their wellbeing?" As noted earlier, this question cannot be answered from a knowledge of the correlation. Indeed, I would suggest that answering this question requires a definition of "impaired wellbeing." If, for example, we know that individuals who score 17 or more on a Beck Depression Inventory (Beck, Steer, & Brown, 1996) may require treatment, we can use this value to establish cut points for the number of hours worked based on our knowledge of the relationship between hours worked and depression.

Doing so would require large-scale (i.e., national) data that allows for the operationalization of wellbeing using a standardized instrument, thereby providing the ability to establish norms. Procedures for establishing cut points are well established in the selection literature (e.g., Catano, Wisener, & Hackett, 2012) and coupled with large scale population data offer the possibility of generating evidence-based guidelines for the management of workplace stressors.

Summary and conclusion

The growing recognition of the need to create healthy workplaces has resulted in numerous programs and interventions designed to improve employee wellbeing. However, many of these programs are subject to cursory evaluation only and are not based on empirical evidence. In this chapter I have argued for the need to adopt an evidence-based approach to employee wellbeing in organizations. Such an approach must consider methodological details, such as how to measure wellbeing and what kind of research is required to justify program implementation. However, an evidence-based approach may also require researchers to change their orientation to research. In particular, a focus on identifying critical levels of organizational stressors appears to be one mechanism with which to identify empirically based standards designed to promote employee wellbeing. Doing so requires a focus on description (i.e., normative samples, understanding the dynamics of constructs and relationships) rather than a single-minded focus on statistical inference. However, solid descriptive data coupled with well-conducted intervention studies offer our strongest possibility of moving toward evidence-based practice and enhancing employee wellbeing.

References

Able Minded Solutions. (2010). *Return to Work and Accommodations for Workers on Disability Leave for Mental Disorders*. Human Solutions Report.

American Institute of Stress. (2005). *Workplace Stress.*" Available at: www.stress.org/workplace-stress/ (accessed 27 August 2015).

Austin, J. T., Scherbaum, C. A., & Mahlman, R. A. (2002). History of research methods in industrial and organizational psychology: Measurement, design, analysis. In: S. G. Rogelberg (eds.), *Handbook of Research Methods in Industrial and Organizational Psychology.* Malden, MA: Blackwell, 1–33.

Baba, V. V., & HakemZadeh, F. (2012). Toward a theory of evidence based decision making. *Management Decision (Emerald)*, 50(5), 832–867.

Baba, V. V., Jamal, M., & Tourigny, L. (1998). Work and mental health: A decade in Canadian research. *Canadian Psychology*, 39, 94–107.

Baicker, K., Cutler, D., & Song, Z. (2010). Workplace wellness programs can generate saving. *Health Affairs*, 29(2), 1–8.

Barton, J., & Folkard, S. (1993). Advancing versus delaying systems. *Ergonomics*, 36, 59–64.

Baysari, M. T., Caponecchia, C., McIntosh, A. S., & Wilson, J. R. (2009). Classification of errors contributing to rail incidents and accidents: A comparison of two human error identification techniques. *Safety Science*, 47, 948–957.

Beck, A., Steer, R., & Brown, G. (1996). *The Beck Depression Inventory – Second Edition Manual.* San Antonio, TX: The Psychological Corporation.

Briner, R., Denyer, D., & Rousseau, D. (2009). Evidence-based management: Concept cleanup time? *Academy of Management Perspectives*, 23, 19–32.

Briner, R., & Rousseau, D. (2011). Evidence-based I–O psychology: Not there yet. *Industrial and Organizational Psychology: Perspectives on Science and Practice*, 4, 3–22.

Broadbent, D. E., Cooper, P. F., FitzGerald, P., & Parkes, K. R. (1982). The Cognitive Failures Questionnaire (CFQ) and its correlates. *British Journal of Clinical Psychology*, 21(1), 1–16.

Canadian Medical Association. (2013). *Mental Health.* Available at: www.cma.ca/En/Pages/mental-health.aspx (accessed 3 August 2015).

Cannon, W. B. (1915). *Bodily Changes in Pain, Hunger, Fear and Rage: An Account of Recent Researches into the Function of Emotional Excitement.* New York: D. Appleton & Co.

Catano, V. M., Wisener, W., & Hackett, R. (2012). *Selection and Recruitment in Canada* (6th ed.). Toronto, ON: Nelson Publishing.

Center for Disease Control. (2014). *Workplace Health Promotion: Depression.* Available at: www.cdc.gov/workplacehealthpromotion/health-strategies/depression/index.html (accessed 11 August 2015).

Chan, D. (1998). The conceptualization and analysis of change over time: An integrative approach incorporating longitudinal mean and covariance structures analysis (LMACS) and multiple indicator latent growth modeling (MLGM). *Organizational Research Methods*, 1(4), 421–483.

Chan, D. (2011). Advances in analytical strategies. In: S. Zedeck (ed.), *APA Handbook of Industrial and Organizational Psychology: Volume 1 Developing and Building the Organization.* Washington, DC: APA Books.

Charlier, S., Brown, K., & Rynes, S. (2011). Teaching evidence-based management in MBA programs: What evidence is there? *Academy of Management Learning & Education*, 10(2), 222–236.

Cook, T. D., & Campbell, D. T. (1979). *Quasi-Experimentation: Design and Analysis for Field Settings.* Boston: Houghton Mifflin.

Darr, W., & Johns, G. (2008). Work strain, health, and absenteeism: A meta-analysis. *Journal of Occupational Health Psychology*, 13, 293–318.

Day, A., Kelloway, E. K., & Hurrell, J. J. (eds.). (2014) *Workplace Well-being: How to Build a Psychologically Health Workplace.* Malden, MA: Wiley.

Dimoff, J. K., & Kelloway, E. K. (2013). Bridging the gap: Workplace mental health research in Canada. *Canadian Psychology/Psychologie Canadienne*, 54, 203.

Dimoff, J. K., & Kelloway, E. K. (in press). Leaders as resources: How managers and supervisors can socially support employees towards better mental health and wellbeing. In: E. K. Kelloway, K. Nielsen, & J. K. Dimoff (eds.), *Leading to Occupational Health and Safety.* Wiley.

Dimoff, J. K., Kelloway, E. K., & MacLellan, A. S. (2014). Health and performance: Science or advocacy? *Journal of Organizational Effectiveness: People and Performance*, 1, 316–334.

Doyle, A. C. (1892). *The Adventures of Sherlock Holmes.* London, UK: George Newnes Ltd.

Ettner, S. L., & Grzywacz, J. G. (2001). Workers' perceptions of how jobs affect health: A social ecological perspective. *Journal of Occupational Health Psychology*, 6, 101–113.

Furnham, A. (2008). HR professionals' beliefs about, and knowledge of, assessment techniques and psychometric tests. *International Journal of Selection and Assessment*, 16(3), 300–305.

Ganster, D. C., & Rosen, C. C. (2013). Work stress and employee health: A multidisciplinary review. *Journal of Management*, 39(5), 1085–1122. doi:10.1177/0149206313475815.

Gardner, R. C., & Neufeld, R. W. J. (2013). What the correlation coefficient really tells us about the individual? *Canadian Journal of Behavioral Science*, 45(4), 313–319.

Garst, H., Frese, M., & Molenaar, P. C. M. (2000). The temporal factor of change in stressor-strain relationships: A growth curve model on a longitudinal study in East Germany. *Journal of Applied Psychology*, 85, 417–438.

Goetzel, R. Z., & Ozminkowski, R. J. (2008). The health and cost benefits of work site health-promotion programs. *Annual Review of Public Health,* 29, 303–323.

Goetzel, R. Z., Ozminkowski, R. J., Sederer, L. I., & Mark, T. L. (2002). The business case for quality mental health services: Why employers should care about the mental health and well-being of their employees. *Journal of Occupational and Environmental Medicine*, 44, 320–330.

Goetzel, R. Z., Roemer, E. C., Liss-Levinson, R. C., & Samoly, D. K. (2008). *Workplace Health Promotion: Policy Recommendations that Encourage Employers to Support Health improvement Programs for Their Workers.* A paper commissioned by Partnership for Prevention, Emory University. Available at: www.prevent.org/data/files/initiatives/workplacehealtpromotionpolicyrecommendations.pdf

Golembiewski, R. T., Billingsley, K., & Yeager, S. (1976). Measuring change and persistence in human affairs: Types of change generated by OD designs. *Journal of Applied Behavioral Science*, 12, 133–157.

Gray, M. J., Elhai, J. D., & Schmidt, L. O. (2007). Trauma professionals' attitudes toward and utilization of evidence-supported practices. *Behavior Modification*, 31, 732–768.

Hakel, M. (1983). *Making It Happen: Designing Research with Implementation in Mind.* Thousand Oaks, CA: SAGE Publications.

Hardy, G. E., Woods, D., & Wall, T. D. (2003). The impact of psychological distress on absence from work. *Journal of Applied Psychology*, 88, 306–314.

Harvey, S., Kelloway, E. K., & Duncan-Leiper, L. (2003). Trust in management as a buffer of the relationships between overload and strain. *Journal of Occupational Health Psychology*, 8, 306–315.

Hemsley-Brown, J., & Oplatka, I. (2005). Bridging the research-practice gap: Barriers and facilitators to research use among school principals from England and Israel. *International Journal of Public Sector Management*, 18(5), 424–446.

Henke, R. M., Goetzel, R. Z., McHugh, J., & Isaac, F. (2011). Recent experience in health promotion at Johnson & Johnson: Lower health spending, strong return on investment. *Health Affairs*, 30(3), 490–499.

Hobbs, A., Williamson, A., & Van Dongen, H. P. (2010). A circadian rhythm in skill-based errors in aviation maintenance. *Chronobiology International*, 27, 304–316.

Hunt, J., & Eisenberg, D. (2010). Mental health problems and help-seeking behavior among college students. *Journal of Adolescent Health*, 46, 3–10.

Jex, S. M. (1998). *Stress and Job Performance: Theory Research and Implications for Managerial Practice.* Thousand Oaks, CA: SAGE Publications.

Johns, G. (1991). Substantive and methodological constraints on behavior and attitudes in organizational research. *Organizational Behavior and Human Decision Processes*, 49, 80–104.

Karinika-Murray, M., & Biron, C. (eds.). (2015). *Derailed Organizational Interventions for Stress and Well-Being: Confessions of Failure and Solutions for Success.* New York: Springer.

Kelloway, E. K. (2014). *Using Mplus for Structural Equation Modeling: A Researcher's Guide* (2nd ed.). Thousand Oaks, CA: SAGE Publications.

Kelloway, E. K., & Barling, J. (1994). Stress, control, well-being, and marital satisfaction: A causal correlational analysis. In: G. P. Keita & J. J. Hurrell (eds.), *Job Stress in a Changing Workforce: Investigating Gender, Diversity, and Family Issues.* Washington, DC: American Psychological Association, 241–252.

Kelloway, E. K., & Day, A. L. (2005). Building healthy organizations: What we know so far. *Canadian Journal of Behavioural Science*, 37, 223–236.

Kelloway, E. K., & Francis, L. (2012). Longitudinal research and data analysis. In: R. Sinclair, M. Wang, & L. Tetrick (eds.), *Research Methods in Occupational Health Psychology.* New York: Routledge, 374–394.

Kelloway, E. K., & Gottlieb, B. H. (1998). The effect of alternative work arrangements on women's well-being. *Women's Health: Research on Gender, Behavior, & Policy*, 4, 1–18.

Kelly, P. J., Deane, F. P., & Lovett, M. (2012). Using the theory of planned behavior to examine residential substance abuse workers' intention to use evidence-based practices. *Psychology of Addictive Behaviours*, 26, 661–664.

Kessler, R. C., Borges, G., & Walters, E. E. (1999). Prevalence of and risk factors for lifetime suicide attempts in the National Comorbidity Survey. *Archives of General Psychiatry*, 56, 617–626.

Konz, S. (1998). Work/rest: Part I – Guidelines for the practitioner. *International Journal of Industrial Ergonomics*, 22, 67–71.

Lilienfeld, S., Ritschel, L., Lynn, S., Cautin, R., & Latzman, R. (2013). Why many clinical psychologists are resistant to evidence-based practice: Root causes and constructive remedies. *Clinical Psychology Review*, 33, 883–900.

Linnan, L., Bowling, M., Childress, J., Lindsay, G., Blakey, C., Pronk, S., . . . & Royall, P. (2008). Results of the 2004 national worksite health promotion survey. *American Journal of Public Health*, 98, 1503–1509.

MacCallum, R. C., Zhang, S., Preacher, K. J., & Rucker, D. D. (2002). On the practice of dichotomization of quantitative variables. *Psychological Methods*, 7, 19–40.

McDaid, D. (2011). *Making the Long-Term Economic Case for Investing in Mental Health to Contribute to Sustainability*. European Union. Available at: http://ec.europa.eu/health/mental_health/docs/long_term_sustainability_en.pdf

McEwen, B. S., & Stellar, E. (1993). Stress and the individual: Mechanisms leading to disease. *Archives of Internal Medicine*, 153, 2093–2101.

Mental Health Commission of Canada [MHCC] (2012). *Changing Directions, Changing Lives: The Mental Health Strategy for Canada*. Calgary, AB.

Mills, P. R., Kessler, R. C., Cooper, J., & Sullivan, S. (2007). Impact of a health promotion program on employee health risks and work productivity. *American Journal of Health Promotion*, 22(1), 45–53.

Nagashima, S., Suwazono, Y., Okubo, Y., Uetani, M., Kobayashi, E., Kido, T., & Nogawa, K. (2007). Working hours and mental and physical fatigue in Japanese workers. *Occupational Medicine*, 57, 449–452.

Ng, T. W. H., & Feldman, D. C. (2008). Long work hours: A social identity perspective on meta-analytic data. *Journal of Organizational Behavior*, 29, 853–880.

Park, J., Kim, Y., Chung, H. K., & Hisanaga, N. (2001). Long working hours and subjective fatigue symptoms. *Industrial Health*, 39, 250–254.

Pfeffer, J., & Sutton, R. (2006). Evidence-based management. *Harvard Business Review*, 84, 63–74.

Pitariu, A. H., & Ployhart, R. E. (2010). Explaining change: Theorizing and testing dynamic mediated longitudinal relationships. *Journal of Management*, 36, 405–429.

Ployhart, R. E., & Vandenberg, R. K. (2010). Longitudinal research: The theory, design, and analysis of change. *Journal of Management*, 36, 94–120.

Podsakoff, P. M., MacKenzie, S. B., Lee, J.-Y., & Podsakoff, N. P. (2003). Common method biases in behavioral research: A critical review of the literature and recommended remedies. *Journal of Applied Psychology*, 88, 879–903.

Reynolds, G. S., & Lehman, W. E. (2003). Levels of substance use and willingness to use the employee assistance program. *The Journal of Behavioral Health Services & Research*, 30, 238–248.

Rosel, J., & Plewis, I. (2008). Longitudinal data analysis with structural equations. *Methodology*, 4, 37–50.

Rousseau, D. (2006). Is there such a thing as "evidence-based management"? *Academy of Management Review*, 31(2), 256–269.

Rousseau, D., & Barends, E. (2011). Becoming an evidence-based HR practitioner. *Human Resource Management Journal*, 21(3), 221–235.

Russell, J. A. (1979). Affective space is bipolar. *Journal of Personality and Social Psychology*, 37, 345–356.

Russell, J. A. (1980). A circumplex model of affect. *Journal of Personality and Social Psychology*, 39, 1161–1178.

Rynes, S., Colbert, A., & Brown, K. (2002). HR professionals' beliefs about effective human resource practices: Correspondence between research and practice. *Human Resource Management*, 41, 149–174.

Rynes, S., Giluk, T., & Brown, K. (2007). The very separate worlds of academic and practitioner periodicals in human resource management: Implications for evidence-based management. *Academy of Management Journal*, 50(5), 987–1008.

Sackett, D. L., Strauss, S. E., Richardson, W. S., Rosenberg, W., & Haynes, R. B. (2000). *Evidence Based Medicine: How to Practice and Teach EBM* (2nd ed.). Edinburgh: Churchill Livingstone.

Salminen, S., & Tallberg, T. (1996). Human errors in fatal and serious occupational accidents in Finland. *Ergonomics*, 39(7), 980–988. doi:10.1080/00140139608964518.

Sapolsky, R. M. (1994). Individual differences and the stress response. *Seminars in Neuroscience*, 6, 261–269. doi:10.1006/smns.1994.1033.

Sauter, S., Lim, S., & Murphy, L. (1996). Organizational health: A new paradigm for occupational stress research at NIOSH. *Japanese Journal of Occupational Mental Health*, 4(4), 248–254.

Sauter, S. L., Murphy, L. R., & Hurrell, Jr., J. J. (1990). Prevention of work-related psychological disorders. *American Psychologist*, 45, 1146–1153.

Schat, A., & Kelloway, E. K. (2000). Effects of perceived control on the outcomes of workplace aggression and violence. *Journal of Occupational Health Psychology*, 5, 386–402.

Smith, R. (1991). Where is the wisdom? . . . . The poverty of medical evidence. *British Medical Journal*, 303, 798–799.

Sparks, K., Cooper, C., Fried, Y., & Shirom, A. (1997). The effects of hours of work on health: A meta-analytic review. *Journal of Occupational and Organizational Psychology*, 70, 391–408.

Spurgeon, A., Harrington, J. M., & Cooper, C. L. (1997). Health and safety problems associated with long working hours: A review of the current position. *Occupational and Environmental Medicine*, 54(6), 367–375.

Stone-Romero, E. (2011). Research strategies in industrial and organizational psychology: Non-experimental, quasi-experimental, and randomized experimental research in special purpose and nonspecial purpose settings. In: S. Zedeck (ed.), *APA Handbook of Industrial and Organizational Psychology, Volume 1: Building and Developing the Organization*. Washington, DC: APA Books, 37–72.

Trimpop, R., Kirkcaldy, B., Athanasou, J., & Cooper, C. L. (2000). Individual differences in working hours, work perceptions and accident rates in veterinary surgeries. *Work and Stress*, 14(2), 181–188.

VanKatwyk, P., Fox, S., Spector, P., & Kelloway, E. K. (2000). Using the Job-Related Affective Well-Being Scale (JAWS) to investigate affective response to work stressors. *Journal of Occupational Health Psychology*, 5, 219–230.

Wallace, J. C., & Chen, G. (2005). Development and validation of a work-specific measure of cognitive failure: Implications for occupational safety. *Journal of Occupational and Organizational Psychology*, 78, 615–632.

Walshe, K., & Rundall, T. G. (2001). Evidence-based management: From theory to practice in health care. *Milbank Quarterly*, 79, 429–457.

Wang, J., & Patten, S. (2001). Perceived work stress and major depression in the Canadian employed population, 20–49 years old. *Journal of Occupational Health Psychology*, 6, 283–289.

Warr, P. B. (1987). *Work, Unemployment, and Menial Health*. Oxford, UK: Oxford University Press.

Wong, J., & Kelloway, E. K. (2015). Sleep and safety. In: J. Barling, C. M. Barnes, E. Carleton, & D. T. Wagar (eds.), *Work and Sleep*. Oxford: Oxford University Press, 171–192.

Wong, J. H. K., & Kelloway, E. K. (2016). What happens at work stays at work? Workplace supervisory social interactions and blood pressure outcomes. *Journal of Occupational Health Psychology*, 21, 133–141.

World Health Organization. (2004). *The Summary Report on Promoting Mental Health: Concepts, Emerging Evidence, and Practice*. Geneva, Switzerland: World Health Organization.

Zapf, D., Dormann, C., & Frese, M. (1996). Longitudinal studies in organizational stress research: A review of the literature with reference to methodological issues. *Journal of Occupational Health Psychology*, 1, 145–169.

Part II
Personal qualities contributing to wellbeing

7

Character, personality, and psychological wellbeing

Thomas A. Wright and Dorothy Klotz

Introduction

> Beginning of the teaching for life,
> The instructions for wellbeing. . . . .
> Knowing how to answer one who speaks,
> To reply to one who sends a message.

The instruction of Amenemope, prologue, c. 11th century BC

Jackie Robinson, who in 1947 broke the color line in Major League baseball, knew how to answer Brooklyn Dodgers President and General Manager Branch Rickey when they first spoke face-to-face in New York on August 28, 1945. At the time, Robinson was playing shortstop for the Kansas City Monarchs of the old Negro Leagues. This first meeting between Rickey and Robinson has taken on the status of legend over the passing years. After exchanging initial greetings, Rickey got down to business and asked Robinson if he was capable of playing baseball in the Major Leagues. Robinson stated that he had played professional baseball for only a year and candidly noted that he didn't know how the Negro Leagues compared with the Minor Leagues talent wise, let alone the Major Leagues.

Branch Rickey then got right to the point. He spoke of the many barriers to be broken by the first Negro in the Major Leagues. He spoke of bigotry and hate and how to fight them. He spoke of the great opportunity to do a noble thing and how to accomplish it. As the story goes, Rickey went to great lengths to dramatically impersonate both the words and actions of possible bigots (Kahn, 2014). He did so not only out of a desire to provide Robinson with a realistic job preview (cf. Premack & Wanous, 1985), but also as a way of assessing Robinson's general wellbeing and gaining insights into his personality and character. When Rickey thought that he had sufficiently upset Robinson, he asked if he still wanted to play in the Major Leagues. Robinson's response was short and emphatic: "Certainly." Once this commitment was established, Rickey, a deeply devout man and reader of the Bible, constantly remonstrated with Robinson his need to "turn the other cheek" to the expected verbal and possibly physical abuse that Robinson would face. According to Kahn (2014): "At one point Robinson said, 'Are you looking for someone who doesn't have the courage to fight back?' 'No,' Rickey said. 'I am looking for someone who has the courage to *not* fight back.'" (p. 107).

It was widely considered in both the Major Leagues and Negro press that Robinson was not the most talented player in the Negro Leagues. Branch Rickey was apparently in agreement with that assessment. While a superb all-around athlete in football, basketball and track at the University of California, Los Angeles, Robinson batted only .097 playing shortstop for the Bruins in the spring of 1940 (Kahn, 2014). As a result, many felt that the honor of most talented Negro League player should go to either Don Newcombe or Roy Campanella. But while Robinson may not have been the most talented or even the best, he was selected by Rickey because his personality and strength of character indicated that he was the most "suitable" choice to succeed. For example, Don Newcombe was considered to be too young and not mature enough to withstand the pressure that was sure to come. A winner of 27 games in his best season, Newcombe later waged a battle with alcoholism that undoubtedly shortened his hugely promising Major League pitching career. This battle would have certainly made Newcombe a highly problematic first choice to integrate Major League Baseball. Likewise, Roy Campanella while also younger than Robinson (in this case a positive), was not considered to have a strong enough personality to weather the extreme abuse expected to be heaped upon whoever was chosen to break the Major League color barrier.

Robinson proved to be the best choice for the integration of professional baseball. He went on to play 10 seasons with the Brooklyn Dodgers and was elected to the Baseball Hall of Fame. However, being the first came with serious costs. Due partly to his family history, but also partly the result of the extreme abuse he suffered early on in his Major League career, Robinson developed heart disease, and, almost blind from diabetes, died of a heart attack at 53.

Robinson's story, from an important part of American history, is highly relevant to this chapter on character, personality, and psychological wellbeing. As we will see, while distinct from psychological wellbeing, aspects of one's character and personality play an integral role in determining not only one's current psychological wellbeing, but also can be instrumental in various intervention strategies charged with the goal of enhancing psychological wellbeing.

We begin our discussion with a brief overview of what constitutes one's character, personality, and psychological wellbeing. As a point of reference, the discussion of character will focus on the "master" or "cardinal" strengths of character. These "elevated" character strengths include valor, industry, integrity, critical thinking (wisdom), and self-regulation (Wright, 2015). Our discussion of personality will focus on the "Big Five" personality traits of extraversion, agreeableness, conscientiousness, openness, and stability (neuroticism) (Soto & John, 2008). Next, the framework for the role of character and personality in determining individual psychological wellbeing is provided. The chapter closes with suggestions for future research directions.

What character is and is not

As this chapter is being prepared in the winter of 2016, the presidential political primaries in the United States are rapidly heating up. In particular, and in both major political parties, the voting public is increasingly questioning the character of many of these presidential candidates. Unfortunately, many of the candidates fail to actually define character, instead simply asserting that they have "it" while their opponents do not have "it." Our politicians are not alone in their vague definitions; the topic of character raises numerous considerations (Wright & Goodstein, 2007). For example, almost 100 years ago, a leading industrial psychologist, Raymond Filter (1921), noted in the *Journal of Applied Psychology* that, "The looseness of meanings attached to names of character traits demands first consideration" (p. 297). Strong sentiments for someone who then failed to provide even a rudimentary definition of character! Obviously, constructing an acceptable definition of character has been no small accomplishment for scholars over the intervening years, given that a number of supposedly related terms – such as virtue, values, personality, and themes – are consistently used interchangeably. As a consequence, these terms have all too frequently been confounded in the literature (Peterson & Seligman, 2004; Wright & Lauer, 2013). While a detailed comparison/contrast analysis of each of these terms is beyond the scope of this chapter, it is worthwhile to briefly consider how character has been previously considered.

Throughout the ages, traditional views of character have been influenced by a wide variety of sources (Wright & Lauer, 2013). These sources include Aristotelian thought; Judeo-Christian beliefs (as especially expressed in Saint Paul's faith, hope, and charity); such Eastern philosophies as Confucianism; and the more modern, secular approaches proposed by utilitarian, justice, and social contract models (Hunter, 2000; Peterson & Seligman, 2004; Wright, 2015; Wright & Goodstein, 2007). Reflective of all these perspectives, *Webster's Unabridged Dictionary* (1989) defines character as "the aggregate of features and traits that form the apparent individual nature of some person or thing" and refers to its adherence to "moral qualities, ethical standards, principles and the like." Considered together, these traditional definitions of character typically contain not only moral, but also social dimensions. As a result, character is best considered as a multidimensional construct (Peterson & Park, 2006; Wright & Huang, 2008). A number of scholars agree that the following three character dimensions are the most widely accepted throughout recorded history: moral discipline, moral attachment, and moral autonomy (Hunter, 2000; Wright & Goodstein, 2007).

An individual exhibits *moral discipline* if he or she suppresses individual, personal needs for those of a communitarian "greater good" considered at the group, organization, or societal levels. A case study analysis of the successful entrepreneur and professional actor, Gus Rethwisch, highlights the need to be disciplined (Wright, 2014a). Rethwisch dramatically discussed both the need and his willingness to sacrifice his personal life for the betterment of his organization through working 12 or more hours per day, seven days a week for more than 10 years! Jackie Robinson had to demonstrate a strong measure of moral discipline when he learned that a number of his future Brooklyn Dodgers teammates had circulated a petition during his first spring training stating that they would not play on the same team with him. Amazingly, Robinson did not allow this to adversely affect his day-to-day relationships with his teammates. How does one develop such a level of self-discipline and restraint? Emanating from both Eastern and Western communitarian tradition, one approach to developing moral discipline is the concept of a silent retreat. Whatever the duration, a period of silent meditation and reflection can be used to help a person discern his or her vocation(s) in life. Forced into near isolation from his teammates during his first season, Robinson had to look inward and draw the strength needed to not only survive, but prosper.

Also compatible with the communitarian idea of a greater societal good is *moral attachment*, the second element of character. Moral attachment is reflective of the confirmation of our commitments to someone or something greater than us (Wright & Goodstein, 2007). Hunter (2000) succinctly describes this as "the embrace of an ideal that attracts us, draws us, animates us, and inspires us" (p. 16). While a stated goal of many organizations, institutions of higher learning would appear to have a unique opportunity to operationalize the notion of the university as "family" toward the end of helping various stakeholders form a sense of attachment to something greater than ourselves (Wright, 2015; Wright & Wefald, 2012). Only from this development of a sense of family can one hope to inspire in university employees, students, and also ourselves a true feeling of service and community involvement or what the Jesuits term as *homines pro aliis*. Along with his desire to play in the Major Leagues and provide economic stability to his wife and family, Robinson also was justifiably proud of being the first African American to play in the modern Major Leagues. He realized that his sacrifice would benefit a wave of future African American ballplayers (such as Henry Aaron, Ernie Banks, Roy Campanella, Larry Doby, Elston Howard, Monte Irvin, Don Newcombe, and Willie Mays). Robinson felt strongly about this attachment to others, composing his own epitaph to read, "A life is important only in the impact it has on other lives" (Kahn, 2014, p. 275).

The third component of character is *moral autonomy*. An individual exhibits moral autonomy if she or he has the capacity to freely make ethical decisions (Hunter, 2000; Wright & Huang, 2008). Autonomy means that a person has *both* the necessary discretion and the skills of judgment at his or her disposal to freely act morally (Wright, 2015). In particular, moral autonomy suggests the dual notions of individual responsibility and free will (Hunter, 2000; Wright & Goodstein, 2007). Deeply rooted in a number of both Eastern and Western spiritual traditions is the end goal of developing a strong sense of empowerment to freely accept and exercise responsibility for one's actions. Again using a Jesuit framework, what better example of this acceptance is the young Ignatius of Loyola surrendering his freedom to his higher power and dedicating his skills and abilities to the furtherance of the Lord's work (Hellwig, 1991).

Jackie Robinson's discretion and moral-based skills of judgment not only benefitted him during his athletic career, but also in his later life. For example, he became the first African American vice president of a major American corporation, *Chock Full o' Nuts*. In recognition of his good moral character and many professional accomplishments, Robinson was posthumously awarded the highest civilian honors bestowed by the US Congress and by the President, the Congressional Gold Medal and the Presidential Medal of Freedom.

Incorporating the three "moral components" of discipline, attachment, and autonomy, character is clearly distinguishable from values (Gentile, 2010; Wright & Quick, 2011a), themes (Buckingham & Clifton, 2001), and personality (Wright & Lauer, 2013). In particular, character is shaped by an individual's convictions and is best evidenced by the ability to persist in those convictions even in the face of strong temptation or moral challenge (Hunter, 2000; Wright, 2015). Building on these three dimensions, Wright and his colleagues have defined character "as those interpenetrable and habitual qualities within individuals, and applicable to organizations that both constrain and lead them to desire and pursue personal and societal good" (Wright, 2015; Wright & Goodstein, 2007, p. 932).

Peterson and Seligman's (2004) Values-In-Action-Inventory of Strengths (VIA-IS) is currently the most popular classification framework for measuring character strength. The VIA-IS is a 240-item self-report questionnaire that uses 5-point Likert scales to measure the degree to which respondents endorse strength-relevant statements about themselves (1 = very much unlike me through 5 = very much like me). Based upon a primarily Internet-generated sample of approximately 3 million respondents, Peterson and Seligman, and their colleagues, have identified 24 strengths of character. Included among these character strengths are the five widely recognized "master" or "cardinal" strengths of character: valor, industry, integrity, critical thinking (wisdom), and self-regulation. These five strengths have been consistently considered as "elevated" or preeminent in nature both over time and across cultures (Wright & Goodstein, 2007). As we will see, these strengths of character are particularly informative when considered in the context of their possible relationships with personality and psychological wellbeing. We next briefly examine what personality *is* and *is not*.

Personality is not character

Interestingly, in his quest to determine what constitutes the construct of personality, the famous psychologist Gordon Allport both singlehandedly and dramatically set back the study of character from applied and social science research (Allport, 1921, 1927, 1937). In particular, Allport and his colleagues (Allport, 1921, 1927; Allport & Vernon, 1930) argued that whereas the study of personality was well within the domain of psychological investigation, character as traditionally viewed was most appropriately the subject matter of philosophy, not psychology. More recently, and as applied to organizational scholarship, the study of character has not been consistently well received (see Wright, 2015 for a further discussion of this topic). The traits of "personality" so ardently sought by Allport and his colleagues for psychological investigation were ostensibly "objective" entities, which Allport named "neuropsychic structures." Allport's goal was quite straightforward: to completely strip these objective entities of any moral significance (Peterson & Seligman, 2004, p. 55). To that end, Allport (1961) preferred "to define character as personality evaluated and personality . . . as character devalued" (p. 32). Allport's viewpoint quickly became the prevailing approach in the psychological sciences, although John Dewey (1922) was one famous dissenter. As a result, the traditional view of character, emphasizing both a moral and social component, all but vanished from psychological and applied research until recently, with the work of Peterson and Seligman (2004), and Wright and his colleagues (Wright, 2015; Wright & Huang, 2008; Wright & Quick, 2011a).

Distinct from this traditional view of character, according to James and Mazerolle (2002), personality is best considered as being composed of "dynamic mental structures and coordinated mental processes that determine individuals' emotional and behavioral adjustments to their environments" (p. 1) More specifically, "mental structures" refer to one's needs, self-image, and aspects of memory, while "mental processes" refer to one's ability to reason and how one perceives one's environment. While subject to change over time, these mental structures exhibit a measure of consistency over one's life course. Roughly 30 years ago, Buss and Finn (1987) provided a still-accurate portrayal of the trait approach to personality research in noting that "several generations of research on personality have yielded numerous traits in a confusing array that begs for organization" (p. 432) How numerous were these traits? Even as far back as the 1930s, Allport and Odbert (1936) assembled an astounding total of 17,953 personality-descriptive adjectives. Later, Cattell (1947) submitted Allport and Odbert's list to a series of factor analyses. Cattell then used a variety of methods to reduce these descriptors to 4,504 "real" traits and then further to 171 trait names. A series of factor analyses by Cattell produced his 16 "source traits" or primary factors for personality. Cattell's landmark research is highly instrumental in the development of the widely used Big Five personality traits: extraversion, agreeableness, conscientiousness, openness, and stability (neuroticism) (Soto & John, 2008). But Branch Rickey had a much more parsimonious, but very accurate, one-word description of Jackie Robinson's personality: "Adventure!" (Kahn, 2014, p. 203). Next, we turn to a discussion of psychological wellbeing.

Psychological wellbeing

One of the most persistent topics of both scholarly and practical interest remains the mysteries surrounding the pursuit of "happiness" or "wellbeing" (Russell, 1930; Wright & Huang, 2012). Although not isomorphic constructs, these terms have typically been used interchangeably, with academic scholars invariably using the "umbrella" term *wellbeing* and the general public preferring the term *happiness*. As a consequence, the terms tend to lack both precision and clarity (Diener, 1984; Diener, Suh, Lucas, & Smith, 1999; Wright & Cropanzano, 2007). While this is beyond the scope of the present chapter discussion, the lead author and his colleagues, along with a number of other organizational scholars, have spent considerable time and effort attempting to better understand the many "faces" of employee "happiness" and "wellbeing" (Ashkanasy, 2011; Cropanzano & Wright, 2001, 2011; Diener et al., 1999; Staw & Barsade, 1993; Warr, 1990; Warr & Clapton, 2010; Wright, 2005, 2014b). For example, as noted by Cropanzano and Wright (2011) and Wright (2014b), part of the conceptual confusion involving scholarly investigation of "happiness" and "wellbeing" involves the conceptual space occupied by other, related concepts.

As shown in Figure 7.1, some terms illustrate concepts that are both broad and inclusive, while other terms refer to concepts that are narrow and more focused in nature (Wright, 2014b). The top of Figure 7.1 lists several of the names attributed to general concepts. Besides the word *happiness* itself, we also find such terms as *flourishing* (e.g., Fredrickson, 2009; Seligman, 2011) and Aristotle's original term *eudaimonia* (e.g., Deci & Ryan, 2008). When reference is made to broad conceptualizations of happiness, the terms *emotional wellbeing* and *subjective wellbeing* come most readily to mind (Diener, 2006; Wright, 2014b). In fact, as considered by Diener (2000), subjective wellbeing is a monolithic entity and is best considered as a latent, higher-order construct composed of a wide spectrum of "people's cognitive and affective evaluations of their lives" (p. 34).

At the bottom of Figure 7.1 are several concepts that are narrower in their conceptual space (Wright, 2014b). These narrow, more precise descriptors include such concepts as "hope" (Luthans & Youssef, 2007), "job satisfaction" (Wright & Cropanzano, 1998), "life satisfaction" (Diener, Emmons, Larsen, & Griffin, 1985), and "psychological wellbeing" (Wright & Bonett, 2007; Wright & Cropanzano, 2000), among others. Considered in its entirety, Figure 7.1 categorizes one set of general concepts (e.g., subjective wellbeing, happiness) and a second set of more specific concepts (e.g., job satisfaction, life satisfaction, positive affect, negative affect, psychological wellbeing).

With such varied definitional options, one can readily see how these terms became such eclectic ideas. Adding to the confusion, some researchers use the narrow concepts to define the more general terms. For example, both Andrews and Withey (1976) and Ryan and Deci (2001) present a view of subjective wellbeing that combines life satisfaction and pleasurable affect (for a further discussion, see Cropanzano & Wright, 2011; Wright, 2014b). For this reason, conceptual models can differ to the extent that they employ different subsets of the available components. Building upon the Figure 7.1 framework and expanding upon earlier work (Cropanzano & Wright, 2001; Wright, 2005; Wright & Cropanzano, 2007), and especially an unpublished manuscript (Cropanzano & Wright, 2011), Wright (2014b) summarized a four faces of happiness taxonomic model organizing the various research perspectives. As discussed in more detail by Wright

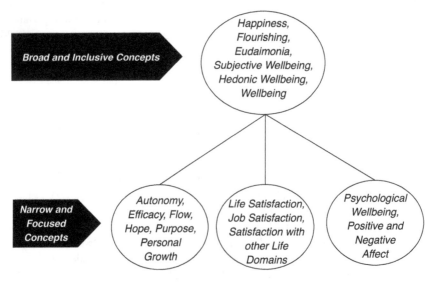

Figure 7.1   Broad and narrow concepts of wellbeing
Source: Adapted from Cropanzano & Wright (2011); Wright (2014b).

(2014b, p. 1156), happiness has a minimum of four definitional categories or faces: (1) objective life conditions; (2) eudaimonic wellbeing; (3) life (and job) satisfaction; and (4) emotion-based wellbeing. It is important to note that each of these faces is best considered as a grouping or category of connected ideas.

In brief, Category 1 is best considered as composed of such objective life conditions as diet, education, employment status, health, and income. Category 2 encompasses the Aristotelian concept of *eudaimonic* wellbeing (Ryan & Deci, 2001). Simply put, this view of "happiness" can be best considered as a multidimensional concept composed of such aspects as *meaning* (Seligman, 2002), *flow* (Csikszentmihalyi, 2003), and *life purpose* (Ryff, 1989). Alternatively, Category 3 highlights the two primary satisfaction domains, life (Diener et al., 1985) and job satisfaction (Wright & Cropanzano, 2000). It is important to note that life and job satisfaction are evaluative judgments, with both having strong cognitive components (Wright, 2014b). Finally, and the focus of our present wellbeing discussion, the Category 4 classification refers to such aspects of emotion-based wellbeing as positive and negative affect, and psychological wellbeing.

However conceptualized, wellbeing has three primary defining characteristics: First, wellbeing is a phenomenological event (Diener, 1994). People are psychologically well when they subjectively believe themselves to be so. Second, wellbeing involves how we feel, experience, and process various forms or patterns of emotion. In particular, psychologically well individuals are more prone to experience positive emotions and less prone to experience negative emotions. Third, wellbeing is best considered as a global judgment. This means that wellbeing refers to one's life in the aggregate, that is, considered as a whole. These are important distinctions from such other "happiness" constructs as job satisfaction (Wright & Cropanzano, 2000). Despite this conceptual confusion, and irrespective of how wellbeing is defined, organizational researchers have long been aware of the extensive costs in both human and financial terms attributable to dysfunctional wellbeing.

Depression, loss of self-esteem, hypertension, alcoholism, and illicit drug consumption are associated with both work and nonwork-related dysfunctional wellbeing (Quick, Wright, Adkins, Nelson, & Quick, 2013). In turn, these variables have been shown to be adversely related with a number of work outcomes. Of special relevance, in the workplace psychological wellbeing has consistently been related with such individual and organizational health and betterment indicators as job performance, employee retention, and cardiovascular health. We now turn to the extant body of applied research examining the relationships among the five "master" or "cardinal" strengths of character, the Big Five personality traits, and psychological wellbeing.

Character, personality, and psychological wellbeing

Our first "master" strength of character, valor, involves not shrinking from threat, challenge, difficulty, or pain. Valor can be distinguished between physical and moral dimensions. Taken together, a person of valor is *both* willing *and* able to confront danger and act rightly in the face of both severe opposition and consequence (Peterson & Seligman, 2004; Wright, Quick, Hannah, & Hargrove, 2017). Proposed relationships among valor and the Big Five personality traits are difficult to ascertain, given that the Big Five traits do not have an apparent "risk orientation" (Harvey, Erdos, & Turnbull, 2009). More specifically, the manifestations of valor typically require some aspect of risk or danger to be present. However, each of the Big Five personality traits of extraversion, agreeableness, conscientiousness, openness, and stability (neuroticism) are best considered as low-risk traits (Digman, 1990; Harvey et al., 2009; Peterson & Seligman, 2004).

The proposed positive relationship between valor and psychological wellbeing (Wright & Quick, 2011b) has interesting implications regarding research on whistleblowers. Employees who report misconduct often suffer "severe retaliation" from the organization (Rothschild & Miethe, 1999; Wright & Lauer, 2013). For example, whistleblowers are often fired from their job, have trouble obtaining future employment, are harassed by colleagues at work, experience various forms of physical and emotional stress, and even contemplate suicide (Near & Miceli, 1996; Wright & Lauer, 2014). Since these types of job strains have been shown to be negatively related to psychological wellbeing (Karimi, Karimi, & Nouri, 2011), it would appear that valorous, whistleblowing employees need to have a reservoir of positive psychological wellbeing to survive (cf. Wright & Hobfoll, 2004).

Peterson and Seligman (2004) define persistence or industry as the "Voluntary continuation of a goal-directed action in spite of obstacles, difficulties, or discouragement" (p. 229). Thus, an industrious individual is one who persists in a course of action despite possible setbacks and takes pride in completing tasks. Dewitte and Schouwenberg (2002) incorporated the Big Five, Lay's general procrastination scale, and a modified "impulsivity scale" (which measured perseverance) to investigate the procrastination tendencies of freshman college students. The findings indicated that procrastinators tended to score low on both "perseverance" and the Big Five trait of conscientiousness. The positive relationship between perseverance and conscientiousness has been consistently obtained in a number of studies (cf. Duckworth, Peterson, Matthews, & Kelly, 2007; MacCann, Duckworth, & Roberts, 2009). However, the relationships among perseverance and the remaining four Big Five traits are not as consistent.

Using a three-experiment framework, Riediger and Freund (2004) found a positive relationship between perseverance and psychological wellbeing. In particular, successful goal attainment or overcoming obstacles obstructing goal attainment (perseverance) were found to be positively associated with psychological wellbeing. Alternatively, circumstances interfering with goal attainment, such as a lack of resources or ineffectual goal attainment strategies, were found to be negatively associated with wellbeing. These findings are consistent with other research investigating the role of goal attainment on wellbeing (Emmons, Keyes, & Haidt, 2003). We further note that the benefits of persevering behavior on the psychological wellbeing of individuals experiencing such health-related ailments as cancer (Ferrell, Smith, Cullinane, & Melancon, 2003), rheumatoid arthritis (Lambert, Lambert, Klipple, & Mewshaw, 1989), and HIV/AIDS (Goodman, Chesney, & Tipton, 1995) have been well documented.

According to Peterson and Seligman (2004 integrity captures "a character trait in which people are true to themselves, accurately representing – privately and publicly – their internal states, intentions, and commitment" (p. 249). Regarding the possibility of a relationship among integrity and the various Big Five personality trait relationships, Wright and Quick (2011b) found their measure of integrity to be positively related with extraversion, agreeableness, conscientiousness, and openness, four of the Big Five personality traits. Alternatively, they found a negative relationship between integrity and the Big Five trait of stability (neuroticism). In an interesting twist, Ashton, Lee, and Son (2000) suggest the possibility of considering integrity as a sixth "Big" personality trait. They propose their novel research question based upon the more robust relationships among such factors as integrity, trustworthiness, truthfulness, and values when compared to the typically weaker associations among integrity and the actual Big Five personality traits.

Preliminary results from a study by Yeh, Lorenz, Wickrama, Conger, and Elder (2006) suggest a possible relationship between integrity and psychological wellbeing. More specifically, Yeh et al. (2006) examined a number of factors hypothesized to be correlated with marital success. First, they found that spousal integrity was a primary contributor to the overall wellbeing of the relationship itself. Second, a successful overall relationship was seen as being beneficial to the wellbeing of each member of the relationship. Finally, an increased effort to be honest with one's spouse was also found to be conducive to strengthening a struggling relationship. These findings are consistent with Wright and Quick's (2011b) suggestion of a relationship between integrity and psychological wellbeing.

Peterson and Seligman (2004) consider critical thinking as "The willingness to search actively for evidence against one's favored beliefs, plans or goals, and to weigh such evidence fairly when it is available" (p. 144). Thus, unlike non–critical thinkers, critical thinkers are able to reevaluate and adjust strongly held attitudes, opinions, or beliefs if presented with logically based contradictory evidence. To date, consistent relationships among critical thinking, conscientiousness, extraversion, and stability (neuroticism) remain to be established. The possible relationship of critical thinking with openness and agreeableness is more promising (Peterson & Seligman, 2004). However, additional research is needed to further examine possible relationships among critical thinking and the Big Five personality traits.

The basis also exists to suggest a relationship between critical thinking and psychological wellbeing. In a study of orchestra students, Wu (2010) proposed that the more an individual's critical-thinking abilities are developed, the greater the possible benefit to psychological wellbeing. More specifically, subjects were asked to report their feelings toward playing in the school band versus playing in an orchestra. Students preferred the orchestra over the school band because the orchestra required more practice and for the students to reflect more deeply about their music.

Peterson and Seligman (2004) define self-regulation as the way that "a person exerts control over his or her own responses so as to pursue goals and live up to standards. These responses include thoughts, emotions, impulses, performances and other behaviors" (p. 500). Regarding the Big Five, two personality traits in particular – agreeableness and conscientiousness – have consistently been shown to be related to self-regulation. In particular, conscientiousness has a number of attributes that personify self-regulatory attitudes and behaviors such as the effortful control of attention, the ability to mindfully manage specific behaviors, the ability to choose one behavior over another, and the capacity to be persistent (cf. Rothbart, Chew, & Gartstein, 2001). Jensen-Campbell, Knack, Waldrip, and Campbell (2007) hypothesized that conscientiousness is related to an individual's ability to control his or her anger. As hypothesized, individuals who were high in conscientiousness were more able to effectively control feelings of anger and aggression. Regarding agreeableness, Tobin, Graziano, and Vanman (2000) examined the ability of college students to regulate their emotions under various circumstances. As expected, their results indicated that agreeableness was positively related to the students' ability to regulate their emotions. We next suggest several research directions for scholars interested in further examining possible relationships among character, personality, and psychological wellbeing.

Future research directions

Building on Peterson and Seligman's (2004) character taxonomy and incorporating a focus group approach, the lead author and his colleagues (Wright, 2011, 2015; Wright & Quick, 2011a) have developed a number of "top five" signature strength profiles for success (from Peterson & Seligman's population of all 24 VIA-IS strengths) that respondents (both MBA and undergraduate business students as well as actual business practitioners) consider most beneficial in achieving success in a growing number of work occupations (Wright & Lauer, 2013; Wright & Quick, 2011a). These include top five signature strength profiles for being an effective business student and such occupations as manager, college president, entrepreneur, nurse, athletic coach, sales/marketing, accountant, engineer, social worker, elementary school teacher, and politician, among others. For example, when queried as to what top five strengths are most beneficial for being a successful college business student, both actual students and business practitioners alike consistently list the following five strengths: love of learning, industry, critical thinking, citizenship, and curiosity.

Fascinating patterns have been suggested across focus groups for a number of occupations. As one example, the top five signature strength profile for success as a manager includes leadership, social intelligence, fairness, critical thinking, and integrity. Along with becoming a manager, many students express a career interest in the field of sales/marketing (Wright, 2015). A consistent top five signature strength profile for success emerges, with zest consistently rated as the necessary top signature strength, followed by the strengths of character: social intelligence, creativity, humor, and curiosity. The field of nursing is interesting as it is the only occupation to date in which the strength of kindness is listed as one of the top five signature strengths. Jackie Robinson's life as a "first" in so many arenas well-personified the importance of demonstrating each of the cardinal or master strengths of character. However, the top five signature strength profiles to be successful in other professions, such as nursing, are different. Future research on the possibility of occupation-specific top five character strength profiles would benefit from the incorporation of mixed method designs integrating the collection and analysis of both quantitative *and* qualitative data (Wright & Sweeney, 2016).

Research is now needed to test the role of "good" character as a defining feature for individual wellbeing and achievement. While subject to further investigation and verification, preliminary research indicates that actual top five student character profiles are consistently and significantly at variance from their proposed or ideal profiles. Highly relevant to this discussion, many students self-rate integrity as one of their top five strengths of character. However, student cheating is at an all-time high. Upwards of 88% of millennial students admit that they have cheated in school, with the modal response regarding how many times they have cheated at an astonishing 100 plus (Wright, 2004). Similarly, students (as well as actual management practitioners) rank social intelligence as being one of the top strengths necessary to be an effective manager. Love of learning is considered as one of the top five character strengths to be an effective MBA student. However, both of these strengths of character are actually among the least commonly self-reported by the hundreds of students surveyed by the lead author. Finally, business students self-rate themselves low in self-regulation and valor, strengths that are highly valued in a number of occupations. These preliminary findings indicate the possibility that actual student character profiles may not provide an optimal fit with the necessary requirements of such sought after occupations as accountant, entrepreneur, financial professional, and sales and marketing, among many others.

Regarding the notion of employee fit with the job, organization, or occupation, management scholars have long been intrigued with how to better optimize the degree of fit between the employee and the organization (French, Caplan, & Harrison, 1982). This level of congruence between an individual employee's skills and abilities and her or his work requirements has been formalized as Person-Environment (P-E) fit theory (Joyce, Slocum, & Von Glinow, 1982). Alternatively, P-E fit theory proposes that the wellbeing of both the individual and his or her organization is negatively impacted when there is an incongruent fit between the characteristics or demands of the job and the characteristics of the employee. While numerous conceptualizations of fit have been suggested and investigated over the years, the roles of character strength profiles, employee personality, and psychological wellbeing have not received adequate attention (Wright, 2015). For example, when considered in the context of character strength profiles, there are a wide range of topics within the domain of P-E fit theory that can inform our research interests. The concept of character strength profile holds much promise for not only what we research, but also how we teach.

While it has provided an initial attempt to conceptualize strength of character, Peterson and Seligman's (2004) work has been increasingly criticized on *both* conceptual and psychometric grounds (Wright, 2015; Wright & Lauer, 2013). Conceptually, this framework has been questioned regarding whether a number of their purported 24 strengths, while certainly positive attributes, are actually aspects or strengths of character. For example, creativity, curiosity, humor, social intelligence, and zest are lacking in a moral dimension, which has been traditionally understood as central to any definition of character (cf., Hunter, 2000). Psychometrically, Wright and Quick (2011a) raised a number of issues, including the possibility that certain VIA-IS instrument strengths of character may suffer from gender bias. In addition, Wright (2015) has suggested the need for additional research to determine if the VIA-IS scales have adequate internal consistency (Cronbach alpha coefficients > .70), along with indications of content and construct validity. Finally, the sheer size of the instrument, a robust 240 items, imposes severe time constraints on many potential test takers. Considered together, these challenges suggest the need for an instrument that is narrower in scope (< 24 scales), with fewer items per subscale, that demonstrates both adequate scale internal consistency and acceptable content and construct validity.

Over time, wellbeing has come to mean any number of things to various people. In organizational research, wellbeing has been considered as positive and negative affect; mental health; emotional exhaustion; job and life satisfaction; dispositional affect; and emotional, subjective, and psychological wellbeing (Wright & Doherty, 1998; Wright & Huang, 2012). This diversity in terminology stimulated Rath and Harter (2010) to very loosely define the construct as "all the things that are important to how we think about and experience our lives" (p. 137). At the extreme, even the *same* measure has been considered differently. As one example, Berkman's (1971) *Index of Psychological Wellbeing* has been referred to in the literature as "mental health" (Wright & Bonett, 1992), "dispositional affect" (Wright & Staw, 1999), and "psychological wellbeing" (Wright & Cropanzano, 2000). A number of scholars, including the lead author and his colleagues (Cropanzano & Wright, 2001; Wright, 2005, 2014; Wright & Cropanzano, 2007), have increasingly called for greater conceptual rigor regarding what constitutes psychological wellbeing. The "four faces" taxonomy approach is one such attempt (cf. Wright, 2014b).

Building upon this taxonomy, we suggest that future research consider the role of psychological wellbeing at not only the individual, but also the social, organizational, and societal levels. For example, given that team or group behavior is best considered in the context of emotional experience and social exchange (Emich & Wright, 2016), we propose the possibility of a group or team "wellbeing contagion" effect. Team members exhibiting positive displays of wellbeing and such strengths of character as industry, integrity, and valor, may through their actions also stimulate the display of these positive strengths in other group members. One important implication is that team members can affect each other, both for the good as well as the bad. Therefore, before adding new team members, the utmost care should be given to how these new additions to the team will influence various team processes already in place. Encouraging situations where character strength, personality traits, and psychological wellbeing are most beneficially coupled is obviously a scenario that is highly beneficial to both employees and their employer.

Concluding thoughts

This chapter undertook several objectives. First, we began our discussion with a brief overview of what constitutes one's character, personality, and psychological wellbeing. Our discussion of character focused on the "master" or "cardinal" strengths of character, including valor, industry, integrity, critical thinking (wisdom), and self-regulation (Wright, 2015). The discussion of personality highlighted the Big Five personality traits of extraversion, agreeableness, conscientiousness, openness, and stability (neuroticism) (Soto & John, 2008). Our discussion on psychological wellbeing focused on differentiating psychological wellbeing from overall wellbeing and happiness. Through the incorporation of such public figures as Jackie Robinson, we provided a framework for the role of character and personality in determining individual psychological wellbeing. The chapter closed with several suggestions for future research directions. To paraphrase Branch Rickey's description of Jackie Robinson, research in the area of character, personality, and psychological wellbeing should truly be an exciting adventure for all who choose to be involved.

References

Allport, G. W. (1921). Personality and character. *Psychological Bulletin*, 18, 441–455.

Allport, G. W. (1927). Concepts of trait and personality. *Psychological Bulletin*, 24, 284–293.

Allport, G. W. (1937). *Personality: A Psychological Interpretation*. New York: Holt.

Allport, G. W. (1961). *Pattern and Growth in Personality*. New York: Holt, Rinehart & Winston.

Allport, G. W., & Odbert, H. S. (1936). *Trait-Names: A Psycho-Lexical Study*. Psychological Monographs, 47 (Serial No. 211).

Allport, G. W., & Vernon, P. (1930). The field of personality. *Psychological Bulletin*, 27, 677–730.

Andrews, F. M., & Withey, S. R. (1976). *Social Indicators of Well-Being*. New York: Plenum Press.

Ashkanasy, N. M. (2011). International happiness: A multilevel perspective. *Academy of Management Perspectives*, 25, 23–29.

Ashton, M. C., Lee, K., & Son, C. (2000). Honesty as the sixth factor of personality: Correlations with Machiavellianism, primary psychopathy, and social adroitness. *European Journal of Personality*, 14, 359–368.

Berkman, P. L. (1971). Life stress and psychological well-being: A replication of Langer's analysis in the midtown Manhattan study. *Journal of Health and Social Behavior*, 12, 35–45.

Buckingham, M., & Clifton, D. O. (2001). *Now, Discover Your Strengths*. New York: Free Press.

Buss, A. H., & Finn, S. E. (1987). Classification of personality traits. *Journal of Personality and Social Psychology*, 52, 432–444.

Cattell, R. B. (1947). Confirmation and classification of primary personality factors. *Psychometrika*, 12, 197–220.

Cropanzano, R., & Wright, T. A. (2001). When a "happy" worker is really a "productive" worker: A review and further refinement of the happy-productive worker thesis. *Consulting Psychology Journal: Practice and Research*, 53, 182–199.

Cropanzano, R., & Wright, T. A. (2011). *The Four Faces of Happiness*. Unpublished manuscript.

Csíkszentmihályi, M. (2003). *Good Business: Leadership, Flow, and the Making of Meaning*. New York: Penguin Books.

Deci, E. L., & Ryan, R. M. (2008). Hedonia, eudaimonia, and well-being: An introduction. *Journal of Happiness Studies*, 9, 1–11.

Dewey, J. (1922). *Human Nature and Conduct*. New York: Henry Holt and Company.

Dewitte, S., & Schouwenberg, H. C. (2002). Procrastination, temptation, and incentives: The struggle between present and the future in procrastinators and the punctual. *European Journal of Personality*, 16, 469–489.

Diener, E. (1984). Subjective well-being. *Psychological Bulletin*, 95, 542–575.

Diener, E. (1994). Assessing subjective well-being: Progress and opportunities. *Social Indicators Research*, 31, 103–107.

Diener, E. (2000). Subjective well-being: The science of happiness and a proposal for a national index. *American Psychologist*, 55, 34–43.

Diener, E. (2006). Guidelines for national indicators of subjective well-being and ill-being. *Applied Research in Quality of Life*, 1, 151–157.

Diener, E., Emmons, R. A., Larsen, R. J., & Griffin, S. (1985). The satisfaction with life scale. *Journal of Personality Assessment*, 49, 71–75.

Diener, E., Suh, E. M., Lucas, R. E., & Smith, H. L. (1999). Subjective well-being: Three decades of progress. *Psychological Bulletin*, 125, 276–302.

Digman, J. M. (1990). Personality structure: Emergence of the five-factor model. *Annual Review of Psychology*, 41, 417–440.

Duckworth, A. L., Peterson, C., Matthews, M. D., & Kelly, D. R. (2007). Grit: Perseverance and passion for long term goals. *Journal of Personality and Social Psychology*, 92, 1087–1101.

Emich, K., & Wright, T. A. (2016). The "I's" in team: The importance of individual members to team success. *Organizational Dynamics*, 45, 2–10.

Emmons, R. A., Keyes, C. L. M., & Haidt, J. (2003). Personal goals, life meaning, and virtue: Wellsprings of a positive life. *Flourishing: Positive Psychology & the Life Well-Lived*, 335, 105–128.

Ferrell, B., Smith, S. L., Cullinane, C. A., & Melancon, C. (2003). Psychological well-being and quality of life in ovarian cancer survivors. *Cancer*, 98, 1061–1071.

Filter, R. O. (1921). An experimental study of character traits. *Journal of Applied Psychology*, 5, 297–317.

Fredrickson, B. L. (2009). *Positivity*. New York: Crown Publishers.

French, J. R. P. Jr., Caplan, R. D., & Harrison, R. V. (1982). *The Mechanisms of Job Stress and Strain*. London: Wiley.

Gentile, M. C. (2010). *Giving Voice to Values: How to Speak Your Mind When You Know What's Right*. New Haven, CT: Yale University Press.

Goodman, E., Chesney, M. A., & Tipton, A. C. (1995). Relationship of optimism, knowledge, attitudes, and beliefs to use of HIV antibody testing by at-risk female adolescents. *Psychosomatic Medicine*, 57, 541–547.

Harvey, J., Erdos, G., & Turnbull, L. (2009). How do we perceive heroes? *Journal of Risk Research*, 12, 313–327.

Hellwig, M. K. (1991). *Finding God in All Things: A Spirituality for Today*. Excerpted from *Living the Mission: A Book of Meditations, Prayers and Insights from the University of San Francisco Community* (2013). San Francisco: University of San Francisco Press (originally published in Sojourners Magazine, December, 1991).

Hunter, J. W. (2000). *The Death of Character: Moral Education in an Age without Good or Evil*. New York: Basic Books.

James, L. R., & Mazerolle, M. D. (2002). *Personality in Work Organizations*. Thousand Oaks, CA: Sage.

Jensen-Campbell, L. A., Knack, J. M., Waldrip, A. M., & Campbell, S. D. (2007). Do Big Five personality traits associated with self-control influence the regulation of anger and aggression? *Journal of Research in Personality*, 41, 403–424.

Joyce, W., Slocum, J. W. Jr., & Von Glinow, M. A. (1982). Person-situation interaction: Competing models of fit. *Journal of Organizational Behavior*, 3, 265–280.

Kahn, R. (2014). *Rickey & Robinson: The True, Untold Story of the Integration of Baseball*. New York: Rodale.

Karimi, L., Karimi, H., & Nouri, A. (2011). Predicting employees' well-being using work-family conflict and job strain models. *Journal of the International Society for the Investigation of Stress*, 27, 111–122.

Lambert, V. A., Lambert, C. E., Klipple, G. L., & Mewshaw, E. A. (1989). Social support, hardiness and psychological well-being in women with arthritis. *Journal of Nursing Scholarship*, 21, 128–131.

Luthans, F., & Youssef, C. M. (2007). Emerging Positive Organizational Behavior. *Journal of Management*, 33, 321–349.

MacCann, C., Duckworth, A. L., & Roberts, R. D. (2009). Empirical identification of the major facets of conscientiousness. *Learning and Individual Differences*, 9, 451–458.

Near, J. P., & Miceli, M. P. (1996). Whistle-blowing: Myth and reality. *Journal of Management*, 22, 507–526.

Peterson, C., & Park, N. (2006). Character strengths in organizations. *Journal of Organizational Behavior*, 27, 1149–1154.

Peterson, C., & Seligman, M. E. P. (2004). *Character Strengths and Virtues: A Handbook and Classification*. New York: Oxford University Press/Washington, DC: American Psychological Association.

Premack, S. L., & Wanous, J. P. (1985). A meta-analysis of realistic job preview experiments. *Journal of Applied Psychology*, 70, 706–719.

Quick, J. C., Wright, T. A., Adkins, J. A., Nelson, D. L., & Quick, J. D. (2013). *Preventive Stress Management in Organizations* (2nd ed.). Washington, DC: American Psychological Association.

Rath, T., & Harter, J. (2010). *Well-being: The Five Essential Elements*. New York: Gallup Press.

Riediger, M., & Freund, A.M. (2004). Interference and facilitation among personal goals: Differential associations with subjective well-being and persistent goal pursuit. *Personality and Social Psychology Bulletin*, 30, 1511–1523.

Rothbart, M. K., Chew, K. H., & Gartstein, M. A. (2001). Assessment of temperament in early development. In: L. T. Singer & P. S. Sanford (eds.), *Biobehavioral Assessment of the Infant*. New York: Guilford Press, 190–208.

Rothschild, J., & Miethe, T. D. (1999). Whistle-blower disclosures and management retaliation: The battle to control information about organization corruption. *Work and Occupations*, 26, 107–128.

Russell, B. (1930). *The Conquest of Happiness*. New York: Liveright.

Ryan, R. M., & Deci, E. L. (2001). On happiness and human potentials: A review of research on hedonic and eudaimonic well-being. *Annual Review of Psychology*, 52, 141–166.

Ryff, C. D. (1989). Happiness is everything, or is it? Explorations on the meaning of psychological well-being. *Journal of Personality and Social Psychology*, 57, 1069–1081.

Seligman, M. E. P. (2002). *Authentic Happiness.* New York: Free Press.

Seligman, M. E. P. (2011). *Flourish: A Visionary New Understanding of Happiness and Well-Being.* New York: Free Press.

Soto, C. J., & John, O. P. (2008). Ten facet scales for the Big Five Inventory: Convergence with NEO PI-R facets, self-peer agreement, and discriminant validity. *Journal of Research in Personality*, 43, 84–90.

Staw, B. M., & Barsade, S. G. (1993). Affect and managerial performance: A test of the sadder-but-wiser vs. happier-and-smarter hypotheses. *Administrative Science Quarterly*, 38, 304–331.

Tobin, R. M., Graziano, W. G., & Vanman, E. J. (2000). Personality, emotional experience, and efforts to control emotions. *Journal of Personality & Social Psychology*, 79, 656–669.

Warr, P. (1990). The measurement of well-being and other aspects of mental health. *Journal of Occupational Psychology*, 63, 193–210.

Warr, P., & Clapton, G. (2010). *The Joy of Work? Jobs, Happiness, and You.* East Sussex, UK: Routledge.

Webster. (1989). *Webster's Ninth New Collegiate Dictionary.* Springfield, MA: Merriam-Webster, Inc.

Wright, T. A. (2004). When a student blows the whistle [on himself]: A personal experience essay on 'delayed' integrity in a classroom setting. *Journal of Management Inquiry*, 13, 291–306.

Wright, T. A. (2005). The role of "happiness" in organizational research: Past, present and future directions. In: P. L. Perrewé & D. C. Ganster (eds.), *Research in Occupational Stress and Well Being* (Vol. 4). Amsterdam, NL: Elsevier, 221–264.

Wright, T. A. (2011). Character assessment is business ethics education. In: D. G. Fisher & D. L. Swanson (eds.), *Toward Assessing Business Ethics Education.* Charlotte, NC: Information Age Publishing, 361–380.

Wright, T. A. (2014a). When character and entrepreneurship meet: A view from the world of sport. *Journal of Business and Management*, 20, 5–23.

Wright, T. A. (2014b). Putting your best 'face' forward: The role of emotion-based well-being in organizational behavior. *Journal of Organizational Behavior*, 35, 1153–1168.

Wright, T. A. (2015). Distinguished scholar invited essay: Reflections on the role of character in business education and student leadership development. *Journal of Leadership & Organizational Studies*, 22, 253–264.

Wright, T. A., & Bonett, D. G. (1992). The effect of turnover on work satisfaction and mental health: Support for a situational perspective. *Journal of Organizational Behavior*, 13, 603–615.

Wright, T. A., & Bonett, D. G. (2007). Job satisfaction and psychological well-being as non-additive predictors of workplace turnover. *Journal of Management*, 33, 141–160.

Wright, T. A., & Cropanzano, R. (1998). Emotional exhaustion as a predictor of job performance and turnover. *Journal of Applied Psychology*, 83, 486–493.

Wright, T. A., & Cropanzano, R. (2000). Psychological well-being and job satisfaction as predictors of job performance. *Journal Occupational Health Psychology*, 5, 84–94.

Wright, T. A., & Cropanzano, R. (2007). The happy/productive worker thesis revisited. In: J. Martocchio (ed.), *Research in Personnel and Human Resource Management* (Vol. 26). Amsterdam: Elsevier Ltd, 269–313.

Wright, T. A., & Doherty, E. M. (1998). Organizational behavior 'rediscovers' the role of emotional well-being. *Journal of Organizational Behavior*, 19, 481–485.

Wright, T. A., & Goodstein, J. (2007). Character is not "dead" in management research: A review of individual character and organizational-level virtue. *Journal of Management*, 33, 928–958.

Wright, T. A., & Hobfoll, S. E. (2004). Commitment, psychological well-being and job performance: An examination of conservation of resources (COR) theory and job burnout. *Journal of Business and Management*, 9, 389–406.

Wright, T. A., & Huang, C.-C. (2008). Character is organizational research: Past directions and future prospects. *Journal of Organizational Behavior*, 29, 981–987.

Wright, T. A., & Huang, C.-C. (2012). The many benefits of employee well-being in organizational research. *Journal of Organizational Behavior*, 33, 1188–1192.

Wright, T. A., & Lauer, T. (2013). What is character and why it really does matter. *Organizational Dynamics*, 42, 25–34.

Wright, T. A., & Lauer, T. (2014). Character and well-being. In: C. L. Cooper & P. Y. Chen (eds.), *Wellbeing: A Complete Reference Guide* (Vol. 111). Oxford, UK: Wiley-Blackwell, 159–174.

Wright, T. A., & Quick, J. C. (2011a). The role of character in ethical leadership research. *The Leadership Quarterly*, 22, 975–978.

Wright, T. A., & Quick, J. C. (2011b). *A Review of Individual Character and Organizational-Level Virtue, Scale Development and Preliminary Results: Technical Report.* Contract No. W911SD-09-P-0581, 28 Mar-2011, USACA, United States Military Academy. West Point, NY 10996–1514.

Wright, T. A., Quick, J. C., Hannah, S. T., & Hargrove, M. B. (2017). Best practice recommendations for scale construction in organizational research: The development and validation of the character strength inventory (CSI). *Journal of Organizational Behavior,* In press.

Wright, T. A., & Staw, B. M. (1999). Affect and favorable work outcomes: Two longitudinal tests of the happy-productive worker thesis. *Journal of Organizational Behavior,* 20, 1–23.

Wright, T. A., & Sweeney, D. A. (2016). The call for an increased role of replication, extension and mixed methods study designs in organizational research. *Journal of Organizational Behavior,* 37, 480–486.

Wright, T. A., & Wefald, A. J. (2012). Leadership in an academic setting: A view from the top. *Journal of Management Inquiry,* 21, 180–186.

Wu, C. H. (2010). Meanings of music making experiences among second-generation Chinese-American string students. *Dissertation Abstracts International Section A: Humanistic and Social Sciences,* 71(6-A).

Yeh, H. C., Lorenz, F. O., Wickrama, K. A. S., Conger, R. D., & Elder, G. H. (2006). Relationships among sexual satisfaction, marital quality, and marital instability at midlife. *Journal of Family Psychology,* 20, 339–343.

8

Work characteristics, work-specific wellbeing, and employee sleep

Christopher J. Budnick and Larissa K. Barber

Introduction

During a typical day, the majority of employed people's time is spent on two activities: work and sleep. For example, working Americans ages 25–54 spend 37% (8.9 hours) of their day on work-related activities and about 32% of their time sleeping (7.7 hours; "Charts from the American Time Use Survey," 2015). Although exact work and sleep hours vary, other countries (i.e., France, Germany, Japan, Britain, and Turkey) observe similar trends ("A day in the life," 2011). Consequently, work and sleep have significant implications for wellbeing among the working population.

In this chapter, we discuss the interplay between work, sleep, and wellbeing. First, we discuss key indicators of wellbeing in the work context. Wellbeing is defined in many ways; thus, we specify the wellbeing outcomes under investigation in this review. Then, we present a guiding model of the links between work, sleep, and wellbeing for our review. Next, we discuss directions for future research based on critical gaps in the literature. We close with practical implications for employees, organizations, and interventions.

Wellbeing in the work context

The concept and measurement of wellbeing is diverse, but can be divided into context-free and context-specific wellbeing (Warr, 1994). Context-free or general wellbeing typically is parsed into subjective and psychological wellbeing (Keyes, Shmotkin, & Ryff, 2002; Ryan & Deci, 2001). The former refers to *hedonic* wellbeing, which encompasses happiness. The latter represents *eudemonic* wellbeing and emphasizes human potential and growth. Although the study of context-free wellbeing has provided insights about the antecedents and consequences of individual wellbeing, we focus on individual wellbeing specifically within the work context for this chapter (i.e., work-specific wellbeing; Warr, 1994).

The work context can contribute and detract from employee wellbeing during both work and nonwork hours through a variety of relationships. Expanding on earlier conceptualizations, Warr (1994) discusses four key dimensions of work-specific wellbeing: pleasure-displeasure, enthusiasm-depression, anxiety-comfort, and fatigue-vigor. Supporting this model, research has identified four common outcomes that are acceptable indicators of wellbeing in the work context (Rothmann, 2008). The first is *job satisfaction* (pleasure-displeasure), which describes one's level of contentment and positive feelings toward the job (Judge & Kammeyer-Mueller, 2012). *Work burnout* (fatigue-vigor) is comprised of feelings related to low energy/exhaustion, loss of motivation, and feelings of ineffectiveness towards one's work (Schaufeli, Leiter, & Maslach, 2009). *Work engagement* (enthusiasm-depression) is characterized by high energy, dedication, and absorption in one's work (Bakker, Schaufeli, Leiter, & Taris, 2008). Lastly, *occupational stress* (anxiety-comfort) refers to the experience of high negative arousal and tension combined with low pleasure when facing work demands (Rothmann, 2008). People with high work-specific wellbeing are those who report more job satisfaction and work engagement, as well as less burnout and occupational stress (Rothmann, 2008). We use this model of work-specific wellbeing to focus on key work-related wellbeing outcomes in our literature review.

The intersection of work, sleep, and wellbeing

Sleep competes with work and nonwork activities (i.e., time with family and personal leisure) because individuals have a finite amount of time to allocate toward daily activities (Barnes, Wagner, & Ghumman, 2012). Thus, increases in work time – in addition to nonwork obligations – often contribute to employees sleeping fewer than the six to nine hours required for optimal daily functioning (Ferrara & De Gennaro, 2001; Luckhaupt, Tak, & Calvert, 2010). Sleep is critical for repairing and replenishing vital physiological systems (Banks & Dinges, 2007); therefore, employee sleep issues can also affect employees' work-specific wellbeing and organizational effectiveness (Barnes, 2012; Barnes, Jiang, & Lepak, 2016). These findings underscore the important intersection between work, sleep, and wellbeing.

Figure 8.1 shows our guiding framework for organizing this chapter, based on the Job-Demands Resources (JD-R) model (Bakker & Demerouti, 2007). The JD-R model incorporates various theoretical perspectives to explain how work demands and resources affect employee wellbeing through *health impairment* (i.e., burnout and occupational stress) and *motivational* (i.e., job satisfaction and work engagement) processes. Sleep's role in this model is behavioral – it is neither a demand nor a resource. In occupational stress theories, sleep behaviors (i.e., quality and quantity) represent strategies for recovery in both the health impairment and motivational process (Barber, 2014). That is, sleep is a way to replenish physiological and psychological functioning (Barber, Munz, Bagsby, & Powell, 2010; Barber & Munz, 2011). Sleep is a critical process in the daily recovery from work demands that can affect individuals' psychological states before returning to work the next day (Demerouti, Bakker, Geurts, & Taris, 2009).

Given that the relationships between job demands, resources, and wellbeing are confirmed empirically (Nixon, Mazzola, Bauer, Krueger, & Spector, 2011; Robbins, Ford, & Tetrick, 2012), we focus on sleep-related links only in our model in Figure 8.1. First, we discuss whether work demands and resources influence employee sleep (Link 1). We then examine whether employee sleep issues influence subsequent work demands and resources (Link 2). We also discuss whether employees' work-specific wellbeing influences their sleep, because work demands and resources affect wellbeing (Link 3). We close by examining whether employee sleep issues influence employees' work-specific wellbeing (Link 4).

Most research examining the relationships among job demands, resources, sleep, and wellbeing have been collected only at one point in time (cross-sectional). Such research designs make teasing apart causal ordering assertions from theoretical models difficult. This chapter focuses on empirical designs that provide stronger evidence of causality by examining how changes in one variable may precede changes in another. We focus on three commonly studied causal models:

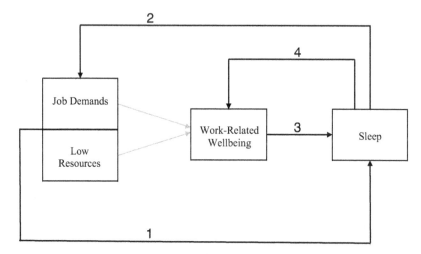

Figure 8.1 Guiding framework: links in black are discussed throughout the chapter; links in gray are already well represented in the literature, and therefore, are not discussed in-depth

the normal causal model, the reverse causal model, and the reciprocal causal model. The *normal causal model* holds that job demands and resources influence sleep (Link 1) and that work-related wellbeing influences sleep (Link 3). The *reverse causal model* holds that sleep affects job demands and resources (Link 2) and wellbeing (Link 4). The *reciprocal model* represents both of the previous pathways. In the following sections, we discuss research informing each model based on experimental, quasi-experimental, and longitudinal designs.

Link 1: Job characteristics (demands/resources) and sleep

Although the JD-R model assumes that different jobs and job roles will present unique stressors, it postulates two general categories that encapsulate all job-related characteristics regardless of a job position's uniqueness: job demands and job resources. In this section, we discuss each of these characteristics, as well as empirical research supporting links between demand/resource characteristics and sleep.

Job demands

Job demands are the "physical, psychological, social, or organizational aspects of the job that require sustained physical and/or psychological (cognitive and emotional) effort or skills and are therefore associated with certain physiological and/or psychological costs" (Bakker & Demerouti, 2007, p. 312). Time pressure, work overload, physically demanding environments, and emotional labor are each examples of job demands. Although not inherently negative, job demands become stressors when employees cannot adequately recover from the effort required to respond to those demands. Consequently, increased job demands predict more employee exhaustion and sickness absences (Bakker, Demerouti, & Schaufeli, 2003; Bakker, Demerouti, & Verbeke, 2004), which suggests that job demands might inhibit employees' ability to recover adequately. Of particular interest to this review is whether job demands inhibit recovery by reducing employee sleep quality and/or quantity. In fact, job demands are reported to increase the odds of suffering disturbed sleep (Åkerstedt et al., 2002). For example, Swedish office workers experienced decreased sleep quality during a high workload week compared to a low workload week (Dahlgren, Kecklund, & Åkerstedt, 2005).

High workloads are not the only job demands that influence employee sleep, and various job demands may influence employee sleep differently. For example, research using objective measurement (i.e., actigraphy) found that employees exhibited greater sleep disturbances following increased social stressors at work, even after accounting for time pressure (a job demand; Pereira & Elfering, 2014). Other research has explored whether occupational stress results in sleep issues across one year for employees without preexisting sleep issues (Linton, 2004). At the one-year follow-up, psychosocial stress at work more than doubled the odds of a new sleep problem. Taken together, these findings support the causal model link of work characteristics (i.e., job demands) predicting employees' subsequent sleep episodes.

Job resources

Job resources are the physical, psychological, social, or organizational aspects instrumental for achieving work-related goals because they stimulate personal growth or development (Bakker & Demerouti, 2007). Adequate compensation, job security, social support, and autonomy are examples of job resources. In the JD-R model, the Conservation of Resources (COR) perspective is used to explain why resources are linked to work engagement outcomes through the motivational process. COR argues that the "acquisition and facilitation of resources" is a central human motivation; people are driven to gain and protect resources while also deterring loss (Hobfoll, 2002, p. 312). Research demonstrates that employees' resources predict their work engagement (Schaufeli & Bakker, 2004). More resources tend to facilitate favorable outcomes for employees in high-stress contexts, result in more active goal-directed behaviors, and lead to better psychological outcomes (Hobfoll, 2002).

Given resources' inherent value, any threat to those resources should be experienced as stressful and could potentially disrupt subsequent sleep episodes. For example, when two hospitals decided to incorporate mandatory pay decreases, researchers used a quasi-experimental longitudinal design to capture changes in nonclinical insomnia. Supervisors at one hospital received interactional justice training. Overall, insomnia significantly increased for all nurses experiencing pay reductions, but for nurses with supervisors trained in interactional justice, that insomnia was significantly lower immediately following training and after six months (Greenberg, 2006). Using supervisory roles to provide social resources (interpersonal and informational justice) reduced the negative impact of pay reductions (resource loss) on nurses' sleep. However, nurses who lacked those social resources exhibited sleep problems to a greater degree. Other longitudinal work reports that low organizational justice levels predict self-reported health, which sleep partially explains (Elovainio, Kivimäki, Vahtera, Keltikangas-Järvinen, & Virtanen, 2003). In other words, organizational justice levels predicted employee sleep, which in part explained the influence of organizational justice on self-reported health two years later. Resources could also offset the negative effect of job demands on sleep to some degree. As discussed next, the JD-R model recognizes that job demands and resources interact to influence important outcomes.

Job demands-resources interaction

Whereas job demands can negatively influence employees through the health impairment process, job resources might buffer against those negative effects through motivational avenues. For example, although high levels of work overload, emotional demands, physical demands, and work-life balance disruptions typically result in higher burnout levels (i.e., health impairment), those factors did not affect burnout levels for employees who possessed a high-quality relationship with their supervisor or high levels of autonomy, feedback, or social support (i.e., motivational processes; Bakker, Demerouti, & Euwema, 2005). Although that study leaves unclear the exact psychological processes underlying the interaction between each unique job demand and resource, job demands and resources did generally interact to affect employees' health and behavior in the workplace (see also Xanthopoulou, Bakker, Demerouti, & Schaufeli, 2007a; Xanthopoulou et al., 2007b). Job demands can impair employees' health, and job resources protect employees' health by buffering that relationship to some extent.

Job demands also disrupt employee sleep, and it is likely not surprising that job resources can protect employee sleep by weakening the job demands to sleep relationship. Increased job demands coupled with decreased job resources resulted in more sleep issues in one study (Greubel & Kecklund, 2011), suggesting that increasing job resources could reduce sleep issues resulting from job demands. Consistent with that assertion, employees have reduced odds of disturbed sleep when social support (Åkerstedt et al., 2002) and job autonomy (Knudsen, Ducharme, & Roman, 2007) levels are high. In fact, cumulative exposure to low job demands and high perceived control (i.e., resource) levels facilitate the highest sleep quality (de Lange et al., 2009). Moreover, employees in roles with simultaneously high demands and low resources (control) exhibited significantly lower sleep quality relative to employees in roles with low demands and high control across one year. When employees moved from less stressful (i.e., low demands, high resources) into more stressful positions (i.e., high demands, low resources), sleep complaints significantly increased. Yet sleep quality did not meaningfully improve when moving from a more stressful into a less stressful position (de Lange et al., 2009).

Consistent with the JD-R model, high levels of job demands (e.g., work overload, role conflict) without the necessary resources (e.g., social support, autonomy) can result in sleep issues. Alternatively, low job demands (e.g., challenging but not overwhelming workload, role clarity) with adequate or excess resources (e.g., social support, autonomy) facilitate improved sleep. Thus improving employee sleep might involve reducing both job demands (e.g., distributing large workloads across a team) and increasing job resources (e.g., encouraging a supportive versus competitive environment). Focusing on building resources to manage demands might improve employee sleep and facilitate next-day performance, especially because resources may be particularly beneficial when job demands are low.

Link 2: Feedback loop of sleep to job demands and resources

Even though the job demand and resource interaction seems to influence employee sleep directly, employee sleep might also influence how workers perceive their subsequent job demands and resources. Less research has focused on a feedback loop wherein sleep can alter job demands and resources (i.e., the reverse causal model). However, two mechanisms could explain how sleep influences work characteristics: First, poor sleep may change tangible levels of job demands or resources at work. Without effective recovery from sleep, employees may struggle to manage new job demands because of decreased self-regulatory ability (Barnes, 2012; Wagner, Barnes, Lim, & Ferris, 2012). In turn, this behavioral ineffectiveness can lead to an increasing cycle of more work and less energy to catch up. Second, poor sleep may not change work characteristics themselves, but key appraisals of work characteristics. According to the transactional model of stress (Lazarus & Folkman, 1984), employees differ on whether they find job demands threatening (as opposed to challenging; primary appraisal) and whether they believe they have adequate resources for managing a particular job demand (secondary appraisal). Sleep may change these appraisals by increasing interpretations of threat in the work environment (Barber & Budnick, 2015) or leaving employees feeling they are less able to manage demands effectively. For example, employees who experience sleep issues interpret incoming information more negatively on the following workday due to a poor mood (Scott & Judge, 2006; Sonnentag, Binnewies, & Mojza, 2008). Additionally, people who are sleepy tend to have more negative ratings of unfair work environments (Barber & Budnick, 2015).

Sleep and changes in job demands and resources

One longitudinal study exploring the job demands, resources (i.e., job control), and sleep relationships sampled Dutch employees across three years (de Lange et al., 2009). After one year, increased job demands significantly predicted reduced sleep quality and higher fatigue. Similarly, job control (a resource) predicted sleep quality one year later. As job control increased, sleep complaints and fatigue decreased. Even though those authors concluded that the normal causal model best explained their observations, their results also suggested the presence of a reciprocal relationship. However, any reversed or reciprocal causal effects were likely limited by the long lag between data collection waves (i.e., three years). Given less time between data collections, the reverse or reciprocal models might have explained the data better than the normal causal model.

Other researchers have also reported evidence for the normal causal model over the reciprocal model. For example, a two-wave longitudinal study of the influence of job demands (e.g., working fast, working intensively, too much effort, conflicting demands) and job resources (e.g., social support, decision authority) on sleep behaviors (e.g., sleep disturbances, awakening problems) among Swedish employees indicated that job demands led to more sleep disturbances, although the observed relationship was weak (Hanson et al., 2011). The reverse sleep-to–job demands relationship was not observed, which is consistent with other longitudinal research (Pereira & Elfering, 2014). However, there was a reciprocal relationship between job resources (i.e., decision authority) and awakening problems. Employees with greater decision authority (i.e., autonomy) reported fewer subsequent awakening problems, and employees who had fewer problems awakening reported higher subsequent decision authority. Similarly, decreased social support predicted more awakening problems two years later and more awakening problems predicted reports of lower social support two years later (Hanson et al., 2011).

Although job demands increase presleep arousal that disrupts sleep (Morin, Rodrigue, & Ivers, 2003), job resources seem to both influence and be influenced by employee sleep. For example, medical residents' sleep loss heightened negative emotions and fatigue after stressful daytime events, and reduced positive emotion following positive events (Zohar, Tzischinsky, Epstein, & Lavie, 2005). Due to increased negative affect poor sleeping employees might interpret those job demands as particularly stressful. Relative to good sleepers, poor sleepers tend to experience an equivalent frequency of minor daily hassles but report those hassles as more stressful (Morin et al., 2003). Sleepy employees might perceive themselves as possessing fewer resources to meet demands, which leave sleepy employees overaroused and unable to fall asleep during nonwork hours.

Together, these results suggest that there are an insufficient number of high-quality empirical studies from which to firmly conclude how job demands, resources, and employee sleep causally associate (Van Laethem, Beckers, Kompier, Dijksterhuis, & Geurts, 2013). This is because disentangling the causal relationships between work, recovery, and sickness absences is a focal research challenge (de Lange et al., 2009). We suggest that researchers examine the causal relationships between work characteristics, work-specific wellbeing, and employee health maintenance, including both recovery (e.g., sleep) and preventative behaviors (e.g., regular physicals).

Link 3: Work-specific wellbeing and sleep

Job satisfaction as a predictor of sleep

An employee's job satisfaction can be considered an evaluative state that reflects contentment with and positive feelings about her or his job (Judge & Kammeyer-Mueller, 2012). Evidence bearing on job satisfaction's direct link to sleep episodes has yet to emerge. As discussed subsequently, the limited evidence available examines the reverse causal path that sleep directly affects job satisfaction, but job satisfaction does not influence sleep. However, extant evidence suggests that this would be a profitable avenue to pursue, considering that job satisfaction meaningfully varies both between and within individuals (Judge & Kammeyer-Mueller, 2012; Scott & Judge, 2006). Although many factors could account for that variability, Affective Events Theory proposes that emotional reactions to environmental events might determine or alter work attitudes, such as job satisfaction (Weiss & Cropanzano, 1996). Employees who have positive experiences in the work environment might report higher job satisfaction, judge their own performance as stronger, and/or generalize those positive feelings to others in the work environment (Fisher, 2002). The same processes might apply to employees experiencing negative work environment events. They might experience less satisfaction, judge their performance as poorer, and/or generalize those negative feelings to others in the environment. Moreover, those negative feelings might increase physiological (e.g., increased heart rate) or psychological (e.g., cognitive perseveration) activation to disrupt subsequent sleep. Future sleep research examining job satisfaction will help broaden our understanding of whether wellbeing influences employee sleep.

Occupational stress as a predictor of sleep

Similar to job satisfaction, the occupational stress and employee sleep relationship has not received much research attention. Research tends to focus more on the occurrence of stressors themselves (i.e., job demands) rather than perceptions of anxiety and tension arising from job demands (i.e., occupational strains/stress). In addition, many measures used to assess occupational stress are fairly nonspecific regarding the source of strain. For example, studies may measure anxiety and tension or health complaints and link them to workplace stressors, but those reported strains could also originate from other life events. There is also reason to believe that reports of occupational stress may better predict sleep issues than reports of stressor events themselves. Consistent with Effort Recovery Theory (Meijman & Mulder, 1998) and Allostatic Load Theory (McEwen, 2006), occupational stress likely increases both physiological (e.g., increased heart rate) and psychological (e.g., rumination) activation, which interferes with relaxation that is necessary for restful sleep (Åkerstedt, 2006; Åkerstedt, Nilsson, & Kecklund, 2009). For example, physiological and psychological arousal states have linked anxiety and tension experienced throughout the day to sleep disturbances (Åkerstedt, Kecklund, & Axelsson, 2007; Sadeh, Keinan, & Daon, 2004; Wuyts et al., 2012). However, considerably more research is needed that specifically examines reports of tension/anxiety due to occupational sources in relation to sleep.

Burnout as a predictor of sleep

Employees under sustained and prolonged occupational stress can develop burnout, another marker of work-specific wellbeing (Rothmann, 2008). Burnout is an extreme and persistent state of reduced work-specific wellbeing because it is an enduring response to a chronically stressful emotional and interpersonal work environment (Maslach, Schaufeli, & Leiter, 2001). Employees suffering burnout experience increased exhaustion and cynicism coupled with decreased self-efficacy (Maslach et al., 2001). Employees experiencing burnout are more frequently absent, have greater intentions to quit, and a higher probability of actual resignation. When performing on the job, employees suffering from burnout are less productive and effective (Maslach et al., 2001). In tandem with burnout, sleep issues also can reduce employee productivity and effectiveness directly (Belenky et al., 2003; Van Dongen, Rogers, & Dinges, 2003).

If burnout fosters sleep issues, then any negative consequences are likely additively compounded; indeed, research demonstrates that burnout and sleep issues are related (de Beer, Pienaar, & Rothmann, 2014; Ekstedt et al., 2006; Grossi, Perski, Evengård, Blomkvist, & Orth-Gomér, 2003). For example, de Beer et al. (2014) found that white-collar financial workers residing in Africa who experienced the most burnout also reported the most sleep difficulties. Employees suffering burnout also have reported increased subjective state sleepiness during the daytime, and tend to exhibit more arousals and greater sleep fragmentation while asleep (Ekstedt et al., 2006). The existing research indicates that burnout disrupts sleep.

Work engagement as a predictor of sleep

Work engagement refers to a "positive, fulfilling, work-related state of mind that is characterized by vigor, dedication, and absorption" (Schaufeli & Bakker, 2004, p. 295). Research suggests that job resources positively relate to work engagement, whereas job demands and engagement exhibited variable relationships depending on whether demands were classified as hindrances or challenges (Crawford, LePine, & Rich, 2010). Specifically, hindrances (e.g., organizational politics, lack of job security, role ambiguity) tend to be associated with less engagement while challenges (e.g., workload, time pressure, responsibility) are associated with more engagement. In other work, recovery from demands also plays a role in work engagement. Morning recovery predicts work engagement on the same day; in turn daily work engagement predicts postwork recovery (Sonnentag, Mojza, Demerouti, & Bakker, 2012).

Morning recovery levels likely are influenced by employee sleep (Demerouti et al., 2009). Employees with poorer sleep should feel less recovered at the start of the next workday, which could reduce work engagement that day. On days when employees experience less morning recovery, they might enter the workday with fewer personal resources (e.g., cognitive energy) resulting in lower work engagement. Theory suggests that recovery and work engagement may also reciprocally relate. As an employee's morning recovery improves, that employee should experience greater work engagement that restricts decreases in his or her recovery levels at the end of the day (Sonnentag et al., 2012). Ending the workday with higher recovery levels might help employees recover further that evening as they might have sufficient personal resources to counteract any work-to-home spillover. However, most empirical work – even using longitudinal methods, such as daily diaries – does not use analyses exploring lagged effects to test the directionality of relationships.

Link 4: Feedback loop of sleep to work-related wellbeing

Sleep as a predictor of job satisfaction

Although limited, research on sleep's ability to predict job satisfaction is emerging. For example, a three-week experience-sampling study found that nonclinical insomnia and job satisfaction were negatively associated within individuals (Scott & Judge, 2006). Whether an employee experiences more or less satisfaction appears to depend on how well she or he slept. Recently, two studies (one using experience-sampling methodology) found that sleep predicts organizational citizenship behaviors, with job satisfaction partially accounting for that relationship (Barnes, Jiang, & Lepak, 2013). Thus it appears that poor sleep decreases job satisfaction, which influences subsequent behaviors directed at organizations and their representatives. One caveat is that neither of those studies provided clear evidence concerning causality based on their cross-sectional analysis strategy. Combined with the lack of research examining job satisfaction's ability to predict sleep, future research should consider the temporal separation of all focal study variables and how they mutually influence each other.

Sleep as a predictor of occupational stress

Not only might poor wellbeing (i.e., occupational stress, burnout) cause sleep issues, but sleep issues might reduce work-specific wellbeing (i.e., increase occupational stress, burnout) by facilitating threat appraisals and/or inhibiting resource availability appraisals. For example, a two-wave longitudinal study of Dutch employees tested the normal, reverse, and reciprocal causal models on occupational stress (i.e., wellbeing) and sleep quality with the addition of perseverative cognition as the mediating mechanism (Van Laethem et al., 2015). Interestingly, the initial results did not support the normal causal model. The relationship between occupational stress at the first measurement and sleep quality at the second was not statistically significant. The reverse causal path was supported. Poor sleep quality was associated with increased occupational stress one year later. Yet after including perseverative cognition as the mediating mechanism, evidence for reciprocal relationships between occupational stress and sleep quality emerged (Van Laethem et al., 2015). Occupational stress predicted perseverative cognitions, and perseverative cognitions predicted subsequent sleep quality. Similarly, sleep quality predicted occupational stress, which predicted perseverative cognitions, resulting in a reciprocal cycle. Employees experiencing increased job demands seemed to ruminate on that stress, which disrupted that night's sleep. The day following insufficient sleep, an employee might perform poorly at work, resulting in increased workload and stress, which might be appraised as especially stressful (Morin et al., 2003). Therefore, employees experiencing sleep issues might appraise the environment and incoming information negatively due to poor sleep (Van Laethem et al., 2015), experience those stressors as particularly intense (Morin et al., 2003), and be less able to self-regulate or reframe those appraisals (Barnes, 2012).

Sleep as a predictor of burnout

As burnout results from chronic occupational stress, sleep issues also might contribute to burnout through stressor appraisals. During a two-year prospective study, employees indicating insufficient sleep (less than six hours) had greater odds of developing burnout (Söderström Jeding, Ekstedt, & Perski, 2012). Similarly, Taiwanese nurses sleeping fewer than six hours per working day had significantly higher odds of developing personal, client-related, and work-related burnout. In fact, work by Chin and colleagues observed a positive association between insufficient sleep and client-related burnout (Chin, Guo, Hung, Yang, & Shiao, 2015), suggesting that burnout might be particularly likely for service providers who sleep poorly.

Whereas sleep difficulties might arise from burnout, impaired sleep might result in burnout, or they could mutually influence each other (de Beer et al., 2014). Over time, employees experiencing chronic burnout and chronic sleep difficulties might develop insomnia. Some research reports that burnout (i.e., reduced work-related wellbeing) is positively associated with insomnia (Armon, Shirom, Shapira, & Melamed, 2008); consequently, sleep problems slow burnout recovery (Sonnenschein, Sorbi, van Doornen, Schaufeli, & Maas, 2007), leading to the suggestion that burnout and sleep difficulties might intensify each other (Armon, 2009). Therefore, impaired sleep might be both an antecedent and a consequence of burnout, as the reciprocal causal model suggests (de Beer et al., 2014).

Sleep as a predictor of work engagement

Although strong empirical designs conducive to causal interpretations have yet to emerge concerning the direct link of work engagement to employee sleep, emerging work suggests a direct causal link whereby employee and supervisor sleep influences employees' next-day work engagement. Correlational research with daily diary data provides initial evidence consistent with this assertion by reporting a moderate relationship between sleep disturbances and work engagement (Hallberg & Schaufeli, 2006), although a theoretical rationale for that relationship is not proposed. Later research adopted a self-regulatory framework as a theoretical mechanism explaining the relationship between employee sleep and work engagement. Individuals who exhibited poor sleep hygiene tended to report lower self-regulatory capacity, experience more subjective job-related strain, and report lower work engagement relative to individuals with better sleep hygiene. The negative sleep and work engagement relationship was attributed to individuals' perception that they had few resources to expend on adaptive self-regulation (Barber, Grawitch, & Munz, 2013). Supervisor sleep also seems important to employee work engagement. One study found that supervisor sleep quality predicted daily abusive supervision behaviors, and a reduction in self-regulatory capacity due to sleep loss accounted for that relationship. That research also observed indirect relationships from supervisor sleep quality to employee unit work engagement through daily leader self-regulatory capacity and daily abusive supervision behaviors (Barnes, Lucianetti, Bhave, & Christian, 2015). Although much work remains, these initial studies provide some empirical support suggesting a direct link between sleep (both employee and supervisor) and employees' next-day work engagement.

Future research directions

Sleep has recently emerged as an important organizational research factor. Although early research focused on sleep's influence on task completion, research is now investigating how employee sleep issues affect the organizational environment and the employee. A noteworthy strength of the research to date is its global comprehensiveness. Researchers across cultures and nations are examining the influence of sleep on the workplace and finding consistent results. The global importance of sleep on multinational organizational structures and their employees is likely to increase in the near future, given the ongoing globalization of the economic marketplace. However, sleep's recent addition to the complex of workplace influences leaves much work remaining to adequately understand sleep's influence on employees and organizations. In the next sections, we discuss some of the many avenues through which future research could yield useful information.

Stronger research designs

The majority of research examining work characteristics, sleep, and wellbeing relationships is correlational, as is expected when a research stream initially emerges. However, the body of correlational evidence has accumulated to a point where it is time to move beyond simple associations to identify the directionality of relationships, which will require the use of stronger research designs (i.e., experimental, quasi-experimental, and longitudinal). Although some researchers have used stronger designs, the available research remains sparse and equivocal concerning the causal relationships among work characteristics, sleep, and employee wellbeing. Some researchers concluded that the normal causal model best explained the relationship between job demands and employee sleep, but reverse and reciprocal causal models also adequately explained those observations (de Lange et al., 2009; Hanson et al., 2011). In other research, job resources did not appear to directly influence employee sleep (the normal causal model); rather, sleep influenced job resources directly, and after accounting for cognitive perseveration, reciprocally (Van Laethem et al., 2015).

The longitudinal studies published to date have incorporated relatively long measurement gaps over many months or even years. Researchers undertaking longitudinal research should consider the appropriate period in which to capture the expected effects. Research might observe the strongest reverse causal relationships during shorter time frames. Sleep is bound to the circadian cycle of approximately 24 hours (Carlson, 2012). Any detrimental effects of poor sleep are mostly eliminated following sufficient rest (Sallinen et al., 2008). Therefore, the influences of sleep on job demands/resources or wellbeing may be best explored through daily diary studies.

Diary studies have participants report on the focal variables at least once a day for multiple consecutive days. For example, Nägel and Sonnentag (2013) used a diary study to examine daily changes in exercise, sleep duration, personal resources, and emotional exhaustion. Participants in that research completed surveys each day assessing those factors, which allowed a within-person examination of their influences. Using that approach they showed that exercise following work was positively associated with personal resources on the next day, but only when sleep duration was longer than an individual's average sleep duration. Those increased personal resources then predicted less emotional exhaustion after the following workday (Nägel & Sonnentag, 2013). Thus, this diary study demonstrated a daily interaction between sleep and exercise to predict resources and exhaustion the following day, which a longer measurement gap likely would have missed. Although work using daily diary research is growing (Fisher & To, 2012), most research examining work, sleep, and wellbeing relationships tends to use analytical methods that do not disentangle directionality of relationships. To draw stronger conclusions regarding causality, we encourage researchers to use analytical strategies that explicitly test lagged relationships in longitudinal designs, such as growth curve analyses (Duckworth, Tsukayama, & May, 2010).

Ecological momentary assessment (EMA) is another method that captures momentary behaviors, psychological states, self-reported symptoms, or physiological states during normal daily functioning (Beal & Weiss, 2003; Ebner-Priemer & Trull, 2009). Individuals report their current affect, behavior, thoughts, or other factors of interest multiple times daily for at least one week (Fisher & To, 2012). EMA designs have several strengths: They provide real-time reports that might reduce recall biases to improve reporting accuracy. In addition, EMA captures important states or behaviors that vary over time, and EMA's repeated measurements can uncover dynamically occurring processes and context-specific relationships. However, EMA designs also present some difficulties. For example, EMA designs also require more effort from participants, which can contribute to increased attrition and/or smaller sample sizes. Similar to recommendations for daily diary methods, we encourage researchers to adopt analytical strategies that capitalize on testing relationship directionality to help further theoretical models.

Measurement techniques

Self-report methodologies dominate the literature concerning work characteristics, work-specific wellbeing, and employee sleep. Corroborating those self-reports with objective measurements is important work for future research. Actigraphs – small devices worn on the wrist that measure movement and light exposure – are quickly becoming the "gold standard" of objective measurement for organizational sleep research conducted outside of the laboratory. Software provided with actigraphs uses algorithms to provide estimates of daily activity and sleep periods. In field research or naturalistic settings, actigraphy is considered both a useful and valid method of objectively assessing sleep-wake cycles as compared to self-reports (Sadeh, 2011); therefore, actigraphy is a commonly employed measurement technique amongst organizational researchers interested in sleep's influence on various outcomes (Barber & Budnick, 2015; Barnes, Schaubroeck, Huth, & Ghumman, 2011; Wagner et al., 2012).

Alternatively, consumer-marketed activity trackers (e.g., Fitbit, Jawbone UP) might provide another rich data source. Many consumer-marketed activity trackers purport to assess sleep length and efficiency, with some even advertising the ability to identify light versus deep sleep cycles (e.g., the Jawbone UP), in addition to tracking activity levels. Recent releases also offer optical heart rate sensors that provide heart rate measurements averaged over five-minute intervals. As these devices are designed for continuous wear, they may provide a large amount of objective data at the daily and even hourly level. However, these devices are now only beginning to emerge in the marketplace, and both their reliability and validity remain questionable. Prior to use in future research, preliminary testing should confirm consumer-marketed activity trackers' reliability and validity.

Moderators and mediators

Occupational stress fosters rumination that decreases employee sleep quality, and rumination is a strong statistical predictor of sleep complaints (Kompier, Taris, & van Veldhoven, 2012). Other research reports similar findings (Van Laethem et al., 2015). Individuals with a proclivity toward rumination should exhibit a stronger relationship between job demands, resources, work-specific wellbeing, and sleep. Therefore, individual differences could moderate and mediate the causal relationship between work characteristics, sleep, and employees' wellbeing. Additionally, understanding how causal relationships differ depending on third factors (e.g., gender, personality) will assist future intervention development, and assist organizations with improving employee wellbeing and organizational functioning.

For example, social anxiety may be key a moderator in the work, sleep, and wellbeing link. Individuals with high levels of social anxiety tend to cognitively perseverate on social interactions more than lower-scoring individuals (Hofman, 2007). Following a stressful work event, socially anxious workers may engage in greater rumination over that event, resulting in increased psychological (e.g., rumination) and physiological (e.g., increased heartrate) activation. If that activation disrupts the subsequent sleep episode, these individuals may be more likely to interpret work experiences negatively the next day. In other words, the relationship between work characteristics and employee sleep might be explained by rumination, and that mediated relationship should be stronger for individuals with a greater proclivity toward rumination (e.g., socially anxious individuals).

Alternatively, individuals who ruminate less might be less likely to experience sleep difficulties. Exploratory research suggests that individuals scoring higher in positive affectivity and optimism tend to have better sleep quality, even when stress levels are high (Norlander, Johansson, & Bood, 2005). A beneficial direction for future research is not only to determine when negative effects result from the job demands/resources, work-specific wellbeing, and sleep relationships, but also to identify the factors that ameliorate or exacerbate those effects. Future research should consider both positive and negative traits and states, and their various combinations.

Finally, the components of work-specific wellbeing likely have differential effects on sleep or may mutually influence each other. Future research could determine which of those indicators exerts the strongest influence on sleep; alternatively, sleep may influence some wellbeing indicators more than others. Additionally, the interaction between work-specific wellbeing indicators should be explored. When work stress and burnout are at high levels, work-specific wellbeing should be lowest. High levels of job satisfaction and engagement might attenuate those effects on wellbeing. When wellbeing is low, then employee sleep might suffer. Employees suffering poor sleep might be less engaged and less satisfied at work. When sleeping poorly, employees also might experience increased stress, which could be more likely to lead to burnout. This could set up a cycle whereby job demands disrupt sleep both directly and indirectly through decreased wellbeing. In turn, sleep disruption then could increase job demands by reducing work performance through cognitive or self-regulatory deficits, which might indirectly decrease wellbeing through those job demands. Future research incorporating longitudinal designs with multiple and frequent measurement points could provide valuable information pertaining to the temporal relationships between job demands, resources, work-specific wellbeing, and employee sleep.

Practical implications

Our review of the literature addressing work characteristics, sleep, and wellbeing has a number of implications for both organizations and employees. At the organizational level, limiting work-related stress is one method of potentially facilitating employees' recovery and sleep, which represents a primary intervention strategy (Kossek, Hammer, Kelly, & Moen, 2014). Even though meta-analysis indicates that organizational interventions are rare (Richardson & Rothstein, 2008), work redesign might be one helpful method of intervening to reduce work-related stress. Organizational interventions focused on increasing employees' resources effectively reduced employees' reported stress (Richardson & Rothstein, 2008). For example, instituting flexible work schedules that allow employees to take breaks whenever they feel particularly stressed could reduce emotional reactivity following disruptive work events (Zohar et al., 2005) and maximize employees' self-control throughout the workday (Tyler & Burns, 2008).

Nevertheless, stressors cannot be completely eliminated or even predicted in all occupations (e.g., emergency response personnel; Van Laethem et al., 2015). In such cases, organizations can facilitate recovery indirectly through secondary intervention strategies. For example, providing employees with sleep hygiene training might be effective (Budnick & Barber, 2015; Van Laethem et al., 2015). Example practices include keeping a consistent sleep schedule, avoiding bright lights (especially of the blue spectrum; Chang et al., 2012), exercise, and stimulants within three hours of sleeping. Consistently getting a sufficient amount of sleep can also decrease stress in as little as one week (Barber & Munz, 2011). Individuals with better sleep hygiene practices also tend to have fewer stressor appraisals resulting in greater wellbeing (Barber, Rupprecht, & Munz, 2013). Simply knowing about effective sleep hygiene practices can also contribute to improved sleep (Brown, Buboltz, & Soper, 2006), making this a low-cost, low-effort intervention to use.

Additionally, helping individuals learn how to engage in effective recovery practices at home can help improve sleep. Recovery experiences at home include psychological detachment (not thinking about work), relaxation, mastery (feelings of increased competence), and control over leisure time. Employees who received a training program on recovery experiences reported higher sleep quality up to three weeks after the training session compared to untrained employees (Hahn, Binnewies, Sonnentag, & Mojza, 2011). Other potential stress management programs that can be used at work or at home include mindful awareness practices (e.g., mindfulness-based stress reduction and mindfulness-based cognitive therapy; Vibe et al., 2013; Siegel, 2007). Mindfulness-trained employees report lower emotional exhaustion and higher job satisfaction, both compared to a control group and compared to their pretraining exhaustion and satisfaction levels.

A subsequent experimental field study confirmed those results. Employees who self-trained in mindfulness reported significantly lower emotional exhaustion and higher job satisfaction relative to a no-training control (Hülsheger, Alberts, Feinholdt, & Lang, 2013). A variety of studies demonstrate that relaxation (e.g., meditation) training, cognitive-behavioral (e.g., cognitive reframing) training, and interventions focused on increasing employee resources each effectively reduced employee stress (Richardson & Rothstein, 2008), which may also help improve employee sleep.

Conclusion

We are only beginning to understand the interrelationships among work characteristics, work-specific wellbeing, and sleep. Although an abundance of past research shows relationships among these variables, most evidence is derived from cross-sectional designs that do not clarify the directionality of these relationships. Initial evidence from stronger designs (i.e., longitudinal, experimental, quasi-experimental) suggests that job demands detrimentally affect sleep and that job resources attenuate this relationship to some extent. However, other evidence seems to indicate the presence of reverse or reciprocal causal relationships; that is, sleep may also contribute to perceptions of demands and resources. We encourage stronger research designs in conjunction with statistical analyses focusing on lagged effects (i.e., growth curve analyzes) to help better understand relationships among work, sleep, and wellbeing.

References

A Day in the Life [WWW Document]. (2011). Available at: www.economist.com/blogs/dailychart/2011/04/time_use (accessed 22 March 2016).

Åkerstedt, T. (2006). Psychosocial stress and impaired sleep. *Scandinavian Journal of Work, Environment & Health, 32,* 493–501. doi:10.5271/sjweh.1054.

Åkerstedt, T., Kecklund, G., & Axelsson, J. (2007). Impaired sleep after bedtime stress and worries. *Biological Psychology, 76,* 170–173. doi:10.1016/j.biopsycho.2007.07.010.

Åkerstedt, T., Knutsson, A., Westerholm, P., Theorell, T., Alfredsson, L., & Kecklund, G. (2002). Sleep disturbances, work stress and work hours. *Journal of Psychosomatic Research, 53,* 741–748. doi:10.1016/S0022–3999(02)00333–1.

Åkerstedt, T., Nilsson, P. M., & Kecklund, G. (2009). Sleep and recovery. In: S. Sonnentag, P. L. Perrewe, & D. C. Gangster (eds.), *Current Perspectives on Job-Stress Recovery, Research in Occupational Stress and Well-Being.* Bingley, UK: JAI Press/Emerald Group Publishing Limited, 205–247.

Armon, G. (2009). Do burnout and insomnia predict each other's levels of change over time independently of the job demand control–support (JDC–S) model? *Stress and Health, 25,* 333–342. doi:10.1002/smi.1266.

Armon, G., Shirom, A., Shapira, I., & Melamed, S. (2008). On the nature of burnout-insomnia relationships: A prospective study of employed adults. *Journal of Psychosomatic Research, 65,* 5–12. doi:10.1016/j.jpsychores.2008.01.012.

Bakker, A. B., & Demerouti, E. (2007). The Job Demands-Resources model: State of the art. *Journal of Managerial Psychology, 22,* 309–328. doi:10.1108/02683940710733115.

Bakker, A. B., Demerouti, E., & Euwema, M. C. (2005). Job resources buffer the impact of job demands on burnout. *Journal of Occupational Health Psychology, 10,* 170–180. doi:10.1037/1076–8998.10.2.170.

Bakker, A. B., Demerouti, E., & Schaufeli, W. (2003). Dual processes at work in a call centre: An application of the job demands – Resources model. *European Journal of Work and Organizational Psychology, 12,* 393–417. doi:10.1080/13594320344000165.

Bakker, A. B., Demerouti, E., & Verbeke, W. (2004). Using the Job Demands–Resources model to predict burnout and performance. *Human Resource Management, 43,* 83–104. doi:10.1002/hrm.20004.

Bakker, A. B., Schaufeli, W. B., Leiter, M. P., & Taris, T. W. (2008). Work engagement: An emerging concept in occupational health psychology. *Work & Stress, 22,* 187–200. doi:10.1080/02678370802393649.

Banks, S., & Dinges, D. F. (2007). Behavioral and physiological consequences of sleep restriction. *Journal of Clinical Sleep Medicine, 3,* 519–528.

Barber, L. K. (2014). Conceptualizations of sleep in stress theory: Exciting new directions. *Stress Health*, 30, 431–432. doi:10.1002/smi.2598.

Barber, L. K., & Budnick, C. J. (2015). Turning molehills into mountains: Sleepiness increases workplace interpretive bias. *Journal of Organizational Behavior*, 36, 360–381. doi:10.1002/job.1992.

Barber, L., Grawitch, M. J., & Munz, D. C. (2013). Are better sleepers more engaged workers? A self-regulatory approach to sleep hygiene and work engagement. *Stress Health*, 29, 307–316. doi:10.1002/smi.2468.

Barber, L. K., & Munz, D. C. (2011). Consistent-sufficient sleep predicts improvements in self-regulatory performance and psychological strain. *Stress and Health*, 27, 314–324. doi:10.1002/smi.1364.

Barber, L. K., Munz, D. C., Bagsby, P. G., & Powell, E. D. (2010). Sleep consistency and sufficiency: Are both necessary for less psychological strain? *Stress and Health*, 26, 186–193. doi:10.1002/smi.1292.

Barber, L. K., Rupprecht, E. A., & Munz, D. C. (2013). Sleep habits may undermine well-being through the stressor appraisal process. *Journal of Happiness Studies*, 15, 285–299. doi:10.1007/s10902–013–9422–2.

Barnes, C. M. (2012). Working in our sleep: Sleep and self-regulation in organizations. *Organizational Psychology Review*, 2, 234–257. doi:10.1177/2041386612450181.

Barnes, C. M., Ghumman, S., & Scott, B. A. (2013). Sleep and organizational citizenship behavior: The mediating role of job satisfaction. *Journal of Occupational Health Psychology*, 18, 16–26. doi:10.1037/a0030349.

Barnes, C. M., Jiang, K., & Lepak, D. P. (2016). Sabotaging the benefits of our own human capital: Work unit characteristics and sleep. *Journal of Applied Psychology*, 101, 209–221. doi:10.1037/apl0000042.

Barnes, C. M., Lucianetti, L., Bhave, D. P., & Christian, M. S. (2015). "You wouldn't like me when I'm sleepy": Leaders' sleep, daily abusive supervision, and work unit engagement. *The Academy of Management Journal*, 58, 1419–1437. doi:10.5465/amj.2013.1063.

Barnes, C. M., Schaubroeck, J., Huth, M., & Ghumman, S. (2011). Lack of sleep and unethical conduct. *Organizational Behavior and Human Decision Processes*, 115, 169–180. doi:10.1016/j.obhdp.2011.01.009.

Barnes, C. M., Wagner, D. T., & Ghumman, S. (2012). Borrowing from sleep to pay work and family: Expanding time-based conflict to the broader nonwork domain. *Personnel Psychology*, 65, 789–819. doi:10.1111/peps.12002.

Beal, D. J., & Weiss, H. M. (2003). Methods of ecological momentary assessment in organizational research. *Organizational Research Methods*, 6, 440–464. doi:10.1177/1094428103257361.

Belenky, G., Wesensten, N. J., Thorne, D. R., Thomas, M. L., Sing, H. C., Redmond, D. P., . . . & Balkin, T. J. (2003). Patterns of performance degradation and restoration during sleep restriction and subsequent recovery: A sleep dose-response study. *Journal of Sleep Research*, 12, 1–12. doi:10.1046/j.1365–2869.2003.00337.x.

Brown, F. C., Buboltz, W. C., & Soper, B. (2006). Development and Evaluation of the Sleep Treatment and Education Program for Students (STEPS). *Journal of American College Health*, 54, 231–237. doi:10.3200/JACH.54.4.231–237.

Budnick, C. J., & Barber, L. K. (2015). Behind sleepy eyes: Implications of sleep loss for organizations and employees. *Translational Issues in Psychological Science*, 1, 89–96. doi:10.1037/tps0000014.

Carlson, N. R. (2012). *Physiology of Behavior* (11 ed.). Boston: Pearson.

Chang, A. M., Santhi, N., St Hilaire, M., Gronfier, C., Bradstreet, D. S., Duffy, J. F., . . . & Czeisler, C. A. (2012). Human responses to bright light of different durations. *The Journal of Physiology*, 590, 3103–3112. doi:10.1113/jphysiol.2011.226555.

Charts from the American Time Use Survey [WWW Document]. (2015). Available at: www.bls.gov/tus/charts/home.htm (accessed 22 March 2016).

Chin, W., Guo, Y. L., Hung, Y. J., Yang, C. Y., & Shiao, J. S. C. (2015). Short sleep duration is dose-dependently related to job strain and burnout in nurses: A cross sectional survey. *International Journal of Nursing Studies*, 52, 297–306. doi:10.1016/j.ijnurstu.2014.09.003.

Crawford, E. R., LePine, J. A., & Rich, B. L. (2010). Linking job demands and resources to employee engagement and burnout: A theoretical extension and meta-analytic test. *Journal of Applied Psychology*, 95, 834–848. doi:10.1037/a0019364.

Dahlgren, A., Kecklund, G., & Åkerstedt, T. (2005). Different levels of work-related stress and the effects on sleep, fatigue and cortisol. *Scandinavian Journal of Work, Environment & Health*, 31, 277–285.

de Beer, L. T., Pienaar, J., & Rothmann, S. (2014). Job burnout's relationship with sleep difficulties in the presence of control variables: A self-report study. *South African Journal of Psychology*, 44, 454–466. doi:10.1177/0081246314538249.

de Lange, A. H., Kompier, M. A. J., Taris, T. W., Geurts, S. A. E., Beckers, D. G. J., Houtman, I. L. D., & Bongers, P. M. (2009). A hard day's night: A longitudinal study on the relationships among job demands and job control, sleep quality and fatigue. *Journal of Sleep Research*, 18, 374–383. doi:10.1111/j.1365–2869.2009.00735.x.

Demerouti, E., Bakker, A. B., Geurts, S. A. E., & Taris, T. W. (2009). Daily recovery from work-related effort during non-work time. In: S. Sonnentag, P. L. Perrew, & D. C. Ganster (eds.), *Current Perspectives on Job-Stress Recovery, Research in Occupational Stress and Well Being*. Bingley, UK: JAI Press/Emerald Group Publishing, 85–123.

Duckworth, A. L., Tsukayama, E., & May, H. (2010). Establishing causality using longitudinal hierarchical linear modeling: An illustration predicting achievement from self-control. *Social Psychological and Personality Science*, 1, 311–317. doi:10.1177/1948550609359707.

Ebner-Priemer, U. W., & Trull, T. J. (2009). Ecological momentary assessment of mood disorders and mood dysregulation. *Psychological Assessment*, 21, 463–475. doi:10.1037/a0017075.

Ekstedt, M., Söderström, M., Åkerstedt, T., Nilsson, J., Søndergaard, H.-P., & Aleksander, P. (2006). Disturbed sleep and fatigue in occupational burnout. *Scandinavian Journal of Work, Environment & Health*, 32, 121–131. doi:10.5271/sjweh.987.

Elovainio, M., Kivimäki, M., Vahtera, J., Keltikangas-Järvinen, L., & Virtanen, M. (2003). Sleeping problems and health behaviors as mediators between organizational justice and health. *Health Psychology*, 22, 287–293. doi:10.1037/0278–6133.22.3.287.

Ferrara, M., & De Gennaro, L. (2001). How much sleep do we need? *Sleep Medicine Reviews*, 5, 155–179. doi:10.1053/smrv.2000.0138.

Fisher, C. D. (2002). Antecedents and consequences of real-time affective reactions at work. *Motivation and Emotion*, 26, 3–30. doi:10.1023/A:1015190007468.

Fisher, C. D., & To, M. L. (2012). Using experience sampling methodology in organizational behavior. *Journal of Organizational Behavior*, 33, 865–877. doi:10.1002/job.1803.

Greenberg, J. (2006). Losing sleep over organizational injustice: Attenuating insomniac reactions to underpayment inequity with supervisory training in interactional justice. *Journal of Applied Psychology*, 91, 58–69. doi:10.1037/0021–9010.91.1.58.

Greubel, J., & Kecklund, G. (2011). The impact of organizational changes on work stress, sleep, recovery and health. *Industrial Health*, 49, 353–364. doi:10.2486/indhealth.MS1211.

Grossi, G., Perski, A., Evengård, B., Blomkvist, V., & Orth-Gomér, K. (2003). Physiological correlates of burnout among women. *Journal of Psychosomatic Research*, 55, 309–316. doi:10.1016/S0022–3999(02)00633–5.

Hahn, V. C., Binnewies, C., Sonnentag, S., & Mojza, E. J. (2011). Learning how to recover from job stress: Effects of a recovery training program on recovery, recovery-related self-efficacy, and well-being. *Journal of Occupational Health Psychology*, 16, 202–216. doi:10.1037/a0022169.

Hallberg, U. E., & Schaufeli, W. B. (2006). "Same same" but different? *European Psychologist*, 11, 119–127. doi:10.1027/1016–9040.11.2.119.

Hanson, L. L. M., Åkerstedt, T., Näswall, K., Leineweber, C., Theorell, T., & Westerlund, H. (2011). Cross-lagged relationships between workplace demands, control, support, and sleep problems. *Sleep*, 34, 1403–1410. doi:10.5665/sleep.1288.

Hobfoll, S. E. (2002). Social and psychological resources and adaptation. *Review of General Psychology*, 6, 307–324. doi:10.1037/1089–2680.6.4.307.

Hofman, S. G. (2007). Cognitive factors that maintain social anxiety disorder: A comprehensive model and its treatment implications. *Cognitive Behaviour Therapy*, 36, 193–209. doi:10.1080/16506070701421313.

Hülsheger, U. R., Alberts, H. J. E. M., Feinholdt, A., & Lang, J. W. B. (2013). Benefits of mindfulness at work: The role of mindfulness in emotion regulation, emotional exhaustion, and job satisfaction. *Journal of Applied Psychology*, 98, 310–325. doi:10.1037/a0031313.

Judge, T. A., & Kammeyer-Mueller, J. D. (2012). Job attitudes. *Annual Review of Psychology*, 63, 341–367. doi:10.1146/annurev-psych-120710–100511.

Keyes, C. L. M., Shmotkin, D., & Ryff, C. D. (2002). Optimizing well-being: The empirical encounter of two traditions. *Journal of Personality and Social Psychology*, 82, 1007–1022. doi:10.1037/0022–3514.82.6.1007.

Knudsen, H. K., Ducharme, L. J., & Roman, P. M. (2007). Job stress and poor sleep quality: Data from an American sample of full-time workers. *Social Science & Medicine*, 64, 1997–2007. doi:10.1016/j.socscimed.2007.02.020.

Kompier, M. A., Taris, T. W., & van Veldhoven, M. (2012). Tossing and turning – Insomnia in relation to occupational stress, rumination, fatigue, and well-being. *Scandinavian Journal of Work, Environment & Health*, 38, 238–246.

Kossek, E. E., Hammer, L. B., Kelly, E. L., & Moen, P. (2014). Designing work, family & health organizational change initiatives. *Organizational Dynamics*, 43, 53–63. doi:10.1016/j.orgdyn.2013.10.007.

Lazarus, R. S., & Folkman, S. (1984). *Stress, Appraisal, and Coping*. New York: Springer Publishing Company.

Linton, S. J. (2004). Does work stress predict insomnia? A prospective study. *British Journal of Health Psychology*, 9, 127–136. doi:10.1348/135910704773891005.

Luckhaupt, S. E., Tak, S., & Calvert, G. M. (2010). The prevalence of short sleep duration by industry and occupation in the National Health Interview Survey. *Sleep*, 33, 149–159.

Maslach, C., Schaufeli, W. B., & Leiter, M. P. (2001). Job burnout. *Annual Review of Psychology*, 52, 397–422. doi:10.1146/annurev.psych.52.1.397.

McEwen, B. S. (2006). Sleep deprivation as a neurobiologic and physiologic stressor: Allostasis and allostatic load. Metabolism, *Sleep: Biological and Medical Perspectives*, 55(Supplement 2), S20–S23. doi:10.1016/j.metabol.2006.07.008.

Meijman, T. F., & Mulder, G. (1998). Psychological aspects of workload. In: P. J. D. Drenth, H. Thierry, & C. J. de Wolff (eds.), *Handbook of Work and Organizational, Volume 2: Work Psychology* (2nd ed.). Erlbaum, UK: Psychology Press/Hove, UK: Taylor & Francis, 5–33.

Morin, C. M., Rodrigue, S., & Ivers, H. (2003). Role of stress, arousal, and coping skills in primary insomnia. *Psychosomatic Medicine*, 65, 259–267.

Nägel, I. J., & Sonnentag, S. (2013). Exercise and sleep predict personal resources in employees' daily lives. *Applied Psychology: Health and Well-Being* 5, 348–368. doi:10.1111/aphw.12014.

Nixon, A. E., Mazzola, J. J., Bauer, J., Krueger, J. R., & Spector, P. E. (2011). Can work make you sick? A meta-analysis of the relationships between job stressors and physical symptoms. *Work & Stress*, 25, 1–22. doi:10.1080/02678373.2011.569175.

Norlander, T., Johansson, Å., & Bood, S. Å. (2005). The affective personality: Its relation to quality of sleep, well-being and stress. *Social Behavior and Personality: An International Journal*, 33, 709–722. doi:10.2224/sbp.2005.33.7.709.

Pereira, D., & Elfering, A. (2014). Social stressors at work, sleep quality and psychosomatic health complaints – A longitudinal ambulatory field study. *Stress Health*, 30, 43–52. doi:10.1002/smi.2494.

Richardson, K. M., & Rothstein, H. R. (2008). Effects of occupational stress management intervention programs: A meta-analysis. *Journal of Occupational Health Psychology*, 13, 69–93. doi:10.1037/1076-8998.13.1.69.

Robbins, J. M., Ford, M. T., & Tetrick, L. E. (2012). Perceived unfairness and employee health: A meta-analytic integration. *Journal of Applied Psychology*, 97, 235–272. doi:10.1037/a0025408.

Rothmann, S. (2008). Job satisfaction, occupational stress, burnout and work engagement as components of work-related wellbeing. *SA Journal of Industrial Psychology*, 34. doi:10.4102/sajip.v34i3.424.

Ryan, R. M., & Deci, E. L. (2001). On happiness and human potentials: A review of research on hedonic and eudaimonic well-being. *Annual Review of Psychology*, 52, 141–166. doi:10.1146/annurev.psych.52.1.141.

Sadeh, A. (2011). The role and validity of actigraphy in sleep medicine: An update. *Sleep Medicine Reviews*, 15, 259–267. doi:10.1016/j.smrv.2010.10.001.

Sadeh, A., Keinan, G., & Daon, K. (2004). Effects of stress on sleep: The moderating role of coping style. *Health Psychology*, 23, 542–545. doi:10.1037/0278-6133.23.5.542.

Sallinen, M., Holm, A., Hiltunen, J., Hirvonen, K., Härmä, M., Koskelo, J., . . . & Müller, K. (2008). Recovery of cognitive performance from sleep debt: Do a short rest pause and a single recovery night help? *Chronobiology International*, 25, 279–296. doi:10.1080/07420520802107106.

Schaufeli, W. B., & Bakker, A. B. (2004). Job demands, job resources, and their relationship with burnout and engagement: A multi-sample study. *Journal of Organizational Behavior*, 25, 293–315. doi:10.1002/job.248.

Schaufeli, W. B., Leiter, M. P., & Maslach, C. (2009). Burnout: 35 years of research and practice. *Career Development International*, 14, 204–220. doi:10.1108/13620430910966406.

Scott, B. A., & Judge, T. A. (2006). Insomnia, emotions, and job satisfaction: A multilevel study. *Journal of Management*, 32, 622–645. doi:10.1177/0149206306289762.

Siegel, D. J. (2007). *The Mindful Brain: Reflection and Attunement in the Cultivation of Well-Being* (Norton Series on Interpersonal Neurobiology). New York: W. W. Norton & Company.

Söderström, M., Jeding, K., Ekstedt, M., & Perski, A. (2012). Insufficient sleep predicts clinical burnout. *Journal of Occupational Health Psychology*, 17, 175–183. doi: 10.1037/a0027518.

Sonnenschein, M., Sorbi, M. J., van Doornen, L. J. P., Schaufeli, W. B., & Maas, C. J. M. (2007). Evidence that impaired sleep recovery may complicate burnout improvement independently of depressive mood. *Journal of Psychosomatic Research*, 62, 487–494. doi:10.1016/j.jpsychores.2006.11.011.

Sonnentag, S., Binnewies, C., & Mojza, E. J. (2008). "Did you have a nice evening?" A day-level study on recovery experiences, sleep, and affect. *Journal of Applied Psychology*, 93, 674–684. doi:10.1037/0021–9010.93.3.674.

Sonnentag, S., Mojza, E. J., Demerouti, E., & Bakker, A. B. (2012). Reciprocal relations between recovery and work engagement: The moderating role of job stressors. *Journal of Applied Psychology*, 97, 842–853. doi:10.1037/a0028292.

Tyler, J. M., & Burns, K. C. (2008). After depletion: The replenishment of the self's regulatory resources. *Self and Identity*, 7, 305–321. doi:10.1080/15298860701799997.

Van Dongen, H. P., Rogers, N. L., & Dinges, D. F. (2003). Sleep debt: Theoretical and empirical issues. *Sleep and Biological Rhythms*, 1, 5–13. doi:10.1046/j.1446–9235.2003.00006.x.

Van Laethem, M., Beckers, D. G. J., Kompier, M. A. J., Dijksterhuis, A. P., & Geurts, S. A. E. (2013). Psychosocial work characteristics and sleep quality: A systematic review of longitudinal and intervention research. *Scandinavian Journal of Work, Environment & Health*, 39, 535–549.

Van Laethem, M., Beckers, D. G. J., Kompier, M. A. J., Kecklund, G., van den Bossche, S. N. J., & Geurts, S. A. E. (2015). Bidirectional relations between work-related stress, sleep quality and perseverative cognition. *Journal of Psychosomatic Research*, 79, 391–398. doi:10.1016/j.jpsychores.2015.08.011.

Vibe, M. de, Solhaug, I., Tyssen, R., Friborg, O., Rosenvinge, J. H., Sørlie, T., & Bjørndal, A. (2013). Mindfulness training for stress management: A randomised controlled study of medical and psychology students. *BMC Medical Education*, 13, 1–11. doi:10.1186/1472–6920–13–107.

Wagner, D. T., Barnes, C. M., Lim, V. K. G., & Ferris, D. L. (2012). Lost sleep and cyberloafing: Evidence from the laboratory and a daylight saving time quasi-experiment. *Journal of Applied Psychology*, 97, 1068–1076. doi: 10.1037/a0027557.

Warr, P. (1994). A conceptual framework for the study of work and mental health. *Work & Stress*, 8, 84–97. doi:10.1080/02678379408259982.

Weiss, H. M., & Cropanzano, R. (1996). Affective events theory: A theoretical discussion of the structure, causes and consequences of affective experiences at work. In: B. M. Staw & L. L. Cummings (eds.), *Research in Organizational Behavior: An Annual Series of Analytical Essays and Critical Reviews* (Vol. 18). Oxford: Elsevier Science/JAI Press, 1–74.

Wuyts, J., De Valck, E., Vandekerckhove, M., Pattyn, N., Bulckaert, A., Berckmans, D., . . . & Cluydts, R. (2012). The influence of pre-sleep cognitive arousal on sleep onset processes. *International Journal of Psychophysiology*, 83, 8–15. doi:10.1016/j.ijpsycho.2011.09.016.

Xanthopoulou, D., Bakker, A. B., Demerouti, E., & Schaufeli, W. B. (2007a). The role of personal resources in the Job Demands–Resources model. *International Journal of Stress Management*, 14, 121–141. doi:10.1037/1072–5245.14.2.121.

Xanthopoulou, D., Bakker, A. B., Dollard, M. F., Demerouti, E., Schaufeli, W. B., & Schreurs, P. J. G. (2007b). When do job demands particularly predict burnout?: The moderating role of job resources. *Journal of Managerial Psychology*, 22, 766. doi:10.1108/02683940710837714.

Zohar, D., Tzischinsky, O., Epstein, R., & Lavie, P. (2005). The effects of sleep loss on medical residents' emotional reactions to work events: A cognitive-energy model. *Sleep*, 28, 47–54.

Part III
Job insecurity and organizational wellbeing

9

Economic stressors and wellbeing at work

Multilevel considerations

Tahira M. Probst, Robert R. Sinclair, and Janelle H. Cheung

Introduction

The economic crisis of 2007–2008 was arguably one of the most important global threats to individual wellbeing of the last couple of decades. This crisis produced worldwide economic instability, leading to thousands of mass layoff events, increased long-term unemployment, and, among those fortunate to keep their jobs, greater uncertainty about their future employment prospects (Grusky, Western, & Wimer, 2011). Not surprisingly then, many studies link the recession to declines in physical and psychological wellbeing (Burgard & Kalousova, 2015; Frone, 2016; Modrek, Hamad, & Cullen, 2015; Piovani & Aydiner-Avasr, 2015; Van Hal, 2015). Although some research has associated recessions with some beneficial health outcomes (Burgard & Kalousova, 2015), recessions and the economic stressors they produce are generally regarded as an important threat to wellbeing. These threats are particularly strong for more vulnerable workers (e.g., unemployed, low income, older) as evidence suggests they have been more adversely affected by the recession (Eurofund, 2012). The Eurofund report also notes that in the aftermath of the recession, workers have become increasingly skeptical about the motives of their governments. Similar trends can be observed in the United States, where trust in government is close to an all-time low (Pew Research Center, 2013). Thus, the economic crisis can be viewed as a major societal event that not only resulted in short-term economic concerns but also lasting changes in perceptions of social institutions.

Some sectors and some countries are now showing signs of recovery. A recent *Wall Street Journal* article (Zumbrun, 2016) noted that in the United States, starting incomes for college graduates have been steadily growing and unemployment rates have been steadily falling, although starting incomes for those without a college degree continue to decline. Similarly, although still higher than prior to the recession, unemployment in Eurozone countries has steadily declined since 2013 (Trading Economics, nd.). Despite signs of optimism, concerns about economic stress are still widespread. A recent survey by Healthways (2014) estimated that 23% of participants in Organization for Economic Cooperation and Development Member States described themselves as "suffering" financially. Similarly, annual surveys of Americans conducted by the American Psychological Association (APA; American Psychological Association, 2013, 2015) routinely place money and work as top economic concerns, with financial issues influencing many of the other top concerns reported (e.g., family and health concerns). In fact, the most recent APA report noted that more than 7 in 10 Americans feel stress about money, with more than 1 in 5 reporting extreme stress about money. Even in periods of economic growth, a significant percentage of any workforce may be described as "working poor" – people who are employed but whose income is close to or below poverty thresholds (Bond & Galinsky, 2011). Such findings highlight that economic concerns always are among top threats to health and wellbeing, and should therefore be an important priority for wellbeing research.

One of the particular challenges of advancing the economic stress literature is that individual experience of economic stress is influenced by the interaction of multiple systems at different levels of analysis (Sinclair, Sears, Probst, & Zajack, 2010). In other words, the experience of economic stress may be heavily influenced by the nature of events and processes in one's occupation, culture, or local community. Incorporating such contextual effects into economic stress research raises theoretical and methodological questions that have received relatively little attention in the occupational health literature. Johns (2006) defined context as "situational opportunities and constraints that affect the occurrence and meaning of organizational behavior as well as functional relationships between variables" (p. 36). In relation to economic stress, contextual effects may be viewed as top-down cross-level factors with direct and/or moderating effects on individual level variables. Johns (2006) also noted that contextual factors can have unusual or unexpected effects on relationships, including curvilinear effects, reversed causality, or changes in the sign of a relationship. Understanding the nature of such contextual effects is a particularly important challenge for economic stress research.

To help address these issues, our chapter has three goals. First, we present an overview of economic stress literature, including a typology of economic stress constructs and a discussion of theoretical issues in economic stress literature. Next, we discuss empirical literature on the consequences of various economic stressors, individual differences in economic stressors, and the nascent literature on multilevel economic stressors. Finally, we describe a series of conceptual issues in this literature and conclude by presenting an agenda for future multilevel research on economic stressors in occupational health psychology.

Defining economic stress

Voydanoff (1990) described economic distress as "aspects of economic life that are potential stressors for individuals and families" (p. 1102). She proposed four broad categories of economic stress measures based on distinctions between employment and income stressors and between objective and subjective stressors (Probst, 2004; Sinclair et al., 2010). Thus, *employment instability* is an objective indicator of employment status, with examples of employment instability including unemployment status, unemployment duration, underemployment, and downward mobility. Similarly, *employment uncertainty* refers to subjective indicators of employment stability with the most common example being job insecurity (Probst, 2004). *Economic deprivation* refers to objective income-related stressors such as the inability to meet financial needs (e.g., because of insufficient income) and/or loss of current income. Finally, subjective indicators of *economic strain* include perceptions of one's financial status and perceived income adequacy.

Theoretical explanations for economic stress effects

There are numerous theories that provide explanations for why exposure to economic stressors leads to adverse effects. Given the tangible and intangible benefits associated with employment and income, it is perhaps not surprising that most relevant theories emphasize a resource-based approach to understanding economic stressors as significant determinants of stress and subsequent wellbeing. In this section we discuss four of the most commonly cited theories: Hobfoll's (1989) Conservation of Resources (COR) theory, Fryer's (1986) Agency Restriction model, Jahoda's (1981) Latent Deprivation theory (LDT), and Warr's (1987) Vitamin model.

According to COR theory (Hobfoll, 1989), people are motivated to maintain (i.e., conserve) valued resources. Such resources can be objects (e.g., house, car, boat), personal characteristics (e.g., self-esteem, optimism, resilience), conditions (e.g., seniority, tenure, managerial status), or energies (e.g., time, money, and knowledge). These are considered resources either because they are valued by individuals or because they serve as a means to obtain other valued resources. For example, stable employment could operate as a condition resource not only because employees value employment in itself, but also because employment brings salary, social status, and respect. Importantly, when resources are lost, perceived to be lost, or threatened with loss, individuals can be expected to experience psychological stress and subsequent strain outcomes.

In a similar vein, Fryer's Agency Restriction model (1986) suggests that monetary resources allow individuals to exercise their personal agency (e.g., make decisions on their own lives, make plans for the future). As a result, when a lack of monetary resources occurs (e.g., due to unemployment or underemployment), the coping ability and personal agency of employees is restricted, consequently leading to poorer wellbeing. Whereas COR theory is a broader theoretical foundation, the Agency Restriction model can be used to support more domain-specific hypotheses in relation to economic stress.

Jahoda's (1981) LDT is one of the primary theoretical perspectives used in past studies in understanding the relationship between economic stressors, specifically employment status, and health. LDT is similar to Hobfoll's broader COR theory such that they both conceptualize the importance of resources as the driving force of one's health and wellbeing, or that the loss of resources can lead to distress. According to Jahoda (1981), employment provides both manifest and latent resources. Manifest resources are associated with economic factors, such as income and other financial resources. Latent resources of employment are associated with psychological needs. The latent functions of work are (1) a time structure, (2) participation in a collective purpose, (3) enlarged social contacts, (4) personal status and identity, and (5) regular activity (Jahoda, 1981; Raito & Lahelma, 2015).

LDT theorizes that the loss of employment can lead to the loss of both manifest and latent resources of work, but it is the deprivation of latent resources that predominantly leads to effects on individual health and wellbeing. This argument is based on evidence supporting that individuals have deep-seated needs for the various latent functions of work, and the fulfillment of these internal needs is conducive to sustaining health and wellbeing (Jahoda, 1982; Paul & Batinic, 2010). Thus, in short, LDT suggests that the loss of employment causes psychological distress because it deprives individuals of the latent resources employment provides.

Finally, just as individuals require vitamins for maintaining their physical health, Warr (1987) proposed there are nine "vitamins" that individuals need for psychological health: opportunity for control, opportunity for skill use, externally generated goals, variety, environmental clarity, availability of money, physical security, opportunity for interpersonal contact, and valued social position. Many of these "vitamins" (similar to the needs identified in Jahoda's LDT) are threatened under conditions of economic stress. For example, organizational conditions that prompt worries about job insecurity are often accompanied by lack of control over the future of one's position and a lack of communication by upper management about the future of one's position – or indeed the future fate of the company. Similarly, loss of one's job is often accompanied by a perceived loss of social position and opportunities for interpersonal interactions.

Although a large body of research has found support for these resource-based models, they differ somewhat in the extent to which they have been used as the foundation for predicting outcomes of economic stressors. For example, COR theory has perhaps been used most broadly, serving as the rationale for predicting outcomes of job insecurity (De Cuyper, Mäkikangas, Kinnunen, Mauno, & De Witte, 2012; Vander Elst, Van den Broeck, De Cuyper, & De Witte, 2014), underemployment (Feldman & Ng, 2013), unemployment (Huffman, Culbertson, Wayment, & Irving, 2015; Lim, Chen, Aw, & Tan, 2016), and financial stress (Lim et al., 2016). On the other hand, although multiple empirical studies have supported LDT, most focus on the association between unemployment and latent deprivation – finding that such deprivation negatively affects individuals' mental health and wellbeing (e.g., Ervasti & Venetoklis, 2010; Hoare & Machin, 2010; Huffman et al., 2015; McKee-Ryan, Song, Wanberg, & Kinicki, 2005; Paul & Batinic, 2010; Selenko, Batinic, & Paul, 2011; Waters & Moore, 2002). Similarly, Fryer's Agency Restriction theory would seem to be more applicable to understanding the impact of financial stressors such as economic deprivation and perceived financial inadequacy. Indeed, Fryer (1992) specifically emphasized the role of financial deprivation as a primary cause of the psychological distress associated with unemployment. Although Warr's Vitamin model has been applied to many different job stressors, within the economic stress domain it has been most commonly utilized to predict outcomes of unemployment (e.g., Broomhall & Winefield, 1990; Halvorsen, 1998) and job insecurity (e.g., De Cuyper & De Witte, 2006; De Cuyper, Notelaers, & De Witte, 2009; Probst, 2005). In the next section, we consider in greater detail these empirical findings demonstrating the myriad adverse effects of economic stress.

Empirical research on the outcomes of economic stress

Individual-level outcomes of economic stress

Most economic stress research in occupational health has focused on three types of employment stressors, particularly unemployment, underemployment, and job insecurity (Probst, 2004). In each case, summaries of the literature highlight the importance of these phenomena. Regarding unemployment, McKee-Ryan et al. (2005) reviewed more than 100 studies concerning the physical and psychological effects of unemployment. They concluded that mental health outcomes were poor for the unemployed in cross-sectional comparisons to the employed, and that physical and mental health improved for the unemployed when they subsequently regained employment. Although there was some evidence suggesting physical health effects of unemployment, they found far fewer studies of physical health as compared with mental health and in some cases meta-analytic confidence interval estimates for physical health effects included 0. Thus, the evidence relating unemployment to psychological wellbeing is fairly strong, although more attention is needed to physical health outcomes.

Job insecurity has been the subject of two meta-analytic reviews (Cheng & Chan, 2008; Sverke, Hellgren, & Näswall, 2002). In the first, Sverke et al. (2002) reviewed 19 studies of job insecurity and physical health, with an attenuation-corrected average correlation of − .16, and 37 studies linking job insecurity to mental health, with a corrected average correlation of − .24. They examined moderating effects of measure type and occupation on these relationships but found no differences for the health-related outcomes. In a follow-up review, Cheng and Chan (2008) reviewed 44 studies of physical health and 77 studies of psychological health, obtaining slightly larger effects (corrected correlations of − .23 and − .28, for physical and psychological health, respectively). With the larger set of studies, Cheng and Chan were able to conduct additional moderator analyses and found somewhat stronger effects of job insecurity on physical health for longer-tenured employees, stronger effects of job insecurity on both physical and mental health for older employees, and no differences in health outcomes by gender.

McKee-Ryan and Harvey (2011) conducted a qualitative review of the literature on underemployment. Their review supported a link between underemployment and wellbeing outcomes such as psychosomatic symptoms, depression, reduced mental health, and lower optimism. Although there have been a few additional studies since this review (e.g., Konrad, Moore, Ng, Doherty, & Breward, 2013; Roh, Chang, Kim, & Nam, 2014), compared with unemployment and job insecurity literature, there is far less attention to underemployment in the empirical literature on employee health and wellbeing. Existing literature supports the importance of underemployment, but more research is clearly needed.

Numerous studies, across several disciplines, demonstrate links of objective and subjective financial stressors with health outcomes (examples include Adler, Epel, Castellazzo, & Ickovics, 2000; Anderson, Kraus, Galinsky, & Keltner, 2012; Boyce, Brown, & Moore, 2010; Boyce, Wood, Banks, Clark, & Brown, 2013; Chou, Chi, & Chow, 2004; Deaton, 2008; Litwin & Sapir, 2009; Lyons & Yilmazer, 2005; Starrin, Åslund, & Nilsson, 2009; Whelan, 1992; Whelan & Maître, 2007; Wood, Boyce, Moore, & Brown, 2012). Although much of this research assumes that financial stressors exert a causal influence on ill health, Lyons and Yilmazert (2005) found stronger evidence for the reverse causal path that ill health creates financial stress. There is comparatively less financial research specifically on occupational health (Sinclair & Cheung, in press), but studies have shown links between economic deprivation and Occupational Health Psychology-relevant individual outcomes such as work-family conflict, depressive symptoms, and poorer health and wellbeing, and organizational outcomes such as job attitudes, job performance, work-family conflict (Brett, Cron, & Slocum, 1995; Chou et al., 2004; Ford, 2011; George & Brief, 1990; Shaw & Gupta, 2001).

Moderating effect of individual differences

Individual differences (i.e., personality, temperament) can change the way individuals respond to both employment- and income-related stressors (e.g., Boyce & Wood, 2011; Creed, Muller, & Machin, 2001; Roskies, Louis-Guerin, & Fournier, 1993). It is important to consider such differences to gain a more comprehensive understanding of the nature of how people respond to economic stressors.

Past empirical findings generally support that individuals who have more positive cognitive styles tend to experience less negative outcomes from economic stressors. For example, Lau and Knardahl (2008) found that job insecurity has a stronger effect on mental distress among individuals who have lower general self-efficacy. Judge, Hurst, and Simon (2009) concluded that individuals with more positive core self-evaluations are less likely to experience financial strain because they are more optimistic and calm when appraising their financial situations, and they are less susceptible to strain in general. Similarly, Selenko and Batinic's (2011) findings revealed that self-efficacy buffered the effects of financial strain on mental health, such that debtors who are more confident about their ability to cope with debts are less affected by financial strain; while Keese (2012) found that individuals with higher external locus of control tend to feel less constrained by debt burdens.

Additionally, Boyce and Wood (2011) found that individuals who are more conscientious are more likely to gain satisfaction from income increases than those who are less conscientious. This is probably because conscientious individuals are better financial planners, which would enable them to derive greater utility from their income, or that they are more driven and motivated to accumulate wealth. Specifically within employment settings, employees' dispositional tendencies to experience negative emotions (i.e., negative affectivity) were found to affect how they perceive their pay satisfaction and organizational commitment, and their voluntary turnover behaviors (Panaccio, Vandenberghe, & Ayed, 2014).

There are, however, studies suggesting that domain-specific personality traits should be measured to understand specifically how individuals cope with the threat of specific economic stressors. For example, Schreurs, van Emmerik, Notelaers, and De Witte (2010) recommended future studies to use domain-specific individual difference constructs, such as job-search self-efficacy or perceived employability, as opposed to general self-efficacy, as moderators of the relationship between job insecurity and health. Moreover, Boyce and Wood (2011) suggested that some general personality indicators, such as openness to experience, may not change economic stress perceptions because employment and income are not important to everyone. The extent to which a person is open to experiences is probably more likely to affect perceptions of nonmonetary resources, such as interpersonal relations and cultural experiences (Boyce & Wood, 2011). This highlights the importance of continued research on economic stress–individual differences interactions, as well as further development of theoretical reasoning for such individual differences as moderators of economic stress–wellbeing relationships.

Contextual and cross-level interaction effects

The relationship between economic stress and health outcomes can be attributed to both individual-level experiences and aggregate-level contextual influences (Brand, 2015; Burgard & Kalousova, 2015; Jiang, Probst, & Sinclair, 2013; Sinclair et al., 2010). In order to more fully account for the effects of economic stress, a multilevel perspective should be adopted in order to examine the interconnection of different levels (e.g., individual, organization, community, macroeconomic). Such research should examine the distinct contributions of variables at multiple levels of analysis to health outcomes as well as cross-level interactions in which aggregate conditions/contexts may moderate the effects of individual experiences of economic stress on health, wellbeing, and work-related outcomes.

As noted earlier, contexts matter because they are "situational opportunities and constraints that affect the occurrence and meaning of organizational behavior as well as functional relationships between variables" (Johns, 2006, p. 36). They are important to consider also because individuals tend to evaluate their experiences based on their relative position in the circumstances they are in (Brand, 2015). For example, experiences of economic stress may change depending on workers' relative position in the labor market. Economic adversity may be more stressful or incite greater perceived deprivation among those who are more economically advantaged, whereas it may be a relatively normative experience for some disadvantaged workers (Brand, 2015).

Burgard and Kalousova (2015) reviewed the recession literature and concluded that aggregate-level changes due to the recession can influence how individuals respond to economic stress. For example, the aggregate-level deceleration of business and industrial activities associated with recessions can affect individual responses to job losses or reduced pay. Moreover, recessions can cause community-level declines in health (e.g., limited availability and affordability of health-relevant infrastructure; reduced funding to medical care services) and subsequently lead to long-term negative impact on individual health status (Burgard & Kalousova, 2015; Reeves, Basu, McKee, Marmot, & Stuckler, 2013; Suhrcke et al., 2011). Other macro-level determinants, such as occupational structure, policy changes and economic developments, can also change how economic stress is perceived. For example, globalization of labor may lead to a decline in job security among low-wage workers (Burgard & Lin, 2013). Similarly, Jiang et al. (2013) found that projected occupational outlook estimates of the extent to which occupations were growing or declining were predictive of individual-level perceptions of job insecurity. Thus, higher-level occupational and economic variables can have main effects on lower-level individual perceptions of economic stress and outcomes.

Some empirical evidence also supports organization-level influences on the effects of economic stress among workers. For example, Debus, König, and Kleinmann (2011) found that company-level performance explained a significant proportion of variance in individual-level job insecurity perceptions, again supporting the importance of considering multilevel main effects and interactions when studying economic stress (Shoss & Probst, 2012).

With regard to contextual influences on the relationship between economic stress and work-related outcomes (i.e., cross-level moderating effects), Debus, Probst, König, and Kleinmann (2012) investigated how country-level values of uncertainty avoidance and societal safety nets (i.e., labor market security index and income security index) influenced the relationship of job insecurity with job satisfaction and organizational commitment. They found that country-level economic security measures buffered the effects of job insecurity on job attitudes, thus supporting the use of country-level policies or governmental interventions in minimizing the negative consequences of economic stress (Burgard & Kalousova, 2015). Ford and Wooldridge (2012) also found that industry-level economic measures, specifically industry revenue growth, can explain workers' job satisfaction through higher levels of autonomy, enrichment, and support from supervisors.

In yet another interesting study, Van De Vliert, Yperen, and Thierry (2008) discussed the interesting idea of climato-economics, which reflects the idea that a country's living conditions – defined by its economy and its weather – influence residents' motives and behaviors. They argued that wages are more necessary in harsh climates (i.e., extreme high/low temperatures) because they provide resources to overcome hardships associated with a harsh climate (e.g., needing better shelter, food storage, transportation). They also argued that working for money was more important in poor countries because goods that enable homeostasis (i.e., thermal comfort, nutrition, health) are more salient and desirable. They found higher levels of wage importance in countries with cold winters (but not in countries with hot summers). They also found a national wealth by cold winter interaction, with the strongest importance of wages in poor countries with cold winters.

Finally, Cifuentes and colleagues (Cifuentes et al., 2008) investigated the link between country-level economic inequality and depression operationalizing inequity with the well-known GINI index, which expresses inequity as a 0 to 1 score based on the distribution of incomes in a region, with 0 reflecting perfect equity (i.e., everyone has the same income) and 1 reflecting cases where one person holds all the income (see Bellù & Liberati, 2006). They also compared countries on a measure of human development (a composite of literacy, life expectancy, school enrollment, and Gross Domestic Product developed by the United Nations [2002]) and found that depression was associated with societal inequity in more highly developed countries. This study, along with the others discussed earlier, illustrates the range of possible approaches for investigating multilevel models of economic stress and highlights the need for continued research in various contextual factors (e.g., economic, social, and health) at different levels of analysis (e.g., community, county, industry, and national).

Key debates

While the literature review clearly indicates that a multilevel approach to the study of economic stress is potentially fruitful, there remain a number of key debates that have yet to be resolved, such as the appropriate levels of analysis, the range of practically meaningful effect sizes that can be attributed to distal contexts (e.g., national), and disparities in effect sizes as a function of the level of aggregation (e.g., community vs. individual-level outcomes). Foremost, however, is the need for comprehensive theoretical explanations for linking contextual effects to individual processes. Industrial/organizational research on these topics tends to rely on theories operating at the individual, group, and organizational levels of analysis because those are the points of intervention where the field typically focuses. Theories regarding the explanatory mechanisms for more distal effects stemming from the community or national level contexts are somewhat less utilized. However, two theories typically used to support individual-level relationships appear to have great promise, namely COR theory (Hobfoll, 1989) and Relative Deprivation (Davis, 1959; Merton & Kitt, 1950; Smith, Pettigrew, Pippin, & Bialosiewicz, 2012). Interestingly, they may suggest somewhat competing hypotheses regarding the expected impact of contextual variables.

Although variants of resource-based theories span many different disciplines (e.g., cognitive psychology, Kahneman, 1973; community psychology, Tilman, 1982; economics, Olalla, 1999), they all acknowledge that resources operate as key determinants of individual adaptation. Perhaps more importantly, COR theory extends prior resource-based theories by specifically predicting that stress will be a function of an individual's subjective perceptions of an event (such as unemployment, underemployment, job insecurity, or financial deprivation) coupled with the objective contextual circumstances that might objectively threaten those resources and/or provide sources of support to buffer the potential loss of those individual-level resources. Indeed, Hobfoll, Briggs, and Wells (1995) specifically discuss the notion of community-level resources (e.g., availability of employment opportunities, government financing, dislocated worker programs) operating to impact individual-level outcomes and reactions to stress. Similarly, organizational researchers have used COR theory as a rationale for contextual effects operating at the community (Zajack, 2010) and country levels (Debus et al., 2012).

Given the focus on and primacy of resource acquisition and maintenance, COR theory would predict that individuals with access to greater resources at the community or national levels should be less likely to experience adverse wellbeing outcomes in response to economic stress, because they may perceive that there are more opportunities to readily replace their lost or threatened resources within their community or societal context. For example, a community that has strong job-placement service centers, or a country that provides a robust social safety net in the event of unemployment, would theoretically lead to fewer individual-level negative reactions to that unemployment event compared to individuals in communities or nations with fewer such resources.

On the other hand, Relative Deprivation theory (Davis, 1959; Merton & Kitt, 1950; see also a recent review by Smith et al., 2012) would predict that the relationship between economic stress and wellbeing might be exacerbated for individuals who live in more positive community contexts (whether defined at the local, regional, or national levels) because the overall positive wellbeing of their community might intensify their sense of financial and/or employment deprivation compared to others in their social context. Indeed, recent research by Jiang, Probst, and Benson (2014) found that employees who perceived a loss of resources due to budgetary cuts had *more negative* reactions when they were in a work context that had suffered *fewer overall budget cuts*, compared to employees with the *same* individual-level perceptions of loss but in a more adverse work context (i.e., one that had suffered more budget cuts). Thus, rather than the effects of resource loss being exacerbated when it occurred at both the individual and contextual levels, it was instead worst when individual loss occurred within the context of less group-level loss. Similarly, a number of studies have shown that objective income *rank* (i.e., based on one's income standing relative to others in their region) explain health outcomes better than absolute measures of income or wealth (e.g., Boyce et al., 2010; Daly, Boyce, & Wood, 2015). This comports with the Finances-Shame model developed by Starrin and colleagues (Starrin & Jönsson, 2006; Starrin et al., 2009), which suggests that financial hardship coupled with the shame and stigmatization associated with financial hardship that leads to adverse health outcomes. In other words, how individuals view themselves (and how they think others view them) within their particular socio-economic context can result in perceived social stigmatization and loss of valued social position.

Together, these theories and multilevel studies provide a mixed picture of the extent to which the higher-level context affects individual-level processes in response to economic stress, with some suggesting resources at the community context can attenuate individual-level negative outcomes, and others suggesting that relative standing and position (or changes in these) may better explain the impact of economic stress on health and wellbeing. Clearly, more research and additional theoretical development is needed to have a better understanding of the link between contextual effects and individual processes.

Emerging agenda

In addition to a need for greater theoretical development, there are other emerging agendas for future basic and applied research in the area of economic stress. On a basic level, certain economic stressors have received far more attention in the literature than others. Research on unemployment goes back decades, to the early part of the 20th century (Rowntree & Lasker, 1911), whereas the notion of underemployment as a psychological (rather than just economic phenomenon) was not recognized until the early 1970s (Toppen, 1971) and job insecurity research did not begin in earnest until the seminal article by Greenhalgh and Rosenblatt (1984). Since then, thousands of articles have been written on these employment-related economic stressors. Far less attention, however, has been paid to the income-related stressors of economic deprivation and economic strain (including perceived financial inadequacy and financial stress), particularly as they apply to organizational contexts and work-related outcomes. For example, little is known about the occupational outcomes of financial stress beyond research on determinants and outcomes of pay satisfaction, although early research was suggestive of relative deprivation effects (Sweeney, McFarlin, & Inderrieden, 1990).

More pertinent to the current chapter, there is scant evidence regarding the impact of contextual variables on individual-level work and occupational health outcomes of income- and employment-related stress. This has been noted by researchers in other disciplines as well. Operating from a sociological perspective, Burgard and Kalousova (2015) reviewed the sometimes contradictory empirical findings relating economic recession to individual-versus-aggregate-level poor health outcomes. Whereas physical and mental health outcomes appear to worsen as macroeconomic conditions worsen (Catalano & Hartig, 2004; Modrek, Stuckler, McKee, Cullen, & Basu, 2013), economic recession has generally been linked to overall *lower* mortality levels (Ruhm, 2003). Burgard and Kalousova concluded that a multilevel perspective is needed that explicitly considers pathways and roles played by individuals, their families, employers, community contexts, and governmental policy environments in understanding these individual-level outcomes.

Thus, as noted in other writings (e.g., Jiang et al., 2013; Shoss & Probst, 2012; Sinclair et al., 2010), we will reiterate our earlier calls for additional research on workgroup-, organizational-, community-, cultural-, and national-level variables in order to better delineate how variables at these contextual levels can impact our understanding of individual-level reactions to economic stress. Toward that end, there is a need for synergistic efforts involving researchers from public health, community health, sociology, economics, occupational health, and organizational psychology. The development and testing of theoretically sound multilevel models would greatly benefit from such collaborative interdisciplinary research teams.

Finally, as the body of evidence suggesting that variables operating at different levels impact individual-level outcomes of economic stress continues to grow, this indicates that there are potentially numerous fruitful points of intervention at each of those levels. This begs the question of what such interventions might look like within workgroup, organizational, occupational, community, and/or national contexts. For example, although organizational psychologists might focus on the individual, workgroup, and organization as points of intervention, research indicates that economic policy differences at even the most distal national level can predict individual-level responses to economic stressors (e.g., Debus et al., 2012). This reaffirms the need for a multidisciplinary approach to the development of interventions and governmental and economic policies at these higher levels of context. Such collaboration will also allow us to better understand how higher-level influences such as financial crises (or conversely, economic recovery) might impact organizational-level variables (layoff vs. hiring trends) and subsequent interactions between supervisors, managers, coworkers, and employees.

Conclusion

We began our chapter by noting that the individual experience of economic stress is influenced by multiple interacting systems operating at different levels ranging from the individual, workgroup, and organizational levels to the community, national, and societal levels. Intentional modeling of such contextual effects within the occupational health and economic stress literatures is sparse. To begin to rectify this gap and spur future researchers to take into account multilevel considerations, we reviewed the nascent literature on multilevel economic stressors, described theoretical foundations that may be used to develop testable research hypotheses, and discussed the need for greater interdisciplinary collaboration to most effectively prevent and/or attenuate the adverse effects of economic stress.

References

Adler, N. E., Epel, E. S., Castellazzo, G., & Ickovics, J. R. (2000). Relationship of subjective and objective social status with psychological and physiological functioning: Preliminary data in healthy white women. *Health Psychology*, 19, 536–592.

American Psychological Association (2013). *Stress in America*. Retrieved from American Psychological Association website: www.apa.org/news/press/releases/stress/2013/highlights.aspx

American Psychological Association (2015) *Stress in America*. Retrieved from American Psychological Association website: www.apa.org/news/press/releases/stress/2014/stress-report.pdf

Anderson, C., Kraus, M. W., Galinsky, A. D., & Keltner, D. (2012). The local-ladder effect: Social status and subjective well-being. *Psychological Science*, 23, 764–771.

Bellù, L., Giovanni, & Liberati, P. (2006). *Inequality The Gini Index*. Food and Agriculture Organization of the United Nations, EasyPol Module 42. Available at: www.fao.org/docs/up/easypol/329/gini_index_040en.pdf (accessed 12 December 2014).

Bond, J. T., & Galinsky, E. (2011). *Low Income Employees in the U.S.* New York: Families and Work Institute.

Boyce, C. J., Brown, G. D. A., & Moore, S. C. (2010). Money and happiness: Rank of income, not income, affects life satisfaction. *Psychological Science*, 21, 471–475.

Boyce, C. J., & Wood, A. M. (2011). Personality and the marginal utility of income: Personality interacts with increases in household income to determine life satisfaction. *Journal of Economic Behavior & Organization*, 78, 183–191.

Boyce, C. J., Wood, A. M., Banks, J., Clark, A. E., & Brown, G. D. A. (2013). Money, well-being, and loss aversion: Does an income loss have a greater effect on well-being than an equivalent income gain? *Psychological Science*, 24, 2557–2562.

Brand, J. E. (2015). The far-reaching impact of job loss and unemployment. *Annual Review of Sociology*, 41, 359–375.

Brett, J. F., Cron, W. L., & Slocum, J. W. (1995). Economic dependency on work: A moderator of the relationship between organizational commitment and performance. *The Academy of Management Journal*, 38, 261–271.

Broomhall, H. S., & Winefield, A. H. (1990). A comparison of the affective well-being of young and middle-aged unemployed men matched for length of unemployment. *British Journal of Medical Psychology*, 63(1), 43–52.

Burgard, S. A., & Kalousova, L. (2015). Effects of the Great Recession: Health and well-being. *Annual Review of Sociology*, 41, 181–201. doi:10.1146/annurev-soc-073014–112204.

Burgard, S. A., & Lin, K. Y. (2013). Bad jobs, bad health? How work and work conditions contribute to health disparities. *American Behavioral Scientist*, 57(8) 1105–1127. doi:10.1177/0002764213487347.

Catalano, R., & Hartig, T. (2004). Economic predictors of admissions to inpatient psychiatric treatment in Sweden. *Social Psychiatry and Psychiatric Epidemiology*, 39(4), 305–310.

Cheng, G. H., & Chan, D. K. (2008). Who suffers more from job insecurity? A meta-analytic review. *Applied Psychology: An International Review*, 57, 272–303.

Chou, K.-L., Chi, I., & Chow, N. W. S. (2004). Sources of income and depression in elderly Hong Kong Chinese: Mediating and moderating effects of social support and financial strain. *Aging & Mental Health*, 8, 212–221.

Cifuentes, M., Sembajwe, G., Tak, S., Gore, R., Kriebel, D., & Punnett, L. (2008). The association of major depressive episodes with income inequality and the human development index. *Social Science & Medicine*, 67, 529–539.

Creed, P. A., Muller, J., & Machin, M. A. (2001). The role of satisfaction with occupational status, neuroticism, financial strain and categories of experience in predicting mental health in the unemployed. *Personality and Individual Differences*, 30, 435–447.

Daly, M., Boyce, C., & Wood, A. (2015). A social rank explanation of how money influences health. *Health Psychology*, 34(3), 222–230.

Davis, J. A. (1959). A formal interpretation of the theory of relative deprivation. *Sociometry*, 22, 280–296.

Deaton, A. (2008). Income, health and well-being around the world: Evidence from the Gallup World Poll. *Journal of Economic Perspectives*, 22, 53–72.

De Cuyper, N., & De Witte, H. (2006). The impact of job insecurity and contract type on attitudes, well-being and behavioural reports: A psychological contract perspective. *Journal of Occupational and Organizational Psychology*, 79, 395–409.

De Cuyper, N., Mäkikangas, A., Kinnunen, U., Mauno, S., & Witte, H. D. (2012). Cross-lagged associations between perceived external employability, job insecurity, and exhaustion: Testing gain and loss spirals according to the Conservation of Resources Theory. *Journal of Organizational Behavior*, 33(6), 770–788.

De Cuyper, N., Notelaers, G., & De Witte, H. (2009). Job insecurity and employability in fixed-term contractors, agency workers, and permanent workers: Associations with job satisfaction and affective organizational commitment. *Journal of Occupational Health Psychology*, 14(2), 193–205.

Debus, M. E., König, C., & Kleinmann, M. (April 2011). *The Building Blocks of Job Insecurity Perceptions: The Impact of Company Performance and Personality on Perceived Job Insecurity*. Poster presented at the annual conference of the Society for Industrial and Organizational Psychology, Chicago, IL.

Debus, M. E., Probst, T. M., König, C. J., & Kleinmann, M. (2012). Catch me if I fall! Enacted uncertainty avoidance and the social safety net a country-level moderators in the job-insecurity-job attitudes link. *Journal of Applied Psychology*, 97, 690–698.

Ervasti, H., & Venetoklis, T. (2010). Unemployment and subjective well-being: An empirical test of deprivation theory, incentive paradigm and financial strain approach. *Acta Sociologica*, 53, 119–138.

Eurofund. (2012). *Third European Quality of Life Survey – Quality of Life in Europe: Impacts of the Crisis*. Publications Office of the European Union, Luxembourg. doi:10.2806/42471.

Feldman, D. C., & Ng, T. W. H. (2013). Theoretical approaches to the study of job transitions. In: N. W. Schmitt & S. Highhouse (eds.), *Handbook of Psychology, Volume 12: Industrial and Organizational Psychology* (2nd ed.). Hoboken, NJ: John Wiley & Sons, 292–307.

Ford, M. T. (2011). Linking household income and work-family conflict: A moderated mediation study. *Stress and Health*, 27, 144–162.

Ford, M. T., & Wooldridge, J. D. (2012). Industry growth, work role characteristics, and job satisfaction: A cross-level mediation model. *Journal of Occupational Health Psychology*, 17, 492–504.

Frone, M. R. (2016). The great recession and employee alcohol use: A U.S. population study. *Psychology of Addictive Behaviors*, 30, 158–167.

Fryer, D. (1986). Employment deprivation and personal agency during unemployment: A critical discussion of Jahoda's explanation of the psychological effects of unemployment. *Social Behavior*, 1(1), 3–23.

Fryer, D. (1992). Psychological or material deprivation: Why does unemployment have mental health consequences? In: E. McLoughlin (ed.), *Understanding Unemployment: New Perspectives on Active Labour Market Policies*. New York: Routledge, 103–125.

George, J., & Brief, A. (1990). The economic instrumentality of work: An examination of the moderating effects of financial requirements and sex on the pay-life satisfaction relationship. *Journal of Vocational Behavior*, 37, 357–368.

Greenhalgh, L., & Rosenblatt, Z. (1984). Job insecurity: Toward conceptual clarity. *The Academy of Management Review*, 9(3), 438–448.

Grusky, D. B., Western, B., & Wimer, C. (2011). The consequences of the great recession. In: D. B. Grusky, B. Western, & C. Wimer (eds.), *The Great Recession*. New York: Russell Sage Foundation, 3–20.

Halvorsen, K. (1998). Impact of re-employment on psychological distress among long-term unemployed. *Acta Sociologica*, 41(2–3), 227–242.

Healthways. (2014). *State of Global Well-Being: Results of the Gallup-Healthways Global Well-Being Index.* Franklin, TN: Healthways, Inc. Available at: www.healthwaysaustralia.com.au/pdf/Gallup_Healthways_State_of_Global_Report.pdf (accessed 18 March 2016).

Hoare, P. N., & Machin, M. A. (2010). The impact of reemployment on access to the latent and manifest benefits of employment and mental health. *Journal of Occupational and Organizational Psychology*, 83, 759–770.

Hobfoll, S. E. (1989). Conservation of resources: A new attempt at conceptualizing stress. *American Psychologist*, 44(3), 513–524. doi:10.1037/0003-066X.44.3.513.

Hobfoll, S. E., Briggs, S., & Wells, J. (1995). Community stress and resources: Actions and reactions. In: S. E. Hobfoll & M. W. deVries, (eds.), *Extreme stress and communities: Impact and intervention*. New York: Kluwer Academic/Plenum Publishers, 137–158. doi:10.1007/978-94-015-8486-9_6.

Huffman, A. H., Culbertson, S. S., Wayment, H. A., & Irving, L. H. (2015). Resource replacement and psychological well-being during unemployment: The role of family support. *Journal of Vocational Behavior*, 89, 74–82.

Jahoda, M. (1981). Work, employment, and unemployment: Values, theories, and approaches in social research. *American Psychologist*, 36, 184–191.

Jahoda, M. (1982). *Employment and Unemployment: A Social-Psychological Analysis*. Cambridge, UK: Cambridge University Press.

Jiang, L., Probst, T. M., & Benson, W. L. (2014). Why me? The frog-pond effect, relative deprivation and individual outcomes in the face of budget cuts. *Work & Stress*, 28, 387–403.

Jiang, L., Probst, T., & Sinclair, R. R. (2013). Perceiving and responding to job insecurity: The importance of multilevel contexts. In: A. G. Antoniou & C. L. Cooper (eds.), *The Psychology of the Recession on the Workplace*. Northampton, MA: Edward Elgar Publishing, 176–195.

Johns, G. (2006). The essential impact of context on organizational behavior. *Academy of Management Journal*, 31, 386–408.

Judge, T. A., Hurst, C., & Simon, L. S. (2009). Does it pay to be smart, attractive, or confident (or all three)? Relationships among general mental ability, physical attractiveness, core self-evaluations, and income. *Journal of Applied Psychology*, 94, 742–755.

Kahneman, D. (1973). *Attention and Effort*. Englewood Cliffs, NJ: Prentice-Hall.

Keese, M. (2012). Who feels constrained by high debt burdens? Subjective vs. objective measures of household debt. *Journal of Economic Psychology*, 33, 125–141.

Konrad, A. M., Moore, M. E., Ng, E. S. W., Doherty, A. J., & Breward, K. (2013). Temporary work, underemployment and workplace accommodations: Relationship to well-being for workers with disabilities. *British Journal of Management*, 24, 367–382.

Lau, B., & Knardahl, S. (2008). Perceived job insecurity, job predictability, personality, and health. *Journal of Occupational and Environmental Medicine*, 50, 172–181.

Lim, V. K. G., Chen, D., Aw, S. S. Y., & Tan, M. (2016). Unemployed and exhausted? Job-search fatigue and reemployment quality. *Journal of Vocational Behavior*, 92, 68–78.

Litwin, H., & Sapir, E. V. (2009). Perceived income adequacy among older adults in 12 countries: Findings from the survey of health, ageing, and retirement in Europe. *The Gerontologist*, 49, 397–406.

Lyons, A. C., & Yilmazert, T. (2005). Health and financial strain: Evidence from the survey of consumer finances. *Southern Economic Journal*, 71, 873–890.

McKee-Ryan, F. M., & Harvey, J. (2011). "I have a job, but . . . ": A review of underemployment. *Journal of Management*, 37, 962–996.

McKee-Ryan, F. M., Song, Z., Wanberg, C. R., & Kinicki, A. J. (2005). Psychological and physical well-being during unemployment: A meta-analytic study. *Journal of Applied Psychology*, 90, 53–76.

Merton, R. K., & Kitt, A. S. (1950). Contributions to the theory of reference group behavior. In: R. K. Merton & P. F. Lazarsfeld (eds.), *Continuities in Social Research: Studies in the Scope and Method of "The American Soldier"*. Glencoe, IL: Free Press, 40–105.

Modrek, S., Hamad, R., & Cullen, M. R. (2015). Psychological well-being during the Great Recession. Changes in mental health utilization in an occupational cohort. *American Journal of Public Health*, 105, 304–310.

Modrek, S., Stuckler, D., McKee, M., Cullen, M. R., & Basu, S. (2013). A review of health consequences of recessions internationally and a synthesis of the US response during the Great Recession. *Public Health Review*, 35, 1–31.

Olalla, M. (1999). The resource-based theory and human resources. *International Advances in Economic Research*, 5, 84–92.

Panaccio, A., Vandenberghe, C., & Ayed, A. K. B. (2014). The role of negative affectivity in the relationship between pay satisfaction, affective and continuance commitment and voluntary turnover: A moderated mediation model. *Human Relations*, 67, 821–848.

Paul, K. I., & Batinic, B. (2010). The need for work: Jahoda's latent functions of employment in a representative sample of the German population. *Journal of Organizational Behavior*, 31, 45–64.

Pew Research Center. (2013). *Trust in Government Nears Record Low, But Most Federal Agencies Are Viewed Favorably 62% Have Positive View of Federal Workers.* Available at: www.people-press.org/files/legacy-pdf/10-18-13%20Trust%20in%20Govt%20Update.pdf (accessed 21 March 2016).

Piovani, C., & Aydiner-Avasr, N. (2015). The 2008/09 economic crisis: The impact on psychological well-being in the USA. *Forum for Social Economics*, 44, 18–45.

Probst, T. M. (2004). Job insecurity: Exploring a new threat to employee safety. In: J. Barling and M. Frone (eds), *The Psychology of Workplace Safety*. Washington, DC: American Psychological Association, 63–80

Probst, T. M. (2005). Countering the negative effects of job insecurity through participative decision making: Lessons from the demand-control model. *Journal of Occupational Health Psychology*, 10(4), 320–329.

Raito, P., & Lahelma, E. (2015). Coping with unemployment among journalists and managers. *Work, Employment and Society*, 29, 720–737.

Reeves, A., Basu, S., McKee, M., Marmot, M., & Stuckler, D. (2013). *Journal of the Royal Society of Medicine*, 106, 432–436.

Roh, Y., Chang, J. Y., Kim, M., & Nam, S. (2014). The effects of income and skill utilization on the underemployed's self-esteem, mental health, and life satisfaction. *Journal of Employment Counseling*, 51, 125–141.

Roskies, E., Louis-Guerin, C., & Fournier, C. (1993). Coping with job insecurity: How does personality make a difference. *Journal of Organizational Behavior*, 14, 617–630.

Rowntree, B. S., & Lasker, B. (1911). *Unemployment: A Social Study*. London, UK: MacMillan.

Ruhm, C. J. (2003). Good times make you sick. *Journal of Health Economics*, 22(4), 637–658.

Schreurs, B., van Emmerik, H., Notelaers, G., & De Witte, H. (2010). Job insecurity and employee health: The buffering potential of job control and job self-efficacy. *Work & Stress*, 24, 56–72.

Selenko, E., & Batinic, B. (2011). Beyond debt. A moderator analysis of the relationship between perceived financial strain and mental health. *Social Science & Medicine*, 73, 1725–1732.

Selenko, E., Batinic, B., & Paul, K. (2011). Does latent deprivation lead to psychological distress? Investigating Jahoda's model in a four-wave study. *Journal of Occupational and Organizational Psychology*, 84, 723–740.

Shaw, J. D., & Gupta, N. (2001). Pay fairness and employee outcomes: Exacerbation and attenuation effects of financial need. *Journal of Occupational and Organizational Psychology*, 74(3), 299–320. doi:10.1348/096317901167370.

Shoss, M. K., & Probst, T. M. (2012). Multilevel outcomes of economic stress: An agenda for future research. In: P. L. Perrewé, J. R. B. Halbesleben, & C. C. Rosen (eds.), *The Role of the Economic Crisis on Occupational Stress and Well-Being: Research in Occupational Stress and Well-Being* (Vol. 10). Bingley, UK: Emerald Group Publishing Limited, 43–86.

Sinclair, R. R., & Cheung, J. H. (in press). Money matters: Recommendations for financial stress research in occupational health psychology. *Stress & Health*, 32(3), 181–193.

Sinclair, R. R., Sears, L. E., Probst, T., & Zajack, M. (2010). A multilevel model of economic stress and employee well-being. In: J. Houdmont & S. Leka (eds.), *Contemporary Occupational Health Psychology: Global Perspectives on Research and Practice*. Chichester: Wiley-Blackwell, 1–20.

Smith, H. J., Pettigrew, T. F., Pippin, G. M., & Bialosiewicz, S. (2012). Relative deprivation: A theoretical and meta-analytic review. *Personality and Social Psychology Review*, 16, 203–232.

Starrin, B., Åslund, C., & Nilsson, K. W. (2009). Financial stress, shaming experiences, and psychosocial ill-health: Studies into the finances-shame model. *Social Indicators Research*, 91, 283–298.

Starrin, B., & Jönsson, L. R. (2006). The finances-shame model and the relation between unemployment and health. In: T. Kieselbach, A. H. Winefield, C. Boyd, & S. Anderson (eds.), *Unemployment and Health: International and Interdisciplinary Perspectives*. Bowen Hills, Queensland: Australian Academic Press, 75–97.

Suhrcke, M., Stuckler, D., Suk, J. E., Desai, M., Senek, M., McKee, M., . . . & Semenza, J. C. (2011). The impact of economic crises on communicable disease transmission and control: A systematic review of the evidence. *PLoS ONE*, 6, e20724.

Sverke, M., Hellgren, J., & Näswall, K. (2002). No security: A meta-analysis and review of job insecurity and its consequences. *Journal of Occupational Health Psychology*, 7, 242–264.

Sweeney, P. D., McFarlin, D. B., & Inderrieden, E. J. (1990). Using relative deprivation theory to explain satisfaction with income and pay level: A multistudy examination. *Academy of Management Journal*, 33(2), 423–436.

Tilman, D. (1982). *Resource Competition and Community Structure*. Princeton, NJ: Princeton University Press.

Toppen, J. T. (1971). Underemployment: Economic or psychological? *Psychological Reports*, 28(1), 111–122.

Trading Economics. (nd.). *Euro Area Unemployment Rate: 2005–2016*. Available at: www.tradingeconomics.com/euro-area/unemployment-rate (accessed 23 March 2016).

United Nations Development Programme. (2002). *Human Development Report 2002. Deepening Democracy in a Fragmented World*. Oxford and New York: Oxford University Press.

Vander Elst, T., Van den Broeck, A., De Cuyper, N., & De Witte, H. (2014). On the reciprocal relationship between job insecurity and employee well-being: Mediation by perceived control? *Journal of Occupational and Organizational Psychology*, 87(4), 671–693.

Van De Vliert, E., Van Yperen, N. W., & Thierry, H. (2008). Are wages more important for employees in poorer countries with harsher climates? *Journal of Organizational Behavior*, 29, 79–94.

Van Hal, G. (2015). The true cost of the economic crisis on psychological well-being: A review. *Psychological Research and Behavior Management*, 8, 17–25.

Voydanoff, P. (1990). Economic distress and family relations: A review of the eighties. *Journal of Marriage and the Family*, 52(4), 1099–1115.

Warr, P. B. (1987). *Work, Unemployment, and Mental Health*. Oxford, UK: Clarendon Press.

Waters, L. E., & Moore, K. A. (2002). Reducing latent deprivation during unemployment: The role of meaningful leisure activity. *Journal of Occupational and Organizational Psychology*, 75, 15–32.

Whelan, C. T. (1992). The role of income, life-style deprivation and financial strain in mediating the impact of unemployment on psychological distress: Evidence from the Republic of Ireland. *Journal of Occupational and Organizational Psychology*, 65, 331–344.

Whelan, C. T., & Maître, B. (2007). Measuring material deprivation with EU-SILC: Lessons from the Irish survey. *European Societies*, 9(2), 147–173. doi: 10.1080/14616690701217767.

Wood, A. M., Boyce, C. J., Moore, S. C., & Brown, G. D. A. (2012). An evolutionary based social rank explanation of why low income predicts mental distress: A 17 year cohort study of 30,000 people. *Journal of Affective Disorders*, 136, 882–888.

Zajack, M. (2010). *Multilevel Antecedents of Economic Stress*. Unpublished doctoral dissertation. Clemson University, SC.

Zumbrun, J. (2016). Income for recent graduates the highest in over a decade. *Wall Street Journal*, January 29. Available at: www.wsj.com/articles/ny-fed-report-finds-rising-incomes-falling-unemployment-for-young-college-graduates-1454079989 (accessed 23 March 2016).

10

Long working hours and presenteeism in Asia

A cultural psychological analysis

Luo Lu and Chun-Yi Chou

Long working hours: the global context

The concern about working hours in Western society can be traced back to the 18th century, at the wake of the Industrial Revolution (Cross, 1990). Following innovations in automation, workers needed to keep up with the timing of machine operation, hence the scheduling of working hours became extremely important. However, workers' wages were low and they needed to work long hours in order to maintain a subsistence existence (Cross, 1990). With the commencement of the trade union movement, working hours became an important issue in employee-employer relations, while academics began to put forward evidence and arguments for the health hazards of excessively long working hours. Consequently, the International Labour Organization (ILO) announced the Hours of Work Convention in 1919, which was the first specification of working hours, followed by the Weekly Rest Convention in 1921; the UN General Assembly passed the International Covenant on Economic, Social, and Cultural Rights in 1966.

All of these policy interventions underlined the belief that reasonable legislative restrictions should be imposed on working hours in order to safeguard employee health and work-life balance. Subsequently, a series of policies and acts to shorten working hours were formulated in various developed countries. With the help of governmental intervention and protection, working hours gradually declined in the West. Nevertheless, in the mid to late 1970s, the concept of flexible working arrangements was proposed as a necessary stimulus for economic competition (WHO, 2006), and working hours once again faced new challenges. Flexible working arrangements have enabled more flexible working hours, but also increased the risk of employees being exposed to excessively short or long working hours. Furthermore, the formulation of national legislation and supervision of working hours became more difficult. For example, a survey by the ILO discovered that in 2000, the proportion of employees working long hours (≥ 50 hours per week) was higher than that in 1987 in countries such as Italy, Finland, Britain, Australia, America, New Zealand, and Japan (Messenger, 2004). Thus, although research on working hours is not new, it does need to expand its scope to respond to emerging challenges in the global economic era.

During the 1970s in Japan, there was an outbreak in cases of sudden deaths of employees due to overwork. The phrase *karoshi* (or "death from overwork") began to be widely used in 1982, following the publication of the book entitled *Karoshi* by three physicians (Kanai, 2006). Public awareness was raised in Japanese society and relevant studies were published, which resulted in the accumulation of a large quantity of epidemiological evidence on the relationship between working hours and health. In recent years, numerous news reports on *karoshi* and overtime work have emerged. In 2010, the media reported at great length about the suspected *karoshi* of a 29-year-old engineer in the high-tech industry due to overtime work. This incident once again sparked an extensive public debate on overwork and overtime work. According to statistics from the Dow Jones (2011) news archive, a total of 166 news reports pertaining to "overtime work" were filed between January 2011 and April 2011, which is many times higher than the isolated cases reported in the past. In the 2010 World Competitiveness Yearbook released by the International Institute for Management Development (IMD) in Switzerland, Taiwan was ranked 14 (out of 59) countries in the average working hours, which mount to 2,074 hours per year. The 2009 human resources survey by the Executive Yuan Directorate-General of Budget, Accounting and Statistics (DGBAS) in Taiwan indicated that 17.6% of employed persons worked more than 50 hours per week.

Much of the data to date rely on *average working hours* to illustrate the trends of change in working hours over the years. While average working hours reflect an overall picture of employees' commitment of working time in Taiwan, the causes and consequences of such long working hours in Asia still need to be explained. As Social Cognitive Theory (SCT) postulates, behavioral manifestations depend on the continuous and mutual influences among the external environment, personal cognition, and past behaviors (Bandura, 1993). Therefore, the same behavior (e.g., long working hours) will have different meanings in different locations, different cultural contexts, and for different people. In the following analysis, we will thus place the behavior of working long hours within the Chinese cultural context along with the Confucian root to better understand its meaning and the relevant situational facilitators/constraints.

Long working hours in Confucian Asia

The definition of overtime work changes with the context and situation, and there is no clear and uniform regulation internationally. In legal terms, overtime work refers to work performed beyond the legal "normal working hours" per week or per day (OECD, 1998), which then gives rise to the problems of paid and unpaid overtime work. Another legal interpretation of "overtime work" refers to work beyond the "maximum working hours" per week or per day, or working hours agreed in collective bargaining. In this case, "overtime work" refers to work that violates the legislative restrictions imposed on "maximum working hours" (McCann, 2005). Since each country has its own restrictions in terms of "normal working hours" and "maximum working hours," it is difficult to clearly demarcate the boundaries of overtime work. Nonetheless, the majority of developed countries have set the limit of "normal working hours per week" at 40 hours, and that of "maximum working hours per week" at 48 hours.

The definition of overtime work in academic research has also varied across countries and academic disciplines. In contrast to the customary phrase *overtime work* used in legal terms, the phrase *long working hours* often appears in research, which has a similar meaning to overtime work. For example, in a Korean study, 40–47 working hours per week were categorized as "intermediate working hours," 49–59 hours per week as "long working hours," and over 60 hours per week as "very long working hours" (Park, Yi, & Kim, 2010). Whereas a Spanish study defined "long working hours" as over 60 hours per week for men, and over 50 hours per week for women (Pimenta et al., 2009).

In addition, studies have adopted hours per day as the unit, and defined "long working hours" as working more than 12 hours per day (Dembe, Erickson, Delbos, & Banks, 2005) or more than

10 hours per day (Nakanishi, Nakamura, Ichikawa, Suzuki, & Tatara, 1999); while another study asked employees a single question on whether they engaged in overtime work, soliciting workers' subjective judgment, without providing any objective references (Fredriksson et al., 1999).

Adhering to the Taiwanese Labour Standards Act, we hereby define "long working hours" as working over 49 hours per week, and "very long working hours" as over 60 hours, which provide objective indicators for our understanding of the current state of working time commitment in Taiwan. However, we will also take into account employees' subjective perceptions of workload. As shown in the aforementioned studies, the concept of "working hours" is not in a static state, but is in a constant flux reflecting the continuous interactions between employees and their environment. Various considerations, including those by employees, supervisors, employers, and government policy-makers all conspire to make the decision on working time as much a personal choice as a socially sanctioned act.

Why people choose to work long hours

The reasons why people work for long hours encompass an often complex interaction between workplace constraints, institutional regulations, incentives, working conditions, cultural values, macroeconomic climate, and personal motivations. So far, we lack a comprehensive theory to encompass both personal and environmental factors implicated in this perplexing phenomenon (Figart & Golden, 1998).

Porter (2004) distinguished two motivations for working long hours, pointing out that a person may work long hours because of their joy in the work. This is the behavior of a constructive, highly committed person. However, one may also be compelled to work long hours, using it as a defensive strategy to avoid repercussions such as tarnished image or risk of being laid off in organizational downsizing. Thus, the driving forces behind long working hours can at least be dichotomized into constructive and compulsive ones.

In view of the growing literature on long working hours, we believe that the field may benefit from theory-building efforts as well as theory-testing research. We thus anchor the basic model in the SCT perspective, as we believe that SCT as an overarching theory with a social-psychological thrust may help to explain the differential reactivity in stress and adaptation in general, and long working hours and presenteeism in particular. Presenteeism refers to the act of showing up for work when one is ill (Johns, 2012), or more precisely defined and measured as sickness presenteeism (Lu, Peng, Lin, & Cooper, 2014). Presenteeism may thus be regarded as an extreme case of long working hours. Although what proportion of long working hours is attributable to presenteeism is yet unknown, presenteeism has undoubtedly exacerbated the problem of overwork. In a nutshell, SCT describes the triadic reciprocal determinism among the environment (e.g., working conditions), the individual (e.g., self-efficacy), and behavior (e.g., long working hours, presenteeism). SCT advocates that individuals tend to undertake behaviors that they believe will result in a "better" outcome. Defined as the belief in one's competence to cope with a broad range of stressful or challenging demands, general self-efficacy thus is a very important factor in shaping the meaning that people ascribe to situations (Bandura, 1997).

Long working hours: adopting the SCT perspective

The basic tenet of SCT is that behavior is controlled by the person through the cognitive processes, and by the environment through facilitators and constraints in the external social situations. Specifically, to recognize the mutual, interacting influences among individuals, their behaviors, and environments, Bandura (1986) advocated *triadic reciprocal determinism* among (1) personal

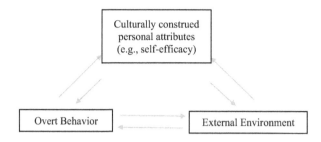

Figure 10.1 Triadic reciprocal causation

attributes, such as internal cognitive and affective states and physical attributes; (2) external environment factors, such as working conditions; and (3) overt behavior (as distinct from internal and physical qualities of the person). In this scheme, external environmental factors, personal attributes, and overt behavior all operate as interlocking mechanisms that affect one another bidirectionally.

Self-efficacy as a key construct in SCT does not come in only an individualistic form nor with a build-in value system. How people's belief of self-efficacy is developed, the forms it takes, the ways it is exercised, and the purposes it serves vary cross-culturally. More specifically, there is both cultural commonality in basic agentic capacities and mechanisms of operation, and diversity in cultivating these inherent capacities. Cultural variations emerge from universalized capacities through the influence of social practices reflecting shared values and norms, incentive systems, role prescriptions, and pervasive modeling of distinctive styles of thinking and behaving (Bandura, 2012). Accordingly, we need to take into consideration the cultural influences in construing self-efficacy, as well as the mutual, dynamic interactions among personal attributes, behavior, and environment, their to fully understand long working hours in Asia (see Figure 10.1).

Some researchers have acknowledged that the behavior of presenteeism results from the interaction of the person and the environment (e.g., Johns, 2010; Lu, Cooper, & Lin, 2013); the SCT theorists however, go further arguing that the behavior should be considered as a co-determinant of the person-environment transaction, rather than the byproduct of it (c.f. Bandura, 1986). In other words, the act of presenteeism, for example, should be seen as a part of the triadic reciprocal determinism that provides feedback to personal attributes and subsequently influences the environment. Adopting this model of triadic reciprocal causality, we will explain and explore interactions and intersections among self-efficacy, external environment, and overt behavior, in the context of long working hours and presenteeism.

A culturally construed personal attribute: self-efficacy

Self-efficacy is a key construct in SCT, which is deeply rooted in the conceptions of the self. The self encompasses culture-specific ideas of the person to formulate how one sees oneself (Lu, 2003). The self is pivotal to cultivate the fundamental beliefs of the individual, including one's self-efficacy, outcome expectations, and goals, postulated as the major psychosocial mechanisms in the SCT.

While the Western self evolved and developed under the Western cultural heritage, which is characterized by individualism and exchange relationships, the Chinese self is immersed in the Confucian cultural heritage, which sanctions the interpersonal relationships prototyped as the

"Five Cardinal Relationships" (*Wu Lun*). Such culturally decreed Chinese interpersonal bonds go far beyond the social contracts of exchange relationships by emphasizing collective welfare, diligent role performance, and rigorous self-cultivation (Lu, 2015). Thus, to get a fuller understanding of the self-efficacy of Chinese people, we need to unravel the unique features of the Chinese self as shaped by the Confucian cultural heritage.

The Chinese self

Mandated and molded by culture, the self refers to a constellation of thoughts, beliefs, feelings, and actions related to how one views oneself. Cultural psychologists, East and West, have exerted concerted efforts to understand the mutual construction between the culture and the self. As an example of such intellectual endeavor, Lu conducted a series of studies (e.g., Lu, 2003, 2007, 2008) on the Chinese self to uncover the essence of the self for contemporary Chinese people. Lu then proposed the theory of the "Chinese bicultural self," postulating that the self of contemporary Chinese people consists of both individual- and social-orientated self systems. Subsequent empirical research supported the claim that the two selves not only coexist but also operate harmoniously to reflect the agentic will of the individual (Lu, 2005, 2008, 2009; Lu, Chang, Kao, & Cooper, 2015; Lu, Cooper, Kao, Chang et al., 2010; Lu & Yang, 2005, 2006; Yang, & Lu, 2005).

In a nutshell, the individual-oriented self is originally conceived in the Western cultural tradition and rooted in the Western individualistic value system, which stresses the complete realization of the true self through consistency and integration. Also, the boundary between the self and others is relatively clear and rigid, and the ultimate goal is for individuals to fully realize their self-potential and achieve self-transcendence. This self system is most evident in modern Western societies (e.g., North America and Europe) and recently implanted onto the Chinese people from the West in the processes of social changes and globalization. In contrast, the social-oriented self has a long history in the Chinese cultural tradition and is rooted in Confucianism, which regards the self as being embedded within interpersonal social networks, or the "Five Cardinal Relationships" (*Wu Lun*). Confucianism stresses the interdependent, relational, and collective nature of interpersonal relationships, emphasizes similarities with others, and suppresses the unique self. The self that is cultivated within this context is flexible, changeable, and more focused on holistic views, which results in multi-faceted external behaviors, to achieve the flexible handling of different situational demands. The boundary between the self and others is flexible and variable; individuals might even continuously pursue the expansion of the self to include others for moral growth. Such a conception of the self is still widely prevalent in modern Chinese societies (e.g., Taiwan, Mainland China, Hong Kong, and Singapore), and those historically influenced by the Confucian teachings (e.g., Japan, Korea, and Vietnam).

A more detailed investigation of the social practices of the self has revealed three underlying dimensions: self–society relations, self–group relations, and self–other relations (Lu, 2007, 2008). Due to space constraint, we will briefly describe the contrasts between the two self systems: the social-oriented self and the individual-oriented self. Regarding self–society relations, the social-oriented self focuses on societal rules and norms, and emphasize cohesion between the self and the society. Individuals are thus compelled to display appropriate behavior in order to conform to the environment, and to fulfill the roles they have been assigned in order to obtain social affirmation. In contrast, the individual-oriented self focuses on fully realizing individual potential, and emphasizes the control and domination of the self over the environment. Individuals' behaviors are thus guided by their own needs and desires rather than norms and requirements of their society. Self-enhancement and self-growth are viewed as pathways to obtain self-respect and social esteem.

Regarding self–group relations, the social-oriented self emphasizes the integration of the individual into the group, in order to become a part of the group, and then trying his or her best to fulfill ascribed roles. The goals and wellbeing of the group are regarded as the priority, whereby individual interests might even be sacrificed in order to maintain the harmony and integrity of the group. In contrast, the individual-oriented self tends to focus on maintaining the independence rather than integration of individuals with the group. This implies that individuals normally give precedence to self-interest in deciding their behaviors. Individuals are also sanctioned to rely on themselves for everything, to be self-sufficient, self-contained, and autonomous. Furthermore, individual goals should take priority over group goals, and personal wellbeing should be the most important consideration.

Finally, regarding self–other relations, the social-oriented self regards interdependence as the essence of human society, advocating that humans cannot live in isolation from others. Strong emphasis is placed on interpersonal sharing and interpersonal affect, forming the psychological foundation for role obligations. Individuals should display polite and reasonable behaviors in order to conform to social norms, being keenly sensitive to the evaluations and responses of others, and regarding these as the basis of self-knowledge. In contrast, the individual-oriented self regards social relations as exchanges, with personal wellbeing at their core. Honest expression of personal preferences, feelings, and needs form the foundation of interpersonal relationships, and personal goals are achieved through fair competition with an emphasis on rationality. Self-knowledge is mainly attained through self-exploration, with a lesser regard for the evaluations of others.

In summary, the self of contemporary Chinese people can be regarded as a product of interactions and integration between these two different orientations, which in turn determines the mental models for interpreting the external environment. Although the influence of Western culture is undeniable (manifesting through the operation of the individual-oriented self), the strong imprint of the Chinese cultural tradition still manifests itself as the dominant self system, that is the social-oriented self. Thus the prevalent Chinese self is different from the prevalent Western self, in terms of its endorsed values, beliefs, cognition, affect, and social behaviors (Lu, 2015).

Accordingly, Chinese strategies of executing human agency are different from Western strategies. Chinese people emphasize the congruence of individual growth and social values and accept the results, whether good or bad (Lu & Gilmour, 2004a, 2004b). In a Chinese society, the pursuit of self-interest is acceptable or legitimate only after one fulfills one's social duties. In contrast, Western cultures encourage one to pursue personal needs, rights, and talents (Geertz, 1975). The vastly different mentalities of Chinese and Western people should be underscored when interpreting the exercise of human agency. In the analysis of the roles of personal determinants within the triadic causal system, SCT highlights a variety of cognitive, vicarious, self-regulatory, and self-reflective processes (Bandura, 1986). We will now focus on Chinese self-efficacy to elaborate its part in these processes.

Chinese self-efficacy

Self-efficacy is concerned with people's beliefs in their capabilities to mobilize the motivation, cognitive resources, and course of action needed to exercise control over the task at hand to produce given attainments (Bandura, 1997). It should be defined in the context of relevant and appropriate behaviors in specific situations, which renders the cultural influences on construing and practicing of the self salient (James, 1995). Self-efficacy exerts its influence through four major processes – *cognitive, motivational, affective,* and *selective* – to affect the behaviors that control and construct environments. Also, the impact of most environmental influences on human beings is through these processes, which give meaning and valence to external events (Bandura, 1993). We hereby elaborate the operation of the Chinese self-efficacy basing on the aforementioned Chinese bicultural self (e.g., Lu, 2003, 2005, 2008) to illustrate the influence of Chinese culture.

First, the *cognitive* processes work well under the condition that human behavior, which is purposive, is regulated by forethought embodying cognized goals (Bandura, 1993). A major function of thought or forethought is to enable people to predict events and to develop ways to control those events that affect their lives. Forethoughts are construed from the observed environmental events in the world around people and the outcomes given actions produced, in short, from the interaction between external macro environment at present and the behaviors feedbacks before (Bandura, 1986). Based on the theory of bicultural self mentioned earlier, Chinese people with a strong social orientation are more concerned about being part of society. On the one hand, they abide by social norms, even outperforming what is expected. Thus, they may consider themselves devoting to work and attaining diligent role performance as their responsibilities, realizing the value of being societal members, also as a way of exercising self-cultivation. On the other hand, even when they have not yet totally internalized these societal values, they may still force themselves to "act out" devotion to work, in order to avoid being excluded or sanctioned by others. Redding (1993) found that working long hours was not only highly praised as a Confucian virtue, but also tolerated as a necessary evil for raising a family, or even regarded as an insurance policy for job security and career advancement. Therefore, the cognitive processes, or more specifically, the forethoughts of Chinese people pertaining to time commitment at work, encompass the broader self including family, organization and society at large.

Second, people *motivate* themselves and guide their actions anticipatorily by the exercise of forethought, as mentioned earlier. They form beliefs about what they can do, and anticipate likely outcomes of prospective actions (Bandura, 1993). The motivational processes of self-efficacy beliefs operate in three forms: as casual attributions, outcome expectancies, and cognized goals of cognitive motivation.

The social orientation in the Chinese self mentioned earlier emphasizes that people are embedded in complicated relationships and sensitive to others' appraisals and responses, which are the foundation of knowing who they are. As such, the outcome expectations involve the imagined consequences of performing particular behaviors ("if I do this, what will others think?"). Chinese people are expected to give precedence to others' appraisals and the collective welfare rather than their own individual preferences. Therefore, Chinese employees would be more concerned for the reputation or profitability of the organization than their own welfare. Furthermore, as Chinese employees see themselves as part of the larger society and value harmonious relationships with coworkers, employers, and even stakeholders outside of the organization, they tend to act in a way that commands appreciation by others, such as working long hours, or working when ill.

Baker-McClearn, Greasley, Dale, and Griffith (2010) conducted interviews in nine Western organizations and identified two triggering factors of the act of presenteeism, termed "personal motivations" and "workplace pressures." Personal motivations include work values and beliefs such as "no one else can do the job," "loyalty to own professional image," and "obligation and commitment to colleagues, clients, and organizations." Workplace pressures refer to the organization's attendance policy, management style, and prevailing workplace culture.

Building on their work, Lu, Lin, and Cooper (2013) combined qualitative interviews with quantitative psychometric methods to contrast two underlying motives of coming to work when ill: approach and avoidance motives. Driven by approach motives, employees choose to attend work while sick because they believe that they should overcome their discomfort to be loyal to their jobs, coworkers, and customers. Driven by avoidance motives, employees force themselves to work because of the fear of financial loss or the backlash of social disapproval. This conceptual distinction is useful to map out the different psychological mechanisms that trigger the same overt behavioral manifestations of the act of presenteeism.

Third, the *affective processes* explain how people's beliefs in their capabilities will affect how much stress and depression they experience in threatening or difficult situations, as well as their level of motivation to act under such circumstances (Bandura, 1993). People who believe they can exercise control over undesirable situations do not conjure up disturbing thought patterns; but those who believe they cannot manage threats experience high anxiety arousal. Worse, they dwell on their coping deficiencies, and view many aspects of their environment as fraught with danger.

In other words, a low sense of efficacy to exercise control produces depression as well as anxiety in stressful encounters. More specifically, the efficacy route to depression is through a low sense of social efficacy. This is because people who judge themselves to be socially efficacious seek out and cultivate social relationships that provide models on how to manage difficult situations, cushion the adverse effects of chronic stressors, and bring satisfaction to people's lives (Bandura, 1993). In this vein, compared with people in the West, Chinese people in essence are more embedded in social relations, relying more on support from their social networks. Furthermore, social contagion and role modeling are more prevalent among Chinese people. As the virtues of endurance and perseverance are highly praised in a Chinese society, Chinese employees may play the role of hardworking and perseverant workers to gain trust from employers and coworkers, which in turn enhances their social efficacy.

Finally, the *selection process* points out that the choices people make allows them to cultivate different competencies, interests, and social networks, which determine life courses. People choose to enter situations in which they expect success (Bandura, 1989). For Chinese people, it is beneficial for them to put themselves in situations conducive to social virtues, such as ones that solicit acts of perseverance and hardworking, or those meeting others' expectations. In the work context, people with mastery goals seek out challenging situations at work as a means to growth and self-fulfillment, while people with performance goals avoid all possibility of being unfavorably judged by others. It thus follows that mastery goals encourage people to commit presenteeism as a proof of personal strength, as a show of devotion to work, expressing vigor, dedication, and absorption, whereas performance goals compel people to commit presenteeism to avoid personal failure and social disapproval. The intricate interplays among self-efficacy beliefs, outcome expectations, and goals deserve more research attention, and may hold the key to understand the complex self-regulation mechanisms in the practice of human agency, when long working hours and presenteeism occur.

Overt behaviors: working long hours and presenteeism

To reiterate, working long hours as a prevalent observable act, and presenteeism as its extreme form, may be driven by different motives. More importantly perhaps is the fact that these different motivational processes subsequently lead to different outcomes for employees and organizations (Lu, Cooper et al., 2013; Lu, Lin et al., 2013). These findings suggest that other mechanisms may be in effect linking motivations, behaviors, and consequences.

Mirroring the reasoning for presenteeism as "approach motives" most likely developed from the employees' sense of enjoyment, pleasure, and excitement obtained through their work, such psychological gains from work enable them to devote themselves to their work for extended time. However, individuals might also engage in long working hours due to desires for social recognition and approval, or to avoid the sense of guilt caused by the violation of social code of diligence, similar to the "avoidance motives" soliciting presenteeism. Furthermore, feelings of job insecurity and external economic pressures that necessitate the act of presenteeism may also solicit the behavior of working long hours, with a depletion of wellbeing.

Existing studies on long working hours have mostly focused on the evolution of working hours and its health consequences (e.g., Dembe et al., 2005; Kanai, 2006; van der Hulst, 2003), largely overlooking its causes and processes leading to (health) outcomes. We will thus use presenteeism (i.e., continuing to work when ill) as a special case of working long hours, to illustrate the potential of adopting the perspective of SCT, especially its view of the agentic interaction between the person and the environment. Hopefully, this will shed more light on the cultural context of long working hours and presenteeism.

The concept of presenteeism has been popularized in the West over the last two decades, and has attracted academic interests spanning from health-related fields to organizational research. Health care professionals have explored the alleged consequences of working in a state of sub-optimal health, such as reduced performance or productivity, prolonged physical discomfort, and the risk of aggravated health problems in the future (Collins et al., 2005; Turpin et al., 2004). Organizational researchers continued to consolidate evidence from more diverse workplaces and using more rigorous social science research methods (e.g., Johns, 2011; Robertson & Cooper, 2011). Relevant research is still in the embryonic stage, mostly involving clarification of the definition and developing appropriate assessments of both the behavior and its alleged consequences. Social researchers have attempted to disentangle the behavior from its consequences, in order to ensure a more precise operation of the concept (Johns, 2012). In this chapter we have also viewed presenteeism as an overt behavior or an act that pertains to employees forcing themselves to attend work even when they feel physical discomfort that qualifies for sick leave (Cooper & Lu, 2016). We thus exclude the antecedents and consequences of this behavior from the definition of presenteeism. We will hereby isolate the behavior and explore the behavioral motivation and consequences within a unified theoretical approach to systematically mapping out key mechanisms involved in the developmental process of presenteeism.

Although presenteeism has attracted increased attention in the field of management in recent years, the majority are cross-sectional studies. Nevertheless, these studies have consistently shown that presenteeism is negatively related to personal and organizational consequences. Specifically, findings indicated that the higher the frequency of presenteeism, the worse was employees' health status (Johns, 2010), and the lower the organizational productivity (Burton, Morrison, & Wertheimer, 2003). Results from one longitudinal study corroborated the above findings. Demerouti, Le Blanc, Bakker, Schaufeli, and Hox (2009) have shown that presenteeism increased nurses' depersonalization, while emotional exhaustion and presenteeism had a reciprocal effect over time. That is, nurses who displayed high presenteeism had higher levels of emotional exhaustion. This caused individuals to mobilize available resources for self-protection, which further caused a decline in physical and mental health, and increased the frequency of presenteeism, thereby resulting in a vicious cycle.

As illustrated in this longitudinal study, the majority of research on presenteeism limits outcome variables to one or more dimensions of job burnout (Cooper & Lu, 2016). It is thus imperative for both academic research and management practice to encompass the wider array of effects of presenteeism on individual physical and mental states, work attitudes, job performance, and other organizational indicators. For instance, in a two-wave study with Taiwanese employees, Lu, Lin et al. (2013) examined consequence indicators including employees' physical health, mental health, and work attitudes. The results showed that presenteeism was negatively related to all of the health and work-related consequences, both immediately and over an extended period of time. This study improves on existing research in the health care tradition by clearly defining presenteeism as an act, which then enables an estimate of the "net" contribution of this act on the impacts of wellbeing and productivity. Furthermore, this study shows that the impact of presenteeism on Chinese employees is similar to that in Western countries (Aronsson, Gustafsson, & Dallner, 2000; Caverley, Cunningham, & MacGregor, 2007; Claus & Johan, 2008; Elstad & Vabo, 2008). That is, although hardworking is regarded as virtuous in Chinese culture, overwork, especially under a suboptimal health state, can still claim heavy costs both on the individual and the organization.

Pertaining to the underlying theoretical perspective, current research on presenteeism mostly adopts the Recovery model and/or Conservation of Resources (COR) theory. According to the Recovery model, presenteeism deprives individuals of the chance of recovery, and increases their physical and mental load, thereby causing their health to deteriorate. This causes more intense physical and mental exhaustion, thereby further increasing the likelihood of presenteeism, thus resulting in a vicious cycle (e.g., Bergström, Bodin, Hagberg, Aronsson, & Josephson, 2009; Johns, 2011). The COR theory proposes that presenteeism causes individuals to mobilize available resources for self-protection, which reduces work efficiency and increases workload, thereby increasing the possibility of producing burnout and reducing work satisfaction in the long-term (Baker-McClearn et al., 2010). Both theoretical perspectives can account for some of the consequences of presenteeism, especially those outcomes related to health and wellbeing. However, both fall short on the role of individual as a human agent.

As observed earlier, existing research has assumed that presenteeism is a stable and passive state, thus largely overlooking the human influence on behaviors. These studies portray individuals as passive recipients of information conveyed in the environment, without agency for change and interaction. This view neglects the transformational potentials of individual differences, let alone cultural differences. Interestingly, Lu, Lin et al. (2013) conducted a two-wave longitudinal study demonstrating that the consequences of presenteeism indeed varied across cultures. As opposed to Western studies consistently showing a negative relation between presenteeism and job performance, in Asia presenteeism did not predict job performance. One of the reasons might be that Eastern cultures construe different meanings of presenteeism. As employees in Asia often regard their work team as a big family, they thus may view presenteeism as an act of duty, which then renders its relationship with job performance unstable.

Furthermore, cultural differences in the context of presenteeism have also been observed in relation to supervisory support. Baker-McClearn et al. (2010) interviewed employees of private and public sector organizations in the United Kingdom and found that supervisory support enabled employees to feel more reassured about taking sick leave, and was a major factor of the attendance decision. In contrast, prevailing Confucian cultural norms in Asia hold that diligence and perseverance are not only desirable work attitudes adhering to the expectations of the society, but also concrete deeds that would elevate individuals to a higher moral standing. Under this cultural context, employees might regard presenteeism as an appropriate and desirable behavior to attain social approval, and thus opt to report to work rather than taking sick leave. Moreover, individuals might also view presenteeism as an obligation to their organization and team members, using this act to convey the sincerity of self-sacrificing for the greater good.

These findings pertaining to cultural variations on both motivations and consequences of presenteeism underline the interactions between the individual and the environment. Both the self-views and decrees of the social environment are potent: presenteeism is a behavior imbued with cultural implications, though the overt act is universal. Different historical and cultural backgrounds will endow presenteeism with different meanings and significance. Therefore, we need to explore this behavior within the specific cultural context, specifically from the perspective of cultural self-views. In the next section we apply the earlier mentioned theory of the Chinese self to long working hours in general and presenteeism in particular, to rediscover the importance of human agency. Affirming that each individual has the ability to interact with the environment will enable us to more precisely analyze and interpret the meanings and implications of such apparent work diligence within the unique cultural realm of Confucian Asia.

Interaction of Chinese self-efficacy and the environment

Whether encouraged by the hardworking Chinese culture, or pressured by the fierce global competition and economic recession, long working hours has become a prevailing trend in Taiwan. For example, a survey with a national representative sample in Taiwan revealed a striking average work week of 48.96 hours (Lu, 2011), well exceeding the then-legal cap of 84 hours over two weeks (a 40-hour-week commenced in Taiwan on January 1, 2016).

As reviewed earlier, the existing research on long working hours and presenteeism has largely overlooked personal psychological mechanisms relative to contextual work factors. The triadic causal system proposed in the SCT fills this void as it highlights a variety of cognitive, vicarious, self-regulatory, and self-reflective processes as psychosocial mechanisms linking the person with the environment (Bandura, 1986).

Confucianism has a long history in Asia, and Taiwan in particular has inherited its traditional values and abided by the essence of the *Wu Lun*. The underlying doctrine states that the father–son relationship should form the foundation of all relationships, which metaphorically expands to relationships of monarch–subject, friends, brothers, and husband–wife. These are vertical intersecting relationships that reinforce the idea that people do not exist as independent individuals but are defined through their relationships with others. People are embedded within interpersonal relationships, and thus become a part of their society. Each person has his or her own duties, and fulfilling them becomes the life goal. These cultural values are as stable as ammonites, hidden within the crevices of rock piles (Levi-Strauss, 1955). They are gradually internalized along with participation in chartered social activities, and are naturally practiced in daily life, shaping and influencing behaviors (Hwang, 1995; Yang & Lu, 2005).

The Chinese self practiced in the workplace within this cultural context can be observed in the subtle interactions between supervisors and subordinates. Both parties interact beyond the balanced reciprocity and "one-to-one" relationships ascribed in Western social exchange theory. Chinese supervisors have a fatherly concern over the life of their subordinates, and believes that it is their natural duty to care about both the work and personal lives of their subordinates. At the opposite side, Chinese subordinates play the role of sons, internalize the idea of "reciprocity" (*bao*), and embrace the mentality of "repaying a drop of water with a gushing stream." Therefore, they exert behaviors of dedicated service, sacrifice, obedience, and voluntary cooperation, and are willing to double their efforts to complete their tasks (Cheng, Chou, Wu, Huang, & Farh, 2004; Lin & Cheng, 2012; Liu, 1996; Tzeng & Jiang, 2012). Both parties thus exceed the role expectations in an instrumental relationship, and establish an affective basis for their interactions in and outside of the work realm. Hence, when they experience concern, care, compassion, or kindness from the other party, they will naturally exhibit reciprocal behaviors, thereby reflecting "emotional reciprocity" in actual practice (Liu, 1996). Furthermore, subordinates' diligent and dedicated contributions to work will earn coveted high praises from the supervisors (Cooper & Lu, 2016).

Thus when Chines employees are faced with intense economic competition confounded with the pressure of industrial structural changes, there might be even more reasons for them to invest more time in work: (1) to embrace the spirit of facing hard times together, viewing personal sacrifice for the organization as a show of solidarity, and thus working harder out of loyalty and gratitude for the supervisors' kindness; (2) to exchange their behavior of working long hours for the reward of not being fired by their supervisors; (3) to demonstrate sincere love and enthusiasm for their work by voluntarily working long hours. These cultural directives will help us to understand the differential meanings and implications of long working hours and presenteeism between Asian and Western societies.

Unfortunately, systematic research on long working hours in Asia is very rare. Most existing studies have only recorded the phenomenon, and viewed long working hours as a byproduct of economic development. These studies have overlooked the cultural context and neglected the agency of the self in exhibiting behaviors. In the next section, we will adopt SCT as an overarching analytical framework treating individuals as agents with the ability to interact with the environment, to propose some directions for future research, especially those centered on the causes and consequences of long working hours in contemporary Chinese societies.

It is worth noting that self-efficacy does create task-mastery experiences, which in turn raise self-efficacy. That is, when an individual competently accomplishes a particular task, such as perseveres to compete a task regardless of hardship, such an experience can become absorbed in the overall achievement of the task (Sweetman & Luthan, 2010). This rewarding experience may also contribute to the persistent culture of long working hours in Taiwan.

Conclusion and future research directions

Although academic interests on long working hours have been developed and evolved in the West for a long time, we still have a long road to go to uncover the culturally relevant factors and facts of this phenomenon in Asia, especially in societies under Confucian influences, such as China, Taiwan, Japan, and Korea. A noticeable feature of this area of research is the lack of comprehensive theoretical frameworks with which to recognize the agentic essence of human being, the interactions and intersections among people (who are carrying their own history), and the environment they encounter at the present time. It is insufficient to see people as merely reactive information receivers and universally the same; the agentic nature of human and what makes a human (i.e., self-views) need to be acknowledged and incorporated into theory building.

The problem of lack of an overarching theory is compounded by researchers' belief of cultural universality when researchers take Western-developed theories and concepts for granted without considering the possible cultural impact on the individuals who commit to work long hours. The dynamic model adopted from the SCT in this chapter helps to organize concerted efforts to focus on the interactive dynamism of the agentic human being, the environment, and the overt behavior. First, we have endeavored to understand the cultural impact on individuals in construing his or her self-views and in turn the belief of self-efficacy. We then have applied this culturally sensitive analysis to elaborate on the Chinese bicultural self, which plays an important role in committing to work long hours. The cultural-level analysis enables us to have a deeper understanding of the complicated interplay of culture at a macro level and choice of working hours at a microlevel (as an individual decision).

More research is still needed to better understand the agentic role of human beings. Any comprehensive way to realize the human act should incorporate the personal and social foci within the causal structure. Specifically, sociostructural influences may operate through various psychological processes to produce behavioral effects. Thus, research on long working hours needs to focus not only on the external environment, such as economic recession or organization downsizing (Bluestone & Rose, 1998; Fenwick & Tausig, 2001; Landers, Rebitzer, & Taylor, 1996), but also – maybe more – on people's cognitive processes, acknowledging that people are sentient, purposive beings (Bandura, 2001). It is a fact that even when faced with mounting tasks, people act attentively to make desired things happen rather than simply succumb to demands of the situation. That is, people actively evaluate actions, set goals, and motivate themselves to perform and regulate chosen behaviors. Adopting the SCT perspective, we acknowledge that people are not only the reactors to the environment, but also producers. Through this agentic action, people figure out ways to adapt to social environmental constraints, redesign their behaviors, and create the situation they desire. Accordingly, working long hours can be understood in a similar frame of fluidity and dynamism.

Pertaining to the practical implications for working long hours, we need to focus more on employees in the "Confucian cultural circle," including China, Taiwan, Hong Kong, Japan, Korea, and Singapore, as the cultural thrust for working long hours is the most salient in these societies. We cannot overstate the need to incorporate the Chinese self in the unraveling of the triadic dynamism involved in long working hours and presenteeism when Chinese employees are increasingly confronted with challenging work situations.

Acknowledgements

In writing this chapter, the corresponding author was supported by a grant from the Ministry of Science and Technology, Taiwan, MOST103–2410-H-002–195-SS3.

References

Aronsson, G., Gustafsson, K., & Dallner, M. (2000). Sick but yet at work: An empirical study of sickness presenteeism. *Journal of Epidemiological Community Health*, 54, 502–509.

Baker-McClearn, D., Greasley, K., Dale, J., & Griffith, F. (2010). Absence management and presenteeism: The pressures on employees to attend work and the impact of attendance on performance. *Human Resource Management Journal*, 20(3), 311–328.

Bandura, A. (1986). *Social Foundations of Thought and Action: A Social Cognitive Theory*. Englewood Cliffs, NJ: Prentice-Hall, Inc.

Bandura, A. (1989). Human agency in Social Cognitive Theory. *American Psychologist*, 44(9), 1175–1184.

Bandura, A. (1993). Perceived self-efficacy in cognitive development and functioning. *Educational Psychologist*, 28(2), 117–148.

Bandura, A. (1997). *Self-Efficacy: The Exercise of Control*. New York: Freeman.

Bandura, A. (2001). Social cognitive theory: An agentic perspective. *Annual Review of Psychology*, 52(1), 1–26.

Bandura, A. (2012). On the functional properties of perceived self-efficacy revisited. *Journal of Management*, 38(1), 9–44.

Bergström, G., Bodin, L., Hagberg, J., Aronsson, G., & Josephson, M. (2009). Sickness presenteeism today, sickness absenteeism tomorrow? A prospective study on sickness presenteeism and future sickness absenteeism. *Journal of Occupational and Environmental Medicine*, 51(6), 629–638.

Bluestone, B., & Rose, S. (1998). The macroeconomics of work time. *Review of Social Economy*, 56(4), 425–441.

Burton, W. N., Morrison, A., & Wertheimer, A. I. (2003). Pharmaceuticals and worker productivity loss: A critical review of the literature. *Journal of Occupational and Environmental Medicine*, 45(6), 610–621.

Caverley, N., Cunningham, J. B., & MacGregor, J. N. (2007). Sickness presenteeism, sickness absenteeism, and health following restructuring in a public service organization. *Journal of Management Studies*, 44(2), 304–319.

Cheng, B. S., Chou, L. F., Wu, T. Y., Huang, M. P., & Farh, J. L. (2004). Paternalistic leadership and subordinate responses: Establishing a leadership model in Chinese organizations. *Asian Journal of Social Psychology*, 7, 89–117.

Claus, D. H., & Johan, H. A. (2008). Going ill to work – What personal circumstances, attitudes and work-related factors are associated with sickness presenteeism? *Social Science & Medicine*, 67(6), 956–964.

Collins, J. J., Baase, C. M., Sharda, C. E., Ozminkowski, R. J., Nicholson, S., Billotti, G. M., & Berger, M. L. (2005). The assessment of chronic health conditions on work performance, absence, and total economic impact for employers. *Journal of Occupational and Environmental Medicine*, 47, 547–557.

Cooper, C. L., & Lu, L. (2016). Presenteeism as a global phenonmenon: Unraveling the psychosocial mechanisms from the perspective of Social Cognitive Theory. *Cross Cultural and Strategic Management*, 23(2), 216–231.

Cross, G. (1990). *A Social History of Leisure since 1600*. Alberta, Canada: Venture Publishing, Inc.

Dembe, A. E., Erickson, J. B., Delbos, R. G., & Banks, S. M. (2005). The impact of overtime and long work hours on occupational injuries and illness: New evidence from the United States. *Occupational and Environmental Medicine*, 62, 588–597.

Demerouti, E., Le Blanc, P. M., Bakker, A. B., Schaufeli, W. B., & Hox, J. (2009). Present but sick: A three-wave study on job demands, presenteeism and burnout. *Career Development International*, 14(1), 50–68.

Directorate-General of Budget, Accounting and Statistics (DGBAS). (2009). *National Income of The Republic of China*. Executive Yuan, ROC.

Dow Jones. (2011). *Dow Jones Sustainability Group Index: Performance and Attributes*. Available at: www.sustainability-index.com/performance.cfm (accessed 22 February 2016).

Elstad, J. I., & Vabo, M. (2008). Job stress, sickness absence and sickness presenteeism in Nordic elderly care. *Scandinavian Journal of Public Health*, 36(5), 467–474.

Fenwick, R., & Tausig, M. (2001). Scheduling stress family and health outcomes of shift work and schedule control. *American Behavioral Scientist*, 44(7), 1179–1198.

Figart, D. M., & Golden, L. (1998). The social economics of work time: Introduction. *Review of Social Economy*, 56(4), 411–424.

Fredriksson, K., Alfredsson, L., Köster, M., Thorbjörnsson, C. B., Toomingas, A., Torgén, M., & Kilbom, A. (1999). Risk factors for neck and upper limb disorders: Results from 24 years of follow up. *Occupational and Environmental Medicine*, 56(1), 59–66.

Geertz, C. (1975). On the Nature of Anthropological Understanding: Not extraordinary empathy but readily observable symbolic forms enable the anthropologist to grasp the unarticulated concepts that inform the lives and cultures of other peoples. *American Scientist*, 63(1), 47–53.

Hwang, K. K. (1995). *Knowledge and Action: A Social Psychological Interpretation of Chinese Cultural Tradition* (in Chinese). Taipei: Psychological Publication Co.

International Institute for Management Development (IMD). (2010). *The World Competitiveness Yearbook*. Lausanne: International Institute for Management Development.

James, L. (1995). *Media, Communication, and Culture: A Global Approach*. New York: Columbia University Press.

Johns, G. (2010). Presenteeism in the workplace: A review and research agenda. *Journal of Organizational Behavior*, 31, 519–542.

Johns, G. (2011). Attendance dynamics at work: The antecedents and correlates of presenteeism, absenteeism, and productivity loss. *Journal of Occupational Health Psychology*, 16(4), 483–500.

Johns, G. (2012). Presenteeism: A short history and a cautionary tale. *Contemporary Occupational Health Psychology: Global Perspectives on Research and Practice*, 2, 204–220.

Kanai, A. (2006). Economic and employment conditions, karoshi (work to death) and the trend of studies on workaholism in Japan. In: R. J. Burke (ed.), *Research Companion to Working Time and Work Addiction*. Cheltenham, UK: Edward Elgar, 158–172.

Landers, R. M., Rebitzer, J. B., & Taylor, L. J. (1996). Rat race redux: Adverse selection in the determination of work hours in law firms. *The American Economic Review*, 86, 3229–3248.

Lévi-Strauss, C. (1955). The structural study of myth. *The Journal of American Folklore*, 68(270), 428–444.

Lin, T. T., & Cheng, B. S. (2012). Life-and work-oriented considerate behaviors of leaders in Chinese organizations: The dual dimensions of benevolent leadership. *Indigenous Psychological Research in Chinese Societies*, 37, 253–302.

Liu, C. M. (1996). Affective Bao in organizations: Some preliminary points of view. *Chinese Journal of Applied Psychology*, 5, 1–34.

Lu, L. (2003). Defining the self-other relation: The emergence of a composite self. *Indigenous Psychological Research in Chinese Societies*, 20, 139–207.

Lu, L. (2005). In pursuit of happiness: The cultural psychological study of SWB. *Chinese Journal of Psychology*, 47, 99–112.

Lu, L. (2007). The individual- and social-oriented self views: Conceptual analysis and empirical assessment. *US-China Education Review*, 4, 1–24.

Lu, L. (2008). The individual- and social-oriented Chinese bicultural self: Testing the theory. *Journal of Social Psychology*, 148, 347–374.

Lu, L. (2009). I or we: Family socialization values in a national probability sample in Taiwan. *Asian Journal of Social Psychology*, 12, 95–100.

Lu, L. (2011). Working hours and personal preference among Taiwanese employees. *International Journal of Workplace Health Management*, 4(3), 244–256.

Lu, L. (2015). The associations between the fit of desired and actual working time and work attitudes: A comparison between different social welfare regimes. *International Journal of Commerce and Strategy*, 7(1), 19–34.

Lu, L., Chang, T. T., Kao, S. F., & Cooper, C. L. (2015). Testing an integrated model of the work-family interface in Chinese employees: A longitudinal study. *Asian Journal of Social Psychology*, 18, 12–21.

Lu, L., Cooper, C., Kao, S. F., Chang, T. T., Allen, T. D., Lapierre, L. M., O'Driscoll, M. P., Poelmans, S.A.Y.,Sanchez, J. I. & Spector, P. E. (2010). Cross-cultural differences in work-to-family conflict and role satisfaction: A Taiwanese-British comparison. *Human Resource Management*, 49, 67–85.

Lu, L., Cooper, C. L., & Lin, H. Y. (2013). A cross-cultural examination of presenteeism and supervisory support. *Career Development International*, 18(5), 440–456.

Lu, L., & Gilmour, R. (2004a). Culture and conceptions of happiness: Individual oriented and social oriented SWB. *Journal of Happiness Studies*, 5(3), 269–291.

Lu, L., & Gilmour, R. (2004b). Culture, self and ways to achieve SWB: A cross-cultural analysis. *Journal of Psychology in Chinese Societies*, 5(1), 51–79.

Lu, L., Lin, H. Y., & Cooper, C. L. (2013). Unhealthy and present: Motives and consequences of the act of presenteeism among Taiwanese employees. *Journal of Occupational Health Psychology*, 18(4), 406–416.

Lu, L., Peng, S. Q., Lin, H. Y., & Cooper, C. L. (2014). Presenteeism and health over time among Chinese employees: The moderating role of self-efficacy. *Work & Stress*, 28(2), 165–178.

Lu, L., & Yang, K. S. (2005). Individual- and social-oriented views of self-actualization: Conceptual analysis and preliminary empirical exploration. *Indigenous Psychological Research in Chinese Societies*, 23, 3–69.

Lu, L., & Yang, K. S. (2006). The emergence and composition of the traditional-modern bicultural self of people in contemporary Taiwanese societies. *Asian Journal of Social Psychology*, 9, 167–175.

McCann, D. (2005). *Working Time Laws: A Global Perspective. Findings from the ILO's Conditions of Work and Employment Database*. Geneva, Switzerland: International Labour Organization.

Messenger, J. C. (2004). *Working Time and Workers' Preferences in Industrialized Countries: Finding the Balance.* Abingdon/New York: Routledge.

Nakanishi, N., Nakamura, K., Ichikawa, S., Suzuki, K., & Tatara, K. (1999). Lifestyle and the development of hypertension: A 3-year follow-up study of middle-aged Japanese male office workers. *Occupational Medicine*, 49(2), 109–114.

OECD. (1998). *Working Hours: Latest Trends and Policy Initiatives*. OECD Employment Outlook, Paris, France: OECD, 153–188.

Park, J., Yi, Y., & Kim, Y. (2010). Weekly work hours and stress complaints of workers in Korea. *American Journal of Industrial Medicine*, 53(11), 1135–1141.

Pimenta, A. M., Beunza, J. J., Bes-Rastrollo, M., Alonso, A., López, C. N., Velásquez-Meléndez, G. Martínez-González, M. A. (2009). Work hours and incidence of hypertension among Spanish University graduates: The Seguimiento Universidad de Navarra prospective cohort. *Journal of Hypertension*, 27(1), 34–40.

Porter, G. (2004). Work, work ethic, work excess. *Journal of Organizational Change Management*, 17(5), 424–439.

Redding, S. (1993). *The Spirit of Chinese Capitalism*. New York: De Gruyter.

Robertson, I., & Cooper, C. L. (2011). *Well-Being: Productivity and Happiness at Work*. Hampshire, UK: Palgrave Macmillan.

Sweetman, D., & Luthans, F. (2010). The power of positive psychology: Psychological capital and work engagement. In: A. B. Bakker & M. P. Leiter (eds.), *Work Engagement: A Handbook of Essential Theory and Research*. New York: Psychology Press, 54–68.

Turpin, R. S., Ozminkowski, R. J., Sharda, C. E., Collins, J. J., Berger, M. L., & Billotti, G. M., & Nicholson, S. (2004). Reliability and validity of the Stanford Presenteeism Scale. *Journal of Occupational and Environmental Medicine*, 46, 1123–1133.

Tzeng, C. W., & Jiang, D. Y. (2012). The relationships between employee motivation and political skill: The moderating effects of Bao. *Research in Applied Psychology*, 53, 207–212.

van der Hulst, M. (2003). Long work hours and health. *Scandinavian Journal of Work, Environment & Health*, 29(3), 171–188.

WHO. (2006). *Employment Conditions and Health Inequalities*. www.who.int/social_determinants/themes/employmentconditions/en/

Yang, K. S., & Lu, L. (2005). Social – vs. Individual -oriented self-actualizers: Conceptual analysis and empirical assessment of their psychological characteristics. *Indigenous Psychological Research in Chinese Societies*, 23, 71–143.

11

Workplace incivility

A critical review and agenda for research and practice

Ashlyn M. Patterson, Alexandra C. Chris, and
M. Gloria González-Morales[1]

Introduction

Have you ever been interrupted during a meeting? Has a coworker ever doubted your judgment on something over which you had responsibility? Although these behaviors may seem insignificant, they are examples of workplace incivility. Other examples of uncivil behaviors include: withholding information, ignoring or excluding someone, putting someone down, or addressing a coworker in unprofessional terms (Cortina, Kabat-Farr, Leskinen, Huerta, & Magley, 2013; Cortina, Magley, Williams, & Langhout, 2001; Pearson & Porath, 2009).

Workplace incivility is defined as "low-intensity deviant behavior[s], with ambiguous intent to harm the target, in violation of workplace norms for mutual respect" (Andersson & Pearson, 1999, p. 457).

Low-intensity means that incivility consists of behaviors that are of lower magnitude of force and are often appraised as frustrating, annoying, and offensive but not threatening (Cortina & Magley, 2009; Glomb, 2002). *Deviant behavior* involves behavior that violates organizational norms and threatens the wellbeing of an organization, its members, or both (Robinson & Bennett, 1995). More specifically, incivility violates organizational norms for *mutual respect*. Last, incivility is characterized by an *ambiguous intent to harm*. In other words, an employee may deliberately be uncivil with the intent to harm, or may accidentally be uncivil due to ignorance, oversight, or personality (Lim, Cortina, & Magley, 2008; Pearson, Andersson, & Porath, 2000).

Evidence suggests that uncivil behaviors do not happen infrequently. For example, 75% of 1,711 university employees reported experiencing incivility within the past year (Cortina & Magley, 2009). In a sample of 612 nurses, 67.5% reported experiencing incivility from their supervisor and 77.6% reported experiencing incivility from coworkers within the month prior to completing the survey (Laschinger, Leiter, Day, & Gilin, 2009).

Focus of the chapter and important clarifications

We conducted a systematic literature search to identify all relevant published research. We conducted searches in three databases: PsycInfo, Proquest Dissertations and Theses, and Business Source Complete. We used four key words: incivility, uncivil, civility, rude, and searched in abstracts from 1999 to October 2015. This resulted in 116 peer-reviewed journal articles that we used to guide our critical review of the field. This chapter does not intend to provide an exhaustive review as other published sources such as Schilpzand, de Pater, and Erez (2016) cover that content. In this chapter, after describing the incivility construct and the main empirical findings, we focus on a discussion of key ideas that have important implications for the emerging agenda of incivility in both research and practice.

Incivility is a relational construct that involves various organizational actors (e.g., targets, witnesses). First, targets are individuals who report that they have experienced uncivil acts by others. Second, witnesses are individuals who report that they are aware of or have observed the enactment of uncivil acts towards others. Third, victims are individuals who report that they feel victimized by these behaviors or acts (as targets or witnesses). Fourth, we use the label *enactor,* instead of perpetrator, to refer to those who are perceived as performing uncivil acts. According to the English dictionary, to perpetrate is to carry out or commit a harmful, illegal, or immoral act. Given that the intent of incivility is inherently ambiguous, we use the term *enactor* as opposed to *perpetrator,* which assumes ill intent.

Incivility: what it is and what it is not

Workplace incivility differs from and overlaps with other forms of workplace mistreatment or deviant behavior that occurs in organizations (Andersson & Pearson, 1999), such as social undermining, bullying/mobbing, abusive supervision, interpersonal conflict, and microaggression. Although all of these behaviors fall under a broad category of mistreatment, each form of behavior has distinguishing characteristics.

Differentiating incivility from its related constructs is necessary to better understand incivility's nomological network. In order to differentiate these constructs we follow Hershcovis's (2011) model of workplace aggression, which includes five variables that differentiate mistreatment variables from one another: frequency, intensity, intent, perceived invisibility, and power relationship. *Uncivil behaviors* are characterized by low intensity and ambiguous intent. Frequency or visibility does not define incivility per se and uncivil behaviors can be enacted, experienced, or witnessed by peers, subordinates, and supervisors.

Bullying is a form of high intensity, intentional, persistent, and frequent negative behavior to which an employee is repeatedly exposed (e.g., abuse, offensive statements, social exclusion, teasing; Einarsen, 2000). *Social undermining* includes intentionally harmful behaviors such as diminishing others' work-related success, negatively influencing others' reputations, and interfering with others' positive relationships at work (Duffy, Ganster, & Pagon, 2002). Whereas bullying and social undermining intentionally seek to harm a specific target (Duffy, Ganster, Shaw, Johnson, & Pagon, 2006; Hershcovis, 2011), uncivil behaviors are not necessarily committed with the intent to harm.

Interpersonal conflict is conceptualized as a source of stress in organizations that involves disagreements between employees (Spector & Jex, 1998). According to Hershcovis (2011) this construct, in theory, does not have any defining features in terms of intensity, intent, frequency, invisibility or power distance. However, its operationalization (e.g., "How often are people rude to you at work?"; "How often do other people do nasty things to you at work?") indicates that interpersonal conflict is not only comprised of disagreements but, similar to incivility, the behaviors violate norms of respect and may or may not be intentional. Unlike incivility, the intent does not have to be ambiguous.

Abusive supervision is defined as sustained enactment of hostile verbal and nonverbal behaviors by a supervisor towards subordinates (Tepper, 2000). It explicitly excludes physical acts, but includes other behaviors that are frequent (or sustained) and intentional. Additionally, this behavior requires the existence of a formal power relationship. Given these defining aspects, abusive supervision involves higher intensity and intentionality than incivility from supervisors.

Another form of mistreatment that occurs in organizations and that can be confounded with incivility is referred to as *microaggression*, a subtle form of discrimination. More specifically, microaggressions are defined as intentional or unintentional "daily verbal, behavioral or environmental indignities" (Nadal, 2008, p. 23) that express hostile attitudes towards individuals of targeted groups. Microaggression is similar to incivility as both forms of mistreatment can be unintentional and of low intensity; however, microaggression is specifically directed at oppressed and stereotyped groups based on gender, sexual orientation, ethnicity, race, etc.

In sum, intent and intensity are the defining factors of mistreatment experienced as incivility. When mistreatment is experienced as low in intensity and the intent is not clear, an individual may experience victimization through incivility. Frequency, visibility, and power relationships are not defining characteristics of incivility; however, if we take these characteristics into account, high frequency may clarify attributions of intent, high visibility can make the perception of victimization more intense, and power distance may turn an initial uncivil behavior into abusive supervision.

Antecedents of incivility

Experiencing incivility

When considering the antecedents of incivility, we discuss predictors of *experiencing* incivility and predictors of *engaging* in incivility. Currently there is limited research examining the variables that predict the experience of incivility. This may be due to the fact that exploring "target traits" may be construed as victim blaming.

Nonetheless, researchers have examined personality characteristics that are positively related to reports of experiencing incivility. Milam, Spitzmueller, and Penney (2009) found that individuals high in neuroticism reported experiencing more workplace incivility than those low in neuroticism. Given that neuroticism is characterized by worrying, nervousness, and insecurity, ambiguous events may appear more threatening to individuals high in neuroticism (Milam et al., 2009). Similar results have been found in relation to trait negative affect (Naimon, Mullins, & Osatuke, 2013).

Furthermore, research has found that individuals low in agreeableness are more likely to experience incivility (Milam et al., 2009; Naimon et al., 2013). Individuals who are low in agreeableness are often viewed as confrontational, surly, and argumentative (Graziano, Jensen-Campbell, & Hair, 1996). Similarly, Trudel and Reio (2011) found that those with a dominating management style (i.e., competitive and lacking concern for others' needs) were more likely to be targets of incivility, whereas employees with an integrating management style (i.e., collaborative) were less likely to be targets. This increased likelihood may be due to the fact that their personality style leads them to more frequently experience incivility by others.

Race and gender may also be related to the likelihood of becoming a target. In a three-study paper, Cortina et al. (2013) examined whether gender and race affected vulnerability to uncivil treatment; they found that being female was related to increased risk of experiencing incivility in a sample of government employees and a sample from the US military. In a sample of employees from a US law enforcement agency, Cortina et al. (2013) found that being a member of a minority race was related to increased risk for experiencing incivility. Moreover, an interaction effect was found in the US military sample suggesting that African American women face higher risk for uncivil treatment than African American men or Whites of either gender. According to Cortina's (2008) theory of selective incivility, the experience of incivility by minority groups may be an example of modern discrimination.

Enacting incivility

Empirical evidence suggests that dispositional differences as well as a lack of psychological resources are related to higher reports of incivility enactment. For example, research has found that trait negative affect (Reio & Ghosh, 2009), attachment anxiety (Leiter, Day, & Price, 2015), low levels of psychological capital (Roberts, Scherer, & Bowyer, 2011), and having a dominant conflict management style or a nonintegrative conflict management style (Trudel & Reio, 2011) are related to incivility enactment.

Other variables that predict enacted incivility are related to stressful working conditions, such as high levels of job demands, work overload (Gallus, Bunk, Matthews, Barnes-Farrell, & Magley, 2014; van Jaarsveld, Walker, & Skarlicki, 2010), and exhaustion (Blau & Andersson, 2005; van Jaarsveld et al., 2010). Similarly, low social exchange contexts in which employees experience low perceptions of distributive justice or low job satisfaction (Blau & Andersson, 2005) have also been related to the enactment of uncivil behaviors. In a longitudinal study, Blau (2007) examined employee responses to a potential worksite closure and consequent job loss. The findings indicated that contract violation, low distributive justice, and the grieving states of anger and low acceptance predicted enacted incivility.

Interestingly, traits that are beneficial for performance – such as having a strong obsessive passion for work (Birkeland & Nerstad, 2016), achievement orientation, and self-efficacy to resolve conflict directly (Liu, Steve Chi, Friedman, & Tsai, 2009) – have been related to the enactment of uncivil behaviors. These characteristics may align with other studies that suggest that power and organizational status contribute to workplace incivility. For example, Pearson and colleagues (Pearson et al., 2000; Pearson & Porath, 2005) found that individuals with more power have more opportunities to be uncivil and are more likely to get away with such behavior.

Contextual factors such as group norms can also facilitate the enactment of uncivil behavior (Estes & Wang, 2008). Individuals have a need to belong (Baumeister & Leary, 1995) and to be accepted by in-group members. Employees working in teams often conform to the group's norms (Cortina, 2008) in order to fulfill their desire to be accepted by other team members (in-group). Thus, if coworkers promote or model uncivil behaviors, other employees are likely to follow (Cortina, 2008).

Inherent biases resulting from cognitive and affective events have also been used to explain subtle forms of discriminatory behavior such as selective incivility. According to Cortina (2008) there are two processes that help to explain the enactment of selective incivility towards minority groups. From an affective perspective, members of the in-group are perceived with positive affective biases, whereas those in the out-group are perceived with negative feelings (Cortina, 2008). Given that minorities are more likely to be categorized as out-group members, negative affect towards the out-group may prompt employees to be uncivil towards minority groups. From a cognitive perspective, individuals often rely on stereotypes to make judgments about people around them. For example, career women and Asians are often stereotyped as having low warmth and overly high competence (Cortina, 2008). These stereotypes generate feelings of hostility and envy that lead to behaving with incivility. Both affective and cognitive factors can operate at the conscious or unconscious level; consequently, those who engage in selective incivility may or may not be aware of their biases.

Finally, values, standards, and norms at the organizational level also influence the enactment of incivility. Organizations that do not place a strong emphasis on general workplace respect or do not set standards regarding acceptable employee behavior are likely to experience higher levels of incivility (Estes & Wang, 2008). Gallus et al. (2014) found that a lack of workplace policies (e.g., "there are no company guidelines on how to treat each other" and "there is no training about how coworkers are supposed to treat each other") predicted the enactment of uncivil behavior. Moreover, Harold and Holtz (2015) suggested that in the absence of a proactive leader, workplaces may become informal and lack clear norms, which Andersson and Pearson (1999) theorized may contribute to workplace incivility. Indeed, Harold and Holtz (2015) found that passive leadership had a direct effect on enacted incivility. In fact, a recent cross-sectional study found that passive leadership had a direct effect on enacted incivility (Harold & Holtz, 2015). Therefore, factors such as organizational culture and values, management philosophy, and leadership style are related to group norms and individual uncivil behaviors.

Consequences of incivility

Given that incivility is a low-intensity phenomenon, any single act of incivility may be perceived as harmless (Caza & Cortina, 2007). However, incivility has severe consequences for individuals and for organizations. Individuals who experience incivility have reported losing time worrying about the uncivil experience (Pearson, 1999), increased negative affectivity (Ghosh, Dierkes, & Falletta, 2011; Zhou, Yan, Che, & Meier, 2015), and symptoms of burnout (Leiter, Laschinger, Day, & Gilin Oore, 2011; Leiter, Nicholson, Patterson, & Laschinger, 2012; Sliter, Jex, Wolford, & McInnerney, 2010).[2] A daily diary study found that participants had higher levels of stress on days that they experienced incivility, but that high supervisor support attenuated this relationship (Beattie & Griffin, 2014a).

Experiencing incivility is also related to work attitudes and behaviors that have negative consequences for organizations. For example, experienced incivility is related to reduced job satisfaction (Blau & Andersson, 2005; Cortina et al., 2001; Lim et al., 2008), organizational commitment (Walsh, Magley, Reeves, Davies-Schrils, Marmet, & Gallus, 2012), and increased turnover intentions (Cortina et al., 2001; Lim et al., 2008). Employees who experience incivility at work also report intentionally reducing their work effort (Pearson & Porath, 2005) and engaging in more counterproductive work behaviors (Sakurai & Jex, 2012).

The incivility spiral theory (Andersson & Pearson, 1999) suggests that individuals who are treated uncivilly will reciprocate with incivility. For example, in a daily diary study Meier and Gross (2015) found that experiencing incivility from a supervisor predicted enacted incivility towards the supervisor when the interactions occurred on the same day. This suggests that the individual enacting the uncivil behavior also experiences consequences. Other consequences of enacting incivility include being distrusted by others (Scott, Restubog, & Zagenczyk, 2013), and experiencing exclusion (Scott et al., 2013) and ostracism (Gray, Carter, & Sears, 2017).

The incivility spiral and other spreading mechanisms

One of the main problems with uncivil behaviors is that they can spread and spiral up (i.e., incivility spirals) or spill over to other parts of the organization and beyond. Pearson et al. (2000) identified several ways in which incivility can spread through an organization, most notably through a *nonescalating uncivil exchange* and an *escalating spiral*. In a nonescalating uncivil exchange, employees engage in uncivil behavior towards one another; however, the behaviors do not escalate into more intense forms of mistreatment (e.g., bullying). For example, Employee A may interrupt Employee B during a meeting, causing Employee B to in turn ignore Employee A.

Andersson and Pearson (1999) theorized that the desire to retaliate in a nonescalating spiral is driven by feelings of negative affect. In other words, experiencing incivility leads to feelings of state negative affect, which in turn triggers the desire for reciprocation. Manegold (2015) conducted a daily diary study and found that experienced incivility predicted enacted incivility and that this relationship was mediated by a desire for revenge. Additionally, Ghosh et al. (2011) examined a nonescalating exchange in mentoring relationships using a cross-sectional design. They found that negative affect experienced by mentees mediated the relationship between perceptions of mentor incivility and engagement in mentee incivility toward their mentor.

In an escalating spiral, the experience of incivility over time is theorized to lead to a tipping point whereby the uncivil behavior no longer has an ambiguous intent to harm (Andersson & Pearson, 1999). When individuals perceive incivility as a direct attack on them, they are more likely to respond with stronger acts of aggression (Pearson, Andersson, & Wegner, 2001). Andersson and Pearson (1999) theorized that the desire to reciprocate in a more aggressive manner is driven by feelings of anger (rather than negative affect); however, this proposition has yet to be empirically tested.

The *nonescalating uncivil exchange* and the *escalating spiral* are the two most common explanations for the spread of incivility; however, Pearson et al. (2000) proposed several other ways incivility could spread beyond the enactor and target. For example, *indirect displacement* occurs when witnessing an uncivil exchange between Employee A and Employee B leads Employee C to model that behavior and enact incivility towards Employee D. *Direct displacement* occurs when two employees engage in a nonescalating uncivil exchange and displace their desire to reciprocate onto additional uninvolved employees. Finally, witnessing incivility and listening to hearsay can increase the likelihood of incivility through *word-of-mouth*.

Both the indirect displacement and word-of-mouth explanations (Pearson et al., 2000) involve the role of witnesses in the spread of incivility. Experimental research suggests that witnessing incivility leads to lower engagement in helping behavior and reduced task performance (Porath & Erez, 2007, 2009). Porath and Erez (2007, 2009) proposed that these relationships are mediated by feelings of negative affect and/or disruptions in cognition. Moreover, Totterdell, Hershcovis, Niven, Reich, and Stride (2012) found that hospital staff felt significantly more emotionally drained after witnessing an unpleasant interaction compared to a pleasant one. Witnessing incivility can also affect external organizational actors; for example, Porath, MacInnis, and Folkes (2010) found that witnessing an uncivil reprimand between employees caused consumers to make negative generalizations about the organization as a whole.

The effects of incivility can also extend beyond the workplace. For example, Lim and Lee (2011) found that supervisor incivility was related to increased work-to-family conflict. In another study, Ferguson (2012) studied 190 couples and found that incivility experienced at work was negatively related to targets' marital satisfaction and their partners' marital satisfaction and was positively related to the partners' family to-work conflict. Moreover, partners' perceptions of *the stress that the employee transmits from the work domain to the family domain mediated the relations between* workplace incivility and personal life outcomes of both targets and partners (Ferguson, 2012). These studies suggest that the negative effects of incivility can extend beyond targets themselves onto family members' wellbeing.

Similarly, the negative effects of incivility on employees over time have negative implications for the organization. An uncivil work environment can reduce the effectiveness of teams because employees may be less likely to cooperate and collaborate. As incivility spreads, it can slowly seep into and become ingrained in an organization's culture. Decreased employee work effort and productivity leads to poor organizational performance and wellbeing (Pearson & Porath, 2005).

Causal direction of antecedents and outcomes

Although constructs are theorized to be antecedents or outcomes of incivility, the research conducted is often cross-sectional, making it difficult to tease apart these relationships. Especially when examining the relationship between experienced and enacted incivility, a cross-sectional design is inadequate in determining the directionality and causation of a potential spiral.

Sparse longitudinal research has examined the antecedents and outcomes of incivility using time frames that vary in length ranging from six months to four years (e.g., Birkeland & Nerstad, 2016; Blau & Andersson, 2005; Meier & Spector, 2013). Specifically examining the daily experience of incivility (e.g., diary studies) is another underutilized methodology. Meier and Spector (2013) suggest that the effects of incivility may be short-lived; thus, the use of diary studies may tap into the fluctuation more than cross-sectional or longer time-frame studies.

Experimental research in this area is also limited and consists of two main focuses: having people witness incivility (that is staged) or having people recall personal experiences of incivility. Experimental designs allow researchers to isolate the effects of incivility on outcome variables, such as task performance; however, manipulation checks are important to ensure participants noticed the incivility. In the following section we highlight the points and issues that require further research, especially longitudinal and experimental designs.

Key tensions, future research and practical implications

The subjective nature of experiencing incivility

Given the ambiguous nature of incivility, the thresholds for what a violation of norms consists of can vary among individuals. For example, Montgomery, Kane, and Vance (2004) had students view a video and rate the extent to which certain behaviors were appropriate; they found that female students, compared to males, rated more behaviors as inappropriate and uncivil. Individual and cultural factors may be related to differences regarding the meaning of "norms of respect" and their violation.

Individual factors

Varying responses to incivility can be partially explained in how people appraise, interpret, and cope with uncivil situations. For example, Beattie and Griffin (2014b) examined employees' reactions to incivility over eight days in a one-month period. They found that targets' perceived severity of an uncivil experience predicted whether or not they engaged in negative behaviors towards the instigator, negative behaviors towards others, support seeking, and forgiveness on a given day. Cortina and Magley (2009) identified five coping profiles among employees from a federal judicial circuit: support seekers, detachers, minimizers, prosocial conflict avoiders, and assertive conflict avoiders. Each profile group appraised uncivil events differently and coped in different ways (Cortina & Magley, 2009). Bunk and Magley (2013) explored patterns regarding how individuals cognitively and emotionally respond to experiencing incivility. They found that employees typically fall into one of four clusters: indifferent, angry victims, positive outlook, and emotionally resilient. Each group reported different emotional responses to incivility. For example, the indifferent group reported the lowest levels of all emotions (e.g., anger, guilt, frustration), while the emotionally resilient group reported the highest levels of guilt (Bunk & Magley, 2013). Research is still needed to identify how the appraisal of uncivil events and coping strategies are related to experiences of victimization and subsequent negative outcomes.

Contextual factors: the virtual workplace

The subjective process of experiencing incivility may be affected by the amount of information that individuals have about the intentions of the enactor. Lim and Teo (2009) defined cyber incivility as "communicative behavior exhibited in computer-mediated interactions that violate workplace norms of mutual respect" (p. 419). Behaviors related specifically to email etiquette include: making demeaning remarks about an individual through email, not replying to an email at all, ignoring a request that one has received through email, and using email for discussions that would require face-to-face dialogue. Byron (2008) theorized that compared to face-to-face incivility, cyber incivility may be more confusing to interpret because emotions are particularly difficult to accurately convey through email. Given that incivility is an ambiguous behavior, eliminating cues such as body language, pitch, tone, and rate of speech can result in cyber incivility being more difficult to interpret (Giumetti, McKibben, Hatfield, Schroeder, & Kowalski, 2012). Moreover, when an employee receives an uncivil email there is little opportunity to seek clarification or feedback.

Lim and Teo (2009) found that the experience of cyber incivility from a supervisor was negatively related to employee commitment and job satisfaction, and positively related to workplace deviance and intention to quit. Francis, Holmvall, and O'Brien (2015) also found that when employees received an uncivil email (compared to neutral email), they were more likely to respond with more incivility (in email form), especially during times of high workload. Further research on incivility in virtual work situations can help us understand the subjective interpretation process involved in experiencing incivility.

Cultural factors

The subjective nature of incivility is tightly connected to the concept of culture. In Schilpzand et al.'s (2016) review of the literature, they indicate that workplace incivility exists and has similar negative consequences worldwide.[3] However, because cultural values influence our perceptions (Markus & Kitayama, 1991; Triandis, 1995) certain behaviors may be considered uncivil in one culture but not in another. For example, being ignored by a supervisor may be less uncivil in a culture where power distance is high than in a culture where power distance is low (Schilpzand et al., 2016). In high power–distance cultures unequal distribution of power is the norm; consequently, being ignored by someone of higher power may be considered within the boundaries of norms of respect.

There has been some research examining the role of cultural orientation in predicting the enactment of incivility as well as the experiences of incivility. For example, Liu et al. (2009) found that people with a high collectivism orientation were less likely to be uncivil than individuals with a low collectivism orientation. They also found that a collectivist orientation mitigates the effects of individual-level factors (direct conflict self efficacy and individual achievement orientation) on the enactment of incivility. Furthermore, in a study examining the outcomes of incivility, Welbourne, Gangadharan, and Sariol (2015) found that the effect of experienced incivility on burnout was weaker among employees with strong horizontal collectivist values (i.e., values emphasizing sociability and warm interpersonal relations) than among employees with strong horizontal individualist values (i.e., values emphasizing self-reliance). Further research examining how cultural orientation relates to incivility is needed.

The measurement of incivility

Brief summary of existing measures

The majority of research examining the experience of incivility has utilized the Workplace Incivility Scale (WIS; Cortina et al., 2001), a seven-item scale that asks participants to indicate the frequency with which they have experienced different discrete uncivil behaviors from their supervisors or coworkers during the past five years (e.g., have you been in a situation where any of your supervisors or coworkers: made demeaning or derogatory remarks to you? Ignored or excluded you from professional camaraderie?). Similar to the WIS, the Uncivil Workplace Behavior questionnaire (Martin & Hine, 2005) is comprised of 20 items with frequency response scales related to hostility, privacy invasion, exclusionary behavior, and gossiping. Leiter, Day, and Laschinger's (2013) Straightforward Incivility Scale consists of five general uncivil behaviors (e.g., ignored, excluded, spoken rudely) to be responded to on a frequency scale. Other researchers have developed their own questionnaires or adapted other more overt mistreatment scales such as the Interpersonal Conflict at Work scale (Spector & Jex, 1998), the Leymann Inventory of Psychological Terror (Leymann, 1990), and the Workplace Aggression Research Questionnaire (Neuman & Keashly, 2002).

In order to measure enacted incivility, Blau and Andersson (2005) used the content from the WIS (Cortina et al., 2001) but flipped the perspective: respondents report how often they have exhibited seven uncivil behaviors to someone (e.g., coworker, other employee, supervisor) at work in the past year. Similarly, the Straightforward Incivility Scale (Leiter et al., 2013) has also been validated as a measure of enacted incivility. Researchers have also developed measures to assess customer related incivility (Customer Incivility Scale by Burnfield, Clark, Devendorf, & Jex, 2004; van Jaarsveld et al., 2010).

For a detailed review of the instruments developed to measure incivility, we refer the reader to Schilpzand et al. (2016). In the present chapter we focus on describing the limitations of extant measurement approaches and suggest opportunities for future research and practical applications.

Discrete behaviors as measures

First, current incivility measures are based on discrete "rude" behaviors. This is potentially problematic because laundry lists of behaviors will never be exhaustive enough to capture the full breadth of incivility. Cortina et al.'s (2001) scale includes seven specific uncivil behaviors, and even though Cortina et al. (2013) updated the WIS to include five additional items in order to assess the construct domain more fully, it is always possible that other specific uncivil behaviors are not being captured. In addition, it is not clear if commission (putting down others or being condescending) and omission behaviors (ignoring or excluding someone) are equivalent.

Moreover, not all items apply to all enactors or targets. For example, ignoring or excluding someone from professional camaraderie is not applicable when measuring instigated incivility towards patients or service recipients. To address this limitation, specific study measures are created (e.g., van Jaarsveld et al., 2010) but the resulting wide variety of instruments makes it difficult to interpret and analyze incivility scholarship as a whole (Schilpzand et al., 2016).

One of the defining features of incivility is that it violates workplace norms for mutual respect. In terms of organizational context, addressing someone in unprofessional terms may not be considered rude in workplaces with relaxed norms about interpersonal treatment. Also, existing incivility scales have been developed and validated in a specific cultural context: Western and Anglo-Saxon countries. Blau and Andersson's (2005) and Cortina et al.'s (2001) measures were validated in the United States, Martin and Hine's (2005) in Australia, and Leiter et al.'s (2013) in Canada. Because the norms for appropriate behavior vary, not only from one organization to another, but also from one culture to another, it is essential to ensure that the behavioral items used to assess incivility are indeed considered uncivil or rude in each specific culture or organization. Again this approach would lead to the proliferation of country, culture, or organization specific nonequivalent measures.

In fact, the problems described earlier are conceptual limitations derived from the method-ological characteristics of formative measurement. As discussed by Hershcovis and Reich (2013), most instruments that operationalize different workplace mistreatment constructs using forma-tive measures, instead of reflective measures, involve aggregating responses to different discrete behaviors into one average score. In theory, formative measures should "form" and cause varia-tion in the construct or the latent variable. Formative measures are typically used for constructs made up of specific component variables, such as socioeconomic status (SES). For example, if SES is defined in terms of occupation, education, and income (Hauser & Goldberger, 1971; Marsden, 1982), SES will increase when an individual completes university, even if occupation and income remain the same. Changes in the indicators cause changes in the construct, whereas changes in the construct do not cause changes in all of the indicators. Therefore, an increase in SES does not necessarily imply a simultaneous change in all the indicators. In contrast to formative measures, reflective measures represent reflections, or manifestations of a construct (Fornell & Bookstein, 1982), meaning that variation in the construct causes variation in all of the measurement items (Bollen, 1989). Reflective measures consist of items that are highly correlated and interchange-able (Edwards, 2011).

The most commonly used incivility scales are formative in nature because they are made up of distinct uncivil behaviors that are not necessarily correlated. Variation in the latent variable, incivility, does not necessarily imply variation in all of the items because the items are not neces-sarily related to one another. If an individual reports being put down by others, that individual will not necessarily report that he or she has been ignored by others. In contrast, in a reflective scale, a high score on one item should imply a high score on the other items.

Given that incivility scales are formative in nature, it is questionable whether an average score is an accurate representation of the amount of incivility experienced/enacted. When items are aggregated into an index score, it is assumed that the items are perceived as equal in severity. However, there is no evidence to suggest that making demeaning, rude, or derogatory remarks is psychologically equivalent to addressing someone in unprofessional terms. A high score on one item may not be equivalent to a high score on another item. For example, suppose participants respond to the WIS on a Likert scale from 0 (*never*) to 4 (*many times*). A participant who responds to six incivility items with a 0 (*never*) and one incivility item with a 4 (*many times*) would receive an average score of .57 out of a possible 4. This suggests that the participant is experiencing low levels of incivility when in reality he or she has experienced very high levels of one form of uncivil behavior.

Therefore, averaging frequency responses of context-dependent discrete behaviors does not perfectly capture the magnitude of incivility. Given that incivility is conceptually defined as a behavior that violates norms of respect, we should generate reflective measurement approaches that capture the experience or enactment of disrespectful behavior (defined generally as violation of contextual norms) that may be interpreted as potentially harmful, have high internal consis-tency, and are not dependent on the type of actor, organizational context, or culture.

Targets and enactors

Researchers typically assess incivility either without differentiating between enactors or targets, or by differentiating them in measurement but collapsing them in the analyses (e.g., Blau & Anders-son, 2005; Harold & Holtz, 2015; Liu et al., 2009; Nicholson & Griffin, 2015; Roberts et al., 2011; Sayers, Sears, Kelly, & Harbke, 2011; Taylor & Kluemper, 2012). This is problematic because the effect sizes of the correlates of incivility may vary depending on who instigates or experiences the incivility. For example, being put down by a supervisor may have greater consequences for wellbeing than being put down by a coworker. Additionally, what causes people to treat a coworker uncivilly may be different from what causes people to be uncivil towards a supervisor. That being said, there are studies in which specific targets/enactors are differentiated (e.g., Ghosh et al., 2011; Kern & Grandey, 2009; Leiter et al., 2011; Lim & Lee, 2011; Meier & Gross, 2015; Meier & Semmer, 2013; Reio, 2011; Sakurai & Jex, 2012; Sliter et al., 2010; van Jaarsveld et al., 2010; Walker, van Jaarsveld, & Skarlicki, 2014).

Following Hershcovis's model (2011) described earlier, we can differentiate incivility from other aggression constructs by examining intent and power distance, two factors that help characterize the mistreatment behavior or the victimizing experience. By using experimental, longitudinal, or diary-based methodologies, researchers can study factors that predict the reciprocal interactions between actors as a function of intent and power distance. For example, studying intent of supervisor-enacted behaviors would clarify how supervisors' actions become less ambiguous and how an initial uncivil experience morphs into abusive supervision. Studying a similar phenomenon between coworkers, however, may yield very different results. Given the advantages of this approach, future research should be methodologically designed to better differentiate targets and enactors.

Multilevel approaches to incivility

Organizations are naturally multilevel systems (e.g., individual, teams, organization) and research should reflect this. Constructs at higher levels (e.g., climate) can have important effects on how individuals choose to behave, perform, and engage with one another day-to-day in a top-down process (Kozlowski & Klein, 2000). In contrast, constructs at lower levels (e.g., individual behaviors of employees) can converge over time and manifest as group or team phenomena in a bottom-up process. However, the majority of measurement and research on incivility has occurred at the individual level, assessing individual-level predictors (e.g., age, gender, personality) and outcomes (e.g., job satisfaction, organizational commitment, burnout) of incivility.

Although not common, exploring the effects of incivility is possible at other organizational levels. For example, Lim et al. (2008) argued that incivility is a "type of work stressor that can be experienced at a personal level (being a direct target) as well as a characteristic of the work environment that can manifest at the group level" (p. 96).

Griffin (2010) was also interested in a group-level measure of incivility. She defined *environmental incivility* as the mean individual experience of incivility within an organization; both within-organization reliability and between-organization differences were found, justifying the aggregation of individual experienced incivility into a measure of environmental incivility. Using multilevel analysis, data showed environmental incivility significantly predicted the extent to which employees intend to remain in the organization, *over and above* the effect of individual experienced incivility (Griffin, 2010). The effect can be partially attributed to the fact that the presence of a shared stressor (i.e., organizational incivility) increases the likelihood that employees witness or hear about incivility from other employees, causing an "empathic crossover of attitudes, emotions, and behaviors" (Griffin, 2010, p. 311). Thus, experiencing incivility and having a shared stressor of environmental incivility had an impact on employees' intent to remain in their organization.

Future research should continue to explore how incivility can be measured at higher levels of analysis, using specific composition models to test the theoretical mechanisms through which this construct emerges at different organizational levels (i.e., team, department, branch) and how top-down or bottom-up processes work.

Practical approaches at the organizational level

The multilevel perspective is particularly important when we consider practical approaches to address incivility in the workplace. Given the interpersonal nature of the phenomenon, it is appropriate to consider team-level interventions. For example, within the health care sector, Osatuke, Moore, Ward, Dyrenforth, and Belton (2009) developed an intervention called Civility, Respect, and Engagement in the Workforce (CREW). The intervention is aimed at workgroups and involves weekly discussions led by a facilitator and supported by an educational tool kit. The trained facilitator leads the group in the process of identifying their strengths and weaknesses related to civility. CREW is designed to be customizable, so depending on a group's strengths and weaknesses, specific discussion around civility varies greatly (Osatuke et al., 2009). Core themes, such as defining civility, creating clear communication, and establishing ground rules for civility, are present in all groups (Leiter et al., 2011; Osatuke et al., 2009).

When the six-month CREW intervention was implemented at various Veterans Health Administration facilities, it was shown to improve employee civility ratings from preintervention to postintervention (Osatuke et al., 2009). Among a sample of Canadian health care workers, the CREW intervention was also effective in reducing incivility, burnout, and absences, and increasing civility and trust in management among intervention participants (Leiter et al., 2011; Leiter, Day, Gilin Oore, & Laschinger, 2012).

Other than the CREW intervention, practical suggestions and case studies aimed at reducing workplace incivility have yet to be empirically tested. More evidence-based applications of the research are still needed to determine the best methods for effectively reducing incivility in the workplace. A practical and central characteristic of the CREW intervention is that the procedure is based on flipping a negatively framed problem, incivility, to a positively framed solution, civility. The following section discusses the construct of civility and proposes the integration of both civility and incivility in future research and practice.

Workplace civility

In their seminal paper, Andersson and Pearson (1999) defined workplace *civility* as "behavior involving politeness and regard for others in the workplace, within workplace norms for respect" (p. 454). The majority of research published since 1999, however, has focused on incivility rather than civility. The rise in positive psychology and the need for organizations to promote the positive (i.e., civility) rather than reduce the negative (i.e., incivility) may help to explain the recent increase in workplace civility research.

What is the relationship between workplace incivility and civility? Initial research suggests these two constructs are related yet independent. Leiter et al. (2012) used the Job Demands–Resources model (Demerouti, Bakker, Nachreiner, & Schaufeli, 2001) to explain how workplace incivility represents a workplace demand while workplace civility represents a workplace resource. In support of their model, they found that supervisor civility was related to professional efficacy and work engagement; in contrast, supervisor incivility was related to burnout. Leiter et al. (2011) also found moderate negative correlations between civility and incivility.

As mentioned earlier, this positive take on (in)civility allows organizations to frame the "problem" in a positive and constructive way. For example, in 2013, the Mental Health Commission of Canada launched a National Standard for Psychological Health and Safety in the Workplace. "Civility and Respect" is one of the 13 factors identified as determinants of psychological health and safety. According to the guide, in order to promote civility and respect at work, employers should (1) create and communicate a policy declaring the commitment of the organization to ensure a respectful and civil work environment, and (2) educate staff and leaders about expectations regarding civil behavior, and train them to model respectful behavior and to manage conflict.

But does it pay to be civil? Using Social Network Analysis, Porath, Gerbasi, and Schorch (2015) examined the effects of civility on advice, leadership, and performance. They found that employees who perceived a coworker to be "civil" were more likely to view that coworker as a leader and seek out advice from him or her. Porath et al. (2015) also found that civil employees were perceived as more competent, warmer, and possessing more leadership qualities compared to their uncivil or even neutral counterparts. In turn, all of these positive benefits of civility (e.g., leadership qualities, competence) are associated with increased performance for the civil employee (Porath et al., 2015).

Civility has also been studied as a group-level construct related to norms. Walsh et al. (2012) found that positive civility norms were related to increased job satisfaction, supervisor satisfaction, coworker satisfaction, and affective commitment. McGonagle, Walsh, Kath, and Morrow (2014) also found that positive civility norms encourage respectful behaviors, promote helping, and facilitate communication within workgroups. Future research should continue to explore the emergence and maintenance of civil workplace climates and how civility norms are related to individual-level experiences of civility, incivility, and their outcomes.

Moving forward, it is important to further explore the civility–incivility link. For example, what are the implications of a workplace that is characterized by both civility and incivility? As workplace civility continues to emerge as a construct, it is also important to connect it to other similar constructs. For example, how is workplace civility related to perceptions of respect, interpersonal justice, perceived coworker support, or organizational citizenship behaviors? Examining these relationships is important in determining what value workplace civility adds to the academic literature on positive organizational behavior.

In terms of practical approaches, elucidating these relationships would inform how we may obtain desired or undesired effects on one aspect if we tackle or ignore a related issue. For example, if civility and coworker support are closely related, it would make sense to first address basic issues related to lack of coworker support before we can obtain changes in the development of civility norms and behaviors.

Reflections on the purpose of enacting incivility and theoretical perspectives

Given the high prevalence rates of experienced incivility, there is a need to acknowledge that most employees engage in behaviors that can be experienced by others as uncivil. Therefore, one of the unanswered questions is why individuals behave in rude or uncivil ways towards others. What is the purpose of incivility? We argue that a diverse set of purposes makes the phenomenon of enactment of incivility qualitatively unique. As a result, different models and theories may apply depending on the purpose or utility of incivility. In turn, researchers need to carefully select the theories they use and practitioners should think critically about the best initiatives to address incivility.

Pressure to conform

Incivility is a low-intensity and ambiguous phenomenon and can be used to pressure group members to behave in certain ways or to conform to group norms. For example, an individual (Person A) may ignore or avoid interacting with a coworker (Person B) because in the past

Person B took credit for Person A's work (this Person is an "idea thief"). Ignoring and avoiding someone at work is considered uncivil; however, such uncivil behavior may be a punishing reaction towards a damaging behavior (e.g., stealing someone's idea) that deviates from the group's norms around cooperation and performance. The uncivil behavior of ignoring pressures the idea thief (Person B) to conform to group norms of cooperation.

Studying incivility in terms of norm-conformity pressure can open the research space to the consideration of how different types of norms make incivility and civility more or less likely. For example, conflict management norms that prescribe the avoidance of direct confrontation may encourage the use of ambiguous and subtle nonconfrontational behaviors that could be labeled as passive-aggressive incivility. These passive-aggressive uncivil behaviors may not be seen as uncivil by the group because they adhere to the prescribed conflict management norms; however, they can be experienced by the target as uncivil because they are potentially disruptive in terms of norms of mutual respect. In terms of research, this means that the study of group norms – not only around respect, but also around interpersonal relationships – can help us understand the mechanisms explaining the enactment and experience of incivility.

In terms of practical applications, recommendations that are limited to the creation of respect norms are incomplete and require a more comprehensive analysis, with a focus on group norms and processes such as communication or leadership. For example, Gedro and Wang (2013) implemented a short civility-training program at a college in the United States. Their training program included educating employees about the language and framework of incivility, bullying, and related terms, discussing how uncivil behaviors can be conceptualized subjectively and individually, and applying this knowledge to case studies. They reported that after completion of training, employees were better able to communicate their concerns around incivility at work; however, this was never empirically tested (Gedro & Wang, 2013).

Management of resources

Interpersonal relationships in the workplace are extremely complex, and the enactment and experience of incivility has been studied in a very simplistic way, assuming that incivility is only "perpetrated" by "bad" people in the workplace. Future research should examine how the enactment of incivility is different from behaving in a more neutral manner towards coworkers that individuals do not like or trust. For example, is it uncivil if an individual fails to invite a coworker to lunch (i.e., nonwork time) if he or she does not like the coworker? From a normative perspective, it is important to question if this is a violation of norms of respect, or if it is related to other types of norms such as organizational citizenship expectations. From a work stress and recovery perspective, this behavior can be conceptualized as a protective behavior for mental health in which lunch is seen as an opportunity to replenish resources and recover before returning to work. If that is the case, is avoiding someone at lunch an intentionally ambiguous harmful act?

Research indicates that lack of resources, as well as high levels of stress and demands, are predictors of uncivil enactment. Therefore it would make sense to use stress models, instead of harassment or aggression models that tend to demonize the enactor, to study incivility in contexts of high demands and low resources. In practice, this implies the need to address the source of stress and lack of resources instead of focusing on creating strong policies and procedures about uncivil behavior.

Subtle discrimination

Finally, people may be uncivil in order to enact their prejudiced attitudes towards minorities. In the current cultural context, overt sexism or racism have evolved into selective incivility in order to bypass the modern norms against explicit racism or sexism. Researchers should study how selective incivility is different from nonselective incivility and other subtle and ambiguous discriminatory behaviors. In this case, theoretical approaches based on stress theories would not be as useful as extant models of workplace discrimination, implicit racism/sexism and workplace aggression or mistreatment.

In terms of practical applications, strong policies and procedures around incivility and other forms of mistreatment may be one of the necessary initiatives to address this situation. For example, Bandow and Hunter (2008) summarized advice from two managers at large corporate US organizations and an attorney in the US military. They suggested that policies around uncivil behavior should define uncivil behavior, describe expected behavior, identify complaint procedures, include options for remedies, and outline consequences for retaliation. In addition, organizations need to take into consideration laws to ensure legality and enforceability (Bandow & Hunter, 2008).

Based on this discussion of "purposes," we propose that a careful analysis and assessment of the situation, the context, and the actors is essential for researchers to advance our knowledge about incivility and for practitioners to propose evidence-based approaches that align with the needs of the organization.

Summary and conclusion

After more than 15 years of research on workplace incivility, we have a reasonably clear picture of its definition, prevalence, consequences, and predictors. In addition, we have come to understand that it is a subjective phenomenon that involves different actors, contextual information, and higher-level constructs such as groups norms or organizational climate. In order to advance our understanding of incivility, this chapter highlights several points of tension and opportunities to explore more complex and comprehensive questions.

First, there is a need for further development of measurement instruments (i.e., reflective measurement) that capture the subjectivity (i.e., contextual and cultural factors) and complexity of the phenomenon (i.e., the role of different actors). Second, research and practice approaches should take into account the natural multilevel structure of organizations and the normative processes that take place within each level. Third, a complete picture of incivility can be provided only if we understand its flip side: civility and respect in the workplace.

Finally, the theoretical models used to study the incivility-civility phenomenon and to design organizational initiatives to address the issue should be guided by a more complex understanding of the purpose and utility of "uncivil" behaviors. Depending on the background of the scholar or practitioner, incivility is described, studied, and addressed using different theoretical models (e.g., discrimination models, mistreatment models, stress models). However, a careful analysis of the motives and functions of the interpersonal behaviors of interest will help scholars and practitioners decide the theoretical model that best fits the phenomenon and guide research questions, methodological designs, and intervention approaches.

Notes

1 These authors contributed equally to this work.
2 For a more detailed review, please see Leiter and Patterson (2014).
3 The reader can refer to this source for an extensive list of countries and samples in which incivility has been studied: Schilpzand et al. (2016).

References

Andersson, L. M., & Pearson, C. M. (1999). Tit for tat? The spiraling effect of incivility in the workplace. *Academy of Management Review*, 24(3), 452–471.

Bandow, D., & Hunter, D. (2008). Developing policies about uncivil workplace behavior. *Business Communication Quarterly*, 71(1), 103–106.

Baumeister, R. F., & Leary, M. R. (1995). The need to belong: Desire for interpersonal attachments as a fundamental human motivation. *Psychological Bulletin*, 117(3), 497–529.

Beattie, L., & Griffin, B. (2014a). Day-level fluctuations in stress and engagement in response to workplace incivility: A diary study. *Work & Stress*, 28(2), 124–142.

Beattie, L., & Griffin, B. (2014b). Accounting for within-person differences in how people respond to daily incivility at work. *Journal of Occupational and Organizational Psychology*, 87(3), 625–644.

Birkeland, I. K., & Nerstad, C. (2016). Incivility is (not) the very essence of love: Passion for work and incivility instigation. *Journal of Occupational Health Psychology*, 21(1), 1–14.

Blau, G. (2007). Partially testing a process model for understanding victim responses to an anticipated work-site closure. *Journal of Vocational Behavior*, 71(3), 401–428.

Blau, G., & Andersson, L. (2005). Testing a measure of instigated workplace incivility. *Journal of Occupational and Organizational Psychology*, 78(4), 595–614.

Bollen, K. A. (1989). *Structural Equations with Latent Variables*. Oxford: John Wiley & Sons.

Bunk, J. A., & Magley, V. J. (2013). The role of appraisals and emotions in understanding experiences of workplace incivility. *Journal of Occupational Health Psychology*, 18(1), 87–105.

Burnfield, J. L., Clark, O. L., Devendorf, S. A., & Jex, S. M. (2004). *Understanding Workplace Incivility: Scale Development and Validation*. 19th Annual Conference of the Society for Industrial and Organizational Psychology, Chicago.

Byron, K. (2008). Carrying too heavy a load? The communication and miscommunication of emotion by email. *Academy of Management Review*, 33(2), 309–327.

Caza, B. B., & Cortina, L. M. (2007). From insult to injury: Explaining the impact of incivility. *Basic and Applied Social Psychology*, 29(4), 335–350.

Cortina, L. M. (2008). Unseen injustice: Incivility as modern discrimination in organizations. *Academy of Management Review*, 33(1), 55–75.

Cortina, L. M., Kabat-Farr, D., Leskinen, E. A., Huerta, M., & Magley, V. J. (2013). Selective incivility as modern discrimination in organizations evidence and impact. *Journal of Management*, 39(6), 1579–1605.

Cortina, L. M., & Magley, V. J. (2009). Patterns and profiles of response to incivility in the workplace. *Journal of Occupational Health Psychology*, 14(3), 272–288.

Cortina, L. M., Magley, V. J., Williams, J. H., & Langhout, R. D. (2001). Incivility in the workplace: Incidence and impact. *Journal of Occupational Health Psychology*, 6(1), 64–80.

Demerouti, E., Bakker, A. B., Nachreiner, F., & Schaufeli, W. B. (2001). The Job Demands–Resources model of burnout. *Journal of Applied Psychology*, 86(3), 499–512.

Duffy, M. K., Ganster, D. C., & Pagon, M. (2002). Social undermining in the workplace. *Academy of Management Journal*, 45(2), 331–351.

Duffy, M. K., Ganster, D. C., Shaw, J. D., Johnson, J. L., & Pagon, M. (2006). The social context of undermining behavior at work. *Organizational Behavior and Human Decision Processes*, 101(1), 105–126.

Edwards, J. R. (2011). The fallacy of formative measurement. *Organizational Research Methods*, 14(2), 370–388.

Einarsen, S. (2000). Harassment and bullying at work: A review of the Scandinavian approach. *Aggression and Violent Behavior*, 5(4), 379–401.

Estes, B., & Wang, J. (2008). Workplace incivility: Impacts on individual and organizational performance. *Human Resource Development Review*, 7(2), 216–240.

Ferguson, M. (2012). You cannot leave it at the office: Spillover and crossover of coworker incivility. *Journal of Organizational Behavior*, 33(4), 571–588.

Fornell, C., & Bookstein, F. L. (1982). Two structural equation models: LISREL and PLS applied to consumer exit-voice theory. *Journal of Marketing Research*, 19(4), 440–452.

Francis, L., Holmvall, C. M., & O'Brien, L. E. (2015). The influence of workload and civility of treatment on the perpetration of email incivility. *Computers in Human Behavior*, 46, 191–201.

Gallus, J. A., Bunk, J. A., Matthews, R. A., Barnes-Farrell, J. L., & Magley, V. J. (2014). An eye for an eye? Exploring the relationship between workplace incivility experiences and perpetration. *Journal of Occupational Health Psychology*, 19(2), 143–154.

Gedro, J., & Wang, J. (2013). Creating civil and respectful organizations through the scholar-practitioner bridge. *Advances in Developing Human Resources*, 15(3), 284–295.

Ghosh, R., Dierkes, S., & Falletta, S. (2011). Incivility spiral in mentoring relationships: Reconceptualizing negative mentoring as deviant workplace behavior. *Advances in Developing Human Resources*, 13(1), 22–39.

Giumetti, G. W., McKibben, E. S., Hatfield, A. L., Schroeder, A. N., & Kowalski, R. M. (2012). Cyber incivility@ work: The new age of interpersonal deviance. *Cyberpsychology, Behavior, and Social Networking*, 15(3), 148–154.

Glomb, T. M. (2002). Workplace anger and aggression: Informing conceptual models with data from specific encounters. *Journal of Occupational Health Psychology*, 7(1), 20–36.

Gray, C. J., Carter, N. T., & Sears, K. L. (2017). The UWBQ-I: An adaption and validation of a measure of instigated incivility. *Journal of Business and Psychology*, 32(1), 21–39.

Graziano, W. G., Jensen-Campbell, L. A., & Hair, E. C. (1996). Perceiving interpersonal conflict and reacting to it: The case for agreeableness. *Journal of Personality and Social Psychology*, 70(4), 820–835.

Griffin, B. (2010). Multilevel relationships between organizational-level incivility, justice and intention to stay. *Work & Stress*, 24(4), 309–323.

Harold, C. M., & Holtz, B. C. (2015). The effects of passive leadership on workplace incivility. *Journal of Organizational Behavior*, 36(1), 16–38.

Hauser, R. M., & Goldberger, A. S. (1971). The treatment of unobservable variables in path analysis. *Sociological Methodology*, 3(1), 81–117.

Hershcovis, M. S. (2011). "Incivility, social undermining, bullying. . . oh my!": A call to reconcile constructs within workplace aggression research. *Journal of Organizational Behavior*, 32(3), 499–519.

Hershcovis, M. S., & Reich, T. C. (2013). Integrating workplace aggression research: Relational, contextual, and method considerations. *Journal of Organizational Behavior*, 34(S1), S26–S42.

Kern, J. H., & Grandey, A. A. (2009). Customer incivility as a social stressor: The role of race and racial identity for service employees. *Journal of Occupational Health Psychology*, 14(1), 46–57.

Kozlowski, S. W., & Klein, K. J. (2000). A multilevel approach to theory and research in organizations: Contextual, temporal, and emergent processes. In: K. J. Klein & S. W. J. Kozlowski (eds.), *Multilevel Theory, Research, and Methods in Organizations: Foundations, Extensions and New Directions*. San Francisco: Jossey-Bass Inc., 3–90.

Laschinger, H. K. S., Leiter, M., Day, A., & Gilin, D. (2009). Workplace empowerment, incivility, and burnout: Impact on staff nurse recruitment and retention outcomes. *Journal of Nursing Management*, 17(3), 302–311.

Leiter, M. P., Day, A., Gilin Oore, D., & Laschinger, H. K. S. (2012). Getting better and staying better: Assessing civility, incivility, distress, and job attitudes one year after a civility intervention. *Journal of Occupational Health Psychology*, 17(4), 425–434.

Leiter, M. P., Day, A., & Laschinger, H. K. S. (May 2013). *Validating a Measure of Incivility at Work: How Trust Moderates the Relationship of Received to Instigated Incivility*. M. P. Leiter, Chair, Links between experienced and instigated mistreatment in health care work. Symposium presented at 16th Congress of the European Association of Work and Organizational Psychology, Münster, Germany.

Leiter, M. P., Day, A., & Price, L. (2015). Attachment styles at work: Measurement, collegial relationships, and burnout. *Burnout Research*, 2(1), 25–35.

Leiter, M. P., Laschinger, H. K. S., Day, A., & Gilin Oore, D. (2011). The impact of civility interventions on employee social behavior, distress, and attitudes. *Journal of Applied Psychology*, 96(6), 1258–1274.

Leiter, M. P., Nicholson, R., Patterson, A. M., & Laschinger, H. K. S. (2012). Workplace relationships as demands and resources: A model of burnout and work engagement. *Ciencia & Trabajo Journal*, 13, 143–151.

Leiter, M. P., & Patterson, A. M. (2014). Respectful workplaces. In: A. Day, E. K. Kelloway, & J. J. Hurrell Jr. (eds.), *Workplace Well-Being: How to Build Psychologically Healthy Workplaces*. West Sussex, UK: Wiley-Blackwell, 205–225.

Leymann, H. (1990). Mobbing and psychological terror at workplaces. *Violence and Victims*, 5(2), 119–126.

Lim, S., Cortina, L. M., & Magley, V. J. (2008). Personal and workgroup incivility: Impact on work and health outcomes. *Journal of Applied Psychology*, 93(1), 95–107.

Lim, S., & Lee, A. (2011). Work and nonwork outcomes of workplace incivility: Does family support help? *Journal of Occupational Health Psychology*, 16(1), 95–111.

Lim, V. K., & Teo, T. S. (2009). Mind your E-manners: Impact of cyber incivility on employees' work attitude and behavior. *Information & Management*, 46(8), 419–425.

Liu, W., Steve Chi, S. C., Friedman, R., & Tsai, M. H. (2009). Explaining incivility in the workplace: The effects of personality and culture. *Negotiation and Conflict Management Research*, 2(2), 164–184.

Manegold, J. G. (2015). Negative social exchange among coworkers: Examining a multilevel process model of incivility. *Academy of Management Annual Meeting Proceedings*, 1, 14916.

Markus, H. R., & Kitayama, S. (1991). Culture and the self: Implications for cognition, emotion, and motivation. *Psychological Review*, 98(2), 224–253.

Marsden, P. V. (1982). A note on block variables in multiequation models. *Social Science Research*, 11(2), 127–140.

Martin, R. J., & Hine, D. W. (2005). Development and validation of the uncivil workplace behavior questionnaire. *Journal of Occupational Health Psychology*, 10(4), 477–490.

McGonagle, A. K., Walsh, B. M., Kath, L. M., & Morrow, S. L. (2014). Civility norms, safety climate, and safety outcomes: A preliminary investigation. *Journal of Occupational Health Psychology*, 19(4), 437–452.

Meier, L. L., & Gross, S. (2015). Episodes of incivility between subordinates and supervisors: Examining the role of self-control and time with an interaction-record diary study. *Journal of Organizational Behavior*, 36(8), 1096–1113.

Meier, L. L., & Semmer, N. K. (2013). Lack of reciprocity, narcissism, anger, and instigated workplace incivility: A moderated mediation model. *European Journal of Work and Organizational Psychology*, 22(4), 461–475.

Meier, L. L., & Spector, P. E. (2013). Reciprocal effects of work stressors and counterproductive work behavior: A five-wave longitudinal study. *Journal of Applied Psychology*, 98(3), 529–539.

Milam, A. C., Spitzmueller, C., & Penney, L. M. (2009). Investigating individual differences among targets of workplace incivility. *Journal of Occupational Health Psychology*, 14(1), 58–69.

Montgomery, K., Kane, K., & Vance, C. M. (2004). Accounting for differences in norms of respect: A study of assessments of incivility through the lenses of race and gender. *Group & Organization Management*, 29(2), 248–268.

Nadal, K. L. (2008). Preventing racial, ethnic, gender, sexual minority, disability, and religious microaggressions: Recommendations for promoting positive mental health. *Prevention in Counseling Psychology: Theory, Research, Practice and Training*, 2(1), 22–27.

Naimon, E. C., Mullins, M. E., & Osatuke, K. (2013). The effects of personality and spirituality on workplace incivility perceptions. *Journal of Management, Spirituality & Religion*, 10(1), 91–110.

Neuman, J. H., & Keashly, L. (2002). *Workplace Aggression Research Questionnaire (WAR-Q)*. Unpublished manuscript.

Nicholson, T., & Griffin, B. (2015). Here today but not gone tomorrow: Incivility affects after-work and next-day recovery. *Journal of Occupational Health Psychology*, 20(2), 218–225.

Osatuke, K., Moore, S. C., Ward, C., Dyrenforth, S. R., & Belton, L. (2009). Civility, Respect, Engagement in the Workforce (CREW): Nationwide organization development intervention at veterans health administration. *The Journal of Applied Behavioral Science*, 45(3), 384–410.

Pearson, C. M. (1999). Rude managers make for bad business. *Workforce*, 78(3), 18.

Pearson, C. M., Andersson, L. M., & Porath, C. L. (2000). Assessing and attacking workplace incivility. *Organizational Dynamics*, 29(2), 123–137.

Pearson, C. M., Andersson, L. M., & Wegner, J. W. (2001). When workers flout convention: A study of workplace incivility. *Human Relations*, 54(11), 1387–1419.

Pearson, C. M., & Porath, C. L. (2005). On the nature, consequences and remedies of workplace incivility: No time for "nice"? Think again. *The Academy of Management Executive*, 19(1), 7–18.

Pearson, C. M., & Porath, C. L. (2009). *The Cost of Bad Behavior: How Incivility Is Damaging Your Business and What To Do about It*. New York: Penguin Group.

Porath, C. L., & Erez, A. (2007). Does rudeness really matter? The effects of rudeness on task performance and helpfulness. *Academy of Management Journal*, 50(5), 1181–1197.

Porath, C. L., & Erez, A. (2009). Overlooked but not untouched: How rudeness reduces onlookers' performance on routine and creative tasks. *Organizational Behavior and Human Decision Processes*, 109(1), 29–44.

Porath, C. L., Gerbasi, A., & Schorch, S. L. (2015). The effects of civility on advice, leadership, and performance. *Journal of Applied Psychology*, 100(5), 1527–1541.

Porath, C. L., MacInnis, D., & Folkes, V. (2010). Witnessing incivility among employees: Effects on consumer anger and negative inferences about companies. *Journal of Consumer Research*, 37(2), 292–303.

Reio, T. G. (2011). Supervisor and coworker incivility: Testing the work frustration-aggression model. *Advances in Developing Human Resources*, 13(1), 54–68.

Reio, T. G., & Ghosh, R. (2009). Antecedents and outcomes of workplace incivility: Implications for human resource development research and practice. *Human Resource Development Quarterly*, 20(3), 237–264.

Roberts, S. J., Scherer, L. L., & Bowyer, C. J. (2011). Job stress and incivility: What role does psychological capital play? *Journal of Leadership & Organizational Studies*, 18(4), 449–458.

Robinson, S. L., & Bennett, R. J. (1995). A typology of deviant workplace behaviors: A multidimensional scaling study. *Academy of Management Journal*, 38(2), 555–572.

Sakurai, K., & Jex, S. M. (2012). Coworker incivility and incivility targets' work effort and counterproductive work behaviors: The moderating role of supervisor social support. *Journal of Occupational Health Psychology*, 17(2), 150–161.

Sayers, J. K., Sears, K. L., Kelly, K. M., & Harbke, C. R. (2011). When employees engage in workplace incivility: The interactive effect of psychological contract violation and organizational justice. *Employee Responsibilities and Rights Journal*, 23(4), 269–283.

Schilpzand, P., de Pater, I. E., & Erez, A. (2016). Workplace incivility: A review of the literature and agenda for future research. *Journal of Organizational Behavior*, 37, S57–S88.

Scott, K. L., Restubog, S. L. D., & Zagenczyk, T. J. (2013). A social exchange-based model of the antecedents of workplace exclusion. *Journal of Applied Psychology*, 98(1), 37–48.

Sliter, M., Jex, S., Wolford, K., & McInnerney, J. (2010). How rude! Emotional labor as a mediator between customer incivility and employee outcomes. *Journal of Occupational Health Psychology*, 15(4), 468–481.

Spector, P. E., & Jex, S. M. (1998). Development of four self-report measures of job stressors and strain: Interpersonal conflict at work scale, organizational constraints scale, quantitative workload inventory, and physical symptoms inventory. *Journal of Occupational Health Psychology*, 3(4), 356–367.

Taylor, S. G., & Kluemper, D. H. (2012). Linking perceptions of role stress and incivility to workplace aggression: The moderating role of personality. *Journal of Occupational Health Psychology*, 17(3), 316–329.

Tepper, B. J. (2000). Consequences of abusive supervision. *Academy of Management Journal*, 43(2), 178–190.

Totterdell, P., Hershcovis, M. S., Niven, K., Reich, T. C., & Stride, C. (2012). Can employees be emotionally drained by witnessing unpleasant interactions between coworkers? A diary study of induced emotion regulation. *Work & Stress*, 26(2), 112–129.

Triandis, H. C. (1995). *Individualism and Collectivism*. New York: Simon & Schuster.

Trudel, J., & Reio, T. G. (2011). Managing workplace incivility: The role of conflict management styles – Antecedent or antidote? *Human Resource Development Quarterly*, 22(4), 395–423.

van Jaarsveld, D. D., Walker, D. D., & Skarlicki, D. P. (2010). The role of job demands and emotional exhaustion in the relationship between customer and employee incivility. *Journal of Management*, 36(6), 1468–1504.

Walker, D. D., van Jaarsveld, D. D., & Skarlicki, D. P. (2014). Exploring the effects of individual customer incivility encounters on employee incivility: The moderating roles of entity (in) civility and negative affectivity. *Journal of Applied Psychology*, 99(1), 151–161.

Walsh, B. M., Magley, V. J., Reeves, D. W., Davies-Schrils, K. A., Marmet, M. D., & Gallus, J. A. (2012). Assessing workgroup norms for civility: The development of the Civility Norms Questionnaire-Brief. *Journal of Business and Psychology*, 27(4), 407–420.

Welbourne, J. L., Gangadharan, A., & Sariol, A. M. (2015). Ethnicity and cultural values as predictors of the occurrence and impact of experienced workplace incivility. *Journal of Occupational Health Psychology*, 20(2), 205–217.

Zhou, Z. E., Yan, Y., Che, X. X., & Meier, L. L. (2015). Effect of workplace incivility on end-of-work negative affect: Examining individual and organizational moderators in a daily diary study. *Journal of Occupational Health Psychology*, 20(1), 117–130.

Part IV
Workplace supports for wellbeing

12

Wellbeing and design at the office

Christopher T. Boyko and Rachel Cooper

Introduction

Imagine yourself at your office desk, working on a computer. The glare from the screen is somewhat straining your eyes, so you look up for a bit of a rest. Out the nearby window, you see two colleagues sitting underneath a tree, having lunch. You wish to text them to say that you will join them shortly. Next to you are your mobile phone, a free Wi-Fi hotspot, and a potted plant with aromatic flowers in full bloom that remind you of a holiday abroad. As you type on your phone, you can hear the general din of other colleagues, happily chatting in the background about work-related matters. Although you are in a wide-open space, you feel like there is enough privacy to work (and text) without being overlooked. You are contented with being able to work in such an environment, for it makes you more productive.

This scenario suggests that the environment in which we work can influence *how* we work. Design factors, such as lighting, noise, views from windows, privacy and access to "green" things (e.g., plants, parks), all play an important part in our work experience as well as impact our subjective wellbeing or illbeing, depending on the circumstances. A further observation regarding the scenario suggests that *where* we work is changing. Although the description of the work environment implies a more traditional office space, the scenario could be realized almost anywhere in which people find themselves working digitally, such as a coffee shop, a coworking space, or even a rented hotel room (Laing, 2014). These new options and opportunities may give people more freedom to work and be productive, but are these environments best-suited to our wellbeing? If not, what can design decision-makers do to improve working environments in nontraditional spaces to enhance wellbeing and minimize illbeing?

This chapter aims to uncover the answers to these questions in two parts. The first part will examine the relationships between the design factors in traditional office environments already mentioned and subjective wellbeing and illbeing. The second part will apply this knowledge to nontraditional work environments, forecasting what will need to be in place to increase wellbeing. The chapter will end with some recommendations to ensure that wellbeing is considered through design wherever people wish to work.

Relationships between design factors in traditional office environments and wellbeing/illbeing

Having an attractive workplace (Kaplan, 1993; Maslow & Mintz, 1956) that also is comfortable and allows for social interaction may result in more productive employees with enhanced wellbeing. What makes a workplace environment attractive, comfortable, and conducive to social interaction will vary from place to place, with different features emphasized and others minimized. Often, though, workplace settings get this wrong: features that increase wellbeing are absent and the features that amplify illbeing are present in spades. In addition, the inability for employees to control the features and conditions in which they work may lead to further illbeing, including heightened levels of individual stress (Cohen, Evans, Stokols, & Krantz, 1991).

For the purposes of this chapter, *wellbeing* refers to a positive mental, physical, and social state that happens when basic needs are met (e.g., access to water and food), when individuals achieve a sense of purpose, and when they feel capable of attaining important personal goals and participate in society (Defra, 2010). *Illbeing* refers to a state of anxiety or worry, negative affect, and bodily complaints that arise from an inability to control and plan one's life, a decreased sense of personal competence, and poor socioeconomic and family circumstances (Headey, 1992; Headey, Holstrom, & Wearing, 1984, 1985). Illbeing also may involve depression, dissatisfaction with self, low self-esteem, or pessimism (Scheff, 1999). Wellbeing and illbeing are not opposites of one another; rather, they have different roots and causes, are found to be associated with different variables (Bradburn, 1969; Bradburn & Caplovitz, 1965; Headey et al., 1984, 1985), and may be impacted in different ways, temporally (Diener & Emmons, 1985). Finally, *workplaces* are "any premises or part of premises which are not domestic premises and are made available to any person as a place of work" (Health and Safety Executive, 1993). This may include business parks, private paths, roads on industrial estates, and common parts of shared buildings.

Although there are many features of workplaces that can impact wellbeing and illbeing (e.g., expectation of high productivity), such as workplace ergonomics,[1] this chapter focuses on four fundamental, physical environment features – noise and air quality; lighting; windows, views, and nature; and privacy – demonstrating through empirical evidence that the physical work environment plays an important role in the physical and psychological wellbeing of employees.[2] While the evidence presented is robust, the reader should consider that most of the research discussed in this chapter pertains to more traditional workplace environments, such as offices and factories; research on wellbeing in other, less traditional workplaces, such as the home, coffee shops, and trains, has been scant (cf. Laing, 2014). Furthermore, the relationships offered are mostly correlational and, as such, do not imply causation between the variables (Cooper, Boyko, & Codinhoto, 2008). Klitzman and Stellman (1989) also suggest that, while the impact of physical work environments on wellbeing has been studied directly, much research focusses on the intermediate role of other variables, including employee attitudes and satisfaction and turnover, in the relationship between workplaces and health.

Noise and air quality

Although advances in architecture and interior design have resulted in thermal, ventilation, and other engineering improvements in office environments (Salter, Powell, Begault, & Alavarado, 2003), poor acoustics and ambient noise continue to afflict workers (Treasure, 2012). In fact, internal acoustics is the feature of office environments with whom employers are most dissatisfied, according to an evaluation of 142 commercial buildings in the United States (Jensen, Arens, & Zagreus, 2005; see also Oldman, 2014, for similar results). Sounds from building reverberations, machines, people, and other sources can lead to difficulties with communication (e.g., speech privacy, Sundstrom, Town, Rice, Osborn, & Brill, 1994), concentration (Perham, Banbury, & Jones, 2007), productivity, and wellbeing.

Regarding wellbeing, office workplace environments that are noisy can contribute to stress (Abbot, 2004; Ahasan, Mohiuddin, Vayrynen, Ironkannas, & Quddus, 1999; Akerstert & Landstrom, 1998; Barreto, Swerdlow, Smith, & Higgins, 1997; Bayo, Garcia, & Garcia, 1995; Cohen, 1969; Kahn, 1981; Kryter, 1972; Menaghan & Merves, 1984; Norbeck, 1985; Oseland & Hodsman, 2015), distress (Klitzman & Stellman, 1989), general anxiety (Cohen, 1969), emotional exhaustion or burnout (Topf & Dillon, 1988), unhappiness (Loscocco & Spitze, 1990), illness (Abbott, 2004), and annoyance (Oseland & Hodsman, 2015). Within nonoffice work environments, loud noise also may contribute to illbeing. In factories and similar settings (e.g., weaving mills) where noise levels exceed the recommended noise exposure limits, workers can experience moderate to high levels of perceived stress (Burns, Sun, Fobil, & Neitzel, 2016), changes in mood and anxiety (Granati, Angelepi, & Lenzi, 1959; Melamed, Najenson, Luz, Jucha, & Green, 1988), negative affect, nervous reactions and additional symptoms on mental health checklists (e.g., social dysfunction; McDonald, 1989).

Like noise, air quality has been linked with illbeing. Klitzman and Stellman (1989) found that poor air quality strongly predicted psychological stress in their study of nonmanagerial officer employees in four different North American locations (see also Cohen, 1984). Poor air quality also may contribute to "sick building syndrome," which occurs in workers who inhabit particular buildings. The most common symptoms are physical – such as headaches, tiredness, and itchy eyes and skin – but psychological symptoms, including stress (Jukes, 2000, as cited in McCoy, 2002) and anxiety (Nakazawa et al., 2005) may occur as well.

Light and lighting

Regarding light and lighting, research has been undertaken that explores the influence of color temperatures on wellbeing. Knez and Enmarker (1998) discovered that artificial light in the workplace can alter mood, with gender acting as a mediating factor. In their research, males preferred cool colors (bluish-white lighting) whereas females preferred warmer colors (reddish lighting). Mills et al. (2007) found a positive relationship between cooler color temperatures and general feelings of wellbeing, with a nearly 14% improvement in mental health among employees working in a shift-work call center that contained more blue-spectrum lighting. Finally, Partonen and Lönnqvist (2000) concluded that exposure to bright lights in an office during winter alleviated distress and improved health-related quality of life among healthy office workers.

Additional variables related to light and lighting appear to impact wellbeing, such as control over lighting, amount of direct and indirect lighting, and sunlight. Having control over lighting, particularly as a result of having a dimmer switch, is associated with higher ratings of environmental satisfaction, lighting quality, and self-rated productivity as well as the prevention of feelings of hopelessness and powerlessness (Barnes, 1981; Boyce, Veitch, Newsham, Myer, & Hunter, 2003). Employees who were more satisfied with lighting also report being happier and more comfortable with their work and their surroundings (Boyce et al., 2003). Furthermore, altering the amount of direct and indirect lighting in offices (from 100% direct lighting to 100% indirect lighting with variations in between), did not lead to positive impacts on office workers' wellbeing (Fostervold & Nersveen, 2008). Concerning sunlight, Leather, Pyrgas, Beale, and Lawrence (1998) found a positive correlation between the level of sunlight penetration in windows in terms of area and general wellbeing, job satisfaction, and employees' negative intentions to quit.

Windows, views, and nature

The presence of these three features in office environments generally contribute to wellbeing and their absence to illbeing. With respect to indoor plants, scholars have found that workers experience increases in their wellbeing, and in the attractiveness and perceived comfort of their workplace, when greenery is nearby. These findings occur even if employee productivity fails to improve (Kaplan, 1993; Larsen, Adams, Deal, Kweon, & Tyler, 1998; Shoemaker, Randall, Relf, & Geller, 1992). Additional wellbeing benefits include decreases in psychophysiological stress responses and more positive mood evaluations (Shibata & Suzuki, 2004), although Bringsli-mark, Hartig, and Grindal Patil (2007) found that indoor plants were not significantly associated with perceived stress.

In terms of windows and wellbeing, it has been found that not having access to windows at work may lead to claustrophobia, depression, feelings of isolation and restriction, job dissat-isfaction, and tension (Finnegan & Solomon, 1981; Ruys, 1970; Sundstrom, 1986). In particular, employees undertaking routine or sedentary tasks in sedentary work environments may feel more bothered about not having windows than those who work in more active jobs (Collins, 1975; Wyon & Nilsson, 1980), as the psychological simulation that comes with having windows will be absent. Office administrators and clerical staff who worked in windowless offices also reported feeling less positive about their working conditions and jobs (Finnegan & Solomon, 1981), and more depressed, tense, and restricted (Ruys, 1970) than those in offices with windows. Moreover, when faced without the prospect of not having windows, workers often compensate by sur-rounding themselves with visual materials containing nature themes (e.g., posters on walls), more so than people in offices with windows (Heerwagen & Orians, 1986).

Having access to windows, then, is important, as are the views from them. Research on dwellings has shown that window views significantly impact life and environmental satisfaction (Kaplan, 1983, 1985; see also anecdotal research about how windows provide "psychological relief" from pain, discomfort, and oppression, Goodrich, 1986; Heerwagen, 1986). In office set-tings, views from windows can provide a restorative value from work-related stress (Heerwagen, 1990; Kaplan et al., 1988). However, what is seen from windows becomes important: Kaplan et al. (1988) found that workers who see only built-up features, such as roads and buildings, may suffer from higher levels of work-related stress and lower levels of job satisfaction compared with workers who can see natural elements or have no view. Indeed, being able to see nature outside the window can mediate the influence of work-related stress and negligibly improves wellbe-ing (Leather et al., 1988; see also Moore, 1981, Ulrich, 1984, and West, 1986, who suggest that the quantity of natural elements viewed from windows is important). Nonetheless, the desire to give employees views from windows needs to be balanced with potential incursions on exposure and privacy, particularly if people are working with sensitive materials (e.g., employee records) (Heerwagen, 1990).

Privacy

Privacy in the workplace is not always something that can be guaranteed, and the design of office environments may do little to improve these perceptions. Klitzman and Stellman (1989) found that lack of visual and acoustic (or architectural) privacy – along with other features of the physical office environment – was positively related to psychological distress and negatively associated with satisfaction. Sundstrom, Burt, and Kamp (1980; cf. Brennan, Chugh, & Kline, 2002) also discovered that office workers with architectural privacy who rated their workspaces as private reported less noise and distraction, and less perceptions of crowding, than did those working in less-private spaces. That is, participants preferred quiet, enclosed, and visually inaccessible workspaces with few and far away colleagues. In fact, if given the choice between having privacy or being able to access people and other spaces regardless of time and place, the former was generally preferred. The uncertainty of moving around to different workspaces at different times of the day – often the preserve of open-plan offices – is perceived by some to be stressful. Nonetheless, other employees enjoy the sense of freedom and mobility from being accessible (Oommen, Knowles, & Zhao, 2008). One factor that might mediate the relationship between stress (or illbeing in general) and privacy within the office environment is perceived lack of control to change one's surroundings when auditory and personal privacy is lacking (McCarrey, Peterson, Edwards, & Kumiz, 1974).

Applying evidence to nontraditional work environments

Each of the four physical environment features described, of course, are interdependent, yet very dependent on the quality of the design and fabric of the workplace, as well as the type, quality, layout of furniture, and equipment used within it. However, for a number of reasons, the office as a work environment is fundamentally changing the nature of work, technology, and the needs of organizations. First, we can look at the emergence of the so-called knowledge worker (Drucker, 1968). The term was linked to work that relied on knowledge, ideas, and creativity as opposed to production and manual skills. It has been adopted widely alongside that of other terms, such as the *knowledge economy* and the often-interchangeable *information worker* (Brinkley, Fauth, Mahdon, & Theodoropolou, 2009). In a study in 2009, The Work Foundation estimated that the United Kingdom has a 30–30–40 workforce: 30% in jobs with high knowledge content, 30% in jobs with some knowledge content, and 40% in jobs with less knowledge content. The foundation also classified jobs into several categories: leaders and innovators, experts and analysts, information handlers, care and welfare workers, servers and sellers, maintenance and logistics operators, and assistants and clerks. Leaders and innovators, and experts and analysts, were top in knowledge content, but the remaining jobs all had knowledge content to some degree.

Many of these knowledge workers sit in open-plan offices, originally designed to address the need for greater efficiency, worker flexibility, and higher office-worker density while simultaneously lowering expenses by not having as many partition walls (Kaarlela-Tuomaala, Helenius, Keskinen, & Hongisto, 2009). In the late 20th century, however, research led to the characterization of workers and their working patterns, and informed more sophisticated design. For example, Duffy (1997) recommended an office design comprising four differing workspaces that supported four types of workers and working patterns, based upon dimensions of autonomy and interaction:

- *The hive* for solo working (e.g., telesales requiring low interaction and low autonomy). Therefore, individual workstations, or a simple open-plan.
- *The cell* for concentrated working (e.g., lawyers requiring low interaction and high autonomy). Therefore, cellular offices or a highly screened open-plan.
- *The den* for group working (e.g., workers in the media requiring high interaction and low autonomy). Therefore, team space, or meeting and work spaces.
- *The club* for knowledge working (e.g., workers in advertising requiring high interaction and high autonomy). Therefore, multiple task space, or diverse, flexible spaces.

Whether the resulting open-place space conformed to these principles depended mainly on the building layout; the skills of architects and interior designers; and suppliers of office furniture. For example, the classic telesales environment has been criticized as soulless, mundane, and factory-like (Fleming & Spicer, 2004), whilst the den and the club approaches often have been an excuse for not providing dedicated desks or moving people about the office, frequently known as hot-desking (Bell, 2010).

Whilst many organizations continue to desire a workforce that is productive, efficient, and effective, knowledge workers in particular are expected also to be creative and innovative. Open-plan offices are viewed as efficient from the perspective of space reduction, but they also have been recognized as an opportunity to generate creativity through employee engagement, both formally and accidentally (e.g., at the water cooler). With the rise of the knowledge economy, the digital sector, and innovation as a driver in competitiveness, many look to successful organizations, such as Google and Apple, for inspiration, as they have deliberately designed collaborative, creative environments. These environments tend to use the first principles of good light, good air quality, spaciousness views, autonomy, and both public and private space, and build on them by introducing "creative" devices (e.g., novel furniture, judicious use of color). Although many organizations do not have the capital, capacity, or vision to create such environments, digital technology has released the knowledge worker from the office and fostered new workers and new ways of working. Since Duffy's classification, there have been further changes in the nature of knowledge work and, therefore, in the roles and tasks that knowledge workers undertake. Greene and Myerson (2011) undertook a study that classified workers as the Anchor, Connector, Gatherer, and Navigator:

- *The Anchor* is the iconic, sedentary office worker, someone who is reliably in the office every day and likely to be found at his or her desk during this time. Anchors describe their desk as "an extension of home." A sense of ownership combined with the ritual of arriving to the same space each day is very important to them; therefore, their requirement is for comfort.
- *The Connector* is the "needle and thread" within an organization. Connectors typically spend half of their time in different places around the building: in meeting rooms, in the café or at colleagues' desks; therefore, their requirement is for use of different spaces.
- *The Gatherer* relies on many relationships generated away from the office. Spending around half the week away from the office at different appointments, Gatherers can be found at client or customer offices, at other sites, or using neutral, "third space" locations such as cafés or members clubs. It is more likely that they will travel regionally than globally; with the office remaining a central fulcrum in their week. They bring back information, business, and important new relationships to the office; therefore, their requirement is for a shared desk or hot desk when they are in the office.
- *The Navigator* incorporates a range of different types of knowledge worker who are rarely in the office. For example, the contractor who is employed on a project basis, the nomad salesman who comes into the office a few times a month, and the consultant who arrives for a meeting and needs access to a space where he or she can sit down and use a laptop; therefore, their requirement is for offices to feel welcome.

The common factor in the development of these categories of work and worker is that technology has liberated the worker. The laptop, the tablet, and the mobile phone – and the ubiquitous networks they use (Duffy, 2000) – have meant that the information and the knowledge are either on a hard drive, a cloud, or in conversations, both digital and physical. Many employees now work at home, in coffee shops, and on trains and transport intersections, such as train stations and airports. Their office is their laptop, and the characteristics of these ways of working include:

- Being highly mobile and nomadic in their work patterns;
- Using multiple, shared-group work settings;

- Using diverse, task-based spaces;
- Having extended and erratic periods of working;
- Varied patterns of sometimes high-density space use;
- More shared and temporary ownership of settings within the office, combined with tele-working and homeworking.

(Laing, 2006, p. 33).

So how do we apply the basic needs of wellbeing to these new workers and their working environments? What basic characteristics related to the four, fundamental physical environment features of lighting, air quality, noise levels, views of nature, and privacy can we expect, and who is responsible for ensuring they are available?

It is well known that lack of control in the workplace is a source of stress; this is usually associated with control over one's tasks and levels of autonomy (Siegrist, 2009). However, control of one's environment, freedom to move, and privacy within that environment also are factors in stress (Cohen et al., 1991). So perhaps we might conclude that, because knowledge workers are no longer bound to the office and can choose where they sit to work on their laptop or have their meetings, this element of control is a major contributor to their own levels of control and thus personal wellbeing. In fact, these workers should have relatively high levels of satisfaction and general health and wellbeing. However, no research into this new workforce has examined this new style of work, as well as the choice between quality of environment and the actual environments chosen and the long-term health implications for the workforce. For example, is it better to sit at a small table on the street outside a café with free Internet, hunched over, inhaling carbon dioxide and other particulates, yet with a view of a park on the other side of the road? Or is better to be in an office with no views, but good air quality and light? We do not have the evidence either way. What we do know is that, in this case, the city is the office and the design of public and semi-public spaces will have an ongoing impact on our physical health and wellbeing. In the case of a workforce that is mobile and agile, who is responsible for employee health and wellbeing? It will be important to ensure that the location and manner of working is conducive to a healthy working environment. Therefore, wherever that is, it should provide the fundamental needs of good light, views of nature and greenspace, appropriate noise levels, good air quality, and privacy.

Conclusions and recommendations

This chapter began with a discussion of four, fundamental physical environment features that influence the wellbeing and illbeing of people at work. With this knowledge at hand, the authors then explored how the office and office worker have been changing – and continue to change – with the advent of new places in which to work, new technologies, and new mobility patterns. The authors believe that, wherever and however people will be doing their jobs in the future, there still will need to be emphasis placed on getting the four fundamentals of environmental wellbeing right so that workers can be productive and happy. But where does the obligation lie in guaranteeing that these four fundamentals are considered properly?

The question of responsibility for delivering these new types of work environment and ensuring the wellbeing of the workforce lies in the combination of the business/employer, the city/town planners, and the individual. There are a number of perspectives:

- From a human resources perspective, the employer must consider the extent of agile and mobile working that it expects from its employees, the impact this working has on the employee, and the ability for employees to work safely and be able to choose appropriate, supportive environments whilst working on the move.

- Cities wishing to host a thriving economy may need to look beyond town planning and development incentives to consider the whole city – its buildings and its public spaces – as "the office." Planners need to work with developers to think about cities as a series of spaces that provide working space, digital space, quiet and contemplative space, and communal space, all with good air quality, good light, noise control, and views that are both green and uplifting aesthetically. In so doing, cities will embody environmental benefits, social benefits, and creative benefits for its mobile working citizens as well as everyone else.
- Private-sector businesses (such as restaurants, cafés, hotels, and transport operators) that offer Internet access and space for mobile working need to consider the level of responsibility levels for privacy, in particular digital and physical spaces, thinking about the four fundamentals of wellbeing in the office. If these fundamental features are delivered, they have the dual benefit of providing healthy environments for their own staff and customers in general. A "kitemark"[3] for healthy working spaces would enable businesses to promote their provision, generate positive PR, and increase customer recognition.
- Clearly, individuals who wish to undertake mobile and nomadic working have a choice and a responsibility to consider the environments that they work in. But do they always make good choices? Do they know what is best? Whether the office is the home, the city, or various forms of transportation, guidelines for healthy working environments aimed at nomadic and mobile workforce are needed.

Ensuring positive wellbeing for the knowledge/office worker in the future will still need to take into account the four fundamentals of environmental wellbeing; noise and air quality, light, views, and privacy. However, responsibility for delivering these fundamentals is increasingly complex, and the people, organizations, and places that take it seriously will be the ones with the most productive, healthiest, and happiest workforce and community.

Notes

1 According to Wilson (2000), "Ergonomics is the theoretical and fundamental understanding of human behavior and performance in purposeful interacting socio-technical systems, and the application of that understanding to design of interactions in the context of real settings" (p. 560).
2 Many of the studies presented in this chapter come from Cooper et al. (2008).
3 A kitemark is a UK product and service quality certification mark, owned and operated by the British Standards Institution (www.bsigroup.com/en-GB/kitemark/).

References

Abbott, D. (2004). Calming the office cacophony. *The Safety and Health Practitioner*, 22(1), 34–36.
Ahasan, M. R., Mohiuddin, G., Vayrynen, S., Ironkannas, H., & Quddus, R. (1999). Work-related problems in metal handling tasks in Bangladesh: Obstacles to the development of safety and health measures. *Ergonomics*, 42(2), 385–396.
Akerstert, T., & Landstrom, U. (1998). Workplace countermeasures of night shift fatigue. *International Journal of Industrial Ergonomics*, 21(3–4), 167–178.
Barnes, R. D. (1981). Perceived freedom and control in the built environment. In: J. H. Harvey (ed.), *Cognition, Social Behaviour, and the Environment*. Hillsdale, NJ: Erlbaum, 409–422.
Barreto, S. M., Swerdlow, A. J., Smith, P. G., & Higgins, C. D. (1997). Risk of death from motor-vehicle injury in Brazilian steelworkers: A nested case-control study. *International Journal of Epidemiology*, 26(4), 814–821.

Bayo, M. V., Garcia, A. M., & Garcia, A. (1995). Noise levels in an urban hospital and workers' subjective responses. *Archives of Environmental Health*, 50(3), 247–251.

Bell, A. (2010). *Re-Imagining the Office: The New Workplace Challenge*. Surrey, UK: Gower.

Boyce, P. R., Veitch, J. A., Newsham, G. R., Myer, M., & Hunter, C. (2003). *Lighting Quality and Office Work: A Field Simulation Study*. Richmond, WA: Pacific Northwest National Laboratory.

Bradburn, N. M. (1969). *The Structure of Psychological Well-Being*. Chicago: Aldine.

Bradburn, N. M., & Caplovitz, D. (1965). *Reports on Happiness: A Pilot Study*. Chicago: Aldine.

Brennan, A., Chugh, J. S., & Kline, T. (2002). Traditional versus open office design: A longitudinal field study. *Environment and Behavior*, 34(3), 279–299.

Bringslimark, T., Hartig, T., & Grindal Patil, G. (2007). Psychological benefits of indoor plants in workplaces: Putting experimental results into context. *HortScience*, 42(3), 581–587.

Brinkley, I., Fauth, R., Mahdon, M., & Theodoropolou, S. (2009). *Knowledge Workers and Knowledge Work*. London, UK: The Work Foundation.

Burns, K. N., Sun, K., Fobil, J. N., & Neitzel, R. L. (2016). Heart rate, stress, and occupational noise exposure among electronic waste recycling workers. *International Journal of Environmental Research and Public Health*, 13(1), 140. doi:10.3390/ijerph13010140.

Cohen, A. (1969). Effects of noise on psychological state. In: W. D. Ward & J. E. Fricke (eds.), *Noise as a Public Health Hazard*. Washington, DC: American Speech and Hearing Association, 74–88.

Cohen, B. F. G. (ed.). (1984). *Human Aspects of Office Automation*. New York, NY: Elsevier.

Cohen, S., Evans, G., Stokols, D., & Krantz, D. (1991). *Behavior, Health and Environmental Stress*. New York: Plenum.

Collins, B. L. (1975). *Windows and People: A Literature Survey*. National Bureau of Standards, Washington, DC: US Government Printing Office.

Cooper, R., Boyko, C., & Codinhoto, R. (2008). *State-of-Science Review: SR-DR2. The Effect of the Physical Environment on Mental Wellbeing*. London: Government Office for Science.

Department for Environment, Food and Rural Affairs (DEFRA). (2010). *Measuring Progress: Sustainable Development Indicators 2010*. London, UK: DEFRA.

Diener, E., & Emmons, R. A. (1985). The independence of positive and negative affect. *Journal of Personality and Social Psychology*, 47(5), 1105–1117.

Drucker, P. F. (1968). *The Age of Discontinuity: Guidelines to Our Changing Society*. London, UK: Transaction Publishers.

Duffy, F. (1997). *The New Office*. London, UK: Conran Octopus.

Duffy, F. (2000). Design and facilities management in a time of change. *Facilities*, 18(10/11/12), 371–375.

Finnegan, M. C., & Solomon, L. Z. (1981). Work attitudes in windowed vs. windowless environments. *Journal of Social Psychology*, 115(2), 291–292.

Fleming, P., & Spicer, A. (2004). 'You can checkout anytime, but you can never leave': Spatial boundaries in a high commitment organization. *Human Relations*, 57(1), 75–94.

Fostervold, K. I., & Nersveen, J. (2008). Proportions of direct and indirect indoor lighting – The effect on health, well-being and cognitive performance of office workers. *Lighting Research and Technology*, 40(3), 175–200.

Goodrich, R. (1986). The perceived office: The office environments experienced by its users. In: J. Wineman (ed.), *Behavioral Issues in Office Design*. New York: Van Nostrand Reinhold, 109–133.

Granati, A., Angelepi, F., & Lenzi, R. (1959). L'influenza dei rumori sul sistema nervosa. *Folio Medica*, 42, 1313–1325.

Greene, C., & Myerson, J. (2011). Space for thought: Designing for knowledge workers. *Facilities*, 29(1/2), 19–30.

Headey, B. (1992). Subjective well-being: Revisions to dynamic equilibrium theory using national panel data and panel regression methods. *Social Indicators Research*, 79(3), 369–403.

Headey, B., Holstrom, E., & Wearing, A. (1984). Well-being and ill-being: Different dimensions. *Social Indicators Research*, 14(2), 115–139.

Headey, B., Holstrom, E., & Wearing, A. (1985). Models of well-being and ill-being. *Social Indicators Research*, 17(3), 211–234.

Health and Safety Executive. (1993). *Workplace (Health, Safety & Welfare) Regulations 1992*. London, UK: HM Government.

Heerwagen, J. (1986). Windowscapes: The role of nature in the view from the window. In: E. J. Bales & R. McCluney (eds.), *Proceedings of the International Daylighting Conference Long Beach, CA*. Atlanta, GA: American Society of Heating, Refrigerating, and Air-Conditioning Engineers, Inc., 352–355.

Heerwagen, J. (1990). The psychological impacts of windows and window design. In: R. I. Selby, K. H. Anthony, J. Choi, & B. Orland (eds.), *Proceedings of the Twenty-First Annual Environmental Design Research Association Conference, Urbana-Champaign, IL.* Edmond, OK: EDRA, 269–280.

Heerwagen, J., & Orians, G. (1986). Adaptations to windowlessness: A study of the use of visual decor in windowed and windowless offices. *Environment and Behavior*, 18(5), 623–639.

Jensen, K. L., Arens, E., & Zagreus, L. (2005). Acoustical quality in office workstations, as assessed by occupant surveys. In: F. Wang (ed.), *Proceedings of Indoor Air 2005, Beijing, China.* Santa Cruz, CA: International Society of Indoor Air Quality and Climate, 2401–2405.

Kaarlela-Tuomaala, A., Helenius, R., Keskinen, E., & Hongisto, V. (2009). Effects of acoustic environment on work in private office rooms and open-plan offices – Longitudinal study during relocation. *Ergonomics*, 52(11), 1423–1444.

Kahn, R. L. (1981). *Work and Health.* New York: Wiley.

Kaplan, R. (1983). The role of nature in the urban context. In: I. Altman & J. F. Wohlwill (eds.), *Behavior and the Natural Environment.* New York: Plenum Press, 127–161

Kaplan, R. (1985). Nature at the doorstep: Residential satisfaction and the nearby environment. *Journal of Architecture and Planning Research*, 2(2), 115–127.

Kaplan, R. (1993). The role of nature in the context of the workplace. *Landscape and Urban Planning*, 26(1–4), 193–201.

Kaplan, S., Talbot, J., & Kaplan, R. (1988). Coping with daily hassles: The impact of nearby nature on the work environment., Washington, DC: U.S. Government Printing Office, Project Report, U.S. Forest Service, North Central Forest Experiment Station, Urban Forestry Unit Cooperative Agreement, 23-85-08.

Klitzman, S., & Stellman, J. M. (1989). The impact of the physical environment on the psychological well-being of office workers. *Social Science and Medicine*, 29(6), 733–742.

Knez, I., & Enmarker, I. (1998). Effects of office lighting on mood and cognitive performance and a gender effect in work-related judgement. *Environment and Behavior*, 30(4), 553–567.

Kryter, K. D. (1972). Non auditory effects of environmental noise. *American Journal of Public Health*, 62(3), 389–398.

Laing, A. (2006). New patterns of work: The design of the office. In: J. Worthington (ed.), *Reinventing the Workplace* (2nd ed.). Oxford: Architectural Press, 29–49.

Laing, A. (2014). *Work and Workplaces in the Digital City.* New York: The Center for Urban Real Estate at Columbia University.

Larsen, L., Adams, J., Deal, B., Kweon, B.-S., & Tyler, E. (1998). Plants in the workplace: The effects of plant density on productivity, attitudes and perceptions. *Environment and Behavior*, 30(3), 261–281.

Leather, P., Pyrgas, M., Beale, D., & Lawrence, C. (1998). Windows in the workplace: Sunlight, view and occupational stress. *Environment and Behavior*, 30(6), 739–762.

Loscocco, K. A., & Spitze, G. (1990). Working conditions, social support, and the well-being of female and male factory workers. *Journal of Health and Social Behavior*, 31(December), 313–327.

Maslow, A. H., & Mintz, N. L. (1956). Effects of esthetic surroundings: 1. Initial shortterm effects of three esthetic conditions upon perceiving 'energy' and 'well-being' in faces. *Journal of Psychology*, 41(2), 247–254.

McCarrey, M. W., Peterson, L., Edwards, S., & Kumiz, P. V. (1974). Landscape office attitudes: Reflections of perceived degree of control over transactions with the environment. *Journal of Applied Psychology*, 59(3), 401–403.

McCoy, J. M. (2002). Work environments. In: R. B. Bechtel & A. Churchman (eds.), *Handbook of Environmental Psychology.* New York: John Wiley & Sons, 443–460.

McDonald, N. (1989). Jobs and their environment: The psychological impact of work in noise. *The Irish Journal of Psychology*, 10(1), 33–50.

Melamed, S., Najenson, T., Luz, T., Jucha, E., & Green, M. (1988). Noise annoyance, industrial noise exposure and psychological stress symptoms among male and female workers. *Noise*, 88, 315–320.

Menaghan, E. G., & Merves, E. S. (1984). Coping with occupational problems: The limits of individual efforts. *Journal of Health and Social Behavior*, 25(4), 406–423.

Mills, P. R., Tomkins, S. C., & Schlangen, L. J. M. (2007). The effect of high correlated colour temperature office lighting on employee wellbeing and work performance. *Journal of Circadian Rhythms*, 5, 2.

Moore, O. (1981). A prison environment's effect on health care service demands. *Journal of Environmental Systems*, 11, 17–34.

Nakazawa, H., Ikeda, H., Yamashita, T., Hara, I., Kumai, Y., Endo, G., & Endo, Y. (2005). A case of sick building syndrome in a Japanese office worker. *Industrial Health*, 43(2), 341–345.

Norbeck, J. S. (1985). Perceived job stress, job satisfaction, and psychological symptoms in critical care nursing. *Research in Nursing and Health*, 8(3), 253–259.

Oldman, T. (2014). 2013 Q4 summary. *Leesman Review*, 12, 6–7.

Oommen, V. G., Knowles, M., & Zhao, I. (2008). Should health service managers embrace open plan work environments? A review. *Asia Pacific Journal of Health Management*, 3(2), 37–43.

Oseland, N., & Hodsman, P. (2015). *Planning for Psychoacoustics: A Psychological Approach to Resolving Office Noise Distraction*. Available at: http://workplaceunlimited.com/Ecophon%20Psychoacoustics%20 v4.5.pdf (accessed 29 January 2016).

Partonen, T., & Lönnqvist, J. (2000). Bright light improves vitality and alleviates distress in healthy people. *Journal of Affective Disorders*, 57(1–3), 55–61.

Perham, N., Banbury, S., & Jones, D. M. (2007). Do realistic reverberation levels reduce auditory distraction? *Applied Cognitive Psychology*, 21(7), 839–847.

Ruys, T. (1970). *Windowless Offices*. MA thesis, University of Washington, Seattle.

Salter, C., Powell, K., Begault, D., & Alavarado, R. (2003). *Case Studies of a Method for Predicting Speech Privacy in the Contemporary Workplace*. Berkeley, CA: Center for the Built Environment, University of California, Berkeley.

Scheff, T. J. (1999). *Being Mentally Ill* (3rd ed.). New York: Aldine de Gruyter.

Shibata, S., & Suzuki, N. (2004). Effects of an indoor plant on creative task performance and mood. *Scandinavian Journal of Psychology*, 45(5), 373–381.

Shoemaker, C. A., Randall, K., Relf, P. D., & Geller, E. S. (1992). Relationships between plants, behaviour, and attitudes in an office environment. *HortTechnology*, 2(2), 205–206.

Siegrist, J. (2009). Job control & rewards. In: S. Cartwright & C. Cooper (eds.), *Oxford Handbook of Organizational Wellbeing*. Oxford, UK: Oxford University Press, 109–133.

Sundstrom, E. (1986). *Workplaces: The psychology of the physical environment in offices and factories*. New York: Cambridge University Press.

Sundstrom, E., Burt, R. E., & Kamp, D. (1980). Privacy at work: Architectural correlates of job satisfaction and job performance. *Academy of Management Journal*, 23(1), 101–117.

Sundstrom, E., Town, J. P., Rice, R. W., Osborn, D. P., & Brill, M. (1994). Office noise, satisfaction and performance. *Environment and Behavior*, 26(2), 195–222.

Topf, M., & Dillon, E. (1988). Noise-induced stress as a predictor of burnout in critical care nurses. *Heart Lung*, 17(5), 567–574.

Treasure, J. (2012). *Building in Sound: Biamp Systems White Paper*. Beaverton, OR: Biamp Systems.

Ulrich, R. S. (1984). View through a window may influence the recovery from surgery. *Science*, 224(4647), 420–421.

West, M. J. (1986). *Landscape Views and Stress Responses in the Prison Environment*. Unpublished Master's thesis, University of Washington, Seattle.

Wilson, J. R. (2000). Fundamentals of ergonomics in theory and practice. *Applied Ergonomics*, 31(11), 557–567.

Wyon, D. P., & Nilsson, I. (1980). Human experience of windowless environments in factories, offices, shops, and colleges in Sweden. In: J. Krochmann (ed.), *Proceedings of the Symposium on Daylight: Physical, Psychological and Architectural Aspects*. Berlin, Germany: Institut für Lichttechnik der TU Berlin, 216–225.

13

Workplace empowerment and employee health and wellbeing

Heather Spence Laschinger and Emily Read

Introduction

The link between workplace empowerment and employee health and wellbeing has gained considerable attention over the last few decades as organizations recognize the benefits of supporting employees' ability to accomplish their work in a meaningful way and, thus, contribute to organizational effectiveness (Bowen & Lawler, 1995). The notion of employee empowerment evolved from a change in management thinking from a top-down command and control model to greater employee involvement in conditions that affect their work (Bowen & Lawler, 1995). Over the last two decades, both structural empowerment, which refers to employees' access to organizational structures needed to accomplish their work (Bowen & Lawler, 1995; Kanter, 1977, 1993), and psychological empowerment, which refers to employees' internal motivational orientation towards their job (Spreitzer, 1995; Thomas & Velthouse, 1990), have been studied in a wide variety of organizational settings. Results from this body of research have consistently demonstrated the important role that workplace empowerment plays for employees and organizations alike. This chapter focuses in particular on the role of workplace empowerment in fostering employee health and wellbeing. In it we summarize research linking structural and psychological empowerment to both positive and negative workplace wellbeing and describe evidence-based empowerment strategies that can be used by leaders to ensure optimal workplace health.

Workplace empowerment theory

The concept of organizational empowerment addresses employees' feeling of power and agency within their organization (Kanter, 1977, 1993). Two theoretical approaches to empowerment are described in the organizational literature. The structural approach (Kanter, 1977, 1993) describes organizational conditions within work settings that enable employees' to accomplish their work and focuses on objective aspects of the job (Kraimer, Seibert, & Liden, 1999). The other approach, psychological empowerment, focuses on employees' cognitive motivational responses to conditions experienced in their work environments (Conger & Kunungo, 1988; Kraimer et al., 1999; Spreitzer, 1995). According to Bowen and Lawler (1995), management efforts to build an empowering state of mind require strategies that focus on both structural and psychological empowerment.

Kanter's structural empowerment theory

According to Kanter (1977, 1993), *power* refers to the ability to mobilize resources and to get things done in the work setting, as opposed to the traditional view of power as coercion or control. Employees are empowered when their work environment is structured in such a way that they have access to the resources (e.g., time, supplies, equipment), information (e.g., policies, procedures, contacts), and support (e.g., encouragement, constructive feedback, advice) they need in order to do their job effectively, as well as access to opportunities for challenging work, skill and knowledge development, and professional growth. These "empowerment tools" depend on formal and informal systems within the work environment. Formal power is defined by jobs that are visible and essential to organizational goals, and that entail greater autonomy and control over work processes. *Informal power* refers to the quality of relationships between employees and their superiors and colleagues, as well as other individuals at lower levels in the organization that facilitate accomplishment of work goals. Employees with high formal and informal power are more able to make or influence decisions, mobilize resources, and accomplish their work. Employees with access to these sources of structural power are said to be *structurally empowered* and are therefore able to contribute to the overall productivity of the organization (Kanter, 1979).

Psychological empowerment theory

Psychological empowerment is a multidimensional concept that captures how employees experience working in empowering work environments (Kraimer et al., 1999). According to Thomas and Velthouse (1990), psychological empowerment is comprised of four dimensions: meaning (the value employees attribute to their work), competence (self-efficacy beliefs related to work accomplishment), self-determination (autonomy and choice in how work is accomplished), and impact (degree to which one can influence decisions and outcomes at work). Employees who are psychologically empowered are motivated to accomplish their work; and they feel that they play an active and valuable role in shaping their work, and that they contribute in a meaningful way to their organization.

Integrated models of empowerment: linking structural and psychological empowerment

The majority of studies we identified focused on only one type of empowerment. However, several empowerment scholars have tested models that incorporated both structural and psychological empowerment, and their combined effect on employee and organizational outcomes, to obtain a more comprehensive explanation of empowerment (Kraimer et al., 1999; Laschinger, Finegan, & Wilk, 2011; Seibert, Silver, & Randolph, 2004; Spreitzer, 2008). This logical link between structural and psychological empowerment was first suggested by Bowen and Lawler (1995) and is consistent with Kanter's (1977, 1993) proposition that when situations are structured in a way that enables employees to accomplish their work, they will feel empowered. That is, they are more likely to experience greater meaning in their work, and greater sense of control, competence, and influence in their work setting (psychological empowerment). Consequently, they respond positively by mobilizing the resources at their disposal in order to achieve successful outcomes at work.

Related research

Laschinger et al. (2011; Laschinger, Finegan, & Wilk, 2009) identified structural empowerment as a key antecedent to psychological empowerment, suggesting that psychological empowerment is an important mechanism through which structurally empowering work environments influence employee and organizational outcomes. The link between structural and psychological empowerment has been supported among staff nurses (Chang, Shih, & Lin, 2010; Laschinger et al., 2001), nurse managers (Laschinger, Purdy, & Almost, 2007), and new graduate nurses (Smith, Andrusyszyn, & Laschinger, 2010). A few studies in the general management literature have supported this link (Kraimer et al., 1999; Spreitzer, 2008). For instance, Kraimer et al. (1999) and Seibert, et al. (2004) found that jobs characterized by structures that foster employees' ability to accomplish their work were positively associated with employees' perceptions of psychological empowerment. Spreitzer (2008) also found that organizational characteristics similar to Kanter's structural empowerment factors were an important part of the nomological network for psychological empowerment. Taken together, these studies provide theoretical and empirical evidence that structural empowerment establishes the working conditions necessary for psychological empowerment to develop and thrive (Chang et al., 2010; Laschinger et al., 2001).

Workplace empowerment and employee health and wellbeing

The links between structural and psychological empowerment and employee health and wellbeing have been supported in numerous studies. In this section, we discuss the evidence linking workplace empowerment to specific health outcomes (mental and physical health) and to broader aspects of positive workplace wellbeing (work engagement organizational commitment, job and career satisfaction and turnover intentions) and negative workplace wellbeing (job stress, job strain and burnout).

Specific health effects of structural and psychological empowerment

Employee mental and physical health has been linked with empowerment in the workplace in a variety of occupational groups. Structural empowerment has been linked to poor occupational mental health ($r = -.69$; Laschinger & Havens, 1997), greater mental health symptoms ($r = -.29$; Wing, Regan, & Laschinger, 2015), and physical health symptoms (Laschinger, Almost, Purdy, & Kim, 2004; Laschinger & Finegan, 2005). In their study of nurse managers, Laschinger et al. (2004) found that structural empowerment was associated with higher energy levels ($r = .22 - .33$) and fewer negative physical health symptoms ($r = -.18 - -.28$). Structural empowerment was also significantly related to fewer depressive symptoms ($r = -.25 - -.33$). In another study, Laschinger and Finegan (2005) found that staff nurses' perceptions of structural empowerment were related to these same outcomes among staff nurses through their effect on perceptions of person–job fit and burnout. Read and Laschinger (2015) found a significant relationship between structural empowerment and mental health symptoms ($r = -.18$) and that social capital (quality of workplace relationships) was an important mechanism through which structural empowerment influenced employee mental health. These studies demonstrate the positive effect that empowerment has on workplace relationships and, ultimately, worker wellbeing.

Research has also shown that empowerment is associated with lower levels of bullying and incivility, which are associated with mental and physical health of employees (Read & Laschinger, 2013). Laschinger et al. (2010) found that structural empowerment had a significant negative effect on workplace bullying ($\beta = -.25$), which was subsequently related to lower burnout, a well-established predictor of poor mental and physical health. Similarly, Laschinger, Leiter, and Day (2009) showed that incivility from coworkers ($r = -.18$) and immediate supervisors ($r = -.26$) were associated with poor mental health among nurses. In another study, Laschinger et al. (2013) found that incivility from coworkers, supervisors, and physicians were all significantly related to increased mental health symptoms among nurses, and that personal resiliency moderated the effect of coworker incivility on frequency of mental health symptoms. This latter finding highlights the protective effect that intrapersonal resources in addition to organizational conditions have on employee health. These studies demonstrate the important role of structurally empowering working conditions in mitigating the negative health effects of workplace mistreatment.

Psychological empowerment has also been shown to have an impact on employee mental and physical health. Laschinger et al. (2004) found that psychological empowerment was significantly related to higher energy levels and fewer physical symptoms as well as significantly lower levels of depressive symptomology. Taştan (2013) found that each of the four components of psychological empowerment were significantly related to Turkish teachers' work-related psychological wellbeing (including anxiety and depression). The meaning component of psychological empowerment had the strongest effect ($\beta = .49$), followed by self-determination ($\beta = .40$), impact ($\beta = .27$), and competency ($\beta = .23$). In Krishnan's (2012) study of managers, psychological empowerment was significantly related to meaning in life ($r = .56$) and overall wellbeing ($r = .40$). Finally, Holdsworth and Cartwright (2003) found that low-autonomy jobs were significantly associated with lower levels of psychological empowerment and poor mental and physical health. These studies support the relationship between psychological empowerment and wellbeing, and highlight the important role that empowering work plays in employee health.

Not surprisingly, burnout has been shown to be a key mediator between empowerment and mental and physical health outcomes. Laschinger and Finegan (2005) found that structural empowerment positively influenced nurses' perceptions of person–job fit, resulting in lower levels of burnout. Burnout, in turn, was significantly related to decreased energy levels and increased frequency of physical and depressive symptoms. This study demonstrated the positive effect of structural empowerment on mental and physical health through its influence on person–job fit and burnout. Structural empowerment has been consistently linked to burnout across numerous studies of nurses (Guo et al., 2015; Laschinger, Finegan, & Wilk, 2011; Laschinger, Grau, Finegan, & Wilk, 2010)

Broader workplace wellbeing empowerment outcomes

Structural empowerment (Kanter, 1977, 1993), has been linked to numerous positive outcomes associated with employee wellbeing, such as work engagement, and job and career satisfaction (Osthus, 2007; Pineau Stam, Laschinger, Regan, & Wong, 2015; Talucci et al., 2015). Low levels of structural empowerment have also been linked to higher levels of negative workplace wellbeing, such as job strain (Laschinger et al., 2001), work stress (Lautizi, Laschinger, & Ravazzolo, 2009), burnout (Laschinger, Wong, & Grau, 2013), and job and career turnover intentions (Cai & Zhou, 2009; Laschinger, 2012; Nedd, 2006).

Similarly, psychological empowerment (Porath et al., 2012; Spreitzer, 1995) has been shown to play a positive role in employees' workplace wellbeing. Psychological empowerment is related to greater work engagement (Bhatnagar, 2012) and job satisfaction, and lower turnover intentions (Laschinger, Finegan et al., 2009). It has also been linked to lower levels of work stress (Holdsworth & Cartwright, 2003), job strain (Spreitzer, Kizilos, & Nason, 1997), and burnout (Boudrias, Morin, & Brodeur, 2012; Laschinger et al., 2011).

In addition to reducing detrimental job-related health outcomes, empowerment also has beneficial outcomes that deserve attention. The advent of the Positive Organizational Scholarship movement in the early 2000s has been influential in shifting the focus of organizational research towards examining positive phenomena such as job satisfaction, work engagement, and organizational commitment. While it is important to understand the role of workplace empowerment in reducing negative employee health outcomes, it is also valuable to recognize the role it plays in creating healthy work environments where employees can not only survive, but also thrive. Job satisfaction, work engagement, and organizational commitment represent key characteristics of employees who are thriving and motivated in their jobs.

Work satisfaction

Employee job satisfaction is an important indicator of employee wellbeing. Structural empowerment has been linked to nurses' job satisfaction in numerous studies. For instance, Laschinger et al. (2011) found that structural empowerment had a direct effect on nurses' job satisfaction (β = .30). Similar findings were reported among new graduate nurses (β = .49) (Pineau Stam et al., 2015). Other studies have found significant associations between structural empowerment and job satisfaction among nurses in Canada (r = .24 − .61) (Laschinger, 2012; Laschinger et al., 2016; Laschinger, Leiter, Day, & Gilen, 2009) and nurses in China (r = .56) (Cai & Zhou, 2009). Read and Laschinger (2015) found that empowerment was positively related to a sense of community at work (social capital), which, in turn, had a positive effect on new graduate nurses' job satisfaction. Cicolini, Comparcini, and Simonetti's (2014) recent systematic review provided conclusive evidence that structural empowerment is a statistically significant predictor of nurses' job satisfaction across numerous studies.

Outside of nursing, Orgambídez-Ramos and Borrego-Ales (2014) found strong relationships between structural empowerment and professors' job satisfaction (r = .25 − .57 for each empowerment dimension). Among general employees in Norway, Østhus (2007) found that task discretion (a form of employee power) was positively related to job satisfaction (r = .34) and negatively related to extensive work demands (r = − .10), job insecurity (r = − 0.11), and work-related health problems (r = − 0.12).

Psychological empowerment has also been linked to worker job satisfaction. Several studies by Larrabee and colleagues have found that psychological empowerment is significantly related to nurses' job satisfaction (Larrabee et al., 2003, 2010; Morrison, Jones, & Fuller, 1997). Koberg, Boss, Senjem, and Goodman (1999) also revealed significant associations between psychological empowerment and job satisfaction among general hospital employees (r = .60). In a recent systematic review, Cicolini et al (2014) also provided evidence that psychological empowerment was an important predictor of nurses' job satisfaction and that structural empowerment had a significant influence on nurses' feelings of psychological empowerment.

Outside of nursing and health care, a national survey of Australian workers by Savery and Luks (2001) found that employee job satisfaction was significantly related to the amount of influence a worker had over their job and decisions that directly affect him or her, supporting the idea that impact and self-determination components of psychological empowerment are particularly important for job satisfaction. Among call center agents, Holdsworth and Cartwright (2003) found that self-determination (β = .716), meaning (β = .24) and impact (β = − .30) were predictors of overall job satisfaction. This is consistent with Khany and Tazik's (2015) study of English teachers in Iran, which showed that teachers' psychological empowerment had a significant direct effect on their job satisfaction (β = .48). Similar results were found by Carless (2004) among customer service employees (β = .83).

Work engagement

Work engagement is a relatively new construct in the literature that has gained considerable empirical support across occupational groups. Work engagement refers to a "positive, fulfilling work-related state of mind that is characterized by vigor, dedication, and absorption" (Schaufeli, Bakker, & Salanova, 2006, p. 702). According to Schaufeli et al. (2006), work engagement is not simply the opposite of burnout, but a unique construct on its own – albeit negatively correlated. It is also reasonable to expect that employees when feel empowered to accomplish their work in a meaningful way, they will feel more engaged with their work. Studies linking empowerment to work engagement are described in the following paragraphs.

Positive links between workplace empowerment and work engagement have been demonstrated in a number of studies. Boamah and Laschinger (2014) found that structural empowerment was a significant predictor of work engagement (β = .45) among new graduate nurses, as did Cziraki and Laschinger (2015) in a study of staff nurses (β = .31). They found that structural empowerment was significantly related to work engagement (r = .44) and mediated the relationship between leader-empowering behaviors and work engagement. Greco, Laschinger, and Wong (2006) and Cho, Laschinger, and Wong. (2006) also linked structural empowerment to engagement, although using a different measure of work engagement. Outside of nursing, Xanthopoulou et al. (2007) showed that both job resources similar to structural empowerment and personal resources similar to psychological empowerment) had positive effects on work engagement (β = .43 for job resources and β = .29 for personal resources). Psychological empowerment is also related to work engagement. Wang and Liu (2015) showed that support for professional practice positively influenced staff nurses' psychological empowerment (β =.46), which subsequently led to greater engagement with their work (β = .54). This is consistent with previous findings showing that nurses' work engagement was positively influenced by structural empowerment (β =.51), and subsequently, greater effectiveness at work (β = .39; Laschinger, Wilk, Cho, & Greco, 2009). Macsinga et al. (2015) also found that psychological empowerment was an important factor related to work engagement (β = .35). A study of managers from Indian manufacturing industries showed that psychological empowerment had a significant positive effect on work engagement (β = .65), leading to increased innovation (β = .28) and lower turnover intentions (β = − .10; Bhatnagar, 2012). DiNapoli et al. (2016) established significant relationships between both structural and psychological empowerment, and work engagement. Together, these studies show that employees who experience their working conditions as structurally empowering tend to be more energized, dedicated, and absorbed in their work, leading to positive outcomes for employees and their organizations.

Organizational commitment

Another important indicator of employees' job-related health and wellbeing is organizational commitment, which refers to employees' psychological attachment to their workplace organization (Meyer & Allen, 1991). Affective commitment – an employee's feelings of affiliation, identification, and belonging – is a particularly important barometer of employee attachment to an organization. Other forms of commitment such as normative commitment (feelings of duty or obligation) and continuance commitment (lack of alternatives) may not necessarily represent positive feelings towards one's organization. Not surprisingly, most studies of organizational commitment have focused on the affective component.

Many studies have found a positive relationship between workplace empowerment and affective organizational commitment. In nursing, structural empowerment has been significantly related to affective commitment in studies of acute-case staff nurses (Wilson & Laschinger, 1994), long-term care nurses (DeCicco, Laschinger, & Kerr, 2006), new graduate nurses (Smith et al., 2010), and nurse managers (Laschinger et al., 2004). Proenca (2007) found that US health care employees working in teams characterized by clear goals, team-based (vs. individual) rewards, and an appropriate mix of complementary skills and expertise had positive effects on psychological empowerment (β = .28), which in turn was a significant predictor of affective commitment (β = .43). In a multilevel study of staff nurses, Laschinger et al. (2009) found that nurses who worked on structurally empowering hospital units had higher levels of psychological empowerment (β = .67) and that both forms of empowerment had significant positive effects on their commitment to the organization (β = .39). In this study, leader member exchange was a precursor to structural empowerment (β = .29), highlighting the important role of leaders in establishing empowering working conditions. Similar findings were demonstrated by Boonyarit, Chomphupart, and Arin (2010) who showed that, among teachers in Thailand, transformational leadership was related to both structural and psychological empowerment, which in turn were significant predictors of organizational commitment.

Overall, research to date suggests that structurally empowering work environments positively influence employees' psychological empowerment, and that both forms of empowerment can increase feelings of commitment towards their workplace organization and their job satisfaction. Consistent with Kanter's (1977, 1993) theory of structural empowerment and Spreitzer's (1995) theory of psychological empowerment, recent work has demonstrated that people value meaningful work and autonomy in their jobs (Benz & Frey, 2008). Meaning and autonomy, in turn, are associated with increased organizational commitment (Meyer, Stanley, & Parfyonova, 2012), job satisfaction (Savery & Luks, 2001), and psychological health benefits (Britt, Adler, & Bartone, 2001). Thus, workplace empowerment, which structures the workplace in ways that increase employee autonomy and motivation, is a logical precursor to employee engagement and commitment.

Effects of empowerment on negative aspects of workplace wellbeing

Working conditions have a potent effect on the health and wellbeing of employees through their influence on job stress, job strain, and burnout. Key theoretical perspectives that inform our understanding of how work environments influence these outcomes include Karasek's (1979) Job Strain model (also referred to as the Job Demands–Control model), Siegrist's (1996) Effort-Reward Imbalance (ERI) theory, and the Job Demands–Resources (JD-R) model (Bakker & Demerouti, 2007). In the Job Strain model, Karasek (1979) proposed that the interaction between an employee's job control (e.g., degree of freedom to make decisions at work) and job demands play a key role in determining employee job strain. Specifically, when job demands are high and job control is low, job strain is likely to result. In the ERI model (Siegrist, 1996), job strain is thought to result from an imbalance between job demands (employee effort) and rewards (such as one's salary, status, etc.). Finally in the JD-R model, job strain is the result of an imbalance between job demands and job resources available to meet those demands (Bakker & Demerouti, 2007). Importantly, the JD-R model also emphasizes that when job resources are sufficient to meet job demands, employee motivation and engagement are likely to result.

Aligning with these related theoretical perspectives, structural empowerment can be thought of as a set of organizational job resources that employees need to meet the demands of their jobs. Structurally empowering work environments that provide workers with the resources, information, support, and opportunities to meet the demands of their job is one way that managers can reduce stressful working conditions and mitigate the negative effects of burnout on employee mental and physical health. This is consistent with the JD-R model (Bakker & Demerouti, 2007; Schaufeli, Bakker, & van Rhenen, 2009), which proposes that job stress and burnout result from an imbalance between job demands and job resources. Xanthopoulou et al. (2007) also suggested that personal resources play an important role in determining how employees respond to work demands, and that given adequate job resources, employees are able to be more effective, engaged, and feel that their work is meaningful. Consistent with Karasek's (1979) work, structurally empowering work environments also provide employees with increased control and autonomy over their work, contributing to lower levels of job strain that comes from feelings of powerlessness to act. Finally, from an ERI perspective, empowering working conditions reward employees for a job well done through positive feedback (support) from coworkers and managers, and opportunities to learn and develop new skills and knowledge.

Empirically, the importance of both structurally empowering work environments and employees' psychological empowerment in preventing job strain and burnout have been supported by several studies. For example, structural empowerment has been associated with increased job strain ($\beta = -.17$) (Guo et al., 2015) and decreased burnout among both new and experienced nurses ($r = -.21 - -.58$) (Gilbert, Laschinger, & Leiter, 2010; Laschinger et al., 2013; Laschinger et al., 2011). Greco et al. (2006) also found that person-job fit was an additional mechanism through which structural empowerment influenced burnout. Thus, structural empowerment has been shown not only to have a direct effect on job strain and burnout, but also to influence employee perceptions of how well their job matches with their expectations ($\beta = .67$), with greater alignment (i.e., person–job fit) leading to decreased burnout ($\beta = -.54$).

Research has also examined the effect of psychological empowerment on workplace stress, job strain, and burnout. Spreitzer (1995) found that of the four components of psychological empowerment, meaning, and competence were important predictors of job strain, with meaning increasing job strain ($\beta = .14$), and competence decreasing it ($\beta = -.26$). In a study of service employees in Israel, Ben-Zur and Yagil (2005) examined the effect of psychological empowerment on aggression from customers, emotion- and problem-focused coping, and burnout. Their results showed that empowerment had a significant negative effect on aggression ($\beta = -.31$) and depersonalization ($\beta = -.20$), and a positive effect on personal accomplishment ($\beta = .41$), and that aggression from customers was positively related to exhaustion ($\beta = .27$), and depersonalization ($\beta = .32$) components of burnout. In a study of hotel and restaurant employees in India, transformational leadership and psychological empowerment were associated with lower levels of job stress ($\beta = -.15$ and $\beta = -.15$, respectively; Gill, Flaschner, & Bhutani, 2010). Others have shown links between psychological empowerment and burnout and employee psychosomatic complaints (Jourdain & Chênevert, 2010), and employees' intention to leave (Jourdain & Chênevert, 2010; Laschinger et al., 2014). Avey, Luthans, and Youssef (2010), on the other hand, did not find a significant relationship between psychological empowerment and cynicism in a heterogeneous sample of US workers, though they did find a significant negative association with intention to quit one's job. In this study, psychological capital was also included, potentially diminishing the unique variance explained by psychological capital. Overall, though, past studies show that, like structural empowerment, psychological empowerment helps employees cope with demanding people and stressful situations at work.

Perhaps most valuable in understanding the effects of structural and psychological empowerment on job stress and burnout are studies that have looked at both forms of empowerment together. One of the first studies to do so was Laschinger et al. (2001), who found that structural empowerment was a significant predictor of psychological empowerment ($\beta = .85$), which, in turn, was related to lower levels of job strain among staff nurses ($\beta = -.57$). Although they did not explicitly use structural empowerment in their study, Xanthopoulou et al. (2007) found that access to job resources that align with Kanter's (1977, 1993) empowerment structures – such as professional development (opportunity), social support (support), autonomy (informal power), and supervisory coaching (support) – were positively related to employees' intrapersonal resources of optimism, organization-based self-esteem, and self-efficacy (overlapping with psychological empowerment), which in turn was associated with lower levels of exhaustion.

In sum, there is considerable evidence that employees react positively to structurally empowering work environments by feeling more psychologically empowered and that both of these forms of workplace empowerment are important factors influencing job stress, job strain, and burnout.

Implications for organizations

Workplace empowerment is an important characteristic of healthy work environments that support employee wellbeing and productivity. Leaders play a vital role in establishing and maintaining working conditions that empower employees to accomplish their work effectively, while remaining engaged, committed, and achieving high levels of health and wellbeing. The strong relationship between empowerment and wellbeing outcomes found in studies reviewed in this chapter suggests that managers can employ structural empowerment strategies to improve employee health and wellbeing. Structural empowerment has shown to be positively related to positive health-related outcomes and negatively related to negative ones. Thus, a practical approach for managers to empower employees and enhance their work-related wellbeing lies in ensuring access to the four empowerment structures identified by Kanter (1993, 1977).

Laschinger and Grau (2012) provide an excellent starting point for evidence-informed strategies that managers can employ to create empowering work environments. In light of the strong relationships between structural and psychological empowerment in the literature, strategies to increase structural empowerment are likely to increase psychological empowerment, and, ultimately, enhance employee health and wellbeing while reducing the incidence of negative outcomes such as burnout, job strain, and ill health. The following strategies will focus primarily on structural empowerment strategies that managers can use to promote positive health outcomes, with the premise that these same strategies will simultaneously reduce negative health and wellbeing-related outcomes.

Access to information

Providing employees with timely and transparent information is an important empowerment strategy. For example, by communicating organizational goals clearly, staff will understand the current status of the organization and the vision for the future. In addition, providing employees with open access to technical knowledge will help them perform their job more effectively. We recommend that leaders use multiple methods of communication with staff (e.g., one-on-one discussions, staff meetings, huddles, emails, and newsletters) and work to build and strengthen positive relationships with staff through relational (vs. merely transactional) leadership styles. Regular contact with employees may help leaders communicate more effectively with employees, leading to greater feelings of work effectiveness and workplace wellbeing.

Access to support

Another empowerment strategy is to provide ongoing support in the work environment. In day-to-day operations, managers should make themselves visible and be available to meet with employees, providing them with opportunities to discuss concerns. Employees should also be provided with recognition for their achievements in meaningful ways. Another way that managers can provide support is by encouraging collaboration and collegiality among staff, and providing access to additional resources when needed. By providing formal and informal support in these ways, managers help employees accomplish their work and meet their emotional and social needs, which are likely to contribute to a sense of wellbeing and have a positive effect on their mental and physical health.

Access to resources

Providing adequate resources is vital to ensure that employees are able to perform their jobs effectively. These include supplies, equipment, and personnel required to successfully accomplish the work at hand. Consistent with the JD-R model and related research, it is reasonable to expect that when employees have access to the job resources that they need to meet the demands of their job, they will be motivated and engaged, and will experience positive health and wellbeing outcomes as a result. Moreover, they will be less likely to experience job strain and burnout, and the detrimental effects on employee health and wellbeing that accompany working conditions where job demands outweigh job resources.

Access to opportunities to learn and grow

It is important for leaders to encourage and provide access to advanced education and life-long learning for staff. Supporting professional training and development opportunities helps to ensure that the organization is keeping up with new ideas and best practices and also meets employee needs for fulfillment and growth. Theoretically, these empowering management strategies derived from Kanter's theory should result in greater psychological empowerment. In other words, by creating environments that are both structurally and psychologically empowering, managers contribute to employee health and wellbeing.

Avenues for future research

Despite considerable evidence linking workplace empowerment to employee health and wellbeing outcomes, relatively few studies have examined the direct impact of empowerment on employee mental and physical health, with the majority of research to date focusing on related outcomes such as burnout, engagement, and affective organizational commitment. Moreover, there are currently no studies examining the link between empowerment and physiological indicators of employee health such as cortisol and C-reactive protein levels, ambulatory or resting blood pressure, heart rate variability, serotonin levels, etc. While collecting physiological data is expensive and challenging, future research examining the links between workplace empowerment and physiological measures of employee health would add to our current knowledge about workplace empowerment. In addition, heightened interest in and availability of self-health monitoring technologies may make studies of this nature more feasible in the coming years.

Further research using more robust research designs (longitudinal and experimental) is needed to provide evidence-based direction for management seeking to create an empowered and healthy workforce. For example, longitudinal studies could examine the influence of structural and psychological empowerment on employee health and wellbeing over different stages of one's career (e.g., during onboarding and newcomer socialization, mid-career, and late career). This would provide a better understanding of the expected trajectory of workplace-related health outcomes as employees age and of the role empowerment plays in this process. As identified by

Seibert et al. (2004), group and multilevel studies examining the role of unit-level empowerment comprise another promising area of research that deserves more attention. Similar to the concept of structural empowerment, Seibert and colleagues found that empowerment climate, "a shared perception regarding the extent to which an organization makes use of structures, policies, and practices supporting employee empowerment" (p. 334), was an important group-level antecedent to psychological empowerment, which, in turn, positively influenced employee performance and job satisfaction. Laschinger, Nosko, Wilk, and Finegan (2014) found that staff nurses who worked on more structurally empowered hospital units also perceived higher levels of support for professional practice, leading to increased unit effectiveness and, ultimately, improved job satisfaction. In this study, nurses' psychological capital was also a significant factor contributing to their job satisfaction. In another study, Laschinger et al. (2009) showed that unit-level structural empowerment had a positive effect on nurses' psychological empowerment, and that both forms of empowerment increased organizational commitment. These studies, though few in number, show that there are important multilevel relationships between structural and psychological empowerment relevant to employees' job-related wellbeing. Given these results and those from numerous cross-sectional studies reviewed in this chapter, research examining the cross-level effects of structural and psychological empowerment on nurses' physical and mental health outcomes – as well as key mediators such as workplace bullying, incivility, and burnout – is a logical next step to advance our understanding of the role that empowerment plays in employee health and wellbeing.

Conclusion

Research to date provides substantial support for the link between workplace empowerment and employee health and job-related wellbeing. Workplace empowerment sets the stage for employees to be engaged in meaningful and productive work, leading to feelings of self-determination, competence, and the ability to make an impact in their work setting. The combination of structural and psychological empowerment has been shown to reduce job stress and burnout, thereby creating a more satisfied and healthy workforce. Organizations and managers play a critical role in creating structurally empowering work environments and fostering employees' psychological empowerment. Therefore, every effort should be made to implement and support initiatives to enhance employee access to workplace empowerment structures and investment in psychological empowerment of employees.

References

Avey, J. B., Luthans, F., & Youssef, C. M. (2010). The additive value of positive psychological capital in predicting work attitudes and behaviors. *Journal of Management*, 36(2), 430–452. doi: 10.1177/0149206308329961

Bakker, A. B., & Demerouti, E. (2007). The Job Demands–Resources model: State of the art. *Journal of Managerial Psychology*, 22(3), 309–328. doi: 10.1108/02683940710733115

Benz, M., & Frey, B. S. (2008). The value of doing what you like: Evidence from the self-employed in 23 countries. *Journal of Economic Behavior and Organization*, 68(3–4), 445–455. doi:10.1016/j.jebo.2006.10.014

Ben-Zur, H., & Yagil, D. (2005). The relationship between empowerment, aggressive behaviours of customers, coping, and burnout. *European Journal of Work and Organizational Psychology*, 14(1), 81–99. doi: 10.1080/13594320444000281

Bhatnagar, J. (2012). Management of innovation: Role of psychological empowerment, work engagement and turnover intention in the Indian context. *The International Journal of Human Resource Management*, 23(5), 928–951. doi: 10.1080/09585192.2012.651313

Boamah, S., & Laschinger, H. (2014). Engaging new nurses: The role of psychological capital and workplace empowerment. *Journal of Research in Nursing*, 20(4), 265–277. doi: 10.1177/1744987114527302

Boonyarit, I., Chomphupart, S., & Arin, N. (2010). Leadership, empowerment, and attitude outcomes. *The Journal of Behavioral Science*, 5(1), 1–14.

Boudrias, J. S., Morin, A. J. S., & Brodeur, M. M. (2012). Role of psychological empowerment in the reduction of burnout in Canadian healthcare workers. *Nursing and Health Sciences*, 14(1), 8–17. doi: 10.1111/j.1442-2018.2011.00650.x

Bowen, D. E., & Lawler, E. E. (1995). Empowering service employees. *Sloan Management Review*, 36(4), 73–79.

Britt, T. W., Adler, A. B., & Bartone, P. T. (2001). Deriving benefits from stressful events: The role of engagement in meaningful work and hardiness. *Journal of Occupational Health Psychology*, 6(1), 53–63.

Cai, C., & Zhou, Z. (2009). Structural empowerment, job satisfaction, and turnover intention of Chinese clinical nurses. *Nursing and Health Sciences*, 11(4), 397–403. doi: 10.1111/j.1442-2018.2009.00470.x

Carless, S. A. (2004). Does psychological empowerment mediate the relationship between psychological climate and job satisfaction? *Journal of Business and Psychology*, 18(4), 405–425.

Chang, L.-C., Shih, C.-H., & Lin, S.-M. (2010). The mediating role of psychological empowerment on job satisfaction and organizational commitment for school health nurses: A cross-sectional questionnaire survey. *International Journal of Nursing Studies*, 47(4), 427–433. doi: 10.1016/j.ijnurstu.2009.09.007

Cho, J., Laschinger, H. S., & Wong, C. (2006). Workplace empowerment, work engagement and organizational commitment of new graduate nurses. *Nursing Leadership*, 19(3), 43–60.

Cicolini, G., Comparcini, D., & Simonetti, V. (2014). Workplace empowerment and nurses' job satisfaction: A systematic literature review. *Journal of Nursing Management*, 22(7), 855–871. doi: 10.1111/jonm.12028

Conger, J. A., & Kanungo, R. N. (1988). The empowerment process: Integrating theory and practice. *Academy of Management Review*, 13(3), 471–482.

Cziraki, K., & Laschinger, H. K. S. (2015). Leader empowering behaviours and work engagement: The mediating role of structural empowerment. *Canadian Journal of Nursing Leadership*, 28(3), 10–22.

DeCicco, J., Laschinger, H., & Kerr, M. (2006). Perceptions of empowerment and respect: Effect on nurses' organizational commitment in nursing homes. *Journal of Gerontological Nursing*, 32(5), 49–56.

DiNapoli, J. M., O'Flaherty, D., Musil, C., Clavelle, J. T., & Fitzpatrick, J. J. (2016). The relationship of clinical nurses' perceptions of structural and psychological empowerment and engagement on their unit. *The Journal of Nursing Administration*, 46(2), 95–100. doi: 10.1097/NNA.0000000000000302

Gilbert, S., Laschinger, H. K. S., & Leiter, M. (2010). The mediating effect of burnout on the relationship between structural empowerment and organizational citizenship behaviours. *Journal of Nursing Management*, 18(3), 339–348. doi: 10.1111/j.1365-2834.2010.01074.x

Gill, A., Flaschner, A. B., & Bhutani, S. (2010). The impact of transformational leadership and empowerment on employee job stress. *Business and Economics Journal*, 18, 1060–1072.

Greco, P., Laschinger, H. K. S., & Wong, C. (2006). Leader empowering behaviours, staff nurse empowerment and work engagement/burnout. *Nursing Leadership (Toronto, Ont.)*, 19(4), 41–56.

Guo, J. Chen, J., Fu, J., Ge, X., Chen, M., & Liu, Y. (2015). Structural empowerment, job stress and burnout of nurses in China. *Applied Nursing Research*. doi: 10.1016/j.apnr.2015.12.007

Holdsworth, L., & Cartwright, S. (2003). Empowerment, stress and satisfaction: An exploratory study of a call centre. *Leadership & Organization Development Journal*, 24(3), 131–140. doi: 10.1108/01437730310469552

Jourdain, G., & Chênevert, D. (2010). Job demands–resources, burnout and intention to leave the nursing profession: A questionnaire survey. *International Journal of Nursing Studies*, 47(6), 709–722. doi: 10.1016/j.ijnurstu.2009.11.007

Kanter, R. M. (1977). *Men and Women of the Corporation*. New York: Basic Books.

Kanter, R. M. (1979). Power failure in management circuits. *Harvard Business Review,* 57(4), 65–75.

Kanter, R. M. (1993). *Men and Women of the Corporation* (2nd ed.). New York: Basic Books.

Karasek, R. A. (1979). Job demands, job decision latitude, and mental strain: Implications for job redesign. *Administrative Science Quarterly*, 24(2), 285–308.

Khany, R., & Tazik, K. (2015). On the relationship between psychological empowerment, trust, and Iranian EFL teachers' job satisfaction: The case of secondary school teachers. *Journal of Career Assessment*, 1–18. doi: 10.1177/1069072714565362

Koberg, C. S., Boss, R. W., Senjem, J. C., & Goodman, E. A. (1999). Antecedents and outcomes of empowerment: Empirical evidence from the health care industry. *Group & Organization Management*, 24(1), 71–91.

Kraimer, M. L., Seibert, S. E., & Liden, R. C. (1999). Psychological empowerment as a multidimensional construct: A test of construct validity. *Educational and Psychological Measurement*, 59(1), 127–142.

Krishnan, V. R. (2012). Transformational leadership and personal outcomes: empowerment as mediator. *Leadership & Organization Development Journal*, 33(6), 550–563. doi: 10.1108/01437731211253019

Larrabee, J. H., Janney, M. A., Ostrow, C. L., Withrow, M. L., Hobbs, G. R., & Burant, C. (2003). Predicting registered nurse job satisfaction and intent to leave. *Journal of Nursing Administration*, 33(5), 271–283.

Larrabee, J. H., Wu, Y., Persily, C. A., Simoni, P. S., Johnston, P. A., Marcischak, T. L., . . . & Gladden, S. D. (2010). Influence of stress resiliency on RN job satisfaction and intent to stay. *Western Journal of Nursing Research*, 32(1), 81–102. doi: 10.1177/0193945909343293

Laschinger, H. K. S. (2012). Job and career satisfaction and turnover intentions of newly graduated nurses. Journal of Nursing Management, 20(4), 472–484. doi: 10.1111/j.1365-2834.2011.01293.x

Laschinger, H. K. S., Almost, J., Purdy, N., & Kim, J.(2004). Predictors of nurse managers' health in Canadian restructured healthcare settings. *Nursing Leadership (Toronto, Ont.)*, 17(4), 88–105.

Laschinger, H. K. S., Cummings, G., Leiter, M., Wong, C., MacPhee, M., Ritchie, J., . . . & Young-Ritchie, C. (2016). Starting Out: A time-lagged study of new graduate nurses' transition to practice. *International Journal of Nursing Studies*, 57, 82–95. doi: 10.1016/j.ijnurstu.2016.01.005

Laschinger, H. K. S., Finegan, J., & Wilk, P. (2001). Impact of structural and psychological empowerment on job strain in nursing work settings expanding Kanter's Model. *Journal of Nursing Administration*, 31(5), 260–272.

Laschinger, H. K. S., Finegan, J., & Wilk, P. (2009). Context matters: The impact of unit leadership and empowerment on nurses' organizational commitment. *Journal of Nursing Administration*, 39(5), 228–235. doi: 10.1097/NNA.0b013e3181a23d2b

Laschinger, H. K. S., Finegan, J., & Wilk, P. (2011). Situational and dispositional influences on nurses' workplace well-being: The role of empowering unit leadership. *Nursing Research*, 60(2), 124–131. doi: 10.1097/NNR.0b013e318209782e

Laschinger, H. K. S., & Grau, A. L. (2012). The influence of personal dispositional factors and organizational resources on workplace violence, burnout, and health outcomes in new graduate nurses: A cross-sectional study. *International Journal of Nursing Studies*, 49(3), 282–291. doi: 10.1016/j.ijnurstu.2011.09.004

Laschinger, H. K. S. Grau, A. L., Finegan, J., & Wilk, P. (2010). New graduate nurses' experiences of bullying and burnout in hospital settings. *Journal of Advanced Nursing*, 66(12), 2732–2742. doi: 10.1111/j.1365-2648.2010.05420.x

Laschinger, H. K. S., & Havens, D. S. (1997). The effect of workplace empowerment on staff nurses' occupational mental health and work effectiveness. *Journal of Nursing Administration*, 27(6), 42–49.

Laschinger, H. K. S., Nosko, A., Wilk, P., & Finegan, J. (2014). Effects of unit empowerment and perceived support for professional nursing practice on unit effectiveness and individual nurse well-being: A time-lagged study. *International Journal of Nursing Studies*, 51(12), 1615–1623. doi: 10.1016/j.ijnurstu.2014.04.010

Laschinger, H. K. S., Purdy, N., & Almost, J. (2007). The impact of leader-member exchange quality, empowerment, and core self-evaluation on nurse manager's job satisfaction. *Journal of Nursing Administration*, 37(5), 221–229. doi: 10.1097/01.NNA.0000269746.63007.08

Laschinger, H. K. S., Wilk, P., Cho, J., & Greco, P. (2009). Empowerment, engagement and perceived effectiveness in nursing work environments: Does experience matter? *Journal of Nursing Management*, 17(5), 636–646. doi: 10.1111/j.1365-2834.2008.00907.x

Laschinger, H. K. S., Wong, C. A., & Grau, A. L. (2013). Authentic leadership, empowerment and burnout: A comparison in new graduates and experienced nurses. *Journal of Nursing Management*, 21(3), 541–552. doi: 10.1111/j.1365-2834.2012.01375.x

Lautizi, M., Laschinger, H. K. S., & Ravazzolo, S. (2009). Workplace empowerment, job satisfaction and job stress among Italian mental health nurses: An exploratory study. *Journal of Nursing Management*, 17(4), 446–452. doi: 10.1111/j.1365-2834.2009.00984.x

Macsinga, I., Sulea, C., Sârbescu, P., Fischmann, G., & Dumitru, C. (2015). Engaged, committed and helpful employees: The role of psychological empowerment. *The Journal of Psychology*, 149(3), 263–276. doi: 10.1080/00223980.2013.874323

Meyer, J. P., & Allen, N. J. (1991). A three-component model conceptualization of organizational commitment. *Human Resource Management Review*, 1(1), 61–89.

Meyer, J. P., Stanley, L. J., & Parfyonova, N. M. (2012). Employee commitment in context: The nature and implication of commitment profiles. *Journal of Vocational Behavior*, 80(1), 1–16. doi: 10.1016/j.jvb.2011.07.002

Morrison, R. S., Jones, L., & Fuller, B. (1997). The relation between leadership style and empowerment on job satisfaction of nurses. *Journal of Nursing Administration*, 27(5), 27–34.

Nedd, N. (2006). Perceptions of empowerment and intent to stay. *Nursing Economics*, 24(1), 13–18.

Orgambídez-Ramos, A., & Borrego-Alés, Y. (2014). Empowering employees: Structural empowerment as antecedent of job satisfaction in university settings. *Psychological Thought*, 7(1), 28–36. doi: 10.5964/psyct.v7i1.88

Østhus, S. (2007). For better or worse? Workplace changes and the health and well-being of Norwegian workers. *Work, Employment & Society*, 21(4), 731–750. doi: 10.1177/0950017007082881

Pineau Stam, L. M., Spence Laschinger, H. K., Regan, S., & Wong, C. A. (2015). The influence of personal and workplace resources on new graduate nurses' job satisfaction. *Journal of Nursing Management*, 23(2), 190–199. doi: 10.1111/jonm.12113

Porath, C., Spreitzer, G., Gibson, C., & Garnett, F. G. (2012). Thriving at work: Toward its measurement, construct validation, and theoretical refinement. *Journal of Organizational Behavior*, 33(2), 250–275. doi: 10.1002/job.756

Proenca, E. J. (2007). Team dynamics and team empowerment in health care organizations. *Health Care Management Review*, 32(4), 370–378. doi: 10.1097/01.HMR.0000296786.29718.86

Read, E., & Laschinger, H. K. (2013). Correlates of new graduate nurses' experiences of workplace mistreatment. *Journal of Nursing Administration*, 43(4), 221–228. doi: 10.1097/NNA.0b013e3182895a90

Read, E. A., & Laschinger, H. K. S. (2015). The influence of authentic leadership and empowerment on nurses' relational social capital, mental health and job satisfaction over the first year of practice. *Journal of Advanced Nursing*, 71(7), 1611–1623. doi:10.1111/jan.12625

Savery, L. K., & Luks, J. A. (2001). The relationship between empowerment, job satisfaction and reported stress levels: Some Australian evidence. *Leadership & Organization Development Journal*, 22(3), 97–104.

Schaufeli, W. B., Bakker, A. B., & Salanova, M. (2006). The measurement of short questionnaire, a cross-national study. *Educational and Psychological Measurement*, 66(4), 701–716. doi: 10.1177/0013164405282471

Schaufeli, W. B., Bakker, A. B., & van Rhenen, W. (2009). How changes in job demands and resources predict burnout, work engagement, and sickness absenteeism. *Journal of Organizational Behavior*, 30, 893–917. doi: 10.1002/job.595

Seibert, S. E., Silver, S. R., & Randolph, W. A. (2004). Taking empowerment to the next level: A multiple-level model of empowerment, performance, and satisfaction. *Academy of Management Journal*, 47(3), 332–349. www.jstor.org/stable/20159585

Siegrist, J. (1996). Adverse health effects of high-effort/low-reward conditions. *Journal of Occupational Health Psychology*, 1(1), 27–41.

Smith, L. M., Andrusyszyn, M. A., & Laschinger, H. K. S. (2010). Effects of workplace incivility and empowerment on newly-graduated nurses' organizational commitment. *Journal of Nursing Management*, 18(8), 1004–1015. doi: 10.1111/j.1365-2834.2010.01165.x

Spreitzer, G. M. (1995). Academy of management psychological empowerment in the workplace: Dimensions, measurement, and validation psychological empowerment in the and validation. *The Academy of Management Review*, 38(5), 1442–1465.

Spreitzer, G. M. (2008). Taking stock: A review of more than twenty years of research on empowerment at work. In: J. Barling & C. L. Cooper (eds.), *The Sage Handbook of Organizational Behaviour*. Trowbridge, Wiltshire: The Cromwell Press, 55–72.

Spreitzer, G. M., Kizilos, M. A., & Nason, S. W. (1997). A dimensional analysis of the relationship between psychological empowerment and effectiveness, satisfaction, and strain. *Journal of Management*, 23(5), 679.

Talucci, C., Rega, M. L., Sili, A., Vellone, E., Tartaglini, D., Galletti, C., & Alvaro, R. (2015). Structural empowerment and job satisfaction among nurses coordinators: A pilot study. *Professioni Inferieristiche*, 68(3), 143–150. doi: 10.7429/pi.2015.683143

Taştan, S. B. (2013). The relationship between psychological empowerment and psychological well being: the role of self-efficacy perception and social support. *Öneri Dergisi*, 10(40), 139–154.

Thomas, K. W., & Velthouse, B. A. (1990). Cognitive elements of empowerment: An "interpretive" model of intrinsic task motivation. *Academy of Management Journal*, 15(4), 666–681.

Wang, S., & Liu, Y. (2015). Impact of professional nursing practice environment and psychological empowerment on nurses' work engagement: Test of structural equation modelling. *Journal of Nursing Management*, 23(3), 287–296. doi: 10.1111/jonm.12124

Wilson, B., & Laschinger, H. K. S. (1994). Staff nurse perception of job empowerment and organizational commitment: A test of Ranter's theory of structural power in organizations. *Journal of Nursing Administration*, 24(4S), 39–47.

Wing, T., Regan, S., & Laschinger, H. K. S. (2015). The influence of empowerment and incivility on the mental health of new graduate nurses. *Journal of Nursing Management*, 23(5), 632–643. doi: 10.1111/jonm.12190

Xanthopoulou, D., Bakker, A. B., Demerouti, E., & Schaufeli, W. B. (2007). The role of personal resources in the Job Demands–Resources model. *International Journal of Stress Management*, 14(2), 121–141. doi: 10.1037/1072-5245.14.2.121

14

Coworking communities as enablers of thriving at work

Gretchen Spreitzer, Peter Bacevice, and Lyndon Garrett

Introduction

We've been studying what enables people to *thrive at work* for the last 10 years. Our research made an interesting turn a couple years ago when an alumnus contacted us after learning of our program of research on human thriving at work. He suggested if we wanted to learn about how organizations can enable higher levels of thriving at work, we should be studying coworking spaces. Our initial response was, "What in the world are coworking spaces?" We were not familiar with the new organizational form – a kind of collaborative workspace for freelance and remote workers to join in a professional work community. We were intrigued because while past research on thriving at work has focused on examining organizational factors that promote thriving in traditional workplaces, where employees have limited control over when, where, and with whom they work, coworking provides a unique case where workers are able to participate in creating the workplace and work routines that best fit their needs, or that best enable them to thrive. In fact, traditional organizations pay their employees to come to work, but in the world of coworking, workers are paying money to be able to come work in these spaces. What is attracting people to be associated with this new form of work organization and what insights might they have for enabling employee thriving at work?

In our research in many different contexts – from blue-collar work to knowledge work – we found that people typically report moderate levels of thriving, averaging 4–5 on a 7-point scale. However, when we measured thriving in coworking spaces, we were surprised to find members reporting levels of thriving substantially higher, approaching 6 on a 7-point scale – more than a full point higher. We were keen to learn about how coworking is inspiring such high levels of thriving at work and whether those factors might be relevant to helping employees working in traditional organizations to also thrive at high levels. And so our research journey on how characteristics of coworking spaces may enable high levels of thriving began.

In this chapter, we begin by defining thriving at work and demonstrating why it is a construct of interest for a volume on wellbeing. Then we describe what we already know about how organizations can enable more human thriving at work. We then introduce the phenomenon of coworking and describe what new insights these workspaces may offer for enabling thriving at work in all kinds of work contexts and situations.

What is thriving at work and why care about it?

Thriving is a desirable subjective experience, defined as "the psychological state in which individuals experience both a sense of vitality and a sense of learning at work" (Spreitzer, Sutcliffe, Dutton, Sonenshein, & Grant, 2005, p. 538). When thriving, individuals feel energized at the same time that they are growing and getting better at what they do. Thriving is the opposite of languishing (i.e., being stuck, caught in a rut, or failing to make progress). Consistent with prior work (e.g., Carmeli & Spreitzer, 2009; Spreitzer et al., 2005), thriving is conceptualized as a continuum where people are more or less thriving at any point in time. Further, Porath et al.'s (2011) construct validation study provided evidence that thriving is a psychological state and not an individual disposition. Specifically, they demonstrated significant within-person variation in the level of thriving across contexts and time periods.

The vitality component of thriving refers to the positive feeling of being energetic (Nix, Ryan, Manly, & Deci, 1999) and a having a zest for life (Miller & Stiver, 1997); it is captured in the broader interdisciplinary literature on thriving by a variety of labels, including flourishing (O'Leary, 1998), being intrinsically animated or energized (Benson & Scales, 2009; Norlander, Von Schedvin, & Archer, 2005; Poorman, 2002), and "living life fully" (Haight, Barba, Tesh, & Courts, 2002, p. 16). The learning component of thriving refers to the sense that one is acquiring and can apply knowledge and skills (Carver, 1998; Elliott & Dweck, 1988), and appears in the thriving literature under labels such as successful adaptation and growth (Ickovics & Park, 1998; O'Leary, 1998), self-generativity (Taylor, 2004), and the development of the self (Benson & Scales, 2009; Saakvitne, Tennen, & Affleck, 1998).

Consistent with Spreitzer et al.'s (2005) conceptualization of thriving, while each dimension – vitality and learning – signals a marker of thriving, the joint experience of both dimensions together is necessary in order for optimal psychological development. Ryff (1989), for example, suggests that development is comprised of learning (i.e., expanding in ways that reflect enhanced self-knowledge and effectiveness) and vitality (not feeling stagnated, bored, or disinterested). Likewise, Carver (1998) conceives of thriving as the psychological experience of growth in a positive capacity (i.e., a constructive or forward direction) that energizes and enlivens (Hartman & Zimberoff, 2007). Thus, the two dimensions reflect prior psychological research that highlights the importance of considering both dimensions of human development simultaneously.

When thriving, individuals are not merely surviving (Saakvitne et al., 1998) or getting by (Benson & Scales, 2009), but instead they are growing (Calhoun & Tedeschi, 1998; Joseph & Linley, 2008) and moving forward on an upward trajectory (Hall et al., 2009). While some researchers emphasize thriving more specifically as growth in response to trauma or crisis (i.e., akin to posttraumatic growth or resilience; Carver, 1998; Ickovics & Park, 1998), others see thriving as an everyday experience regarding how people interact with their environment (Blankenship, 1998).

As most working adults spend a large portion of their waking hours at work, it is important to consider how people do or do not experience thriving at work. Work is often considered a domain of life that is depleting or energy draining (Sonnentag & Zijlstra, 2006), but the emerging body of literature on Positive Organizational Scholarship is turning our attention to the potential for work to be "life-giving" and energy producing (Cameron & Spreitzer, 2012), such as by promoting the experience of thriving at work. Moreover, we have also found a positive spillover from thriving at work to thriving in other more personal aspects of life (Porath, Spreitzer, Gibson, & Garnett, 2012).

Prior research has found that, in addition to benefiting the individual, thriving is predictive of important work-related outcomes including job performance, reduced burnout, health, and career development initiative (Porath et al., 2012). Thriving individuals are also more proactive and creative in the doing of their work (Carmeli & Spreitzer, 2009). Thriving can also be a buffer for negative dynamics in work environments. For example, Gerbasi, Porath, Spreitzer, Brown, and Cross (forthcoming) found that thriving positively moderated the negative relationship between de-energizing relationships at work and job performance. Clearly, thriving is attractive to both individuals and to organizations – yet most individuals report wanting to improve their thriving in the workplace. In fact, when asked to share a time at work when they were thriving, the great majority will describe a past, rather than a current, work experience. This leads us to ask what organizations and leaders can do to enhance workers' experiences of thriving at work.

What can organizations do to enable more human thriving at work?

Prior research has found a number of enablers and disablers of human thriving at work. Drawing from theoretical work by Spreitzer et al. (2005), Porath, Spreitzer, and Gibson (2008) identified four organizational design features that enabled thriving at work. They found that more decision-making discretion (or empowerment), greater transparency in information sharing, a culture of civility, and more performance feedback all increased employee perceptions of thriving at work. These elements of a high-involvement or high-performance work system (Lawler, Mohrman & Ledford, 1998) are enablers of human thriving at work. In addition, Niessen, Sonnentag, and Sach (2013) found that when employees experience more meaning in their everyday work, they are more likely to report thriving at the end of the workday, because meaning at work increases exploration and task-focused behaviors. Other resources Niessen et al. (2013) were also found to enable thriving were positive relationships and knowledge. Most recently, Cullen, Gerbasi, and Chrobot-Mason (in press) found that when individuals experience more role overload and role ambiguity, they report lower levels of thriving at work.

While these findings are helpful, clearly there is still much to be learned about how organizations, leaders, and even individuals can enable thriving at work. We know little about how peers and teammate behaviors can enable or inhibit feeling of thriving at work. We know little about how environments with significant volatility or undergoing change influence thriving at work. We also do not know about how thriving can be manifest at a collective level in teams or units. Perhaps studying thriving at work in coworking spaces might help advance a research agenda on enabling human thriving at work. In the next section, we explain more about what the coworking phenomenon entails and why it may be of interest.

What is coworking and why care?

Much of the existing research on thriving at work is conducted in large organizational settings. But the evolving nature of knowledge work, the loosening of organizational boundaries, and the evolution of relationships between people and organizational social systems has invited a broader examination of what it means to thrive at work in a more flexible context. In today's work environment, time and place are less likely to constrain when and where people work. Technology has provided knowledge workers with more tools for working in more mobile and flexible ways. These changes are likely to create new relationships among organizational actors, and they heighten the fluidity of organizational structure while reconfiguring the physical, social, and mental boundaries of organizations (Hernes, 2004). As more knowledge workers self-identify as "gig workers," freelancers, mobile workers, remote workers, teleworkers, contract workers, and part-time workers, we witness a decrease in the number of people tied to an assigned desk at a fixed place in time with a fixed community of colleagues and a predictable set of interpersonal interactions. So in order to understand what it means to thrive at work, we had to broaden our definition what it means to be "at work."

In recent years, coworking has emerged as a new workplace phenomenon that gives structure and community to an otherwise loosely coupled array of relationships among workers, those with whom they collaborate, and the organizations with which they identify. As Fiol and Romanelli (2013) note in their paper about the emergence of new organizational forms,

> significant research has empirically documented that a strong collective identity that is self-defining for members is a key determinant of their commitment to collective action and their ability to follow through even on failing collective projects that they might otherwise abandon.
>
> *(p. 603)*

This statement describes what we observe in the commitment of coworking space members toward creating a sustaining structure and community that defines and legitimizes new and more flexible ways of working in today's economic landscape.

Coworking is a way of working that supports freelancers, remote workers/telecommuters, entrepreneurs, and other independent workers in a shared work environment (Garrett, Spreitzer, & Bacevice, 2014). The number of coworking spaces worldwide has risen over the past few years from 1,417 in February 2012 to 2,490 in February 2013. Globally, the number reached the 6,000 mark by the end of 2014 – serving nearly 300,000 people (as reported by Deskmag.com).

Typically, coworking spaces are designed to inspire creativity and encourage collaboration (Allen & Henn, 2007; Elsbach & Bechky, 2007; Laing & Bacevice, 2013; Price, 2007; West & Wind, 2007) through open and collaborative floor plans, access to natural light, big open tables or desks (as opposed to cubicles or closed offices), common areas, social spaces, and quiet rooms for work requiring concentration. Coworking spaces usually charge a daily fee for public use of the space (including access to shared amenities such as Wi-Fi and printing), or a monthly fee to become a member. Membership in these spaces typically includes access to the space, so members can come and go 24/7; access to community events; and access to an online community presence. Membership at some spaces also involves having a voice in decisions regarding the management of the community and space, and participating in the maintenance and upkeep of the space.

The "market" for coworking is rooted in the philosophy of *collaborative consumption* (Botsman & Rogers, 2010) where values around community and trust are deeply embedded. Collaborative consumption involves sharing, bartering, lending, trading, and renting goods and services often processed through the use of social media technology. People who pay to work from coworking spaces are inherently sharing tangible group resources (real estate, office technology, office supplies, coffee, and food) and intangible group resources (expertise and networking contacts). In their study of collaborative consumption, Albinsson and Perera (2012) found that people participate in market-based sharing, in part, to feel a connection to others in a community but to also trade in nontangible services and skills. Coworking spaces embody multiple prosocial market-based behaviors in that members share and contribute to the costs of real estate, office supplies, and Internet access. Prosocial behaviors such as heedful relating (Spreitzer et al., 2005), nurturing of high-quality connections (Dutton & Heaphy, 2003), and promoting a culture of trust (Adler, 2001) are common in coworking communities.

What new insights does coworking provide about how organizations can enable thriving at work?

We offer several reasons why the experience of coworking enables independent and remote workers to thrive in their work, especially beyond the earlier findings articulated earlier. We surveyed more than 200 coworkers in more than 25 spaces around the United States and in Europe about their experience of coworking. We matched their responses to information about the design and amenities of the coworking space, as captured from our coding of information on their websites.

In the popular press, some reporters conclude that it is the amenities and aesthetics of coworking spaces that set these spaces above traditional work environments. Indeed, physical features and amenities are an essential component of coworking spaces because they facilitate professional, productive work. But they are not the key reason why people join coworking spaces and in fact are found to have a relatively minor effect on coworkers' experiences of thriving. Instead, we find that the two most important factors for why coworking enables high levels of thriving are (1) the flexibility and autonomy they provide and (2) the community they create. We describe each factor in turn.

Flexibility and autonomy

In coworking spaces, members are invited to help take responsibility for the space by volunteering for jobs such as cleaning duty, restocking supplies, welcoming prospective members, or planning social events. This invitation to actively coconstruct and maintain the community enables independent workers to craft the kind of work environment that will meet their needs (Garrett et al., 2014; Grant & Parker, 2009). Prior theoretical work had conceptualized thriving as cocreated by individuals and the work organizations. Given their organic design and democratic governance, coworking spaces enable this kind of cocreation that is so important for the experience of thriving. For example, in one coworking space that we studied, in Michigan, members desired a workspace that offered both quiet and collaborative possibilities. Some members desired more quiet options for working and making telephone calls. So they raised money and helped design phone booth-like structures to be constructed so they could have the kind of space that truly met their work needs. In another space that we visited, members wanted to host evenings where members could binge watch favorite series together. Rather than waiting for a social director to organize something, one member took it upon herself to organize regular watching events for interested members. This event planning was energizing to the member who organized the events and also created stronger bonds with other members who shared this common quirky interest.

Traditional work environments can also give employees even more control to self-structure their work activities in time and place. Some companies are adopting flexible work policies that provide more autonomy to employees to structure their own work schedules and to self-manage the pacing of their day-to-day routines. Technology initiatives such as "bring your own device" programs even let employees use their personal technologies (i.e., laptops, tablets, mobile phones) for doing their jobs, provided they meet basic organizational security requirements (Miller, Voas, & Hurlburt, 2012). Such changes, which provide employees with greater opportunities for self-management, reflect new realities of organizational coordination.

In terms of flexibility, technology has provided workers with tools that enable them to work anywhere and anytime by largely eliminating the temporal and spatial constraints associated with various types of work. The last decade has witnessed the advent of robust and ubiquitous wireless connectivity, mobile applications, and the falling costs of mobile computing, which has only recently untethered knowledge workers' tools of production from fixed place. Today, the accelerating pace of technological change has painted a new landscape in the nature of knowledge work. Technological innovations have provided people with new levels of flexibility and autonomy in when, how, and where they do their work.

Today, we see a growing portion of the workforce who are agentic autonomous workers who work for an organization but in a virtual setting beyond the purview of constant supervision. Workplaces are increasingly adopting flexible work policies that allow people to be based elsewhere and telecommute either full time or part time. The increasing number of flexible work policies in large traditional firms signals a shift toward changing workplace norms and practices (see Gittleman, Horrigan, & Joyce, 1998; Kalleberg, 2001). Coworking communities support these remote workers who might otherwise be working in physical isolation from home.

HR policies in some companies are evolving to reset expectations with managers and employees about roles and responsibilities in work environments where flexibility supersedes in-person "face time" (Kelly & Kalev, 2006). Additionally, corporate IT departments are increasingly supporting virtual collaboration as a way to keep people connected to one another and to information when they are not physically present in the same location. These trends make it easier for workers to work remotely from traditional office settings. The overall decoupling of work from fixed time and place impacts the social structures of work. In some ways, the changes described here provide the means to connect people in more ways than previously possible. Information and communication technologies as well as social media undoubtedly facilitate interactions that form the basis of distributed project teams – within large organizations with teams of people working together around the globe and among freelancers and independent workers. Organizational and technological changes are necessary structural antecedents for coworking, but it is necessary to consider other relational variables that help us differentiate between coworking and other ways of working.

The flexibility and autonomy related to work, which people exercise through the organization of coworking communities, stretch the physical, social, and mental boundaries of organizational activity (Hernes, 2004). The ability to work from anywhere stretches the physical boundaries of organizations beyond the container of specified buildings into a constellation of places that include coworking spaces. Social boundaries are stretched as people negotiate new norms of interaction and connectivity with remote colleagues working elsewhere and proximate colleagues situated side-by-side in the same coworking space. Mental boundaries are stretched as individuals establish new workplace engagement rituals and share new experiences that legitimize the norms of work. Scholars (i.e., Lefebvre, 1974; Soja, 1985; Walker, 1985) have theorized about the social production of space and the notion of space as an organizing variable of economic and organizational activity. Coworking creates a new order for a growing and diverse segment of the workforce where time and space no longer normatively define how workers should work, but workers nevertheless benefit from some form of routine that is enacted. It is to this end that coworking reorders the spatial construction of organization, and in so doing, provides a platform for flexibility and autonomy that contributes to thriving.

Community

A second key reason why coworking spaces enable thriving is that they provide a community where members share networks, ideas, and social events (Garrett et al., 2014). In a work environment where people are decoupled from fixed time and place, the nature of work relationships can change. On the one hand, having the ability to separate from others with whom we have ongoing close interactions helps overcome what Sennett (1977) describes as a paradox of sociability – or the notion that one must have a way to escape from those with whom one would become friends. Having the ability to literally take a break from relationships actually strengthens them. Instead of being compelled to be in the presence of the same people every day, we strengthen our relationships when we return to each other naturally and when it makes sense to do so. On the other hand, separation can bring isolation and make people feel as though they are missing out. Coworking's rise as a phenomenon coincides with the evolution of work and the desire of people to seek out an alternative social structuring of work activities. Gore, Leuwerke, and Krumboltz (2002) argue that the technologically enabled "boundaryless" lives many of us live through the ordering of our work leads us to search for community in new areas. This, in part, describes the ascent of coworking.

As society becomes increasingly global and virtually connected, attention is shifting to the quality of relationships available in community, viewing community as a mode of relating rather than simply a structure to organize activity (Calhoun, 1998). What is important about community, more than the structural form, is the sense of relatedness and connectedness that holds a group together (Kim & Kaplan, 2004; McMillan & Chavis, 1986). Bellah, Madson, Sullivan, Swidler, and Tipton (1985) define community as "a group of people who are socially interdependent, who participate together in discussion and decision making, and who share certain practices that both define the community and are nurtured by it" (p. 333). Although existing research on workplace communities – namely communities of practice, occupational communities, and open-source communities (Brown & Duguid, 2000; Hargadon & Bechky, 2006; van Maanen & Barley, 1984) – helps guide our understanding of the coworking phenomenon, coworking may be evolving into its own archetype of community that goes beyond contemporary perspectives on work communities.

Given that a range of people – including remote workers from various organizations, independent entrepreneurs, and other professionals – share space in a coworking space, trust must allay any concerns that sensitive business information will be leaked or used inappropriately by other members. Coworking spaces establish community rules and norms for members, and members sometimes have a say in who gets to be a part of the community as a mechanism for nurturing and sustaining a trust-based safe space for work to happen and knowledge to be shared among people. Coworking establishes a work environment that provides people with the trust and security of working in corporate office or an individual home office, while simultaneously supporting people with opportunities for community and exposure to new ideas. Coworking communities also provide members freedom to choose when, where, and how they work.

Once individuals assimilate into a coworking space, they are given the capacity and the room to enact whatever authentic form of community is mutually desired within it. This is an important value proposition for the coworking business model. Unlike traditional flexible or shared offices marketed to freelance professionals and telecommuters, coworking's angle toward the cultivation of community can be portrayed as a kind of social movement (Zald & Ash, 1966) defined by liberating people from negative work experiences (Jones, Sundsted, & Bacigalupo, 2009) and helping them find purpose and community through their work (Hurst, 2014). A large number of coworking spaces subscribe to the Coworking Manifesto (www.coworkingmanifesto. com) and abide by a set of core values including community, openness, accessibility, collaboration, and sustainability. This manifesto and its inherent advocacy fit well with the typical activities found during the creation stage of a new form of organization (Lawrence & Suddaby, 2006). With movement toward a peer-to-peer, community-based, collaborative consumption economy (seen through such services as Zipcar or Airbnb; Sacks, 2011), we see evidence of new business models in a shared economy. The initial success of coworking spaces indicates that independent and remote workers are willing to pay for access to a more authentic form of community in their professional lives. All of these angles offer insights into creating a sustainable business model for coworking spaces that can enable more human thriving for independent workers.

Conclusion

The emergence of coworking coincides with major economic shifts and the impact that those shifts have had on traditionally office-based knowledge work. In recent years, ubiquitous and increasingly cheaper and more powerful technology has provided people with a means to untether their work from a fixed time and place – allowing them to fully exploit the value their own intellectual means of production. The same technology has provided a growing number of freelance workers and people who work remotely from traditional organizations a means to connect with one another and with employers, other organizations, and project opportunities. While the proliferation of information and communication technologies has provided people with a means to virtually connect with one another in a structural way, this same proliferation has had an isolating effect in that technology can also be a barrier to the growth of relational ties as the need for physical colocation in the context of work diminishes. Coworking represents an effort to resocialize virtual and remote work while providing individuals with some elements of organizational structure and community through a unique archetypal form. The dual benefits of flexibility/autonomy and community enable coworkers to thrive at unprecedented levels. Traditional organizations that seek to enable their own employees' thriving would do well to learn from coworking spaces.

References

Adler, P. (2001). Market, hierarchy, and trust: The knowledge economy and the future of capitalism. *Organization Science*, 12(2), 215–234.

Albinsson, P., & Yasanthi Perera, B. (2012). Alternative marketplaces in the 21st century: Building community through sharing events. *Journal of Consumer Behaviour*, 11(4), 303–315.

Allen, T., & Henn, G. (2007). *The Organization and Architecture of Innovation*. Amsterdam: Elsevier.

Bellah, R. N., Madson, N., Sullivan, W. M., Swidler, A., & Tipton, S. M. (1985). *Habits of the Heart: Individualism and Commitment in American Life*. Berkeley, CA: University of California Press.

Benson, P., & Scales, P. (2009). The definition and preliminary measurement of thriving in adolescence. *The Journal of Positive Psychology*, 4, 85–104.

Blankenship, K. (1998). A race, class, and gender analysis of thriving. *Journal of Social Issues*, 54(2), 393–404.

Botsman, R., & Rogers, R. (2010). *What's Mine Is Yours: The Rise of Collaborative Consumption*. New York: HarperCollins.

Brown, J., & Duguid, P. (2000). *The Social Life of Information*. Boston: Harvard Business School Press.

Calhoun, C. (1998). Community without propinquity revisited: Communications technology and the transformation of the urban public sphere. *Sociological Inquiry*, 68(3), 373–397.

Calhoun, L., & Tedeschi, R. (1998). Beyond recovery from trauma: Implications for clinical practice and research. *Journal of Social Issues*, 54(2), 357–371.

Cameron, K., & Spreitzer, G. (eds.). (2012). *Oxford Handbook of Positive Organizational Scholarship*. New York: Oxford University Press.

Carmeli, A., & Spreitzer, G. (2009). Trust, connectivity, and thriving: Implications for innovative work behavior. *Journal of Creative Behavior*, 43(3), 169–191.

Carver, C. S. (1998). Resilience and thriving: Issues, models, and linkages. *Journal of Social Issues*, 54(2), 245–266.

Cullen, K., Gerbasi, A., & Chrobot-Mason, D. (in press). Thriving in central network positions: The role of political skills. *Journal of Management*.

Dutton, J., & Heaphy, E. (2003). The power of high quality connections. In: K. Cameron, J. Dutton, & R. Quinn (eds.), *Positive Organizational Scholarship* (1st ed.). San Francisco: Berrett-Koehler Publishers, 263–278.

Elliott, E. S., & Dweck, C. S. (1988). Goals: An approach to motivation and achievement. *Journal of Personality and Social Psychology*, 54, 5–12.

Elsbach, K., & Bechky, B. (2007). It's more than a desk: Working smarter through leveraged office design. *California Management Review*, 49(2), 80–101.

Fiol, C. M., & Romanelli, E. (2013). Before identity: The emergence of new organizational forms. *Organization Science*, 23(3), 597–611.

Garrett, L., Spreitzer, G., & Bacevice, P. (2014). Co-constructing a sense of community at work: The emergence of community in coworking spaces. *Academy of Management Proceedings*, 2014(1), 14004–14004.

Gerbasi, A., Porath, C. L., Parker, A., Spreitzer, G., & Cross, R. (2015). Destructive de-energizing relationships: How thriving buffers their effect on performance. *Journal of Applied Psychology*, 100(5), 1423–1433.

Gittleman, M., Horrigan, M., & Joyce, M. (1998). "Flexible" workplace practices: Evidence from a Nationally Representative Survey. *Industrial and Labor Relations Review*, 52(1), 99.

Gore, P. A., Leuwerke, W. C., & Krumboltz, J. D. (2002). Technologically enriched and boundaryless lives: Time for a paradigm upgrade. *The Counseling Psychologist*, 30(6), 847–857.

Grant, A., & Parker, S. (2009). 7 Redesigning work design theories: The rise of relational and proactive perspectives. *The Academy of Management Annals*, 3(1), 317–375.

Haight, B., Barba, B., Tesh, A., & Courts, N. (2002). Thriving: A life span theory. *Journal of Gerontological Nursing*, 28, 14–22.

Hall, J., Roman, M. W., Thomas, S. P., Brown Travi, C., Powell, J., Tennison, C., & McArthur, P. M. (2009). Thriving as becoming resolute in narrative of women surviving childhood maltreatment. *American Journal of Orthopsychiatry*, 79(3), 375–386.

Hargadon, A., & Bechky, B. (2006). When collections of creatives become creative collectives: A field study of problem solving at work. *Organization Science*, 17(4), 484–500.

Hartman, D., & Zimberoff, D. (2007). Posttraumatic growth and thriving with heart-centered therapies. *Journal of Heart-Centered Therapies*, 10, 65–85.

Hernes, T. (2004). *The Spatial Construction of Organization*. Philadelphia: John Benjamins Publishing Company.

Hurst, A. (2014). *The Purpose Economy*. Boise: Elevate.

Ickovics, J., & Park, C. (1998). Paradigm shift: Why a focus on health is important. *Journal of Social Issues*, 54(2), 237–244.

Jones, D., Sundsted, T., & Bacigalupo, T. (2009). *I'm Outta Here!* Brooklyn: Not an MBA Press.

Joseph, S., & Linley, A. (2008). *Trauma, Recovery and Growth: Positive Psychological Perspectives on Posttraumatic Stress*. Hoboken, NJ: John Wiley and Sons.

Kalleberg, A. (2001). Organizing flexibility: The flexible firm in a new century. *British Journal of Industrial Relations*, 39(4), 479–504.

Kelly, E. L., & Kalev, A. (2006). Managing flexible work arrangements in US organizations: Formalized discretion or "a right to ask." *Socio-Economic Review*, 4(3), 379–416.

Kim, J., & Kaplan, R. (2004). Physical and psychological factors in sense of community: New urbanist Kentlands and nearby orchard village. *Environment and Behavior*, 36(3), 313–340.

Laing, A., & Bacevice, P. (2013). Using design to drive organizational performance and innovation in the corporate workplace: Implications for interprofessional environments. *Journal of Interprofessional Care*, 27(S2), 37–45.

Lawler, E. E., Mohrman, S. A., Ledford, G. E. (1998). *Strategies for High Performance Organizations: The CEO Report*. San Francisco: Jossey-Bass.

Lawrence, T., & Suddaby, R. (2006). Institutions and institutional work. In: S. Clegg, C. Hardy, T. Lawrence, & W. Nord (eds.), *The SAGE Handbook of Organization Studies* (2nd ed.). London: Sage, 215.

Lefebvre, H. (1991 [1974]). *The Production of Space*. Translated by Donald Nicholson-Smith. Cambridge, MA: Basil Blackwell.

McMillan, D., & Chavis, D. (1986). Sense of community: A definition and theory. *Journal of Community Psychology*, 14(1), 6–23.

Miller, J. B., & Stiver, I. P. (1997). *The Healing Connection: How Women form Relationships in Therapy and in Life*. Boston: Beacon Press.

Miller, K. W., Voas, J., & Hurlburt, G. F. (2012). BYOD: Security and privacy considerations. *IT Professional*, 14(5), 53–55.

Niessen, C., Sonnentag, S., & Sach, F. (2012). Thriving at work—A diary study. *Journal of Organizational Behavior*, 33(4), 468–487.

Nix, G., Ryan, R. M., Manly, J., & Deci, E. L. (1999). Revitalization through self-regulation: The effects of autonomous and controlled motivation on happiness and vitality. *Journal of Experimental Social Psychology*, 35(3), 266–284.

Norlander, T., von Schedvin, H., & Archer, T. (2005). Thriving as a function of affective personality: Relation to personality factors, coping strategies and stress. *Anxiety, Stress, and Coping*, 18, 105–116.

O'Leary, V. (1998). Strength in the face of adversity: Individual and social thriving. *Journal of Social Issues*, 54, 425–446.

Poorman, P. (2002). Perceptions of thriving by women who have experiences abuse or status-related oppression. *Psychology of Women Quarterly*, 26, 51–62.

Porath, C., Spreitzer, G., & Gibson, C. (2008). *Antecedents and Consequences of Thriving at Work: A Study of Six Organizations*. Working paper. University of Southern California.

Porath, C. L., Spreitzer, G., Gibson, C., & Garnett, F. S. (2012). Thriving in the workplace: Towards its measurement, construct validation, and theoretical refinement. *Journal of Organizational Behavior*, 33(2), 250–271.

Price, I. (2007). Lean assets: New language for new workplaces. *California Management Review*, 49(2), 102–118.

Ryff, C. D. (1989). Happiness is everything, or is it – Explorations on the meaning of psychological well-being. *Journal of Personality and Social Psychology*, 5, 1069–1081.

Saakvitne, K. W., Tennen, H., & Affleck, G. (1998). Exploring thriving in the context of clinical trauma theory: Constructivist self-developmental theory. *Journal of Social Issues*, 54(2), 279–299.

Sacks, D. (2011). The sharing economy. *Fast Company*, 155, 88–131.

Sennett, R. (1977). *The Fall of Public Man*. New York: Knopf.

Soja, E. W. (1985). The spatiality of social life: Towards a transformative retheorisation. In: D. Gregory & J. Urry (eds.), *Social Relations and Spatial Structures*. New York: St. Martin's Press, 90–127.

Sonnentag, S., & Zijlstra, F. R. H. (2006). Job characteristics and off-job time activities as predictors of need for recovery, well-being, and fatigue. *Journal of Applied Psychology*, 91, 330–350.

Spreitzer, G., Sutcliffe, K., Dutton, J., Sonenshein, S., & Grant, A. (2005). A socially embedded model of thriving at work. *Organization Science*, 16(5), 537–549.

Taylor, J. (2004). Moving from surviving to thriving: African American women recovering from intimate male partner abuse. *Research and Theory for Nursing Practice: An International Journal*, 18, 35–50.

Van Maanen, J., & Barley, S. (1984). Occupational communities: Culture and control in organizations. In: B. Staw & L. Cummings (ed.), *Research in Organizational Behavior* (6th ed.). Greeniwch: JAI Press, 287–365.

Walker, R. A. (1985). Class, division of labour and employment in space. In: D. Gregory & J. Urry (eds.), *Social Relations and Spatial Structures*. New York: St. Martin's Press, 164–189.

West, A., & Wind, Y. (2007). Putting the organization on wheels: Workplace design at SEI. *California Management Review*, 49(2), 138–153.

Zald, M., & Ash, R. (1966). Social movement organizations: Growth, decay and change. *Social Forces*, 44(3), 327.

15

The long-hours culture

Implications for health and wellbeing

Marian N. Ruderman, Cathleen Clerkin, and Jennifer J. Deal

Introduction

The modern workplace is not a particularly healthy place. The advent of email-linked smartphones, global commerce and teams, and the global economic slowdown has put pressure on organizations to have staffing as lean (and cheap) as possible; subsequently, employees are working longer hours and taking on additional responsibilities, which in turn is taking a mental, emotional, and physical toll (Brom, Buruck, Horváth, Richter, & Leiter, 2015; Burke & Cooper, 2008). In short, the expanding workweek is becoming a modern-day psychological job hazard. Although it may not be as obvious a hazard as a slippery floor or faulty equipment, the downside to the trend of working longer hours is very real. The long hours spent working pose a significant threat to wellbeing (Van der Hulst, 2003) and health (Kivimäki et al., 2015), and in rare cases can even be fatal (Burke & Cooper, 2008). Moreover, while people often espouse long hours to increase production, contrary to popular belief, more hours at work do not necessarily lead to greater productivity (Pencavel, 2014).

In this chapter we explore the threat posed by modern workplace expectations for long hours and the impact of long hours on health and wellbeing. We also describe psychological mechanisms linking jobs to health and wellbeing using the Job Demands–Resources (JD-R) model (Demerouti et al., 2001), and propose strategies of psychological recovery and renewal that can help mitigate the effects of the current workplace culture.

Factors that contribute to long-hours culture

The International Labor Organization (ILO) established international labor standards on working hours nearly a century ago – declaring that work hours should be limited to eight-hour workdays and 48 hour work weeks (ILO, 1919). At the time, leaders were optimistic that this was a first step in a declining workweek, with some predicting that, in a few generations, work hours might drop to three hours a day (Lee, McCann & Messenger, 2007). While work-life balance has improved in many countries and industries since 1919, this prediction of a continuous decline in work hours has obviously not come true. In fact, work cultures that encourage long work hours seem to be on the rise.

Today, many professionals, managers, and executives work hours well over the international limit proposed by the ILO. For example, Saad (2014) reported a Gallup poll that showed salaried employees work 49 hours per week on average, with 25% working 50–59 hours and 25% working 60+ hours a week. According to the National Bureau of Economic Research, there has been an increase in work hours in the United States since the 1970s. The trend is strongest among highly educated, highly paid workers – a notable distinction given that, in previous decades, this group was less likely to work long hours (Kuhn & Lozano, 2008). This shift toward longer hours is not limited to the United States: 34% of managers surveyed in Europe reported working more than 60 hours a week, and more than half said that they worked more hours in 2007 than they did in 2000 (Burke & Cooper, 2008). Moreover, global studies of workplace hours commonly report that Asian countries such as South Korea, Hong Kong, and Thailand have the longest work hours of them all (Hitchcock, Dick, Russo, & Schmit, 2004). A recent estimate by the ILO suggests that about 20% of people worldwide work beyond the 48-hour week (Burke & Cooper, 2008).

There are a number of factors that may contribute to today's long-hours work culture. One reason is that the boundaries of the work day have been virtually eliminated as a result of smartphones. Mobile devices increase the permeability of the boundary between work and the rest of life, making it possible for workers to be available to colleagues and clients whenever they are awake, regardless of where they are (Kossek & Lautsch, 2012; Kossek, Ruderman, Braddy, & Hannum, 2012). With this permeability comes expectations from others to be available at all times, making it difficult to psychologically detach from work. For example, people who carry smartphones engage with the workplace approximately 72 hours a week (13.5 hours per work day, and an additional five hours on the weekends; Deal, 2013). Although smartphones and other mobile devices give people more latitude over when and where they work, social expectations mitigate against that sense of control by encouraging working all the time, in every place. Some argue that smartphones are even addictive, resulting in a reduced sense of volitional control (Bianchi & Phillips, 2005; Lee, Chang, Lin, & Cheng, 2014).

Smartphones also place a mental burden on those who carry them because they hold the possibility of doing work. It is likely that the option to do work activates the Zeigarnik Effect – the inability to completely forget about something when it is left incomplete. The Zeigarnik Effect is more likely to be activated when completing the task is possible (Greist-Bousquet & Schiffman, 1992). Since the work of executives, managers, and professionals is rarely completed, and since they have the option to continue to make progress on the work because of the availability of the workplace through the smartphone (or laptop, etc.), their brains are likely to nudge them to work even after they have moved on to other activities (Baumeister & Bushman, 2008). Difficulties in separating from work are linked to high fatigue (Kinnunen, Feldt, Siltaloppi, & Sonnentag, 2011).

Another factor associated with the long-hours work culture is the increase in workload in response to global competition as trade barriers fall and transaction costs decline. New global competitors are entering previously local markets. In response, companies are facing intense pressure, which gets communicated to employees as a reason to work longer and harder. Domestic organizations are now forced to compete against companies from around the world. Additionally, new talent analytic approaches for monitoring productivity, now called *talent optimization systems,* are creating pressure for improved performance (Jones, 2014). The continual push for productivity can render jobs more complex, making it difficult for workers to experience a sense of mastery over the situation.

Related to the increased competition, globalization is also increasing the span of operations contributing to a long-hours culture. The need to coordinate work across multiple time zones increases the length of the workday. For example, a day may start with meetings originating from

Asia and end with meetings originating from the United States, requiring participation at work over a 12-hour span. Organizations are expected to provide 24-hour service, resulting in a much more intense work environment. Consequently, workers are expected to work "flexibly" to meet these demands. Generally, flexibility is thought to make a positive difference – but it can be a double-edged sword, with greater options for the time and place of work contributing to the pressure to always be responsive. The ability to connect with almost anyone anywhere constitutes a new complexity in job demands and can inhibit feelings of control and competence.

Impact of long-hours culture on health and wellbeing

Originally intended to boost productivity, the culture of long hours is now associated with threats to the psychological and physiological health of employees (Green, 2008). Most people are aware of the hours they are working, but are not necessarily fully aware of how these factors influence psychological and physiological functioning. One of the most notable effects of the long-hours culture is that employees are not getting enough recovery time (Sonnentag, 2003). Recovery time is defined as the time needed to return to baseline levels of wellbeing after experiencing a demanding workload (Meijman & Mulder, 1998). Just as athletes need recovery time for dealing with overworked muscles, so do workers need mental and emotional recovery time for stress associated with excessive hours.

Not surprisingly, constant work and lack of recovery time has led to increased stress – which is now recognized as a global health issue by the World Health Organization (2004). People everywhere are stressed, and a large portion of the stress is about work. Work is burdening the body by chronically activating the autonomic nervous system's "fight, flight, freeze" response. This response is supposed to be a short-term emergency response to help humans deal with immediate threat (Sapolsky, 2004). However, it is maladaptive in the modern long-hours culture where threats are experienced over a long time period rather than in short bursts. This chronic activation can contribute to physical diseases such as cardiovascular disease, diabetes, and autoimmune disorders (Weiss, Haber, Horowitz, Stuart, & Wolfe, 2009).

Studies conducted over the past few years by the American Psychological Association (2014, 2015) clearly show that the levels of stress felt by people of all ages is high. They find that about one-third of respondents report feeling isolated, and almost as many say that their stress level has affected their physical and mental health (American Psychological Association, 2015). Though many people report using stress management techniques, they tend to choose more sedentary activities such as surfing the Internet, watching television or movies, and eating, rather than more physical activities that would be more supportive of a healthy lifestyle (American Psychological Association, 2015).

Long work hours also inhibit physical and mental recovery by limiting sleep time. According to a study of 444,306 Americans by the Centers for Disease Control, many adults aren't getting as much sleep as is recommended (Centers for Disease Control, 2012). Recent surveys suggest that approximately 19.5% of Americans and 15% of Europeans report feeling sleepy during the day (Ohayon, 2012; Ohayon, Priest, Zulley, Smime, & Paiva, 2002). Sleep deprivation can lead to decreased short-term and long-term memory, diminished focus, and slower responses, all of which can make it difficult to make decisions and learn from mistakes (Walker, Stickgold, Alsop, Gaab, & Schlaug, 2005). Prolonged sleep deprivation, such as one might experience in a career of working long hours, can cause notable damage to physical wellness, including higher risks of accidents, diabetes, heart disease, and hypertension (King et al., 2008; Knutson, Ryden, Mander, & Van Cauter, 2006; Williamson & Feyer, 2000). Sleep also plays a role in mood regulation, and lack of sleep can lead to anxiety and hostility (Connolly, Ruderman, & Leslie, 2014).

Recent research on the effects of sleep deprivation on cognition and decision making highlight just how detrimental long work hours can be to performance and health. For instance, one study found that approximately 25% of ICU errors made in the hospital by first-year medical interns could be accounted for by sleep deprivation caused by long work hours (Lockley et al., 2004). Another study found that individuals who stayed awake for 24 hours straight had cognitive and motor impairment similar to individuals with a blood alcohol level of 0.10 – well above the legal limit of intoxication in most Western countries (Williamson & Feyer, 2000). Difficulty in mood and emotion regulation caused by sleep deprivation could also make it hard to communicate effectively and engage in the interpersonal processes necessary for successful workplace interactions (Connolly et al., 2014). In addition to the negative short-term effects of insufficient sleep, long-term sleep deprivation is likely to lead to increased sick days, medical bills, leaves of absence, and damage to long-term organizational success.

In addition to working too many hours, getting too little sleep, and being stressed, many employees get too little exercise. The World Health Organization estimates that globally around 31% of adults were insufficiently active in 2008 and that a major reason for this is the increased sedentary behavior in modern occupations (World Health Organization, 2016). Moreover, this trend seems to be escalating: the Physical Activity Council's (2016) survey of 10,778 Americans estimates that in 2015 around 28% of Americans ages 6 and older lived a sedentary lifestyle – up 18% from 2007. This is particularly troubling given that it is well documented that lack of physical movement and activities increases the risk for a myriad of health issues including high blood pressure, cardiovascular disease, and obesity.

Part of the problem is that the way work is organized often results in people being too sedentary. Employees in professional, managerial, and executive positions in organizations spend a large part of their day sitting: sitting at a computer, sitting in meetings, sitting at lunch. In many cases people can live their lives in such a way that minimal day-to-day physical activity is required. Many try to increase their physical activity through exercise regimes, but getting exercise in brief bursts isn't enough. While it is important to exercise, simply put, sitting too much (as people typically do at work) is unhealthy (Owen, Sparling, Healy, Dunstan, & Matthews, 2010). As long as most work is done sitting down at a computer or desk this is going to continue to be a health concern for employees and organizations.

Fundamentally, working too many hours isn't healthy, mentally, emotionally, socially, or physically. Moreover, the factors mentioned earlier all damage one's ability to perform well at work through decreased focus, emotional regulation, decision making, and physical fitness. To further understand the underlying mechanisms that link long-hours work culture and health and wellbeing, we turn to the JD–R model.

The JD-R model

According to the JD-R model, the psychological characteristics associated with any job situation can be described by two characteristics: the job demands, or what the job requires psychologically and physiologically; and job resources, or the aspects of the job that help to achieve work goals, stimulate learning, and reduce job demands (Bakker, Demerouti, de Boer, & Schaufeli, 2003; Demerouti et al., 2001). Job resources help provide the motivation and the energy to work. Aspects of a job that help employees achieve work goals, provide benefits, or stimulate learning, are job resources because they increase energy and improve skills and success.

A critical assumption of the model is that both job demands and job resources influence health impairment and motivational processes. When jobs have enough resources to support demands, health is maintained. However, when job demands overwhelm the amount of resources available, negative consequences occur. Thus, job demands are not stressors in and of themselves but become so when they exhaust employees' mental and physical resources, thereby depleting energy and strength and impairing physical and mental health. Consequently, stress reduction and health protection can be achieved not only by decreasing work demands (stressors), but also by increasing the personal resources of employees through job resources.

Organizational cultures that promote long work hours cause two levels of damage to employees' wellbeing – both increasing demands and depleting resources. For instance, mobile devices increase job demands, which results in job expansion, which creates increased need for resources. However, due to increased time demands, there is little time for recovery or to replenish the resources needed to carry the expanded load. This imbalance decreases the likelihood of meeting work goals due to insufficient capacity, which then further depletes energy. Thus, a long-hours culture essentially is a culture of high demand and little renewal of resources, creating a vicious cycle. The next section of this chapter describes recommendations for breaking this cycle and helping individuals perform at their best in the workplace.

Recovery practices: replenishing resources to create a culture of health

The purpose of the rest of this chapter is to present some solutions that can be implemented by organizations and individuals to help counter the negative impact of the current 24/7 work culture. Our recommendations build on the idea that psychological and physiological resources depleted by the long-hours culture can be replenished though psychological, emotional, and physiological recovery strategies. The strategies for renewal are drawn broadly from recent research on affective neuroscience and positive psychology. We believe such an interdisciplinary approach is needed to understand the various impacts of long-hours culture and to inform possible solutions.

Following Kinnunen et al. (2011), we consider recovery an important mechanism that can buffer against the negative effects of long-hours work culture on health. Recovery refers to the process in which a person's functioning returns to the prestressor baseline (Craig & Cooper, 1992; Meijman & Mulder, 1998). Inadequate recovery from a stressful situation requires an individual to put in extra effort to get through routine tasks, which may lead to depleted resources and deteriorating wellbeing over time (Demerouti, Bakker, Geurts, & Taris, 2009). Therefore, increasing resources through recovery processes lessens the impact of expanding job demands because they improve the capacity to respond to job demands (Sonnentag & Fritz, 2007).

Resource recovery has potential to ameliorate the negative effects of work on health (Demerouti et al., 2009). We've organized our treatment of ways to build resources into five practices: sleep, mindfulness, physical movement, social connections, and positivity. The strategies described in these sections are drawn from positive psychology, neuroscience, and contemplative practices. Each resource category includes steps individuals can take to increase their own resources, as well as recommendations for organizations looking for preventative interventions to mitigate the effects of overwork. These practices are ways organizations and employees can foster recuperation from the long-work hours culture.

Sleep recovery practices

Perhaps the most direct way that long work hours impact health and wellbeing is by eroding one's ability to get a good night's sleep. This is particularly problematic as a growing body of research shows that sleep is a key factor in the ability to perform optimally in the workplace. Sleep is the most natural form of recovery.

Because sleep is so critical both to functioning effectively and to recovery, creating a workplace environment that protects and promotes sleep is one of the most important ways to cultivate a culture of health and wellbeing within an organization. Workplaces should encourage employees to get 7–8 hours of sleep, and should manage hours and workloads to ensure that this is possible. For those brief periods when long hours are necessary, organizations can help employees take advantage of alternative sleep schedules to improve recovery. According to the National Sleep Foundation (2016), short "power" naps are an effective way to reap some of the benefits of sleep when people are not able to get enough sleep overnight. Because of how sleep cycles work, a 15–20 minute nap is likely to leave one feeling alert and refreshed, while a longer nap might leave one feeling groggy and dazed (Mednick & Ehrman, 2006). Organizations can encourage a "pro-napping" culture by providing nap pods (such as those provided at Google), ostrich pillows (pillows creating the feeling of "sticking your head in the sand"), and napping rooms. In positions where employees travel a great deal, jet lag may become an issue. In those cases organizations should be mindful and allow enough time so staff can fully recover from jet lag and return to their standard sleep schedule.

Additionally, good sleep practices can be taught in the workplace as part of developmental initiatives. Sleep experts recommend creating sleep routines and avoiding stimulants to promote optimal sleep. The human body operates according to circadian rhythms, and simply going to sleep at the same time every day can facilitate faster sleep onset and higher-quality rest. Similarly, engaging in relaxation activities near bedtime, such as taking a warm bath, listening to soothing music, or practicing meditative techniques can speed up sleep onset.

Conversely, exposure to stimulation near bedtime can inhibit sleep, even after one is in bed and feels ready for sleep. Physically, brains and bodies need time to "power down" and too much stimulation can interfere with this process. For instance, exercising or working near bedtime can prevent sleep onset because the brain and body are active and unable to suddenly turn off (Connolly et al., 2014). Moreover, exposure to "blue light" (such as that emitted by smartphones and tablets) can suppress melatonin production and cause alertness (West et al., 2011), and late-night interaction with technology can delay sleep. Finally, alcohol intake can also inhibit rest. While alcohol causes initial drowsiness, it also interferes with REM (rapid eye movement) sleep, and exacerbates daytime sleepiness (Roehrs & Roth, 2001).

To improve sleeping habits, organizations can proactively teach employees about the importance of sleep as a source of energy and educate employees on how to sleep better. Educators and trainers can add content about sleep into curriculum development and delivery. Universities can add a component about sleep into management courses. According to sleep experts, sleep deprivation can be avoided through disciplined sleep hygiene (Payne, 2015). Additionally, individuals can learn about sleep on their own initiative and take control of their sleep practices without the organization being involved. There are numerous self-help systems available. Improving sleep practices can increase the perception of control by adding cognitive resources.

Mindfulness recovery practices

Mindfulness can be defined as "paying attention, in a particular way, on purpose, without judgment" (Kabat-Zinn, 1994, p. 4). Mindfulness is increasingly important in today's always-on, multitasking-heavy, global and digital workforce because it may help individuals stay calm and focused, without letting ruminations about the past, worries about the future, or preoccupation with other facets of life interfere with the present moment. While mindfulness has origins in Eastern religions and traditions, uses of mindfulness in the workplace are secular.

A growing body of research has demonstrated that mindfulness is a successful intervention for increasing both physiological health and psychological and emotional wellbeing. There is evidence that mindfulness can reduce cortisol levels (Carlson, Campbell, Garland, & Grossman, 2007), enhance immune function (Davidson et al., 2003), decrease blood pressure (McCraty, 2003), and help cope with chronic pain (Baer, 2003). Mindfulness breathing meditation and Mindfulness-Based Cognitive Therapy (MBCT) have been linked to decreased illness, depressive symptoms, and anxiety, and increased stress management (Davidson et al, 2003; Fredrickson, Cohn, Coffey, Pek, & Finkel, 2008; Kuyken et al., 2008). Psychologically, there is evidence that mindfulness can enhance attentional control (Jha, Krompinger, & Baime, 2007), working memory, and emotion regulation (Bishop et al., 2004; Brown & Ryan, 2003).

Recently, research on mindfulness interventions in the workplace has shown that mindfulness can improve a wide variety of workplace outcomes including social relationships, resiliency, task performance, enjoyment, and subjective wellbeing (See Hyland, Lee, & Mills, 2015 for a review). From Google, to General Mills, to eBay, to the US Army, some of the biggest and most successful organizations in the world are starting to implement mindfulness programs and practices as a way to help employees cope with longer work hours and stressful and demanding work environments. Workplace mindfulness training is currently evolving into its own field, and a number of institutes and organizations have begun to create their own mindfulness training programs (e.g., The Institute for Mindful Leadership, The Potential Project). Many organizations are also beginning to create their own mindfulness curriculum (e.g., Harvard Pilgrim's Mind the Moment program, Google's Search Inside Yourself Leadership Institute), and there are also apps and Internet-based approaches for learning mindfulness.

There are a number of different tools and practices that can be used to facilitate mindfulness, most of which involve some form or level of meditation. Common practices include mindful breathing exercises, loving-kindness meditation, mindful walking, mindful eating, body scans, mindful journaling, metaphor techniques, and mindful coaching (Kabat-Zinn, 1994; Moran, 2011). The different approaches may be combined and used in different ways, and the techniques are taught with different levels of formality and context. Though the details may differ, all these methods serve as a way to anchor the mind and increase focus and clarity on the present moment without judgment. While most of these practices have roots outside of professional organizations, thanks to the recent "mindful revolution," many of these practices are have begun being implemented in organizational contexts (Hyland et al., 2015; Pickert, 2014).

Successful mindful workplace initiatives tend to be flexible and multimodal (offering a combination of in-person courses, one-day retreats, and online materials and modules, etc.), allowing employees to work around their busy schedules and find their own combination of practices. They also tend to offer different types of mindfulness tools (e.g., guided meditation, mindful yoga classes, and silent retreats) to allow individuals to participate in the method of mindfulness that works best for them. However, it should be noted, that one of the main critiques of workplace mindfulness programs is that it is unclear how far mindfulness programs can be "watered down" and still produce positive outcomes (Ruderman & Clerkin, 2015). Mindfulness is something that takes practice and patience, and employees who go into mindfulness trainings without the proper mind frame and dedication are unlikely to reap many rewards. Like sleep, mindfulness is a practice that individuals can take up on their own, and is a particularly useful tool in dealing with the chronic stress because mindfulness helps individuals to recover.

Physical movement recovery practices

As noted previously, one of the current issues with modern long-hours work culture is that it is largely sedentary. Therefore, in addition to using up time that could be spent at the gym, long-hours work culture also drains the resources that come with having a physically healthy body.

This is cost is substantial, considering that the benefits of physical movement and body-based practices are well known. Research has demonstrated that physical movement can reduce stress and increase memory, energy, mood, and cognitive performance (McDowell-Larsen, 2012). In one study, four months of yoga were found to significantly improve psychological and physiological stress, mood, blood pressure, and heart rate as much as cognitive behavior therapy (Granath, Ingvarsson, von Thiele, & Lundberg, 2006). A review of the literature shows that different forms of exercise moderate cognitive decline in aging (Bherer, Erickson, & Liu-Ambrose, 2013).

Physical wellness is a growing concern in organizations as lack of fitness affects health care costs, and work time lost to illness affects productivity. In addition to organizations encouraging fitness generally, activities such as yoga, tai-chi, and other mind-body connection practices are increasingly being incorporated into organizations as a way to relieve an overworked and high-stressed workforce (Gelles, 2012).

Physical activities also have the added benefit of increasing blood flow and helping burn off cortisol (a hormone that is released during times of stress). This is particularly important in long hours/high stress work environments where employees are constantly stressed and rarely have enough downtime to recover. The body responds to environmental stressors by secreting hormones, increasing heart rate, and preparing to fight, flee, or freeze. Since people can't typically act on these instincts and burn off the cortisol while at work, an excess of cortisol is left in the system that over the long term can damage health.

Physical action allows the body to mimic the physical "fight or flight" reaction and reduce the cortisol load. Evans (2015), calls this "Playing It Out." The Playing It Out method emphasizes the importance of short bursts of intense movement during the workday to help use up cortisol, allowing the body to get back to equilibrium (Evans, 2015). This practice of physically dealing with energy and stress can take multiple forms – running on a treadmill or up stairs, punching a punching bag, etc. The key is that the activity must be intense enough to use up the excess cortisol. This is a very literal form of recovery.

Incorporating physical activities and/or body-based practices into the workplace can be straight forward. Physical techniques provide a way to burn off stress related to challenging workplace environments, and help keep employees' bodies physically healthy, thereby lowering medical costs to the organization and decreasing the amount of sick leave taken by employees. There is also developmental value in educating employees about physical health, as it can be a tool to improve their work, help with emotion regulation, improve their health, and cope with stress.

Social connection recovery practices

Humans are intrinsically social beings, and a growing body of research shows that social connection is important not only for physical survival, but also for psychological wellbeing and cognitive flourishing (e.g., Siegel, 2012). Socially driven constructs such as social support, social ties, networking, social integration, and teamwork have all been linked to improved performance and health outcomes both within organizational contexts and in society in general. Building social connections in the workplace can help buffer against the stress and fatigue of long-hours work culture and is an important job resource.

There is an abundance of research on the positive effect of relationships on cognitive and neurophysiological health and wellbeing. For instance, longitudinal data from the Health and Retirement study showed that people with the highest levels of social integration had less cognitive decline and better memory compared to less socially active subjects (Ertel, Glymour, & Berkman, 2008). People who have more diverse types of social ties (regular interaction with family members, friends, coworkers, community members, etc.) are less susceptible to the common cold

(Cohen, Doyle, Skoner, Rabin, & Gwaltney, 1997). Moreover, the effects are contagious. Holding someone's hand can decrease threat-related neural activation during stressful situations (Coan, Schaefer, & Davidson, 2006), and receiving hugs can buffer against physiological stress reactions such as lowered immune systems (Cohen, Janicki-Deverts, Turner, & Doyle, 2015). The positive impacts of social relationships have been demonstrated within workplace contexts as well: even brief interactions been shown to have a positive cardiovascular, neuroendocrine, and immune system effects on individuals in workplace settings (Heaphy & Dutton, 2008).

There are many practices for enhancing social capital and for facilitating relational strategies in the workplace. While much of this work has focused on cultivating healthy social connections with youth, there has been an increasing focus on social connections within the context of organizations. Baker and Dutton (2007) identify two primary classes of practices that can create and sustain social capital in the workplace: reciprocity and high-quality connections (HQCs).

Reciprocity has to do with the exchange of resources between people in large systems. Research on reciprocity shows that people underestimate how willing others are to give, and that once people are given something, they feel compelled to reciprocate (Grant, 2013). Baker has developed reciprocity rings as way to teach leaders about reciprocity, and as a way for organizations to import principles of reciprocity into their systems. During a reciprocity ring session, groups of people are gathered with the express purpose of asking for and giving help. Generally, participants are told that the requests should be important and individuals are encouraged to provide context for their request. After requests are shared, individuals help each other meet their goals, either with direct help, or by facilitating connections to others.

HQCs are connections between people characterized by mutuality, positive regard, and vitality. They stand out as different from low-quality connections because they have a positive and lasting impact on people through heightened positive emotions and enhanced physiological functioning. Dutton calls these *connections* rather than relationships to encompass brief interpersonal encounters as well as those that are long-term (Dutton, 2014). Research shows that HQCs increase individuals' cognitive abilities, adaptability, and resilience by making people feel that they have more capacity for dealing with challenges (Stephens, Heaphy, Carmeli, Spreitzer, & Dutton, 2013). Dutton argues that the four pathways to building HCQs at work are through respectful engagements, task enabling, trusting, and playing (Dutton, 2014).

Social connection techniques have a lot of potential for providing resources in the face of demanding and stressful jobs. As organizations adapt to constant change, strong relationships can be powerful protective features for the individual and the collective during times of stress. Organizational initiatives could explicitly teach, facilitate, and provide opportunities for reciprocity and HQCs rather than leaving them to occur by chance. This is also a potentially effective approach for individuals to take regardless of organizational initiatives, because an individual can improve social connections on his or her own without the culture of the organization changing. It is relatively easy for one person to demonstrate genuine interest in another at work, and to provide support in times of stress.

Positivity recovery practices

A wealth of research in the fields of positive psychology and the psychology of emotions has shown the benefits and restorative power of positive emotions. Barbara Fredrickson's (2001) broaden-and-build theory of positive emotions contends that the experience of positive emotions broadens the field of awareness and encourages exploratory and creative actions. Positive emotions provide energy and engagement. Over time, positivity can become a resource that is built and strengthened and, in turn, helps build other skills. Fredrickson describes this as an upward spiral in which positive emotions are linked to positive outcomes such as creative thinking, executive brain functioning, and decreased worrying.

This trajectory of positive emotions stands in contrast to negative emotions, which tend to narrow thoughts and the range of possible actions (e.g., the panicky "tunnel vision" that often happens during crisis or threat). With its high level of frustration, the always-on, never-off culture does not necessarily inspire positivity or the "upward spirals" or behaviors Fredrickson (2003) associates with positive emotions. Conversely, long hours, lack of sleep, high demand, and high stress levels are all likely to create the type of negative moods and feelings of threat and crisis that narrows thoughts and responses.

There are, however, ways to increase the likelihood of positive emotions. A growing body of research suggests that positive emotions can be induced (Burton & King, 2004). Positivity induction is not about creating fake positive emotions, rather, it is about paying attention to, and savoring, the positive aspects in one's life that might not otherwise be noted during stressful times. Gratitude is a particularly promising positive emotion to cultivate. A large body of evidence suggests that gratitude is related to wellbeing, and that gratitude interventions can have a positive impact in the workplace (Wood, Froh, & Geraghty, 2010). The gratitude journal is a classic intervention. Essentially, this involves keeping a diary and writing down a few things that one is grateful for and why. The simple act of writing reinforces the positive experience. Other approaches include gratitude visits or writing gratitude letters to others. A meta-analysis on positive interventions suggests that the gratitude visit has the most impact (Wood et al., 2010). In addition to gratitude, other positive emotions include joy, serenity, generosity, interest, awe, love, hope, pride, inspiration, and amusement. These emotions are not typically associated with long hours, however, it is possible to leverage these emotions as well and to make them salient in the work culture.

Interventions based on positivity can be introduced by both organizations and individuals. The field of Positive Organizational Behavior discusses ways of leveraging the power of positive experiences in the workplace. These range from job crafting to conducting self-development activities imagining what one is like at their best. There are a variety of leadership strategies such as fostering compassion, forgiveness, and gratitude that can be used to establish a positive climate (Cameron, 2012).

As with the other ways of building psychological resources, individual employees can work to increase positive emotions in the workplace as well; organizations do not have to sanction positivity interventions for them to happen. There are many ways individuals can access gratitude interventions, be generous, experience joy, cultivate serenity, express interest, have hope, have pride, be inspired, and be amused.

Conclusion

The trend toward working long hours seems to be on the rise in most parts of the world – particularly among successful white-collar employees. This trend is concerning because there are serious documented psychological and physical health risks associated with long-hours work culture. We caution against encouraging employees to work longer and harder – especially given that they are likely to receive diminishing returns for their sacrifice. The "simple" solution is to create organizational cultures that promote working fewer hours. However, given that the current extended workweek seems to be tied to the technology-laden, global 24/7 marketplace, we are aware that this simply solution may not always be feasible.

The JD–R model suggests that when demands cannot be reduced, the next best thing to do is to provide more resources. Therefore, we suggest that organizations – and/or individuals who are not able to work fewer hours (and reduce work demands) – should seek out ways to increase job resources. Specifically, we suggest five recovery practices that should help employees maintain a baseline level of psychological and physiological health. We do not suggest that all five practices have to be used by everyone, or that these recovery techniques are exhaustive or mutually exclusive. Rather, we offer them as examples of what recovery techniques are possible to help buffer against some of the psychological and physiological demands of long-hours work culture. We encourage organizations to think broadly about what practices and techniques would be most beneficial to their specific circumstances in order to provide recovery options and create a culture of health.

References

American Psychological Association. (2014). *Stress in America: Are Teens Adopting Adults' Stress Habits?* Available at: www.apa.org/news/press/releases/stress/2013/stress-report.pdf (accessed 1 February 2016).

American Psychological Association. (2015). *Stress in America: Paying With Our Health.* Available at: www.apa.org/news/press/releases/stress/2014/stress-report.pdf (accessed 1 February 2016).

Baer, R. A. (2003). Mindfulness training as a clinical intervention: A conceptual and empirical Review. *Clinical Psychology: Science and Practice*, 10(2), 125–143.

Baker, W., & Dutton, J. E. (2007). Enabling positive social capital in organizations. In: J. E. Dutton & B. Ragins (eds.), *Exploring Positive Relationships at Work: Building a Theoretical and Research Foundation.* Mahwah, NJ: Lawrence Erlbaum, 325–346.

Bakker, A. B., Demerouti, E., de Boer, E., & Schaufeli, W. (2003). Job demands and job resources as predictors of absence duration and frequency. *Journal of Vocational Behavior*, 62, 341–356.

Baumeister, R. F., & Bushman, B. J. (2008). *Social Psychology and Human Nature.* United States: Thompson Wadsworth.

Bherer, L., Erickson, K. I., & Liu-Ambrose, T. (2013). A Review of the effects of physical activity and exercise on cognitive and brain functions in older adults. *Journal of Aging Research.* doi:10.1155/2013/657508.

Bianchi, A., & Phillips, J. G. (2005). Psychological predictors of problem mobile phone use. *CyberPsychology & Behavior*, 8(1), 39–51.

Bishop, S. R., Lau, M., Shapiro, S., Carlson, L., Anderson, N. D., Carmody, J., . . . & Devins, G. (2004). Mindfulness: A proposed operational definition. *Clinical Psychology: Science and Practice*, 11(3), 230–241.

Brom, S. S., Buruck, G., Horváth, I., Richter, P., & Leiter, M. P. (2015). Areas of worklife as predictors of occupational health – A validation study in two German samples. *Burnout Research*, 2(2), 60–70.

Brown, K. W., & Ryan, R. M. (2003). The benefits of being present: Mindfulness and it's role in psychological well-being. *Journal of Personalty and Social Psychology*, 84(4), 822–848.

Burke, R. J., & Cooper, C. L. (eds.). (2008). *The Long Work Hours Culture: Causes, Consequences and Choices.* Bingley, UK: Emerald Group Publishing.

Burton, C. M., & King, L. A. (2004). The health benefits of writing about intensely positive experiences. *Journal of Research in Personality*, 38, 150–163. doi:10.1016/S0092–6566(03)00058–8.

Cameron, K. (2012). *Positive Leadership Strategies for Extraordinary Performance.* San Francisco: Berrett-Koehler Publishers.

Carlson, L. E., Campbell, T. S., Garland, S. N., & Grossman, P. (2007). Associations among salivary cortisol, melatonin, catecholamines, sleep quality and stress in women with breast cancer and healthy controls. *Journal of Behavioral Medicine*, 30(1), 45–58.

Centers for Disease Control. (2012). *Insufficient Sleep Is a Public Health Problem.* Available at: www.cdc.gov/Features/dsSleep/index.html (accessed 11 January 2016).

Coan, J. A., Schaefer, H. S., & Davidson, R. J. (2006). Lending a hand: Social regulation of the neural response to threat. *Psychological Science*, 17(12), 1032–1039.

Cohen, S., Doyle, W. J., Skoner, D. P., Rabin, B. S., & Gwaltney, J. M. (1997). Social ties and susceptibility to the common cold. *Journal of the American Medical Association*, 277(24), 1940–1944.

Cohen, S., Janicki-Deverts, D., Turner, R. B., & Doyle, W. J. (2015). Does hugging provide stress-buffering social support? A study of susceptibility to upper respiratory infection and illness. *Psychological Science*, 26, 135–147.

Connolly, C., Ruderman, M. N., & Leslie, J. (2014). *Sleep Well, Lead Well: How Better Sleep Can Improve Leadership, Boost Productivity, and Spark Innovation.* White paper. Center for Creative Leadership, Greensboro, NC.

Craig, A., & Cooper, R. E. (1992). Symptoms of acute and chronic fatigue. In: A. P. Smith & D. M. Jones (eds.), *Handbook of Human Performance (Volume 3): State and Trait*. London: Academic Press Limited, 289–340.

Davidson, R. J., Kabat-Zinn, J., Schumacher, J., Rosenkrantz, M., Muller, D., Santorelli, S., . . . & Sheridan, J. (2003). Alterations in brain and immune function produced by mindfulness meditation. *Psychosomatic Medicine*, 65(4), 564–570.

Deal, J. J. (2013). *Always on, Never Done? Don't Blame the Smartphone*. Center for Creative Leadership. Available at: http://insights.ccl.org/wp-content/uploads/2015/04/AlwaysOn.pdf (accessed 12 January 2016).

Demerouti, E., Bakker, A. B., Geurts, A. E. G., & Taris, T. W. (2009). Daily recovery from work-related effort during non-worktime. In: S. Sonnentag, P. L. Perrewé, & D. C. Ganster (eds.), *Current Perspectives on Job-Stress Recovery: Research in Occupational Stress and Well Being* (Vol. 7). Bingley, UK: JAI Press, 85–123.

Demerouti, E., Bakker, A. B., Nachreiner, F., & Schaufeli, W. B. (2001). The Job Demands–Resources model of burnout. *Journal of Applied Psychology*, 86, 499–512.

Dutton, J. (October 2, 2014). *How to Be a Positive Leader through Building High Quality Connections*. Power-Point slides. Center for Positive Organizations, University of Michigan.

Ertel, K. M., Glymour, M., & Berkman, L. F. (2008). Effects of social integration on preserving memory function in a nationally representative US elderly population. *American Journal of Public Health*, 98(7), 1215–1220.

Evans, J. C. (2015). *The Resiliency Revolution: Your Stress Solution for Life 60 Seconds at a Time*. Minneapolis, MN: Wise Ink Creative Publishing.

Fredrickson, B. (2001). The role of positive emotions in positive psychology – The broaden-and-build theory of positive emotions. *American Psychologist*, 56, 218–226.

Fredrickson, B. (2003). The value of positive emotions: The emerging science of positive psychology is coming to understand why it's good to feel good. *American Scientist*, 91, 330–335.

Fredrickson, B. L., Cohn, M. A., Coffey, K. A., Pek, J., & Finkel, S. M. (2008). Open hearts build lives: Positive emotions, induced through loving-kindness meditation, build consequential personal resources. *Journal of Personality and Social Psychology*, 95, 1045–1062.

Gelles, D. (2012). The mind business. *FT Magazine*, August 24. Available at: www.ft.com/intl/cms/s/2/d9cb7940-ebea-11e1-985a-00144feab49a.html (accessed 20 March 2016).

Granath, J., Ingvarsson, S., von Thiele, U., & Lundberg, U. (2006). Stress management: A randomized study of cognitive behavioural therapy and yoga. *Cognitive Behaviour Therapy*, 35(1), 3–10.

Grant, Adam. (2013). *Give and Take: A Revolutionary Approach to Success*. New York: Viking Adult.

Green, F. (2008). Work effort and worker well-being in the age of affluence. In: R. J. Burke & C. L. Cooper (eds.), *The Long Work Hours Culture: Causes, Consequences and Choices*. Bingley, UK: Emerald Group Publishing Limited, 115–135.

Greist-Bousquet, S., & Schiffman, N. (1992). The effect of task interruption and closure on perceived duration. *Bulletin of the Psychonomic Society*, 30(1), 9–11.

Heaphy, E. D., & Dutton, J. E. (2008). Positive social interactions and the human body at work: Linking organizations and physiology. *Academy of Management Review*, 33(1), 137–162.

Hitchcock, E. M., Dick, R. B., Russo, J. M., & Schmit, J. M. (2004). *Overtime and Extended Work Shifts: Recent Findings on Illnesses, Injuries, and Health Behaviors*. Cincinnati, OH: US Department of Health and Human Services, Centers for Disease Control and Prevention, National Institute for Occupational Safety and Health, Publication 2004-143, 1–37.

Hyland, P. K., Lee, R. A., & Mills, M. J. (2015). Mindfulness at work: A new approach to improving individual and organizational performance. *Industrial and Organizational Psychology*, 8(4), 576–602.

International Labor Organization. (1919). *Hours of Work (Industry)*. Convention, 1919 (No. 1). Available at: www.ilo.org/dyn/normlex/en/f?p=NORMLEXPUB:12100:0::NO::P12100_ILO_CODE:C001 (accessed March 20, 2016).

Jha, A. P., Krompinger, J., & Baime, M. J. (2007). Mindfulness training modifies subsystems of attention. *Cognitive, Affective, & Behavioral Neuroscience*, 7(2), 109–119.

Jones, K. (2014). *Talent Management Systems 2014: Market Analysis, Trends and Provider Profiles*. Oakland, CA: Bersin by Deloitte.

Kabat-Zinn, J. (1994). *Wherever You Go, There You Are: Mindfulness Meditation in Everyday Life*. New York: Hyperion.

King, C. R., Knutson, K. L., Rathouz, P. J., Sidney, S., Liu, K., & Lauderdale, D. S. (2008). Short sleep duration and incident coronary artery calcification. *Journal of the American Medical Association*, 300(24), 2859–2866.

Kinnunen, U., Feldt, T., Siltaloppi, M., & Sonnentag, S. (2011). Job demands-resources model in the context of recovery: Testing recovery experiences as mediators. *European Journal of Work and Organizational Psychology*, 20(6), 805–832.

Kivimäki, M., Jokela, M., Nyberg, S. T., Singh-Manoux, A., Fransson, E. I., Alfredsson, L., Bjorner, J. B., . . . & Virtanen, M. for the IPD-Work Consortium (2015). Long working hours and risk of coronomary heart disease and stroke: A systematic review and meta-analysis of published and unpublished data for 603, 838 individuals. *The Lancet,* 386(10005), 1739–1746. doi.10.1016/S0140–6736(15) 60295–1.

Knutson, K. L., Ryden, A. M., Mander, B. A., & Van Cauter, E. (2006). Role of sleep duration and quality in the risk and severity of type 2 diabetes mellitus. *Archives of Internal Medicine*, 166(16), 1768–1774. doi:10.1001/archinte.166.16.1768.

Kossek, E. E., & Lautsch, B. A. (2012). Work–family boundary management styles in organizations: A cross-level model. *Organizational Psychology Review*, 2(2), 152–171.

Kossek, E. E., Ruderman, M. N., Braddy, P. W., & Hannum, K. M. (2012). Work-nonwork boundary management profiles: A person-centered approach. *Journal of Vocational Behavior*, 81(1), 112–128.

Kuhn, P., & Lozano, F. (2008). The expanding workweek? Understanding trends in long work hours among U.S. men, 1979–2006. *Journal of Labor Economics*, 26(2), 311–343.

Kuyken, W., Byford, S., Taylor, R. S., Watkins, E., Holden, E., White, K., . . . & Teasdale, J. D. (2008). Mindfulness-based cognitive therapy to prevent relapse in recurrent depression. *Journal of Consulting and Clinical Psychology*, 76, 966–978.

Lee, S., McCann, D., & Messenger, J. C. (2007). *Working time around the world: Trends in working hours, laws and policies in a global comparative perspective* (pdf). London and New York: Routledge.

Lee, Y., Chang, C., Lin, Y., & Cheng, Z. (2014). The dark side of smartphone usage: Psychological traits, compulsive behavior and technostress. *Computers in Human Behavior*, 31, 373–383.

Lockley, S. W., Cronin, J. W., Evans, E. E., Cade, B. E., Lee, C. J., Landrigan, C. P., . . . & Czeisler, C. A. (2004). Effect of reducing interns' weekly work hours on sleep and attentional failures. *New England Journal of Medicine*, 351(18), 1829–1837.

McCraty, R. (2003). *Heart–Brain Neurodynamics: The Making of Emotions*. Publication No. 03–015. Boulder Creek, CA: HeartMath Research Center, Institute of HeartMath. Available at: http://store.heartmath.org/store/e-books/heart-brain-neurodynamics (accessed 24 March 2016).

McDowell-Larsen, S. (2012). *The Care and Feeding of the Leader's Brain*. Greensboro, NC: Center for Creative Leadership.

Mednick, S. C., & Ehrman, M. (2006). *Take a Nap!: Change Your Life*. New York: Workman Publishing.

Meijman, T. F., & Mulder, G. (1998). Psychological aspects of workload. In: P. J. D. Drenthe & H. Thierry (eds.), *Handbook of Work and Organizational Psychology: Volume 2. Work Psychology*. Hove, UK: Psychology Press, 5–33.

Moran, D. J. (2011). ACT for Leadership: Using acceptance and commitment training to develop crisis-resilient change managers. *The International Journal of Behavioral Consultation and Therapy*, 7(1), 68–77.

National Sleep Foundation. (2016). *Napping*. Available at: https://sleepfoundation.org/sleep-topics/napping/page/0/3 (accessed 30 March 2016).

Ohayon, M. M. (2012). Determining the level of sleepiness in the American population and its correlates. *Journal of Psychiatric Research*, 46(4), 422–427.

Ohayon, M. M., Priest, R. G., Zulley, J., Smime, S., & Paiva, T. (2002). Prevalence of narcolepsy symptom-atology and diagnosis in the European general population. *Neurology*, 58(12), 1826–1833.

Owen, N., Sparling, P. B., Healy, G. N., Dunstan, D. W., Matthews, C. E. (2010). Sedentary behavior: Emerging evidence for a new health risk. *Mayo Clinic Proceedings*, 85(12), 1138–1141. Available at: www.ncbi.nlm.nih.gov/pmc/articles/PMC2996155/

Payne, J. (2015). *The Neuroscience of Being Your Best Self: Leading (and Living) Well*. Presentation. Executive Development Round Table, Boston, MA.

Pencavel, J. (2014). *The Productivity of Working Hours*. Bonn, Germany: IZA. Available at: http://ftp.iza.org/dp8129.pdf

Physical Activity Council. (2016). *2016 Participation Report*. Available at: http://physicalactivitycouncil.com/pdfs/current.pdf

Pickert, K. (2014). The mindful revolution. *Time*, February 3, 40–49.

Roehrs, T., & Roth, T. (2001). Sleep, sleepiness, and alcohol use. *Alcohol Research and Health*, 25(2), 101–109.

Ruderman, M. N., & Clerkin, C. (2015). Using mindfulness to improve high potential development. *Industrial and Organizational Psychology*, 8(4), 694–698.

Saad, L. (2014). *The "40-Hour" Workweek Is Actually Longer – By Seven Hours*. Available at: www.gallup.com/poll/175286/hour-workweek-actually-longer-seven-hours.aspx (Accessed 8 January 2015).

Sapolsky, R. M. (2004). *Why Zebras Don't Get Ulcers: The Acclaimed Guide to Stress, Stress-Related Diseases, and Coping*. New York: Macmillan.

Siegel, D. J. (2012). *Pocket Guide to Interpersonal Neurobiology: An Integrative Handbook of the Mind* (Norton Series on Interpersonal Neurobiology). New York: WW Norton & Company.

Sonnentag, S. (2003). Recovery, work engagement, and proactive behavior: A new look at the interface between nonwork and work. *Journal of Applied Psychology*, 88(3), 518–528.

Sonnentag, S., & Fritz, C. (2007). The recovery experience questionnaire: Development and validation of a measure for assessing recuperation and unwinding from work. *Journal of Occupational Health Psychology*, 12, 204–221.

Stephens, J. P., Heaphy, E. D., Carmeli, A., Spreitzer, G. M., & Dutton, J. E. (2013). Relationship quality and virtuousness: Emotional carrying capacity as a source of individual and team resilience. *The Journal of Applied Behavioral Science*, 49(1), 13–41.

Van der Hulst, M. (2003). Long work hours and health. *Scandinavian Journal of Work, Environment and Health*, 29(3), 171–188.

Walker, M. P., Stickgold, R., Alsop, D., Gaab, N., & Schlaug, G. (2005). Sleep-dependent motor memory plasticity in the human brain. *Neuroscience*, 133(4), 911–917.

Weiss, S. J., Haber, J., Horowitz, J. A., Stuart, G. W., & Wolfe, B. (2009). The inextricable nature of mental and physical health: Implications for integrative care. *Journal of the American Psychiatric Nurses Association*, 15(6), 371–382. doi:10.1177/1078390309352513.

West, K. E., Jablonski, M. R., Warfield, B., Cecil, K. S., James, M., Ayers, M. A., . . . & Hanifin, J. P. (2011). Blue light from light-emitting diodes elicits a dose-dependent suppression of melatonin in humans. *Journal of Applied Physiology*, 110(3), 619–626.

Williamson, A. M., & Feyer, A. M. (2000). Moderate sleep deprivation produces impairments in cognitive and motor performance equivalent to legally prescribed levels of alcohol intoxication. *Occupational and Environmental Medicine*, 57(10), 649–655.

Wood, A. M., Froh, J. J., & Geraghty, A. W. (2010). Gratitude and well-being: A review and theoretical integration. *Clinical Psychology Review*, 30, 890–905.

World Health Organization. (2004). *Work Organization & Stress: Systematic Problem Approaches for Employers, Managers and Trade Union Representatives*. World Health Organization: Protecting Workers' Health Series No 3. 2004. Available at: www.who.int/occupational_health/publications/pwh3rev.pdf

World Health Organization. (2016). *Physical Inactivity: A Global Public Health Problem*. Available at: www.who.int/dietphysicalactivity/factsheet_inactivity/en/

16

Rethinking work-life balance and wellbeing

The perspectives of fathers

Clare Stovell, David Collinson, Caroline Gatrell, and Laura Radcliffe

Introduction

> Priscilla and I are starting to get ready for our daughter's arrival. We've been picking out our favorite childhood books and toys.
>
> We've also been thinking about how we're going to take time off during the first months of her life. This is a very personal decision, and I've decided to take 2 months of paternity leave when our daughter arrives.
>
> Studies show that when working parents take time to be with their newborns, outcomes are better for the children and families. At Facebook we offer our US employees up to 4 months of paid maternity or paternity leave which they can take throughout the year.
>
> *Mark Zuckerberg (2015)*

At the end of 2015, celebrating the birth of his daughter Maxima, Mark Zuckerberg, Chief Executive of Facebook, announced that he was taking two months' paternity leave so that he could spend time with his new family. His post on Facebook indicated his view that engagement with newborn children has a positive effect on wellbeing, from the perspective of both parents and of children.

In this chapter, we examine work-life balance and wellbeing from the perspective of fathers and fatherhood. In the 21st century, strong arguments have been made within the literature on work-life balance for more research specifically on fatherhood and wellbeing (Duckworth & Buzzanell, 2009; Friedman, 2015; Gatrell, Burnett, Cooper, & Sparrow, 2013; James, 2014). For example, Ranson (2012) claims that there has been too much focus on working mothers and not enough attention paid to what she terms "working fathers." The fact that such a term is not in common usage demonstrates the extent to which fathers have been omitted from discussions about balancing work and family life.

Explorations of work-life balance and wellbeing have tended to focus on how women interpret and prioritize their commitments to family and employment: what social economist Catherine Hakim terms maternal "preference" (Hakim, 1995, 1998, 2000, 2003; see also Gatrell, 2005). Perhaps this focus on mothers has led to a relative lack of understanding regarding fathers' work-life balance, their work-family preferences, and the impact these have on wellbeing, particularly with regard to their relationships and masculine identities (Holter, 2007). Where studies have focused on men and work-life balance, the majority have looked at their employment and the impact of long-hours cultures on men's wellbeing (Worrall & Cooper, 1999) with less focus on men's paternal roles (Burnett, Gatrell, Cooper, & Sparrow, 2013). Conceivably, women have been the main focus of work-family research because they have been most affected by the issues of juggling the "dual burden" of paid employment and child care (Hochschild, 1989). Why should we now be turning our attention to fathers?

Huffman, Olson, O'Gara Jr, and King (2014) argue that fathers' work-life balance needs to be studied because fathers tend to have the least balance between the two domains of work and home, as, on average, they spend longer hours in the workplace than mothers. Breadwinning continues to play an important part in constructing masculine identity and typically leads to employment being prioritized over family life (Collinson & Hearn, 2014). This is perpetuated by a growth in firms expecting a "total commitment" working culture (Kvande, 2009) and the fact that men in Britain work some of the longest hours in Europe (Lewis & Lamb, 2007). Although research suggests that hours spent in paid employment are not in themselves associated with negative wellbeing or conflict between work and family roles (Bianchi & Milkie, 2010), there is evidence that many men are unhappy with their work-life balance and would like more involvement in child care (Dermott, 2008; Kaufman & Uhlenberg, 2000; Milkie, Mattingly, Nomaguchi, Bianchi, & Robinson, 2004). It is important to consider the negative impact this has on fathers' wellbeing. Unmet desires to spend time with children cause emotional strain and long working hours are associated with stress and health problems (Byrne, 2005).

Despite the persistence of the male breadwinning norm, there is increasing pressure to be an "involved" father who not only cares *about* his children, but cares *for* them too (Eräranta & Moisander, 2011; Kimmel, 1993). Paternal time spent on child care has increased (Dermott, 2008; Lewis & Lamb, 2007; O'Brien, 2005) and, thanks to the introduction of shared parental leave in 2015, fathers in Britain arguably have more opportunities than ever to balance family and paid work. Fathering practices are also being changed by the recession and technological advances. Rising unemployment and job insecurity have resulted in more fathers spending time at home (Buzzanell & Turner, 2003), while increases in flexible and home working blur the boundaries between work and domestic life (Halford, 2006). This trend of increased father involvement exposes men to the issue of work-life conflict and the associated risks of burnout and reduced wellbeing (Aycan & Eskin, 2005).

Gaining a greater understanding of fathers' work-life balance is particularly important because their needs are less understood and, as a consequence, they receive little support. Fathers' work-life conflict is exacerbated by the fact that workplaces do not appear to have adapted to the changing trends in fathering practices. Several studies have found that organizations restrict men from considering greater involvement in family life and are unsupportive if male employees do attempt to scale back their work hours for child care (Burnett et al., 2013). Lack of support from organizations has been a consistent finding in the work-life balance literature focusing on women (Cahusac & Kanji, 2014). However, research suggests that men and women have very different experiences and needs regarding work-life balance policies in the workplace (Blithe, 2015).

There is a broad consensus that a well-balanced division between work and family is beneficial for wellbeing (see Graham & Dixon, 2014; James, 2014). Research focusing on men in particular has found that higher levels of work-life balance are associated with more positive attitudes and increased work performance (Perrone, Wright, & Jackson, 2009), while investing in family is associated with a higher quality of life for fathers (Aumann, Galinsky, & Matos, 2011). However, work-life conflict and poor work-life balance have been found to have a negative impact on the wellbeing of both men and women cross-nationally (Graham & Dixon, 2014; Lunau, Bambra,

Eikemo, van der Wel, & Dragano, 2014). The dimensions of wellbeing affected include mental health, marital satisfaction, and parental role performance (Aycan & Eskin, 2005). In their summary of the literature, Allen, Herst, Bruck, and Sutton (2000) showed that conflict caused by work impacting on family life is linked to strain, depression, somatic problems, and burnout.

Changes in fathers' work-family situations also have a knock-on effect on women and children's wellbeing. Research shows that children benefit from spending time with their parents, and some studies point to particular benefits of fathering involvement (Lewis & Lamb, 2003). Understanding the work-life conflicts of both parents is important because research suggests there is an interaction between partners' levels of work-life balance and wellbeing. This can take the form of spillover, where moods originating in one domain spill over into another (Williams & Alliger, 1994), and crossover, where the emotions, mood, and dispositions of one partner cross over to the other (Westman, Brough, & Kalliath, 2009). For example, fathers' stress at work can be passed on to mothers and cause them to feel greater work-life conflict (Bakker, Westman, & Schaufeli, 2007; Bakker, Westman, & van Emmerik, 2009). Partners can also have a positive effect on work-family issues. Work-life conflict can be improved by a partner providing support both practically (sharing child care and housework) and emotionally (supporting career moves and showing interest in their work, for example) (Bianchi & Milkie, 2010).

Understanding fathers' constraints to achieving better work-life balance has positive repercussions not only at the level of individual households but for society in general, as men's involvement in child care is believed to play a crucial role in combating the stalling of the gender revolution (Haas & O'Brien, 2010). To date, while women's labor market participation has increased, women (and especially mothers) still undertake the lion's share of child care and housework – a situation not assisted by the still limited access to paternity leave and flexible working for fathers in Britain. Scholars argue that without symmetrical change, in which men also increase involvement in housework and child care, equality between the sexes cannot be achieved (England, 2010; Friedman, 2015; Haas & O'Brien, 2010). When men share domestic work, they improve women's work-life balance and wellbeing by reducing the "dual burden" phenomenon and allowing women to invest more in their careers. Furthermore, wider uptake of work-life balance provision by both genders may encourage organizations to take policies more seriously and reduce the negative connotations associated with working flexibly or taking leave (Blithe, 2015).

Although the work-life balance literature focusing on fathers is still in its infancy in comparison to that looking at mothers, the last decade has seen a dramatic increase in the amount of research explicitly investigating fathers' experiences. Despite this, even recent studies continue to claim that they are "one of the first" looking at fathers in relation to work-life balance (for example, Huffman et al., 2014). The reason that the proliferation of work in this area has not been acknowledged could be due to a tendency for some work-life balance researchers to refer primarily to literature from within their own discipline (Gatrell et al., 2013, see also Hearn and Niemistö, (2012)). In this chapter we collate the growing body of cross-disciplinary research on fathers' work-life balance experiences and their impact on wellbeing in order to consolidate this knowledge and recognize the contributions that have been made. We begin by considering fathers' experiences of their work and family roles and go on to look at the difficulties they face with regards to achieving balance between the two domains.

Research on fathers' work-life balance and wellbeing

Although work-life balance has traditionally been considered a maternal issue, focus has turned increasingly to fathers' levels of balance and their attitudes, needs, and desires regarding the division of paid work and family life. Research suggests that how men allocate their time, in practice, may not necessarily be a reflection of their preferences. Fathers' unmet desires have negative implications for wellbeing.

Fathers' work-life balance preferences

Much research on work-life balance preferences has included only fathers by implication. For example, Hakim's preference theory (1995, 1998, 2000, 2003) argues that women's lack of representation in the workplace can be explained by their desire to prioritize family life over work. However, although she claims her theory is applicable to both sexes, her data are focused primarily on women (see Hakim, 2000, 2003, for limited data on men). She works on the assumption that the persistence of the male breadwinner is due to men having a homogenous orientation towards work (Hakim, 2000) – but is this the case? Research that has specifically studied male participants suggests that their work-life balance preferences may be more complex.

Kimmel's (1993) article "What do men want?" was one of the first in the work-family domain to focus exclusively on men and take their work-life preferences seriously. Kimmel outlines the change in male working identity from the dedicated breadwinner of the fifties, Whyte's (1956) "Organization Man," who strove for a stable, suburban lifestyle, to the competitive and individualistic "New Organization Man" (Hanan, 1971) of the seventies and eighties, and, finally, to the "New Man" of the nineties and beyond who strives to combine both work and family demands, while also looking for personal meaning (Beck & Beck-Gernsheim, 1995). Kimmel claims this last shift away from an identity based on work and providing was brought about by economic decline and women's entrance into the work force. The New Man discourse problematizes the role of the father as breadwinner and primarily work orientated. At the same time, it opens up the issues of work-life balance to men in that the involved father "balances his career with home life in order to promote equal opportunities for his partner in the labor market and to form stronger, closer, and personally more rewarding relationships with his children" (Eräranta & Moisander, 2011, p. 518). Recent studies show that men, more often than women (Milkie et al., 2004), express preferences for spending more time with their family (Dermott, 2008; Kanji & Samuel, 2015; Kaufman & Uhlenberg, 2000; Merla, 2008). Although this is likely to be linked to gender differences in working hours, it reveals that fathers experience imbalance between their work and family roles, and have an unmet desire for more time with their children. The proportion of men saying that work-life balance is important for them has also increased, and more than half of fathers state that opportunities for flexibility are important to them (Tipping, Chanfreau, Perry, & Tait, 2012). These findings question the idea that men have a homogenous preference for work.

Fathers' desires for greater involvement in the family role are more nuanced than some research suggests. Duckworth and Buzzanell (2009) have challenged the tendency in the literature to view the balance of work and life in terms of having a preference for either one or the other. They found that fathers were more likely to have a "both/and" rather than "either/or" discourse when discussing their work-family preferences and priorities (see also Radcliffe & Cassell, 2014). In contrast with Hakim's (2000) assumption of men's homogenous work preference, they found evidence of "family first" priorities held by all the fathers they interviewed. Richardson, Moyer, and Goldberg's (2012) study of the work-family issues encountered by gay fathers also suggests that men can have an orientation towards both family and work, and suggests that work-family preferences are not fixed. Richardson et al. found that the fathers' work orientations were fluid: prior to having children, many of the fathers described themselves as firmly work-oriented; however, once they were responsible for child care, their priorities shifted dramatically.

There is therefore evidence that fathers have a preference for spending more time with family and that work-life balance is important to them. However, this reported preference has been challenged by some scholars. Kimmel points out that "the desire to change is often more rhetorical than real" (1993, p. 55) and argues that men recognize they "need" to be more involved, but this does not necessarily mean they "want" to. More recently, Campbell and van Wanrooy's (2013) qualitative study into working time preferences found that when respondents were given the opportunity to talk at length, their main attitude was one of ambivalence due to multiple and conflicting ideas about working hours. Furthermore, much research fails to problematize the concept of preference itself and regards stated preferences as stable and measurable. It is also important to consider the great variety within fathers' preferences and work-family experiences. Class, nationality, ethnicity, age, religion, sexual preference, and occupation are related to considerable differences in the amount of time fathers can, and would like to, dedicate to paid work and family.

How fathers experience work-life balance in practice

While there is evidence of fathers wanting greater work-life balance and involvement in child care, research shows that the degree to which this is being achieved is limited (Scott & Clery, 2013). The model of the full-time male breadwinner remains deeply ingrained in workplace cultures and this acts as a social constraint, preventing fathers from achieving work-life balance (Moen & Yu, 2000). Britons spend more hours at work than employees in most other European countries and those who work the longest hours are most likely to be men (Byrne, 2005; Tipping et al., 2012). Even when men do take on flexible working, this does not necessarily improve their work-life balance. Although most part-time workers are women, more men than women work from home. Unlike part-time work, home working is actually associated with longer working hours and intrusion on family life, which leads to greater work-life conflict (Bell & Bryson, 2005; Russell, O'Connell, & McGinnity, 2009).

The nature of employment also has an important influence on levels of work-life balance. Paradoxically, when men are given greater control over their hours at work, this does not necessarily increase family time and can have a negative impact on wellbeing (Kanji & Samuel, 2015). Despite enhancing flexibility and autonomy, being self-employed has been found to create more work-life conflict, not less (Schieman, Whitestone, & Van Gundy, 2006). Meanwhile, Kvande (2009) studied the work-life balance of Norwegian fathers in knowledge industries and law firms, and found that their independence and freedom to take leave when they wished actually resulted in them "choosing" to spend more time at work. The "total commitment" culture in these workplaces, combined with the importance of teamwork and exceeding client expectations, created pressure to work long hours and made it difficult to take time off. This conflicted with their desire, and that of the Norwegian government, for fathers' greater involvement in child care. Those in demanding jobs or those who have high degrees of authority are most vulnerable to conflict, overload, and stress (Moen & Yu, 2000; Schieman & Reid, 2009) despite having higher earnings and more nonroutine work, which are two factors usually positively associated with health. Schieman and Reid (2009) argue that this is because the positive effects of authority are frequently offset by greater work-life conflict.

Working long hours prevents fathers from spending time with their family and achieving balance. However, there is also evidence of fathers experiencing conflict associated with combining work and family roles, and debate about the extent to which this impacts on their wellbeing. Although women have been found to experience greater work-life conflict, the gender difference tends to be small, and a considerable number of working fathers struggle to manage work and family obligations (Leineweber, Baltzer, Hanson, & Westerlund, 2013; Parker & Wang, 2013). In the United States, Hill (2005) found that men worked long hours, but also had significant involvement in household responsibilities. Despite this dual burden, fathers reported less work-life conflict and better wellbeing than mothers. In contrast, some studies have found that men actually experience greater work-life conflict and poorer work-life balance than women (Galinsky, Aumann, & Bond, 2011; Lunau et al., 2014; Nomaguchi, Milkie, & Bianchi, 2005). Although Nomaguchi et al. (2005) found that men experienced greater work-life conflict, they concur with Hill (2005) that time deficits appeared to be associated with lower wellbeing only in women. They posit that this is due to women being under greater social pressure to be devoted to family. Keene and Reynolds (2005) suggest that men are less likely to experience conflict because their partners are taking on the majority of domestic duties. Although men's desire to be involved with raising their children and their hours of child care have increased (Kan, Sullivan, & Gershuny, 2011), there has been little change in men's involvement in domestic chores. Women continue to take on the brunt of cooking, cleaning, and laundry regardless of their hours in paid work (Gershuny, Bittman, & Brice, 2005).

There is also evidence to suggest that work-life conflict does have a negative impact on wellbeing for men. In a study revealing higher levels of psychological distress in single fathers compared to those who were partnered, Janzen and Kelly (2012) discovered that the greater level of work-life conflict experienced by single fathers was the most important factor in explaining the differences in mental wellbeing. Cooklin et al. (2015) also found that work-life conflict was associated with increased distress for fathers. Their nationally representative study of more than 3,000 fathers in Australia showed that men's tendency to stay in full-time work after the birth of a child had a negative impact on their mental health. According to Leineweber et al. (2013), work-life conflict has a negative effect on wellbeing for both men and women, but there are gender differences in how this is manifested. Both men and women have increased risk of emotional exhaustion, however, men are more likely to experience problem drinking and women are more likely to report poor health.

To summarize, research shows that despite claiming a desire for greater work-life balance and involvement in child care, employed fathers in developed economies are spending increasingly long hours in paid employment. There is a general consensus that fathers experience "competing devotions" between work and family roles (Halrynjo, 2009) and this has been shown to have a negative impact on their wellbeing.

What prevents fathers from achieving work-life balance?

As we have seen, the gap between preferred hours and actual hours in paid work is greater for fathers than mothers, and this is due to the fact that they often appear less able or willing to cut back on paid work (Bianchi & Raley, 2005; Moen & Yu, 2000). However, Gregory and Milner (2009) remind us that preferences are shaped by perceived constraints as well as values and desires. We look at two constraints that affect fathers' ability to reduce their hours in paid work: pressure to conform to traditional conceptions of masculinity, and organizational cultures that are unsupportive of men's family role.

The importance of masculine identity and norms

The discrepancy between fathers' preferences regarding their allocation of time and their actual work-life balance appears to be closely linked to gender norms and notions of masculinity. Writing in the seventies, Pleck (1977) argued that reducing time at work is not enough to improve men's work-family balance, as ideology must first be challenged. He revealed the important place that breadwinning holds in the male identity and the purpose that employment gives to many men's lives. Pleck predicted that only once gender ideologies changed would men's time in employment become the more significant barrier to increased domestic involvement. To some extent, gender segregation has decreased and ideologies have become more egalitarian (Scott & Clery, 2013), but the male breadwinning identity is still prevalent. More recently, Thomas and Linstead (2002) studied a large sample of middle managers and found that status and success at work were important for men's identity and self-worth. When interviewing men about their work-life balance, Blithe (2015) found that although they were anxious not to appear to support traditional gender roles, many saw being a family breadwinner as an important part of their identity "as men." Additionally, many mentioned that their wife had "natural" caring tendencies (Miller, 2011) and this gave her a greater right to time out of work, thereby framing a traditional approach in modern, benevolent terms (Gaunt, 2013).

Continuing social expectations for fathers to be family providers shape their intentions and work-life balance decisions. There is a positive relationship between traditional gender role beliefs in fathers and their hours spent in paid work (Huffman et al., 2014). McLaughlin and Muldoon (2014) reveal that those men who are most comfortable with a breadwinning identity do not experience work-life conflict, as they feel they are sufficiently meeting their role as a father by providing. Building a fathering identity around a discourse of male breadwinning helps solve the dilemma of being invested in one's children while remaining a committed employee, and may be used by employees to justify sacrifices at home (Thomas & Linstead, 2002). Indeed, many highly masculine workplace cultures (as well as subcultures and countercultures) emphasize and celebrate family breadwinner identities as a fundamental expression of what it means to be a "real man" (Cockburn, 1983; Collinson, 1992). The importance of breadwinning in masculine identity and the social pressure for fathers to provide for their family may explain Kaufman and Uhlenberg's (2000) finding that fathers generally have a stronger work attachment than men without children. Traditional visions of masculinity are important throughout the life course, and fathers' lack of work-life balance can be rooted in decisions made long before having children. Vandello, Hettinger, Bosson, and Siddiqi (2013) found that, although men and women both value work-life balance at the beginning of their careers, men are less likely to seek or expect flexibility, due to fears about being seen as less masculine. This sets the scene for reduced work-life balance for men later in life.

The continuing importance of breadwinning for fathering identity is in conflict with new expectations regarding involvement in child care (Aumann et al., 2011; McLaughlin & Muldoon, 2014; Ranson, 2012). Pressure to provide for one's family and be successful at work is contrasted with fears of neglecting family responsibilities, missing out on children's formative years, and damaging relationships with partners. Although, individually, many women experience similar conflicts between work and family pressures, there is more cultural acceptance of women prioritizing family over work. Involved fathering and better work-life balance can be threatening to masculine identity, as they challenge traditional gender roles. Prentice and Carranza's (2002) study of gender stereotypes found that "the incompatibility of new fatherhood ideals and traditional definitions of masculinity were readily apparent, as was a keen reluctance on the part of these fathers to behave contrary to traditional gender roles for fear of negative repercussions" (p. 446). Not fitting in with conventional masculine ideals and norms can have negative repercussions on emotional wellbeing, due to the impact on relationships with other men and subsequent damage to social networks.

The centrality of breadwinning to fathers' identities has been questioned, however. Kimmel (1993) states that during an economic downturn, involvement in child care can provide fathers with the feelings of identity and fulfilment usually found at work. Buzzanell and Turner's (2003) research into men's identity and work-family management following job loss also found that emotion work was important for maintaining fathers' wellbeing. Spending time on child care created positive feelings and gave emotions of normalcy. However, somewhat in contrast to Kimmel, they found that sustaining a breadwinning identity while out of paid work was still important for asserting masculinity and status, and child care was not enough to replace these needs. We can also question whether a breadwinning identity still applies to men only. Reynolds and Aletraris (2007) found that only women wanted to reduce their hours when work impacted on family. However, contrary to the authors' expectations, conflict in the other direction (family interfering with work) made women want to increase their work hours. The researchers suggest that this negative reaction to family life encroaching on work is due to the fact that, as for men, work commitment plays an important role in women's identity.

Regardless of these debates, it would appear that breadwinning remains a powerful concept for fathers and encourages them to prioritize work over family life, thus causing imbalance. In this sense, new expectations of greater paternal involvement are at odds with traditional visions of masculinity and the importance of work in masculine identity. These tensions in identity and issues of imbalance can have a negative impact on wellbeing.

How organizations consider fathers' work-life balance

The literature suggests that organizations play a crucial role in preventing fathers from achieving their desired level of work-life balance, while Allard, Haas, and Hwang (2011) go so far as to claim that organizations are the *main* culprits for men's work-life conflict. Workplaces are frequently criticized for doing little to improve work-life balance, particularly in times of recession, and organizational support appears to be particularly lacking for fathers.

Several scholars point to a failure by organizations to adapt to changes in the work-family situations of their employees and to the rise of dual-earning households (Blithe, 2015; Coltrane, Miller, DeHaan, & Stewart, 2013). Currently, many workplace cultures remain rooted in the assumption that employees have someone (by implication, a woman) at home full-time to deal with family demands (Thomas & Linstead, 2002) and this results in conventions of long hours and presenteeism (Kvande, 2009). As a result of expectations of "total commitment," there is a considerable long-term penalty to career progression and earnings for anyone who reduces his or her hours (Burnett et al., 2013; Holter, 2007; Kimmel, 1993). That has been referred to as a "flexibility stigma" (Coltrane et al., 2013). Research focusing on male employees has found that those who take advantage of flexible working or leave for family reasons risk long-term wage penalties (Coltrane et al., 2013) and may be perceived as less committed, less serious about their work, and less deserving of a raise (Vandello et al., 2013).

While organizational pressure on employees to be committed to work and the suppression of family and home life has been well documented in the literature on women's inequality in the workplace (Blair-Loy, 2006), research looking at perceptions of leave-takers suggests that fathers who seek greater involvement in home life may be particularly penalized at work. Allen and Russell (1999) found that male employees who took leave for family reasons were less likely to be perceived as committed to their work or deserving of reward than female employees, while the participants in Wayne and Cordeiro's (2003) study considered men as less likely to be altruistic at work than women who took leave. This is most likely due to the conflict with expectations of male breadwinning (Burnett et al., 2013) and the fact that flexible working has been associated with being less masculine (Vandello et al., 2013), making men who use work-life balance provisions appear gender deviant. However, these assumptions have been challenged by longitudinal research on the actual outcomes of leave taking on long-term earnings, which suggests that "the consequences of privileging family care over work obligations appear to carry similar penalties for men and women" (Coltrane et al., 2013, p. 298). Regardless of whether the flexibility stigma is greater for men, a result of the lack of organizational support for men's work-life balance, fathers' needs are rarely considered (Burnett et al., 2013) and, as a result of the lack of organizational support for men's work-life balance, changes in men's work-family orientations often start at home and are brought to jobs rather than the other way round (Holter, 2007).

Even if fathers take the risk of sacrificing career progression and decide to increase their involvement in child care, they are likely to find it difficult to negotiate a flexible working arrangement due to gender differences in the application of work-life balance policies. Burnett et al. (2013) found that fathers were aware of work-life balance initiatives, but were excluded or discouraged from using them by their employers, who often considered these initiatives to be reserved exclusively for women. The gay fathers interviewed by Richardson et al. (2012) struggled with workplaces that were unprepared for discussions regarding child care needs that did not involve mothers. McDonald, Brown, and Bradley (2005) identify five reasons why men do not use work-life balance policies when they are available: lack of managerial support for work-life balance, perceptions of negative career consequences, organizational time expectations, the gendered nature of policy utilization, and negative reactions from colleagues without family responsibilities. Interestingly, Lunau et al. (2014) found that family policies were in fact more important to men's work-life balance than women's. They suggest that this is due to the fact that women are more likely to adjust their employment patterns to suit family responsibilities when reconciliation policies (such as child care services, parental leave, support for single parents) are unavailable. The fact that fathers are less likely to take advantage of work-life balance policies may lead to them having greater issues with wellbeing. Greenhaus, Collins, and Shaw (2003) found that wellbeing can be improved by work-life initiatives that allow employees to have greater involvement at home, and Burke (2010) concludes that this is the case for both men and women.

Due to the problematic nature of organizational work-life balance policies for fathers, many resort to unofficial measures for fulfilling family responsibilities, such as using holiday allowance or sick leave. The individual characters of managers therefore have a considerable impact on men's ability to achieve work-life balance and wellbeing (Kvande, 2009), as a sympathetic supervisor is more likely to allow informal flexibility and leave arrangements. Unofficial leave taking and supportive colleagues have been found to be more effective than formal policies alone (Behson, 2005; Burnett et al., 2013; Lewis & Cooper, 2005; Richardson et al., 2012). Tracy and Rivera (2010) found that male executives' personal views regarding the gender division of labor and preferences for work-life balance (a large number were self-confessed workaholics) dictated the way they interpreted and reacted to employees' requests for leave. These executives were clear about their expectations for women to take on domestic responsibilities, yet they were unlikely to support male employees who requested leave or flexibility for family demands, failing to recognize that fathers' wellbeing might be inextricably bound up in family as well as employment demands.

Given that work-life policies are difficult to implement without company support, Kvande (2009) concludes that fathers need legitimization for leave taking and are unlikely to "opt-in" to work-family policies, unless they are provided nationally by a welfare state and also supported at an organizational level. Burnett et al. (2013) also highlight the impact of organizational attitudes towards fathers, but argue that policies are not effective for changing social behavior. They recommend that the work-life balance and wellbeing needs of fathers should receive greater recognition in the workplace, and that employers should be more understanding of the needs of parents.

In summary, organizations influence preferences and provide structural constraints to greater work-life balance. Frequently, success is measured by the number of hours worked and employees are encouraged to prioritize work over family life. Those who wish to dedicate more time to family regardless of these pressures face barriers in the form of unequal application of policy, reduced opportunities for career progression, and unsupportive colleagues. Since many workplace cultures continue to assume a model of male breadwinning, fathers experience greater organizational constraints and lack of support for improving work-life balance.[1]

Conclusion

Calls for more consideration of work-life balance from the perspective of fathers and their wellbeing have been a regular feature of research in the work-family domain (Burnett et al., 2013). This chapter has demonstrated that researchers have responded to these calls, and their work reveals that fathers' experiences of work-life balance (and consequently paternal perspectives on wellbeing) are more complex than previously imagined. Studies that included fathers by implication tended to assume that the integration of work and family was a concern unique to women, and that men had a homogenous preference for work. Instead, due to men's increasing involvement with child care, growing numbers of fathers are experiencing the conflict associated with combining family responsibilities and work. However, such conflicts do not appear to be the primary cause of most fathers' work-life balance issues (or, arguably, the principal threat to paternal wellbeing). For the majority of fathers, work continues to take priority and imbalance comes from an unmet desire to spend more time with family.

While men show evidence of desire for greater work-life balance, this is problematized by the continuing importance of providing in masculine and fathering identities. The ideology of male breadwinning is particularly strong in organizations, which appear outdated in their expectations that only women have child care duties and that the ideal employee is one without domestic responsibilities. Structural constraints, in the form of requirements for total commitment and a lack of organizational support, restrict fathers' ability to achieve work-life balance. Some researchers have also questioned the sincerity of men's stated desires for greater time with family and point to the conflict between modern expectations of increased paternal involvement and the central role work plays in societal notions of success.

Although studies on fathers, wellbeing, and work-life balance have proliferated over the past decade, this remains an emerging field with gaps to fill and assumptions to be challenged. More qualitative research is needed, for example, to better understand fathers' work-life balance preferences and the causes of mismatches in desires and practice. Outside of academia, we need recognition at an organizational level that men's perspectives on fatherhood have changed and that many now have or want greater responsibility for child care. A wholesale shift in employer support for fathers who seek access to family-friendly policies is necessary, and this will enable both men and women to better balance work and child care.

If fathers are constrained from enacting preferences for greater work-life balance, this has a negative effect on wellbeing through stress and mental health issues, as well as potentially impairing relationships with children and partners. The fact that fathers' work-life conflict tends to be centered around unmet desires for more time with family, rather than the dual burden more associated with working mothers, leads to gender differences in the outcomes of conflict on wellbeing (Emslie & Hunt, 2009). As Connell (2005, p. 378) has so aptly observed: "Dropping dead from career-driven stress, or shriveling emotionally from never seeing one's children, is a different issue from exhaustion because of the double shift, or not getting promotion because of career interruptions".

Note

1   When considering work-family research that takes place in organizations, Greenhaus, Parasuraman, and Collins (2001) remind us that it is important to consider the possibility of sampling bias, as those who experience too much work-life conflict are likely to leave the workforce.

References

Allard, K., Haas, L., & Hwang, C. P. (2011). Family-supportive organizational culture and fathers' experiences of work–family conflict in Sweden. *Gender, Work & Organization*, 18(2), 141–157.

Allen, T. D., Herst, D. E. L., Bruck, C. S., & Sutton, M. (2000). Consequences associated with work-to-family conflict: A review and agenda for future research. *Journal of Occupational Health Psychology*, 5(2), 278–308.

Allen, T. D., & Russell, J. E. A. (1999). Parental leave of absence: Some not so family-friendly implications. *Journal of Applied Social Psychology*, 29(1), 166–191.

Aumann, K., Galinsky, E., & Matos, K. (2011). *The New Male Mystique*. New York: Families and Work Institute.

Aycan, Z., & Eskin, M. (2005). Relative contributions of childcare, spousal support, and organizational support in reducing work-family conflict for men and women: The case of Turkey. *Sex Roles*, 53(7–8), 453–471.

Bakker, A. B., Westman, M., & Schaufeli, W. (2007). Crossover of burnout: An experimental design. *European Journal of Work and Organizational Psychology*, 16(2), 220–239.

Bakker, A. B., Westman, M., & van Emmerik, I. J. H. (2009). Advancements in crossover theory. *Journal of Managerial Psychology*, 24(3), 206–219.

Beck, U., & Beck-Gernsheim, E. (1995). *The Normal Chaos of Love*. Cambridge: Polity Press.

Behson, S. J. (2005). The relative contribution of formal and informal organizational work–family support. *Journal of Vocational Behavior*, 66(3), 487–500.

Bell, A., & Bryson, C. (2005). Work-life balance – still a "women's issue"? In: A. Park, J. Curtice, K. Thomson, C. Bromley, M. Phillips, & M. Johnson (eds.), *British Social Attitudes: The 22nd Report*. London: SAGE, 33–62.

Bianchi, S. M., & Milkie, M. A. (2010). Work and family research in the first decade of the 21st century. *Journal of Marriage and Family*, 72(3), 705–725.

Bianchi, S. M., & Raley, S. B. (2005). Time allocation in families. In: S. M. Bianchi, L. M. Casper, & R. B. King (eds.), *Work, Family, Health, and Well-Being*. Philadelphia: Erlbaum, 21–42.

Blair-Loy, M. (2006). *Competing Devotions: Career and Family among Women Executives*. Cambridge, MA: Harvard University Press.

Blithe, S. (2015). *Gender Equality and Work-Life Balance: Glass Handcuffs and Working Men in the US*. New York: Routledge, Taylor & Francis Group.

Burke, R. (2010). Do managerial men benefit from organizational values supporting work-personal life balance? *Gender in Management: An International Journal*, 25(2), 91–99.

Burnett, S. B., Gatrell, C. J., Cooper, C. L., & Sparrow, P. (2013). Fathers at work: A ghost in the organizational machine. *Gender, Work & Organization*, 20(6), 632–646.

Buzzanell, P. M., & Turner, L. H. (2003). Emotion work revealed by job loss discourse: Backgrounding-foregrounding of feelings, construction of normalcy, and (re)instituting of traditional masculinities. *Journal of Applied Communication Research*, 31(1), 27–57.

Byrne, U. (2005). Work-life balance: Why are we talking about it at all? *Business Information Review*, 22(1), 53–59.

Cahusac, E., & Kanji, S. (2014). Giving up: How gendered organizational cultures push mothers out. *Gender, Work & Organization*, 21(1), 57–70.

Campbell, I., & van Wanrooy, B. 2013. Long working hours and working-time preferences: Between desirability and feasibility. *Human Relations*, 66(8): 1131–1155.

Cockburn, C. (1983). *Brothers: Male Dominance and Technological Change*. London: Pluto Press.

Collinson, D. (1992). *Managing the Shopfloor: Subjectivity, Masculinity and Workplace Culture*. Berlin: De Gruyter.

Collinson, D., & Hearn, J. (2014). Taking the obvious apart: Critical approaches to men, masculinities and the gendered dynamics of leadership. In: R. Burke & D. Major (eds.), *Gender in Organizations: Are Men Allies or Adversaries to Women's Career Advancement*. Cheltenham: Edward Elgar Publishing, 73–92.

Coltrane, S., Miller, E. C., DeHaan, T., & Stewart, L. (2013). Fathers and the flexibility stigma. *Journal of Social Issues*, 69(2), 279–302.

Connell, R. W. 2005. A really good husband: Work/life balance, gender equity and social change. *Australian Journal of Social Issues,* 40(3), 369–383.

Cooklin, A. R., Giallo, R., Strazdins, L., Martin, A., Leach, L. S., & Nicholson, J. M. (2015). What matters for working fathers? Job characteristics, work-family conflict and enrichment, and fathers' postpartum mental health in an Australian cohort. *Social Science & Medicine,* 146, 214–222.

Dermott, E. (2008). *Intimate Fatherhood: A Sociological Analysis.* Abingdon: Routledge.

Duckworth, J. D., & Buzzanell, P. M. (2009). Constructing work-life balance and fatherhood: Men's framing of the meanings of both work and family. *Communication Studies,* 60(5), 558–573.

Emslie, C., & Hunt, K. (2009). "Live to work" or "work to live"? A qualitative study of gender and work–life balance among men and women in mid-life. *Gender, Work & Organization,* 16(1), 152–172.

England, P. (2010). The gender revolution uneven and stalled. *Gender & Society,* 24(2), 149–166.

Eräranta, K., & Moisander, J. (2011). Psychological regimes of truth and father identity: Challenges for work/life integration. *Organization Studies,* 32(4), 509–526.

Friedman, S. (2015). Still a "stalled revolution"? Work/family experiences, hegemonic masculinity, and moving toward gender equality. *Sociology Compass,* 9(2), 140–155.

Galinsky, E., Aumann, K., & Bond, J. T. (2011). *Times Are Changing: Gender and Generation at Work and at Home.* New York: Families and Work Institute.

Gatrell, C. (2005). *Hard Labour: The Sociology of Parenthood.* Maidenhead: Open University Press.

Gatrell, C. J., Burnett, S. B., Cooper, C. L., & Sparrow, P. (2013). Work–life balance and parenthood: A comparative review of definitions, equity and enrichment. *International Journal of Management Reviews,* 15(3), 300–316.

Gaunt, R. (2013). Ambivalent sexism and perceptions of men and women who violate gendered family roles. *Community, Work & Family,* 16(4), 401–416.

Gershuny, J., Bittman, M., & Brice, J. (2005). Exit, voice, and suffering: Do couples adapt to changing employment patterns? *Journal of Marriage and Family,* 67(3), 656–665.

Graham, J. A., & Dixon, M. A. (2014). Coaching fathers in conflict: A review of the tensions surrounding the work-family interface. *Journal of Sport Management,* 28(4), 447–456.

Greenhaus, J. H., Collins, K. M., & Shaw, J. D. (2003). The relation between work–family balance and quality of life. *Journal of Vocational Behavior,* 63(3), 510–531.

Greenhaus, J. H., Parasuraman, S., & Collins, K. M. (2001). Career involvement and family involvement as moderators of relationships between work-family conflict and withdrawal from a profession. *Journal of Occupational Health Psychology,* 6(2), 91–100.

Gregory, A., & Milner, S. (2009). Editorial: Work–life balance: A matter of choice? *Gender, Work & Organization,* 16(1), 1–13.

Haas, L., & O'Brien, M. (2010). New observations on how fathers work and care: Introduction to the special issue – Men, work and parenting – Part I. *Fathering: A Journal of Theory, Research, and Practice about Men as Fathers,* 8(3), 271–275.

Hakim, C. (1995). Five feminist myths about women's employment. *The British Journal of Sociology,* 46(3), 429–455.

Hakim, C. (1998). Developing a sociology for the twenty-first century: Preference theory. *The British Journal of Sociology,* 49(1), 137–143.

Hakim, C. (2000). *Work-Lifestyle Choices in the 21st Century: Preference Theory.* New York: Oxford University Press.

Hakim, C. (2003). *Models of the Family in Modern Societies: Ideals and Realities.* Aldershot: Ashgate.

Halford, S. (2006). Collapsing the boundaries? Fatherhood, organization and home-working. *Gender, Work & Organization,* 13(4), 383–402.

Halrynjo, S. (2009). Men's work–life conflict: Career, care and self-realization: Patterns of privileges and dilemmas. *Gender, Work & Organization,* 16(1), 98–125.

Hanan, M. (1971). Make way for the new organization man. *Harvard Business Review,* 49(4), 128–138.

Hearn, J., & Niemistö, C. (2012). Men, "Father managers" and home-work relations. In: P. McDonald & E. Jeanes (eds.), *Men, Wage Work and Family* (Vol. 28). London and New York: Routledge, 95–114.

Hill, E. J. (2005). Work-family facilitation and conflict, working fathers and mothers, work-family stressors and support. *Journal of Family Issues,* 26(6), 793–819.

Hochschild, A. R. (1989). *The Second Shift: Working Parents and the Revolution at Home.* New York: Viking Penguin.

Holter, O. (2007). Men's work and family reconciliation in Europe. *Men and Masculinities,* 9(4), 425–456.

Huffman, A. H., Olson, K. J., O'Gara Jr., T. C., & King, E. B. (2014). Gender role beliefs and fathers' work-family conflict. *Journal of Managerial Psychology*, 29(7), 774–793.

James, A. (2014). Work–life "balance", recession and the gendered limits to learning and innovation (or, why it pays employers to care). *Gender, Work & Organization*, 21(3), 273–294.

Janzen, B. L., & Kelly, I. W. (2012). Psychological distress among employed fathers: Associations with family structure, work quality, and the work-family interface. *American Journal of Men's Health*, 6(4), 294–302.

Kan, M., Sullivan, O., & Gershuny, J. (2011). Gender convergence in domestic work: Discerning the effects of interactional and institutional barriers from large-scale data. *Sociology*, 45(2), 234–251.

Kanji, S., & Samuel, R. (prepublished 26 August 2015). Male breadwinning revisited: How specialisation, gender role attitudes and work characteristics affect overwork and underwork in Europe. *Sociology*. doi: 10.1177/0038038515596895

Kaufman, G., & Uhlenberg, P. (2000). The influence of parenthood on the work effort of married men and women. *Social Forces*, 78(3), 931–947.

Keene, J. R., & Reynolds, J. R. (2005). The job costs of family demands: Gender differences in negative family-to-work spillover. *Journal of Family Issues*, 26(3), 275–299.

Kimmel, M. S. (1993). What do men want? *Harvard Business Review*, 71(6), 50–63.

Kvande, E. (2009). Work–life balance for fathers in globalized knowledge work. Some insights from the Norwegian context. *Gender, Work & Organization*, 16(1), 58–72.

Leineweber, C., Baltzer, M., Hanson, L. L. M., & Westerlund, H. (2013). Work-family conflict and health in Swedish working women and men: A 2-year prospective analysis (the slosh study). *European Journal of Public Health*, 23(4), 710–716.

Lewis, C., & Lamb, M. E. (2003). Fathers' influences on children's development: The evidence from two-parent families. *European Journal of Psychology of Education*, 18(2), 211–228.

Lewis, C., & Lamb, M. E. (2007). *Understanding Fatherhood*. York: Joseph Rowntree Foundation.

Lewis, S., & Cooper, C. L. (2005). *Work-Life Integration: Case Studies of Organisational Change*. Chichester: John Wiley.

Lunau, T., Bambra, C., Eikemo, T. A., van der Wel, K. A., & Dragano, N. (2014). A balancing act? Work-life balance, health and well-being in European welfare states. *European Journal of Public Health*, 24(3), 422–427.

McDonald, P., Brown, K., & Bradley, L. (2005). Explanations for the provision-utilisation gap in work-life policy. *Women in Management Review*, 20(1), 37–55.

McLaughlin, K., & Muldoon, O. (2014). Father identity, involvement and work–family balance: An in-depth interview study. *Journal of Community & Applied Social Psychology*, 24(5), 439–452.

Merla, L. (2008). Determinants, costs, and meanings of belgian stay-at-home fathers: An international comparison. *Fathering: A Journal of Theory, Research, and Practice about Men as Fathers*, 6(2), 113–132.

Milkie, M. A., Mattingly, M. J., Nomaguchi, K. M., Bianchi, S. M., & Robinson, J. P. (2004). The time squeeze: Parental statuses and feelings about time with children. *Journal of Marriage and Family*, 66(3), 739–761.

Miller, T. (2011). *Making Sense of Fatherhood: Gender, Caring and Work*. Cambridge: Cambridge University Press.

Moen, P., & Yu, Y. (2000). Effective work/ life strategies: Working couples, work conditions, gender, and life quality. *Social Problems*, 47(3), 291–326.

Nomaguchi, K. M., Milkie, M. A., & Bianchi, S. M. (2005). Time strains and psychological well-being: Do dual-earner mothers and fathers differ? *Journal of Family Issues*, 26(6), 756–792.

O'Brien, M. (2005). *Shared Caring: Bringing Fathers into the Frame* (Vol. 18). Manchester: Equal Opportunities Commission.

Parker, K., & Wang, W. (2013). *Modern Parenthood: Roles of Moms and Dads Converge as They Balance Work and Family*. Washington: Pew Research Center.

Perrone, K. M., Wright, S. L., & Jackson, Z. V. (2009). Traditional and nontraditional gender roles and work-family interface for men and women. *Journal of Career Development*, 36(1), 8–24.

Pleck, J. H. (1977). The work-family role system. *Social Problems*, 24(4), 417–427.

Prentice, D. A., & Carranza, E. (2002). What women and men should be, shouldn't be, are allowed to be, and don't have to be: The contents of prescriptive gender stereotypes. *Psychology of Women Quarterly*, 26(4), 269–281.

Radcliffe, L. S., & Cassell, C. (2014). Resolving couples' work–family conflicts: The complexity of decision making and the introduction of a new framework. *Human Relations*, 67(7), 793–819.

Ranson, G. (2012). Men, paid employment and family responsibilities: Conceptualizing the "working father." *Gender, Work & Organization*, 19(6), 741–761.

Reynolds, J., & Aletraris, L. (2007). Work–family conflict, children, and hour mismatches in Australia. *Journal of Family Issues*, 28(6), 749–772.

Richardson, H., Moyer, A., & Goldberg, A. (2012). "You try to be superman and you don't have to be": Gay adoptive fathers' challenges and tensions in balancing work and family. *Fathering: A Journal of Theory, Research, and Practice about Men as Fathers*, 10(3), 314–336.

Russell, H., O'Connell, P. J., & McGinnity, F. (2009). The impact of flexible working arrangements on work–life conflict and work pressure in Ireland. *Gender, Work & Organization*, 16(1), 73–97.

Schieman, S., & Reid, S. (2009). Job authority and health: Unraveling the competing suppression and explanatory influences. *Social Science & Medicine*, 69(11), 1616–1624.

Schieman, S., Whitestone, Y. K., & Van Gundy, K. (2006). The nature of work and the stress of higher status. *Journal of Health and Social Behavior*, 47(3), 242–257.

Scott, J., & Clery, E. (2013). An incomplete revolution. In: A. Park, C. Bryson, E. Clery, J. Curtice, & M. Phillips (eds.), *British Social Attitudes: The 30th Report*. London: NatCen, 115–138.

Thomas, R., & Linstead, A. (2002). Losing the plot? Middle managers and identity. *Organization*, 9(1), 71–93.

Tipping, S., Chanfreau, J., Perry, J., & Tait, C. (2012). *The Fourth Work-Life Balance Employee Survey*. London: Department for Business Innovation and Skills.

Tracy, S. J., & Rivera, K. D. (2010). Endorsing equity and applauding stay-at-home moms: How male voices on work-life reveal aversive sexism and flickers of transformation. *Management Communication Quarterly*, 24(1), 3–43.

Vandello, J. A., Hettinger, V. E., Bosson, J. K., & Siddiqi, J. (2013). When equal isn't really equal: The masculine dilemma of seeking work flexibility. *Journal of Social Issues*, 69(2), 303–321.

Wayne, J. H., & Cordeiro, B. L. (2003). Who is a good organizational citizen? Social perception of male and female employees who use family leave. *Sex Roles*, 49(5), 233–246.

Westman, M., Brough, P., & Kalliath, T. (2009). Expert commentary on work–life balance and crossover of emotions and experiences: Theoretical and practice advancements. *Journal of Organizational Behavior*, 30(5), 587–595.

Whyte, W. H. (1956). *The Organization Man*. New York: Simon and Schuster.

Williams, K. J., & Alliger, G. M. (1994). Role stressors, mood spillover, and perceptions of work-family conflict in employed parents. *The Academy of Management Journal*, 37(4), 837–868.

Worrall, L., & Cooper, C. L. (1999). Working patterns and working hours: Their impact on UK managers. *Leadership & Organization Development Journal*, 20(1), 6–10.

Zuckerberg, M. [Mark] (20 November 2015) Priscilla and I are starting to get ready for our daughter's arrival. . . . [Facebook status update]. Retrieved from www.facebook.com/zuck?lst=503553279%3A4%3A1486998594

Part V
Initiatives to enhance wellbeing

17

Wellbeing coaching

Tim Anstiss and Jonathan Passmore

Introduction

The last 10–15 years have witnessed a growing interest in the science around wellbeing (e.g., Diener, Suh, Lucas, & Smith, 1999; Kahneman, Diener, & Schwarz, 1999; Keyes, Schmotkin, & Ryff, 2002; Seligman, 2011; Stratham & Chase, 2010). Seligman (1998, p. 538) gave the field a boost during his 1998 speech as the president of the American Psychological Association, when he said:

> The field of Psychology has, since World War 2, become a science and practice of healing. It concentrates on repairing damage within a disease model of human functioning. I proposed changing the focus of the science and the profession from repairing the worst things in life to understanding and building the qualities that make life worth living. I call this new orientation Positive Psychology.

Positive psychology has been defined as "the study of the conditions and processes that contribute to the flourishing or optimal functioning of people, groups, and institutions" (Gable & Haidt, 2005, p. 103).

In this chapter we explore how to combine insights from the science of wellbeing and positive psychology with coaching, to help coaches become as effective as possible in helping their clients take steps to protect and improve their wellbeing.

The development of coaching

Over the past two decades the term *coaching* has entered the popular language. However, its frequent use has meant the term has become misused and is often poorly defined. For some, coaching has come to mean almost any conversation where one party is expecting another party to do something. In this sense the term *coaching* has become a substitute for teaching, mentoring, and even instruction. We dispute this view. Instead, we believe coaching is a distinctive and useful methodology, one that has particular value in supporting people to make behavioral change that can enhance their wellbeing and health.

In this chapter we use the term *coaching* to describe a very specific process that is different from teaching, mentoring, and instruction. John Whitmore (1992) a popular writer in the field of coaching, has suggested that coaching is about "unlocking a person's potential to maximise their own performance" (Whitmore, 1992). Whitmore's background in motorsport and subsequent transfer to the world of business consulting has shaped his perspective and thus this definition. When one looks at coaching for health or wellbeing, we feel the definition is more difficult to apply.

In the parallel field of coaching psychology, Anthony Grant and Stephen Palmer have argued that coaching is primarily concerned with enhancing performance in personal life and work, and should be restricted to nonclinical and adult populations: "Coaching psychology is for enhancing performance in work and personal life domains with normal, non-clinical populations, under-pinned by models of coaching, grounded in established therapeutic approaches" (Grant & Palmer, 2002). This perspective, however, has been challenged by other coaching psychologists who have argued that coaching is a future-focused methodology for behavioral change and can be applied more widely, in terms of client groups, as well as presenting issues. (Passmore, Peterson, & Freire, 2013). Publications reflecting this diversity of application and client group have proliferated in the period since 2010. While coaching remains a staple methodology at work to improve performance, it is now also being applied with offenders (McGregor, 2015), learner drivers (Pass-more & Mortimer, 2011), the armed forces (Passmore & Rehman, 2012), and small family busi-ness coaching (Shams & Lane, 2011), as well as to improve health outcomes (Rogers & Maini, 2016), address obesity (Newnham-Kanas, 2011), and improve safety in the oil and gas industry (Passmore, Krauesslar, & Avery, 2015).

Given this proliferation of coaching, Passmore and Fillery-Travis (2011) have offered an alter-native definition for coaching, which can more conveniently be applied across the wide range of applications which coaching is now being applied.

> Coaching is a Socratic, based future focused dialogue between a facilitator (coach) and a participant (coachee/client), where the facilitator uses open questions, active listening, summaries and reflections which are aimed at stimulating the self-awareness and personal responsibility of the participant.
>
> *(Passmore & Fillery-Travis, 2011)*

For wellbeing coaching, however, we might further add to this by suggesting that the role of coaching in this context is not solely about awareness and personal responsibility, and should be towards behavioral outcomes. Increased self-awareness and personal responsibility, combined with new knowledge, can contribute towards enhanced motivation, skill development, and behavioral change, which in turn may then result in improved experience of health and wellbeing.

For the purposes of this chapter therefore we offer the following definition:

> Wellbeing coaching is a Socratic, future-focused, collaborative conversation between a coach and the client, during which the coach uses open questions, affirmations, reflective listening, summaries, and information exchange to stimulate and encourage self-awareness, personal responsibility, and behavioral change thought likely to lead to improved wellbeing outcomes over time.

In short, wellbeing coaching is a Socratic intervention focused on enhancing self-awareness and personal responsibility, with the medium to long-term goal of facilitating behavioral change for improved health and wellbeing outcomes.

The development of coaching research

Unlike for some comparable interventions, research on coaching has been relatively slow to develop. The number of high-quality research studies on coaching remains relatively small when compared to studies on interventions such as motivational interviewing, which in a similar period of development from the early 1990s has been subject to more than 650 randomized controlled trial (RCT) studies. (This means that if motivational interviewing were to be considered a form of coaching, then the empirical support for coaching would dramatically improve – but obviously for certain types of coaching only.)

In our view, this relatively poverty of research into the effectiveness of coaching reflects, in part, the lack of importance placed on evidence-based practice by human resources professionals and managers seeking solutions to issues of performance, development, and wellbeing at work. Compare this with the situation in health care settings in which funders, managers, and clinicians commonly need to justify their decisions and actions in terms of the existing evidence about what is known to be (or is likely to be) effective in particular contexts.

In the field of coaching there are still relatively few high-quality RCT studies – perhaps fewer than 50 published papers across workplace, education, and wellbeing coaching combined. This slow rate of growth compared to other approaches may be explained in part by the limited funding available to support such studies compared with health care interventions, along with the difficulty of securing workplace or education establishment buy-in for a robust evaluation involving different groups of people receiving different interventions, the challenges of reliably measuring outcomes, and a limited pool of academically focused coaching researchers.

It is therefore encouraging to observe an increased use of randomized and controlled experiments in coaching since 2001 (see Grant, Passmore, Cavanagh, & Parker, 2010 for a wider discussion). Anthony Grant has been one of the most active contributors to the research in this area and has published a number of RCT studies. Most have focused on the psychological impact of coaching, workplace learning, and personal performance.

A study by Grant, Curtayne, and Burton (2009) of 41 executives in an Australian public health agency explored the impact of coaching on goal attainment and resilience. The quantitative data showed that coaching enhanced participants goal attainment, resilience, and wellbeing, and decreased stress and depression, when compared to the control condition. The study also indicated that coaching fostered self-confidence, personal insight, and helped the managers to develop their managerial skills.

In a study by Gyllensten and Palmer (2005) with 31 managers from a UK finance organization, the researchers found, compared with a "no-coaching" control group, the use of a coaching intervention was associated with lower levels of anxiety and stress.

There have been a number of other health- and wellbeing-related studies. Taylor (1997) found that solution-focused coaching fostered resilience in medical students. Gattellari et al. (2005) found that peer coaching by general practitioners improved coachees' ability to make informed decisions about prostate-specific antigen screening. Spence, Cavanagh, and Grant (2008) found that goal attainment in a health-coaching program was greater in the coaching condition when compared to an education-only intervention. Duijts, Kant, van den Brandt, and Swaen (2008) examined the effectiveness of coaching as a means of reducing sickness absence due to psychosocial health complaints, showing that coaching can enhance the general wellbeing of employees. On wellbeing outcomes they found significant improvements in health, life satisfaction, burnout, and psychological wellbeing, but no improvement in self-reported sickness absence.

These coaching studies indicate that coaching can improve – indeed, facilitate – goal attainment, reduce anxiety and stress (Grant, 2003), and enhance psychological and subjective wellbeing

(Green, Oades, & Grant, 2006; Spence & Grant, 2007) and resilience, while reducing depression, stress, or anxiety (Green, Grant, & Rynsaardt, 2007).

The development of wellbeing literature

The literature on the psychology of happiness and wellbeing often makes a distinction between two different traditions or "versions" of wellbeing: wellbeing as "feeling good," aka subjective wellbeing or SWB (e.g., Bradburn, 1969; Diener and Emmons, 1984; Kahneman, Diener, & Schwarz, 1999; Lyubomirsky & Lepper, 1999), and wellbeing as good psychological functioning, as "doing well," thriving, and flourishing (e.g., Rogers, 1961; Ryff, 1989,; Waterman, 1993).

Subjective wellbeing, a feeling state akin to "feeling happy" in common parlance, is thought by some (e.g., Bradburn, 1969; Diener & Suh, 1997) to be comprised of three main factors, including two affective or feeling components – relatively frequent positive emotions and relatively infrequent negative emotions (but not their complete absence) – and a more evaluative or cognitive component regarding how well the individual feels his or her life is going, or his or her "satisfaction with life." This suggests that to help clients improve their (subjective) wellbeing, the coach should focus on helping them in three areas: (1) to experience more frequent, more intense, or longer-lasting positive emotional states; (2) to experience less frequent, less intense, or shorter-duration negative emotional states; and (3) to become more satisfied with their lives, either overall or with particular domains of their life.

With regard to wellbeing as doing well (not just feeling good) there is no agreement on the main components of human flourishing, with different authors emphasizing slightly different factors. An early pioneer in this area, Carol Ryff (1989, p. 1069) recognized that there had been insufficient attention paid to "the task of defining the essential features of psychological wellbeing" and has argued (Ryff & Singer, 2008) for the following elements: self-acceptance, purpose in life, environmental mastery, positive relationships, personal growth, and autonomy.

Corey Keyes (2002, 2005, 2009) has taken a "diagnostic" approach to positive human function and has attempted to define human flourishing by the presence of certain clusters of "symptoms" of emotional, psychological, and social wellbeing in a person's life in the previous few weeks. His work has done much to demonstrate that good mental health is indeed more than the mere absence of mental illness, and that good mental health reduces the likelihood of an individual developing a diagnosable mental health problem during the following time period.

Martin Seligman (2011), one of the founders of the positive psychology movement, has argued that the central topic of positive psychology is wellbeing, that the gold standard for measuring wellbeing is flourishing, and that the goal of positive psychology is to increase flourishing (Seligman, 2011, p. 13). He describes five "pillars" of wellbeing, or building blocks for a flourishing life: Positive Emotion, Engagement, positive Relationships, Meaning, and Accomplishment, or PERMA for short.

Another definition of wellbeing is provided in the UK government's Foresight Mental Capital and Wellbeing project (2008, p. 10) in which mental wellbeing is defined as:

> a dynamic state in which the individual is able to develop their potential, work productively and creatively, build strong and positive relationships with others and contribute to their community. It is enhanced when an individual is able to fulfill their personal and social goals and achieve a sense of purpose in society.

Definitions of wellbeing show some overlap with the concept of quality of life, which has been defined by the World Health Organization as:

an individual's perception of their position in life in the context of the culture and value systems in which they live and in relation to their goals, expectations, standards and concerns. It is a broad ranging concept affected in a complex way by the person's physical health, psychological state, personal beliefs, social relationships and their relationship to salient features of their environment.

(World Health Organization, 1997, p. 1)

Of course, ideas about mental health, wellbeing, and flourishing are not new. William James highlighted the issue of a healthy mind as far back as 1902 (James, 1902). Writers such as Abraham Maslow and Carl Rogers within the humanistic tradition highlighted the importance of the well-functioning "self-actualized" person (Maslow, 1954) and the "good life" (Rogers, 1961, p. 186). Rogers believed that each individual strived towards becoming a "fully functioning person" who is open to experience, trusts in his or her own organism, and leads an increasingly existential life (Rogers, 1961, p. 187). Much earlier than, this many philosophical schools of both the East and the West saw as their main task the cultivation and living of a good life, or the best life possible for a human being (Radhakrishman & Moore, 1967; Sharples, 1996; Chan, 1969).

The Flourishing and Engagement at Work model for wellbeing coaching

How might practitioners best draw on the wealth of research from humanistic and positive psychology traditions to help them both think about and apply coaching practice to the issue of wellbeing at work? One helpful framework, developed by Grant and Passmore (Grant et al., 2010), combines ideas from positive psychology for enhancing performance and wellbeing in the workplace with both the work engagement literature (Llorens, Schaufeli, Bakker, & Salanova, 2007) and Keyes' ideas around positive mental health, languishing, and flourishing (Keyes, 2003).

The model in Figure 17.1 assumes that, in organizations, overall performance is closely related to the extent to which individual employees are either flourishing or languishing in life (Wright & Cropanzano, 2004). The model has two dimensions (mental health and workplace engagement), which combine to yield four zones: Flourishing at Work, Acquiescent, Burnout, and Distressed but Functional. We will discuss each of these in turn.

Flourishing at Work zone

Individuals in this zone experience good levels of both mental health and engagement. Many will consider this the ideal or target state. Individuals in this area will be highly involved within their work, have a well-developed sense of work-related meaning, and will be enjoying positive relations with work colleagues.

Acquiescent zone

Individuals in this zone have good mental health but relatively low levels of workplace engagement. It may sound somewhat incongruous that individuals can be "happy" but are disengaged with their work. These individuals may be physically present but not actively engaged with the organization's goals, and they do not find their purpose or meaning within their work. They may be cynical about their work and be at risk of drifting towards a state of languishing. Alternatively, they may consider work as a necessary evil and a mere means to another end, with the bulk of their meaning and purpose in life being derived from activities outside of work such as family, sport, art, or a hobby.

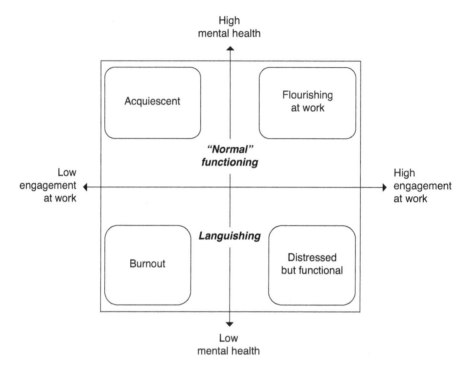

Figure 17.1   The Flourishing and Engagement framework for wellbeing coaching
Source: Adapted from Grant et al., 2010.

Burnout zone

Individuals in this zone have low levels of positive wellbeing and moderate levels of workplace engagement. They have not (yet) developed symptoms of mental ill-health such as stress, anxiety, of depression. These individuals may be trying to become more engaged with their work (perhaps via coaching) or they may be seeking a move to a new role that they believe would offer them more meaning, purpose, engagement, and experience of positive emotions.

Distressed but Functional zone

Individuals in this zone have relatively high levels of workplace engagement and may be seen as high performers, but underneath their performance lies poor emotional health such as depression, anxiety, or stress. Some coaches may struggle working with individuals from this zone, as most coaches are not trained psychologists and may assume that high-functioning individuals are also mentally resilient. Even trained psychologists may not always identify those clients experiencing depression or anxiety disorders. The client may not raise the issue, and coaches thus need to be mindful to signs that can sometimes emerge when discussing motivation, time management, or interpersonal communication difficulties.

Burnout zone

Individuals in this zone are experiencing burnout, possibly also with clinical levels of anxiety, depression, or other mental health problems. Clients in this area have very low levels of workplace engagement, and may feel cynical and experience low levels of self efficacy. It might be argued that individuals in this zone are not suitable candidates for coaching – especially if the coach lacks training and experience in working with clinical issues. However, given the blurred overlap between coaching and therapy found in such methodologies such as Solution Focused Coaching (Grant, 2015), Motivational Interviewing (Anstiss & Passmore, 2013), and Cognitive Behavioral Coaching (CBC; Palmer & Williams, 2013), some coaching approaches may prove very helpful with clients in this zone, enabling them to avoid experiencing the (real or perceived) stigma of having "therapy" while directing their attention and energy towards a future, health, and wellbeing–focused dialogue. Clearly, the boundaries between workplace wellbeing coaching and therapy for a mental health problem can become blurred in this quadrant. We would argue that coaching for clients in this space is best delivered by an experienced psychologist or health professional with experience of using appropriate coaching approaches such as motivational interviewing or cognitive-behavioral coaching for people with mental health problems such as depression, anxiety, and addictive behaviors. However, there are some mental health conditions (e.g., schizophrenia, psychosis) for which there is no evidence that coaching is an appropriate intervention; in these cases, a medical referral would be the most appropriate step for the coach.

The PERMA model for wellbeing coaching

The PERMA model is based on Seligman's five pillars of wellbeing. The model can be used to introduce the topic of wellbeing and flourishing into the conversation, to inform clients about important components of wellbeing, and to explore clients' opinions as to where they may wish to focus their efforts during the coaching process. The model suggests that in order for clients to flourish and to experience higher levels of personal wellbeing, they probably need find ways to:

- Increase their experience of positive emotions.
- Increase their engagement in life.
- Strengthen and deepen their positive relationships.
- Find ways to protect or increase the amount of meaning and purpose in their lives.
- Increase their feelings of achievement and accomplishment.

We will review each of these somewhat overlapping domains in turn.

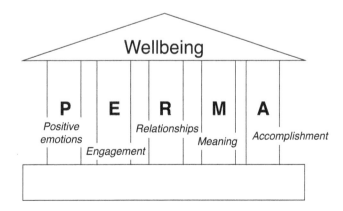

Figure 17.2 The PERMA framework for wellbeing coaching
Source: Based on Seligman, 2010.

Coaching towards increased experience of positive emotions

There are a very wide range of positive feelings that can be experienced, including joy, gratitude, awe, contentment, fun, relaxation, excitement, pleasure, hope, relief, pleasant fatigue, acceptance, forgiveness, connection, etc. There will be a range of things that clients will already being doing in order to experience positive emotions in their lives, and there will also be some things they might do more of so as to increase their experiences of positive emotions.

Some actions may increase more than one positive emotion. For instance, a walk with a friend in a wood or on a hillside may lead to a range of positive feelings such as relaxation, friendship, connection, achievement, appreciation of beauty, pleasure, curiosity, or pleasant fatigue. Watching a movie might lead to such positive feelings of happiness, fun, excitement, elevation, gratitude, nostalgia, or pleasant sadness, depending on which film is selected (Niemiec & Wedding, 2013).

After talking about the importance of positive emotions and how they are currently experienced in a client's life, the coach might then explore with the client options for increasing the future experience of positive emotions – in terms of range, frequency, intensity, and duration – and then agree a plan to strengthen this pillar of wellbeing in the future.

Some actions may might result in the experience of a pleasant emotion quite rapidly – e.g., enjoying a favorite food for dinner, sex (alone or with someone), noticing what went well during the previous 24 hours, or cultivating gratitude. Other behaviors may not be immediately enjoyable at the time (e.g., studying or going to the gym, for some people) but may result an increase in positive emotions in the medium or long term.

Helping the client clarify his or her values or explore and develop her or his strengths may also result in increased levels of positive emotions over time. This may result from the client deepening in self awareness, changing his or her self concept, more fully accepting and valuing who she or he is, using his or her strengths more fully in different areas of life (Niemiec, 2013) or taking actions more fully in line with her or his values (Harris, 2009).

Coaching towards increased engagement in life

Different people find different things engaging: for instance, sport, creating art, viewing art, political activities, spiritual practices, charity work, activities and tasks at work, conservation, studying, playing chess or computer games, visiting a museum, etc. A wellbeing coach might spend some time exploring with the client the kind of activities he or she currently finds engaging, the things she or he used to find engaging but have stopped doing, and the activities she or he might wish to do more of in the future. They might also have the client look forward two to three years and talk about hopes and desires for the future, for example, how she or he might be spending a typical day or week.

Strengths work might also help increase a person's engagement with life. The coach might help the client discover her or his strengths using one or more activities (e.g., online survey, best reflected self, you at your best, etc.), and explore with the client how he or she currently using his or her strengths. They might then explore with the client ways of using strengths more fully at work, at home or in other life areas, perhaps using their strengths in combination.

The coach might also explore with the client the concept of *flow*, the pleasant state in which one becomes immersed or absorbed in a task or activity, losing track of time and perhaps becoming less self-conscious (Csikszentmihalyi, 2002). Ways in which the client might spend more time in flow might be agreed upon.

Coaching towards improved relationships

Positive relationships are among the most important determinants of health and wellbeing (Umberson & Montez, 2010). But positive relationships may not just happen; they may need to be created, developed, and maintained. Skills might also need to be developed to create and maintain positive relationships such as expressing affection and liking, general conversation skills, forgiving, apologizing, listening, assertiveness, affirming, and problem solving (Nelson-Jones, 2006).

The coach might, perhaps, use the GROW model of coaching (Whitmore, 1992) for this pillar (as indeed you might with any of the pillars of wellbeing). For instance, they might ask the client about his or her goals when it comes to relationships. What is it she or he would like to have more of, and what she or he would like to have less of? They might then explore the client's current reality, how things are now, or how things have been recently with regard to important relationships and feelings of connection, friendship, sharing, caring and being cared for, intimacy, arguments and disagreements, companionship, loneliness, and worries. The conversation might then progress to an exploration of the options the client has for increasing the quality or quantity of positive relationships, and perhaps also for reducing his or her exposure to negative, draining, undermining, or abusive relationships over time. Then the conversation might progress to agree with the client the way forwards, the actual steps she or he will take, when and with what support, to increase their experience of positive relationships over time, including any skills that may need to be developed.

Coaching towards increased meaning and purpose

Having good meaning and purpose in life is associated with good health, wellbeing, and resilience (Schaefer et al., 2013). Different people have different levels of meanings and purpose in their lives, and also find meaning and purpose in different activities and ideas. One way to help clients make progress is to help them to clarify their values (Harris, 2009). Values are things that matter to people, things that they feel make for a "good" life, and things that help shape their choices. Despite the importance of values, some people may not be able to clearly articulate what their values are. There are a number of different exercises and activities that the coach can share to help the client reach a deeper understanding of his or her values, including having the client rank values from a list, or sort a deck of value cards into different piles according to how much each value printed on the card matters to him or her. Once values have been clarified, the coach might then explore with the client how these values show up in his or her life at the moment, and how these values have helped to shape some of her or his choices.

Coaching towards achievement and accomplishment

There are two main ways to help a person experience more feelings of accomplishment and achievement. One is to have the client talk about and reflect on previous successes, achievements, and accomplishments. For instance, you may ask someone who has done a good job of bringing up healthy and well-functioning kids to talk about this experience and what she or he feels most proud about from this phase of life, what challenges he or she experienced, and how she or he overcame these. The coach might use affirmations to help the client more fully recognize and appreciate his or her effort, values, or achievement. A second way of helping a client experience greater feelings of achievement or accomplishment is to help him or her make real progress toward valued life goals in the future. The coach might help the client to set one or two value-informed, achievable, long-term, and short-term approach type goals in different life areas, help them develop a plan for reaching those goals, and then help him or her implement the plan and adapt it over time to maximize the changes of goal attainment and the accompanying feelings of achievement and accomplishment.

Conclusions

In this chapter we have briefly discuss the development of coaching and offered a definition of and some ideas around wellbeing coaching. We reviewed the development of coaching and wellbeing research before applying these ideas to wellbeing coaching practice through two models: the Flourishing and Engagement framework and the PERMA framework.

Wellbeing coaching is an emerging field and is relatively underresearched. We believe that theory-driven wellbeing coaching – informed by and incorporating insights, tools, and strategies from coaching psychology, positive psychology, humanistic psychology, solution-focused, cognitive behavioral and motivational interviewing approaches – has the potential to significantly enhance the health, wellbeing, engagement, flourishing, and performance of many people at work, with the added benefit of being a more acceptable form of help, guidance, and support for people struggling in one or more areas of life and who are unwilling to accept counselling or therapy.

References

Anstiss, T., & Passmore, J. (2013). Motivational interviewing. In: J. Passmore, D. Peterson, & T. Freire (ed.), *The Wiley Blackwell Handbook of the Psychology of Coaching & Mentoring*. Chichester: Wiley, 339–364.

Bradburn, N. M. (1969). *The Structure of Psychological Well Being*. Chicago: Aldine.

Chan, W. (1969). *A Source Book in Chines Philosophy*. Princeton: Princeton University Press.

Csikszentmihalyi, M. (2002). *Flow: The Psychology of Happiness*. London: Random House.

Diener, E., & Emmons, R. A. (1984). The independence of positive and negative affect. *Journal of Personality & Social Psychology*, 47, 1105–1117.

Diener, E., & Suh, E. M. (1997). Measuring quality of life: Economic, social and subjective wellbeing: Relative or absolute. *Social Indicators Research*, 28, 195–223.

Diener, E., Suh, E. M., Lucas, R. E., & Smith, H. I. (1999). Subjective well-being: Three decades of progress. *Psychological Bulletin*, 125(2), 276–302.

Duijts, S. F. A. P., Kant, I. P., van den Brandt, P. A. P., & Swaen, G. M. H. P. (2008). Effectiveness of a preventive coaching intervention for employees at risk for sickness absence due to psychosocial health complaints: Results of a randomized controlled trial. *Journal of Occupational & Environmental Medicine*, 50(7), 765–776.

Foresight Mental Capital and Wellbeing Project. (2008). Final Report. *Government Office for Science*. London. Available at: www.gov.uk/government/publications/mental-capital-and-wellbeing-making-the-most-of-ourselves-in-the-21st-century (Accessed 18 February 2017).

Gable, S. L., & Haidt, J. (2005). What (and why) is positive psychology? *Review of General Psychology*, 9(2), 103–110.

Gattellari, M., Donnelly, N., Taylor, N., Meerkin, M., Hirst, G., & Ward, J. (2005). Does "peer coaching" increase GP capacity to promote informed decision making about PSA screening? A cluster randomised trial. *Family Practice*, 22(3), 253–265.

Grant, A. M. (2003). The impact of life coaching on goal attainment, metacognition and mental health. *Social Behavior and Personality: An International Journal*, 31(3), 253–264.

Grant, A. (2015). Solution focused coaching. In: J. Passmore (ed.), *Excellence in Coaching: The Industry Guide*. London: Kogan Page, 94–108

Grant, A. M., Curtayne, L., & Burton, G. (2009). Executive coaching enhances goal attainment, resilience and workplace: A randomized controlled study. *The Journal of Positive Psychology*, 4, 396–407.

Grant, A. M., & Palmer, S. (May 18, 2002). *Coaching Psychology Workshop*. Annual Conference of the Counselling Psychology Division of the BPS, Torquay, UK.

Grant, A. M., Passmore, J., Cavanagh, M. J., & Parker, H. M. (2010). The state of play in coaching today: A comprehensive review of the field. *International Review of Industrial and Organizational Psychology*, 25(1), 125–167.

Green, L. S., Grant, A. M., & Rynsaardt, J. (2007). Evidence-based life coaching for senior high school students: Building hardiness and hope. *International Coaching Psychology Review*, 2(1), 24–32.

Green, L., Oades, L., & Grant, A. (2006). Cognitive-behavioral, solution-focused life coaching: Enhancing goal striving, well-being, and hope. *The Journal of Positive Psychology*, 1(3), 142–149.

Gyllensten, K., & Palmer, S. (2005). Can coaching reduce workplace stress: A quasi experimental study. *International Journal of Evidence Based Coaching and Mentoring*, 3(2), 75–85.

Harris, R. (2009). *ACT Made Simple: An Easy to Read Primer on Acceptance and Commitment Therapy*. Oakland, CA: New Harbinger Publications.

Kahneman, D., Diener, E., & Schwarz, N. (1999). *Well-Being: Foundations of Hedonistic Psychology*. New York: Russell Sage Foundation.

Keyes, C. L. M. (2002). The mental helath continuum: From languishing to flourishing. *Journal of Health and Social Behaviour*, 43, 207–222.

Keyes, C. L. M. (2003). Complete mental health: An agenda for the 21st century. In: C. L. M. Keyes & J. Haidt (eds.), *Flourishing: Positive Psychology and the Life Well-Lived*. Washington, DC: American Psychological Association, 293–312.

Keyes, C. L. M. (2005). Mental illness and / or mental helath? Investigating axioms of the complete state mode of helath. *Journal of Consulting and Clinical Psychology*, 73, 539–548.

Keyes, C. L. M. (2009). The Black-White paradox in helath. Flourishing in the face of social inequality and discriminations. *Journal of Personality*, 77(6), 1677–1706.

Keyes, C. L., Schmotkin, D., & Ryff, C. D. (2002). Optimizing well-being: The empirical encounters of two traditions. *Journal of Personality & Social Psychology*, 82(6), 1007–1022.

Llorens, S., Schaufeli, W., Bakker, A., & Salanova, M. (2007). Does a positive gain spiral of resources, efficacy beliefs and engagement exist? *Computers in Human Behavior*, 23(1), 825–841.

Lyubomirsky, S., & Lepper, H. (1999). A meaure of subjective happiness: Preliminary and construct validity. *Social Indicator Research*, 46, 137–155.

McGregor, C. (2015). *Coaching behind Bars*. New York: Open University Press.

Maslow, A. (1954). *Motivation and Personality*. New York: Harper.

Nelson-Jones, R. (2006). *Human Relationship Skills: Coaching and Self Coaching* (4th ed.). London: Routledge.

Newnham-Kanas, C. E. (2011). *Motivational Coaching: Its Efficacy as an Obesity Intervention and a Profile of Professional Coaches*. Electronic Thesis and Dissertation Repository. Paper 243. Available at: http://ir.lib.uwo.ca/etd/243

Niemiec, R. M. (2013). *Mindfulness and Character Strenths: A Practical Guide to Flourishing*. Gottingen, Germany: Hogrefe.

Niemiec, R. M., & Wedding, D. (2013). *Positive Psychology at the Movies: Using Films to Build Character Strenths and Wellbeing* (2nd ed.). Gottingen, Germany: Hogrefe.

Palmer, S., & Williams, H. (2013). Cognitive behavioural coaching. In: J. Passmore, D. Petersen, & T. Freire (eds.), *The Wiley Blackwell Handbook of the Psychology of Coaching & Mentoring*. Chichester: Wiley, 319–338.

Passmore, J., & Fillery-Travis, A. (2011). A critical review of executive coaching research: A decade of progress and what's to come. *Coaching: An International Journal of Theory, Practice & Research*, 4(2), 70–88. doi:10.1080/17521882.2011.596484.

Passmore, J., Krauesslar, V., & Avery, R. (2015). Safety coaching: A critical literature review of coaching in high hazard industries. *Industrial & Commercial Training*, 47(4), 195–200.

Passmore, J., & Mortimer, L. (2011). The experience of using coaching as a learning technique in learner driver development: An IPA study of adult learning. *International Coaching Psychology Review*, 6(1), 33–45.

Passmore, J., Peterson, D., & Freire, T. (2013). The psychology of coaching & mentoring. In: J. Passmore, D. Peterson, & T. Freire (eds.), *The Wiley-Blackwell Handbook of the Psychology of Coaching and Mentoring*. Chichester: Wiley-Blackwell, 1–12.

Passmore, J., & Rehman, H. (2012). Coaching as a learning methodology – A mixed methods study in driver development – A randomised controlled trial and thematic analysis. *International Coaching Psychology Review*, 7(2), 166–184.

Radhakrishnan, S., & Moore, C. A. (1967). A Source Book in Indian Philosophy. Princeton: Princeton University Press.

Rogers, C. R. (1961). *On Becoming a Person*. Boston: Houghton Mifflin.

Rogers, J., & Maini, A. (2016). *Coaching for Health: Why It Works and How To Do It*. Milton Keynes, UK: Open University Press.

Ryff, C. D. (1989). Happiness is everything, or is it? Exploration on the meaning of psychological wellbeing. *Journal of Personality and Social Psychology*, 57, 1069–1088.

Ryff, C. D., & Singer, B. H. (2008). Know theyself and become what you are: A Eudaimonic approach to psychological well-being. *Journal of Happiness Studies*, 9, 13–39.

Schaefer, S. M., Boylan, J. M., van Reek, C. M., Lapata, R. C., Norris, C. J., Ryff, C. D., & Davidson, R. J. (2013). Purpose in life predicts better emotional recovery from negative stumuli. *PLoS ONE*, 8(11), e80329. doi:10.1371/journal.pone.0080329.

Seligman, M. E. P. (1998). *The President's Address*. American Psychological Association.

Seligman, M. E. P. (2011). *Flourish: A New Understanding of Happiness and Well-Being*. London: Nicholas Brealey Publishing.

Shams, M., & Lane, D. (2011). *Coaching in the Family Owned Business*. London: Karnac.

Sharples, R. W. (1996). *Stoics, Epicureans and Sceptics: An Introduction to Hellenistic Philosophy*. London and New York: Routledge

Spence, G. B., Cavanagh, M. J., & Grant, A. M. (2008). The integration of mindfulness training and health coaching: An exploratory study. *Coaching: An International Journal of Theory, Research and Practice*, 1(2), 145–163.

Spence, G. B., & Grant, A. (2007). Professional and peer life coaching and the enhancement of goal striving and well-being: An exploratory study. *The Journal of Positive Psychology*, 2, 185–194.

Stratham, J., & Chase, E. (2010). *Childhood Wellbeing: A Brief Overview*. London: Childhood Wellbeing Research Centre, Briefing Paper 1.

Taylor, L. M. (1997). *The Relation between Resilience, Coaching, Coping Skills Training, and Perceived Stress during a Career-Threatening Milestone*. [Empirical, Ph.D., WS]. DAI-B 58/05, p. 2738, November 1997.

Umberson, D., & Montez, J. K. (2010). Social Relationships and health: A flashpoint for health. *Journal of Health Social Behaviour*, 51(Supplement), 54–66.

Waterman, A. S. (1993). Two concepts of happiness: Contrasts of personal expressiveness. *Journal of Personality & Social Psychology*, 64(4), 678–691.

Whitmore, J. (1992). *Coaching for Performance*. London: Nicholas Breadley.

World Health Organization (1987). *WHOQOL Measuring Quality of Life*. Geneva. Available at: www.who.int/mental_health/media/68.pdf (Accessed February 2017).

Wright, T. A., & Cropanzano, R. (2004). The role of psychological welling in job performance. *Organisational Dynamics*, 334, 338–351.

18

Work and wellbeing

Creating a psychologically healthy workplace

Matthew J. Grawitch, David W. Ballard, and Kaitlyn R. Erb

Introduction

The literature and popular press abounds with prescriptions for how organizations should seek to enhance the wellbeing of their workforce. From workplace health promotion efforts (e.g., wellness programs, incentives for getting healthy, gym memberships) to work-life initiatives (e.g., flextime, telecommuting, adequate time off) to practices fostering a more positive work environment (e.g., creating a culture of recognition, quirky and playful workspace design, pets in the office) to countless other recommendations, there are certainly ample resources available to assist organizations in thinking through ways to enhance worker wellbeing.

However, most of these recommendations, prescriptions, and suggestions are offered without any serious mention of the importance of context. The uniqueness of a particular organization (e.g., its industry, culture, structure) and its workforce (e.g., education, needs, personality) provides the context within which any attempts to address wellbeing must be considered. For example, when it comes to stress-related initiatives, Grawitch, Ballard, and Erb (2015) argued that "many traditional stress management interventions are created as add-ons that are implemented in parallel to employees' work roles" rather than these practices being designed using "a more strategic approach . . . that emphasizes the improvement of multiple parts of the larger system" (p. 272).

The same can be said of many initiatives designed and/or implemented by organizations to address the issue of workplace wellbeing in general. That is, organizations often implement interventions designed to address wellbeing without first considering how those interventions fit within the larger organizational system. Yet, as the American Psychological Association (APA) Psychologically Healthy Workplace program emphasizes, "there is no 'one-size-fits-all' approach to creating a psychologically healthy workplace" (2015a, para. 4). As such, there is no one best way to address the issue of workplace wellbeing. Rather, an organization should address the issue in a manner consistent with its unique context.

In this chapter, we seek to provide some clarity for organizations considering ways to enhance workplace wellbeing. To that end, we cover three topics in this chapter. First, we develop a definition of workplace wellbeing building on previous research regarding the affective circumplex. Second, we integrate previous research focused on demands, resources, and self-regulation to offer a Dynamic Workplace Wellbeing model focused on explaining four manifestations of workplace wellbeing: engagement, workaholism, exhaustion, and satisfaction. Third, we discuss how workplace wellbeing is influenced by specific external resources: tangible support (psychologically healthy workplace practices), emotional support (psychosocial safety climate), and need fulfillment (Self-Determination Theory). Finally, we offer practical application of various aspects of the Dynamic Workplace Wellbeing model through the lens of organizations that have been recognized through the APA's Psychologically Healthy Workplace Program and a case example of a specific organization.

General wellbeing

Wellbeing has, for better or worse, evolved more as a series of interrelated conceptual constructs rather than with any sort of unified definition (Bradburn, 1969; Diener, 1984; Dodge, Daly, Huyton, & Sanders, 2012; Ryff, 1989). As Dodge et al. (2012) pointed out in their recent review, "researchers have focused on dimensions or descriptions of wellbeing rather than on definitions" (p. 223). This has resulted in the conceptualization and measurement of numerous indicators of wellbeing, some of them more global (e.g., positive and negative affect, life satisfaction) and some of them emphasizing more context-focused wellbeing (e.g., marital satisfaction, job satisfaction; Danna & Griffin, 1999). To add to this effort, Gallup (Rath & Harter, 2010) proposed a list of five focused areas of wellbeing: health, career, interpersonal, financial, and community. Rath and Harter demonstrated that achieving greater levels of wellbeing across these areas can be useful in enhancing overall life satisfaction, and this perspective has become a cornerstone of many contemporary health promotion programs.

When considering the various conceptualizations of wellbeing as defined by Rath and Harter (2010), Diener (2005), and Ryff (1989) and others over the years, wellbeing is perhaps best conceptualized as multi-faceted. Such a conceptualization recognizes that there are multiple levels of wellbeing, including (1) a global level, consisting of a broad, reflective sense of wellbeing that is not isolated to any one aspect of life (e.g., life satisfaction, growth/purpose); (2) a domain-specific level, consisting of an evaluation of some specific aspect of life (e.g., job satisfaction, work engagement, career satisfaction, marital satisfaction); and (3) a momentary level, consisting of cognitive and affective reactions to the various positive and negative experiences people have on a day-to-day basis (e.g., thoughts, emotions). Workplace wellbeing, therefore, may be best described as a domain-specific type of wellbeing, though it may also influence and be influenced by global, momentary, and domain-specific areas of wellbeing.

Defining workplace wellbeing

While it would be easy to define workplace wellbeing as strictly a function of present conditions or as satisfaction with one's work life, such a framing fails to incorporate the critical role motivation plays in the experience of wellbeing and excludes manifestations of wellbeing that stem from the drive for growth and improvement. This differentiation is important because satisfaction relates more to the idea of what we already have, whereas more motivated manifestations of wellbeing (e.g., work engagement) imply that wellbeing can occur as a function of striving toward something more (Macey & Schneider, 2008; Warr & Inceoglu, 2012). The achievement of desired outcomes results in the experience of a level of satisfaction, whereas the motivation to close the discrepancy between one's current state and desired future state results in the experience of engagement.

While traditional perspectives on person–environment fit promote the idea that maximizing fit between individuals and their environment results in increased wellbeing (e.g., Cable &

DeRue, 2002; Hecht & Allen, 2005), that explains one's sense of wellbeing only as it relates to present conditions (Ryff, 1989; Warr & Inceoglu, 2012). In fact, other perspectives on wellbeing, such as Self-Determination Theory and Control Theory, would suggest that discrepancies must exist in order to produce motivated aspects of wellbeing (e.g., Carver & Scheier, 1998, 2011; Ryan & Deci, 2001). Warr and Inceoglu (2012) recently demonstrated that the discrepancy between actual and desired features of a job has differential relationships with job satisfaction and work engagement. They found that when people reported actual levels of important job features (e.g., supportive environment, ethical principles) that were below their desired level of these features, they tended to report lower levels of job satisfaction but higher levels of work engagement. However, when there were fewer differences between actual and desired levels of these features, job satisfaction was higher, but work engagement was lower. They argued that this occurs because job satisfaction is dependent more on what workers perceive they currently experience (i.e., it is more a function of present conditions), whereas engagement is more dependent on what workers perceive they may achieve or obtain in the future (i.e., discrepancy between present and desired conditions).

This phenomenon would be consistent with the dynamic process of self-regulation, especially self-regulation defined through the lens of control theory (e.g., Carver & Scheier, 1998, 2011; Grawitch, Barber, & Justice, 2010). Engagement relates more to the activation of the behavioral approach system (i.e., pursuit of desired positive outcomes), whereas job satisfaction would become more salient once valued outcomes are achieved and maintained. Expanding beyond Warr and Inceoglu's (2012) specific study results, research in self-regulation also suggests that a failure to make sufficient progress toward desired outcomes could stifle motivational energy and produce negative wellbeing consequences (Carver & Scheier, 2011; Grawitch et al., 2010). In research using daily-diary methodology, Amabile and Kramer (2007) found that workers experienced greater positive mood and intrinsic motivation when they reported achieving a goal or making progress toward a goal. Furthermore, in a national poll of US workers, the APA (2014) found that employees who had received recognition within the past six months (obviously a positive experience) were more likely to report higher levels of (1) satisfaction overall with their organization's recognition practices, (2) motivation to work hard, and (3) feeling valued, all of which were related to overall job satisfaction. Therefore, when progress is made toward goals, and when others recognize (and perhaps validate) that progress, employees tend to experience more positive workplace wellbeing.

Bakker and Oerlemans (2010) provided an innovative way of conceptualizing various manifestations of workplace wellbeing when they mapped a variety of constructs onto the affective circumplex (Figure 18.1). Russell (1980, 2003) originally developed and presented a circumplex model of affect that was useful for categorizing affective experiences (i.e., moods, emotions) along two continua: hedonic tone (i.e., the [un]pleasantness of an experience) and activation (i.e., physiological arousal or motivated energy). All affective experiences could thus be categorized using this framework. According to Bakker and Oerlemans (2010), work engagement, or a "positive, fulfilling, work-related state of mind that is characterized by vigor, dedication, and absorption" (Schaufeli, Salanova, González-Romá, & Bakker, 2002, p. 74), is a state in which individuals experience a high level of motivated energy and experience pleasure from the pursuit of their goals. This can be contrasted with job satisfaction, which occurs when individuals experience pleasantness combined with a low level of motivated energy. This would be consistent with a perspective in which job satisfaction is the result of perceived alignment between what individuals value or desire and what they currently possess (consistent with the empirical results presented by Warr & Inceoglu, 2012). When an individual experiences a general level of satisfaction with few discrepancies between actual and desired outcomes, motivation to reduce that discrepancy

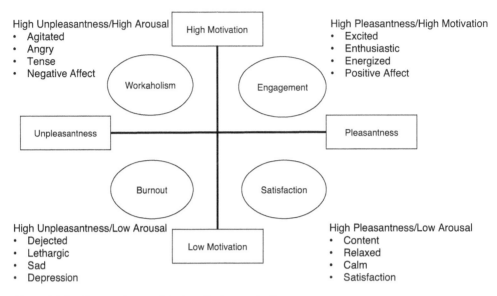

High Unpleasantness/High Arousal
- Agitated
- Angry
- Tense
- Negative Affect

High Motivation

High Pleasantness/High Motivation
- Excited
- Enthusiastic
- Energized
- Positive Affect

Workaholism

Engagement

Unpleasantness

Pleasantness

Burnout

Satisfaction

High Unpleasantness/Low Arousal
- Dejected
- Lethargic
- Sad
- Depression

Low Motivation

High Pleasantness/Low Arousal
- Content
- Relaxed
- Calm
- Satisfaction

Figure 18.1   Circumplex model of wellbeing and affect
Source: Adapted from Bakker and Oerlemans (2010).

will not exist, and therefore, work engagement will be stifled. As such, consistent with the self-regulatory processes of control theory (Carver & Scheier, 1998, 2011; Grawitch et al., 2010), some discrepancy is needed to create motivated energy.

However, motivated energy is not always positive. Workaholism occurs when an individual experiences a high level of motivated energy but experiences unpleasantness as a result of working obsessively hard, above and beyond what is reasonably expected (Schaufeli, Taris, & van Rhenen, 2008). In some ways, this may relate to the difference between being motivated by a desire to excel as opposed to being motivated because of a desire to avoid failing (Poortvliet, Anseel, & Theuwis, 2015). Hence, how workers perceive their work can be the difference between the experience of engagement and workaholism. Finally, burnout is a state of emotional exhaustion and cynicism, composed of a high level of unpleasantness and a low level of motivated energy. It is considered to be the opposite of work engagement (Schaufeli et al., 2002, 2008). Hence, burnout may result when engaged individuals encounter too many demands or lack sufficient support to make progress toward their goals.

In many ways, Bakker and Oerlemans' (2010) mapping of these aspects of workplace wellbeing is consistent with the conceptualization of subjective wellbeing argued by Diener (1984, 2005), who defined subjective wellbeing as the combination of life satisfaction, positive affect, and negative affect. Mapping these characteristics onto the affective circumplex model suggests that life satisfaction occupies the same conceptual space as job satisfaction (i.e., both represent a feeling of contentment), positive affect sits in the same space as work engagement (i.e., both are defined by enthusiasm and excitement), and negative affect inhabits the same space as workaholism (i.e., both are defined by tension and stress). All that is lacking in Diener's conceptualization is a surrogate for the lower left quadrant of Figure 18.1, which could most easily be described as depressive affect and represents the same conceptual space as burnout, defined by feelings of dejection or lethargy.

The affective circumplex model is useful for both conceptualizing the various manifestations of workplace wellbeing and understanding how consistent affective experiences at work (e.g., moments of tension, excitement, contentment, dejection) can contribute to more stable components of workplace wellbeing (i.e., workaholism, work engagement, job satisfaction, burnout). Yet, what drives the experiences that affect workplace wellbeing requires a deeper examination of the Job Demands–Resources (JD-R) model.

The JD-R model

The JD-R model of workplace wellbeing originally espoused the notion that job demands were the primary contributor to the experience of burnout (Demerouti, Bakker, Nachreiner, & Schaufeli, 2001), while resources were the primary contributor to work engagement (Schaufeli & Bakker, 2004). Bakker, Demerouti, and Sanz-Vergel (2014) and Schaufeli and Taris (2014) both provided fairly up-to-date reviews of the JD-R model as it relates to both wellbeing and health, which now includes a differentiation between job resources and personal resources (Schaufeli & Taris, 2014, provided an exhaustive list of demands, resources, and outcomes as well).

Though much of the research has been focused on burnout and engagement, some studies have been conducted to also demonstrate that demands and resources are related to the other two components of workplace wellbeing discussed by Bakker and Oerlemans (2010). Generally, the results suggest that job demands do indeed predict workaholism (Molino, Bakker, & Ghislieri, 2015; Schaufeli et al., 2008) and resources tend to be predictive of job satisfaction (e.g., Cheng, Mauno, & Lee, 2014; Rayton & Yalabik, 2014).

Overall, research conducted using the JD-R model as a theoretical paradigm has produced results that are relatively consistent with the affective circumplex approach to workplace wellbeing. An important takeaway from the research results, though, is that both job demands and job resources are typically defined on the basis of employee perceptions. Hence, two employees in the same work unit could perceive different levels of demands and resources. In addition, as evidenced in Schaufeli and Taris (2014), the emphasis on personal resources has largely focused on individual difference traits (e.g., resilience, extraversion, emotional stability, competencies), as opposed to other more situationally-dependent or supply-oriented resources (e.g., time, energy). These individual difference traits likely influence employee perceptions of job demands and resources (e.g., Grawitch et al., 2010).

The personalized emphasis of the JD-R model has been a key underlying element of interventions focused on job crafting, which Tims, Bakker, and Derks (2012) defined as a way of altering demands and resources in such a way as to reduce the negative impact of demands while increasing the positive impact of resources. In essence, job crafting relies on autonomy and involvement-focused forms of decision making to improve the interface between employees and their workplace, which serves as a key element in other related perspectives (e.g., Self-Determination Theory, Psychologically Healthy Workplace framework; Grawitch, Ledford, Ballard, & Barber, 2009; Ryan & Deci, 2001).

Though the JD-R model provides a solid framework within which to consider the role of demands and resources in the experience of workplace wellbeing, it fails to fully capture the dynamic process of self-regulation. It is largely a work-centric perspective (hence, the use of "job" in the title of the model). In fact, the three recommendations for affecting engagement and burnout discussed by Bakker et al. (2014) were specifically focused on targeting the workplace (e.g., optimizing job demands, increasing job resources) and the employee (i.e., increasing personal resources such as resilience). This is an important issue because the JD-R model fails to fully incorporate the importance of demands and resources that exist outside the workplace but are still likely to affect workplace wellbeing. In addition, the treatment of traits and competencies as universal resources conflicts with much of what we know about person–environment fit (Cable & DeRue, 2002; Tong, Wang, & Peng, 2015), a limitation that can be addressed through an understanding of personal resource allocation.

The Personal Resource Allocation (PRA) framework

Grawitch et al. (2010) introduced a dynamic self-regulation perspective called the PRA framework (Figure 18.2). It proposed that, at any point in time, individuals possess a finite amount of personal resources – which they defined as time, energy, and finances – available for responding to demands (i.e., any activity that competes for resources) they encounter in their daily lives. Individuals choose how to allocate their existing resources in response to those demands. How well people allocate their resources subsequently influences their performance in meeting various demands, and how they appraise their use of resources influences subjective wellbeing. Grawitch et al. also argued that the process can be influenced by a variety of factors, including individual differences (e.g., personality traits, attitudes/interests, demographics), resources external to the individual (e.g., organizational resources, nonwork resources), and person–environment fit.

The PRA framework introduces concepts that offer an important refinement to our understanding of workplace wellbeing. Rather than defining personal resources through the lens of more stable characteristics as the JD-R model does, the PRA framework (1) defines resources at a more basic universal level and (2) recognizes that resources are situationally determined. The PRA framework recognizes that more stable characteristics of the person, such as personality traits and competences, are not universal resources. Rather, they can be advantageous in some situations but irrelevant or even disadvantageous in other situations, which is the hallmark argument of the person–environment fit literature (e.g., Cable & DeRue, 2002; Tong et al., 2015).

Consider the issue of persistence. Though not represented in the list by Schaufeli and Taris (2014), persistence would most likely meet the classification of a personal resource as they defined it. However, previous research has suggested that persistence in the face of impossible tasks is

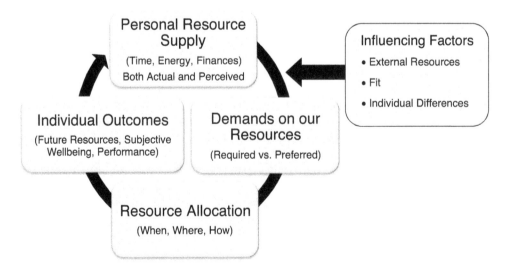

Figure 18.2 The PRA framework

actually maladaptive (e.g., Barber, Grawitch, & Munz, 2012; Wrosch, Scheier, Miller, Schulz, & Carver, 2003). Furthermore, in specific reference to the PRA framework, Barber et al. (2012) noted that "ineffective resource allocation can needlessly deplete one's resources and ability to pursue other, perhaps more attainable, goals" (p. 77). As such, the PRA framework's emphasis on individual differences and person–environment fit as factors that influence personal resources and how they are allocated represents a more dynamic, process-oriented perspective.

Because it is more process and situation focused, the PRA framework emphasizes the allocation of limited personal resources across all life domains, with an emphasis on the allocation of those resources in context (Grawitch et al., 2010). Instead of simply focusing on how much time, energy, or money is required to respond to a demand, the PRA framework also explicitly creates a role for when, where, and how that time, energy, or money is allocated, carving out an important role for autonomy and control, which is an important underlying factor in many self-regulation perspectives (e.g., Control Theory as discussed by Carver & Scheier, 1998, 2011; Self-Determination Theory as discussed by Ryan & Deci, 2001; and Conservation of Resources theory as discussed by Hobfoll, 1989). For example, while multiple demands can require the expenditure of resources, Grawitch and Barber (2013) demonstrated that attempting to respond to those demands simultaneously (i.e., multitasking) can exceed one's attentional capabilities, requiring an inefficient expenditure of resources that increases performance errors; however, responding to one demand before proceeding to a second demand (i.e., sequential task performance) can lead to a more efficient use of one's limited energy, reducing performance errors. Exercising some degree of control over when, where, or how resources are allocated can thus allow more optimal resource allocation.

The role of individual differences

Individual differences can be defined as relatively stable factors that vary among people. From differences in personality traits to variations in nonwork life factors (e.g., marital status, parental status), individual differences bring with them variability in both personal resources (e.g., someone in poor physical health may lack the energy to accomplish certain physical demands) and demands (e.g., a parent has a different set of demands than a nonparent).

Within the context of workplace wellbeing, a review of the factors discussed by Grawitch et al. (2010), Ryan and Deci (2001), and Schaufeli and Taris (2014) suggests that individual differences can largely be broken down into two broad categories: (1) intraindividual factors (e.g., personality traits, race, sex, interests/aptitudes, competencies, health) and (2) nonwork life factors (e.g., marital status, parental status, debt). The JD-R model treats a variety of intraindividual factors (e.g., personality traits, competencies) as a source of personal resources, which implies universal relevance (which, according to person-environment fit perspectives, would not be the case). However, the PRA framework treats individual differences as factors separate from personal resources, recognizing that such factors can sometimes serve as facilitators of effective resource allocation, while at other times they can serve as barriers.

In addition to influencing demands and resources, individual differences, in the form of intraindividual factors, can also lead to more stable influences on workplace wellbeing. For example, theory and research have suggested that both employee engagement and job satisfaction possess some stability across time and context (e.g., Dormann & Zapf, 2001; Macey & Schneider, 2008). In the case of engagement, Hirschfeld and Thomas (2008) argued it is associated with traits with underlying elements that concern human agency, the tendency to exercise more proactive control over surroundings to shape "present circumstances in ways that facilitate the attainment of subsequent [desired] outcomes" (p. 63). In the case of job satisfaction, Dormann and Zapf (2001) argued similarly that individual traits drive people to select themselves into particular situations that subsequently produce some shared elements.

Brauchli, Schaufeli, Jenny, Füllemann, and Bauer (2013) observed that more than half the variance in work engagement and almost half the variance in burnout was stable, in essence representing a more trait-like characteristic. Perhaps most telling was the fact that at least half the variance in job resources and around a third of the variance in job demands also possessed trait-like stability. This is important for two reasons. First, it suggests that work engagement and burnout (and likely the other manifestations of workplace wellbeing) are going to demonstrate some degree of stability over time. Second, it suggests that this may, at least in part, be a function of the stability in perceptions of job demands and job resources.

While the exact amount of observed stability tends to differ across studies, previous research suggests that these individual differences are going to have consequences for workplace wellbeing, and some of the stability in workplace wellbeing is going to occur because employees develop patterns regarding how they perceive their work environment. Hence, to change the pattern of perceptions requires the active involvement of employees, which is why interventions that make employees active participants in constructing their work environment, such as job crafting (Tims et al., 2012), employee involvement (Grawitch et al., 2009), and other approaches, can be effective. Such approaches give employees the autonomy to modify their environment so it fits better with intraindividual and/or nonwork life factors.

An integrated perspective: the dynamic approach to workplace wellbeing

The affective circumplex approach to workplace wellbeing can be integrated with the JD-R model and PRA framework to produce a Dynamic Model of Workplace Wellbeing (Figure 18.3). Following the PRA framework, time, energy, and money form the foundation of our personal resources, while the work domain, nonwork domain, and work-life interface are the primary sources of demands (defined as both things we have to do as well as things we want to do). Personal resources and demands have both objective and subjective qualities to them that are influenced by intraindividual and nonwork life factors. Between our personal resources and our demands exists an area called *External Resources,* which is included in both the PRA framework and the JD-R model. These are actual and perceived resources external to us (e.g., workplace support resources, nonwork support resources) that can: (1) directly influence perceptions of personal resources, demands, and workplace wellbeing (Dollard & Bakker, 2010; Grawitch et al., 2010); (2) moderate the extent to which personal resources and demands influence workplace wellbeing (Dollard & Bakker, 2010); and (3) influence how we allocate our personal resources (e.g., Grawitch et al., 2010). Our perception (i.e., appraisals) of our resources (both internal and external) and demands determines (1) the valence of wellbeing (i.e., positive or negative) and (2) the extent to which we are motivated to act (i.e., high or low arousal). As detailed by Bakker et al. (2014), previous research underlying the JD-R model suggests that a greater number of demands increases the likelihood of unpleasant affective experiences, whereas the presence of greater resources increases the likelihood of pleasant affective experiences. However, this implies that demands are all the same in terms of their centrality to an individual's goals, which previous self-regulation research suggests is not the case (e.g., Carver & Scheier, 2011). In other words, demands stimulate positive affective experiences when they are aligned with our goals, which initiates self-regulatory processes focused on reducing the discrepancy between the current and desired condition (as evidenced by Warr & Inceoglu, 2012). Yet, as noted by Bakker, Hakanen, Demerouti, and Xanthopoulou

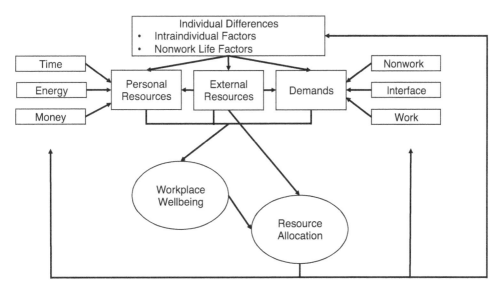

Figure 18.3   Dynamic Model of Workplace Wellbeing

(2007), demands may trigger higher levels of engagement only when employees perceive they have sufficient resources necessary to effectively respond to them.

Therefore, the interaction between perceived demands and resources may ultimately influence the extent to which we experience motivated energy (engagement/workaholism) or unmotivated energy (satisfaction/exhaustion). When tying research on the JD-R model to previous research in self-regulation (i.e., the foundation of the PRA framework), it seems likely that our experience of workplace wellbeing will be influenced by the following appraisals: (1) the presence of perceived demands (high vs. low), (2) the alignment between demands and goals (high vs. low), and (3) the presence of resources (both personal and external) needed to meet demands (high vs. low). Table 18.1 provides possible affective responses on the basis of these appraisals.

Table 18.1 Affective experiences as a function of appraisals

Current Salient Demands	Perceived Goal Alignment of Current Demands	Perceived Current Resources	Affective Experience
High	High	High	Engagement
High	Low	High	Workaholism
High	Low	Low	Exhaustion
High	High	Low	Exhaustion/Temporary Disengagement
Low	High	High	Satisfaction
Low	Low	High	Satisfaction/Neutral Affect
Low	High	Low	Satisfaction
Low	Low	Low	Satisfaction/Neutral Affect

Our experience of wellbeing influences when, where, and how we allocate our resources (e.g., Grawitch et al., 2010, 2015). Because they represent high demands and high resources, more motivated aspects of workplace wellbeing (i.e., workaholism, engagement) result in efforts to allocate resources to particular demands. The difference between work engagement and workaholism, though, can be viewed through the lens of Control Theory (Carver & Scheier, 1998, 2011). Both exist in the presence of higher demands and higher resources, but work engagement occurs when employees perceive alignment between demands and goals, which triggers self-regulatory processes designed to move them toward a desired future condition (Warr & Inceoglu, 2012). In contrast, workaholism occurs when employees do not perceive alignment between demands and goals. This triggers what Carver and Scheier (2011) referred to as "avoidance processes." Before being able to allocate resources toward closing the discrepancy between their current condition and desired future condition, employees must allocate resources toward misaligned demands. As such, they seek to avoid unpleasant outcomes that would result from failing to effectively respond to those demands (Schaufeli et al., 2008).

Less motivated forms of affect, however, occur when demands and resources are themselves misaligned. When demands are high and resources are low, individuals will likely experience exhaustion. As such, they may respond by withdrawing their personal resources or minimizing their allocation of resources to the extent possible (Bolton, Harvey, Grawitch, & Barber, 2012). Yet, when demands are low (thus signaling no need for motivated action) but resources are high, an individual will experience greater satisfaction or contentment (Warr & Inceoglu, 2012).

From a self-regulatory perspective, the workplace wellbeing that employees experience will trigger a behavioral response (i.e., resource allocation decisions), and the effectiveness of that response (in terms of its impact on resources, demands, subjective evaluations, and other factors) will serve as feedback in the wellbeing process (Grawitch et al., 2010). However, workplace wellbeing is not the sole factor that influences resource allocation decisions. Those decisions will also be affected by the presence of various external resources. When examining the list of job resources provided by Schaufeli and Taris (2014), several of them (e.g., social support, autonomy, advancement, team cohesion) serve as support mechanisms that assist employees in allocating their personal resources. For example, consider the availability of flexible scheduling practices in an organization. If employees are motivated to respond to demands that compete for time and energy resources, having access to flexible scheduling can provide them greater latitude in when they respond to those demands (Grawitch & Barber, 2010), increasing the likelihood they can accomplish both. In this way, external resources can serve as a type of support needed to enhance resource allocation effectiveness. It, therefore, becomes an element of the context within which employee resource allocation occurs, setting the boundaries within which resource allocation decisions are made.

Supportive workplace environment as an external resource

A supportive workplace environment is a critical component of workplace wellbeing and resource allocation because it serves as the predominant resource that facilitates workplace wellbeing. In some ways, it represents the broader context in which workplace wellbeing processes occur. The concept of social support has a long history within psychology, and various categorizations of support have been offered since as far back as House (1981). However, Semmer, Elfering, Jacobshagen, Beehr, and Boos (2008) essentially argued that those who provide support will either focus on the other person's emotional needs or will offer some form of tangible assistance. As such, social support can be thought of as falling into two broad categories: emotional (which subsumes appraisal and esteem support) and tangible or instrumental (which subsumes informational support; Semmer et al., 2008; Shakespeare-Finch & Obst, 2011).

Within the context of workplace wellbeing and resource allocation, support can be provided in numerous ways. For example, support can provide the instrumental means of enhancing employees' personal resources, but it can also provide the emotional means for employees to address conflicts between work and nonwork life demands. For the purposes of workplace wellbeing and resource allocation, both are of critical importance. Not only must employees have the tangible means of effectively allocating their resources, but they must also feel supported in doing so.

Tangible support: psychologically healthy workplace practices

Tangible support involves providing employees with the tools, tactics, and capabilities to effectively manage their personal resources in the context of various demands. This can be accomplished by offering support that enhances employees' (1) actual or perceived personal resources, (2) control over actual or perceived demands, or (3) ability to effectively and efficiently allocate their resources toward demands. Grawitch et al. (2015) provided a framework within which to consider various ways of offering tangible support within the context of stress management. Building on the conceptualization of a psychologically healthy workplace as introduced by the APA and reviewed by Grawitch et al. (2006), this tangible support comes from five main types of practices: employee involvement (i.e., autonomy and involvement in decision making), work-life balance (i.e., practices to support work flexibility and help employees meet their nonwork demands), employee growth and development (i.e., training and career development practices), health and safety (i.e., practices intended to promote health, manage disease, or improve safety), and employee recognition (i.e., monetary and nonmonetary rewards and awards; Figure 18.4). These practices can be leveraged to enhance the workplace wellbeing process when they are consistent with the organization's mission and values and they exist within a more broadly supportive organizational environment (they are valued, utilization is encouraged; Grawitch et al., 2015). Table 18.2 provides examples of ways in which various types of psychologically healthy workplace practices can be leveraged to affect the workplace wellbeing process.

Emotional support: psychologically healthy workplace climate

Though psychologically healthy workplace practices can provide the tangible support needed to improve workplace wellbeing, these practices are not likely to produce the intended results unless they exist within a more broadly supportive context. This context provides the emotional support that employees need to utilize the tangible support offered by the individual practices. As an example, consider the issue of training. As described in Table 18.2, training can be leveraged as a way of improving resource allocation competencies, allowing employees to more effectively or efficiently allocate their personal resources in response to demands. However, to be useful, employees have to be able to transfer the knowledge and skills they acquire in a learning environment to their actual jobs (Blume, Ford, Baldwin, & Huang, 2010). Though a variety of factors (e.g., trainee characteristics, training content) can influence this transfer of knowledge and skills, a recent meta-analysis by Blume et al. found that factors that facilitate a supportive work environment (which included transfer climate, supervisor support, and peer support) were all associated with transfer of training. In other words, what people learn in a training environment is more likely to be applied to their jobs when the proper support exists.

Table 18.2 Psychologically healthy workplace practices and workplace wellbeing

Psychologically Healthy Workplace Area	Primary Area(s) of Focus	Example Practice(s)
Employee Involvement	Work Demands	Work Redesign/Job Crafting
	Resource Allocation	Enhanced Job Autonomy
Health and Safety	Personal Resources (Energy)	Wellness Programs
	Nonwork Demands	Disease Management Programs
	Workplace Wellbeing (Exhaustion)	Counseling/Employee Assistant Programs
Employee Growth and Development	Resource Allocation	Job/Contextual Skills Training
Work-Life Balance	Work Demands	Vacation/Leave Time
	Personal Resources (Money)	On-Site Daycare
	Resource Allocation	Flextime/Remote Working
Employee Recognition	Personal Resources (Money)	Promotion/Competitive Wages
	Workplace Wellbeing (Engagement)	Job Crafting/Selection Mechanisms

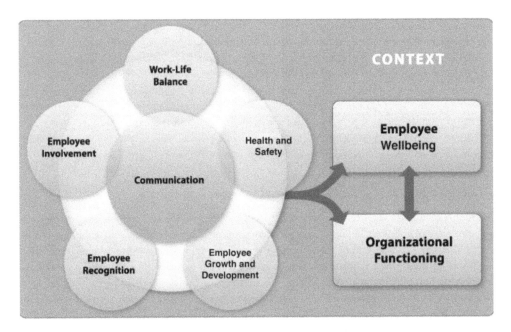

Figure 18.4   The psychologically healthy workplace

That support can be defined in many ways. However, one useful way is to consider it through the lens of climate. Schneider, Ehrhart, and Macey (2013) defined *climate* as "the shared perceptions of and the meaning attached to the policies, practices, and procedures employees experience and the behaviors they observe getting rewarded and that are supported and expected" (p. 362).

Climate is influenced by individual differences, group processes, and organizational structures and practices (Fulmer & Ostroff, 2016) and has been shown to affect workplace wellbeing (Hall, Dollard, & Coward, 2010).

As Schneider et al. (2013) pointed out, there is a difference between the general climate (e.g., organizational climate) and more focused climates that provide an assessment of some specific element of the general climate (e.g., safety climate, health climate). Furthermore, focused climates can differ in their relationship with important outcomes. For example, Dollard and Bakker (2010) defined a psychosocial safety climate as one in which employees perceive a "freedom from psychological and social risk or harm" (p. 580). Hall et al. (2010) subsequently provided an empirical differentiation between psychosocial safety climate and physical safety climate (the extent to which employees perceive an environment that promotes physical safety). They found that psychosocial safety climate added to the prediction of workplace wellbeing over and above physical safety climate.

In the context of workplace wellbeing, psychosocial safety climate represents a critical contextual variable that can influence employee utilization of various psychologically healthy workplace practices and the resulting experience of workplace wellbeing. Hall et al. (2010) described psychosocial safety climate as being driven by employee perceptions of supportive management, the importance placed on psychological health in the workplace, communication, and involvement and participation. Involvement and communication both tie back to the types of practices included in APA's psychologically healthy workplace model (Figure 18.4), while supportive management and the perceived importance of psychological health in the workplace are more generalized aspects of the climate that would be included under context. In addition, Dollard and Bakker (2010) found that psychosocial safety climate was an important factor associated with work demands and work resources; in addition, it served as an external resource that attenuated the positive association between higher emotional demands and the experience of emotional exhaustion.

The bridging of the gap between psychologically healthy workplace practices and the psychosocial safety climate was, in some ways, an element of a study conducted by Grawitch, Trares, and Kohler (2007), at least at the level of individual perceptions. Grawitch et al. found that employee satisfaction with each of the five psychologically healthy workplace practices (see Table 18.2) was a function of the perceived availability of the practice, self-reported participation in the practice, and the perception that the practice was supported by the organization. Employee satisfaction with each of the practices was associated with a variety of workplace wellbeing indicators (i.e., emotional exhaustion, general wellbeing, organizational commitment, and turnover intentions). As further evidence that involvement and communication play a key role in psychosocial safety climate, satisfaction with employee involvement practices was a key linking mechanism connecting the other psychologically healthy workplace practices to workplace wellbeing.

The results of the research conducted by Dollard and Bakker (2010), Grawitch et al. (2007), and Hall et al. (2010) all suggest that the key to understanding the mechanism through which tangible support mechanisms (e.g., psychologically healthy workplace practices) influence the experience of workplace wellbeing resides within an understanding of the emotional support provided by an effective psychosocial safety climate. This harkens back to Kahn's (1990) argument more than 25 years ago regarding the three psychological conditions necessary for engagement: psychological safety, psychological meaningfulness, and psychological availability. An integration of these psychological conditions into the Dynamic Workplace Wellbeing model (Figure 18.3) provides the opportunity to address, in a very practical and comprehensive way, the experience of workplace wellbeing.

Creating the psychological conditions for workplace wellbeing

Kahn's (1990) description of the three psychological conditions necessary for engagement provided a recognition that engagement is a function of the dynamic interplay between employees and their work environment, both in terms of the specific work tasks and the environment within which those tasks are completed. He defined *psychological meaningfulness* as "feeling that one is receiving a return on investments of one's self in a currency of physical, cognitive, or emotional energy" and explained that employees experience this when they feel "worthwhile, useful, and valuable-as though they [make] a difference and [are] not taken for granted" (p. 704). He defined *psychological safety* as "feeling able to show and employ one's self without fear of negative consequences to self-image, status, or career" and explained that people feel safe "in situations in which they [trust] that they will not suffer for their personal engagement" (p. 708). Finally, he defined *psychological availability* as "the sense of having the physical, emotional, or psychological resources to personally engage at a particular moment" and explained that employees should be "more or less available to place their selves fully into role performances depending on how they [cope] with the various demands of both work and nonwork aspects of their lives" (p. 714).

These three psychological conditions all closely align with the Dynamic Workplace Wellbeing model (Figure 18.3) and suggest a practical approach to addressing workplace wellbeing. First, Kahn's psychological availability condition relates very much to the dynamic process of self-regulation that occurs in the allocation of resources to effectively respond to demands. Addressing this aspect of engagement largely involves the provision of tangible support in the form of psychologically healthy workplace practices (Table 18.2). Grawitch et al. (2015) argued that a proper needs assessment can be employed to help identify the specific personal resources, demands, and resource allocation issues that exist. The results of this needs assessment can then be used to develop programs, policies, and practices needed to enhance personal resources, minimize the excessive quantity or intensity of demands, and improve overall resource allocation competencies (e.g., skills, autonomy).

Kahn's (1990) psychological safety condition refers largely to the issues of climate and other factors that fall under the heading of emotional support. Issues such as interpersonal relationships, group and intergroup dynamics, management style and process, and organizational norms should support a positive, constructive work environment. Previous research has suggested that issues such as supportive management, leader inclusiveness, organizational communication, and team climate all contribute to the development of psychological safety (Brown & Leigh, 1996; Hall et al., 2010; Idris, Dollard, Coward, & Dormann, 2012; Nembhard & Edmondson, 2006). Addressing issues related to emotional support, therefore, could involve any of the following: (1) tailoring specific programs, policies, and practices to be consistent with existing management style, group dynamics, and organizational norms; (2) introducing change initiatives to align management style, group dynamics, and organizational systems and processes with psychologically healthy workplace practices; or (3) a combination of tailoring and intervention.

Kahn's (1990) meaningfulness condition relates specifically to the issue of whether employees perceive a return on investment when they allocate their resources to meet particular demands. This relates very specifically to the concept of need fulfillment as discussed as a key element of self-regulation (Carver & Scheier, 1998; Deci & Ryan, 2000; Warr & Inceoglu, 2012). As Deci and Ryan (2000) argued, people are active and growth oriented, and they are motivated to regulate their own behavior, establish meaningful relationships with others, and interact effectively with their environment to develop mastery. As such, Kahn's (1990) psychological availability and psychological safety conditions may help to bring about the experience of psychological meaningfulness, which then helps to bring about the experience of workplace wellbeing.

Practical applications

Employers who view workforce wellbeing as critical to success approach their workplace efforts strategically. Rather than implementing a collection of individual programs and policies, these organizations optimize wellbeing and functioning through comprehensive efforts to provide both tangible external resources and a supportive work environment. The five types of practices that help create a psychologically healthy workplace (i.e., employee involvement, health and safety, employee growth and development, work-life balance, employee recognition) are instrumental in nature and can provide employees with external supports, but utilization of these resources and the resulting impact depend on context.

Practices are more likely to be used effectively when they are consistent with the organization's mission and values and exist in an environment where employees feel supported in using them. For example, in the five organizations that received the APA's 2015 Psychologically Healthy Workplace Award, on average, 79% of employees said their employer promotes and supports a healthy lifestyle (APA, 2016a). At these award-winning companies, regular participation in the organization's health and wellness programs (65%) far exceeds that in the US workforce as a whole (35%).

A supportive climate is also linked to employees' relationship with the organization. In a survey of APA's 2015 award winners, more than 7 out of 10 employees reported that they believe the organization values employee involvement (71%), training and development (78%), work-life balance (77%) and employee recognition (77%; APA, 2016b). In these broadly supportive environments, an average of 92% of employees reported being satisfied with their job, compared to just 71% nationally, and more than 8 in 10 (82%) said they would recommend their organization to others as a good place to work, compared to just 58% in the US workforce (APA, 2016a). These high-performing companies also reported an average turnover rate of just 13% in 2015 – significantly less than the national average of 42%, as estimated by the US Department of Labor – and only 9% of their employees indicated that they intend to seek employment elsewhere within the next year, compared to more than double that number (23%) nationally in the United States (APA, 2016a).

Creating a healthy, high-performing organization requires more than simply offering wellness activities or desirable benefits. One employer that has built psychologically healthy workplace principles into the very norms, values, and beliefs that are part of the organization's culture is Certified Angus Beef (CAB), a three-time recipient of APA's national award.

CAB is a not-for-profit entity owned by the American Angus Association that establishes and monitors quality standards and works with a network of ranchers, restaurants, and retailers to provide consumers with a premium product. The organization's reputation for quality extends to its work environment as well, where business practices are designed to support both employee wellbeing and the bottom line.

Employee involvement

CAB strives to support involvement by valuing employee voice and providing mechanisms for those voices to be heard. From an open-door policy and regular meetings with supervisors to keep the lines of communication open to division retreats, regular brainstorming sessions, and company-sponsored community outreach efforts, employees play an active and enthusiastic role at CAB. By facilitating employee involvement in activities from planning to execution, CAB works to build a sense of family in the organization, as well as supportive relationships among staff members, leadership, and the community.

Health and safety

CAB provides a comprehensive wellness program that includes a health risk assessment, discounted health club memberships, onsite fitness and ergonomic specialists, midday workouts, weight management groups, ergonomic evaluations, yoga, company-provided fitness trackers, blood pressure checks, and fresh fruit in the office.

To address employees' emotional needs, CAB contracts with a clinical psychologist who serves as the organization's emotional wellness specialist and employee assistance program provider. Understanding that stigma can sometimes create a barrier to accessing mental health services, CAB aimed to build a supportive culture from the start. To introduce the psychologist, the organization held a lunchtime learning session and scheduled brief meet-and-greets. The psychologist hosts stress management sessions and quarterly relaxation workshops and provides confidential one-on-one appointments on company time at no cost to employees. By including mental health as part of overall wellbeing, reducing stigma, framing psychological services as a resource to help employees thrive, and providing easy access, CAB is providing both tangible supports and climate that values and supports employee health.

Employee growth and development

Not content merely to have satisfied workers, CAB offers numerous opportunities for employees to grow in their current roles or expand into new ones. Certification programs, conferences, e-learning, job rotation, cross-training, mentoring, training workshops, and tuition reimbursement all promote professional development. In 2011, CAB launched a yearlong leadership development series that is open to all employees. The sessions explore topics designed to help employees promote a supportive environment at CAB, including communication, trust, conflict resolution, and empowerment.

Work-life balance

CAB offers many tangible resources to help employees manage the work-life interface, including flexible schedules, part-time work, and telecommuting, and a generous time-off package with an additional day earned for each year of employment.

A variety of nonwork support resources are also available onsite to help employees more efficiently allocate their resources to meet life's demands. In addition to sessions with the psychologist, CAB-sponsored services include a wellness coach, financial planner, attorney, and concierge, which are available at discounted rates or free of charge.

While the flexible policies and support resources provide tangible benefits, CAB's family-oriented culture emphasizes the autonomy and latitude to attend to life's unexpected demands with the full support of management. The organization also monitors employee business travel and workloads and makes adjustments as needed to promote work-life fit.

Employee recognition

CAB regularly recognizes individuals and teams for their contributions to the organization as well as for professional and personal accomplishments. These occur in person, at biweekly staff breakfasts, and at an annual service awards dinner. CAB also promotes camaraderie and a supportive, family-oriented culture by hosting special events such as patio parties with live music, games, and food.

The bottom line

Since beginning its wellness initiatives, CAB has seen single-digit increases in annual health insurance premiums and a reduction in sick time, saving hundreds of thousands of dollars. The combination of external resources provided through CAB's comprehensive set of workplace practices and a climate that broadly promotes wellbeing and supports employees' emotional needs has helped to create a positive work environment that drives excellent business results. Even during the recent economic recession, CAB maintained record sales and cultivated a reputation as an employer of choice. This has resulted in public accolades, increased employee job candidate referrals, a large volume of high-quality applicants, and low turnover rates.

Through its combination of (1) workplace practices that enhance resources, moderate demands, and facilitate effective resource allocation; (2) a supportive climate that includes positive interpersonal relationships, trust, and a sense of community; and (3) a nurturing environment where employees feel valued and can pursue both personal and professional growth, CAB fosters a psychologically healthy workplace where both employees and the organization can thrive.

Conclusion

The Dynamic Workplace Wellbeing model offers three implications for future research and application. First, it recognizes that employees are going to differ with regard to intraindividual and nonwork life factors that will ultimately impact their workplace wellbeing. Second, it provides the first integration of the JD-R model with the PRA framework and affective circumplex approach to workplace wellbeing, suggesting that there are various combinations of personal resources, external resources, and demands that will produce differences in workplace wellbeing and employee strategies for allocating their personal resources. Third, it provides a delineation of the types of external resources (i.e., tangible, emotional) employers can provide to support effective resource allocation, thus enhancing workplace wellbeing. Obviously, dedicated research is needed to support some of the model's more nuanced linkages, but the model itself represents a theoretical step forward in adding greater sophistication to our understanding of workplace wellbeing, an approach with very practical implications as evidenced by the case example.

References

Amabile, T. M., & Kramer, S. J. (2007). Inner work life: Understanding the subtext of business performance. *Harvard Business Review*, 85, 72–83.

American Psychological Association. (2014). *Employee Recognition Survey*. Available at: www.apaexcellence.org/assets/general/employee-recognition-survey-results.pdf

American Psychological Association. (2015a). *Resources for Employers: Introduction*. Available at: www.apaexcellence.org/resources/creatingahealthyworkplace/

American Psychological Association. (2015b). *2015 Work and Well-Being Survey*. Available at: www.apaexcellence.org/assets/general/2015-work-and-wellbeing-survey-results.pdf

American Psychological Association. (2016a). *Data Reveal the Benefits of a Psychologically Healthy Workplace*. Graph. Available at: www.apaexcellence.org/assets/general/phwa-2016-combined-charts-1–2.pdf

American Psychological Association. (2016b). *Psychologically Healthy Workplaces Value Employees and Communicate Effectively*. Graph. Available at: www.apaexcellence.org/assets/general/phwa-2016-combined-charts-3–4.pdf

Bakker, A. B., Demerouti, E., & Sanz-Vergel, A. I. (2014). Burnout and work engagement: The JD-R approach. *Annual Review of Organizational Psychology and Organizational Behavior*, 1, 389–411.

Bakker, A. B., Hakanen, J. J., Demerouti, E., & Xanthopoulou, D. (2007). Job resources boost work engagement particularly when job demands are high. *Journal of Educational Psychology*, 99, 274–284.

Bakker, A. B., & Oerlemans, W. G. M. (2010). Subjective well-being in organizations. In: K. S. Cameron & G. M. Spreitzer (eds.), *Handbook of Positive Organizational Scholarship*. Oxford: Oxford University Press, 178–189.

Barber, L. K., Grawitch, M. J., & Munz, D. C. (2012). Disengaging from a task: Lower self-control or adaptive self-regulation? *Journal of Individual Differences*, 33(2), 76–82.

Blume, B. D., Ford, J. K., Baldwin, T. T., & Huang, J. L. (2010). Transfer of training: A meta-analytic review. *Journal of Management*, 36(4), 1065–1105.

Bolton, L. R., Harvey, R. D., Grawitch, M. J., & Barber, L. K. (2012). Counterproductive work behaviors in response to emotional exhaustion: A moderated mediational approach. *Stress and Health*, 28(3), 222–233.

Bradburn, N. (1969). *The Structure of Psychological Wellbeing*. Chicago: Aldine.

Brauchli, R., Schaufeli, W. B., Jenny, G. J., Füllemann, D., & Bauer, G. F. (2013). Disentangling stability and change in job resources, job demands, and employee well-being – A three-wave study on the Job-Demands Resources model. *Journal of Vocational Behavior*, 83(2), 117–129.

Brown, S. P., & Leigh, T. W. (1996). A new look at psychological climate and its relationship to job involvement, effort, and performance. *Journal of Applied Psychology*, 81(4), 358–368.

Cable, D. M., & DeRue, D. S. (2002). The convergent and discriminant validity of subjective fit perceptions. *Journal of Applied Psychology*, 87(5), 875–884.

Carver, C. S., & Scheier, M. F. (1998). *On the Self-Regulation of Behavior*. New York: Cambridge University Press.

Carver, C. S., & Scheier, M. F. (2011). Self-regulation of action and affect. In: K. D. Vohs & R. F. Baumeister (eds.), *Handbook of Self-Regulation: Research, Theory, and Applications* (2nd ed.). New York: The Guilford Press, 3–21.

Chen, F. F., Jing, Y., Hayes, A., & Lee, J. M. (2014). Two concepts or two approaches? A bifactor analysis of psychological and subjective well-being. *Journal of Happiness Studies*, 14(3), 1033–1068.

Cheng, T., Mauno, S., & Lee, C. (2014). Do job control, support, and optimism help job insecure employees? A three-wave study of buffering effects on job satisfaction, vigor and work-family enrichment. *Social Indicators Research*, 118(3), 1269–1291.

Danna, K., & Griffin, R. W. (1999). Health and well-being in the workplace: A review and synthesis of the literature. *Journal of Management*, 25(3), 357–384.

Deci, E. L., & Ryan, R. M. (2000). The "what" and "why" of goal pursuits: Human needs and the self-determination of behavior. *Psychological Inquiry*, 11, 227–268.

Demerouti, E., Bakker, A. B., Nachreiner, F., & Schaufeli, W. B. (2001). The job demands–resources model of burnout. *Journal of Applied Psychology*, 86, 499–512.

Diener, E. (1984). Subjective well-being. *Psychological Bulletin*, 95, 542–575.

Diener, E. (2005). *Guidelines for National Indicators of Subjective Well-Being and Ill-Being*. Available at: http://internal.psychology.illinois.edu/~ediener/Documents/Guidelines_for_National_Indicators.pdf

Dodge, R., Daly, A. P., Huyton, J., & Sanders, L. D. (2012). The challenge of defining wellbeing. *International Journal of Wellbeing*, 2(3), 222–235.

Dollard, M. F., & Bakker, A. B. (2010). Psychosocial safety climate as a precursor to conducive work environments, psychological health problems, and employee engagement. *Journal of Occupational and Organizational Psychology*, 83, 579–599.

Dormann, C., & Zapf, D. (2001). Job satisfaction: A meta-analysis of stabilities. *Journal of Organizational Behavior*, 22(5), 483–504.

Fulmer, C. A., & Ostroff, C. (2016). Convergence and emergence in organizations: An integrative framework and review. *Journal of Organizational Behavior*, 37, S122–S145.

Grawitch, M. J., Ballard, D. W., & Erb, K. R. (2015). To be or not to be (stressed): The critical role of a psychologically healthy workplace in effective stress management. *Stress and Health*, 31, 264–273.

Grawitch, M. J., & Barber, L. K. (2010). Work flexibility or non-work support? Mapping the work-life balance research onto a conceptual framework. *Consulting Psychology Journal: Practice and Research*, 62, 169–188.

Grawitch, M. J., & Barber, L. K. (2013). In search of the relationship between polychronicity and multitasking performance: The importance of trait self-control. *Journal of Individual Differences*, 34(4), 222–229.

Grawitch, M. J., Barber, L. K., & Justice, L. (2010). Re-thinking the work-life interface: It's not about balance, it's about resource allocation. *Applied Psychology: Health and Well-Being*, 2, 127–159.

Grawitch, M. J., Gottschalk, M., & Munz, D. C. (2006). The path to a healthy workplace: A critical review linking healthy workplace practices, employee well-being, and organizational improvements. *Consulting Psychology Journal: Practice and Research*, 58, 129–147.

Grawitch, M. J., Ledford, G. E., Ballard, D. W., & Barber, L. K. (2009). Leading the healthy workforce: The integral role of employee involvement. *Consulting Psychology Journal: Practice and Research*, 61, 122–135.

Grawitch, M. J., Trares, S., & Kohler, J. M. (2007). Healthy workplace practices and employee outcomes. *International Journal of Stress Management*, 14(3), 275–293.

Hall, G. B., Dollard, M. F., & Coward, J. (2010). Psychosocial safety climate: Development of the PSC-12. *International Journal of Stress Management*, 17(4), 353–383.

Hecht, T. D., & Allen, N. J. (2005). Exploring links between polychronicity and well-being from the perspective of person–job fit: Does it matter if you prefer to do only one thing at a time? *Organizational Behavior and Human Decision Processes*, 98(2), 155–178.

Hirschfeld, R. R., & Thomas, C. H. (2008). Representations of trait engagement: Integrations, additions, and mechanisms. *Industrial and Organizational Psychology: Perspectives on Science and Practice*, 1(1), 63–66.

Hobfoll, S. E. (1989). Conservation of resources: A new attempt at conceptualizing stress. *American Psychologist*, 44, 513–524.

House, J. S. (1981). *Work Stress and Social Support*. Reading, MA: Addison Wesley.

Idris, M. A., Dollard, M. F., Coward, J., & Dormann, C. (2012). Psychosocial safety climate: Conceptual distinctiveness and effect on job demands and worker psychological health. *Safety Science*, 50, 19–28.

Kahn, W. A. (1990). Psychological conditions of personal engagement and disengagement at work. *Academy of Management Journal*, 33, 692–724.

Macey, W. H., & Schneider, B. (2008). The meaning of employee engagement. *Industrial and Organizational Psychology: Perspectives on Science and Practice*, 1(1), 3–30.

Molino, M., Bakker, A. B., & Ghislieri, C. (2015). The role of workaholism in the Job Demands–Resources model. *Anxiety, Stress, and Coping* (Online First).

Nembhard, I. M., & Edmondson, A. C. (2006). Making it safe: The effects of leader inclusiveness and professional status on psychological safety and improvement efforts in health care teams. *Journal of Organizational Behavior*, 27, 941–966.

Poortvliet, P. M., Anseel, F., & Theuwis, F. (2015). Mastery-approach and mastery-avoidance goals and their relation with exhaustion and engagement at work: The roles of emotional and instrumental support. *Work and Stress*, 29(2), 150–170.

Rath, T., & Harter, J. (2010). *Well-Being: The Five Essential Elements*. New York: Gallup Press.

Rayton, B. A., & Yalabik, Z. Y. (2014). Work engagement, psychological contract breach and job satisfaction. *The International Journal of Human Resource Management*, 25(17), 2382–2400.

Russell, J. A. (1980). A circumplex model of affect. *Journal of Personality and Social Psychology*, 39(6), 1161–1178.

Russell, J. A. (2003). Core affect and the psychological construction of emotion. *Psychological Review*, 110(1), 145–172.

Ryan, R. M., & Deci, E. L. (2001). On happiness and human potentials: A review of research on hedonic and eudaimonic well-being. *Annual Review of Psychology*, 52, 141–166.

Ryff, C. D. (1989). Happiness is everything, or is it? Explorations on the meaning of psychological well-being. *Journal of Personality and Social Psychology*, 57, 1069–1081.

Schaufeli, W. B., & Bakker, A. B. (2004). Job demands, job resources, and their relationship with burnout and engagement: A multi-sample study. *Journal of Organizational Behavior*, 25, 293–315.

Schaufeli, W. B., Salanova, M., González-Romá, V., & Bakker, A. B. (2002). The measurement of engagement and burnout: A two sample confirmatory factor analytic approach. *Journal of Happiness Studies*, 3, 71–92.

Schaufeli, W. B., & Taris, T. W. (2014). A critical review of the Job Demands-Resources Model: Implications for improving work and health. In: G. F. Bauer & O. Hämmig (eds.), *Bridging Occupational, Organizational and Public Health: A Transdisciplinary Approach*. New York: Springer.

Schaufeli, W. B., Taris, T. W., & van Rhenen, W. (2008). Workaholism, burnout, and work engagement: Three of a kind or three different kinds of employee well-being? *Applied Psychology: An International Review*, 57(2), 173–203.

Schneider, B., Ehrhart, M. G., & Macey, M. H. (2013). Organizational climate and culture. *Annual Review of Psychology*, 64, 361–388.

Semmer, N., Elfering, A., Jacobshagen, N., Beehr, T., & Boos, N. (2008). The emotional meaning of social support. *International Journal of Stress Management*, 15, 235–251.

Shakespeare-Finch, J., & Obst, P. L. (2011). The development of the 2-way social support scale: A measure of giving and receiving emotional and instrumental support. *Journal of Personality Assessment*, 93(5), 483–490.

Tims, M., Bakker, A. B., & Derks, D. (2012). The development and validation of the job crafting scale. *Journal of Vocational Behavior*, 80, 173–186.

Tong, J., Wang, L., & Peng, K. (2015). From person-environment misfit to job burnout: Theoretical extensions. *Journal of Managerial Psychology*, 30(2), 169–182.

Warr, P., & Inceoglu, I. (2012). Job engagement, job satisfaction, and contrasting associations with person–job fit. *Journal of Occupational Health Psychology*, 17(2), 129–138.

Wrosch, C., Scheier, M. F., Miller, G. E., Schulz, R., & Carver, C. S. (2003). Adaptive self-regulation of unattainable goals: Goal disengagement, goal re-engagement, and subjective well-being. *Personality and Social Psychology Bulletin*, 29, 1494–1508.

19

Job resources as contributors to wellbeing

Evangelia Demerouti, Machteld Van den Heuvel,
Despoina Xanthopoulou, Lonneke Dubbelt,
and Heather J. Gordon

Introduction

Protecting employees from the unfavorable consequences of work-related, psychosocial risk factors and enhancing their motivation at work should be a main priority, since healthy and happy employees are important assets for organizations (for a review, see Demerouti & Cropanzano, 2010). Work psychology and occupational health literatures suggest that organizations can achieve this goal by designing resourceful work environments (Hackman & Oldham, 1980) since job resources have been found to play a dual role in employee wellbeing (Bakker & Demerouti, 2007; Demerouti, Bakker, Nachreiner, & Schaufeli, 2001). First, job resources help employees manage and deal more effectively with their job demands, thus buffering their detrimental impact on job strain and health. Second, job resources are important in their own right because the availability of resources facilitates goal attainment, thereby enhancing employee motivation, work engagement, and performance. Based on these theoretical assumptions and supportive empirical evidence (for a review, see Bakker, Demerouti, & Sanz-Vergel, 2014), organizations are encouraged to create and sustain resourceful work environments. To this end, recent studies have emphasized the role of the supervisor in this process, since certain leadership styles (e.g., transformational leadership) have been found to promote job resources (e.g., Breevaart, Bakker, Demerouti, Sleebos, & Maduro, 2014; Breevaart, Bakker, Demerouti, & Van den Heuvel, 2015).

Facilitating the creation of resourceful work environments through top-down redesign strategies or leadership processes may seem an important aim for organizations during stable times. Nevertheless, the global financial crisis and its aftermath has created an unstable environment that called for unfavorable changes not aimed at organizational development, but mainly at organizational survival (Petrou, Demerouti, & Xanthopoulou, 2017). These changes imposed threats to employee wellbeing such as job intensification and restrictions in resources (Sinclair, Sears, Probst, & Zajack, 2010). More so, due to these constraints, organizations have been less reluctant to invest in promoting resourceful work environments. Furthermore, these changes have facilitated new ways of working that integrate technological innovations in order to make work processes more efficient and cost effective (Demerouti, Derks, Ten Brummelhuis, & Bakker, 2014). As a result, it becomes less common to work under a supervisor or to interact with a supervisor on a daily basis. This new organizational reality makes the need for proactive employees who can take charge of their working life (Grant & Parker, 2009) more prominent than ever. Employees who act proactively are likely to achieve a better person–job fit, which can facilitate their adaptation to threatening conditions and may enhance their motivation. Self-leadership or self-management (Breevaart, Bakker, & Demerouti, 2014; Manz, 1986) and job crafting (Wrzesniewski & Dutton, 2001) are proactive behaviors that have been found to enable employee wellbeing and better functioning during threatening conditions (Petrou, Demerouti, & Schaufeli, 2015).

Although the enhancement of resourceful work environments is important, traditional top-down job (re)design strategies seem to be scarce or do not respond sufficiently to the current environmental and organizational challenges. Thus, it is of particular theoretical and practical importance to investigate alternative, bottom-up strategies that may supplement top-down approaches in enhancing job resources, and to test their effectiveness. In this chapter, we respond to the question of how organizations may promote resources. After defining the concept of resources, we present recent empirical evidence at the between- and the within-person level of analysis on which leadership styles and behaviors may contribute to promoting job resources. Next, we explain what employees can do to create a better work environment for themselves, and we present evidence showing that employees can be trained to engage in proactive behavioral strategies that can result in enriched work environments. This chapter ends with an overall discussion suggesting that bottom-up interventions that concern employee proactivity may compensate for the lack of top-down, organizational interventions and aid in the creation of resourceful work environments.

Definition and function of (job) resources

Inspection of the term of *resources* in Wikipedia provides the following definition:

> A resource is a source or supply from which benefit is produced. Typically resources are materials, energy, services, staff, knowledge, or other assets that are transformed to produce benefit and in the process may be consumed or made unavailable. Benefits of resource utilization may include increased wealth, meeting needs or wants, proper functioning of a system, or enhanced wellbeing. Resources have three main characteristics: utility, limited availability, and potential for depletion or consumption.
>
> *(Wikipedia, n.d.)*

It is clear from this definition that resources meet several needs and are particularly important for individuals. However, another central characteristic of resources is that they are limited and can be depleted or consumed. One of the first theories on resources, the Conservation of Resources (COR) theory (Hobfoll, 1989, 2002), suggests that individuals have an innate need to acquire and conserve resources. Thus, acquisition of resources is a drive and is linked to human behavior and wellbeing. According to COR theory, resources may be objects (like a good-quality home or computer), conditions (like having a caring partner or nice colleagues), personal characteristics (like positive sense of self and mastery), and energies (like time, money, and knowledge). The loss or potential loss of resources can be stressful for individuals, who may employ other resources to offset the net loss. In contrast, when individuals manage to gain resources and enrich their resource pool, they are likely to feel better and adapt successfully to their environment. Although COR theory was not initially developed for the work context, its principles have been applied to explain work-related wellbeing.

Work-related theories or models that emphasize resources and their role in the work domain are the Job Characteristics model (JCM; Hackman & Oldham, 1980) and the Adequacy of

Resources framework (Bacharach & Bamberger, 1995). The JCM focuses on five specific job characteristics (i.e., skill variety, task identity, task significance, autonomy, and feedback) that have motivating potential when they are present (Hackman & Oldham, 1980). The presence of these five resources enhances job satisfaction and performance because they elicit specific critical psychological states (e.g., meaningfulness of work, responsibility for outcomes, knowledge of results) in employees. This is particularly the case for employees with knowledge and skills, and a high need for self-development. The Adequacy of Resources framework (Bacharach & Bamberger, 1995) suggests that resource inadequacy (i.e., the inability to mobilize resources like information, support, equipment, clients, material) represents a situational constraint. This situational constraint influences the effort and ability that individuals invest in their tasks because it is difficult for them to reach maximum effectiveness. Resource inadequacy hinders individual performance and requires individuals to invest time and effort in mobilizing adequate resources rather than executing their task. Both the JCM and the Adequacy of Resources framework emphasize the role of specific resources at work for motivation and performance.

A work-related model that builds on these insights is the Job Demands–Resources (JD-R) model (Demerouti et al., 2001). At the heart of the JD-R model lies the assumption that even though every occupation may have its own specific risk factors associated with work-related wellbeing, these factors can be classified in two general categories, namely, job demands and job resources (Bakker & Demerouti, 2007). Job demands refer to those physical, psychological, social, or organizational aspects of the job that require sustained physical and/or psychological (cognitive and emotional) effort or skills and are therefore associated with certain physiological and/or psychological costs. Examples are high work pressure, an unfavorable physical environment, and emotionally demanding interactions with clients. Although job demands are not necessarily negative in nature, they may turn into job stressors, when meeting those demands requires immense effort from which the employee cannot recover adequately or cannot adequately cope with. Job resources refer to those physical, psychological, social, or organizational aspects of the job that are either (1) functional in achieving work goals, (2) reducing job demands and the associated physiological and psychological costs, and/or (3) stimulating personal growth, learning, and development. Accordingly, resources are valued in their own right or are valued because they are means to gain or protect other resources. Resources may be located at different levels of analysis: first, the level of the organization (e.g., pay, career opportunities, job security); second, the level of interpersonal and social relations (e.g., supervisor and coworker support, team climate); third, the level of the organization of work (e.g., role clarity participation in decision making), and finally, at the level of the task (e.g., skill variety, task identity, task significance, autonomy, performance feedback).

Another central premise of the JD-R model is that two different psychological processes play a role in the development of job strain and motivation. In the first process, the so-called energetic or health impairment process, poorly designed jobs, and/or chronic job demands (e.g., work overload, emotional demands), exhaust employee's mental and physical resources and may therefore lead to the depletion of energy (i.e., a state of exhaustion) and to health problems (e.g., Demerouti, Bakker, Nachreiner, & Schaufeli, 2000, 2001). The second process is motivational in nature, whereby it is assumed that job resources have the potential to motivate employees and lead to high work engagement, low cynicism, and excellent performance. By definition, job resources may play either an intrinsic motivational role because they foster employee's growth, learning and development, or they may play an extrinsic motivational role because they are instrumental in achieving work goals. In the former case, job resources fulfil basic human needs, such as the need for autonomy, competence, and relatedness (Ryan & Deci, 2000). For instance, proper feedback fosters learning, thereby increasing job competence, whereas job discretion and social support satisfy the need for autonomy and the need to belong, respectively. Job resources may also play an extrinsic motivational role, because work environments that offer many job resources foster the willingness to dedicate one's efforts and abilities to the work task. In that case, it is likely that the task will be completed successfully and that the work goal will be attained. For example, supportive colleagues and proper feedback from one's supervisor increases the likelihood of being successful in achieving one's work goals.

Next to these processes, the interaction between job demands and job resources has been more explicitly tested as a buffer function of resources on the relationship between job demands and work-related outcomes such as job strain and motivation (Bakker, Demerouti, & Euwema, 2005). Moreover, it has been suggested and found that job resources boost employee motivation and work engagement particularly under demanding conditions (i.e., the coping hypothesis; Bakker, Hakanen, Demerouti, & Xanthopoulou, 2007). Which job demands and resources play a role in a certain organization depends upon the specific job characteristics that prevail. Thus, the JD-R model states that different types of job demands and job resources may interact in predicting both job strain and motivation.

Mobilization of job resources

Because job resources are so important for wellbeing and individual functioning at work, the critical question is how they can be generated. We will focus explicitly on two ways that this can be done. The first is through the direct supervisor and the second is through individuals themselves by means of job-crafting behaviors.

Supervisors

Leadership is associated with employee and organizational outcomes, but the mechanisms through which leaders exert their influence on their followers' wellbeing, motivation, and performance have not been adequately addressed in the literature (Avolio, Zhu, Koh, & Bhatia, 2004). Breevaart and colleagues (Breevaart et al., 2015) have conducted a series of studies to investigate whether leaders' behaviors influence employee wellbeing, work engagement, and job performance via their impact on the work environment. Specifically, Breevaart et al. (2015) showed that followers in high-quality Leader Member Exchange (LMX) relationships received more latitude to make decisions about how and when to perform their work (i.e., autonomy), more opportunities to grow and develop (i.e., developmental opportunities), and more social support from their colleagues. In turn, these resources contributed to how engaged followers felt in their work and, consequently, how well they performed their core tasks. Similarly, using data from supervisor-employee dyads, Breevaart et al. (2014) showed that followers have more resources available when their leader is inspiring and attentive of individual needs, and when the leader challenges followers on an intellectual level (i.e., transformational leadership). These resources initiated a motivational process whereby followers became more engaged in their work, because their basic needs were fulfilled. Followers who were more engaged in their work were rated higher on their in-role (i.e., task) performance by their leader.

In a diary study among 61 naval cadets, who completed a diary questionnaire for 34 days on active duty, Breevaart, Bakker, Hetland, Demerouti, Olsen, and Espevik (2014) examined the daily influence of transformational leadership, contingent reward, and active management-by-exception (MBE-active) on followers' daily work engagement. Cadets were more engaged on days that their leader showed more transformational leadership and provided contingent rewards.

MBE-active was unrelated to followers' work engagement. As predicted, transformational leadership and contingent reward contributed to a more favorable work environment (more autonomy and support), while MBE-active resulted in a less favorable work environment (less autonomy) for the cadets. Another longitudinal study that looked at the beneficial effects of resources on employees' change adaptation capabilities, found that LMX predicted employee adaptivity, as well as personal resources – that is, employees' ability to find meaning and to feel valued by the organization (Van den Heuvel, Demerouti, & Bakker, 2013).

These empirical findings suggest that leaders have great potential to contribute to the amount of resources that are available to their employees. Leaders who develop high-quality relationships with their subordinates are likely to promote autonomy or quality coaching in the work environment. In a similar vein, transformational leaders who inspire their followers and show consideration for their problems are likely to provide support and quality feedback. The availability of these job resources enhances followers' motivation and, consequently, their job performance. This may be because employees who work in such environments are more likely to feel that their basic psychological needs are satisfied. For example, having a say over the processes at work satisfies their need for autonomy, while receiving support and quality coaching satisfies their need to belong. Nevertheless, since supervisors may not always be present or willing to facilitate resource allocation, it is important to examine how employees may take responsibility to create a resourceful work environment for themselves.

Individual strategies

Despite the positive impact leaders may have on their followers, due to the current organizational transformations, it is increasingly common to no longer work under the supervision of a leader. Employees are faced with changes in who they report to, and this may jeopardize the benefits of a high-quality LMX relationship as described in the previous section. It is, therefore, vital to examine how employees can manage their own wellbeing, work engagement, and effective functioning at work. One strategy that seems to have potential to manage not only work-related wellbeing but also performance outcomes is self-leadership. Self-leadership is a multi-faceted self-management process through which employees motivate themselves to perform in enjoyable and desirable ways (Houghton & Neck, 2002; Manz, 1986). The construct consists of behavior-focused strategies (e.g., self-observation, self-goal setting), natural reward strategies (e.g., focus on building intrinsically pleasurable or motivating aspects into the working environment), and constructive thought pattern strategies (e.g., positive self-talk). Self-leadership has been found to relate positively to job performance (Prussia, Anderson, & Manz, 1998) and negatively to strain (Unsworth & Mason, 2012) via its positive impact on personal resources such as self-efficacy.

The use of self-leadership strategies can fluctuate from day to day, which was shown in a study that examined how daily fluctuations in the use of self-leadership strategies relate to work engagement and job performance (Breevaart et al., 2014). Using daily diary data from maternity nurses, who generally work without the supervision of a leader, it was found that daily self-management related positively to the resourcefulness of the daily work environment (i.e., more skill variety, feedback, and developmental opportunities) and consequently, to employees' daily work engagement. The aspects of self-management that were related to daily job resources were self-goal setting, self-observation, and self-cueing (i.e., reminding oneself of important goals). These findings indicate that employees may play a vital role in regulating their own motivation and wellbeing using strategies such as self-leadership.

Job crafting

Employees may actively change the design of their jobs by choosing tasks, negotiating a different job content, and assigning meaning to their tasks or jobs (Parker & Ohly, 2008). This process through which employees shape their jobs has been referred to as "job crafting" (Wrzesniewski & Dutton, 2001). Job crafting is defined as the physical and cognitive changes individuals make in their task or relational boundaries. Physical changes refer to changes in the form, scope, or number of job tasks, whereas cognitive changes refer to changing how one sees the job. Wrzesniewski and Dutton (2001) note that job crafting is a phenomenon that is not inherently "good" or "bad" for an organization. Rather, the effects of job crafting behavior depend on the situation.

The central characteristic of job crafting is that employees alter their tasks or other job characteristics on their own initiative (Tims, Bakker, & Derks, 2012). This distinguishes job crafting from other bottom-up redesign approaches such as idiosyncratic deals (i-deals), wherein employees negotiate their work conditions with their employer (Hornung, Rousseau, Glaser, Angerer, & Weigl, 2010), or employee participation in traditional job redesign attempts (Briner & Reynold, 1999; Nadin, Waterson, & Parker, 2001). According to Tims and colleagues (2012), job crafting differs from previously studied proactive constructs because the changes that job crafters make are primarily aimed at improving their person–job fit and work motivation.

In order to capture the "everyday" changes in job characteristics that employees may pursue, some scholars (Petrou, Demerouti, Peeters, Schaufeli, & Hetland, 2012; Tims & Bakker, 2010) theoretically frame the definition of job crafting in the JD–R model (Bakker, 2011; Bakker & Demerouti, 2007; Demerouti et al., 2001). Accordingly, job crafting is defined as the changes that employees can make to balance their job demands and job resources with their personal abilities and needs (cf. Tims & Bakker, 2010). In line with Petrou et al. (2012), job crafting can then be conceptualized as consisting of three behaviors: resource seeking, challenge seeking, and demand reducing. In line with Wrzesniewski and Dutton (2001), Petrou et al. suggest that even in the most stable environments with detailed job descriptions and clear work procedures, individuals can and do adjust the tasks they perform, and mobilize the resources they need to carry out their tasks successfully on a day-to-day basis. In this way, individuals manage their wellbeing and remain healthy and motivated.

Seeking job resources (e.g., feedback, advice from colleagues or the manager, maximizing job autonomy) is a way individuals can cope with job demands, achieve goals, or complete tasks. This is in line with COR theory (Hobfoll, 2001) and empirical findings suggesting that several resource-seeking behaviors, such as feedback seeking (Ashford, Blatt, & Vande Walle, 2003) or social support seeking (Carver, Scheier, & Weintraub, 1989), produce positive outcomes and facilitate employee functioning.

Challenge seeking may include behaviors such as seeking new or more challenging tasks at work, keeping busy during one's work day, or asking for more responsibilities once one has completed assigned tasks. Csikszentmihalyi and Nakamura (1989) argue that when individuals engage in activities offering opportunities for growth, they seek challenges to maintain motivation and avoid boredom.

When individuals reduce demands, they minimize those threatening aspects of the job that are emotionally, mentally, or physically strenuous, they reduce their workload, or they make sure that the work success is not at the cost of their private life. Reducing demands might be a health-protecting coping mechanism when demands are excessively high (Demerouti, 2014). Behaviors similar to reducing demands have been studied in the literature. For example, "task avoidance" has been described as a withdrawal-oriented coping mechanism (Parker & Endler, 1996). Other examples are slow or sloppy work and poor attendance, which are described as counterproductive behaviors (Gruys, 1999). Finally, procrastination can be an "active" behavior similar to task avoidance (Chu & Choi, 2005).

Using the conceptualization of job crafting as a three-dimensional behavior, Petrou et al.'s (2012) diary study showed that job crafting occurs on a daily basis as daily fluctuations of job crafting ranged between 31% (challenges seeking) and 34% (resources seeking) to 78% (demands reducing). Furthermore, there is substantial evidence demonstrating that job crafting relates to employee work engagement. Bakker, Tims, and Derks (2012), in a cross-sectional study, found that seeking structural and social job resources and seeking job challenges were associated with work engagement. Petrou et al. (2012) addressed this relationship on a daily basis and found that day-level seeking challenges (but not resources) associated positively with day-level work engagement, whereas day-level reducing demands associated negatively with day-level work engagement. Additionally, job crafting has been found to relate to job satisfaction. For instance, Tims, Bakker, and Derks (2013) found that employees who crafted their (structural and social resources) job resources reported an increase in job resources, and this increase related positively to increased job satisfaction two months later. However, crafting job demands (i.e., challenging and hindering) was unrelated to job satisfaction over time.

Several empirical studies have provided evidence for the positive relation between job crafting and work performance. Job crafting has been related to other ratings of task performance through work engagement (Bakker et al., 2012; Tims, Bakker, & Derks, 2015). Particularly, seeking resources was found to predict task performance over time (Petrou, Demerouti, & Schaufeli, 2016). On a day level, Demerouti, Bakker, and Halbesleben (2015) found that daily seeking resources associated positively with daily task performance. Yet, daily reducing demands was detrimental for daily task performance and altruism. Although reducing one's work-related demands seems to associate with less favorable outcomes, overall, most studies show that job crafting – and particularly seeking resources and seeking challenges – can help employees to build wellbeing, motivation, and performance at work. It is, therefore, important to focus on interventions that may help employees to actively use job-crafting behaviors.

Interventions to increase wellbeing

Most applied organizational interventions to increase wellbeing and employee functioning are top-down, but only 30% of these attempts are found to be effective (Balogun & Hope Hailey, 2004). Moreover, their focus tends to be either on improving health and wellbeing, or performance, but not both. Researchers have recognized that organizational processes are too complex to be captured under solely strict "traditional" job redesign frameworks of stress management or other top-down organizational interventions (Briner & Reynold, 1999). Bottom-up organizational interventions that use "participatory approaches" emphasize collaboration between employees and management, which is crucial for intervention success (Nielsen, Taris, & Cox, 2010). Bottom-up interventions that take into account the social context (Egan, Bambra, Petticrew, & Whitehead, 2009; Murta, Sanderson, & Oldenburg, 2007; Oakley et al., 2006) and employee input are increasingly applied as a way to improve employee health and wellbeing in the face of the current societal pressures (Kompier & Kristensen, 2001; Le Blanc, Hox, Schaufeli, Taris, & Peeters, 2007; Schaufeli & Enzmann, 1998). To this end, we review bottom-up interventions aimed to boost employee proactive behavior as a way to manage their own wellbeing and motivation at work, and discuss their effectiveness.

The trend towards positive organizational psychology has made researchers emphasize the importance of "positive behavioral change" research and the need to place more attention on this and other change-supporting behaviors (Shoss, Witt, & Vera, 2011; Van den Heuvel, Demerouti, E., & Peeters, 2012). The review by Meyers, van Woerkom, and Bakker (2013) shows that *positive interventions* are effective in increasing positive affective states. However, results have not been conclusive about their effectiveness with regard to functioning at work.

In line with Randall and Nielsen (2012), intervention success in complex environments is significantly determined by the degree of fit between (1) individual employees and the intervention, and (2) the intervention and the work environment, where the intervention is to be implemented. The former referred to as "person–intervention fit" and the latter as "environment–intervention fit." The suitability of an intervention (direct appraisal of "good" or "poor" fit) was found to predict individuals' changes in the working environment (Lazarus & Folkman, 1992; Nielsen, Randall, & Albertsen, 2007). After given the opportunity to fit their jobs in order to match their personal needs and skills, individuals' perceptions of their current work situations improved (Bond & Bunce, 2001). Further, poor intervention–environment fit seems to explain small or nonsignificant intervention effects (LaMontagne, Keegel, Louie, Ostry, & Landsbergis, 2007). From research on person–environment fit, we conclude that interventions that support person–environment fit are more likely to promote a better fit because they empower employees to adjust their job in a way they think is best for them (i.e., within the boundaries of what they can and cannot change), in contrast to the traditional "biomedical" model according to which employees are told (instructed) how to work best.

Thus, tailor-made bottom-up organizational intervention programs are beginning to shift away from the traditional, top-down biomedical model and moving more towards solution-focused, proactive ways in which individual employees can shape their work lives (Nielsen, 2013). One such intervention is job-crafting intervention that focuses on the work environment (i.e., job demands and resources), as well as how individuals react to it (Van den Heuvel et al., 2012; Van den Heuvel, Demerouti, & Peeters, 2015). Job-crafting intervention has been used to stimulate changes in individuals' work engagement, wellbeing, and performance (Demerouti, 2014). The intervention helps employees to develop "self-reinforcing" skills and strategies needed to positively influence their work-related wellbeing, motivation, and performance. In this way, they will be more equipped to deal with future challenges than those employees who have yet to develop them (Seligman, Steen, Park, & Peterson, 2005). Next we describe a number of interventions that focus on job crafting and resources.

Job-crafting interventions

Van den Heuvel et al. (2012, 2015) developed a job-crafting intervention consisting of one day of group training, four weeks of follow-up self-guided job-crafting activities, and a half-day reflection session. Job-crafting intervention aims to increase participants' motivation, wellbeing, and engagement through two different routes: (1) promoting employees' self-directed behavior (e.g., Demerouti, van Eeuwijk, Snelder, & Wild, 2011), and (2) strengthening employees' personal resources such as self-efficacy (e.g., Van den Heuvel et al., 2012, 2015).

The job-crafting intervention consists of the following phases:

1   *Organizing and communicating job crafting*: At this stage, all aspects of the intervention are organized and communicated in consultation with the organization that will apply the job-crafting intervention as a motivational intervention. The organization recruits a group of participants who will attend the intervention on a voluntary basis. The intervention starts with a job-crafting workshop, which consists of a one-day session in small groups of employees. Through various explanations and exercises during the workshop, employees get

to know the concept of job crafting. The workshop concludes with the development of a Personal Crafting Plan (PCP). The PCP consists of specific crafting actions that the participants/employees will formulate and undertake for a period of four weeks.

2   *Getting started with job crafting itself:* In this phase, employees themselves keep a "crafting diary." This is a weekly diary where employees – for a period of four weeks – keep reports of their crafting activities of each week as they have been specified in their PCP. Specifically, during the first week of Van den Heuvel et al.'s (2012) job-crafting intervention, participants were asked to focus on increasing resources (e.g., seeking social support or feedback), while during the second week they were instructed to decrease demands. In the third week, participants were asked to seek job challenges, while during the fourth week they were again asked to increase job resources (e.g., opportunities for development). Moreover, participants were asked to plan time to think about a number of reflection questions every week (e.g., to which extent they have achieved the PCP goals) in order to increase personal resources, for example self-efficacy.

3   *Exchange of experiences:* After participants have crafted their jobs for one month, they meet again to exchange their experiences on the crafting actions. During this reflection session, they discuss successes, problems, and solutions. In this way, employees learn from each other's best practices and in fact coach each other on areas that are in need of improvement. Attention is given to how employees may overcome possible obstacles that hinder their future job-crafting attempts. Participants present their key learnings and tips to each other.

4   *What is the effect?* In this, final phase, the effects of the job-crafting intervention on employee health, wellbeing, and motivational outcomes is examined.

Van den Heuvel et al. (2012, 2015) found indications on the effectiveness of the job-crafting intervention in increasing job resources (i.e., LMX and opportunities for development), and self-efficacy. Also, participants in the experimental group reported more positive emotions and less negative emotions after the intervention. Van den Heuvel et al. (2015) also analyzed within-person, week-level data and found that on weeks that participants used more resource-seeking behaviors, they also reported more developmental opportunities, LMX, and positive affect. On weeks when participants used more reducing-demands behaviors, they reported more positive affect. Taken together, job-crafting intervention seems to have potential to positively influence working conditions, as well as employee wellbeing levels.

Gordon et al. (2014) shortened Van den Heuvel et al.'s (2012, 2015) intervention to three hours and adjusted it by creating Situated Experiential Learning Narratives (SELN) to help stimulate the job-crafting behaviors. SELN were created for this intervention and are based in Benner, Hooper Kyriakidis, and Stannard's (2011) "thinking-in-action" approach, which is usually used in nursing. The intervention also included a participatory approach such that individuals could choose if they wanted to join or not without repercussions (Le Blanc et al., 2007). The intervention was found to be effective not only in directly and indirectly enhancing job-crafting behaviors and wellbeing, but also employees' job performance. Specifically, the intervention was successful in increasing medical specialists' and nurses' work engagement, health, and performance, while also decreasing their exhaustion. Furthermore, the intervention was effective in increasing medical specialists' seeking challenges, which could explain changes in their work-related wellbeing and performance. Moreover, the intervention increased nurses' seeking-resources behaviors, which consequently explained increases in their work engagement. Finally, Dubbelt, Demerouti, and Rispens (2015) adapted Gordon et al.'s (2014) intervention by underlining employees' past job crafting experiences and the way these can be used to facilitate learning new job crafting behaviors. According to Gordon et al.'s (2014) SELN and experiential learning theory, past experiences are stepping stones to learning a new behavior and make it easier for employees to think of ways to apply newly learned behavior (Kolb & Kolb, 2012). Dubbelt et al. (2015) applied the intervention in an academic context with the participation of both academic and administrative staff. The results showed that not only was the intervention effective in increasing work engagement, but it also improved task performance and career satisfaction through seeking resources. More specifically, compared to the control group, the experimental group showed more seeking resources and decreasing demands behaviors after the intervention. Moreover, the intervention directly enhanced participants' work engagement compared to the control group, but also indirectly through an increase in seeking resources. Finally, participants in the experimental group were better able to perform their jobs and grew in career satisfaction because they sought more resources to achieve their goals. Thus, the effect of job crafting goes beyond the job and the work environment, since it also affected positive career outcomes.

Conclusions

The main question that we wanted to address in this chapter was how organizations may increase and promote job resources in order to enhance employee motivation and adaptive functioning in challenging times. To this end, we explained the value of job resources from a theoretical and practical point of view and we presented empirical evidence showing that leaders (and also employees themselves) may engage in behaviors that create resourceful work environments. From a top-down point of view, recent studies at the between- and within-person level of analysis show that transformational leaders that empower and inspire their followers provide resources because they are more supporting, give quality feedback, and allow their subordinates to make autonomous decisions. However, in conditions where these top-down processes are not relevant or are not present, research shows that proactive, bottom-up strategies such as job crafting may also promote resourceful work environments. Importantly, a number of job-crafting interventions to date support the impact that job-crafting strategies (especially seeking resources) can have on enhancing employee wellbeing and performance at work either directly or indirectly through the enrichments of the work environment (Dubbelt et al., 2015; Gordon et al., 2014; Van den Heuvel et al., 2012, 2015). Moreover, a recent study by Vakola, Xanthopoulou, and Demerouti (2016) showed that job-crafting strategies (and particularly resources seeking) promote employee adaptation during organizational changes particularly when influence tactics from the side of management are absent. These results are important because they suggest that job crafting may substitute for the absence of organizational-level attempts to promote resources in a threatening work environment.

Implications for future research

We provided a number of answers regarding the value of job resources for work-related wellbeing, motivation, and performance, as well as regarding the effectiveness of interventions that can boost employee capability of mobilizing resources and/or adapting demands. This relatively new body of research on microlevel interventions brings with it a number of new questions that future studies may focus on. We describe two key issues that need to be addressed.

1 The paradox of leadership: how to leverage the role of the leader in building proactive employees?

From a theoretical point of view, we have addressed the role of the leader as an important top-down resource in organizations. Leaders can empower their followers via transformational leadership behaviors and by building a high-quality exchange relationship. As such, they can be instrumental in providing access to other resources (Yukl, Gordon, & Taber, 2002) and can positively influence employee wellbeing via their own wellbeing (Skakon, Nielsen, Borg, & Guzman, 2010). Following on from this, we emphasized that employees themselves have an important bottom-up role to play in building resources via job-crafting and self-leadership behaviors. Many studies have shown the benefits of these proactive strategies for employee thriving at work. Focusing on the interplay between leader and followers, Breevaart et al. (2014, 2015), in their studies using leader-follower dyads, have shown that leaders can enhance work engagement and performance via the provision of resources and that these benefits hold particularly for employees that feel a high need for leadership. However, as of yet, less is known on how leaders can facilitate proactive behavior such as job crafting or self-leadership in their followers. This is especially important given that many employees are faced with reorganizations that result in new managers or periods in which no manager is present to guide employees at work. These conditions emphasize the urgency for employees to take charge of their own work in order to achieve a better person–job fit. The cost of not being successful in managing oneself could be health complaints or burnout, which is on the rise especially amongst young employees (Muller, Hooftmann, & Houtman, 2015), or disengagement and decreases in motivation. In this context, the paradoxical challenge for leaders is how to stimulate a low need for leadership by facilitating employees' proactive behaviors in order to create flourishing workforces. This is an important area for future research, especially since it seems that levels of job autonomy are on the decline (Muller et al., 2015). This may also mean that future studies will need to focus on developing training specifically tailored to managerial/leadership roles, not only to guide leaders in developing their own proactive behavior, but also to teach them how to coach and mentor their reports in becoming more proactive.

2 When are reducing-demands strategies helpful and when do they hinder wellbeing?

A second question that is emerging and is as of yet unexplored relates to the role of reducing demands in building wellbeing. Some studies have shown that reducing demands brings positive outcomes for employees (e.g., enhanced positive affect; Van den Heuvel et al., 2015), but most studies show that reducing-demands behaviors are in fact related to a decline in wellbeing and motivation (Petrou et al., 2012, 2015, 2017). In cross-sectional studies, these results may indicate that reducing demands is mainly called upon in high-workload settings. Therefore it is not clear whether reducing demand is causing exhaustion, for example, or whether exhaustion forces employees to try reducing their workload. Also, when employees suffer from high work pressures and there are not enough resources to counteract their negative effects, reducing demands may require effort that employees cannot spare. Thus, employees may become depleted and exhausted when applying this strategy. In addition, from our experience as job-crafting trainers, it seems that not all demands can be crafted or altered. For example, demands stemming from top-down decisions during reorganizations or other change efforts often are hard to influence. Attempts to do so may end in frustration and negative affect. Another issue here is that employees may be more or less skilled in crafting their job demands, which may impact the outcomes of this strategy. Reducing demands may require skills like time management, negotiation, and influencing skills. When employees do not have those additional skills, attempts to reduce demands may not work out – or worse, may have a counterproductive effect. For example, when an individual employee starts asserting boundaries at work by saying "no" to new requests coming in from colleagues or supervisors, he or she may provoke negative responses, which may exacerbate the already demanding situation. All in all, it seems wise for employees to initially focus on building resources, even in high-demands situations. Future studies should zoom in on the particular conditions that can cause job-crafting behaviors related to reducing demands to have their intended positive effects on wellbeing (and motivation). Also, future research could look for other types of behaviors that could be adopted within the context of demands reducing but may be more constructive, like for example, task delegation.

This list of issues that future research should pay attention to is by no means exhaustive. There are other points that scholars should consider when trying to explain the outcomes of job-crafting strategies for work-related wellbeing and job performance, for instance, the role of employee personality. Nevertheless, we have tried to capture those topics that appear most prominent on a way forward.

Final conclusion

Evidence for the importance of job resources for employee wellbeing outcomes is growing, especially in demanding times of change and crisis. There is merit in studying how organizations and employees can increase resources in order to prevent burnout and other health complaints. However, as of yet, findings in this space are inconsistent; reducing demands may not always benefit individual workers (cf. Petrou et al., 2012), while boosting resources in the work environment has shown consistent positive results (cf. Bakker et al., 2014).

Therefore, our conclusion is that it is important for organizations to create work environments where employees have access to job resources, including autonomy that allows employees the latitude to craft their jobs in order to achieve a better person–job fit, and ideally, where employees have the opportunity to take part in interventions that help them build proactive behaviors towards that end. Also, organizations should aim to equip their leaders to be able to take on a coaching/transformational role, within which they may stimulate resourceful work environments. Finally, employees should focus on building their own resources, which can start with small actions such as asking for feedback or support. Small steps can lead to big changes in wellbeing and motivation.

References

Ashford, S. J., Blatt, R., & Vande Walle, D. (2003). Reflections on the looking glass: A review of research on feedback seeking behavior in organizations. *Journal of Management*, 29, 773–799.

Avolio, B. J., Zhu, W., Koh, W., & Bhatia, P. (2004). Transformational leadership and organizational commitment: Mediating role of psychological empowerment and moderating role of structural distance. *Journal of Organizational Behavior*, 25, 951–968.

Bacharach, S. B., & Bamberger, P. (1995). Beyond situational constraints: Job resources inadequacy and individual performance at work. *Human Resource Management Review*, 5, 79–102.

Bakker, A. B. (2011). An evidence-based model of work engagement. *Current Directions in Psychological Science*, 20, 265–269.

Bakker, A. B., & Demerouti, E. (2007). The Job Demands–Resources model: State of the art. *Journal of Managerial Psychology*, 22, 309–328.

Bakker, A. B., Demerouti, E., & Euwema, M. C. (2005). Job resources buffer the impact of job demands on burnout. *Journal of Occupational Health Psychology*, 10, 170–180.

Bakker, A. B., Demerouti, E., & Sanz-Vergel, A. I. (2014). Burnout and work engagement: The JD-R approach. *Annual Review of Organizational Psychology and Organizational Behavior*, 1, 389–411.

Bakker, A. B., Hakanen, J. J., Demerouti, E., & Xanthopoulou, D. (2007). Job resources boost work engagement, particularly when job demands are high. *Journal of Educational Psychology*, 99, 274–284.

Bakker, A. B., Tims, M., & Derks, D. (2012). Proactive personality and job performance: The role of job crafting and work engagement. *Human Relations*, 65, 1359–1378.

Balogun, J., & Hailey, V. H. (2004). *Exploring Strategic Change*. London: Prentice Hall.

Benner, P., Hooper Kyriakidis, P., & Stannard, D. (2011). *Clinical Wisdom and Interventions in Acute and Critical Care: A Thinking-in-Action Approach*. New York: Springer Publishing Company.

Breevaart, K., Bakker, A. B., & Demerouti, E. (2014). Daily self-management and employee engagement. *Journal of Vocational Psychology*, 84, 31–38.

Breevaart, K., Bakker, A. B., Demerouti, E., Sleebos, D. M., & Maduro, V. (2014). Uncovering the underlying relationship between transformational leaders and followers' task performance. *Journal of Personnel Psychology*, 13, 194–203.

Breevaart, K., Bakker, A. B., Demerouti, E., & van den Heuvel, M. (2015). Leader-member exchange, work engagement, and job performance. *Journal of Managerial Psychology*, 30, 754–770.

Breevaart, K., Bakker, A. B., Hetland, J., Demerouti, E., Olsen, O. K., & Espevik, R. (2014). Daily transactional and transformational leadership and daily employee engagement. *Journal of Occupational and Organizational Psychology*, 87, 138–157.

Briner, R. B., & Reynolds, S. (1999). The costs, benefits, and limitations of organizational level stress interventions. *Journal of Organizational Behavior*, 20, 647–664.

Bond, F. W., & Bunce, D. (2001). Job control mediates change in a work reorganization intervention for stress reduction. *Journal of Occupational Health Psychology*, 6, 290–302.

Carver, C. S., Scheier, M. F., & Weintraub, J. K. (1989). Assessing coping strategies: A theoretically based approach. *Journal of Personality and Social Psychology*, 56, 267–283.

Chu, A. H. C., & Choi, J. N. (2005). Rethinking procrastination: Positive effects of "active" procrastination behavior on attitudes and performance. *Journal of Social Psychology*, 145, 245–264.

Csikszentmihalyi, M., & Nakamura, J. (1989). The dynamics of intrinsic motivation: A study of adolescents. *Research on Motivation and Education*, 3, 45–71.

Demerouti, E. (2014). Design your own job through job crafting. *European Psychologist*, 19, 237–247. doi:10.1027/1016–9040/a000188.

Demerouti, E., Bakker, A. B., & Halbesleben, J. R. B. (2015). Productive and counterproductive job crafting: A daily diary study. *Journal of Occupational Health Psychology*, 457–469.

Demerouti, E., Bakker, A. B., Nachreiner, F., & Schaufeli, W. B. (2000). A model of burnout and life satisfaction among nurses. *Journal of Advanced Nursing*, 32, 454–464.

Demerouti, E., Bakker, A. B., Nachreiner, F., & Schaufeli, W. B. (2001). The Job Demands–Resources model of burnout. *Journal of Applied Psychology*, 86, 499–512.

Demerouti, E., & Cropanzano, R. (2010). From though to action: Employee work engagement and job performance. In: A. B. Bakker & M. P. Leiter (eds.), *Work Engagement: A Handbook of Essential Theory and Research*. Hove, East Sussex: Psychology Press, 147–163.

Demerouti, E., Derks, D., Ten Brummelhuis, L. L., & Bakker, A. B. (2014). New ways of working: Impact on working conditions, work-family balance, and well-being. In: C. Korunka & P. Hoonakker (eds.), *Impact of ICT on Quality of Working Life*. Dordrecht: Springer, 123–141.

Demerouti, E., Van Eeuwijk, E., Snelder, M., & Wild, U. (2011). Assessing the effects of a "personal effectiveness" training on psychological capital, assertiveness and self-awareness using self-other agreement. *Career Development International*, 16, 60–81.

Dubbelt, L., Demerouti, E., & Rispens, S. (May 2015). *Increasing Career Satisfaction, Work Engagement, and Task Performance Through Job Crafting: An Intervention Study*. Paper presented at the 17th Conference of the European Association of Work and Organizational Psychology (EAWOP), Oslo, Norway.

Egan, M., Bambra, C., Petticrew, M., & Whitehead, M. (2009). Reviewing evidence on complex social interventions: Appraising implementation in systemic revies of the health effects of organisational-level workplace interventions. *Journal of Epidemiology & Community Health*, 63, 4–11.

Gordon, H. J., Demerouti, E., Le Blanc, P. M., Bakker, A. B., Bipp, T., & Verhagen, M. A. M. T. (July 2014). *Bottom-up Job (Re)design: Job Crafting Interventions in Healthcare*. Paper presented at the seventh European Conference on Positive Psychology, Amsterdam, The Netherlands.

Grant, A. M., & Parker, S. K. (2009). Redesigning work design theories: The rise of relational and proactive perspectives. *Academy of Management Annals*, 3, 273–331.

Gruys, M. L. (1999). *The Dimensionality of Deviant Employee Performance in the Workplace*. Unpublished doctoral dissertation, University of Minnesota, Minneapolis, MN, US.

Hackman, J. R., & Oldham, G. R. (1980). *Work Redesign*. Reading: Addison-Wesley.

Hobfoll, S. E. (1989). Conservation of resources: A new attempt at conceptualizing stress. *American Psychologist*, 44, 513–524.

Hobfoll, S. E. (2001). The influence of culture, community, and the nest-self in the stress process: Advancing conservation of resources theory. *Applied Psychology: An International Review*, 50, 337–421.

Hobfoll, S. E. (2002). Social and psychological resources and adaptation. *Review of General Psychology*, 6, 307–324.

Hornung, S., Rousseau, D. M., Glaser, J., Angerer, P., & Weigl, M. (2010). Beyond top-down and bottom-up work redesign: Customizing job content through idiosyncratic deals. *Journal of Organizational Behavior*, 31, 187–215.

Houghton, J. D., & Neck, C. P. (2002). The revised self-leadership questionnaire: Testing a hierarchical factor structure for self-leadership. *Journal of Managerial Psychology*, 17, 672–691.

Kolb, A. Y., & Kolb, D. A. (2012). Experiential learning theory. In: N. M. Seel (ed.), *Encyclopedia of the Sciences of Learning*. New York: Springer, 1215–1219.

Kompier, M. A. J., & Kristensen, T. S. (2001). Organizational work stress interventions in a theoretical, methodological and practical context. In: J. Dunham (ed.), *Stress in the Workplace: Past, Present and Future*. Philadelphia: Whurr Publishers, 164–190.

LaMontagne, A. D., Keegel, T., Louie, A. M., Ostry, A., & Landsbergis, P. A. (2007). A systematic review of the job-stress intervention evaluation literature, 1990–2005. *International Journal of Occupational and Environmental Health*, 13, 268–280.

Lazarus, R., & Folkman, S. (1992). *Stress, Appraisal and Coping*. New York: Springer.

Le Blanc, P. M., Hox, J. J., Schaufeli, W. B., Taris, T., & Peeters, M. C. W. (2007). Take care! The evaluation of a team-based burnout intervention program for oncology care providers. *Journal of Applied Psychology*, 92, 213–227.

Manz, C. (1986). Self-Leadership: Toward an expanded theory of self-influence processes in organizations. *The Academy of Management Review*, 11, 585–600.

Meyers, M. C., Van Woerkom, M., & Bakker, A. B. (2013). The added value of the positive: A literature review of positive psychology interventions in organizations. *European Journal of Work and Organizational Psychology*, 22, 618–632.

Muller, J., Hooftmann, W., & Houtman, I. L. D. (2015). *Netherlands: Steady Decline in Job Autonomy*. Loughlinstown: European Foundation for the Improvement of Living and Working Conditions (Eurofound).

Murta, S. G., Sanderson, K., & Oldenburg, B. (2007). Process evaluation in occupational stress management programs: A systematic review. *American Journal of Health Promotion*, 21, 248–254.

Nadin, S. J., Waterson, P. E., & Parker, S. K. (2001). Participation in job redesign: An evaluation of the use of a sociotechnical tool and its impact. *Human Factors and Ergonomics in Manufacturing*, 11, 53–69.

Nielsen, K. (2013). How can we make organizational interventions work? Employees and line managers as actively crafting interventions. *Human Relations*, 66, 1029–1050.

Nielsen, K., Randall, R., & Albertsen, K. (2007). Participants' appraisals of process issues and the effects of stress management interventions. *Journal of Organizational Behavior*, 28, 793–810.

Nielsen, K., Taris, T., & Cox, T. (2010). The future of organizational interventions: Adressing challenges of today's organizations. *Work & Stress*, 24, 219–233.

Oakley, A., Strange, V., Bonell, C., Allen, E., Stephenson, J., & RIPPLE Study Team. (2006). Process evaluation in randomised controlled trials of complex interventions. British Medical Journal, 332, 413–416.

Parker, J. D. A., & Endler, N. S. (1996). Coping and defense: A historical overview. In: M. Zeidner & N. S. Endler (eds.), *Handbook of Coping: Theory, Research, Applications*. Oxford, UK: John Wiley & Sons, 3–23.

Parker, S. K., & Ohly, S. (2008). Job design and work role demands. In: R. Kanfer, G. Chen, & R. D. Pritchard (eds.), *Work Motivation: Past, Present, and Future. SIOP Frontiers Series*, Hillsdale, NJ: Laurence Erlbaum Associates, 233–284.

Petrou, P., Demerouti, E., Peeters, M. C. W., Schaufeli, W. B., & Hetland, J. (2012). Crafting a job on a daily basis: Contextual correlates and the link to work engagement. *Journal of Organizational Behavior*, 33, 1120–1141.

Petrou, P., Demerouti, E., & Schaufeli, W. B. (2015). Job crafting in changing organizations: Antecedents and implications for exhaustion and performance. *Journal of Occupational Health Psychology*, 20, 470–480.

Petrou, P., Demerouti, E., & Schaufeli, W. B. (2016). Crafting the change: The role of employee job crafting behaviors for successful organizational change. *Journal of Management*, advance online publication.

Petrou, P., Demerouti, E., & Xanthopoulou, D. (2017). Regular versus cutback-related change: The role of employee job crafting in organizational change contexts of different nature. *International Journal of Stress Management*, 24, 62–85

Prussia, G. E., Anderson, J. S., & Manz, C. C. (1998). Self-leadership and performance outcomes: The mediating influence of self-efficacy. *Journal of Organizational Behavior*, 19, 523–538.

Randall, R., & Nielsen, K. (2012). Does the intervention fit? An explanatory model of intervention success and failure in complex organizational environments. In: C. Biron, M. Karanika-Murray, & C. L. Cooper (eds.), *Improving Organizational Interventions for Stress and Well-Being: Addressing Process and Context.* London, UK: Routledge, 120–134.

Ryan, R. M., & Deci, E. L. (2000). Self-determination theory and the facilitation of intrinsic motivation, social development, and well-being. *American Psychologist*, 55, 68–78.

Schaufeli, W., & Enzmann, D. (1998). *The Burnout Companion to Study and Practice: A Critical Analysis.* London: Taylor & Francis.

Seligman, M. E. P., Steen, T. A., Park, N., & Peterson, C. (2005). Positive psychology progress: Empirical validation of interventions. *American Psychologist*, 60, 410–421.

Skakon, J., Nielsen, K., Borg, V., & Guzman, J. (2010). Are leaders' well-being, behaviours and style associated with the affective well-being of their employees? A systematic review of three decades of research. *Work & Stress*, 24, 107–139.

Shoss, M. K., Witt, L. A., & Vera, D. (2011). When does adaptive performance lead to higher task performance? *Journal of Organizational Behavior*, 33, 910–924.

Sinclair, R. R., Sears, L. E., Probst, T., & Zajack, M. (2010). A multilevel model of economic stress and employee wellbeing. In: J. Houdmont & S. Leka (eds.), *Contemporary Occupational Health Psychology: Global Perspectives on Research and Practice.* Oxford, UK: Wiley-Blackwell, 1–20.

Tims, M., & Bakker, A. B. (2010). Job crafting: Towards a new model of individual job redesign. *South-African Journal of Industrial Psychology*, 36, 1–9.

Tims, M., Bakker, A. B., & Derks, D. (2012). Development and validation of the job crafting scale. *Journal of Vocational Behavior*, 80, 173–186.

Tims, M., Bakker, A. B., & Derks, D. (2013). The impact of job crafting on job demands, job resources, and well-being. *Journal of Occupational Health Psychology,* 18, 230–240.

Tims, M., Bakker, A. B., & Derks, D. (2015). Job crafting and job performance: A longitudinal study. *European Journal of Work and Organizational Psychology*, 24, 914–928.

Unsworth, K. L., & Mason, C. M. (2012). Help yourself: The mechanisms through which a self-leadership intervention influences strain. *Journal of Occupational Health Psychology*, 17, 235–246.

Vakola, M., Xanthopoulou, D., & Demerouti, E. (2017). Are job crafters prone to embrace a top-down organizational change on a daily basis? The moderating role of influence tactics. Manuscript submitted for publication.

Van den Heuvel, M., Demerouti, E., & Bakker, A. B. (2013). How psychological resources facilitate adaptation to organizational change. *European Journal of Work and Organizational Psychology*, 23, 847–858.

Van den Heuvel, M., Demerouti, E., & Peeters, M. C. W. (2012). Succesvol job craften door middel van een groepstraining [Successfull job crafting with the help of a group training]. In: J. de Jonge & M. C. W. Peeters (eds.), *Scherp in werk: Motivatie, zelfsturing en inzetbaarheid op het werk.* Utrecht: Van Gorcum, 27–49.

Van den Heuvel, M., Demerouti, E., & Peeters, M. C. W. (2015). The job crafting intervention: Effects on job resources, self-efficacy and affective well-being. *Journal of Occupational and Organizational Psychology*, 88, 511–532.

Wikipedia. (n.d.). Resource. Available at: https://en.wikipedia.org/wiki/Resource (accessed 16 March 2016).

Wrzesniewski, A., & Dutton, J. E. (2001). Crafting a job: Revisioning employees as active crafters of their work. *Academy of Management Review*, 26, 179–201.

Yukl, G., Gordon, A., & Taber, T. (2002). A hierarchical taxonomy of leadership behavior: Integrating a half century of behavior research. *Journal of Leadership and Organization Studies*, 9, 15–32.

20

Stress management techniques in the workplace

Oi Ling Siu

Introduction

Stress is a common problem that can affect anyone, anytime. It occurs when the pressure to succeed overtakes one's ability to cope (Cooper & Palmer, 2000). Stress is dependent on individual confidence and experience, along with the ability to handle situations that may seem important or threatening. In contemporary society, workplace stress has progressively become more recognized and been taken more seriously as a risk factor for chronic disease, poor quality of life, and injury (Umanodan et al., 2009). Globalization, technology innovation, work intensification, and other factors have all contributed to increased work pressure and workplace stress. As advocated by Kalliath et al. (2014), there are three main reasons why occupational stress should be addressed: financial reasons, health and performance reasons, and social reasons. Employees' workplace stress creates a significant burden for organizations through costs such as higher absenteeism, lower productivity, higher turnover rates, and health benefit costs (Walinga & Rowe, 2013). Employees experiencing work stress have been shown to develop negative health conditions such as diabetes, increased cholesterol levels, depression, and high blood pressure (Schulz et al., 2012). Furthermore, occupational stress is found to be related to workplace violence such as bullying and harassment. Therefore, it is of utmost importance to cope with workplace stress before more serious consequences arise. Apart from coping with stress at an individual level, stress management in the workplace has gained a lot of attention, since healthy employees are key to business success. This chapter will provide an overview of different stress management techniques and interventions at individual as well as organizational levels.

Stress management interventions

A number of interventions have been developed to help employees cope with work-related stress. Job stress is defined as "a situation wherein job-related factors interact with the worker to change his or her psychological and/or physiological condition such that the person is forced to deviate from normal functioning" (Newman & Beehr, 1979, p. 1). Interventions applicable to coping with job stress are generally broken down into three stages in the stress process: primary, secondary, and tertiary levels of intervention (Murphy, 1988).

Primary prevention is concerned with taking action to reduce or eliminate stressors (i.e., sources of stress) and positively promoting a supportive and healthy work environment. This stress reduction stage is the most proactive approach of stress management interventions.

Secondary prevention is concerned with the prompt detection and management of depression and anxiety by increasing self-awareness and improving stress management skills. This stage involves stress management training.

Tertiary prevention is concerned with the rehabilitation and recovery process of those individuals who have suffered or are suffering from serious ill health as a result of stress. This final stage focuses on counselling and debriefing, and involves employee assistance programs.

To develop an effective and comprehensive organizational policy on stress, employers need to integrate these three approaches. In this chapter, we will present stress management techniques that have been developed to help employees overcome their stress symptoms before they progress and before professional help becomes necessary. The techniques discussed include cognitive behavior therapy, mindfulness-based interventions, relaxation through yoga and meditation, the organizational approach, and the comprehensive approach.

Cognitive behavior therapy

Psychological problems such as stress have been linked to faulty patterns of thinking and behavior (Enright, 1997). In cognitive behavior therapy, therapist and patient together aim to identify patterns of thinking and behavior underlying the patient's problems. Initially used to treat depression, cognitive behavior therapy nowadays addresses a wide range of mental health issues. The main goal of cognitive behavior therapy is to reduce stress by conducting stress management interventions (De Vente, Kamphuis, Emmelkamp, & Blonk, 2008). According to cognitive behavior theory, negative thinking and abnormal behavior do not cause negative psychological symptoms, but instead intensify and maintain emotional problems (Enright, 1997). Therefore, cognitive behavior therapy introduces coping strategies for individuals to adjust their cognition and behavior.

The ABCDE model of stress

The major theory underlying cognitive behavior therapy is the ABCDE model, which is basically an addition to the ABC model put forward and developed by Albert Ellis (Cooper & Palmer, 2000). The ABCDE model of stress is depicted in Figure 20.1.

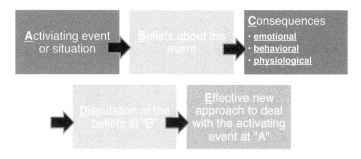

Figure 20.1 The ABCDE model of stress

According to the ABCDE model, individuals experience undesirable *activating* events, which prompt either rational (i.e., healthy and functional) or irrational (i.e., unhealthy and dysfunctional) *beliefs*. Irrational beliefs result in emotional, behavioral and physiological *consequences*. Emotional consequences may include anxiety and fear, behavioral consequences may include aggressiveness, and physiological consequences may include heart conditions. In cognitive behavior therapy an intervention is introduced at this stage to *dispute* clients' irrational beliefs and replace them with *effective* new approaches to deal with the activating event, thereby reducing individuals' level of stress (Watson & Dodd, 1984).

Research support for cognitive behavior therapy

Flaxman and Bond studied how employee stress management training improved health behavior (Flaxman & Bond, 2010). They provided three treatment categories: time management training, muscular relaxation training, and individual counseling or group therapy. Their results showed that cognitive behavior therapy benefited employees who were initially distressed, especially benefiting initially highly distressed participants (Flaxman & Bond, 2010).

Further support for the effectiveness of cognitive behavior therapies was provided by Willert, Thulstrup, Hertz, and Bonde (2009). The researchers conducted group-based interventions, including an introduction of the therapy, dealing with dysfunctional thinking, and teaching of effective communication techniques. For ethical reasons, the researchers allowed the wait-list control group to join the treatments, thereby flawing the comparison. Another methodological issue with this research was that only one follow-up was conducted three months after the treatment. Thus, although positive treatment results were found, the gap between treatment and follow-up was too short to determine long-term effects. Still, the study is another indication for the usefulness of cognitive behavior therapy.

Another study, conducted by De Vente et al. (2008), investigated five treatment modules for work-related stress complaints. The researchers provided treatments to employees on sickness leave due to work-related stress. Work-related stress was defined as a state caused by job stressors and included complaints such as distress and burnout resulting from anxiety, depression, exhaustion, and other factors (De Vente et al., 2008). In this study, the researchers applied influential theory, which is similar to transactional theory, stating that the environment and personal characteristics influence the method an individual may use when faced with stressful situations (De Vente et al., 2008). Those methods include social and problem-solving skills: the better those skills are, the shorter the duration of stress and the fewer related problems. This study provided a series of promising treatment modules aiming to reduce stress by educating patients how to cope with stress through cognitive-behavioral interventions that should be further investigated in future research. Treatments included the following five modules (De Vente et al., 2008):

- *Psychoeducation* informs the individual on how certain lifestyles and habits can lead to increased stress-related problems.
- *Cognitive restructuring* pinpoints any negative emotions or thoughts and attempts to alter people's mindset.
- *Time management* and *goal setting* help individuals create strategies to restructure their mindsets in both the long- and short-term.
- *Assertiveness skills training* improves social skills and teaches participants to say "no," thereby showing them better ways of handling social situations.

- *Evaluation* and *relapse prevention* refer to the individual's capability of handling the identified stress factors and the determination to conduct solid action to prevent negative stress responses from further worsening or reoccurring.

Although the researchers could not find support for the effectiveness of cognitive behavior therapy in dealing with work-related stress, research support for one of their five treatment modules, psychoeducation, was provided by Shimazu, Kawakami, Irimajiri, Sakamoto, and Amano (2005). They designed a website for employees with the intention of making psychoeducation available in a convenient, geographically independent, and inexpensive way to help individuals cope with occupational stress. The goal of this study was to observe the effect of psychoeducation towards self-efficacy, problem-solving behavior, stress responses, and job satisfaction. Topics included cognitive preparation and motivation, skill acquisition and rehearsal, and application (Shimazu et al., 2005). After each unit of learning, questions had to be answered correctly in order to move on. Results indicated an increase in self-efficacy and job satisfaction; however, only short-term effects were measured and hence long-term effectiveness still needs to be assessed.

Meditation

Another technique that has been proposed to help employees manage work-related stress is meditation. Meditation aims to decrease tension and stress of individuals by teaching them the idea of "letting go" (Richardson & Rothstein, 2008, p. 88), allowing them to shift their attention from sources of stress and to put them aside. Meditation utilizes passive techniques focusing on the removal of certain emotions and behaviors that may further coincide with stress and create health problems (Richardson & Rothstein, 2008).

Yoga is a special form of movement-based meditation that has been introduced as a relaxation technique for stress management (Edwards, Mischoulon, Rapaport, Stussman, & Weber, 2013; Kabat-Zinn, 2009). Hartfiel, Havenhand, Khalsa, Clarke, and Krayer (2011) examined how yoga may affect the wellbeing and resilience of stressed individuals in their workplace. For their study they recruited a small, self-selected sample of 17 females and three males. In this research, *wellbeing* was defined as individual behavior that shows positive work engagement, productiveness, and pleasure, while *stress* was defined as the incapability of individuals to manage their wellbeing in a difficult situation. *Resiliency* referred to individuals' capability of achieving success, though faced with pressure and difficulties. The sample was divided into one group participating in yoga and a wait-list control group. Dru Yoga style classes were conducted weekly for six weeks, each class lasting 60 minutes. This type of yoga targets flowing movements, directs breathing, and introduces relaxation techniques that require visualization (Hartfiel et al., 2011). Within each class, the practice was broken down into four target areas:

- activation exercises
- energy-block release sequences
- postures
- relaxation

After six weeks of training, the researchers found significant differences between the two groups. Those who participated in yoga showed improvements in most of the measures of the Profile of Mood States – Bipolar (POMS-Bi) and Inventory of Positive Psychological Attitudes (IPPA). Measures that indicated the effectiveness of yoga included clear-mindedness, composure, elation, energy, and confidence. Additionally, findings indicated a positive effect towards participants' work behavior and attitude when facing stressful and threatening situations. Therefore, this study showed that yoga was indeed effective in terms of improving wellbeing and resilience to stress, even if it was a short practice. In order to proceed with this technique, it is important for employers to encourage this practice, whether it is sponsoring employees with classes at other facilities or to provide classes for employees at the workplace.

Although Hartfiel et al.'s (2011) study did include posture, they did not specify how posture promotes relaxation. This was examined by Melville, Chang, Colagiuri, Marshall, and Cheema (2012). Participants were instructed to follow yoga postures for 15 minutes. A second group performed guided meditation practice for the same amount of time while seated in the office workspace. A third group was included as control group. The researchers measured perceived stress, blood pressure, respiration rate, and heart rate. Participants who practiced yoga postures and who practiced meditation showed significant decreases in perceived levels of stress compared to the control group. In addition, the meditation group showed significant improvements in terms of blood pressure as compared to the control group. The respiration rate decreased similarly for both yoga postures and meditation groups, while it increased for the control group compared to the yoga group. Finally, the yoga posture group showed increased heart rate, whereas the meditation group showed decreased heart rate compared to the control group. Overall, no significant difference was found between the effects of yoga postures and meditation. However, results indicated that both techniques were effective in reducing and improving physiological and psychological factors causing stress.

Mindfulness

Mindfulness-based interventions have been increasingly popular in organizational settings. They are believed to aid individuals who are chronically suffering from stress and distress in their workplace. *Mindfulness* conveys the meaning of "to see with discernment" (Shapiro, Astin, Bishop, & Cordova, 2005, p. 165). It allows individuals to be in the present moment without any thoughts or feelings towards the situation, to remain in a calm state without making any judgments (Shapiro et al., 2005). Mindfulness engages the individual mentally in terms of how to react to stressful situations by providing healthier coping strategies outside of negative personal thoughts, feelings, and emotions.

Mindfulness-based interventions have been incorporated into several treatments for mental and physical health (Virgili, 2015). Mindfulness-based stress reduction (MBSR) is one of the most well-known interventions, developed from the traditional Buddhist mindfulness meditation. MBSR normally takes place in an eight-week duration with two hours of interaction per week, followed by six hours of silent retreat, and 45-minute sessions at home (six days per week) for formal and informal mindfulness meditation. The traditional MBSR provides instructions on formal mindfulness practices, which include sitting meditation, waking meditation, mindful yoga, and body scan. Additionally, there are sessions that help apply the skills to everyday situations and threats being faced.

MBSR has also been applied to health care professionals (Shapiro et al., 2005). Although health care professionals help clients with health problems, they may face severe stress issues themselves. Professionals who are impacted by stress may have higher chances of depression, lower rates of job satisfaction, lower engagement, and distress. Shapiro et al. (2005) used MBSR in a study designed to determine its short-term effects on reducing stress in health care professionals. The intervention was designed to help professionals become aware of their thoughts, feelings, and body sensations. The program included one session per week, with eight two-hour sessions in total. The mindfulness technique was broken down into four procedures:

- Sitting meditation: focuses on breathing while being aware of thoughts, emotions, and body sensations
- Body scan: moves the attention from toes to head, analyzing the different sensations
- Hatha yoga: a practice composed of stretches and posture awareness that produces a structured and strong musculoskeletal system
- Three-minute breathing space: focuses on breathing and the current state

Comparison of participants before and after treatment indicated that the eight-week MBSR program was effective in reducing participants' stress. It showed increases in quality of life and self-compassion, along with reduced job burnout and psychological distress. It also showed improvement in job satisfaction, which is likely to improve health care professionals' work engagement and also to benefit clients. However, no significant difference was found between participants and the control group, which might be due to the small sample size. Still, the technique is promising in yielding significant improvements in future studies if larger sample sizes are examined.

While Shapiro et al. (2005) focused on general health professionals, Cohen-Katz, Wiley, Capuano, Baker, and Shapiro (2005) investigated the effects of MBSR for nurses, specifically in regards to stress and burnout. The results are summarized in Table 20.1. Taken together, the findings indicate that MBSR was successful in decreasing burnout and psychological distress while increasing quality of life and self-compassion for the nurses.

Another profession prone to stress is teaching. Teachers have to balance managing the behavior of children along with providing academic guidance to them. Due to the pressure of engaging in the classroom, stress may negatively impact the productiveness and effectiveness of teachers. Years of stress piled up due to factors such as ineffective time management and inappropriate

Table 20.1 The effects of MBSR for nurses

Measure	Measured Variables	Findings: Pre- vs. Post- Intervention	Findings: Treatment vs. Control Group
Maslach Burnout Inventory	Burnout	Decrease	Negative trend, but no significant difference
Perceived Stress Scale	Perceived stress	Decrease	significant decrease for treatment over control group
Brief Symptom Inventor	Psychological distress	Decrease	Negative trend, but no significant difference
Mindfulness Attention Awareness Scale	Mindfulness awareness and attention	Increase	No significant difference
Self-Compassion Scale	Self-compassion	Increase	Significant increase for treatment group over control group
Satisfaction With Life Scale	Life Satisfaction	Increase	Positive trend, no significant difference

student behavior, among others, may easily result in burnout. Thus, it is important to decrease teachers' stress and burnout, since they control the classroom and the wellbeing of students both academically and socially. It is important for teachers to face lower emotional exhaustion and psychological distress, while showing higher engagement, in order to provide students with the best teaching and support. In the study conducted by Flook, Goldberg, Pinger, Bonus, and Davidson (2013), instead of the general MBSR used to apply mindfulness skills, a modified MBSR program was implemented. The modified program included a training that was specifically designed for teachers, requiring additional sessions, and including flexible practice times as well as applicable activities developed to meet the needs of specific schools (Flook et al., 2013). The effectiveness of mindfulness applicable to teachers was measured by psychological distress, mindfulness, self-compassion, burnout, and teacher classroom behavior. After the intervention, it became evident that teachers' mindfulness and self-compassion increased, while psychological symptoms and burnout decreased; in addition, strong improvements in their teaching behavior emerged. Teachers who did not undergo treatment were predicted to continue to experience physiological stress, as was indeed indicated by their low morning cortisol levels. Moreover, teachers who did not receive treatment tended to show lower modes of accomplishment due to stress, reducing their motivation to engage in the classroom.

Siu, Cooper, and Phillips (2014) reported two secondary intervention studies in Hong Kong that focused on stress management and adopted a positive psychology approach. The first intervention study was conducted among health care workers to reduce burnout and enhance work wellbeing (job satisfaction, physical/psychological symptoms) and positive emotions. A one-group pretest-posttest design was adopted and 1,034 health care employees were recruited from hospitals to participate in a two-day training course held in 17 separate classes. The results obtained from paired t-tests consistently demonstrated an improvement in work-related wellbeing and a reduction in burnout after the training. The second intervention study was designed to investigate whether the improvements were specifically caused by the intervention. This second study adopted a quasi-experimental method with a control group, also using a pretest-posttest design, and with an additional aim of improving the recovery experiences. The experimental group comprised 50 teachers, and the control group comprised 48. The results show that teachers in the experimental group scored significantly higher in recovery experiences (particularly mastery) compared to those in the control group.

Recently, based on self-regulation theory, Long and Christian (2015) examined whether and how work-related self-regulatory variables such as mindfulness buffer retaliatory responses to perceived injustice at work. Their study, examining both undergraduate students in a lab setting and employees in an online survey, showed that mindfulness mitigated the process underlying the injustice–retaliation relationship. Specifically, mindfulness buffered the influence of injustice on rumination and outward negative emotions, which alternatively lead to reduced retaliation.

Furthermore, a pilot study by Cruess et al. (2015) explored whether a brief stress management session would reduce acute distress and buffer physiological responses – i.e., salivary assays of cortisol (sCORT) and alpha-amylase (sAA) – to a social stress test. In this study 120 healthy young adults were randomly assigned to one of three conditions: a brief enhanced-mindfulness intervention, a somatic-relaxation intervention, and an attention-only control group. Afterwards all participants underwent a standardized social stress test. Both subjective and physiological measures were assessed at three time points: before the intervention, after the intervention, and after the social stress test. Results showed that one session of stress management strategies decreased acute subjective distress and immediately buffered physiological responses to social stress.

Multicomponent intervention

While many studies focus on one intervention, the combination of two or more methods may be most effective in certain situations. This type of intervention presented here is a combination of passive and active coping skills to achieve and maintain a balance in the mind-body system (van der Klink, Blonk, Schene, & Van Dijk, 2001). Achieving psychological and physical balance is important because both the brain and the body work towards improving the person as a whole. Granath, Ingvarsson, von Thiele, and Lundberg (2006) incorporated two methods:

1   Yoga: back treatment, basic movements, balancing body, energy, and mind, and to release tension on shoulders, neck, and head (conducted weekly)
2   Cognitive behavioral program: provided knowledge on relaxation, discussion of home assignments that included case studies and daily drills, psychoeducation and management techniques, such as problem solving, goal setting, and time management

The researchers measured psychological and physiological states before and after the treatment among 33 employees (26 women and 7 men) from a Swedish company. Participants were randomly assigned to either the yoga or cognitive behavior therapy condition, in either a mixed or all-female group (totaling four groups). Psychological states included stress and behavior, anger control, and quality of life, while for physiological state heart rate and blood pressure were measured.

Overall, both interventions showed similar results, with neither one being more effective than the other, supporting both stress management interventions. Therefore, it is advisable to use both techniques together since they focus on different aspects of the individual. The combination of mental relaxation (cognitive behavior therapy) and physical relaxation (yoga) may lead to better results and would be important to further explore in future research.

Another multicomponent intervention was examined by Umanodan et al. (2009). The first set of variables focused on stress and self-efficacy. Umanodan et al. defined self-efficacy as an individual's belief in his or her ability in terms of achievement and success. The second set of variables measured psychological distress, physical complaints, and job performance. The intervention was divided into six sessions:

1   Progressive muscular relaxation training and introduction of psychological stress theory: how relaxing one's muscles can ease tension and anxiety; highlighting potential stress factors and the importance of coping
2   Time management: how to properly schedule work within working hours
3   Goal setting: teaching participants to work towards a small goal one step at a time, instead of rushing towards the big goal that may eventually cause stress if unable to achieve
4   Communication skills: being able to express their own thoughts and feelings through proper communication with other individuals
5   Causal attributions: how to deal with negative views on problems
6   Irrational-dysfunctional belief: modification of given negative evaluations

Results indicated significant effects for the first set of variables focusing on stress and self-efficacy, and none for the second set measuring psychological distress, physical complaints, and job performance. Findings suggest that the multicomponent intervention can effectively improve knowledge and professional efficacy, although job control appears to act as a modifying factor.

Furthermore, the intervention showed promising results in reducing psychological distress and improving job performance.

In order to target both mind and body, Wolever et al. (2012) designed a stress reduction intervention combining both a Viniyoga stress reduction program and two versions of MBSR. The intervention was implemented among a total of 239 employees of a US-based insurance carrier. Participants were divided among four categories: Viniyoga (90 participants), in-class and online MBSR (96 participants), and control (53 participants). The Viniyoga stress reduction program ran for 12 weeks, with one-hour sessions per week. It aimed at reducing stress by teaching *asanas* (yogic postures), breathing techniques, and relaxation techniques for self-practice at home (Wolever et al., 2012). Half of the 90 participants in the yoga condition were given a DVD for self-practice at home, however the data indicated no difference in results compared to those who did not receive a DVD, which is why the groups were later combined for analysis. The two mindfulness programs were identical in content and designed to influence individuals to be nonjudgmental based on understanding their own feelings, thoughts, and emotions. The first 12-week Mindfulness at Work program was conducted for a total of 14 hours (Wolever et al., 2012). The second program, conducted virtually, also took place for 12 weeks with one-hour sessions per week and a two-hour intensive session during week 10 (Wolever et al., 2012). Overall, results showed that participants in the mind-body intervention had reduced stress, better quality of sleep, and an improved heart-rhythm coherence ratio of heart-rate variability, indicated by measuring the pulse rate. The in-class versus online mindfulness programs produced equivalent results. Though the results were significant, further studies are needed to determine whether the interventions can reduce other outcomes like resignation and sick leave.

Organizational approach

While the interventions presented this far targeted individual problems, the intervention introduced now targets the organization as a whole, suggesting that the atmosphere of the workplace can also affect the individual's mental health. Basically, organizations should target stressor reduction, adopting a primary intervention approach designed to reduce or eliminate stressors. Instead of focusing on individual approaches that do not provide long-term results, this intervention focuses on the environment the individual is a part of on a daily basis (Dollard & Gordon, 2014). At the first stage, diagnosis of stressors should be conducted. Reflecting on how employees feel can be a first step in adjusting organizational development to limit employees' negative perception of changes. Elo, Ervasti, Kuosma, and Mattila (2008) conducted a study that attempted to reduce stressors at the workplace. This organizational intervention included five steps:

1   Participants provide feedback for the researchers on the work environment via a survey in order to have a brief assessment of the present situation.
2   Based on the feedback, one-time five-hour training sessions for supervisors are designed and conducted. This training includes group discussions on how to avoid negative feedback and to come up with possible solutions.
3   Work conferences are conducted that introduce methods on goal setting, future development, and evaluation of the current actions. This first session lasted two workdays, with a half day to follow up.
4   Leadership training for the supervisors are conducted, which takes seven and a half days. Including the management level is important for the success of the program, since management provides guidance and support for employees in terms of managing stress and burnout.

5   The last step is optional for participants, including lectures and guided discussions on topics related to physical exercise and well-being, plus recreational excursions.

Results did not show an improvement of the work environment as hypothesized. Some suggestions to the management necessary to improve the work environment were lower work demands and improvement of their decision-making skills. Throughout the study, communication between employees did improve, but no significant changes were found in the wellbeing of employees (Elo et al., 2008, p. 20).

Employee assistance programs (EAPs) adopting a tertiary intervention approach are another organizational strategy, one that aims to treat stressed employees to recover and resume duty. EAPs focus on counselling and debriefing services to employees who are experiencing or have experienced stress.

Comprehensive approach

Organizational health practitioners and work stress researchers believe that interventions designed for individuals, such as counseling and meditation, have overlooked the possibility that job conditions and work environments may also cause stress. Focusing on the individual may be misunderstood as blaming the individual instead of uncovering root causes of stress like insufficient work training or negative management productivity (Noblet & LaMontagne, 2006). It has also been implied that many significant results found in favor of individual interventions reduce stress in the short term only, while in the long term there are no beneficial effects for organizations.

In their theoretical paper, Noblet and LaMontagne (2006) introduced a comprehensive stress prevention program targeting organizational factors and individual characteristics that contribute to the experience of stress for employees. Following DeFrank and Cooper's (1987) typology of stress interventions, Noblet and LaMontagne (2006) classified interventions according to organizational level:

1   Individual-level intervention: helps individuals enrich their knowledge by introducing coping strategies relevant to stress-related situations, includes meditation and yoga to help relax the body and mind, and support with time management and future goals.
2   Combination of the individual and organization-based measures: includes relationships amongst colleagues, workplace environment, and role clarification (Noblet & LaMontagne, 2006). Problems have to be encountered before the solutions can be implemented.
3   Physical, organizational, and social environments: modifications to prevent increased stress.

According to Noblet and LaMontage (2006), benefits of the comprehensive stress prevention program include positive outcomes for the individual (e.g., in terms of higher work engagement and job satisfaction) and for the organization (e.g., improved job performance and fewer sick leaves). In order to reduce employee stress, it is important to consider both the individual and the direct impacts of working conditions on health as well as employees' ability to live a "healthy" lifestyle.

Regarding organization-based interventions, two fundamental models are Karasek and Theorell's Demand-Control-Support (DCS) model and Siergest's Effort-Reward Imbalance (ERI) model (Noblet & LaMontagne, 2006). DCS measures job control and social support to determine job performance and impact on health, while ERI determines the relationship between the effort given and the gains to be received.

These models were the theoretical bases for Limm et al.'s (2011) study, which included 154 lower- and middle-level managers from an international manufacturing plant in Germany. This sample group was composed of 99% males, who were divided into an intervention (75 participants) and a control group (79 participants). The intervention designed for this group specifically targeted four items:

- improve employee ability to label stressors;
- improve employee ability to handle stressful situations;
- be able to impact the work environment;
- create a mutual bond between the employees to support each other.

The intervention consisted of eight group-orientated teaching units lasting 90 minutes each over the course of two consecutive days. Three to six months after the initial training, two additional sessions of 180 minutes each were held to refresh what had previously been taught. In those sessions, participants completed empathy exercises during which they were asked to remember individual situations in which they experienced workplace stress and share them with the group. Working together, the group then searched for solutions. During this group process, the experienced trainer introduced several coping tools, such as how to deal with negative emotions and interpersonal conflict. Results showed a greater reduction of self-reported stress reactivity and sympathetic nervous system activation for the intervention as compared to the control group. Differences in cortisol levels could not be documented. The intervention group showed a trend of reduced anxiety and depression, though results were not significant. Positive effects in terms of ERI and mental health parameters were still present in the intervention group one year later.

Summary evaluation on stress management studies

Most of the studies that have been introduced in this chapter have the common problem of small sample size, which should be addressed in future research. Sample sizes have been moderately small and taken from a small percentage of the larger population. In order to achieve more accurate results, researchers should examine broader samples for their studies. For example, instead of focusing on teachers or nurses in one community, using a national sample of teachers and nurses will generate a well-balanced set of data. Studies should also choose a balanced sample with an equal amount of female and male participants, since results may differ by gender. Most of the studies in this review were conducted in person, however the studies that were conducted online showed promising results. Online intervention programs are applicable to different schedules and convenient for participants with geographical limitations. Therefore, programs of this type can offer an effective, yet cost-efficient solution for individuals and organizations. Given these promising results, online interventions should be considered by health insurance companies as a more affordable, yet potentially equally effective option for their customers. Though the main goal is to reduce stressors, this is only possible if the intervention is affordable for the majority of employees.

Yoga was found to be a successful intervention that helped the body and mind relax through specific practices (e.g., Hartfiel et al., 2011). The stretching techniques appear to help participants let go of their stress and put it aside. However, yoga interventions last only for a certain number of weeks and researchers cannot influence who will continue practicing yoga. Some may decide to stop after the treatment because they already feel improvement, but that may cause relapse. Since it is important for the techniques to be continued, providing yoga classes for a company or workplace may be a solution. Oftentimes, the study results provided were collected pre- and posttreatment, which indicates only the improvements for that short period of time. Thus, data should be collected after a longer period of time to determine whether the treatment was actually effective for those who decide to continue with yoga practices and for those who chose to stop, or whether it was only efficient for the short duration of the treatment. Another issue for yoga interventions was that a handful of the participants who agreed to take part in the study wanted to participate in yoga prior to the initiation of the study; therefore, it is a possibility that their interest in yoga generated the predicted results. If there were a balance between those who want to do yoga and those who do not, the results would potentially be more accurate. Finally, some studies like Hatfield et al. (2011) were limited in that a specific gender was overrepresented in their sample (i.e., in this case females). For future studies, it is important to have an equal amount of both genders as participants since male participants may generate different results compared to females.

Mindfulness-based intervention has shown positive results in decreasing factors such as burnout, psychological distress, and increasing self-compassion levels. Mindfulness is not a one-step procedure; it requires determination and discipline along with the right attitude in order to succeed. It is a useful practice that should continue posttreatment in order to obtain the best results. The modified MBSR (mMBSR) showed significant results amongst teachers. Further, the continuation of the mMBSR intervention was believed to positively impact the development of teachers (Flook et al., 2013). The healthier the teachers, the more beneficial it is for the students in the classroom. While attempting to improve the wellbeing of teachers, it will also help if students receive a brief training on how they can help change the classroom environment as well. Additionally, given the positive results from mMBSR for teachers, other forms of mMBSR should be created for different professionals to enhance their work behavior, thoughts, feelings, and emotions in order to contribute to a better environment and atmosphere for those around. Mindfulness-based intervention is also cost-effective and affordable for most organizations. However, most studies have shown the short-term effects of MBSR and have not investigated followup assessments over a longer period of time. Results were significant for those who participated in mindfulness right after the treatment, but it is uncertain how long it will last and whether continuing this treatment is necessary.

A recommendation from Limm's study (2011) was to combine the individual behavior approach with the organizational approach. In addition to improving individual wellbeing, facilitating communication between employees is also extremely important. More positive interactions between employees will create a better working environment for them. In addition, encouraging social bonds within the workplace will allow employees to positively encourage and support one another if any stressors occur. Also, similar to other studies, a longer follow-up is necessary to determine long-term effects. If these interventions are unsuccessful in the long run, it is necessary to modify current interventions until they successfully help reduce stress in the workplace, and to prevent mental health issues from worsening. However, neither Limm et al.'s (2011) study nor Wolever et al.'s (2012) study found significant reductions in depressive symptoms among affected individuals. Mino, Babazono, Tsuda, and Yasuda (2006) found support for the effectiveness of cognitive behavior therapy and suggest that successful reduction of symptoms depends on the specific situation in which the intervention is used.

Conclusion

Stress is a serious issue for both employees and organizations, and it cannot be neglected. It is important to aid stressed individuals by teaching them coping strategies in order to prevent their mental health from deteriorating. Individuals should be supported in learning how to deal with stress by changing their behavior as well as dysfunctional attitudes and beliefs. Stress should not be dealt with only when it becomes noticeable, because by then it has already affected the individual and possibly the organization. Therefore, it is necessary for employers to encourage their employees to manage their stress well by providing workshops that help them to acknowledge stress prior to noticing symptoms. The main interventions introduced in the literature review were cognitive behavior therapy, mindfulness-based interventions, relaxation through yoga and meditation, organizational approach, and the comprehensive approach. Different techniques may be more appropriate in terms of guiding individuals to prevent psychological and physical illnesses depending on the situation and the level of stress being faced. However, it is most ideal to combine individual approaches with organizational approaches to target the body and mind together. The best results include helping the individual, while targeting the workplace environment as a large contributor to stress. Overall, acknowledging the importance of dealing with stress and implementing measures to prevent negative consequences is key.

References

Cohen-Katz, J., Wiley, D. S., Capuano, T., Baker, D. M., & Shapiro, S. (2005). The effects of mindfulness-based stress reduction on nurse stress and burnout, Part II: A quantitative and qualitative study. *Holistic Nursing Practice*, 19, 26–35.

Cooper, C. L., & Palmer, S. (2000). *Conquer Your Stress*. London: Chartered Institute of Personnel and Development.

Cruess, D. G., Finitsis, D. J., Smith, A., Goshe, B. M., Burnham, K., Burbridge, C., & O'Leary, K. (2015). Brief stress management reduces acute distress and buffers physiological response to a social stress test. *International Journal of Stress Management*, 22, 270–286.

DeFrank, R. S., & Cooper, C. L. (1987). Worksite stress management interventions: Their effectiveness and conceptualisation. *Journal of Managerial Psychology*, 2, 4–10.

De Vente, W., Kamphuis, J. H., Emmelkamp, P. M., & Blonk, R. W. (2008). Individual and group cognitive-behavioural treatment for work-related stress complaints and sickness absence: A randomized controlled trial. *Journal of Occupational Health Psychology*, 13, 214–225.

Dollard, M. F., & Gordon, J. A. (2014). Evaluation of a participatory risk management work stress intervention. *International Journal of Stress Management*, 21, 27–42.

Edwards, E., Mischoulon, D., Rapaport, M., Stussman, B., & Weber, W. (2013). Building an evidence base in complementary and integrative healthcare for child and adolescent psychiatry. *Child and adolescent psychiatric clinics of North America*, 22, 509–529.

Elo, A. L., Ervasti, J., Kuosma, E., & Mattila, P. (2008). Evaluation of an organizational stress management program in a municipal public works organization. *Journal of Occupational Health Psychology*, 13, 10–23.

Enright, S. J. (1997). Cognitive behaviour therapy – Clinical applications. *British Medical Journal*, 314, 1811–1816.

Flaxman, P. E., & Bond, W. F. (2010). Worksite stress management training: Moderated effects and clinical significance. *Journal of Occupational Health Psychology*, 15, 347–355.

Flook, L., Goldberg, S. B., Pinger, L., Bonus, K., & Davidson, R. J. (2013). Mindfulness for teachers: A pilot study to assess effects on stress, burnout, and teaching efficacy. *Mind, Brain and Education*, 7, 182–195.

Granath, J., Ingvarsson, S., von Thiele, U., & Lundberg, U. (2006). Stress management: A randomized study of cognitive behavioural therapy and yoga. *Cognitive Behaviour Therapy*, 35, 3–10.

Hartfiel, N., Havenhand, J., Khalsa, S. B., Clarke, G., & Krayer, A. (2011). The effectiveness of yoga for the improvement of well-being and resilience to stress in the workplace. *Scandinavian Journal of Work, Environment & Health*, 1, 70–76.

Kabat-Zinn, J. (2009). *Full catastrophe living: Using the wisdom of your body and mind to face stress, pain, and illness*. Crystal Lake, IL: Delta Publishing Company.

Kalliath, T., Brough, P., O'Driscoll, M., Manimala, M., Siu, O. L., & Parker, S. (2014). *Organizational Behaviour: An Organizational Psychology Perspective for the Asia Pacific*. North Ryde: McGraw-Hill Education.

Limm, H., Gündel, H., Heinmüller, M., Marten-Mittag, B., Nater, U. M., Siegrist, J., & Angerer, P. (2011). Stress management interventions in the workplace improve stress reactivity: A randomized controlled trial. *Occupational and Environmental Medicine*, 68, 126–133.

Long, E. C., & Christian, M. S. (2015). Mindfulness buffers retaliatory responses to injustice: A regulatory approach. *Journal of Applied Psychology*, 100, 1409–1422.

Melville, G. W., Chang, D., Colagiuri, B., Marshall, P. W., & Cheema, B. S. (2012). Fifteen minutes of chair-based yoga postures or guided meditation performed in the office can elicit a relaxation response. *Evidence-Based Complementary Alternative Medicine*, 2012, 1–9.

Mino, Y., Babazono, A., Tsuda, T., & Yasuda, N. (2006). Can stress management at the workplace prevent depression? A randomized controlled trial. *Psychotherapy and Psychosomatics*, 75, 177–182.

Murphy, R. (1988). *Social Closure: The Theory of Monopolization and Exclusion*. Oxford: Oxford University Press.

Newman, J. E., & Beehr, T. A. (1979). Personal and organizational strategies for handling job stress: A review of research and opinion. *Personnel Psychology*, 32, 1–43.

Noblet, A., & LaMontagne, A. D. (2006). The role of workplace health promotion in addressing job stress. *Health Promotion International*, 21, 346–353.

Richardson, K. M., & Rothstein, H. R. (2008). Effects of occupational stress management intervention programs: A meta-analysis. *Journal of Occupational Health Psychology*, 13, 69–90.

Schulz, A. J., Mentz, G., Lachance, L., Johnson, J., Gaines, C., & Israel, B. A. (2012). Associations between socioeconomic status and allostatic load: Effects of neighborhood poverty and tests of mediating pathways. *American Journal of Public Health*, 102, 1706–1714.

Shapiro, S. L., Astin, J. A., Bishop, R. S., & Cordova, M. (2005). Mindfulness-based stress reduction for health care professionals: Results from a randomized trial. *International Journal of Stress Management*, 12, 164–176.

Shimazu, A., Kawakami, N., Irimajiri, H., Sakamoto, M., & Amano, S. (2005). Effects of web-based psychoeducation on self-efficacy, problem solving behaviour, stress responses and job satisfaction among workers: A controlled clinical trial. *Journal of Occupational Health Psychology*, 47, 405–413.

Siu, O. L., Cooper, C. L., & Phillips, D. R. (2014). Intervention studies on enhancing work well-being, reducing burnout, and improving recovery experiences among Hong Kong health care workers and teachers. *Special Issue of International Journal of Stress Management*, 21, 69–84.

Umanodan, R., Kobayashi, Y., Nakamura, M., Kotaoka-Higashiguchi, K., Kawakami, N., & Shimazu, A. (2009). Effects of a worksite stress management training program with six short-hour sessions: A controlled trial among Japanese employees. *Journal of Occupational Health Psychology*, 51, 294–302.

Van der Klink, J., Blonk, R. W., Schene, A. H., & Van Dijk, F. (2001). The benefits of interventions for work-related stress. *American Journal of Public Health*, 91, 270–274.

Virgili, M. (2015). Mindfulness-based interventions reduce psychological distress in working adults: A meta-analysis of intervention studies. *Mindfulness*, 6, 326–337.

Walinga, J., & Rowe, W. (2013). Transforming stress in complex work environments: Exploring the capabilities of middle managers in the public sector. *International Journal of Workplace Health Management*, 6, 66–88.

Watson, A. K., & Dodd, C. H. (1984). Alleviating communication apprehension through rational emotive therapy: A comparative evaluation. *Communication Education*, 33, 257–266.

Willert, M. V., Thulstrup, A. M., Hertz, J., & Bonde, J. P. (2009). Changes in stress and coping from a randomized controlled trial of a threemonth stress management intervention. *Scandinavian Journal Work, Environment & Health*, 35, 145–152.

Wolever, R. Q., Bobinet, K. J., McCabe, K., Mackenzie, E. R., Fekete, E., Kusnick, C. A., & Baime, M. (2012). Effective and viable mind-body stress reduction in the workplace: A randomized controlled trial. *Journal of Occupational Health Psychology*, 17, 246–258.

21

Physical activity and workplace wellbeing

Gemma Ryde and Helen Elizabeth Brown

Objectives

After reading this chapter you should be able to answer the following questions:

- What is physical activity?
- How much physical activity should we do?
- Why is physical activity important for wellbeing?
- What are current workplace physical activity trends?
- Why is physically activity important for workplace wellbeing?
- How can we influence physical activity at work?

Physical activity and wellbeing

This first section looks at questions relating to overall physical activity and wellbeing such as what physical activity is, how much physical activity should we do, and why physical activity is important for wellbeing. The second section then goes on to discuss such issues in relation to the workplace.

What is physical activity?

Physical activity is a behavior defined as any bodily movement produced by skeletal muscle action that results in increased energy expenditure above those of resting levels (Caspersen, Powell, & Christenson, 1985). Physical activity includes a wide range of activities from walking and playing tennis to gardening and vacuuming, and typically occurs in four main contexts: occupational (as part of your job), leisure (in your free time), transport (walking or bicycling to and from places), and domestic/home-based activities (household tasks and gardening) (Baecke, Burema, & Frijters, 1982).

Exercise is a subcategory of physical activity that is planned, structured, and repetitive and is performed with the aim of improving or maintaining physical fitness, such as going for a 20-minute run every morning before work (Caspersen et al., 1985). The "dose" of physical activity, or exercise, is described by the characteristics of frequency (number of sessions), duration (length of the activity), and intensity (effort associated with the activity) (Garber et al., 2011; Nelson et al., 2007). The terms *moderate* and *vigorous* are often used to describe the intensity of physical activity. Moderate activity is conceptualized as getting warmer, breathing harder with your heart beating faster, but still able to carry on a conversation, whilst vigorous activity is described as getting warmer and breathing much harder with your heart beating rapidly, making it more difficult to carry on a conversation (Garber et al., 2011; Nelson et al., 2007).

Physical fitness is an attained state consisting of a set of attributes that are either health- or skill-related and that can be measured with specific tests to assess the degree to which people have these attributes (Caspersen et al., 1985). Physical fitness includes cardiorespiratory fitness, muscular strength and endurance, body composition and flexibility, balance, agility, reaction time, and power (Garber et al., 2011). When we exercise, this disrupts our normal homeostasis. Our body therefore adapts to minimize this disruption and becomes more efficient at coping with exercise. This is the process of improving fitness.

The terms *physical activity, fitness,* and *exercise* are related constructs, and are often used interchangeably. For the purposes of this chapter, *physical activity* will be used as an umbrella term and will incorporate both fitness and exercise.

Sedentary behavior, or being sedentary, has also emerged over the past decade as a focus for public health researchers (Hamilton, Healy, Dunstan, Zderic, & Owen, 2008; Levine, Schleusner, & Jensen, 2000; Owen, Bauman, & Brown, 2009; Owen, Leslie, Salmon, & Fotheringham, 2000; Pate, O'Neill, & Lobelo, 2008). Sedentary behavior refers to any waking activity characterized by an energy expenditure of ≤ 1.5 metabolic equivalents *and* a sitting or reclining posture (Barnes et al., 2012). As with physical activity, sedentary behavior occurs in different contexts. These include whilst at work (sitting at your desk or in meetings), watching television, for transport (sitting in the car or on the bus), using a computer at home, and other during leisure activities (reading, having a meal) (Owen et al., 2009). Sedentary behavior should not be confused with *physical inactivity*, which is a term used when an individual is not meeting physical activity guidelines. Someone can be physically active (walk every evening after work), but also sedentary (sit for seven hours whilst at work).

Box 21.1 Physical activity guidelines*

Adults aged 19–64 years should be active daily. Over a week, this activity should add up to at least 2½ hours of moderate intensity activity in bouts of 10 minutes or more. One way to achieve this is to do 30 minutes of moderate activity every day for at least five days a week. You can achieve similar benefits by doing at least 1¼ hours of vigorous intensity activity a week or combinations of both moderate and vigorous intensity activity. In addition, adults should also undertake physical activity to improve muscle strength two or more days a week. All adults should aim to minimize the amount of time spent being sedentary (sitting) for extended periods.

* Based on the current UK guidelines – guidelines are different depending on which country you are in.

How much physical activity should we do?

Physical activity guidelines vary across the world. Box 21.1 shows the current guidelines for the United Kingdom, which are similar to other countries such as the United States and Canada (Department of Health, 2011; Haskell et al., 2007; Warburton, Katzmarzyk, Rhodes, & Shephard, 2007). However, guidelines can evolve as physical activity research develops; for example,

Australian guidelines now suggest we should be achieving double this amount of activity per week (Australian Government Department of Health, 2015). In general, a key message is that any movement is better than no movement. For example, those who currently have very little movement in their day are likely to benefit the most from increasing their activity, even if it is below what the guidelines suggest. Research suggests that even very modest increases in physical activity or light-intensity activity (i.e., not moderate or vigorous) confer health benefits (Carson et al., 2013; Levine, 2002). Such low-intensity activities have been shown to have beneficial effects on cardiovascular disease risk, obesity, diabetes, and all-cause mortality (Villablanca et al., 2015).

Why is physical activity important for wellbeing?

Physical activity is strongly linked to improved physical, social, and mental wellbeing. Physical inactivity is the fourth leading risk factor for global mortality, causing an estimated 3.2 million deaths globally (Lee et al., 2012; World Health Organization, 2010). Importantly, physical activity is not useful only for the prevention of ill-health, but also for the treatment of health problems. Physical activity is associated with improved outcomes for at least 25 chronic medical condition, including premature mortality, cardiovascular disease, stroke, some cancers, Type II diabetes, and osteoporosis (Pedersen & Saltin, 2015; Warburton, Nicol, & Bredin, 2006a, 2006b; Warburton, Charlesworth, Ivey, Nettlefold, & Bredin, 2010). Many of these associations are in an inverse linear dose response manner (i.e., the more physical activity, the less risk) (Lee & Skerrett, 2001).

Physical activity has also been found to be beneficial to mental wellbeing. In a recent meta-analysis investigating physical activity as a treatment for depression, physical activity demonstrated a large significant effect on depression and a significant antidepressant effect (Schuch et al., 2016). Regular physical activity has also been reported to protect against poor mental health, including depression, anxiety, and stress; reduce symptoms of fatigue, somatization, and cognitive decline; and promote positive mental health such as coping, enhanced mood, quality of life, and life satisfaction (Brown et al., 2003; Eime, Young, Harvey, Charity, & Payne, 2013; Fox, 1999; Martinsen, 2008; Paluska & Schwenk, 2000; Penedo & Dahn, 2005; Strohle, 2009; Taylor, Sallis, & Needle, 1985).

Being involved in physical activity is also beneficial for social health. Many physical activities involve participation with other people, such as club- and team-based sport (tennis, football, badminton) and noncompetitive organized physical activity (fitness classes, walking groups). A recent systematic review reported that taking part in club and team-based sport was associated with better psychological and social health outcomes compared to other individual forms of physical activity (Eime et al., 2013). Further, sport at work was found to be important not only for the individual, but also for group cohesion and performance, and organizational benefits including increased work performance (Brinkley, Mcdermott, & Munir, 2017).

Emerging evidence also suggests that sedentary behavior may be associated with poor wellbeing. Sedentary behavior has been shown to be associated with all-cause and cardiovascular disease mortality, cardio-metabolic biomarkers, metabolic syndrome, obesity, Type II diabetes, and depression (Healy, Matthews, Dunstan, Winkler, & Owen, 2011; Thorp, Owen, Neuhaus, & Dunstan, 2011; Tremblay, Colley, Saunders, Healy, & Owen, 2010; Vallance et al., 2011). Understanding the health risks associated with high levels of sedentary behavior may be important, considering that some research suggests these risks are still present after accounting for time spent in moderate to vigorous physical activity (Matthews et al., 2012; Whitfield, Pettee Gabriel, & Kohl, 2013). For example, in a study looking at 240,819 adults, those who achieved seven hours per week of moderate to vigorous physical activity, but also had high television viewing time (seven hours per week), were 50% more likely to die during the 8½year follow-up than those who were as active but sit for less than one hour per week (Matthews et al., 2012). Other studies suggest that physical activity can play a role in attenuating the risk of sitting or that those who are inactive are still at the greatest risk (Asvold et al., 2017; Ekelund et al., 2017; Petersen et al., 2016; Stamatakis et al. 2016). Regardless, the evidence suggests that, sitting less and moving more are likely to be beneficial to wellbeing.

Physical activity and wellbeing in the workplace

In the first section, questions were answered relating to overall physical activity and wellbeing, such as what physical activity is, how much physical activity we should do, and why physical activity is important for wellbeing. In this next section these points are narrowed to focus on physical activity and wellbeing in the workplace and interventions in this area.

What are current workplace physical activity trends?

Total physical activity has declined over the past five decades. Current data from many countries suggest the majority of individuals are insufficiently active, with one in four adults globally not active enough to gain the health benefits associated with being active (World Health Organization, 2015). A study by Ng and Popkin (2012) assessed physical activity in five countries from the early 1960s and projected future trends by examining energy expenditure (Ng & Popkin, 2012). They reported declines in total physical activity in the United States, the United Kingdom, Brazil, China, and India. (In the United States, for example, physical activity decreased by 32% between 1965 and 2009.) This decline in global physical activity is projected to continue and is largely mirrored by an increase in sedentary behavior.

The decrease in overall energy expenditure is largely driven by decreases in occupational physical activity (Ng & Popkin, 2012). Advances in technology and technological innovation within the workplace have created fewer labor-intensive environments, with a significant reduction in the prevalence of labor-orientated jobs, such as goods production and agriculture, and an increase in less active professions, such as service-providing roles (Church et al., 2011). This changing nature of work has led to an increase in workplace sitting. Sedentary behavior at work is more common than in any other context where it might occur; a study by Miller and Brown (2004) showed that occupational sitting time accounted for more than half the time spent sitting each week, with TV or home computer time accounting for only 21% of total sitting time (Miller & Brown, 2004). Although not all occupations involve high levels of sitting, sitting time in office employees is predominantly high. Chau, van der Ploeg, Merom, Chey, and Bauman (2012) report that full-time office employees may sit for approximately six hours per day at work, with 42% of men and 47% of women reporting their jobs as mostly sitting. In our recent work we reported that, relative to total occupational sitting time, employees spend 67% of their work hours sitting at their own desk (Ryde, Brown, Gilson, & Brown, 2014). Attenuating the decline in activity, and reducing workplace sitting, is therefore increasingly important for improving overall levels of physical activity.

Why is physical activity important for workplace outcomes?

What is already known from reading this chapter:

- Physical activity is strongly related to physical, mental and social wellbeing.
- Adults are not active enough to gain health benefits.

- Workplaces can be a setting in which high volumes of sedentary behavior and low amounts of physical activity occur.

Workplaces benefit from healthier, more active employees. Low levels of physical activity in employees are associated with many work-related factors, including reduced productivity (quality and quantity of work) and increased absenteeism, health care costs, disability, work impairment, and musculoskeletal problems (Anderson et al., 2000; Pronk et al., 2004; Pronk, Tan, & O'Connor, 1999; Wang, McDonald, Champagne, & Edington, 2004).

Employees who are regularly physically active have been shown to be more productive (Bernacki & Baun, 1984; Durbeck et al., 1972; Leutzinger & Blanke, 1991; Robison et al., 1992; Voit, 2001). Employers who introduce physical activity programs into the workplace have reported positive effects related to productivity such as job satisfaction and mood (Bernacki & Baun, 1984; Shephard, Cox, & Corey, 1981; Voit, 2001). Workplace wellness initiatives, which include attempts to increase physical activity, can also provide other less-quantifiable benefits. These benefits may include attracting top candidates, improved recruitment and retention of workers, and enhanced corporate image (Pronk, 2014b; Shephard, 1992). For example, a cross-sectional analysis has shown significant positive relationships between pedometer-measured, total daily step counts, and employees' ability to meet demands for quantity, quality, and timeliness of completed work (Puig-Ribera, Gilson, Mckenna, & Brown, 2007).

Another concern for workplaces is that of absenteeism, or the number of sick-leave days taken by employees. Physical inactivity is associated with higher levels of absenteeism (Gebhardt & Crump, 1990; Pender, Smith, & Vernof, 1987; Shephard, 1992). For example, employees who do no physical activity are more likely to be absent for more than seven days annually than those who are physically active for 20 minutes at least once per week, with other studies reporting similar findings (Jacobson & Aldana, 2001; Proper, van den Heuvel, de Vroome, Hildebrandt, & van der Beek, 2006). In a review paper looking at a critical analysis of worksite physical activity programs and their economic benefit, it was suggested that improvements in absenteeism rates could equate to up to 1.4% of payroll costs (Shephard, 1992). When assessing the projected saving of a 10% reduction in physical inactivity, it was estimated that 114,000 working days would be gained, with a lifetime potential opportunity cost savings in workforce production of $12 million (Australian) (Cadilhac et al., 2011).

An emerging issue for employers is presenteeism, the extent to which work is adversely affected as a result of individuals who choose to remain at work despite having physical or psychosocial symptoms or conditions (Chapman, 2005). Conceptualizations of presenteeism indicate that it is not simply the opposite of absenteeism, but rather a reduced ability to work productively (Cooper & Dewe, 2008). A recent policy paper indicated that the costs of presenteeism are between 1.9 and 5.1 times more than those incurred for absenteeism (Sainsbury Centre for Mental Health, 2007). These costs are associated with reduced work output, errors on the job, and failure to meet company standards (Schultz & Edington, 2007). Physical health conditions associated with presenteeism include hypertension and cardiovascular disease, arthritis, diabetes and other metabolic disorders, migraines/headaches, cancer, respiratory infections, asthma, and allergies (Chapman, 2005). Psychosocial conditions include anxiety, chronic fatigue, depression, nervousness, panic attacks, and low energy levels (Chapman, 2005). Some of these psychosocial conditions are reported to be among the most frequent causes of occupational disability whilst at work (Wang, Simon, & Kessler, 2003). As physical activity has a well-established inverse association with many of these physical and psychosocial conditions, it could, therefore, also be inversely associated with presenteeism. Whilst the exact relationship between physical activity and presenteeism is unknown, it should be considered when reviewing the potential benefits of increasing employee physical activity levels (Brown, Gilson, Burton, & Brown, 2011).

How can we influence physical activity at work?

Previously in this chapter, the very clear association between physical activity and workplace wellbeing has been highlighted. Despite strong evidence of the relationship between physical activity and workplace wellbeing, the potential of the workplace to increase physical activity has yet to be realized.

This section aims to provide a practical guide for organizations wishing to increase the physical activity levels of their employees. It starts with an overview of some of the key systematic reviews in this area providing a general summary of the research field. It then goes on to:

1   Highlight some of the most commonly used physical activity interventions in workplaces.
2   Provide tips for best practice to increase the potential success of workplace physical intervention.

Workplaces need to adapt solutions to suit their worksite, which is likely to have its own unique characteristics, employees, and culture (Pronk, 2009). This section provides a starting point for those interested in increasing physical activity and improving workplace wellbeing, with suggestions of further reading.

Workplace physical activity intervention reviews

There is considerable extant evidence appraising the efficacy of workplace physical activity interventions; one paper documented 28 reviews of workplace physical activity programs (Pronk, 2009). The overall findings of these reviews have varied considerably. Whilst some report positive effects of workplace physical activity initiatives (Abraham & Graham-Rowe, 2009; Conn, Hafdahl, Cooper, Brown, & Lusk, 2009; Kahn et al., 2002; Proper et al., 2003b), for others, the findings are less clear (Dishman, Oldenburg, O'Neal, & Shephard, 1998; Engbers, van Poppel, Chin, & van Mechelen, 2005; Malik, Blake, & Suggs, 2014; Marshall, 2004).

Dishman et al., 1998 conducted a meta-analysis to quantify the efficacy of workplace interventions that aimed to increase physical activity (Dishman et al., 1998). Looking at 26 studies and 9,000 subjects, they reported only a small, nonsignificant positive effect of workplace physical activity interventions on physical activity behavior ($r = 0.11$). While this may not appear notable, the authors said cautiously it could be compared to the equivalent of increasing physical activity in six people per 100, which may still be meaningful at a population level. A more recent systematic review offered a similar message, stating that it remains difficult to draw robust conclusions regarding the effect of workplace physical activity interventions on increasing employee physical activity (Malik et al., 2014).

Other researchers have reported more positive findings and suggested that some interventions might be more valuable than others. Abraham and Graham-Row (2009) reported an overall small effect size but suggested that worksite walking interventions were nearly four times as beneficial than other forms of physical activity promotion (Abraham & Graham-Row, 2009). Gilson, McKenna, Puig-Ribera, Brown, and Burton (2008) also suggested that workplace walking interventions using step counters might be effective approaches to increase employee physical activity. They also highlighted positive effects for some active travel initiatives and workplace counselling sessions (Dugdill, Brettle, Hulme, Mccluskey, & Long, 2007). Other strategies or behavior change techniques that are included in many interventions might have potential for influencing employee physical activity. Strategies that have shown promise include goal setting, self-monitoring, and motivational prompts (Abraham & Graham-Row, 2009; Dugdill et al., 2007; Marshall, 2004).

It should be noted that workplaces are complex intervention settings. It has therefore been suggested that whilst the workplace is a good setting for the delivery of physical activity interventions, it is not an ideal setting for conducting high-quality research. The lack of effectiveness reported by some studies may be partially explained by scientific issues relating to poor research design and measurement issues (Dishman et al., 1998; Malik et al., 2014). Many authors have concluded that such results should not suggest workplace physical activity interventions are ineffective but that focus should be paid on increasing the success of interventions that show promise and addressing issues of participation and recruitment (Abraham & Graham-Row, 2009; Ryde, Gilson, Burton, & Brown, 2013).

Commonly used physical activity interventions in workplaces

In this section, commonly used interventions which may work to increase physical activity in employees are reviewed. Each intervention includes a detailed example, including behavior change techniques when reported. The interventions focused on in this section include:

- Walking and activity trackers
- Behavioral counselling
- Stair use
- Active travel
- Sit-stand and activity-permissive desks
- Active by default

Walking and activity trackers: Walking has been described as an ideal form of exercise as it is low impact, free, can be done anywhere, and doesn't require any special equipment. Walking interventions have typically used pedometers or step counters to measure physical activity through steps. Pedometers and step counters are small, inexpensive devices typically attached to the waist that record and display step counts. They provide feedback on the number of steps and may motivate people to be more active and to set goals. They are often used in conjunction with other strategies and behavior-change techniques, such as diaries, goal setting, competitions, motivational emails, websites, and counselling. Individual are generally advised to aim for 10,000 steps per day, based on that fact we typically accumulate 6,000–7,000 steps through the day without a concerted effort, and 3,000 steps per day is about 30 minutes of activity (as per the physical activity guidelines). However, this can be a high target for sedentary employees, with some interventions preferring to set goals based on an employee's starting step count.

In recent years, many mobile phone applications and activity trackers that measure steps and/or physical activity have become available. These allow for automated ways to collect activity data and provide feedback to those using them. A recent review of the evidence assessing their effect on increasing physical activity suggests that there are still many questions surrounding their validity and effectiveness for promoting behavior change (Sullivan & Lachman, 2016). However, this is a promising area that may have a positive impact on workplace physical activity in the future.

Example: University employees (330) from five different campuses across four countries (Canada, Northern Ireland, the United States and two in Australia) took part in an automated website intervention (Walk@Work) that aimed to increase workplace walking by 1,000 steps per day above an employee's starting step count. Employees recorded their starting step counts and the website then generated goals of +1,000, +2,000, and +3,000 steps every two weeks over a 12-week period. Employees entered their step counts throughout the program and were provided with visual feedback on their step progress and whether they were achieving their goals. Employees were also provided with strategies to encourage them to walk more with each new goal, starting with targeting changes in sitting and low intensity, incidental walking (i.e., walking to speak to a colleague instead of sending an email, known as an "active emails," or making mobile calls while walking), short walks of up to 10 minutes during tea/coffee breaks, and finishing with longer, moderate-intensity lunchtime walks longer than 10 minutes. Workplace walking was shown to increase by 25% over the course of the study (Gilson et al., 2013).

Behavioral counselling: Behavioral counselling and other similar interventions are commonly used in workplaces to change employee physical activity behavior. These interventions can vary significantly in intensity and delivery, and range from group sessions to one-on-one counselling. They focus on more than merely educational materials and increasing knowledge, but instead provide the individual with support, knowledge, and guidance to become more active based on their current physical activity levels. Often, behavioral counsellors help employees to set goals and overcome possible barriers to being active. These sessions tend to be driven by theory, employing approaches such as motivational interviewing and cognitive behavioral therapy.

Example: Employees from municipal service departments in Enschede, in the Netherlands ($n = 131$), were provided with seven 20-minute individual consultations by a physiotherapist. Counselling focused primarily on enhancing individual physical activity, with a secondary focus on healthy nutrition habits. Content and style of the counselling was based on employee's readiness to change their physical activity behavior. Sessions included providing general information on lifestyle factors (physical activity, nutrition, alcohol, smoking, work stress, and ergonomics) followed by the creation of a plan to improve physical activity. Progress on this plan was then discussed at the remaining sessions. A positive effect was reported for physical activity (energy expenditure) and for cardio-respiratory fitness (Proper, Hildebrandt, van der Beek, Twisk, & van Mechelen, 2003a).

Stair use: Encouraging employees to use the stairs more at work is a simple way to add movement into the workplace daily routine. Stair-use interventions are typically delivered through point-of-prompt displays, which can be either motivational (posters or banners highlighting the benefits or what can be achieved by stair climbing) or directional (arrows or footprints informing employees of nearby stair-use opportunities). Although some studies have reported limited effect of stair usage on physical activity and that intervention effects in workplaces tend to be short-lived, using a combination of both motivational and directional techniques is more likely to have a positive effect on stair climbing. In addition, several other strategies could be used to improve stage usage and increase longer term use. For example, stairwell enhancements such as artwork, music, interactive paintings, or painting, and replacing doors have shown promise, although there are not many studies on this yet (Boutelle, Jeffery, Murray, & Schmitz, 2001; Swenson & Siegel, 2013; van Nieuw-Amerongen, Kremers, de Vries, & Kok, 2011). After a stair usage initiative has been occurring for a while, revitalizing posters and stair use campaigns may be beneficial. Those who are involved in developing or modifying the workplace environment should look at ways to make using stairs more attractive, such as creating visible and attractive stairwells.

Example: Stairwells in a public health department were decorated with multiple interactive paintings in the stairwells to encourage employee to use the stairs. The paintings were large, two-dimensional pieces that aimed to have employees write, draw, and interact with them (for example, they provided markers with which employees could draw). Paintings included (1) a world map, where people could mark where they were born, where they had visited, and where they wanted to go; (2) storyboards on which people could create and tell their own stories or add on to other people's stories; and (3) the repeated phrase, "Someday I want to ___" where people could fill in the blanks with their own aspirations.

Signs were placed outside the stairwell and elevator, next to existing signage reading replacing "stairs" with "fun stairs" and smiling figure, and next to "In case of fire use stairs," a smiling figure said "In case of fun use stairs." Stair use, relative to stair plus elevator use, increased to 66.2% (compared with 31.5% at baseline) over the six-week intervention period (Swenson & Siegel, 2013).

Active travel: Active travel, or active commuting, is concerned with how employees get to and from work, and can include a mix of public transport and other means such as cycling and/ or walking. Active travel has been shown to contribute greatly towards daily physical activity. It can be easily integrated into existing routines, often more so than leisure-time physical activity. As a potential strategy to increase overall physical activity, workplaces can assist employees to commute more actively and to reduce car usage whilst at work. Possible strategies include creating active travel plans, walking and cycling campaigns, and providing facilities (bike storage, changing rooms, lockers, and showers).

Example: An intervention that aimed to increase walking and cycling to work through a "walk in to work out" pack was tested in 145 employees from three public-sector organizations in Glasgow, Scotland. The pack contained a booklet with information on choosing routes, maintaining personal safety, shower and safe cycle storage information, and useful contacts. It also contained a wall chart diary, a workplace map, distances from local stations, local cycle retailers and outdoor shops, contacts for relevant organizations, local maps, and reflective safety accessories. Authors found that, at six months, employees receiving the intervention were twice as likely to increase walking to work than employees who didn't receive the intervention (Mutrie et al., 2002).

Sit-stand and activity-permissive desks: Replacing conventional seated, static desks with sit-stand desks (i.e., a desk that can be used in both a seated or standing positon and allows users to alternate between postures) may be a potential strategy to reduce sedentary behavior at work. Whilst it should be noted that sit-stand desks don't tend to increase physical activity (typically sitting is replaced with standing), they might offer an alternative for organizations where physical activity interventions are difficult to implement (Alkhajah et al., 2012; Healy et al., 2013). Another option to help increase movement is that of activity-permissive desks. These desks typically include an adapted desk with either a treadmill desks that allow users to walk whilst using their computer, an under-desk portable pedal or stepping devices, or an exercise bike at the desk.

Example: Thirty-six employees from a financial services corporation in Minnesota, the United States, had their preexisting desks replaced with a treadmill desk. The desks could be elevated or lowered (for chair use) using a hydraulic motor at the press of a button and a treadmill ran silently beneath the desk up to a maximum speed of 2 mph. The desks did not force employees to walk but gave them the option if they chose to walk. Those with access to the desk increased their physical activity by 33% at six months and reduced their sedentary behavior by 1 hour 31 minutes per day (Koepp et al., 2013).

Active by default: Interventions that look at creating environments that are active by default may have a positive effect on physical activity. Such interventions are also known as "push," "opt-out," or "nudge" strategies. They typically include short bouts of light activity incorporated into the workday such as integrating physical activity into existing and accepted organizational practices (such as meetings and workshops). These interventions are designed to change sociocultural norms relating to physical activity and to increase visibility around efforts to address physical activity in the workplace. The premise is that physical activity can be introduced to a group of employees gathered for work purposes, relying less on individual motivation for physical activity and utilizing social support. Using societal physical activity promotion has been shown to be effective in community settings (Kahn et al., 2002).

Example: An intervention to incorporate activity breaks into employees daily routine was tested with 449 County Department of Health Services' employees in Los Angeles, the United States. The program, called Lift Off, consisted of a 10-minute physical activity break integrated into meetings and events greater than an hour long, specifically ones with refreshments. The breaks consisted of a series of simple aerobic dance/calisthenics movements with catchy titles (e.g., the Hulk, the Hallelujah, the Knee High), developed by physical activity experts. Employees did not need to change or shower. Materials included video and audiotape, and employees were provided with training on how to deliver the intervention. A company director endorsed the program and circulated a memorandum to senior managers encouraging their inclusion. More than 90% of employees who attended meetings participated, with employees reporting an increased in their perception of workplace support (Yancey et al., 2004).

Best practice for implementing physical activity programs

Those employing strategies to increase physical activity in the workplace setting can also draw lessons from broader health promotion interventions. These can be used as a guide when looking for more information on implementing physical activity initiatives (National Institute for Occupational Safety and Health, 2008; Pronk, 2009, 2014a) and will also be covered in more detail in Chapter 22.

Box 21.2 Workplace physical activity interventions should address the following (ecological approach)

- **Individual factors:** employees' existing physical activity level, skills, knowledge
- **Social context:** corporate culture, colleague relationships, managers' perceptions
- **Organizational factors:** leadership, desire to increase physical activity
- **Policy level:** workplace physical activity policy

Given the complex nature of workplaces, interventions that are multi-faceted may be more effective (Heaney & Goetzel, 1997; Stokols, Pelletier, & Fielding, 1996). This is sometimes known as an ecological approach (see Box 21.2), acknowledging the different levels of influence in the workplace and how these might interact to influence physical activity. For example, there is little point in promoting a walking intervention if the workplace culture does not support employees leaving their desks or access to stairwells is restricted.

Other key points for success when implementing workplace physical activity interventions are outlined below.

Organizational culture and leadership
- Engage with leadership and top management support from the start.
- Engage with mid-level management and other key gatekeepers (those with a responsibility for occupational health and employee wellbeing).

- Identify physical activity enthusiasts or champions who can help drive the agenda.
- Create supportive physical and social environments – improving social norms and social support.
- Use participatory approaches to involve employees and increase ownership of the program.

Program design
- Establish clear aims and objectives for the program.
- Engage employees and management throughout the process.
- Integrate with programs and polices already in place.
- Link to existing business objectives and priorities.
- Link to the social aspects of the workplace and look at how best to use peer champions.
- Consider all levels of the ecological approach (see Box 21.2).
- Consider using techniques that can engage and motivate individuals such as goal setting, feedback, and self-monitoring.
- Consider creative and appealing incentives; for example, providing time off to be physically active.
- Tailor the program to suit the workplaces context and needs.
- Measure outcomes prior to starting and repeat in the future – include physical activity measures and workplace outcomes that link to business objectives and priorities.
- Assess and adjust as the program develops.
- Address the long-term outlook – not just short-term objectives.
- Consider potential privacy and confidentiality issues.

Program implementation
- Start small and scale up.
- Assess the resources required and allocate these.
- Communicate early, often, and effectively.

Resources and program evaluation
- Measure and analyze the progress of the program and its outcomes.
- Make changes as appropriate and ensure any lessons are addressed.

Summary

The aim of this chapter was to explore the relationship between physical activity and wellbeing in the specific context of the workplace. It began by defining physical activity and introducing the related and emerging issue of sedentary behavior. It then outlined current physical activity guidelines, which suggest adults should aim to be active daily (for example, 30 minutes of moderate activity on at least five days a week). Looking at the benefits of physical activity, it reported on the strong relationship between physical activity and improved physical, social, and mental wellbeing, and described evidence to suggest that sedentary behavior might be associated with poor wellbeing. It highlighted key trends in total and occupational physical activity such as declines in total physical activity across the world, mirrored by an increase in sedentary behavior. These issues were then discussed in relation to the workplace, with advances in technology and the changing nature of work leading to an increase in sedentary work environments. Potential benefits of increasing physical activity in employees were discussed, including improved productivity, and reduced absenteeism and presenteeism. Best practices for implementing physical activity programs were then outlined, drawing on learning from the wider workplace wellness literature. Practical advice for those seeking to increase physical activity in their workplace were outlined, and several strategies described that may be of use for those seeking to support healthier, happier, and more productive employees.

References

Abraham, C., & Graham-Row, E. (2009). Are worksite interventions effective in increasing physical activity? A systematic review and meta-analysis. *Health Psychology Review*, 3, 108–144.

Alkhajah, T. A., Reeves, M. M., Eakin, E. G., Winkler, E. A., Owen, N., & Healy, G. N. (2012). Sit-stand workstations: A pilot intervention to reduce office sitting time. *American Journal of Preventive Medicine*, 43, 298–303.

Anderson, D. R., Whitmer, R. W., Goetzel, R. Z., Ozminkowski, R. J., Dunn, R. L., Wasserman, J., . . . & Health Enhancement Research Organization Research, C. (2000). The relationship between modifiable health risks and group-level health care expenditures. Health Enhancement Research Organization (HERO) Research Committee. *The American Journal of Health Promotion*, 15, 45–52.

Asvold, B. O., Midthjell, K., Krokstad, S., Rangul, V., Bauman, A. (2017). Prolonged sitting may increase diabetes risk in physically inactive individuals: An 11 year follow-up of the HUNT Study, Norway. *Diabetologia*. doi: 10.1007/s00125-016-4193-z.

Australian Government Department of Health. (2015). *Make Your Move – Sit Less Be Active for Life!* Available at: www.health.gov.au/internet/main/publishing.nsf/content/F01F92328EDADA5BCA257BF0001E7 20D/$File/brochure%20PA%20Guidelines_A5_18-64yrs.PDF.

Baecke, J. A., Burema, J., & Frijters, J. E. (1982). A short questionnaire for the measurement of habitual physical activity in epidemiological studies. *The American Journal of Clinical Nutrition*, 36, 936–942.

Barnes, J., Behrens, T. K., Benden, M. E., Biddle, S., Bond, D., Brassard, P., . . . & Network, S. B. R. (2012). Letter to the editor: Standardized use of the terms "sedentary" and "sedentary behaviours". *Applied Physiology Nutrition and Metabolism-Physiologie Appliquee Nutrition Et Metabolisme*, 37, 540–542.

Bernacki, E. J., & Baun, W. B. (1984). The relationship of job performance to exercise adherence in a corporate fitness program. *Journal of Occupational and Environmental Medicine*, 26, 529–531.

Boutelle, K. N., Jeffery, R. W., Murray, D. M., & Schmitz, M. K. (2001). Using signs, artwork, and music to promote stair use in a public building. *American Journal of Public Health*, 91, 2004–2006.

Brinkley, A., Mcdermott, H., & Munir, F. (2017). What benefits does team sport hold for the workplace? A systematic review. *Journal of Sports Science*, 35, 136–148.

Brown, D. W., Balluz, L. S., Heath, G. W., Moriarty, D. G., Ford, E. S., Giles, W. H., & Mokdad, A. H. (2003). Associations between recommended levels of physical activity and health-related quality of life – Findings from the 2001 Behavioral Risk Factor Surveillance System (BRFSS) survey. *Preventive Medicine*, 37, 520–528.

Brown, H. E., Gilson, N. D., Burton, N. W., & Brown, W. J. (2011). Does physical activity impact on presenteeism and other indicators of workplace well-being? *Sports Medicine*, 41, 249–262.

Cadilhac, D. A., Cumming, T. B., Sheppard, L., Pearce, D. C., Carter, R., & Magnus, A. (2011). The economic benefits of reducing physical inactivity: An Australian example. International Journal of Behavioral Nutrition and Physical Activity, 8, 99.

Carson, V., Ridgers, N. D., Howard, B. J., Winkler, E. A., Healy, G. N., Owen, N., . . . & Salmon, J. (2013). Light-intensity physical activity and cardiometabolic biomarkers in US adolescents. *PLoS ONE*, 8, e71417.

Caspersen, C. J., Powell, K. E., & Christenson, G. M. (1985). Physical activity, exercise, and physical fitness: Definitions and distinctions for health-related research. *Public Health Reports*, 100, 126–131.

Chapman, L. S. (2005). Presenteeism and its role in worksite health promotion. *The American Journal of Health Promotion*, 19(Supplement), 1–8.

Chau, J. Y., van der Ploeg, H. P., Merom, D., Chey, T., & Bauman, A. E. (2012). Cross-sectional associations between occupational and leisure-time sitting, physical activity and obesity in working adults. *Preventive Medicine*, 54, 195–200.

Church, T. S., Thomas, D. M., Tudor-Locke, C., Katzmarzyk, P. T., Earnest, C. P., Rodarte, R. Q., . . . & Bouchard, C. (2011). Trends over 5 decades in U. S. occupation-related physical activity and their associations with obesity. *PLoS ONE*, 6, e19657.

Conn, V. S., Hafdahl, A. R., Cooper, P. S., Brown, L. M., & Lusk, S. L. (2009). Meta-analysis of workplace physical activity interventions. *American Journal of Preventive Medicine*, 37, 330–339.

Cooper, C., & Dewe, P. (2008). Well-being – Absenteeism, presenteeism, costs and challenges. *Occup Med (Lond)*, 58, 522–524.

Department of Health. (2011). *UK Physical Activity Guidelines*. Available at: www.gov.uk/government/publications/uk-physical-activity-guidelines

Dishman, R. K., Oldenburg, B., O'Neal, H., & Shephard, R. J. (1998). Worksite physical activity interventions. *American Journal of Preventive Medicine*, 15, 344–361.

Dugdill, L., Brettle, A., Hulme, C., Mccluskey, S., & Long, A. F. (2007). Workplace physical activity interventions: A systematic review. *International Journal of Workplace Health Management*, 1, 20–40.

Durbeck, D. C., Heinzelmann, F., Schacter, J., Haskell, W. L., Payne, G. H., Moxley, R. T., 3rd, . . . & Fox, S. M., 3rd. (1972). The National Aeronautics and Space Administration-U.S. Public health service health evaluation and enhancement program: Summary of results. *American Journal of Cardiology*, 30, 784–790.

Eime, R. M., Young, J. A., Harvey, J. T., Charity, M. J., & Payne, W. R. (2013). A systematic review of the psychological and social benefits of participation in sport for adults: Informing development of a conceptual model of health through sport. *International Journal of Behavioral Nutrition and Physical Activity*, 10, 135.

Ekelund, U., Steene-Johannessen, J., Brown, W. J., Fagerland, M. W., Owen, N., Powell, K. E., . . . & Lancet Sedentary Behavior Working Group. (2016). Does physical activity attenuate, or even eliminate, the detrimental association of sitting time with mortality? A harmonised meta-analysis of data from more than 1 million men and women. *Lancet*, 388(10051), 1302–1310.

Engbers, L. H., van Poppel, M. N., Chin, A. P. M. J., & van Mechelen, W. (2005). Worksite health promotion programs with environmental changes: A systematic review. *American Journal of Preventive Medicine*, 29, 61–70.

Fox, K. R. (1999). The influence of physical activity on mental well-being. *Public Health Nutrition*, 2, 411–418.

Garber, C. E., Blissmer, B., Deschenes, M. R., Franklin, B. A., Lamonte, M. J., Lee, I. M., . . . & American College of Sports, M. (2011). American college of sports medicine position stand: Quantity and quality of exercise for developing and maintaining cardiorespiratory, musculoskeletal, and neuromotor fitness in apparently healthy adults: Guidance for prescribing exercise. *Medicine & Science in Sports & Exercise*, 43, 1334–1359.

Gebhardt, D. L., & Crump, C. (1990). Employee fitness and wellness programs in the workplace. American Psychologist, 45, 262–272.

Gilson, N. D., Faulkner, G., Murphy, M. H., Meyer, M. R., Washington, T., Ryde, G. C., . . . & Dillon, K. A. (2013). Walk@Work: An automated intervention to increase walking in university employees not achieving 10,000 daily steps. Preventive Medicine, 56, 283–287.

Gilson, N., McKenna, J., Puig-Ribera, A., Brown, W., & Burton, N. (2008). The International Universities Walking Project: Employee step counts, sitting times and health status. *International Journal of Workplace Health Management,* 1(3), 152–161.

Hamilton, M., Healy, G., Dunstan, D., Zderic, T., & Owen, N. (2008). Too little exercise and too much sitting: Inactivity physiology and the need for new recommendations on sedentary behavior. *Current Cardiovascular Risk Reports*, 2, 292–298.

Haskell, W. L., Lee, I. M., Pate, R. R., Powell, K. E., Blair, S. N., Franklin, B. A., . . . & Bauman, A. (2007). Physical activity and public health: Updated recommendation for adults from the American College of Sports Medicine and the American Heart Association. *Medicine & Science in Sport & Exercise*, 39, 1423–1434.

Healy, G. N., Eakin, E. G., Lamontagne, A. D., Owen, N., Winkler, E. A., Wiesner, G., . . . & Dunstan, D. W. (2013). Reducing sitting time in office workers: Short-term efficacy of a multicomponent intervention. Preventive Medicine, 57, 43–48.

Healy, G. N., Matthews, C. E., Dunstan, D. W., Winkler, E. A., & Owen, N. (2011). Sedentary time and cardio-metabolic biomarkers in US adults: NHANES 2003–06. *European Heart Journal*, 32, 590–597.

Heaney, C. A., & Goetzel, R. Z. (1997). A review of health-related outcomes of multi-component worksite health promotion programs. *The American Journal of Health Promotion*, 11, 290–307.

Jacobson, B. H., & Aldana, S. G. (2001). Relationship between frequency of aerobic activity and illness-related absenteeism in a large employee sample. *Journal of Occupational and Environmental Medicine*, 43, 1019–1025.

Kahn, E. B., Ramsey, L. T., Brownson, R. C., Heath, G. W., Howze, E. H., Powell, K. E., . . . & Corso, P. (2002). The effectiveness of interventions to increase physical activity: A systematic review. *American Journal of Preventive Medicine*, 22, 73–107.

Koepp, G. A., Manohar, C. U., Mccrady-Spitzer, S. K., Ben-Ner, A., Hamann, D. J., Runge, C. F., & Levine, J. A. (2013). Treadmill desks: A 1-year prospective trial. *Obesity (Silver Spring)*, 21, 705–711.

Lee, I. M., Shiroma, E. J., Lobelo, F., Puska, P., Blair, S. N., Katzmarzyk, P. T., & Lancet Physical Activity Series Working, G. (2012). Effect of physical inactivity on major non-communicable diseases worldwide: An analysis of burden of disease and life expectancy. *Lancet*, 380, 219–229.

Lee, I. M., & Skerrett, P. J. (2001). Physical activity and all-cause mortality: What is the dose-response relation? *Medicine & Science in Sports & Exercise*, 33, S459–S471; discussion S493–S494.

Leutzinger, J., & Blanke, D. (1991). The effect of a corporate fitness program on perceived worker productivity. *Health Values*, 15, 20–29.

Levine, J. A. (2002). Non-exercise activity thermogenesis (NEAT). *Best Practice & Research Clinical Endocrinology & Metabolism*, 16, 679–702.

Levine, J. A., Schleusner, S. J., & Jensen, M. D. (2000). Energy expenditure of nonexercise activity. *The American Journal of Clinical Nutrition*, 72, 1451–1454.

Malik, S. H., Blake, H., & Suggs, L. S. (2014). A systematic review of workplace health promotion interventions for increasing physical activity. British Journal of Health Psychology's, 19, 149–180.

Marshall, A. L. (2004). Challenges and opportunities for promoting physical activity in the workplace. *Journal of Science and Medicine in Sport*, 7, 60–66.

Martinsen, E. W. (2008). Physical activity in the prevention and treatment of anxiety and depression. *Nordic Journal of Psychiatry*, 62, 25–29.

Matthews, C. E., George, S. M., Moore, S. C., Bowles, H. R., Blair, A., Park, Y., . . . & Schatzkin, A. (2012). Amount of time spent in sedentary behaviors and cause-specific mortality in US adults. *American Journal of Clinical Nutrition*, 95, 437–445.

Miller, R., & Brown, W. (2004). Steps and sitting in a working population. *International Journal of Behavioral and Medicine*, 11, 219–224.

Mutrie, N., Carney, C., Blamey, A., Crawford, F., Aitchison, T., & Whitelaw, A. (2002). "Walk in to work out": A randomised controlled trial of a self help intervention to promote active commuting. *Journal of Epidemiology and Community Health*, 56, 407–412.

National Institute for Occupational Safety and Health. (2008). *Essential Elements of Effective Workplace Programs and Policies for Improving Worker Health and Wellbeing*. Available at: www.cdc.gov/niosh/twh/essentials.html

Nelson, M. E., Rejeski, W. J., Blair, S. N., Duncan, P. W., Judge, J. O., King, A. C., . . . & Castaneda-Sceppa, C. (2007). Physical activity and public health in older adults: Recommendation from the American College of Sports Medicine and the American Heart Association. *Medicine & Science in Sports & Exercise*, 39, 1435–1445.

Ng, S. W., & Popkin, B. M. (2012). Time use and physical activity: A shift away from movement across the globe. *Obesity Review*, 13, 659–680.

Owen, N., Bauman, A., & Brown, W. (2009). Too much sitting: A novel and important predictor of chronic disease risk? British Journal of Sports Medicine, 43, 81–83.

Owen, N., Leslie, E., Salmon, J., & Fotheringham, M. J. (2000). Environmental determinants of physical activity and sedentary behavior. *Exercise and Sport Sciences Reviews*, 28, 153–158.

Paluska, S. A., & Schwenk, T. L. (2000). Physical activity and mental health – Current concepts. *Sports Medicine*, 29, 167–180.

Pate, R. R., O'Neill, J. R., & Lobelo, F. (2008). The evolving definition of "sedentary." *Exercise and Sport Sciences Reviews*, 36, 173–178.

Pedersen, B. K., & Saltin, B. (2015). Exercise as medicine – Evidence for prescribing exercise as therapy in 26 different chronic diseases. *Scandinavian Journal of Medicine & Science in Sports*, 25, 1–72.

Pender, N. J., Smith, L. C., & Vernof, J. A. (1987). Building better workers. *American Association of Occupational Health Nurses Journal*, 35, 386–390.

Penedo, F. J., & Dahn, J. R. (2005). Exercise and well-being: A review of mental and physical health benefits associated with physical activity. *Current Opinion in Psychiatry*, 18, 189–193.

Petersen, C. B., Bauman, A., Tolstrup, J. S. (2016). Total sitting time and the risk of incident diabetes in Danish adults (the DANHES cohort) over 5 years: A prospective study. *British Journal of Sports Medicine*, 50(22), 1382-1387.

Pronk, N. P. (2009). Physical activity promotion in business and industry: Evidence, context, and recommendations for a national plan. *The Journal of Physical Activity and Health*, 6(Supplement 2), S220–S235.

Pronk, N. P. (2014a). Best practice design principles of worksite health and wellness programs. *ACSM's Health & Fitness Journal*, 18, 42–46.

Pronk, N. P. (2014b). Placing workplace wellness in proper context: Value beyond money. Preventing Chronic Disease, 11, E119.

Pronk, N. P., Martinson, B., Kessler, R. C., Beck, A. L., Simon, G. E., & Wang, P. (2004). The association between work performance and physical activity, cardiorespiratory fitness, and obesity. *The Journal of Occupational and Environmental Medicine*, 46, 19–25.

Pronk, N. P., Tan, A. W., & O'Connor, P. (1999). Obesity, fitness, willingness to communicate and health care costs. *Medicine & Science in Sports & Exercise*, 31, 1535–1543.

Proper, K. I., Hildebrandt, V. H., van der Beek, A. J., Twisk, J. W. R., & van Mechelen, W. (2003a). Effect of individual counseling on physical activity fitness and health – A randomized controlled trial in a workplace setting. *American Journal of Preventive Medicine*, 24, 218–226.

Proper, K. I., Koning, M., van der Beek, A. J., Hildebrandt, V. H., Bosscher, R. J., & van Mechelen, W. (2003b). The effectiveness of worksite physical activity programs on physical activity, physical fitness, and health. *Clinical Journal of Sport Medicine*, 13, 106–117.

Proper, K. I., van den Heuvel, S. G., de Vroome, E. M., Hildebrandt, V. H., & van der Beek, A. J. (2006). Dose-response relation between physical activity and sick leave. British Journal of Sports Medicine, 40, 173–178.

Puig-Ribera, A., Gilson, N., Mckenna, J., & Brown, W. (2007). Walking towards well-being and job performance in a university commuinty: Preliminary analysis of baseline data. *Medicine & Science in Sport & Exercise*, 39, S193.

Robison, J. I., Rogers, M. A., Carlson, J. J., Mavis, B. E., Stachnik, T., Stoffelmayr, B., . . . & van Huss, W. D. (1992). Effects of a 6-month incentive-based exercise program on adherence and work capacity. *Medicine and Science in Sports and Exercise*, 24, 85–93.

Ryde, G. C., Brown, H. E., Gilson, N. D., & Brown, W. J. (2014). Are we chained to our desks? Describing desk-based sitting using a novel measure of occupational sitting. *The Journal of Physical Activity and Health*, 11, 1318–1323.

Ryde, G. C., Gilson, N. D., Burton, N. W., & Brown, W. J. (2013). Recruitment rates in workplace physical activity interventions: Characteristics for success. *American Journal of Health Promotion*, 27, E101–E112.

Sainsbury Centre for Mental Health. (2007). *Mental Health at Work: Developing the Business Case*. Policy Paper 8. Sainsbury Institute for Mental Health, London.

Schuch, F. B., Vancampfort, D., Richards, J., Rosenbaum, S., Ward, P. B., & Stubbs, B. (2016). Exercise as a treatment for depression: A meta-analysis adjusting for publication bias. *Journal of Psychiatric Research*, 77, 42–51.

Schultz, A. B., & Edington, D. W. (2007). Employee health and presenteeism: A systematic review. *The Journal of Occupational Rehabilitation*, 17, 547–579.

Shephard, R. J. (1992). A critical analysis of work-site fitness programs and their postulated economic benefits. *Medicine & Science in Sports & Exercise*, 24, 354–370.

Shephard, R. J., Cox, M., & Corey, P. (1981). Fitness program participation – Its effect on worker performance. *Journal of Occupational and Environmental Medicine*, 23, 359–363.

Stamatakis, E, Pulsford, R. M., Brunner, E. J., Britton, A. R., Bauman, A. E., Biddle, S. JH., Hillsdon, M. (2017). Sitting behaviour is not associated with incident diabetes over 13 years: The Whitehall II cohort study. *British Journal of Sports Medicine*, published online first, doi: 10.1136/bjsports-2016-096723.

Stokols, D., Pelletier, K. R., & Fielding, J. E. (1996). The ecology of work and health: Research and policy directions for the promotion of employee health. Health Education Quarterly, 23, 137–158.

Strohle, A. (2009). Physical activity, exercise, depression and anxiety disorders. *Journal of Neural Transmission*, 116, 777–784.

Sullivan, A. N., & Lachman, M. E. (2016). Behavior change with fitness technology in sedentary adults: A review of the evidence for increasing physical activity. *Frontiers in Public Health,* 4. doi: 10.3389/fpubh.2016.00289

Swenson, T., & Siegel, M. (2013). Increasing stair use in an office worksite through an interactive environmental intervention. *American Journal of Health Promotion*, 27, 323–329.

Taylor, C. B., Sallis, J. F., & Needle, R. (1985). The relation of physical-activity and exercise to mental-health. *Public Health Reports*, 100, 195–202.

Thorp, A. A., Owen, N., Neuhaus, M., & Dunstan, D. W. (2011). Sedentary behaviors and subsequent health outcomes in adults a systematic review of longitudinal studies, 1996–2011. *American Journal of Preventive Medicine*, 41, 207–215.

Tremblay, M. S., Colley, R. C., Saunders, T. J., Healy, G. N., & Owen, N. (2010). Physiological and health implications of a sedentary lifestyle. *Applied Physiology Nutrition and Metabolism*, 35, 725–740.

Vallance, J. K., Winkler, E. A., Gardiner, P. A., Healy, G. N., Lynch, B. M., & Owen, N. (2011). Associations of objectively-assessed physical activity and sedentary time with depression: NHANES (2005–2006). *Preventive Medicine*, 53, 284–288.

van Nieuw-Amerongen, M. E., Kremers, S. P. J., de Vries, N. K., & Kok, G. (2011). The use of prompts, increased accessibility, visibility, and aesthetics of the stairwell to promote stair use in a university building. *Environment and Behavior*, 43, 131–139.

Villablanca, P. A., Alegria, J. R., Mookadam, F., Holmes, D. R., Jr., Wright, R. S., & Levine, J. A. (2015). Nonexercise activity thermogenesis in obesity management. *Mayo Clinic Proceedings*, 90, 509–519.

Voit, S. (2001). Work-site health and fitness programs: Impact on the employee and employer. *Work*, 16, 273–286.

Wang, F., McDonald, T., Champagne, L. J., & Edington, D. W. (2004). Relationship of body mass index and physical activity to health care costs among employees. *Journal of Occupational and Environmental Medicine*, 46, 428–436.

Wang, P. S., Simon, G., & Kessler, R. C. (2003). The economic burden of depression and the cost-effectiveness of treatment. *The International Journal of Methods in Psychiatric Research*, 12, 22–33.

Warburton, D. E. R., Charlesworth, S., Ivey, A., Nettlefold, L., & Bredin, S. S. D. (2010). A systematic review of the evidence for Canada's Physical Activity Guidelines for Adults. *International Journal of Behavioral Nutrition and Physical Activity*, 7, 39. doi: 10.1186/1479-5868-7-39.

Warburton, D. E., Katzmarzyk, P. T., Rhodes, R. E., & Shephard, R. J. (2007). Evidence-informed physical activity guidelines for Canadian adults. Canadian Journal of Public Health, 98(Supplement 2), S16–S68.

Warburton, D. E., Nicol, C. W., & Bredin, S. S. (2006a). Health benefits of physical activity: The evidence. *Canadian Medical Association Journal*, 174, 801–809.

Warburton, D. E. R., Nicol, C. W., & Bredin, S. S. D. (2006b). Prescribing exercise as preventive therapy. *Canadian Medical Association Journal*, 174, 961–974.

Whitfield, G., Pettee Gabriel, K. K., & Kohl, H. W. (2013). Sedentary and active: Self-reported sitting time among marathon and half-marathon participants. *Journal of Physical Activity and Health*, 11, 165–172.

World Health Organization. (2010). Global recommendations on physical activity for health. *Geneva: World Health Organization*.

World Health Organization. (2015). *Physical Activity Fact Sheet N°385*. Available at: www.who.int/media centre/factsheets/fs385/en/

Yancey, A. K., Mccarthy, W. J., Taylor, W. C., Merlo, A., Gewa, C., Weber, M. D., & Fielding, J. E. (2004). The Los Angeles Lift Off: A sociocultural environmental change intervention to integrate physical activity into the workplace. *Preventive Medicine*, 38, 848–856.

22

Essential elements of organizational initiatives to improve workplace wellbeing

Arla Day and Samantha A. Penney

Introduction

Although it is almost axiomatic that workplaces can lead to stress and negative health outcomes among employees, there also has been an emerging body of research demonstrating that workplaces can act as positive health resources and can assist in enhancing employee health and wellbeing (e.g., Danna & Griffin, 1999; Day & Randell, 2014; Grawitch, Gottschalk, & Munz, 2006; Sparks, Faragher, & Cooper, 2001). That is, in addition to the stressors and demands that a job may bring, work also may provide resources such as social relationships, meaning, and training programs that promote wellbeing (Day & Randell, 2014). Moreover, organizations have the ability to change work environments and social contexts to both directly and indirectly improve employee wellbeing.

The models and research presented throughout this book reinforce the notion that there are many prevailing factors that can influence health and wellbeing. For example, based on the wellbeing models presented in Part I, various organizational interventions have been proposed. However, it is important to have a good understanding of why these organizational programs are successful. That is, what are the key elements of successful programs and initiatives? As demonstrated in Part II, individual characteristics also contribute to wellbeing, and thus must be taken into consideration. By taking a holistic approach to wellness and by highlighting the individual-, group-, leader- and organizational-focused elements and resources that can improve employee wellbeing, organizations are able to create positive program outcomes.

Theoretical framework: essential elements of workplace wellness programs

In this chapter, we developed a framework to help identify these essential elements in terms of three core areas that impact the success of wellbeing initiatives: (1) having valid content and a holistic focus of the initiatives, (2) considering contextual factors of the initiatives, and (3) incorporating successful program development and implementation processes (see Figure 22.1). Of these areas, the content of these interventions is an obvious component, taking into consideration the level of focus of the initiative (i.e., focusing on the individual, group, leader, or the

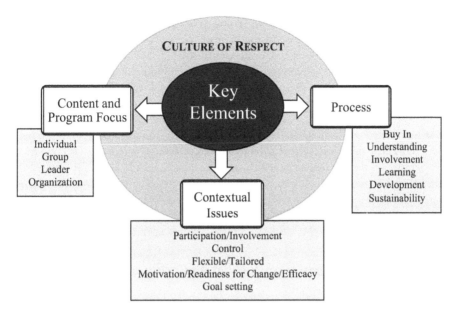

Figure 22.1 Framework to examine essential elements of workplace wellness programs

organization and work context). We also examine some of the contextual issues that may be critical to workplace wellbeing initiatives, such as involving and engaging employees in the initiatives, tailoring the programs to meet individual and organizational needs, ensuring flexibility of the initiatives to meet needs, and emphasizing key training components of goal setting. Using models of intervention development (e.g., Day, 2014; Watson, 2008), we discuss the process of developing and implementing initiatives that is critical to intervention success. Finally, in extending current models of healthy workplaces, we emphasize the core element of respect, as it can be seen as a unifying theme underlying all components in the model.

Using organizations to improve wellbeing

Before examining these components, it is helpful to briefly examine the assumptions as to why it is important for organizations to be involved in improving worker wellbeing in the first place. Given that most people can spend up to a quarter or a third of their adult life at work (Harter, Schmidt, & Keyes, 2003), the organization can influence – either negatively or positively – individual wellbeing. On the one hand, there are significant organizational costs associated with poor employee wellbeing. For example, employee mental health and wellbeing tends to be associated with increased absenteeism, turnover, health care utilization, and poor performance and productivity (Goetzel et al., 2004; Goetzel, Ozminkowski, Sederer, & Mark, 2002; Rongen, Robroek, van Lenthe, & Burdorf, 2013).

On the other hand, organizations have the opportunity to foster employee wellbeing and promote healthy workplaces. Investing in employee health and wellbeing has been associated with reduced sickness absenteeism, accident rates, and turnover as well as improved engagement, resilience, commitment, and productivity (see Cooper & Bevan, 2014, for an overview). Moreover, many organizational leaders view worker wellbeing as simply being part of an ethical responsibility to their employees. Therefore, regardless of the philosophical perspective of organizations (altruism vs. profit), arguments can be made for their involvement in protecting and fostering the wellbeing of their workers. As such, Blake and Lloyd (2008) argued that "improving the health of the working population requires that organizations accept responsibility for workplace wellness, whether for altruistic, philanthropic or egotistical reasons" (p. 450).

Therefore, if organizations are motivated to foster the wellbeing of their employees, it is important to understand what initiatives, or program components, will be effective. Unfortunately, as argued by Parks and Steelman (2008), past research is inconclusive about the benefits, and we don't know the financial and psychosocial contributions of specific wellness program elements. Although there is limited literature that directly assesses the key components of organizational wellness programs, research examining the success of organizational programs and training in general can be applied to wellness initiatives. We also can learn from existing validated wellness programs as guides to identify the key elements by examining their underlying processes and contextual aspects.

Essential elements: intervention content and program focus

An obvious key aspect of increasing the success of any workplace wellness program is ensuring that the program has relevant and valid content. To date, overarching conclusions about the validity of specific content in wellness programs is somewhat limited (Parks & Steelman, 2008). Even if a program demonstrates validity, trying to generalize "valid" content can be challenging because the content may vary across programs, the organizational context may vary, and the specific criteria may vary. Nonetheless, a starting point is to identify successful programs as a means to provide a theoretical framework to examine the key elements more extensively.

Most comprehensive workplace wellbeing initiatives focus on the individual to improve physical and psychological wellbeing through employee-focused activities such as education, prevention, counseling, goal-setting, accountability, and health promotion (Day & Helson, 2016; Parks & Steelman, 2008). Moreover, in addition to these individual-focused programs, it is equally important to focus on the group and social context of work, the role of leaders, and the overall organization.

Individual-focused initiatives

Much of the content of organizational wellness programs tends to involve helping individuals to develop stronger coping skills and resilience, and helping them to improve healthy behaviors and lifestyles. For example, increasing individual resources may involve training in terms of developing resilience and recovery experiences. Resilience is a reaction that occurs when people are faced with change, adversity, or demands, and refers to the ability to cope and to bounce back (Luthans, 2002; Stewart, Reid, & Mangham, 1997). It is related to physical and psychological wellbeing (e.g., Tugade & Fredrickson, 2004), and research has suggested that it can be improved through training (Robertson, Cooper, Sarkar, & Curran, 2015).

Recovery is considered a process of engaging in nonwork activities in order to restore individual wellbeing and resources (Sonnentag & Bayer, 2005). Recovery experiences assist in restoring lost resources as well as preventing further resources from being lost (Sonnentag & Fritz, 2007). Recovery experiences are positively related to employee wellbeing (Sonnentag & Frese, 2003). Workplace interventions can help to increase the frequency of engaging in recovery experiences (e.g., Hahn, Binnewies, Sonnentag, & Mojza, 2011; Stevens, 2010), leading to improved wellbeing.

Similar to the research on these training programs, research conducted on workplace health promotion typically emphasizes changes to individual behavior and lifestyle (i.e., cessation of negative health behaviors, promoting positive health and lifestyle behaviors, and health screening; see Day & Helson, 2016, for a review). There has been some research looking at the effectiveness of programs to address specific issues (e.g., smoking cessation or obesity prevention; Lemmens, Oenema, Knut, & Brug, 2008; Sorensen et al., 2007). However, although we know that programs targeting specific content may be effective, there is no clear understanding of why these individual-focused programs are effective.

Several specific programs incorporate multiple aspects of an individual focused program. For example, HealthWatch is an interactive Web-based intervention tool that provides employees with tools to promote health and wellbeing involving interactive exercises on health promotion and stress management as well as brief assessments on the psychosocial work environment and health, with instant feedback (Hasson, Anderberg, Theorell, & Arnetz, 2005; Hasson & Villaume, 2013). Participating in HealthWatch is associated with improvements in stress- and recovery-related biomarkers and improved perceived ability to manage stress, sleep quality, concentration, and mental energy in comparison to a control group (Hasson et al., 2005).

Similarly, Day, Francis, Stevens, Hurrell, and McGrath (2014) created a 12-week, phone-based coaching program, in which employees talk to their own personal coach every week to help set and achieve personal- and work-related goals to manage life demands and balance work and life responsibilities (Achieving Balance in Life and Employment, or ABLE). Participation in the program was associated with improved life satisfaction, engagement, positive mood, and job satisfaction as well as reduced negative mood, cynicism, perceived stress, and absenteeism in comparison to a wait-list control group. These results were maintained for four months following program completion. These results suggest that a phone-based coaching program may be an effective method to improve individual wellbeing.

Group-focused initiatives

In addition to these initiatives focusing on the individual, there is a movement toward considering work groups and the social context of work as being integral in employee health. Not surprisingly, positive social interactions at work are related to positive health outcomes (e.g., strengthened immune system, cardiovascular activity, and hormonal patterns; Heaphy & Dutton, 2008) as well as to organizational outcomes such as decreased intentions to turnover (Feeley, Hwang, & Barnett, 2008). Similarly, interpersonal compatibility among individuals and their work group/ team (i.e., person–group/team fit) is related to both coworker and job satisfaction (Kristof-Brown, Zimmerman, & Johnson, 2005). Therefore, because social interactions can influence wellbeing, the group context can provide a valuable context for promoting employee wellbeing. For example, the Civility, Respect, and Engagement in the Workplace (CREW) program is designed to target employee incivility (Osatuke, Moore, Ward, Dyrenforth, & Belton, 2009) at a group level by empowering work groups to create common culture norms around civility and goals toward achieving it. CREW has shown success in increasing group civility compared to a control group (Osatuke et al., 2009), as well as increasing coworker civility, respect, job satisfaction, and trust in management, and decreasing supervisor incivility, cynicism, and work absences (Leiter, Laschinger, Day, & Gilin Oore, 2011). Some of the effects were maintained one year later (Leiter, Day, Gilin Oore, & Laschinger, 2012).

Leader-focused initiatives

Leaders also are an integral aspect of wellbeing initiatives and can influence employee wellbeing in many ways: They can foster wellbeing and health by directly supporting employees and providing resources (Day & Nielsen, 2017). They can be role models by engaging in initiatives and healthy behavior. They also can help educate on wellbeing initiatives. For example, several studies have demonstrated that transformational leadership is associated with positive employee wellbeing (Arnold, Turner, Barling, Kelloway, & McKee, 2007; Kelloway, Turner, Barling, & Loughlin, 2012; Nielsen, Yarker, Brenner, Randall, & Borg, 2008) and with other positive employee outcomes, such as employee involvement, influence, meaningfulness of work (Arnold et al., 2007; Nielsen et al., 2008), and organizational commitment (Barling, Weber, & Kelloway, 1996). Therefore, interventions that focus on promoting transformational leadership behaviors should be effective initiatives to improve employee wellbeing.

In order to help leaders provide resources to employees and improve employee wellbeing, it is also necessary to provide support and resources for the leaders themselves. For example, providing leaders with tools to help them respond to employee mental health problems can be an integral component of a holistic organizational wellbeing program. As such, the Mental Health Awareness Training (MHAT) is an education program that was designed to educate leaders to help increase mental health literacy, and help them respond to employee mental health problems (Dimoff & Kelloway, 2013). It has been successful in increasing knowledge of mental health issues, creating more positive attitudes towards mental health, providing leaders with greater self-efficacy to deal with employees with mental health problems, and increasing leaders' intentions to promote mental health in the workplace (Dimoff & Kelloway, 2013).

Organizational-focused initiatives

Finally, wellbeing initiatives may target the work environment in terms of the job, work context, and organization. Job redesign refers to the processes and outcomes of how employees' work is structured and organized (Parker & Wall, 1998) in terms of variety, autonomy, task identity, and feedback (Hackman & Lawler, 1971). Job redesign has been associated with increased wellbeing (e.g., Holman, 2002), job satisfaction (Griffin, 1991), and empowerment (Ugboro, 2006), and decreased stress symptoms and absenteeism rates (Kawakami, Araki, Kawashima, Masumoto, & Hayashi, 1997). Participatory Interventions from an Organizational Perspective (PIOP) is an organizational program that focuses on identifying demands and resources, and subsequently making changes to the way work is designed and managed based on such information in order to improve employee wellbeing (Nielsen, Stage, Abildgaard, & Brauer, 2013). Specifically, through carrying out a series of steps (i.e., planning the intervention design, identifying areas for improvement, developing action plans and improvement initiatives, implementing improvement initiatives, and evaluating the intervention; see Nielsen & Randall, 2012) organizational participatory interventions have been shown to be related to employee outcomes such as wellbeing, social support, and autonomy (Nielsen & Randall, 2012).

These examples of workplace initiatives emphasize the importance of taking a holistic approach to wellbeing by providing individual resources and by modifying the external factors involving groups, leaders, and the organization context. Given this holistic approach to wellbeing, employees are responsible for changing their behaviors and lifestyle, and developing their own internal resources (e.g., resilience), and the organization is responsible for providing healthy workplaces with organizational resources for employees (e.g., fostering supportive group interactions, leadership training, job redesign).

Another critical step involves understanding the reasons as to why programs are successful. Therefore, in trying to understand why these and other workplace wellbeing initiatives are successful, we need to move beyond simply examining the content of the initiatives to creating an organizing framework to study the essential elements of these initiatives by integrating existing organizational healthy workplace models.

Healthy workplace models

Given the importance of these individual-, group-, leader-, and organization-focused initiatives, we use existing models to help integrate these aspects into a holistic view of wellness. We know that the workplace can be a significant source of stress; Sauter, Murphy, and Hurrell (1990) identified work design aspects that could either reduce or contribute to ill health in terms of workload and work pace, work schedule, work roles, job future, social environment, job content, and participation and control. That is, a healthy workplace is one that minimizes the negative aspects as well as promotes positive aspects.

Therefore, a healthy workplace can contribute to employee wellbeing through this process of fostering positive components and minimizing negative components. Warr (2007) argued that several elements are key to worker happiness. Some of the elements address interpersonal relationships at work in terms of having positive contact with other people and having supportive and considerate supervision. Some elements involved job tasks, such as having a manageable workload and goals; having a reasonably clear role; and having variety in the tasks on the job, the skills used in doing the tasks, or even in the location of the job. Several other components may be classified as involving security and control at work, not only in terms of a sense of job security, but also in terms of the freedom to voice ideas and be heard, being involved in changes, having an opportunity to acquire and use skills, and having personal control and discretion over decisions. Other aspects involve the meaning of the work, such that the workers are doing a job that is valued by the organization and believing that they are doing something worthwhile. Overlapping with these components is an overall sense of having safe and comfortable surroundings in which employees are treated fairly.

Recently, the term *psychologically healthy workplace* has been used as an umbrella term to encompass the physical environment, psychological, and social aspects of the organization (Kelloway & Day, 2005), which can provide a framework for understanding and examining worker wellbeing. Similarly, in the Healthy and Resilient Organization (HERO) model, a healthy workplace is defined as one that encompasses healthy organizational resources and practices, healthy employees, and healthy organizational outcomes (Salanova, Llorens, Cifre, & Martinez, 2012). Healthy workplaces support and foster employee psychological and physical wellbeing, maximizing both worker wellbeing goals and organizational efficiency and productive goals (Day & Randell, 2014; Sauter, Lim, & Murphy, 1996).

Interventions that foster a healthy workplace encompass the physical health and safety of employees (e.g., safety hazards; creating a safe and ergonomically designed workplace), specific health promotion initiatives (e.g., knowledge sharing, screening, behavior and lifestyle change; Day & Helson, 2016), and the psychosocial environment involving the multitude of types of social interactions at work (Day & Randell, 2014; e.g., culture of support, respect, and fairness; Kelloway & Day, 2005). These promotion activities/programs can target the individual or the environment (Day & Helson, 2016) and may take a primary (e.g., preventative, workplace redesign), secondary (e.g., change perception, stress management programs), or tertiary approach (e.g., treat symptoms, utilization of health care benefits to treat illness; Cooper & Cartwright, 1994).

Therefore, in taking a holistic view of wellness, these related literatures may be used to provide a framework around employee wellness initiatives, to include creating a safe work environment; fostering work-life balance; developing positive interpersonal relationships and a culture

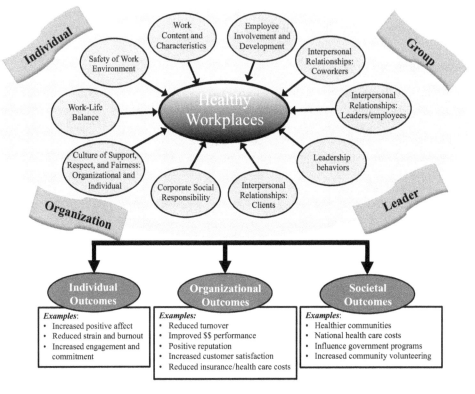

Figure 22.2 Model of psychologically healthy workplaces
Source: From Day & Nielsen, 2017; based on Kelloway & Day, 2005.

of support, respect, and fairness; involving employees at work; developing employees' knowledge, skills, and abilities; emphasizing the importance of giving and corporate social responsibility; and maximizing the positive aspects of the work content and characteristics (Day & Randell, 2014; Kelloway & Day, 2005; see Figure 22.2). We can use these literatures to help us identify where we want to direct our attention in improving workplace wellbeing. That is, because psychologically healthy workplace components tend to be associated with increased wellbeing, and because research has identified some of the components associated with workplace happiness, then any workplace wellness initiative should incorporate one or more of these content areas/components, and try to reduce or eliminate the factors that lead to negative worker outcomes.

This and other healthy workplace models (e.g., Grawitch et al., 2006) implicitly advocate for a holistic perspective by focusing on the individual, group, leader, and overall organization. They also highlight the importance of key constructs such as balance, culture, and interpersonal relationships. Interestingly, there tends to be an absence of explicit suggestions to implement specific initiatives (beside the inclusion of anecdotes or examples). Their lack of focus on specific initiatives may suggest that the initiatives per se may be less important than the overall concepts of health, safety, and respect. That is, although the concept of wellbeing should be important to organizations, there are a variety of specific initiatives that can be developed to support employee wellbeing. Therefore, we may shift our focus from the specific initiatives to the overarching components that would help unify this literature, such as culture.

Culture of respect: the unifying component

Although not always explicitly stated in all models of wellbeing and healthy workplaces, one of their critical assumptions is that a culture of mutual respect can be integral in developing a healthy workplace and in fostering employee wellbeing. Respect at work tends to be associated with employee wellbeing. For example, a positive social environment (including respect) at work is related to wellbeing (Repetti, 1987). Conversely, disrespect and mistreatment at work has negative implications for employee wellbeing (Leiter & Patterson, 2014). As a component of respect, perceived support (i.e., global beliefs about the extent to which the organization values your work and is concerned for your wellbeing; Eisenberger, Huntington, Hutchison, & Sowa, 1986) is negatively related to strain (Rhoades & Eisenberger, 2002) and can buffer the negative effects of work-related stress and strain (Thomas & Ganster, 1995).

Therefore, if there is mutual respect and support among individuals in an organization (workers, leaders, owners), the specific initiatives may be of secondary importance. If leaders respect the opinions of their employees, they will want to involve them in decision making. If leaders are sensitive to the needs of employees, they will want to help employees balance work and nonwork responsibilities, engage in meaningful work, provide opportunities for skills development. Conversely, initiatives that are implemented in an environment that lack this supportive and respectful culture may be met with skepticism by employees or viewed as unnecessary. For example, Sloan and Gruman (1988) argued that employee participation in workplace health promotion programs may be influenced by the organizational climate of perceived supportiveness, and they found that greater perceived supervisor support was associated with increased employee participation. Therefore, the cultural component might be a unifying component that also impacts the conceptual factors of wellbeing initiatives.

In the general training literature, supervisor support can have a strong impact on employees' training success and effectiveness (e.g., Facteau, Dobbins, Russell, Ladd, & Kudisch, 1995; Lim & Johnson, 2002; Switzer, Nagy, Mullins, 2005). Supervisor support tends to be positively related to employee motivation prior to training (Facteau et al., 1995; Switzer et al., 2005), and employees are more likely to participate in training when their supervisors are supportive (Switzer et al., 2005). Similarly, Lim and Johnson (2002) found that supervisor support was one of the strongest variables that influenced training transfer. Specifically, transfer of training was more successful when employees were involved with discussions with supervisors, received positive feedback from supervisors, and when supervisors were familiar with the training and/or participated in the training (Lim & Johnson, 2002).

Similar to the literature on supervisor support, there is evidence in the transfer of training literature to suggest that peer support is important in training. Peer support tends to predict motivation prior to training and transfer of training (Chiaburu & Marinova, 2005), and it is related to greater transfer of training (Clarke, 2002; Facteau et al., 1995; Martin, 2010). Therefore, peer support may make an important contribution to the success of workplace wellbeing programs.

To summarize, having valid and relevant content is an obvious key element in designing any wellbeing initiative. There are several theoretical models that we can use to support our assumptions about what the content of such programs should contain, and current thinking suggests that taking a holistic perspective (in targeting the individual, group, leader, and organization) and having an underlying culture of respect are key to program success (Day & Nielsen, 2017).

Although there is evidence to suggest that certain work factors are important to wellbeing (e.g., transformational leadership is related to employee wellbeing; Arnold et al., 2007), and that certain organizational wellbeing programs are successful (e.g., ABLE, Day, 2014; HealthWatch Hasson et al., 2005), a systematic examination and comparison of the successful components of healthy workplace programs is still lacking. Part of the challenge in identifying success factors in programs is that there is little standardization of programs, in that many may target very specific aspects of wellbeing (or related outcomes). Therefore, in examining the effectiveness of these programs, it is helpful to look at the contextual factors (e.g., valid content, tailored communications, accountability) that may influence the success of wellbeing initiatives.

Essential elements: contextual factors

Given wellness initiatives that have valid content and that are holistic in their breadth of coverage, and given a culture of respect and support, other contextual components of wellbeing programs also can influence program success, such as increasing employee participation, involvement in the development and implementation, allowing employee control over the initiative, having a flexible initiative that can be tailored to the individual, ensuring participant motivation and efficacy, and assisting with goal setting.

Participation, involvement, empowerment, and control

Encouraging participation of all key stakeholders (e.g., employees, leaders) not only in the development of the initiatives, but also in the initiatives themselves may be a key program success factor. In the general health promotion literature, Arneson and Ekberg (2005) argued that empowering individuals is a key component of health promotion. Empowerment involves increasing control over decisions and actions affecting health (World Health Organization, 1986). Research has demonstrated that control tends to be associated with increased psychological health (Noblet, 2003) and psychological functioning (Mikkelsen & Saksvik, 1999).

Related to the idea of empowerment is the issue of participation. Participatory interventions are associated with improved employee wellbeing and increased social support and autonomy (Nielsen & Randall, 2012) as well as improved team functioning and employee wellbeing 12 months following the intervention (Nielsen et al., 2014). Therefore, taking a participatory approach to organizational intervention implementation may be an effective approach to increase employee wellbeing.

Flexibility and tailored programs

It has been suggested that having flexibility in programs to address individual needs and tailoring the program to the individual and organizational level can increase program success. For example, Day et al.'s (2014) ABLE program aimed to address employee needs that existing workshops did not allow, in terms of having sufficient flexibility in their content or timing to accommodate schedules and individual needs of the employee. Qualitative data suggests that having flexibility and control over content that is tailored to the individual is desired and associated with increased program satisfaction (Day et al., 2014).

Motivation, readiness for change, and efficacy

Employee motivation is a key component to the success of any training program. Related to motivation is the concept of readiness for change, which is defined as an attitude toward change that reflects the extent to which one "is cognitively and emotionally inclined to accept, embrace, and adapt a particular plan to purposefully alter the status quo" (Holt, Armenakis, Harris, & Feild, 2007, p. 326). Numerous studies have demonstrated that individual motivation is related to learning and transfer of training (i.e., extent to which the participants applied the material they learned to their job; e.g., Chiaburu & Marinova, 2005; Facteau et al., 1995; Grossman & Salas, 2011) and to the intentions and commitment to transfer their training materials to the job (Machin & Fogarty, 1997).

Failing to assess employees' readiness for change may be a main reason that workplace wellness programs are unsuccessful (Madsen, 2003). This argument is in line with behavior-change models such as Kurt Lewin's three-step model of change (unfreezing, change, refreezing; Lewin, 1947) and Prochaska, Norcross, and DiClemente's (1994) six steps of change (precontemplation, contemplation, preparation, action, maintenance, termination). Both models argue that if the initial steps to behavior change (e.g., unfreezing or contemplation and preparation) do not occur, behavior change or program success is unlikely to occur (Madsen, 2003).

Self-efficacy refers to one's belief in their ability to perform a specific behavior, meet a goal, or cope with a situation (Bandura, 1997). It tends to be related to goals students set for themselves and academic achievement (Zimmerman, Bandura, & Martinez-Pons, 1992) and is a good predictor of job performance (Judge & Bono, 2001). Interventions have been effective at increasing self-efficacy (for an overview, see Gist & Mitchell, 1992). Moreover, self-efficacy may not only impact performance, but it also tends to be positively related to wellbeing (Barlow, Wright, & Cullen, 2002; Magaletta & Oliver, 1999) and negatively related to negative affect, depression, and anxiety (Luszczynska, Scholz, & Schwarzer, 2005). Therefore, programs designed to increase self-efficacy may lead not only to setting higher goals and having better goal attainment, but also to creating higher levels of wellbeing.

Goal setting

Because consciously chosen goals are precursors to actions (Latham, 2012), and consequently, tend to guide human behavior (Mitchell, Thompson, & George-Falvy, 2000), goal setting may be a valuable component in developing programs that focus on individual behavior (such as workplace wellness). Goal-setting theory specifies that goals can influence employee performance (Locke & Latham, 1990), such that compared to individuals without goals, individuals with set goals are better able to focus their attention and action, exert more energy, continue even when faced with failure, and develop better strategies (Locke, Shaw, Saari, & Latham, 1981). In terms of the types of goals, goal setting theory stipulates that specific, difficult, and assigned goals result in higher performance than vague "do your best" goals (Latham & Locke, 2007; Locke & Latham, 1990, 2002). Therefore, it would make sense that any wellbeing intervention that targets individual change may want to incorporate goal setting into the program as a means of increasing success.

In looking at the general training literature, incorporating goal setting may increase skill transfer to one's job (Richman-Hirsch, 2001). For example, in Taylor, Russ-Eft, and Chan's (2005) meta-analysis of behavior modeling training, having a goal-setting component incorporated into the program increased the extent of transfer of training of program materials. Finally, in addition to performance outcomes, goal attainment is positively related to wellbeing (Emmons, 1996; Sheldon & Elliot, 1999). Therefore, the act of setting and attaining goals may, in and of itself, be an essential element of wellbeing.

Essential elements: successful program processes

In addition to the content of the programs and the contextual factors of training and the organization, the actual process can impact the success of workplace wellbeing initiatives. Based on several implementation models of organizational wellness programs (e.g., Canadian Centre for Occupational Health and Safety, n.d.; Cavanagh & Chadwich, 2005; Centers for Disease Control and Prevention, 2012; Watson, 2008), Day (2014) developed the BUILD model, which provides a mnemonic of the essential elements of implementing healthy worker/workplace initiatives to help organizations understand and implement healthy workplace practices by: (1) building buy-in to foster the engagement and participation of stakeholders; (2) understanding the needs and constraints of the organization; (3)implementing the wellbeing initiatives; (4) learning and modifying the program through monitoring and evaluation; and (5) developing and sustaining a long-term plan for wellness (see also Day, Hartling, & Mackie, 2015).

Buy-in

The first critical step of any change initiative or organizational wellness program is to gain the buy-in of all stakeholders by developing commitment to the initiative, ensuring employee participation and involvement, communicating and sharing knowledge, and engaging stakeholders. This process can be helped by having a committee to organize the workload and/or by having a champion for the initiative.

Participation and empowerment are integral contextual aspects of wellbeing initiatives. Interventions aimed at improving employee wellbeing tend to be most successful when they incorporate the participation of employees (Nielsen, Randall, Holten, & Gonzalez, 2010). Participation from employees allows for the opportunity to increase the fit of the initiative with the organizational culture and context, reduce resistance to change, and foster employee control and sense of support and justice (Nielsen et al., 2010). Therefore, during implementation, involving a committee – which ideally consists of the participation of both management and employees – is vital to employee wellbeing program success (e.g., Nielsen et al., 2010). Moreover, interventions that take an organizational participatory approach are related to improved autonomy, social support, and wellbeing postintervention (Nielsen & Randall, 2012).

Understand

Before any initiatives are put in place, the organization should have a good understanding of the unique needs and constraints of its workplace and its workers by conducting some type of a formal or informal needs assessment or gap analysis to identify the specific needs (Arthur, Bennett, Edens, & Bell, 2003; Brown, 2002; Ostroff & Ford, 1989; Salas & Cannon-Bowers, 2001; Watson, 2008). It is critical at this stage to identify any unique demands of the organization, as well as the resources and supports the organization can offer to the initiative and to employees. This component is essential in order to create applicable tailored and flexible programs.

Brown (2002) argued that conducting a needs assessment prior to developing training programs is important to allow organizations to identify problem areas, gain management support for the training, obtain a baseline in order to compare program effectiveness following the implementation of the program, and assess the costs and benefits associated with training. Ironically, despite calls to understand specific organizational and employee needs, very few studies incorporate needs assessments prior to developing or implementing training (Arthur et al., 2003). Needs assessments can be conducted at the organization level (organization analysis to assess the appropriateness of training related to organizational goals), task level (task analysis to assess the skills and knowledge necessary for a trainee to complete a task), or person level (person analysis to assess whether training is needed and whether trainees are ready for training; Brown & Sitzmann,

2011). Although much of this literature targets general training initiatives, the use of these analyses to develop wellness programs may help create valid and sustainable programs.

Related to the issue of understanding needs is the issue of having tailored programs. Although it may not be essential to reinvent new programs, tailoring (customizing interventions, programs, or materials to the unique needs of the individual) tends to result in more effective outcomes (Skinner, Campbell, Rimer, Curry, & Prochaska, 1999). For example, health behavior–change interventions (e.g., weight loss, smoking cessation) have consistently demonstrated that tailored intervention programs are typically more effective than general programs or untailored programs (e.g., Adachi et al., 2007; Meyer et al., 2008). Therefore, understanding the needs of the individual and organization, and either creating new programs or tailoring existing programs to address those needs, should result in better outcomes.

Implement

Once there is buy-in for the concept of a healthy workplace and there is a good understanding of the unique organizational needs and constraints, specific wellness initiatives can be developed and implemented (Day et al., 2015; Watson, 2008). In planning and brainstorming the initiatives, one should look at the strengths of the organization in relation to the unique demands and needs identified. For example, a survey of organizational best practices may be helpful to identify the feasibility and validity of programs that may match the organizational needs. It is essential to continue the involvement of stakeholders and integrate the key contextual factors (e.g., goal setting, tailored programs, participation, and control).

Learn

Many times, organizations stop after implementing a program and simply assume that it was successful. That is, "organizations frequently implement wellness programs to reduce organizational costs and improve morale . . . [but they] rarely evaluate the effectiveness of the programs in meeting these goals" (Parks & Steel, 2008, pp. 58–59), even though program monitoring and evaluation are integral to the intervention process (Kaufman & Keller, 1994; Watson, 2008) in order to understand the effects of the program, provide feedback, to learn about what aspects worked and/or didn't work, and make improvements. Therefore, an evaluation of the processes and mechanisms to assess program effectiveness is important (Cavanagh & Chadwich, 2005; Nielsen & Randall, 2013).

Develop and sustain

Developing the initiatives further so that they can be sustainable and receptive to individual and organizational change is a critical, yet overlooked, component in many programs. Even the most successful programs are susceptible to failure if the momentum and effects can't be sustained. Therefore, the key aspects of a program should include plans to maintain the program (Canadian Centre for Occupational Health and Safety, n.d.) for long-term sustainability (Day, 2014).

Conclusion

Given the amount of time individuals spend at work, and given the influence that work can have over one's health and wellbeing, organizations are in an excellent position to foster employee health and wellbeing. Moreover, because of the direct and indirect costs and benefits associated with employee health and wellbeing, the importance of making an effort towards supporting wellbeing is obvious. However, we don't have conclusive evidence of the utility of workplace wellness programs (Parks & Steelman, 2008) and the question remains: What are the essential components of successful workplace wellbeing initiatives? Although the literature is somewhat lacking in providing direct answers about these essential elements, the general research on training programs and the existing organizational wellness programs provided guidance to develop a framework to help researchers and practitioners understand how to move forward.

In addition to having valid content for each initiative, the research suggests that in order to increase employee wellbeing, organizations should incorporate a holistic approach in which the onus for wellbeing is placed both on the organization (Blake & Lloyd, 2008) and the employee (e.g., Day et al., 2014), incorporating keys aspects of individual programs (e.g., ABLE; Day et al., 2014), group social contexts (e.g., CREW; Leiter et al., 2011), leadership supports and processes (e.g., MHAT; Dimoff & Kelloway, 2013), and organizational change (participatory approach; Nielsen & Randall, 2012). Moreover, by incorporating programs that focus on the individual, group, leaders, and the overall organizational environment, wellbeing becomes incorporated into the culture of the organization, and thus may increase the success of any one initiative. Having a culture that is supportive of wellbeing initiatives is integral to the success of programs. Finally, specific program elements, such as tailoring the content to the individual, encouraging participation/involvement and control over decisions, fostering employee motivation and self-efficacy, incorporating goal setting can add to the success of programs. It is interesting and important to note that these components should not be considered as orthogonal to the culture components: in fact, these components should naturally flow from a respectful culture that supports employee wellbeing.

Essential program elements model and future research

Based on these components, we created a framework to help understand the essential elements of organizational wellbeing programs. Future research is needed to empirically test this framework to help identify these critical components and potentially expand upon it to include other elements. For example, even though our focus is on the individual, group, leaders, and organization, future research may take into consideration how organizations help employees' nonwork wellbeing (e.g., offering employee and family assistance programs – EFAPs – to assist employees and their families with managing nonwork demands such as legal and financial issues or family alcohol abuse). However, the evaluation of the effectiveness of EFAPs has received less attention (Cooper, Dewe, & O'Driscoll, 2010), and although it is typically recognized that changing the social environment helps create and sustain individual change, it is unknown the extent to which having a focus on nonwork social structures is integral to workplace wellbeing programs.

From our review, it appears that it may be the case that the process of designing initiatives is as important, or even more important, than their content. Therefore, consideration needs to be given to the steps of engaging the workplace, assessing the needs and wants of the employees and the organization, developing valid initiatives, assessing their effectiveness, and creating sustainable wellbeing initiatives.

One of the key elements that extends across all components of content, focus, process, and context is the apparent importance of a culture of respect and support in creating successful wellbeing initiatives. That is, without a supportive environment and culture, initiatives may be less successful. Without a culture of mutual trust and respect, programs may not even be developed and offered, and the employees may be less likely to use them and to benefit from them. Although having valid content is obviously important, the lack of a respectful and supportive environment may inhibit program success. Therefore, developing a culture of respect may be 'the' essential element of wellbeing initiatives.

References

Adachi, Y., Sato, C., Yamatsu, K., Ito, S., Adachi, K., & Yamagami, T. (2007). A randomized controlled trial on the long-term effects of a 1-month behavioral weight control program assisted by computer tailored advice. *Behaviour Research and Therapy*, 45(3), 459–470.

Arneson, H., & Ekberg, K. (2005). Evaluation of empowerment processes in a workplace health promotion intervention based on learning in Sweden. *Health Promotion International*, 20(4), 351–359.

Arnold, K. A., Turner, N., Barling, J., Kelloway, E. K., & McKee, M. C. (2007). Transformational leadership and psychological well-being: The mediating role of meaningful work. *Journal of Occupational Health Psychology*, 12(3), 193.

Arthur, W. Jr., Bennett, W. Jr., Edens, P. S., & Bell, S. T. (2003). Effectiveness of training in organizations: A meta-analysis of design and evaluation features. *Journal of Applied Psychology*, 88(2), 234–245.

Bandura, A. (1997). *Self-Efficacy: The Exercise of Control*. New York: Freeman.

Barling, J., Weber, T., & Kelloway, E. K. (1996). Effects of transformational leadership training on attitudinal and financial outcomes: A field experiment. *Journal of Applied Psychology*, 81(6), 827–832.

Barlow, J., Wright, C., & Cullen, L. (2002). A job-seeking self-efficacy scale for people with physical disabilities: Preliminary development and psychometric testing. *British Journal of Guidance and Counselling*, 30(1), 37–53.

Blake, H., & Lloyd, S. (2008). Influencing organisational change in the NHS: Lessons learned from workplace wellness initiatives in practice. *Quality in Primary Care*, 16(6), 449–455.

Brown, J. (2002). Training needs assessment: A must for developing an effective training program. *Public Personnel Management*, 31(4), 569–578.

Brown, K. G., & Sitzmann, T. (2011). Training and employee development for improved performance. In: S. Zedeck (eds.), *APA Handbook of Industrial and Organizational Psychology*. Washington, DC: American Psychological Association, 469–503.

Canadian Centre for Occupational Health and Safety. (nd.). *Workplace Health and Wellness Program: Getting Started*. Available at: www.ccohs.ca/oshanswers/psychosocial/wellness_program.html

Cavanagh, S., & Chadwich, K. (2005). *Health Needs Assessment: A Practical Guide*. London, UK: National Institute for Health and Clinical Excellence.

Centers for Disease Control and Prevention. (2012). *Steps to Wellness: A Guide to Implementing the 2008 Physical Activity Guidelines for Americans in the Workplace*. Available at: www.cdc.gov/nccdphp/dnpao/hwi/downloads/Steps2Wellness_BROCH14_508_Tag508.pdf

Chiaburu, D. S., & Marinova, S. V. (2005). What predicts skill transfer? An exploratory study of goal orientation, training self-efficacy and organizational supports. *International Journal of Training and Development*, 9(2), 110–123.

Clarke, N. (2002). Job/work environment factors influencing training transfer within a human service agency: Some indicative support for Baldwin and Ford's transfer climate construct. *International Journal of Training and Development*, 6(3), 146–162.

Cooper, C. L., & Bevan, S. (2014). Business benefits of a healthy workplace. In: A. Day, E. K. Kelloway, & J. J. Hurrell (eds.), *Workplace Well-Being: How to Build a Psychologically Healthy Workplaces*. West Sussex, UK: John Wiley & Sons, 27–49.

Cooper, C. L., & Cartwright, S. (1994). Healthy mind; healthy organization – A proactive approach to occupational stress. *Human Relations*, 47(4), 455–471.

Cooper, C., Dewe, P., & O'Driscoll, M. (2010). Employee assistance programs: Strengths, challenges and future roles. In: J. Quick & L. Tetrick (eds.), *Handbook of Occupational Health Psychology*. Washington, DC: American Psychological Association, 337–356.

Danna, K., & Griffin, R. W. (1999). Health and well-being in the workplace: A review and synthesis of the literature. *Journal of Management*, 25(3), 357–384.

Day, A. (2014). *Developing Psychologically Healthy Workplaces*. Psychologically Healthy Workplaces Workshop, Halifax, NS, November 20, 2014.

Day, A. L., Francis, L., Stevens, S., Hurrell, J. J., & McGrath, P. (2014). Improving employee health and work-life balance: Developing and validating a coaching-based ABLE (Achieving Balance in Life and Employment) program. In: C. Biron, R. J. Burke, & C. L. Cooper (eds.), *Creating Healthy Workplaces:*

Stress Reduction, Improved Well-Being, and Organizational Effectiveness. Burlington, VT: Gower Publishing Company, 68–90.

Day, A., Hartling, N., & Mackie, B. (2015). The psychologically healthy workplace: Fostering employee well-being & healthy businesses. In: P. Perrewe & J. Meurs (eds.), *Stress and Quality of Working Life.* pp. 199-217. Charlotte, NC: Information Age Publishing.

Day, A. L., & Helson, T. (2016). Workplace health promotion. In: S. Clarke, T. M. Probst, F. W. Guldenmund, & J. Passmore (eds.), *The Wiley Blackwell Handbook of Psychology of Occupational Safety and Workplace Health.* West Sussex, UK: John Wiley & Sons, 337–412.

Day, A. L., & Nielsen, K. (2017). What does our organization do to help our well-being? In: N. Chmiel, F. Fraccaroli, & M. Sverke (eds.), *An Introduction of Work and Organizational Psychology.* Wiley Blackwell.

Day, A. L., & Randell, K. (2014). Building a foundation for psychologically health workplaces and well-being. In: A. Day, E. K. Kelloway, & J. J. Hurrell (eds.), *Workplace Well-Being: How to Build a Psychologically Healthy Workplaces.* West Sussex, UK: John Wiley & Sons, 3–26.

Dimoff, J., & Kelloway, E. K. (2013). *Mental Health Awareness Training.* Paper presented at the European Congress of Psychology, Stockholm, Sweden.

Eisenberger, R., Huntington, R., Hutchison, S., & Sowa, D. (1986). Perceived organizational support. *Journal of Applied Psychology,* 71, 500–507.

Emmons, R. A. (1996). Striving and feeling: Personal goals and subjective well-being. In: P. M. Gollwitzer (ed.), *The Psychological of Action: Linking Cognition and Motivation to Behavior.* New York: Guilford Press, 313–337.

Facteau, J. D., Dobbins, G. H., Russell, J. E., Ladd, R. T., & Kudisch, J. D. (1995). The influence of general perceptions of the training environment on pretraining motivation and perceived training transfer. *Journal of Management,* 21(1), 1–25.

Feeley, T. H., Hwang, J., & Barnett, G. A. (2008). Predicting employee turnover from friendship networks. *Journal of Applied Communication Research,* 36(1), 56–73.

Gist, M. E., & Mitchell, T. R. (1992). Self-efficacy: A theoretical analysis of its determinants and malleability. *Academy of Management Review,* 17(2), 183–211.

Goetzel, R. Z., Long, S. R., Ozminkowski, R. J., Hawkins, K., Wang, S., & Lynch, W. (2004). Health, absence, disability, and presenteeism cost estimates of certain physical and mental health conditions affecting US employers. *Journal of Occupational and Environmental Medicine,* 46(4), 398–412.

Goetzel, R. Z., Ozminkowski, R. J., Sederer, L. I., & Mark, T. L. (2002). The business case for quality mental health services: Why employers should care about the mental health and well-being of their employees. *Journal of Occupational and Environmental Medicine,* 44(4), 320–330.

Grawitch, M. J., Gottschalk, M., & Munz, D. C. (2006). The path to a healthy workplace: A critical review linking healthy workplace practices, employee well-being, and organizational improvements. *Consulting Psychology Journal: Practice and Research,* 58(3), 129–147.

Griffin, R. W. (1991). Research notes. Effects of work redesign on employee perceptions, attitudes, and behaviors: A long-term investigation. *Academy of Management Journal,* 34(2), 425–435.

Grossman, R., & Salas, E. (2011). The transfer of training: What really matters. *International Journal of Training and Development,* 15(2), 103–120.

Hackman, J. R., & Lawler, E. E. (1971). Employee reactions to job characteristics. *Journal of Applied Psychology,* 55(3), 259–286.

Hahn, V. C., Binnewies, C., Sonnentag, S., & Mojza, E. J. (2011). Learning how to recover from job stress: Effects of a recovery training program on recovery, recovery-related self-efficacy, and well-being. *Journal of Occupational Health Psychology,* 16(2), 202–216.

Harter, J. K., Schmidt, F. L., & Keyes, C. L. (2003). Well-being in the workplace and its relationship to business outcomes: A review of the Gallup studies. In: C. L. Keyes & J. Haidt (eds.), *Flourishing: Positive Psychology and the Life Well-Lived.* Washington, DC: American Psychological Association, 205–224.

Hasson, D., Anderberg, U. M., Theorell, T., & Arnetz, B. B. (2005). Psychophysiological effects of a web-based stress management system: A prospective, randomized controlled intervention study of IT and media workers. *BMC Public Health,* 5(1), 78–91.

Hasson, D., & Villaume, K. (2013). An automated and systematic web-based intervention for stress management and organizational health promotion. In: G. Bauer & J. Gregor (eds.), *Salutogenic Organizations and Change the Concepts behind Organizational Health Intervention Research.* New York: Springer, 217–237.

Heaphy, E. D., & Dutton, J. E. (2008). Positive social interactions and the human body at work: Linking organizations and physiology. *Academy of Management Review,* 33(1), 137–162.

Holman, D. (2002). Employee well-being in call centres. *Human Resource Management Journal,* 12(4), 35–50.

Holt, D. T., Armenakis, A. A., Harris, S. G., & Feild, H. S. (2007). Toward a comprehensive definition of readiness for change: A review of research and instrumentation. *Research in Organizational Change and Development*, 16, 289–336.

Judge, T. A., & Bono, J. E. (2001). Relationship of core self-evaluations traits – Self-esteem, generalized self-efficacy, locus of control, and emotional stability – With job satisfaction and job performance: A meta-analysis. *Journal of Applied Psychology*, 86(1), 80–92.

Kaufman, R., & Keller, J. M. (1994). Levels of evaluation: Beyond Kirkpatrick. *Human Resource Development Quarterly*, 5(4), 371–380.

Kawakami, N., Araki, S., Kawashima, M., Masumoto, T., & Hayashi, T. (1997). Effects of work-related stress reduction on depressive symptoms among Japanese blue-collar workers. *Scandinavian Journal of Work, Environment & Health*, 23(1), 54–59.

Kelloway, E. K., & Day, A. L. (2005). Building healthy workplaces: What we know so far. *Canadian Journal of Behavioural Science/Revue canadienne des sciences du comportement*, 37(4), 223–235.

Kelloway, E. K., Turner, N., Barling, J., & Loughlin, C. (2012). Transformational leadership and employee psychological well-being: The mediating role of employee trust in leadership. *Work & Stress*, 26(1), 39–55.

Kristof-Brown, A. L., Zimmerman, R. D., & Johnson, E. C. (2005). Consequences of individual's fit at work: A meta-analysis of person-job, person-organization, person-group, and person-supervisor fit. *Personnel Psychology*, 58, 281–342.

Latham, G. P. (2012). *Work Motivation: History, Theory, Research, and Practices*. Thousand Oaks, CA: Sage Publications, Inc.

Latham, G. P., & Locke, E. A. (2007). New developments in and directions for goal-setting research. *European Psychologist*, 12(4), 290–300.

Leiter, M. P., Day, A., Oore, D. G., & Laschinger, H. K. (2012). Getting better and staying better: Assessing civility, incivility, distress, and job attitudes one year after a civility intervention. *Journal of Occupational Health Psychology*, 17(4), 425–434.

Leiter, M. P., Laschinger, H. K. S., Day, A., & Oore, D. G. (2011). The impact of civility interventions on employee social behavior, distress, and attitudes. *Journal of Applied Psychology*, 96(6), 1258–1274.

Leiter, M. P., & Patterson, A. (2014). Respectful workplaces. In: A. Day, E. K. Kelloway, & J. J. Hurrell (eds.), *Workplace Well-Being: How to Build a Psychologically Healthy Workplaces*. West Sussex, UK: John Wiley & Sons, 205–225.

Lemmens, V. E. P. P., Oenema, A., Klepp, K. I., Henriksen, H. B., & Brug, J. (2008). A systematic review of the evidence regarding efficacy of obesity prevention interventions among adults. *Obesity Reviews*, 9(5), 446–455.

Lewin, K. (1947). Frontiers in group dynamics II. Channels of group life; social planning and action research. *Human Relations*, 1(2), 143–153.

Lim, D. H., & Johnson, S. D. (2002). Trainee perceptions of factors that influence learning transfer. *International Journal of Training and Development*, 6(1), 36–48.

Locke, E. A., & Latham, G. P. (1990). *A Theory of Goal Setting & Task Performance*. Englewood Cliffs, NJ: Prentice-Hall, Inc.

Locke, E. A., & Latham, G. P. (2002). Building a practically useful theory of goal setting and task motivation: A 35-year odyssey. *American Psychologist*, 57(9), 705–717.

Locke, E. A., Shaw, K. N., Saari, L. M., & Latham, G. P. (1981). Goal setting and task performance: 1969–1980. *Psychological Bulletin*, 90(1), 125–152.

Luszczynska, A., Scholz, U., & Schwarzer, R. (2005). The general self-efficacy scale: Multicultural validation studies. *The Journal of Psychology*, 139(5), 439–457.

Luthans, F. (2002). The need for and meaning of Positive Organizational Behavior. *Journal of Organizational Behavior*, 23, 695–706.

Machin, M. A., & Fogarty, G. J. (1997). The effects of self-efficacy, motivation to transfer, and situational constraints on transfer intentions and transfer of training. *Performance Improvement Quarterly*, 10(2), 98–115.

Madsen, S. R. (2003). Wellness in the workplace: Preparing employees for change. *Organization Development Journal*, 21(1), 46–55.

Magaletta, P. R., & Oliver, J. M. (1999). The hope construct, will, and ways: Their relations with self-efficacy, optimism, and general well-being. *Journal of Clinical Psychology*, 55(5), 539–551.

Martin, H. J. (2010). Workplace climate and peer support as determinants of training transfer. *Human Resource Development Quarterly*, 21(1), 87–104.

Meyer, C., Ulbricht, S., Baumeister, S. E., Schumann, A., Rüge, J., Bischof, G., . . . & John, U. (2008). Proactive interventions for smoking cessation in general medical practice: A quasi-randomized controlled trial to examine the efficacy of computer-tailored letters and physician–delivered brief advice. *Addiction*, 103(2), 294–304.

Mikkelsen, A., & Saksvik, P. Ø. (1999). Impact of a participatory organizational intervention on job characteristics and job stress. *International Journal of Health Services*, 29(4), 871–893.

Mitchell, T. R., Thompson, K. R., & George-Falvy, J. (2000). Goal setting: Theory and practice. In: C. L. Cooper & E. A. Locke (eds.), *Industrial and Organizational Psychology: Linking Theory and Practice*. Malden, MA: Blackwell Publishers Ltd, 216–249.

Nielsen, K., Daniels, K., Thiele Schwarz, U., Hasson, H., Hasson, D., & Ogbonnaya, C. (2014). *Are You Ready? The Role of Organizational Readiness for Change When Implementing Interventions to Improve Employee Well-Being*. Paper presented at the International Commission of Occupational Health – Work and Psychosocial Factors, Adelaide, South Australia.

Nielsen, K., & Randall, R. (2012). The importance of employee participation and perceptions of changes in procedures in a teamworking intervention. *Work & Stress*, 26(2), 91–111.

Nielsen, K., & Randall, R. (2013). Opening the black box: Presenting a model for evaluating organizational-level interventions. *European Journal of Work and Organizational Psychology*, 22(5), 601–617.

Nielsen, K., Randall, R., Holten, A. L., & González, E. R. (2010). Conducting organizational-level occupational health interventions: What works? *Work & Stress*, 24(3), 234–259.

Nielsen, K., Stage, M., Abildgaard, J. S., & Brauer, C. V. (2013). Participatory intervention from an organizational perspective: Employees as active agents in a healthy work environment. In: G. F. Bauer & G. J. Jenny (eds.), *Salutogenic Organizations and Change: The Concepts behind Organizational Health Intervention Research*. London, UK: Springer Science & Business Media, pp. 327–350.

Nielsen, K., Yarker, J., Brenner, S. O., Randall, R., & Borg, V. (2008). The importance of transformational leadership style for the well-being of employees working with older people. *Journal of Advanced Nursing*, 63(5), 465–475.

Noblet, A. (2003). Building health promoting work settings: Identifying the relationship between work characteristics and occupational stress in Australia. *Health Promotion International*, 18(4), 351–359.

Osatuke, K., Moore, S. C., Ward, C., Dyrenforth, S. R., & Belton, L. (2009). Civility, Respect, Engagement in the Workforce (CREW) Nationwide organization development intervention at veterans health administration. *The Journal of Applied Behavioral Science*, 45(3), 384–410.

Ostroff, C., & Ford, K. J. (1989). Critical levels of analysis. In: I. L. Arthur, B. Edens, & B. Goldstein (ed.), *Training and Development in Organizations*. San Francisco, CA: Jossey-Bass, 25–62.

Parker, S., & Wall, T. (1998). *Job and Work Design: Organizing Work to Promote Well-Being and Effectiveness*. Thousand Oaks, CA: Sage Publications Inc.

Parks, K. M., & Steelman, L. A. (2008). Organizational wellness programs: A meta-analysis. *Journal of Occupational Health Psychology*, 13(1), 58.

Prochaska, J. O., Norcross, J., & DiClemente, C. (1994). *Changing for Good: The Revolutionary Program that Explains the Stages of Change and Teaches You How to Free Yourself from Bad Habits*. New York: Morrow.

Repetti, R. L. (1987). Individual and common components of the social environment at work and psychological well-being. *Journal of Personality and Social Psychology*, 52(4), 710–720.

Rhoades, L., & Eisenberger, R. (2002). Perceived organizational support: A review of the literature. *Journal of Applied Psychology*, 87(4), 698–714.

Richman-Hirsch, W. L. (2001). Posttraining interventions to enhance transfer: The moderating effects of work environments. *Human Resource Development Quarterly*, 12(2), 105–120.

Robertson, I. T., Cooper, C. L., Sarkar, M., & Curran, T. (2015). Resilience training in the workplace from 2003 to 2014: A systematic review. *Journal of Occupational and Organizational Psychology*, 88(3), 533–562.

Rongen, A., Robroek, S. J., van Lenthe, F. J., & Burdorf, A. (2013). Workplace health promotion: A meta-analysis of effectiveness. *American Journal of Preventive Medicine*, 44(4), 406–415.

Salanova, M., Llorens, S., Cifre, E., & Martínez, I. M. (2012). We need a hero! Toward a validation of the healthy and resilient organization (HERO) model. *Group & Organization Management*, 37(6), 785–822.

Salas, E., & Cannon-Bowers, J. A. (2001). The science of training: A decade of progress. *Annual Review of Psychology*, 52(1), 471–499.

Sauter, S. L., Lim, S. Y., & Murphy, L. R. (1996). Organizational health: A new paradigm for occupational stress research at NIOSH. *Japanese Journal of Occupational Mental Health*, 4(4), 248–254.

Sauter, S. L., Murphy, L. R., & Hurrell, J. J. (1990). Prevention of work-related psychological disorders: A national strategy proposed by the National Institute for Occupational Safety and Health (NIOSH). *American Psychologist*, 45(10), 1146–1158.

Sheldon, K. M., & Elliot, A. J. (1999). Goal striving, need satisfaction, and longitudinal well-being: The self-concordance model. *Journal of Personality and Social Psychology*, 76(3), 482–497.

Skinner, C. S., Campbell, M. K., Rimer, B. K., Curry, S., & Prochaska, J. O. (1999). How effective is tailored print communication? *Annals of Behavioral Medicine*, 21(4), 290–298.

Sloan, R. P., & Gruman, J. C. (1988). Participation in workplace health promotion programs: The contribution of health and organizational factors. *Health Education & Behavior*, 15(3), 269–288.

Sonnentag, S., & Bayer, U. V. (2005). Switching off mentally: Predictors and consequences of psychological detachment from work during off-job time. *Journal of Occupational Health Psychology*, 10(4), 393–414.

Sonnentag, S., & Frese, M. (2003). *Stress in Organizations*. John Wiley & Sons, Inc.

Sonnentag, S., & Fritz, C. (2007). The recovery experience questionnaire: Development and validation of a measure for assessing recuperation and unwinding from work. *Journal of Occupational Health Psychology*, 12(3), 204–221.

Sorensen, G., Barbeau, E. M., Stoddard, A. M., Hunt, M. K., Goldman, R., Smith, A., . . . & Wallace, L. (2007). Tools for health: The efficacy of a tailored intervention targeted for construction laborers. *Cancer Causes & Control*, 18(1), 51–59.

Sparks, K., Faragher, B., & Cooper, C. L. (2001). Well-being and occupational health in the 21st century workplace. *Journal of Occupational and Organizational Psychology*, 74(4), 489–509.

Stevens, S. M. (2010). *Understanding How Employees Unwind after Work: Expanding the Construct of 'Recovery.'* Dissertation Abstracts International, pp. 1–180.

Stewart, M., Reid, G., & Mangham, C. (1997). Fostering children's resilience. *Journal of Pediatric Nursing*, 12, 21–31.

Switzer, K. C., Nagy, M. S., & Mullins, M. E. (2005). The influence of training reputation, managerial support, and self-efficacy on pre-training motivation and perceived training transfer. *Applied HRM Research*, 10(1), 21–34.

Taylor, P. J., Russ-Eft, D. F., & Chan, D. W. (2005). A meta-analytic review of behavior modeling training. *Journal of Applied Psychology*, 90(4), 692–709.

Thomas, L. T., & Ganster, D. C. (1995). Impact of family-supportive work variables on work-family conflict and strain: A control perspective. *Journal of Applied Psychology*, 80(1), 6–15.

Tugade, M. M., & Fredrickson, B. L. (2004). Resilient individuals use positive emotions to bounce back from negative emotional experiences. *Journal of Personality and Social Psychology*, 86(2), 320–333.

Ugboro, I. O. (2006). Organizational commitment, job redesign, employee empowerment and intent to quit among survivors of restructuring and downsizing. *Journal of Behavioral and Applied Management*, 7(3), 232–253.

Warr, P. (2007). *Work, Happiness, and Unhappiness*. Mahwah, NJ: Lawrence Erlbaum Associates, Inc.

Watson, M. (2008). Going for gold: The health promoting general practice. *Quality in Primary Care*, 16(3), 177–185.

World Health Organization. (1986). *Ottawa Charter for Health Promotion*. Ottawa, Canada: First International Health Promotion Conference.

Zimmerman, B. J., Bandura, A., & Martinez-Pons, M. (1992). Self-motivation for academic attainment: The role of self-efficacy beliefs and personal goal setting. *American Educational Research Journal*, 29(3), 663–676.

23

Improving employee wellbeing through leadership development

Maria Karanika-Murray, Henna Hasson,
Ulrica von Thiele Schwarz, and Anne Richter

Introduction

Good leadership is essential for organizational effectiveness and a source of competitive advantage (Day, 2001; Riggio, 2008). Over the last few decades a substantial body of research has been accumulated that shows that leadership is linked to a surprisingly broad array of outcomes of importance to the organization and individual employees. At the same time, the market for leadership development has shown continuous growth, with organizations investing considerable financial and other resources in this. However, there is surprisingly little research that directly and explicitly tests the relationship between leadership development and employee outcomes such as performance and wellbeing. This may be based on an implicit but also erroneous assumption that investment in leadership development will readily translate into desirable employee outcomes, and in particular in terms of the health and wellbeing of employees.

Consequently, the aims of this chapter are to (1) explicate the link between leadership development and employee wellbeing, (2) present a more systematic approach to thinking and planning leadership training that can impact on employees, and in the process (3) develop pointers for research and good practice. First, we will summarize the evidence on the effects of leadership development programs on employee health and wellbeing. Then, we will present ways by which leadership development can be achieved in organizations in order to support employee wellbeing. We will end with a discussion of how the key debates identified can shape future research and practice.

Leadership development: translating findings from leadership research into organizational practice

Leadership is at the heart of organizational life and organizational effectiveness. Several meta-analyses and reviews have documented the effects of leadership on productivity and job satisfaction (e.g., Avolio, Reichard, Hannah, Walumbwa, & Chan, 2009; Gregersen, Kuhnert, Zimber, 2011; Kuoppala, Lamminpää, Liira, & Vainio, 2008; Nyberg & Bernin, 2005; Skakon, Nielsen, Borg, & Guzman, 2010). Leadership development represents a planned and systematic effort to improve the quality of leadership (Groves, 2007) and is a tool for translating these results into organizational practice. Leadership development can be implemented as either a psychosocial intervention (affecting human process and psychosocial aspects of the work situation) or a socio-technical intervention (affecting objective work condition), or both (Kelloway & Barling, 2010). Leadership development initiatives have gained increasing attention in the last decades. For example, an extensive meta-analysis of the impact of leadership identified 200 studies of which 62 could be described as leadership development (Avolio et al., 2009). The assumption behind leadership development is that learned leadership skills and behaviors will be enacted in practice and lead to desirable outcomes.

Compared to other employee outcomes that have been studied in the context of leadership, the effects of leadership on employee health and wellbeing have received comparatively little research attention. The results of available research have been summarized in four reviews (Gregersen et al., 2011; Kuoppala et al., 2008; Nyberg & Bernin, 2005; Skakon et al., 2010). Skakon et al. (2010) demonstrated that a good-quality relationship between leaders and their followers (such as positive leader behaviors whereby the leader supports, empowers, and shows consideration towards employees) is associated with employee wellbeing and lower stress. Whereas some of these studies focus on a specific leadership theory – such as transformational leadership or the two-factor theory of leadership (task or relationship orientated) – others focus on investigating specific leader behaviors, such as providing social support or the opportunity to participate (Gregersen et al., 2011). Transformational leadership, the most popular in this line of research, has been associated with lower stress and higher wellbeing amongst employees (Skakon et al., 2010). These findings have been supported by both cross-sectional as well as longitudinal research. For example, Alimo-Metcalfe, Alban-Metcalfe, Bradley, Mariathasan, and Samele (2008) showed that quality of leadership was linked to employee wellbeing in the long term. Finally, as Kelloway and Barling (2010) noted, leadership development can be used as a primary intervention to improve workplace conditions in the immediate short term and the health and wellbeing of employees in the longer term. Investing in leadership development with the aim to improve employee wellbeing is a natural progression from the research consensus on the link between good leadership and employee wellbeing.

There is a broad variety of activities that have been frequently and effectively used in leadership development to train leaders in leadership skills. Practices commonly used include 360-degree feedback, developmental relationships (coaching, mentoring, and networking), on-the-job assignments, and action learning (e.g., Day, 2001). Other activities include role playing by actors trained to portray a specific leadership style (theater forum), participant role playing, and scenarios/vignettes of specific leadership styles/actions (e.g., Avolio et al., 2009). Training programs can differ to a great extent in terms of intensity: for example, how much time leaders spend training, which can vary from hours to days or even years.

Day (2001) underlines fundamental differences between leader and leadership development that mirror how the definition of leadership has evolved over time and how leadership has been theorized and studied. *Leader development* focuses on developing human capital and the specific skills of individuals in positions of leadership (e.g., leadership-related knowledge, skills, and abilities), whereas *leadership development* operates at a more collective level and is concerned with the development of social capital in organizations (e.g., resources embedded in the connections and relations between individuals). As Day, Fleenor, Atwater, Sturm, and McKee (2014) highlight, "leader development focuses on developing individual leaders whereas leadership development focuses on a process of development that inherently involves multiple individuals (e.g., leaders and followers or among peers in a self-managed work team)" (p. 64). The objective is to go beyond training the leader in specific competencies and to develop leadership as an interactive and reciprocal process that fosters positive relationships and develop a workplace environment that boosts employee wellbeing and "unlocks the entire organization's human asset potential" (Hernez-Broome & Hughes, 2004, p. 29; Day, 2001). However, Day (2001) also emphasizes that one form of development without the other is incomplete. A single focus may even be harmful as it leaves the team and the organization vulnerable to threats posed by complex and adaptive leadership challenges (Heifitz, 1994). Finally, even though Day (2001) differentiates between leader and leadership development, but also highlights the inseparability of the two neither is consistently followed in existing research on leadership training programs. In this chapter we consider results from both leader and leadership development programs.

Outcomes of leadership development

An effective leadership development initiative should result in changes in target leadership attitudes, behaviors, or experience (Avolio et al., 2009). Therefore, the direct outcome of a leadership development is an enhancement of the individuals' leadership (Kelloway & Barling, 2010). In practice, evaluations of leadership development initiatives have documented moderate positive effects (Avolio et al., 2009; Burke & Day, 1986; Collins & Holton, 2004). However, the range of outcomes studied has been heterogeneous, and effects may vary according to the leadership theory that has informed the content of the training in the first place (Avolio et al., 2009). For example, newer theoretical perspectives such as transformational leadership have been more strongly with affective and cognitive outcomes, whereas more traditional approaches, such as those based on relationships and transactions, have been more strongly associated with more proximal target behaviors (Avolio et al., 2009). Moreover, it has been suggested that the combined effects of leadership development programs is greater than the effects of each in isolation (Collins, 2001), indicating an augmentative effect of such programs. Finally, Alimo-Metcalfe and Alban-Metcalfe (2014) offered evidence for the impact of engaging leadership at the organizational level on savings and on cultural change in terms of wellbeing and positive work attitudes – although this study did not examine leadership development, we can surmise that targeted leadership development would yield similar outcomes.

Compared to other types of interventions in workplace health and wellbeing, the ultimate outcome of leadership development is not localized to the participants, but rather includes those who are affected by the leaders – i.e., the employees. Nevertheless, much of the research on the effectiveness of leadership development programs looks at outcomes at the individual leader level, such as changes in leadership behaviors (Riggio, 2008). Even though the aim is to impact upon employees, there is very little direct empirical evidence that leadership trainings can achieve the goal of changing employee outcomes. It is expected that studies that examine changes in immediate knowledge and behavioral outcomes of leadership training will demonstrate high efficiency of leadership training. However, the challenge here is to demonstrate effects on the employees that are more distal; evidence on such effects is very weak and often overlooked in this line of research.

There are several possible reasons for the limited evaluation of leadership development program on employee wellbeing outcomes. One may be the complexity of leadership and leadership development, and their often indirect effects on employee outcomes (Riggio, 2008). For example, it may be necessary for the leader to be able to build trusting relationships, which may result in a better work relationship and, in turn, affect health and wellbeing positively (Avolio et al., 2009; Kelloway & Barling, 2010) – these effects are delayed rather than immediate such that it may not be clear when to time the evaluation of leadership development programs. Several longitudinal measurements may be required, as for example as carried out by Barling, Weber, and Kelloway (1996) who measured leadership and commitment two weeks prior and five months after the training programme. Similar pre- and posttraining evaluation designs have been used in the majority of the published leadership intervention studies. For example, Brown and May (2012) administered a baseline measure of leadership, productivity, and satisfaction, which they assessed again at a 12-month follow-up. When the cause-effect expectations necessitate long-term evaluation of effects, the choice of the time lag is of particular importance, but so far there is little knowledge of what the appropriate time frames or time lags should be (Kelloway & Barling, 2010). Moreover, the effect of leadership development on employee health and wellbeing is complex and implies a chain of events that are expected before the effect appears. It is necessary that employees first notice the differences in their leader. As a result they may change their evaluations and attributions, which may in turn translate into changes in their own behaviors and other desirable outcome variables such as health, wellbeing, or performance (Kelloway & Barling, 2010).

Very few studies have empirically examined the effects of leadership training and development on employee outcomes. An exception is Hasson, von Thiele Schwarz, Holmström, Karanika-Murray, and Tafvelin (2016) who showed that leadership training resulted in improved manager and employee evaluations of organizational learning and safety climate (see also von Thiele Schwarz, Hasson, & Tafvelin, 2016). Other researchers who have investigated components of wellbeing at work are Brown and May (2012) and Hardy et al. (2010), who studied satisfaction with the job and the supervisor over time.

In the absence of direct empirical evidence on the mechanisms by which leadership development may impact on employee wellbeing and health, it is possible to make inferences from the literature on leadership. The impact of leadership on employee outcomes is mainly via three routes: through a direct effect on work practices and resources, an effect via employee perceptions and motivation, and a responsibility for engaging employees and communicating and promoting workplace initiatives for employee wellbeing. Leaders have the power to increase work-related resources or decrease work stressors at the workplace (Kuehnl, Rehfuess, von Elm, Nowak, & Glaser, 2014). They can provide information clues that shape employees' perceptions of their work and foster positive appraisals of the work environment (Griffin, 1981), in turn impacting intrinsic motivation, commitment, and performance (Piccolo & Colquitt, 2006). Leaders can also directly contribute to employees' empowerment and development (Avolio et al., 2009), collective efficacy (Walumbwa, Wang, Lawler, & Shi, 2004), task significance (Graen & Uhl-Bien, 1995), role ambiguity (House, 1996), and perceptions of their work as meaningful (Barling, Turner, Dezan, and Carroll, 2008; Arnold, Turner, Barling, Kelloway, & McKee, 2007). An often-cited mechanism for this effect is trust in the leader (Barling, Turner, Dezan, & Carroll, 2008). Leaders also hold the legitimate and often coercive power to influence employees' work resources and the environment, clarifying roles and providing opportunities for development (Nielsen et al., 2008), reducing job demands and offering tangible support (Leithwood, Menzies, Jantzi, & Leithwood, 1996), shaping perceptions of work characteristics (Karanika-Murray, Bartholomew, Williams, & Cox, 2015), and enabling participation in wellbeing interventions, and providing opportunities for learning (Bezuijen, Dam, Berg, & Thierry, 2010). Moreover, another way by which leadership – in this case transformational leadership – translates into positive or desirable employee outcomes is via changes in employee self-perceptions, emotions, and attitudes (e.g., empowerment or motivation), changes in the perception of the team (e.g., team learning or trust in the team), changes in the perception of the leader (e.g., leader supper or the closeness of the leader member relationship), and in the perception of job and working conditions (e.g., climate, meaningfulness of work or participation) (Tafvelin, 2013).

Moreover, the effects of a leadership development program may also depend on the theoretical foundations on which the content of the program is based. Different foci of leadership development will lead to different outcomes (Avolio et al., 2009). Consequently, to measure the effects of leadership development on the outcome variable, there is a need to specify relevant intervening variables. This requires a complex measurement and modelling procedure to examine and explain *how* leadership development affects outcomes such as health and wellbeing (Kelloway & Barling, 2010). These routes are likely to mirror the routes by which leadership impacts on employee wellbeing, as explicated earlier, but to date there is no relevant available evidence. Moreover, there are practical consequences for developing an intervention, such as the necessity to use change models, as described later in the chapter in order to identify relevant intervening variables and employee outcomes.

Setting of leadership development programs

Similar to other organizational-level interventions for stress and wellbeing, leadership development is often weakly integrated into day-to-day business, highlighting a challenge to better integrate it in organizational life (Nielsen, Randall, Holten, & González, 2010). Leadership development that is predominantly based on classroom experience (leadership training) overlooks the importance of the emotional resonance between the leader and employees, and the importance of developing a supportive and enabling organizational context (Day, 2001; Hernez-Broome & Hughes, 2004). A way to achieve integration between the two is by offering the training to all leaders at all levels within the organization.

For example, Brown and May (2012) describe a leadership development program where all first-line managers of a manufacturing company were offered training in leadership, senior management and employees were involved in creating the content of the program, and senior management were actively involved in communicating and delivering the training. A direct link between improvements in leadership and reward systems was made at the program design stage, with the aim to achieve improvements in both productivity and the organizational culture. As such, and in order to integrate leadership development in line managers' everyday work, the program was evaluated by means of a survey and as part of a regular performance evaluation and salary review. This way of delivering leadership development, by targeting all leaders in the organization, is in contrast to leadership training that targets individual leaders, that is, leaders who themselves choose to take part in the development program. A drawback of this approach is that it may be difficult to take the individual leaders' needs and motives into account. It does, however, also mean that the program can be delivered as an organizational-level intervention, be better integrated in the organization's strategy and goals, and take into account the specific organizational context. This way of delivering leadership development can form part of an organization's normal business, which makes it particularly suitable for improving employee wellbeing.

When leadership development is delivered as an organizational-level intervention and integrated into organizational structures and processes, knowledge of the local context needs to be considered in the design process (Day, 2001). This means that organizational stakeholders should be involved in co-creating the program, as they may offer perspectives which are complementary to those of leadership consultants and researchers. A co-creation process is an approach in which researchers and organizational stakeholders collaborate in designing, conducting, and evaluating an intervention or a program (von Thiele Schwarz, Lundmark, & Hasson, 2016). For example, key stakeholders often have knowledge about the local context that is important for making sure the program fits the context where it is applied, such as the leadership needs in the organization (Block & Manning, 2007; Cleary, Freeman, & Sharrock, 2005). Co-creation underlies the design of leadership development, as described in the next section. Specifically, the next section outlines practical ways to create and deliver leadership development for employee wellbeing.

Designing leadership development programs

Although several theories and empirical evidence connect leadership to employee wellbeing, these do not cover the theory of change that links the leadership development program to changes in leadership behaviors (Kristensen, 2005). Here, we discuss how the design of leadership development programs can be optimized and offer an example of how theory from other fields such as pedagogy, program evaluation, and training transfer can be used to develop an understanding of the chain of effects necessary to demonstrate impact from leadership development to employee outcomes.

From the program evaluation literature, we adopt the use of a program logic model to outline how leadership development can be expected to be linked to employee wellbeing. A program logic is a structured way to describe how activities are hypothesized to relate to a chain of intermediate and target outcomes (Olsen, Legg, & Hasle, 2012). In Table 23.1, we offer a general example of a program logic model for a leadership development program, which is based on previous studies on leadership development programs and the theories of leadership and employee wellbeing.

Using end and intermediate outcomes as design principles

Following principles from pedagogy, the starting point in the design of leadership development program process is not the content – i.e., what activities that should be performed as a part of the program – but rather the outcomes. This is in line with pedagogical theory (e.g., Biggs, 1996) and training evaluation theory (Kirkpatrick, 1998; Kirkpatrick & Kirkpatrick, 2005). Pedagogical models generally focus on learning outcomes, referred to as Level 2 in Kirkpatrick's evaluation model ("Learning Outcomes Among Participating Leaders" in Table 23.1). However,

Table 23.1 A general program logic model for leadership development

Core Inputs in Leadership Development Program	Learning Outcomes Among Participating Leaders	Intermediate Outcomes	Changes in Working Conditions	End Outcomes
Multisource measurement and feedback on leadership behaviors Personal goal setting and action planning Group or individual counselling, mentoring Exemplary leadership practices Lectures, role plays, exercises, discussions about the theoretical leadership model such as transformational leadership and contingent reward	Improved self-awareness of own leadership and followers reactions Improved knowledge, skills and capabilities in transformational leadership and contingent reward Leader-rated increase in transformational leadership behaviors	Employee-rated increase in transformational leadership behaviors	Increased autonomy	Increased employee job satisfaction Increased employee motivation Improved employee health and wellbeing

we suggest starting even further down the stream, with the intervention end outcomes, i.e., Level 4 in Kirkpatrick's model ("Changes in Working Conditions" in Table 23.1). The reason for this is that achieving learning outcomes is generally not sufficient for leadership development. Rather, it is the ability of the participants (the leaders) to transfer that learning to behaviors and the impact of those behaviors that matters most. Thus, the leadership development program needs to support leaders in this transfer, and it needs to be designed in relation to its potential for achieving the end or target outcomes. Therefore, we suggest that the intervention design process should start with reflections on what the desired end outcomes of the intervention are, followed by identification of intermediate outcomes. For example, whereas the end outcomes may be increased job satisfaction and work engagement among employees, the intermediate outcome may be changes in leadership behaviors as perceived by the employees (Lornudd, Bergman, Sandahl, & von Thiele Schwarz, 2016).

In addition, the co-creation process described earlier suggests that the identification of outcomes is conducted in collaboration between researchers and key stakeholders from the organizations (von Thiele Schwarz, Hasson, et al., 2016). The key stakeholders (such as senior managers, employees, and leader participants) have an important role to play in the definition of end outcomes for several reasons. First, they have an implicit understanding of the most relevant outcomes, in terms of both the outcomes that are most important to target and the outcomes that the organization values, and therefore that cannot be jeopardized and should be central to the leader development program. Since the purpose of any organization is to produce services or goods, rather than serve as a venue for producing good leadership and employee wellbeing per se, this step may involve addressing how leader development and the organizations' core tasks are linked. Second, key stakeholders can ensure that the program and its target outcomes are well aligned with other organizational goals. An example of this is presented in Jeon, Simpson, Chenoweth, Cunich, and Kendig (2013), who explicitly designed their leadership development program so that it was congruent with, and incorporated into, the organization's philosophy, policies, leadership, and strategic directions. Third, engaging key stakeholders early in the process is a way to create the buy-in necessary for accepting and taking responsibility for changes that follow from the program. This is part of establishing organizational ownership for the intervention. Fourth, stakeholder engagement paves the way for acceptance of the results of program evaluation. In evaluation, it is well known that key stakeholders that have not been involved in deciding on target outcomes may be less likely to accept the result of an evaluation after it is completed (Leviton, Khan, Rog, Dawkin, & Cotton, 2010).

Identifying learning outcomes

Once the end and intermediate outcomes have been identified, the focus shifts to identifying learning outcomes for the development program – in this case leadership skills and competences, in this case. Informed by leadership theories, learning outcomes may, for instance, include an increase in transformational leader behaviors. However, it may not always, however, be sufficient to assume that transformational leadership behaviors in general will be sufficient. First, different sub-factors of transformational leadership may be relevant in different organizational context (Antonakis, Avolio, & Sivasubramaniam, 2003). Second, as leadership development programs often have the goal of improving leaders' behaviors within a specific domain, such as safety, the learning outcomes may also be more specific. To know what learning outcomes are most relevant, we suggest using adaptive reflection as a structured method, which engages key stakeholders in identifying learning outcomes as well as choosing the learning activities that are most appropriate for reaching those outcomes (Savage, 2011). This method was originally defined for development of courses in higher education but has also been used in occupational health interventions and leader training. Adaptive reflection builds on pedagogical theory, mainly that of Kolb, Biggs, and Bloom (Biggs, 1996; Bloom, Englehart, Frust, Hill & Krathwohl, 1956; Kolb, 1984). Adaptive reflection is conducted in workshops with key stakeholders in an organization. The process starts with individual reflection on which skills, behaviors, and attitudes are required of a leader for achieving the end outcomes in this specific case. The reflections are documented on sticky notes. In the second step, participants gather all sticky notes and, in silence, jointly sort them in in meaningful categories. In the third step, participants jointly find appropriate headings for each category. In the fourth step, each heading is reformulated into a sentence containing an active verb. In this way, the categories become the target learning outcomes.

After the learning outcomes have been identified, the next step is to design the leadership development program prototype, which involves providing the leaders with activities to help them develop the skills, knowledge, and capabilities needed to act. Contextualization is a process that is specific to the category of leadership development programs that targets all leaders in an organization and involves ensuring that the leaders have opportunities to perform the target behavior in their daily praxis in their local setting. The steps are described in the following sections.

Planning the content of the program

Once the outcomes of the leadership development program have been identified, the next step in the adaptive reflection process is to turn attention to what the program needs to entail in order to help the participants develop the leadership capabilities and skills that have been identified. That is, the appropriate content of the program or, borrowing a term from pedagogy, the *learning activities* need to be identified. We will use this term here, to highlight that the content is not important on its own. Rather, the value of the content is determined by its appropriateness as a mean to reach the target outcomes. In pedagogy, this is an important part of constructive alignment (Biggs, 1996). To be able to match learning activities to outcomes, the first step is to gather a pool of possible and available learning activities. This can, for example, be based on previous studies, and on the experience of those who will deliver the intervention as well as the stakeholders who may have knowledge about how certain learning activities fit the current setting. The program logic model that we presented earlier offers examples of activities that are commonly used in leadership development programs. It shows that, generally, participatory approaches and experiential learning such as storytelling and role plays seem to be most common, whereas didactic learning activities are used less often. Activities that use assessment of leadership and feedback on that assessment – for example, involving 360-degree measurements where the leader him- or herself as well as his or her subordinates, colleagues, and superiors rate leadership behaviors – are particularly common.

Once a pool of potential learning activities has been gathered, the next step is to match each learning outcome to a learning activity. Savage (2011) suggests using a matrix for this, with the learning outcomes in the first column and the potential activities in the first row. Going through the matrix, the task is to pick the learning activity that is likely to be most effective to achieve each learning outcome. In this, attention should be paid to the verb used in the learning outcome. The verb indicates the depth of the learning required and should be paired with a learning activities that reflects the degree and level of the learning required. That is, the activities and the learning outcomes should be constructively aligned (Biggs, 1996).

Contextualization to optimize the opportunities to perform the behaviors

Once a prototype program has been designed, it is time to reflect on how well this prototype can be used in the specific organization. Some prior models have described this as a process in which a hypothetical intervention is contextualized to an organization (von Thiele et al., 2016). This process is concerned with assuring that the leaders have opportunities to perform the target behavior in their daily praxis in their local setting. The need to contextualize the program may vary. If a co-designed adaptive reflection process has been followed, minor adaptations may be sufficient. If it instead is a predesigned program, contextualization may involve greater changes or additions to make it work in the involves ensuring context.

The organizational intervention literature emphasizes that success of an intervention is highly influenced by the organizational context in which it takes place and in what way it is implemented (Biron & Karanika-Murray, 2014; Hasson et al., 2016; Karanika-Murray & Biron, 2015). Most prior studies have considered these factors primarily to make sense of intervention outcomes after the implementation. It has, however, been suggested that contextual data should be used up front, for instance in terms of increasing employees' low readiness for change before an intervention rather than using it to explain any contradictory or unexpected results post-intervention (Nielsen, 2013). This is central in the Dynamic Integrated Evaluation (DIEM) model for continuous-change interventions, where it is described as a way to plan for sustainability from the beginning (von Thiele Schwarz, Hasson, et al., 2016). In line with this approach, we suggest that context and implementation factors that may influence the effectiveness of leadership development programs are already managed in the planning stages.

In order to engage key stakeholders in contextualizing the program prototype, we have expanded the adaptive reflection process with an additional final step. In this step, all managers participating in the intervention brainstorm the type of organizational context they would like to see or work in, in order to be able to successfully lead in the way that they identified in the first step of the process. As in the first step, brainstorming is documented on sticky notes and categorized to highlight the main issues of context and implementation. This information can then be fed back to others in the design team (e.g., consultants, researchers, and other organizational stakeholders such as senior managers). The task is to reflect on whether the program logic holds up in this particular organization, and on what changes or additions to the program prototype may be needed to make the program work. For instance, in one of our ongoing leadership development programs, the local stakeholders realized that in addition to training middle managers in change management, so-called informal leaders also needed this training. This resulted in informal leaders participating in some parts of the programs, together with the middle managers.

One benefit of the contextualization is that it might help program participants to transfer the learning from the program into their daily practice. The transfer-of-training literature suggests that in order for transfer to occur, factors related not only to the *individual* but also the *design of the training* and the wider *work environment* (i.e., context) need to be considered (Baldwin & Ford, 1988; Blume, Ford, Baldwin, & Huang, 2010). The program design process that we suggested in the present chapter implies that transfer of training is an issue that cannot and should not be considered after ensuring implementation of a program. Instead, transfer of training is supported throughout all steps of the design process. For example, individual factors such as ability and motivation of participants are considered by engaging participants in the design process, making sure that the content is relevant and matched to their roles and needs. The use of constructive alignment in the design process ensures that the program entails appropriate learning activities (e.g., training design). Finally, the contextualization process targets work environment factors, including removing obstacles to transfer in the organizational context and establishing a favorable social climate in the organization.

Training transfer is commonly viewed as consisting of two dimensions: generalization and maintenance. Generalization involves the extent to which skills and knowledge learned in a training setting are applied in the very different setting of everyday practice. In the program logic outlined earlier, this is reflected in the extent to which not only leaders but also the employees can recognize that a change has taken place. Maintenance captures the extent to which these newly acquired skills persist over time (Blume et al., 2010). Thus, there is a direct link between transfer and sustainability. In designing a leadership development program that has profound impact on an organization, both types of transfer dimensions need to be considered. This should not only be done in a summative evaluative form (i.e., to determine whether transfer has occurred), but also, in line with the DIEM evaluation model presented, we propose using data to continuously develop the program and the transfer process. This means that the design process is not finished once the prototype has been contextualized. Instead, it is still a prototype that may need to be adjusted based on data on how the program functions once it is applied in practice. This includes evaluating and adjusting the program based on how it meets the learning outcomes – both intermediate and end. This is particularly important when the context changes fast, as new obstacles and opportunities appear that can either make or break the program and the transfer of learning. Thus, continuous evaluation is a key part of any leadership development program that is intended to become part of an organization's overall commitment to improving employee wellbeing.

Conclusions

We have discussed how leadership development can be used to support employee wellbeing and presented a procedure for developing and delivering leadership development that is practical and actionable, and also aligned with the organizational goals and context. Although leadership development can be used as an effective intervention for workplace wellbeing (Kelloway & Barling, 2010), for a range of reasons, research and practice are still lagging behind. Accordingly, the potential of leadership development for primary prevention in employee wellbeing and ultimately for supporting healthy workplaces has gone unrecognized. The common assumption is that if leadership has positive effects on employee outcomes such as wellbeing, then training leaders in relevant competencies or behaviors will yield the desirable changes. Unfortunately, the empirical evidence is still forthcoming, and as the literature on learning transfer shows, transfer of learning in contingent on a number of conditions that have to be met for learned behaviors to be transferred into practice.

A number of debates and priorities for future research can be highlighted. First, as mentioned, the focus on leader training on desirable skills and behaviors fails to acknowledge the potential of leadership development as distributed practice and as a means to organizational change. In addition as Alimo-Metcalfe (2012) notes, senior managers (or leaders in senior positions) who tend to be targeted for leadership development and who have substantial influence on organizational culture are also "typically found to be least likely to participate actively in leadership development" (p. 11). Leadership development is more than leader training, and research and practice ought to take a broader scope in order to identify its impact on wellbeing. Second, the scope of leadership development evaluation can similarly be expanded to explicate longer term and more broad-ranging consequences of leadership development. As essential as leadership is to individual behavior and organizational performance alike, most empirical research has taken a myopic view. Third, the narrow approach to leader development as building competencies and optimizing leader behaviors (training the leader) that have the potential to impact on employee wellbeing is nevertheless a good starting point for truly developing leadership throughout the organization

(Day, 2001) that is supportive of employee wellbeing. An integrated and systematic approach such as the one described here can be used for maximum benefit. In reality, practical considerations such as resource and time limitations, and the logistical complexity of leadership development over leader training, can pose barriers that practice should strive to overcome. Fourth, although the absence of evidence is no evidence of absence, the missing link is the transferability of leadership development initiatives to employee wellbeing, on which we need more research. We cannot assume that transferability takes place seamlessly; pursuing a deeper understanding on the mechanisms for these effects is definitely worthwhile. Fifth, a clearer understanding of the role of the organizational context can help to integrate leadership development into normal business and align the two with employee wellbeing. For example, how can policies and practices and a conducive workplace climate support leadership development for employee wellbeing and reinforce leader training? Sixth, so far there has been little or no mention of return on investment (ROI) in relation to leadership development programs, but cost-effectiveness studies can help to strengthen the business case for leadership development as a way to support wellbeing and employee performance. Again, the focus should be on leadership development and the way that leadership is enacted, as opposed to leader training and leader competencies. Such a focus is likely to show higher ROI than a focus on the latter alone since the effects may be indirect and diffused. For example, contrary to expectations, leadership competencies do not predict team productivity (Alimo-Metcalfe, 2012). Finally, implementing the program logic for leadership development as we have described in this chapter and understanding its practical and conceptual nuances can help organizations to further develop actionable practice in leadership development.

Because of its focus on enacting specific skills and behaviors (human capital) in a conducive organizational context (social capital; Day, 2001), leadership development has the power to develop organizations that truly enable employee wellbeing. This is an area in need of further research, and we urge researchers and practitioners to invest in future research resources in order to further explore how leadership development can be optimized for employee wellbeing and organizational effectiveness.

References

Alimo-Metcalfe, B. (2012). The "need to get more for less": a new model of "engaging leadership" and evidence of its effect on team productivity, and staff morale and wellbeing at work. *Management Articles of the Year*, 6. Available at: eprints.lancs.ac.uk/74449/1/Management_Articles_of_the_Year_June_2012_0.pdf#page=6

Alimo-Metcalfe, B., & Alban-Metcalfe, J. (2014). Leading and managing high performing teams. In: L. Tate, E. Donaldson-Feilder, K. Teoh, B. Hug, & G. Everest (eds.), *Implementing Culture Change Within the NHS: Contributions from Occupational Psychology*. Occupational Psychology in Public Policy Group Report, British Psychological Society. Available at: www.bps.org.uk/system/files/user-files/Division%20of%20Occupational%20Psychology/public/17689_cat-1658.pdf

Alimo-Metcalfe, B., Alban-Metcalfe, J., Bradley, M., Mariathasan, J., & Samele, C. (2008). The impact of engaging leadership on performance, attitudes to work and wellbeing at work: A longitudinal study. *Journal of Health Organization and Management*, 22(6), 586–598.

Antonakis, J., Avolio, B. J., & Sivasubramaniam, N. (2003). Context and leadership: An examination of the nine-factor full-range leadership theory using the Multifactor Leadership Questionnaire. *The Leadership Quarterly*, 14(3), 261–295.

Arnold, K. A., Turner, N., Barling, J., Kelloway, E. K., & McKee, M. C. (2007). Transformational leadership and psychological well-being: the mediating role of meaningful work. *Journal of Occupational Health Psychology*, 12(3), 193–203.

Avolio, B. J., Reichard, R. J., Hannah, S. T., Walumbwa, F. O., & Chan, A. (2009). A meta-analytic review of leadership impact research: Experimental and quasi-experimental studies. *The Leadership Quarterly*, 20(5), 764–784.

Baldwin, T. T., & Ford, J. K. (1988). Transfer of training: A review and directions for future research. *Personnel Psychology*, 41, 63–105.

Barling, J., Turner, N., Dezan, H., & Carroll, A. (2008). The nature and consequences of apologies from leaders in organizations. *Academy of Management Proceedings,* Issue 1, 1–6.

Barling, J., Weber, T., & Kelloway, E. K. (1996). Effects of transformational leadership training on attitudinal and financial outcomes: A field experiment. *Journal of Applied Psychology*, 81, 827–832.

Bezuijen, X. M., Dam, K., Berg, P. T., & Thierry, H. (2010). How leaders stimulate employee learning: A leader–member exchange approach. *Journal of Occupational and Organizational Psychology*, 83(3), 673–693.

Biggs, J. (1996). Enhancing teaching through constructive alignment. *Higher Education*, 32, 347–364.

Biron, C., & Karanika-Murray, M. (2014). Process evaluation for organizational stress and well-being interventions: Implications for theory, method, and practice. *International Journal of Stress Management*, 21(1), 85–111.

Blume, B. D., Ford, J. K., Baldwin, T. T., & Huang, J. L. (2010). Transfer of training: A meta-analytic review. *Journal of Management*, 36, 1065–1105.

Block, L. A., & Manning, L. J. (2007). A systemic approach to developing frontline leaders in healthcare. *Leadership in Health Services*, 20(2), 85–96.

Bloom, B., Englehart, M., Furst, E., Hill, W., & Krathwohl, D. (1956). *Taxonomy of educational objectives: The classification of educational goals. Handbook I: Cognitive domain.* New York: David McKay Company.

Brown, W., & May, D. (2012). Organizational change and development: The efficacy of transformational leadership training. *Journal of Management Development*, 31(6), 520–536.

Burke, M. J., & Day, R. R. (1986). A cumulative study of the effectiveness of managerial training. *Journal of Applied Psychology,* 71(2), 232–245.

Cleary, M., Freeman, A., & Sharrock, L. (2005). The development, implementation, and evaluation of a clinical leadership program for mental health nurses. *Issues in Mental Health Nursing*, 26(8), 827–842.

Collins, D. B. (2001). Organizational performance: The future focus of leadership development programs. *Journal of Leadership Studies*, 7(4), 43–54.

Collins, D. B., & Holton, E. F. (2004). The effectiveness of managerial leadership development programs: A meta-analysis of studies from 1982 to 2001. *Human Resource Development Quarterly*, 15(2), 217–248.

Day, D. V. (2001). Leadership development: A review in context. *The Leadership Quarterly*, 11(4), 581–613.

Day, D. V., Fleenor, J. W., Atwater, L. E., Sturm, R. E., & McKee, R. A. (2014). Advances in leader and leadership development: A review of 25 years of research and theory. *The Leadership Quarterly*, 25(1), 63–82.

Graen, G. B., & Uhl-Bien, M. (1995). Relationship-based approach to leadership: Development of leader–member exchange (LMX) theory of leadership over 25 years: Applying a multi-level multi-domain perspective. *The Leadership Quarterly*, 6(2), 219-247.

Gregersen, S., Kuhnert, S., Zimber, A., & Nienhaus, A. (2011). Führungsverhalten und Gesundheit – Zum Stand der Forschung [Leadership behavior and health – The current state of research]. *Gesundheitswesen*, 73, 3–12.

Griffin, R. W. (1981). Supervisory behaviour as a source of perceived task scope. *Journal of Occupational Psychology,* 54, 175–182.

Groves, K. S. (2007). Integrating leadership development and succession planning best practices. *Journal of Management Development*, 26(3), 239–260.

Hardy, L., Arthur, C. A., Jones, G., Shariff, A., Munnoch, K., Isaacs, I., & Allsopp, A. J. (2010). The relationship between transformational leadership behaviors, psychological, and training outcomes in elite military recruits. *The Leadership Quarterly*, 21(1), 20–32.

Hasson, H., von Thiele Schwarz, U., Holmström, S., Karanika-Murray, M., & Tafvelin S. (2016). Improving organizational learning through leadership training. *Journal of Workplace Learning*, 28(3), 115–129.

Heifitz, R. (1994). *Leadership without Easy Answer.* Cambridge, MA: Harvard University.

Hernez-Broome, G., & Hughes, R. L. (2004). Leadership development: Past, present, and future. *People and Strategy*, 27(1), 24.

House, R. J. (1996). Path-goal theory of leadership: Lessons, legacy, and a reformulated theory. *The Leadership Quarterly*, 7(3), 323–352.

Jeon, Y. H., Simpson, J. M., Chenoweth, L., Cunich, M., & Kendig, H. (2013). The effectiveness of an aged care specific leadership and management program on workforce, work environment, and care quality outcomes: Design of a cluster randomised controlled trial. *Implementation Science,* 8(1), 126.

Karanika-Murray, M., Bartholomew, K., Williams, G., & Cox, T. (2015). LMX across levels of leadership: Concurrent influences of line managers and senior management on work characteristics and employee psychological health. *Work & Stress*, 29(1), 57–74.

Karanika-Murray, M., & Biron, C. (Eds.) (2015). *Derailed Organizational Health and Well-Being Interventions: Confessions of Failure, Solutions for Success*. Dordrecht, Netherlands: Springer Science+Business Media.

Kelloway, K., & Barling, J. (2010). Leadership development as an intervention in occupational health psychology." *Work & Stress*, 24, 260–279.

Kirkpatrick, D. L. (1998). *Another Look at Evaluating Training Programmes: Fifty Articles from Training and Development and Technical Training: Magazines Cover the Essentials of Evaluation and Return-on-Investment*. Alexandria, VA: American Society for Training & Development.

Kirkpatrick, D., & Kirkpatrick, J. (2005). *Transferring Learning to Behavior: Using the Four Levels to Improve Performance*. San Francisco, CA: Berrett-Koehler Publishers.

Kolb, D. A. (1984). *Experiential Learning: Experiences as the Source of Learning and Development*. Englewood Cliffs, NJ: Prentice Hall.

Kristensen, T. S. (2005). Intervention studies in occupational epidemiology. *Occupational and Environmental Medicine*, 62, 205–210.

Kuehnl, A., Rehfuess, E., von Elm, E., Nowak, D., & Glaser, J. (2014). Human resource management training of supervisors for improving health and well-being of employees (Protocol), Issue 1. Art. No.: CD010905.

Kuoppala, J., Lamminpää, A., Liira, J., & Vainio, H. (2008). Leadership, job well-being, and health effects – A systematic review and a meta-analysis. *Journal of Occupational and Environmental Medicine*, 50, 904–915.

Leithwood, K., Menzies, T., Jantzi, D., & Leithwood, J. (1996). School restructuring, transformational leadership and the amelioration of teacher burnout. *Anxiety, Stress, and Coping*, 9(3), 199–215.

Leviton, L. C., Khan, L. K., Rog, D., Dawkins, N., & Cotton, D. (2010). Evaluability assessment to improve public health policies, programmes, and practices. Annual Review of Public Health, 31, 213–233.

Lornudd, C., Bergman, D., Sandahl, C., & von Thiele Schwarz, U. (2016). A randomised study of interventions for healthcare managers. *Leadership in Health Services*, 29(4), 358–376.

Nielsen, K. (2013). Review article: How can we make organizational interventions work? Employees and line managers as actively crafting interventions. *Human Relations*, 66(8), 1029–1050.

Nielsen, K., Randall, R., Holten, A.-L., & González, E. R. (2010). Conducting organizational-level occupational health interventions: What works? *Work & Stress*, 24(3), 234–259.

Nielsen, K., Randall, R., Yarker, J., & Brenner, S- O. (2008). The effects of transformational leadership on followers' perceived work characteristics and psychological well-being: A longitudinal study. *Work & Stress*, 22(1), 16–32.

Nyberg, A., Bernin, P., & Theorell, T. (2005). *The Impact of Leadership on the Health of Subordinates*. PhD thesis. Stockholm: National Institute for Working Life [Arbetslivsinstitutet].

Olsen, K., Legg, S., & Hasle, P. (2012). How to use programme theory to evaluate the effectiveness of schemes designed to improve the work environment in small businesses. *Work: A Journal of Prevention, Assessment and Rehabilitation*, 41, 5999–6006.

Piccolo, R. F., & Colquitt, J. A. (2006). Transformational leadership and job behaviors: The mediating role of core job characteristics. *Academy of Management Journal*, 49(2), 327–340.

Riggio, R. E. (2008). Leadership development: The current state and future expectations. *Consulting Psychology Journal: Practice and Research*, 60(4), 383–392.

Savage, C. (2011). *Overcoming Inertia in Medical Education*. Institut för lärande, informatik, management och etik/Deparment of Learning, Informatics, Management and Ethics.

Skakon, J., Nielsen, K., Borg, V., & Guzman, J. (2010). Are leaders' well- being, behaviours and style associated with the affective well-being of their employees? A systematic review of three decades of research. *Work & Stress*, 24, 107–139.

Tafvelin, S. (2013). *The Transformational Leadership Process*. Ph.D. thesis, Umeå University.

Thiele Schwarz, U. von, Hasson. H., & Tafvelin, S. (2016). Leadership training as an occupational health intervention: Improved safety and sustained productivity. *Safety Science*, 81, 35–45.

Thiele Schwarz, U. von, Lundmark, R., & Hasson, H. (2016). The Dynamic Integrated Evaluation Model (DIEM): Achieving sustainability in organizational intervention through a participatory evaluation approach. *Stress & Health* (Special Issue on Organizational health interventions – Advances in evaluation methodology), 32(4), 285–293.

Walumbwa, F. O., Wang, P., Lawler, J. J., & Shi, K. (2004). The role of collective efficacy in the relations between transformational leadership and work outcomes. *Journal of Occupational and Organizational Psychology*, 77(4), 515–530.

24

Participatory approach for a healthy workplace in Japan

Akihito Shimazu and Daniel Goering

Introduction

Work can be stressful for employees, and this stress can be costly to organizations. In fact, a recent nationwide survey conducted in Japan found a high proportion of Japanese workers (61%) as experiencing high levels of anxiety and stress in their daily work lives (Japanese Ministry of Health, Labour, & Welfare, 2013). Figures in the United States are similarly concerning, with data indicating upwards of 80% of all on-the-job injuries and 40% of total employee turnover attributed to work stress (Atkinson, 2004), and roughly 30% of US workers indicating they are currently experiencing burnout (Shanafelt et al., 2012), a mental health condition caused by chronic exposure to work stress (Maslach, 1982). There is a growing body of evidence showing the risks that increased work-related stressors pose to employee mental and physical health, and the subsequent effects this can have on productivity and performance. For instance, several meta-analyses have established a clear link between greater job demands, a key determinant of work-related stress, and both psychological maladies such as burnout ($\rho = .27$, $k = 27$; Crawford, LePine, & Rich, 2010) and physical injuries ($\rho = .13$, $k = 21$; Nahrgang, Morgeson, & Hofmann, 2011). Consequently, burnout may have negative effects on job performance ($\rho = -.25$, weighted average among three burnout dimensions; Swider & Zimmerman, 2010).

Considering the significant link between work-related stress and employee mental and physical wellbeing, it is important to note that the cost is not only to the individual employee. There are significant costs to the organization and society as well. For instance, the estimated cost of workplace injuries and illnesses approximates 4%–5% of Gross Domestic Product worldwide (World Health Organization, 2008). Furthermore, in the United States alone workplace stress may contribute to an estimated $120 billion to $190 billion annually in added healthcare costs to the economy and more than 120,000 deaths in the US workforce (Goh, Pfeffer, & Zenios, 2015).

Although it is difficult to estimate the true costs to individuals and organizations, taking all of the evidence together suggests that finding ways to reduce or at least help manage stress in the workplace is important. This is particularly true as the nature of work continues to become more demanding; as economies develop from manufacturing, to service, to knowledge-based economies, work is becoming more interdependent, dynamic, and complex (Grant & Parker, 2009; Ring & Van de Ven, 1994; Weick, 2005). It is therefore increasingly relevant for organizations to find ways to effectively manage work-related stress. As such, considerable research on stress management strategies and interventions has been conducted over several decades (for one review, see Richardson & Rothstein, 2008). Although a treatment of the theoretical underpinnings of such interventions will be given in the next section, one of the core principles common to them all is to find ways to either reduce demands or increase resources, or a combination of both (Demerouti, Bakker, Nachreiner, & Schaufeli, 2001). Furthermore, interventions can also vary on the types of demands and resources targeted, whether they be physical, psychological, or social in nature. As our main focus is on work-related stress in Japan and other developed nations where the demands of work typically relate more closely to those in service and knowledge-based economies (i.e., less physically demanding), we will focus here on psychosocial factors.

Improving the psychosocial work environment

There are three types of psychosocial factors that moderate the relationship between workplace stressors (e.g., work overload, role conflict) and employee stress-related outcomes (e.g., burnout, physical ailments, mental health problems). The first type is "individual factors," meaning broadly the traits (e.g., neuroticism, dispositional optimism), human capital (e.g., knowledge, skills, abilities), and other personal resources or constraints of an individual. The second type of psychosocial factor relates to those resources or demands outside of work (e.g., life events, work–family conflict). The third type of factor is "supporting factors," which are "physical, social, or organizational aspects of the job" (Xanthopoulou, Bakker, Demerouti, & Schaufeli, 2007, p. 122) that are external to the individual. Each of these types of psychosocial factors can either augment or mitigate employee psychophysiological reactions to workplace stressors.

Related to these psychosocial factors, Tsutsumi and Shimazu (2016) introduced three prevention strategies to help prevent mental health problems at work. The first strategy is self-care training. In self-care training, employees acquire the knowledge and skills necessary to more effectively manage their own stress levels in daily life. It is meant to bolster the level of individual resources (i.e., "individual factors") available to an employee to help mitigate the negative effects of workplace stressors. The second strategy is supervisor training. This strategy targets the "supporting factors" by providing supervisors with information on the potential negative effects to employees of various occupational stress factors as well as techniques on how to support employees and cooperate with occupational health staff members. This strategy is supported by findings which show that buy-in from supervisors appears to be an important aspect of effective implementation of any stress management intervention (Tsutsumi et al., 2005). The third strategy is to improve the workplace environment itself. This type of intervention strategy is preferable (Lamontagne, Keegel, Louie, Ostry, & Landsbergis, 2007) as it typically emphasizes primary prevention, meaning interventions that attempt to alter or reduce the *sources* of workplace stress rather than simply train on skills or provide support to cope with stress (Murphy & Sauter, 2003). By focusing on the organization's work environment, systematic improvements can be made that have lasting effects even after new, untrained employees are hired or existing employees and supervisors are promoted, retire, or otherwise turn over. Indeed an organization-based approach to improve the psychosocial work environment appears to be one of the most effective ways to ensure the mental health of employees (Kawakami & Kobayashi, 2015).

By improving the psychosocial work environment, organizations can proactively improve the working methods, conditions, or design of work to help reduce employee exposure to workplace stressors at the organization or unit level. Such an organization-based approach is proactively preventative as it focuses on designing the social environment or context in which work occurs to induce positive psychological processes (e.g., perceptions of meaning, psychological safety, and availability; Kahn, 1990) prior to workers experiencing what would otherwise be a workplace stressor. In other words, this approach focuses on reducing risk factors at the source (e.g., work overload, unclear meaning in job). It should be noted here, however, that there is evidence to suggest that a combination of intervention strategies, or a "systems approach" in which the work environment is designed to reduce stress risk factors in combination with training workers how to cope with stress to ameliorate its effects, may offer optimal benefits (Lamontagne et al., 2007).

Existing evidence supports the use of organization-based strategies to improve the psycho-social work environment to reduce potential risk factors. For instance, in their meta-analytic review of the relationship between psychosocial work environments and employee mental health, Stansfeld and Candy (2006) found that a combination of high job demands and low decision latitude (i.e., high job strain) as well as a combination of high effort and low reward (i.e., effort-reward imbalance) were the greatest risk factors for employee mental health problems. In the meta-analysis by Lamontagne et al. (2007), organization-based interventions were found to have significant benefits at both the individual and organizational levels whereas individual-focused approaches were beneficial at the individual level only. Furthermore, Yoshikawa et al. (2013) analyzed 17 cases to qualitatively draw up guidelines to improve the psychosocial work environments of organizations. Thus there is growing support for the use of primary intervention strategies focusing on improving the psychosocial factors of the workplace environment.

In the next section of this chapter, we provide practical guidelines on how to implement improvements to the psychosocial work environment. We then provide an explanation of the importance of employee participation in implementing such interventions (i.e., the "participatory approach"). This is followed by a discussion of achieving healthy workplaces, including an overview of the underlying theory. We conclude with a case study as a relevant example of successful implementation of a participatory approach to achieve a healthy workplace in Japan.

Guidelines for improving the psychosocial work environment in Japan

From a practical point of view, it is important to provide evidence-based guidelines on how to implement organization-based stress management interventions effectively. Yoshikawa et al. (2013) reviewed the extant research in the occupational health literature in order to develop guidelines and subsequent recommendations for designing and implementing intervention strategies. We present here an adaptation of Yoshikawa and colleagues' (2013) guidelines. Although these guidelines are perhaps generalizable across multiple cultures and settings, they were proposed specifically with application to workplaces in the Asia Pacific region in mind. As further research explores potential boundary conditions, including various cultural contexts, these guidelines should be modified appropriately based on the best available evidence.

There are four main guidelines, which we summarize here as *preparation, benchmarking, coordinated implementation,* and *continued improvement.* Each of these guidelines is comprised of specific recommendations. The four guidelines should be followed in the order given (i.e., from *preparation* through to *continued improvement*). We also recommend that the specific recommendations found within each guideline be followed in order, as much as possible. However, due to the unique nature and constraints of any given organization, the recommendations within a given guideline may be adapted as necessary to suit specific organizational needs.

Guideline 1: Preparation

The first guideline is *preparation*, which relates to actions taken in order to accurately assess the current work environment and secure buy-in from all levels within the organization. This step is one of the most critical; however, it may also be the most difficult to execute as a degree of consensus is needed from an array of stakeholders, including managers who may be reluctant to alter the status quo (Kawakami & Kobayashi, 2015). One way to resolve some of these barriers is to use a participatory approach (explained in the next section), in which workers are actively engaged in providing feedback to managers regarding existing issues and possible solutions to those issues. This participation has been shown to be an effective way to increase the effectiveness of action plans (Kobayashi, Kaneyoshi, Yokota, & Kawakami, 2008). Therefore, the first specific recommendation within this guideline is to *build consensus on aims and establish a steering group*. By building consensus around a plan to improve the psychosocial work environment, employees, managers, and other stakeholders have a sense of ownership and commitment which will be crucial to successfully executing the plan.

The second specific recommendation in this guideline is to *adopt a problem-solving approach* in lieu of a problem-identifying approach. The focus with a problem-*solving* approach is to not simply identify existing and potential issues, but to propose and discuss *solutions* to those issues. This change in focus from problem identification to problem solving, especially when those solutions are provided via active participation from workers, can help encourage managers to identify the most relevant problems and most feasible solutions based on existing policies or other internal constraints. Organizations that successfully implemented changes to the psychosocial work environment emphasized this approach (Yoshikawa & Kogi, 2010).

Finally, it is important to *elicit proactive involvement from organizational and division heads*, meaning that there is top-down support for the plan as well as cooperation by supporting divisions such as human resources.

In summary, adequate preparation leads to support and concentrated effort on an agreed-upon plan. With support from senior management and supporting divisions, managers can then elicit participation from workers to build consensus on a problem-solving course of action.

Guideline 2: Benchmarking

After adequate *preparation* throughout various levels of the organization, the next step is to engage in *benchmarking* that helps define the basic rules of implementation. Benchmarking is used to develop specific action plans and identify appropriate methods in implementing improvements to the psychosocial work environment. Thus the first recommendation within this guideline is to *refer to good practices inside and outside of the workplace*. This means, for example, referencing existing case studies of similar organizations that have already successfully implemented improvements. There are existing tools in the academic literature that can be used effectively (e.g., Mental Health Action Checklist for a Better Workplace Environment, Kawakami & Kobayashi, 2015; tools designed specifically for small-scale enterprises, Moriguchi, Sakuragi, & Ikeda, 2016).

In addition, as an extension of garnering worker participation in the planning process as part of the *preparation* guideline, the next recommendation is to *continue to facilitate workers' participation* throughout the entire process.

Finally, managers should *list and prioritize a broad range of issues related to workers' mental health* in order to strategically decide on the most feasible solutions and improvement measures to be implemented.

Guideline 3: Coordinated implementation

The next guideline is *coordinated implementation*, wherein the appropriate improvement measures (identified via *benchmarking*) are implemented via coordination at various organizational levels (with the buy-in gained through sufficient *preparation*). The improvement measures are implemented in light of the existing resources and readiness of the organization. Accordingly, the first recommendation is to *take into account the workplace resources* while implementing the improvement measures so as to not unnecessarily disrupt the existing routines, procedures, etc. of the organization. For example, if changes in the environment are made without careful consideration of existing resources (e.g., money, manpower, managers' schedules) and constraints (e.g., time, scope of action plan), then those changes have the possibility of being short-lived or even, ironically, cause unintended stress on the very stakeholders the changes are meant to benefit. Therefore it is recommended that changes be implemented carefully, if not gradually, maintaining consensus and active participation throughout the process.

The next recommendation is to *use appropriate tools to support workers*. These tools do not need to be expensive or time-consuming (Tsutsumi, Nagami, Yoshikawa, Kogi, & Kawakami, 2009). Furthermore, when possible we recommend that already existing workplace mechanisms be used when implementing improvement action plans. For example, many organizations will already have an organizational structure in place to help monitor worker health (e.g., safety committees). Coordination with existing workplace mechanisms is an efficient use of existing resources and helps to ensure sustained commitment to executing and adapting plans to improve the psychosocial work environment in the future. In fact, adoption of a sustainable improvement plan is the fourth and final guideline.

Guideline 4: Continued improvement

The final guideline is to adopt a sustainable, long-term view with continued implementation as the focus; as such, we term this guideline *continued improvement*. One way to ensure sustained effort towards the gradual improvement of the psychosocial work environment is to set intermediate goals and celebrate the gradual improvements obtained throughout the process. In other words, this means continuing to engage in "participatory activities . . . based on a step-by-step problem-solving approach" (Tsutsumi & Shimazu, 2016), which has been shown to be effective (Tsutsumi et al., 2009). This guideline implies a feedback loop in which managers assess improvements using improvement measures while workers continue to provide feedback on existing stressors and solutions; in this way action plans can be adapted as necessary for new or as-yet-unsolved problems.

This cycle of *preparation, benchmarking, coordinated implementation,* and *continued improvement* then perpetuates gradual, sustained improvements in the work environment. A key point to note here is the necessity for participation at every stage of the process. In the next section we discuss the participatory approach in more detail.

Participatory approach

As discussed in the last section, an organization-based approach to employee stress management, where the work environment is designed such to improve the psychosocial factors needed to reduce workplace stressors, is one of the most effective strategies to improve the mental health of workers. This approach has received increased interest by scholars and practitioners, particularly in Japan where organizations are required by law to engage in activities to promote the mental health of employees, with strong guidance towards implementing an organization-based approach (Japanese Ministry of Health, Labour, and Welfare, 2006). Kawakami and Kobayashi (2015) noted several examples of successful implementation of this approach, including Sony's efforts to formalize a health management program for its employees. Implementation of some form of employee mental health care by larger corporations (i.e., with more than 1,000 employees), such as Sony, is very high (> 99%; Ministry of Health, Labour, and Welfare, Japan, 2013). However, implementation in smaller enterprises, such as small- and microscale enterprises in Japan (i.e., fewer than 50 employees) still appears to be low, near 39%. Thus we note the need to further understand the barriers preventing more widespread implementation of strategies to improve the psychosocial work environment of organizations.

A participatory approach is one way to (1) not only increase implementation by organizations currently not engaging in mental health activities but (2) also increase the effectiveness of existing activities (Tsutsumi et al., 2009). A participatory approach is one in which organizations not only apply top-down changes to the psychosocial work environment but simultaneously include bottom-up input and control from employees. In addition, human resources professionals and occupational health professionals work in concert with employees and managers to make risk assessments and develop action plans to proactively prevent, as much as possible, workplace stressors and other risk factors relating to employee health. Involvement by employees is important, because employees are those who are "in the trenches" and likely best understand the potential stressors and other risk factors involved in their job. Involvement by managers is also important, because execution of the intervention action plans requires ownership as well as knowledge of the strategy and process. Finally, involvement by the human resources department, working with health care professionals, is important in order to both comply with existing laws and regulations as well as proactively prevent unnecessary workplace stressors.

Although research on the effectiveness and boundary conditions of the participatory approach to improve the psychosocial work environment is still relatively scant, based on existing evidence, organizations can expect increased employee physical health benefits (Rivilis et al., 2006) as well as mental health benefits (Kobayashi et al., 2008) and increased productivity (Tsutsumi et al., 2009) by following a participatory approach. Furthermore, employees who are encouraged to contribute to the process and provide their input are likely to find the mental health activities to be implemented more meaningful (Reichers, Wanous, & Austin, 1997), and may perhaps perceive the implementation process as being more fair (i.e., procedural justice perceptions). Thus, a participatory approach allows employees and organizational leaders to work together to develop appropriate interventions, and such activities have a higher likelihood of being integrated and adhered to by employees and supervisors alike (Tsutsumi et al., 2009). As for small enterprises, participatory intervention programs have been found to be effective at reducing mental health risk factors (Kogi, 2006). Access to convenient tools customized for small employers will likely make implementation more widespread across Japan (Moriguchi et al., 2016).

Achievement of a healthy workplace

So far, we have referred to how to improve the psychosocial work environment by focusing on a participatory approach. According to a 2012 survey of employee health by the Japanese government (Ministry of Health, Labour, and Welfare, Japan, 2013), only about 26% of employers that were working to promote mental health did so by assessing and improving conditions in the workplace. Current steps to improve conditions in the workplace are primarily intended to identify and decrease stress factors in the workplace that harm mental health and seek to prevent mental health problems. Nevertheless, an overview of the steps that have been taken to improve conditions in the workplace shows that there are several issues with these steps:

1   When steps to improve conditions in the workplace are taken only in select workplaces that pose a risk to health, supervisors are less motivated to take steps to improve conditions and problems are glossed over.
2   When the topic of reducing stress is brought to the fore, workers have trouble staying motivated and, ironically, efforts to deal with stress may lead to stress. In addition, employees in workplaces with less stress (less risk) tend to be less actively involved in efforts to reduce stress (efforts are not applicable to them).
3   Occupational health staff (e.g., occupational physicians, occupational health nurses, and psychologists) are limited in what they can do; they are precluded from initiating independent efforts throughout the company. In addition, the nature of departments, sections, and teams and the existing organizational framework can influence the level of stress and dedication of the organization. There are thus limits and constraints (i.e., both organizational and legal) to what occupational health personnel can do to improve working conditions.

In order to overcome these problems and to conduct activities to improve psychosocial work conditions smoothly, the following changes in viewpoint must be made:

1   Occupational health personnel and management must collaborate more than they have done so in the past. To that end, occupational health personnel and management should set common goals (e.g., invigorating the organization and empowering individuals).
2   Attention must be paid to positive outcomes (e.g., work engagement) as well as negative (e.g., mental and physical disorders, absenteeism, presenteeism).
3   Efforts must both enhance organizational strengths (job resources) and reduce organizational weaknesses (stressors).
4   Efforts to deal with stress must not be implemented in isolation. Instead, efforts to improve the workplace must be included in routine managerial processes.

Internationally, efforts to promote mental health in the workplace are taking an even broader view toward preventing mental health problems and accentuating the more positive aspects of mental health (e.g., work engagement) (World Health Organization, 2017b). With common goals and a common framework, the occupational health department and management can collaborate to deftly initiate efforts to invigorate the organization. An example of a common framework is the Job Demands–Resources model (Figure 24.1) (Schaufeli & Bakker, 2004), which is a key concept in work engagement.

The Job Demands–Resources model consists of two main processes: a motivational process and a health impairment process. In the motivational process (i.e., the bottom portion of Figure 24.1), job resources lead to work engagement and subsequently to positive organizational outcomes (e.g., improved work-related attitudes) and ultimately better health. In the health impairment process (i.e., the top portion of Figure 24.1), job demands (job stressors) lead to burnout that in turn leads to adverse health and ultimately then to detrimental organizational outcomes. We refer readers to Schaufeli and Bakker (2004) for a more detailed description of these processes. Conventional efforts by occupational health have focused on the health impairment process. Those efforts concentrated on reducing stress due to high job demands (burnout) and preventing health problems. Job demands and job resources are the starting points for both the motivational process and the health impairment process. Thus, creating a healthy workplace focuses on reducing job demands and increasing job resources. Increased job resources lead to increased work engagement and reduced burnout, so enhancing and improving job resources is particularly crucial to creating a healthy workplace.

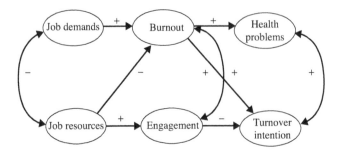

Figure 24.1 The Job Demands–Resource model
Source: Copyright Schaufeli and Bakker, 2004, p. 297.

A case study of efforts to achieve a healthy workplace

This section will describe a case study of efforts to achieve a healthy workplace (details have been altered somewhat for purposes of anonymity without affecting the relevant facts; these efforts are ongoing). Efforts to create a healthier workplace environment were initiated by Company A (a department store chain located in Japan) at its headquarters and at outlets in a major metropolitan area. These efforts involved five processes: (1) informing the health and safety committee of the efforts being initiated, (2) assessment of conditions in the workplace, (3) meetings to report questionnaire results, (4) initiation of efforts to invigorate and improve the workplace, and (5) the extension of those efforts laterally. The first author assisted those efforts as an outside party.

During the second process (i.e., assessment of conditions in the workplace), all of Company A's employees were asked to complete a Web-based version of the new Brief Job Stress Questionnaire (Inoue et al., 2014) in August 2014. Employees individually accessed and completed the questionnaire using a PC or smartphone. Using a Web-based system, occupational health personnel calculated mean values for job demands, organizational resources, stress responses, satisfaction (work and family life), job performance, and work engagement in each workplace. Results were displayed in charts and diagrams: a chart of the overall health of the organization, a job stress assessment diagram, and a radar (spider) chart.

As part of the third process, meetings to report survey results took place twice in October 2014 and were attended by the heads of different workplaces (about 20 members of management). Each meeting took two hours, and 30–40 heads of different workplaces attended each meeting. If the head of a given workplace was unable to attend the meeting, an industrial physician met with the head separately to report the questionnaire results. The meetings to report survey results took place as shown in Table 24.1. Introductory remarks, an explanation of the purpose of the meeting, and a final summary were given by the head of human resources, but all other information in the meeting was provided by the first author.

In a 30-minute lecture, work engagement was described as a positive concept related to mental health in the workplace. Audience members were informed that increased work engagement leads to both improved mental and physical health, and that it invigorates the entire organization thereby creating a healthier workplace. Audience members were informed that work engagement could be increased by enhancing and improving organizational resources (workplace strengths). The survey results were interpreted, with examples from every workplace, and the main aspects of efforts to create a healthy workplace at the organization were explained. Based on results from each workplace, Initiative 1 (identifying workplace strengths and issues) and

Table 24.1 Outline of the meeting to report survey results

	Content	Time (minutes)
1	Introductory remarks (human resources manager)	5
2	Lecture (work engagement and how to achieve a healthy workplace)	30
3	Interpretation of the survey results	25
4	Initiative 1: identifying workplace strengths and issues	25
5	Initiative 2: making an action plan to make a healthier workplace	25
6	Summary and questions and answers	8
7	Clarify next steps (human resources manager)	2

Initiative 2 (making an action plan to create a healthier workplace) were begun. For Initiatives 1 and 2, the head of each workplace filled out a form while referring to the results for that workplace. Conclusions were described, a question-and-answer session was held, and a synopsis was given in order to clarify next steps. During the synopsis, the head of each workplace was asked to submit an action plan on how to improve the health of the organization's workplace to human resources and the occupational health department within two weeks. Drafting of the action plan for each workplace was left to the discretion of the head of that workplace.

As part of the fourth process (i.e., initiation of efforts to invigorate and improve the workplace), the action plans made as part of Initiative 2 in the previous process were submitted to the human resources and occupational health department within two weeks of the conclusion of the meetings to report questionnaire results. Initiatives to execute those action plans were identified and begun. From the end of February to March 2015, the human resources and occupational health departments were informed of the state of efforts to invigorate and improve the organization in each workplace. Case studies of successful efforts were subsequently identified in interim reports. Case studies of successful efforts were provided to devise efforts for the following year, and the lateral extension of those efforts was planned.

In the case study we have just outlined with Company A, work engagement was a key concept for efforts to achieve a healthier work environment within the organization. The fact that increased work engagement leads to improved mental and physical health and that it invigorates the organization was stressed to management and managers. This point was emphasized because conditions in the workplace cannot be improved without the understanding and cooperation of management and key managers in an organization. In fact, in the past conventional efforts to deal with stress in Japanese workplaces have focused on only reducing the difficulty of working in a given workplace (stress factors), and these efforts have typically been spearheaded by the occupational health department. However, interventions that involve how a company is managed or an organization's management policies cannot be implemented by the occupational health department alone, and the occupational health department is limited in the ways it can help employees deal with stress in the workplace. Historically efforts to deal with stress in the workplace in Japan have been primarily focused on reducing the difficulty of working in a given workplace (stress factors); yet without the participation of all organizational levels these efforts have been more likely to be ignored or thwarted by management and workplace managers. In other words, conventional interventions that do not use the participatory approach have tended to be less effective and unsustainable.

In light of these limitations, goals to improve conditions in the workplace need to be set in accordance with the requirements of management and managers and efforts to improve those conditions need to be encouraged by management and managers. Creating a healthy workplace within the organization through increased work engagement leads to better employee health and performance, so collaboration between occupational health and management should be encouraged. Another advantage of such an approach is that it allows the involvement of workplace managers as part of the routine management of an organization. In the company in the case study, occupational health department and human resources jointly initiated efforts – which are ongoing – to invigorate and improve the workplace with common goals (i.e., healthy workplace).

Conclusion

This chapter referred to how to achieve a healthy workplace through the participatory approach. With common goals and a common framework (i.e., healthy workplace), occupational health departments and management can collaborate to deftly initiate efforts to invigorate and improve the organization. In such an event, employee health should be viewed as a valuable business resource, a mindset captured by an increasingly common saying in Japan: "No business wealth without workers' health" (World Health Organization, 2017a). In accordance with this mindset, and based on extant empirical evidence, efforts to encourage health should be incorporated into managerial processes, and individuals should be empowered to participate in making improvements to the workplace. Doing so will help organizations become healthy places for employees to work. Furthermore, this mindset is crucial for encouraging efforts to promote mental health among employers (and particularly small and medium-sized businesses), particularly in Japan. In the future, the authors hope to devise specific techniques and develop tools to achieve a healthy workplace in organizations, and to assemble case studies of successful efforts to invigorate organizations.

References

Atkinson, W. (2004). Stress: Risk management's most serious challenge? *Risk Management*, 51(6), 20–25.

Crawford, E. R., LePine, J. A., & Rich, B. L. (2010). Linking job demands and resources to employee engagement and burnout: A theoretical extension and meta-analytic test. *Journal of Applied Psychology*, 95(5), 834.

Demerouti, E., Bakker, A. B., Nachreiner, F., & Schaufeli, W. B. (2001). The Job Demands–Resources model of burnout. *Journal of Applied Psychology*, 86(3), 499–512.

Goh, J., Pfeffer, J., & Zenios, S. A. (2015). The relationship between workplace stressors and mortality and health costs in the United States. *Management Science*, 62(2), 608-628.

Grant, A. M., & Parker, S. K. (2009). 7 redesigning work design theories: The rise of relational and proactive perspectives. *The Academy of Management Annals*, 3(1), 317–375.

Inoue, A., Kawakami, N., Shimomitsu, T., Tsutsumi, A., Haratani, T., Yoshikawa, T., . . . & Odagiri, Y. (2014). Development of a short questionnaire to measure an extended set of job demands, job resources, and positive health outcomes: The new brief job stress questionnaire. *Industrial Health*, 52, 175–189.

Japanese Ministry of Health, Labour and Welfare. (2006). *The guideline for promotion and maintenance of mental health of workers*. Ministry of Health, Labour and Welfare, Japan, Tokyo (in Japanese). Available at: www.mhlw.go.jp/houdou/2006/03/dl/h0331-1b.pdf.

Japanese Ministry of Health, Labour and Welfare. (2013). *Survey on State of Employees' Health 2012*. Ministry of Health, Labour and Welfare, Japan, Tokyo (in Japanese). Available at: www.mhlw.go.jp/toukei/list/h24–46–50.html

Kahn, W. A. (1990). Psychological conditions of personal engagement and disengagement at work. *Academy of Management Journal*, 33, 692–724.

Kawakami, N., & Kobayashi, Y. (2015). Increasing worker participation: The mental health action checklist. In: M. Karanika-Murray & C. Biron (eds.), *Derailed Organizational Interventions for Stress and Well-Being*. Springer Netherlands, 175–182.

Kobayashi, Y., Kaneyoshi, A., Yokota, A., & Kawakami, N. (2008). Effects of a worker participatory program for improving work environments on job stressors and mental health among workers: A controlled trial. *Journal of Occupational Health*, 50(6), 455–470.

Kogi, K. (2006). Advances in participatory occupational health aimed at good practices in small enterprises and the informal sector. *Industrial Health*, 44(1), 31–34.

Lamontagne, A. D., Keegel, T., Louie, A. M., Ostry, A., Landsbergis, P. A. (2007). A systematic review of the job-stress intervention evaluation literature, 1990–2005. *International Journal of Occupational and Environmental Health*, 13(3), 268–280.

Maslach, C. (1982). *Burnout: The Cost of Caring*. ISHK.

Moriguchi, J., Sakuragi, S., & Ikeda, M. (2016). Improving psychosocial factors in small-scale enterprises in Japan and the Asia-Pacific region. In: A. Shimazu, M. Dollard, R. Nordin, & J. Oakman (eds.), *Psychosocial Factors at Work in the Asia Pacific: From Theory to Practice*. Cham, Switzerland: Springer.

Murphy, L. R., & Sauter, S. L. (2003). The USA perspective: Current issues and trends in the management of work stress. *Australian Psychologist*, 38(2), 151–157.

Nahrgang, J. D., Morgeson, F. P., & Hofmann, D. A. (2011). Safety at work: A meta-analytic investigation of the link between job demands, job resources, burnout, engagement, and safety outcomes. *Journal of Applied Psychology*, 96(1), 71–94.

Reichers, A. E., Wanous, J. P., & Austin, J. T. (1997). Understanding and managing cynicism about organizational change. *The Academy of Management Executive*, 11(1), 48–59.

Richardson, K. M., & Rothstein, H. R. (2008). Effects of occupational stress management intervention programs: A meta-analysis. *Journal of Occupational Health Psychology*, 13(1), 69–93.

Ring, P. S., & Van de Ven, A. H. (1994). Developmental processes of cooperative interorganizational relationships. *Academy of Management Review*, 19(1), 90–118.

Rivilis, I., Cole, D. C., Frazer, M. B., Kerr, M. S., Wells, R. P., & Ibrahim, S. (2006). Evaluation of a participatory ergonomic intervention aimed at improving musculoskeletal health. *American Journal of Industrial Medicine*, 49(10), 801–810.

Schaufeli, W. B., & Bakker, A. B. (2004). Job demands, job resources, and their relationship with burnout and engagement: A multi-sample study. *Journal of Organizational Behavior*, 25, 293–315.

Shanafelt, T. D., Boone, S., Tan, L., Dyrbye, L. N., Sotile, W., Satele, D., . . . & Oreskovich, M. R. (2012). Burnout and satisfaction with work-life balance among US physicians relative to the general US population. *Archives of Internal Medicine*, 172(18), 1377–1385.

Stansfeld, S., & Candy, B. (2006). Psychosocial work environment and mental health – A meta-analytic review. *Scandinavian Journal of Work, Environment & Health*, 32(6), 443–462.

Swider, B. W., & Zimmerman, R. D. (2010). Born to burnout: A meta-analytic path model of personality, job burnout, and work outcomes. *Journal of Vocational Behavior*, 76(3), 487–506.

Tsutsumi, A., Nagami, M., Yoshikawa, T., Kogi, K., & Kawakami, N. (2009). Participatory intervention for workplace improvements on mental health and job performance among blue-collar workers: A cluster randomized controlled trial. *Journal of Occupational and Environmental Medicine*, 51(5), 554–563.

Tsutsumi, A., & Shimazu, A. (2016). Guidelines for primary prevention for mental health at work. In: A. Shimazu, M. Dollard, R. Nordin, & J. Oakman (eds.), *Psychosocial Factors at Work in the Asia Pacific: From Theory to Practice*. Cham, Switzerland: Springer.

Tsutsumi, A., Takao, S., Mineyama, S., Nishiuchi, K., Komatsu, H., & Kawakami, N. (2005). Effects of a supervisory education for positive mental health in the workplace: A quasi-experimental study. *Journal of Occupational Health*, 47(3), 226–235.

Weick, K. E. (2005). Managing the unexpected: Complexity as distributed sensemaking. In: R. R. McDaniel & D. J. Driebe (eds.), *Uncertainty and Surprise in Complex Systems*. Berlin and Heidelberg: Springer, 51–65.

World Health Organization (2017a). *Global Healthy Workplace Model*. Available at: www.who.int/occupational_health/healthy_workplaces

World Health Organization (2017b). *Five Keys to Healthy Workplaces: No Business Wealth without Workers' Health*. Available at: www.who.int/occupational_health/5keys_healthy_workplaces.pdf

World Health Organization. (2008). *Global Strategy on Occupational Health for All: The Way to Health at Work*. Available at: www.who.int/occupational_health/en/

Xanthopoulou, D., Bakker, A. B., Demerouti, E., & Schaufeli, W. B. (2007). The role of personal resources in the Job Demands–Resources model. *International Journal of Stress Management*, 14(2), 121–141.

Yoshikawa, T., & Kogi, K. (2010). Roles in stress prevention of good practices for workplace improvements and the use of action support tool. *Job Stress Research*, 17, 267–274.

Yoshikawa, T., Yoshikawa, E., Tsuchiya, M., Kobayashi, Y., Shimazu, A., Tsutsumi, A., . . . & Kawakami, N. (2013). Development of evidence-based medicine guideline for improving the workplace environment by means of primary job stress prevention. *Job Stress Research*, 20, 135–145.

25

Workplace conflict resolution interventions

Debra Gilin Oore and Norman Dolan

Introduction

An eight-member management consulting firm is developing a bid for a contract to provide leadership assessment and coaching services to a large prospective client. Beth, a new consultant fresh out of business school, wants to lead the project to build her reputation within the company. She is certified to provide personality assessments and believes the proposal bid should center on assessment and feedback to leaders. Mark, a seasoned consultant on the team and sought-after speaker on leadership, expects to lead the project and plans to focus it on leadership coaching – this is, after all, "his area." In the team meeting, Beth and Mark float their different ideas for the proposal's focus. As each senses competition and opposition, they become defensive, vocally critique the other's ideas, and experience frustration, hostility, and anger. After the meeting, Mark hurriedly sends the entire team, ccing the director, an email asserting that leadership coaching is the way to go, he is the person to lead this, and he will send a draft proposal to all. Beth "replies all" with a challenging email – referring to Mark's email as "rash" and "uncollegial" – and says she will circulate a proposal that "actually responds to the client's needs" – and the team should vote between them. Beth and Mark avoid one another, seething, while more derogatory email exchanges continue.

This scenario ticks all the definitional boxes for conflict at work, according to a recently proposed model (LeBlanc, Gilin Oore, & Axelrod, 2014). Beth and Mark have experienced *social discord* (arguments), *interpersonal dissonance* (a sense that things have gone wrong in the relationship), *threat to a core human interest* (Beth: reputation and livelihood; Mark: identity and esteem), and *negative emotion* (LeBlanc et al., 2014). If we instead map the situation to the most widely researched taxonomy of work group conflict types (Jehn, 1995), we can say that Beth and Mark experienced a task conflict (about the work to be done) that quickly escalated to include relational conflict (personality clashes, emotional tension). In the parlance of workplace incivility theory and research, we could instead describe the incident as an *escalatory spiral* from uncivil behaviors (Andersson & Pearson, 1999), to verbal aggression. In this chapter, we use the term *interpersonal conflict at work* to refer to two (or more) employees' mutual experience of a troubling disturbance in their relationship.

Conflict and wellbeing

Interpersonal conflict at work is a risk factor for reduced employee wellbeing. The social support and cohesion of the work group is vital to employees' work functioning (Halbesleben, 2006; Viswesvaran, Sanchez, & Fisher, 1999). For example, in challenging and dangerous work team environments, team cohesion is a strong predictor of team performance (Vianen & De Dreu, 2001). Conversely, team relational conflict correlates with deteriorating employee wellbeing, such as high emotional exhaustion and stress (Giebels & Janssen, 2005). In a meta-analysis of 161 studies, Chiaburu and Harrison (2008) report that negative, antagonistic interactions among coworkers relate to employee withdrawal: greater effort reduction, higher turnover intentions, lower citizenship, and increased counterproductive behaviors directed at peers. If handled poorly, conflicts can escalate into verbal aggression and bullying (Ayoko, Callan, & Härtel, 2003; Skogstad et al., 2007). Applying these findings to our opening vignette, there is a reasonable chance that Beth and Mark's escalating disagreement will spark deviant, aggressive behavior between them, and this toxic spiral can poison the work team by involving others and draining their time and energy.

But what about when conflicts are handled well? Some theorists argue that conflict is a natural and unavoidable human experience (Axelrod & Johnson, 2005; Gilin Oore, Leiter, & LeBlanc, 2015). The transformative theory of conflict, in particular, articulates that in some conflicts we see a positive or upward spiral of connection and understanding between the parties, "from a negative, destructive, alienating and demonizing interaction to one that becomes positive, constructive, connecting, and humanizing, even while conflict and disagreement are continuing" (Bush & Folger, 2005, p. 20). These more positive views of work conflict remind that, under the right circumstances, contention may lead to beneficial insight and growth for the individuals and their relationship.

While empirical evidence of positive outcomes of conflict are less common, they do exist. Task conflict has been shown to increase performance in top management teams and teams performing nonroutine tasks (De Dreu & Weingart, 2003; de Wit, Greer, & Jehn, 2012), and there is evidence of positive, energized emotions in response to mild, frequent task conflict in teams (Todorova, Bear, & Weingart, 2014). Applying this possibility to our opening vignette, it is possible that Mark and Beth can learn to appreciate the other's concerns and see a joint solution that fulfills their superordinate goals of serving the client and building a strong team.

Work conflict represents a tipping point in the social environment of the workplace. If handled poorly, which the current literature suggests is quite common, conflict escalates and becomes both distressing and distracting from job and organizational goals. But when handled well, conflict has the potential to increase performance as well as the depth and meaning of work relationships. What can workplaces do to maximize the chances of a growth spiral, or to minimize a downward spiral, in response to the inevitable experience of interpersonal conflict?

Development of organizational conflict resolution initiatives

The organization has a critical role to play, and leadership is a key determinant in whether work conflict leads to employee distress versus growth. On one hand, when leaders adopt a laissez-faire style and fail to intervene, conflicts are more likely to morph into bullying (Skogstad et al., 2007). On the other hand, when leaders provide support and assistance to those in conflict, it can ameliorate the toll of conflict on workers' emotional exhaustion, absenteeism, and turnover intentions (Giebels & Janssen, 2005). Organizational support for resolving conflict can help veer employees off of the destructive path so they can return to a productive focus on their job and organizational goals.

For much of work life in the 20th century, organizations had virtually no systemic mechanisms to help employees resolve interpersonal conflicts (Roche & Teague, 2012). Unionized and progressive organizations managed formal grievance proceedings, relying on legal action as an option of last resort. These systems were initiated for primarily contractual and "rights-based" complaints, and do not fit well with the "interest-based" goals of relationship repair and gaining mutual understanding in an interpersonal conflict (Bendersky, 2010). A significant downside to these formal dispute resolution systems is that grievances and legal action are extremely costly in both monetary terms (~$100,000 in direct costs per case; Cascio, 2000) and human losses (distress, sick leave, absenteeism, and irreparable damage to organizational relationships; Fox & Stallworth, 2009; Nabatchi & Blomgren Bingham, 2010).

Responding to this problem, the past 20 years have seen exponential growth in alternative dispute resolution practices within organizations that are intended to resolve interpersonal conflicts more effectively (Brubaker et al., 2014; Roche & Teague, 2012). Organizations began offering more comprehensive conflict management systems that could accommodate the resolution of interpersonal conflict through neutral mediators (trained third parties who identify issues and solutions without imposing an outcome) or arbitrators (trained third parties who impose an outcome). Options for conflict resolution have proliferated, to the point that a large menu of conflict interventions is available to organizations. The remainder of this chapter will review these options, describing evidence for what makes implementation more successful, and summarize the existing evidence for benefits versus costs of each approach. We conclude the chapter with recommendations for selecting and implementing right-sized conflict supports for interested organizations.

Specific conflict resolution supports for work wellbeing

The field of occupational health psychology classifies workplace prevention strategies as primary, secondary, or tertiary (Cooper & Cartwright, 1997). In Figure 25.1, we map typical conflict resolution supports onto this continuum by considering how preventive versus reactive the intervention is. Primary prevention strategies for conflict at work aim to prevent the conditions that lead to escalated, intense relational conflict – with the goal of avoiding a problem altogether. Three interventions that organizations offer to employees fall into the primary prevention zone: preventive work-group civility norm interventions, conflict education and awareness, and preventive

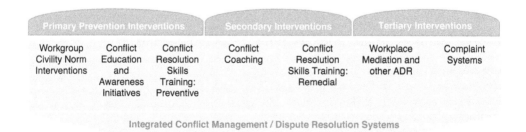

Figure 25.1 Conflict resolution interventions placed on a continuum from most preventive to most reactive

conflict resolution skills training. Secondary interventions are those that help intervene early in the development of interpersonal conflict with the goal of avoiding further escalation and distress. Conflict coaching and conflict resolution skills training to remediate an escalating conflict are examples of secondary conflict interventions. Tertiary interventions try to help individuals recover from an escalated conflict episode, and include workplace mediation and alternative dispute resolution and complaint systems.

Primary conflict prevention interventions

Work group civility interventions

Work group civility interventions are an innovative recent development, with a primary prevention goal: to strengthen social support and civil behavior, while decreasing uncivil behavior. A successfully implemented and tested work-group civility intervention is the Civility, Respect, and Engagement in the Workforce (CREW) initiative. This initiative has been developed and refined in hospital environments, such as the Veterans Health Administration hospitals in the United States (Osatuke et al., 2009) and the public health care system in Canada (Leiter et al., 2011, 2012). CREW is a highly participative, tailored, team-based approach. Participating work groups, with the help of an expert facilitator, work together to define civility and incivility, develop goals for increasing civil and decreasing uncivil behavior in their workplace, and track the work unit's progress on those goals over a six-month period. It is flexible and customized to the work group's needs and desires for the social atmosphere.

Benefits?

The CREW work group civility intervention has shown strong results in quasi-experimental studies. Work groups completing the CREW initiative report more improved civility at the end of the six-month program than control work groups (Osatuke et al., 2009). Confirming this result, an independent second evaluation of the intervention also found increased civility among CREW work groups that carried over into more distal work wellbeing outcomes, such as lower cynicism (a facet of job burnout), higher job satisfaction, higher trust in management, and lower absences (Leiter et al., 2011). Encouragingly, a longitudinal follow-up with CREW work groups showed that the positive group dynamics facilitated by the initiative continued to spiral upwards after the end of the program. Six months after completing CREW, intervention groups showed a continuing trajectory of improvement: civility continued to increase, while supervisor incivility and employee distress continued to decrease (Leiter et al., 2012). Comparison groups showed little change during the same period.

Costs?

Work group civility interventions, such as CREW, with readily available facilitator materials tend to be resource efficient (Osatuke et al., 2009). They are conducted under a "train-the-trainer" model, with a central intervention expert either identified internally or contracted externally. The expert develops, modifies, or gathers the resource materials needed, and liaises with the management team to apply the program to the organization's context. Facilitators must similarly be identified (internally to the organization) or contracted (externally), and trained. Materials include simple self-report surveys and typical meeting supplies (flip charts, whiteboards). Kickoff, midpoint, and follow-up celebrations, and some motivational incentives, entail catering and merchandise costs, but can markedly increase the visibility and enthusiasm for the program (Leiter et al., 2011; Osatuke et al., 2009).

Bottom line for civility interventions

Among other benefits, such as general work engagement and involvement, work group civility interventions can prevent incivility from spiraling to conflict and aggression through the creation of self-generated work group norms and goals for the social environment. Although civility interventions were not devised with conflict prevention explicitly in mind, we believe they nonetheless show strong efficacy for preventing and reducing conflict. Organizations looking to add supports for conflict resolution may find that "an ounce of prevention," in the form of preventive work group civility interventions, is worth "a pound of cure," in terms of relative costs.

Conflict resolution awareness and education

Organizations providing employee health and wellbeing supports through their human resources function commonly conduct group information sessions and workshops to raise awareness of conflict management styles, options, and supports. For example, in our experience consulting and collaborating with organizations in Canada, preventive conflict education and awareness sessions for employees are offered at health care facilities, colleges, and universities (described briefly in LeBlanc, Gilin Oore, Calnan, & Solarz, 2012), and public service organizations. These education and awareness sessions differ from conflict resolution training interventions in that they are short (typically one hour) and do not involve skills training or practice. They simply provide general education about work conflict.

Benefits?

Despite their popularity, there are no existing studies of whether such awareness and education supports actually help employees respond more productively to conflict. Constantino and Merchant (1996) suggest another potential positive outcome: that education initiatives may be especially useful for explaining what alternative dispute resolution entails, when to apply it, and how to gain access to services. They note that education delivered by respected peers and colleagues who can reference practical experience is generally well received.

Costs?

In the event that future empirical studies demonstrate that education/awareness sessions help prevent negative conflict, this would be an extremely cost-effective solution. Typically, internal personnel working on organizational wellbeing fold these duties into their work day, and are able to reach multiple groups in a brief format. Yet it seems unlikely that such short, general information sessions will produce work wellbeing improvements by inoculation against escalatory conflict reactions.

Bottom line for conflict education/awareness workshops

Given the lack of evidence for conflict education and awareness sessions, their most valuable potential is to increase uptake of other, proven conflict interventions. Establishing the efficacy of this commonly provided workplace support would illuminate its best role in organizations' overall conflict management system or workplace wellbeing strategy.

(Preventive) conflict resolution skills training

Conflict resolution skills training can also represent a primary prevention approach. Conflict resolution skills training can range in scope from professional mediation and arbitration training (Bingham, 2004; Neilson & English, 2001) to more generic active listening and direct communication skills (Brinkert, 2016; Phillips, 1999). It also takes the form of "train-the-trainer" interventions. For example, Brinkert (2011) reports a 12-hour intervention among nurse managers training them to provide conflict coaching to their subordinates, with the goal of passing down the skills for nurse peers to resolve interpersonal conflict directly.

Most commonly, conflict resolution skills training interventions directly train employees to resolve their own disputes. Constantino and Merchant (1996) recommend conflict resolution skills training concentrate on understanding and accepting that conflict is present, and imparting listening and communication skills that can be employed in daily interactions. A number of delivery models exist for conflict resolution skills training. These include external trainers employing predetermined curricula (Brinkert, 2016; Brubaker et al., 2014; Lipsky, 2015), external consultants who demonstrate and coach participants during the interventions, and disinterested parties such as internal ombuds offices with oversight capacity to determine and respond to patterns in developing conflict.

Benefits?

Preventive conflict resolution skills training is reported to be very successful in qualitative studies in health care and military sectors. For example, academic health care staff and medical residents who were offered a two-day conflict resolution skills training (Zweibel et al., 2008) reported gaining a more positive outlook on conflict. Trained individuals reported increased ability to solve problems and apply conflict resolution skills, such as interest analysis and communication techniques, 12 months after the training. They also reported using these skills to gain perspective, reduce tension, increase mutual understanding, and build relationships (Zweibel et al., 2008). In a qualitative evaluation of a "train-the-trainer" intervention with nurse managers, both the managers and their subordinates reported enhanced conflict communication efficacy (Brinkert, 2011). This preventive conflict resolution skills training is generally viewed as positive (Brinkert, 2016; Jameson, 2001; Kals & Jiranek, 2012).

The Canadian Armed Forces' experience in delivering conflict resolution training and education was captured recently in an in-depth qualitative interview study (Dolan, 2014). The philosophy behind the program is to help members recognize and deal with emerging conflict, so they remain focused and dedicated to their main operational mandate. The conflict resolution training initiatives of the Canadian Armed Forces include both career-based training and pre–military-deployment training.

Career-based training

The Canadian Armed Forces career-based training approach has an interesting philosophy: to build a critical mass of conflict-competent members trained and skilled in recognizing and responding to potential or emerging conflict (Dolan, 2014). Proponents of the program held that if 25% of Canadian Armed Forces members in a particular area were trained on conflict skills, the skill set and capacity would become self-sustaining; and fewer conflicts would arise between members, and, when they arose, conflicts would be dealt with more effectively. The Canadian Armed Forces therefore developed a series of two-day courses related to dispute resolution and conflict management that were incorporated into the professional development training for all noncommissioned officers. Significant progress was achieved in attaining that critical mass in the noncommissioned officer ranks, with training at various levels being delivered to between 15,000 and 20,000 people per year (Dolan, 2014).

Predeployment training

The Canadian Armed Forces also initiated four-day conflict resolution skills training as part of predeployment training (before leaving for an active combat zone), with the result that 39% of members received training prior to being deployed (Dolan, 2014). Postdeployment evaluation (via interviews with responsible parties) reported significant success in reducing internal friction, increasing mission effectiveness and substantially eliminating instances of members being prematurely returned to their home unit as well as the identification of unresolved disputes (Dolan, 2014). After these initial successes, a similar course was developed for naval warships preparing for long operational deployments at sea. Typically a warship on deployment would experience internal conflict cases at a rate of approximately 30%–40% of the ship's staff membership. Postdeployment evaluation indicated that following the introduction of conflict management training, the number of cases dropped to 2%. These successes are quite striking and bolster our understanding of conflict management training as a strong preventive workforce development tactic.

Costs?

Cost-benefit analyses of preventive conflict resolution programs are not yet widely reported, but we can infer that since the evaluated program examples reviewed here involve from 12 hours to four days, they are costly. The development of strong training content, the hiring and possibly the training of qualified instructors, and the valuable organizational time of both internal trainers, and the trained staff, are significant. However, these costs are balanced by the benefits: evidence from the military field suggests very strong results in terms of wellbeing and efficacy of troops, even – or especially – under pressure and threat.

Bottom line for preventive conflict skills training

Evidence-based, well-designed, and well-conducted conflict resolution skills training appears to be a strong investment in preventing the escalation of conflict, reducing team distress and associated administrative costs, and improving overall performance.

Secondary conflict interventions

Conflict coaching

Brubaker et al. (2014) provide a short history of the rise of conflict coaching interventions offered within broader workplace alternative dispute resolution programs. "Conflict coaching" refers to a family of one-on-one interventions designed to assess leaders' conflict handling abilities, expand their skills, and apply these expanded skills at work (Brubaker et al., 2014). Tools within the realm of "conflict coaching" include conflict assessment, conflict skills training, one-on-one and group role-play coaching, and premediation coaching (and/or facilitated discussions with the other party). In North America, a notable increase in the popularity of conflict coaching approaches may be linked to the widespread introduction of such services within the alternative dispute resolution service of the Canadian Armed Forces in 2001 (Brubaker et al., 2014; Dolan, 2014).

Benefits?

There is a strong rationale for providing such interventions as part of a workplace's total conflict management system (Lipsky, 2015). Given the well-replicated finding in occupational health psychology that severe interpersonal conflicts relate to a host of negative employee wellbeing and efficacy outcomes (Ayoko et al., 2003; Chiaburu & Harrison, 2008; Vianen & De Dreu, 2001), logic dictates that interventions to build conflict handling skill and to help productively resolve these conflicts should avoid unfortunate escalation of employee distress. However, empirical studies examining the efficacy of coaching are just emerging. General executive coaching focused broadly on self-awareness, goal-setting, and feedback has recently garnered empirical support from the first systematic studies of efficacy. Studies indicate that coaching can improve leaders' communication skills and relationships with subordinates (Evers, Brouwers, & Tomic, 2006; Kombarakaran et al., 2008; Luthans & Peterson, 2003). These first rigorous studies of the effects of general executive coaching help validate the coaching approach as a potentially powerful learning tool.

To the best of our knowledge, a recently conducted Canadian study (Gilin Oore et al., 2016) is the only one that has specifically measured the outcomes of conflict-coaching interventions. In this study, university and health care employees at organizations with a dedicated conflict resolution services office completed a quantitative and qualitative survey. Of employees who had experienced a conflict within the year prior to the survey, we compared those who had (1) sought assistance from the conflict resolution service ($n = 136$), the vast majority of which sought conflict coaching, with those who had (2) pursued formal, rights-based resolutions such as union grievances, formal complaints, or legal action instead ($n = 35$). The formal solution group was considered an interesting contrast group because grievances, complaints, and legal action are the standard options available at organizations that do not offer *alternative* dispute resolution.

Our results show that the group that sought alternative conflict resolution services had less self-serving attributions for the conflict, greater process satisfaction, greater self-reported relationship repair, fewer weekly work hours spent on the conflict, and greater self-rated job performance, up to one year after the focal conflict, than did the group who pursued formal action (Gilin Oore et al., 2016). The most helpful aspects of the conflict coaching service mentioned by respondents included the coach providing support and validation (32%), providing advice on how to deal with the focal conflict (17%), providing perspective on the conflict (17%), and self-reflection/self-awareness (10%). Conflict coaching was therefore seen as providing valuable input on one's conflict and helped participants understand, tailor, and modify their conflict approaches. This study provides initial evidence for the relative strength of alternative conflict resolution services to contribute to employee wellbeing and performance.

Costs?

Internal conflict-coaching services, in the model followed by the university and health care organizations in Gilin Oore et al.'s study (2016), involve a commitment of the organization to at least one full-time salary for a conflict resolution professional. In our experience, it is highly advantageous if the program also has a dedicated program administrator for intake, scheduling, and evaluation tracking. Staffing an internal conflict-coaching office in this way, and allowing employees to access the program directly, confidentially, and free of charge, provides excellent preventive access to individual conflict skill improvement.

Bottom line for preventive conflict skills training

We believe the potential for conflict coaching to improve general wellbeing of the workforce is most likely to be realized with this type of widely accessible, individually focused coaching from a qualified expert. It would be less costly, but also markedly less accessible, if upper management contracted a qualified conflict resolution expert from outside the organization to provide conflict coaching to selected employees (for example, selected for special professional development or for remediation of a deficit in conflict resolution ability). We turn to this possibility next.

(Corrective) conflict resolution skills training

As a counterpoint to organizations offering preventive conflict resolution training (such as general developmental career training, or predeployment training for military members as already reviewed), we note that organizations may also offer corrective conflict resolution skills training. Our experience with organizations indicates this is typically a recommended or mandated measure to address a performance deficit of an employee, most commonly a manager or leader for whom conflict resolution – of their own conflicts or the conflicts among their subordinates – is a critical competency required by their role. Such corrective conflict resolution training represents a secondary intervention (Cooper & Cartwright, 1997), because it is offered after conflict has emerged and had some negative impacts.

Benefits?

Although unfortunately (to our knowledge) no organizational efficacy studies have been published for conflict resolution training provided to correct a skills deficiency, we can borrow knowledge from educational and clinical psychology. These disciplines lend themselves well to rigorous experimental methods. The existing literature reports strong results for corrective conflict skills training. For example, newlywed couples randomly assigned to conflict training had a significantly lower separation rate at follow-up (11%) compared with a no-treatment control group (separation rate 24%). Similarly, a nine-hour group conflict-resolution skills training improved couples' self-reported and expert-rated conflict behavior over 12 months, compared to a control group (Worthington et al., 2015). Schoolchildren randomly assigned to comparable length and content of conflict skills training similarly showed gains in their interest-based negotiation, problem-solving, and communication skills in conflict situations as rated by expert raters (Stevahn et al., 1996, 2002). They also reported more positive attitudes about conflict.

Costs?

The need to compensate professional experts for their time to develop and deliver conflict resolution training to identified employees renders targeted expert training moderately costly, but *less* so than making conflict coaching or training services available to a large portion of the workforce. However, such training is not intended nor expected to provide the broad protective or preventive benefits to the workforce as a whole of these more preventive options.

Bottom line for corrective conflict skills training

The best evidence we can borrow from randomized control trials indicates that the cost of well-developed and implemented remedial conflict resolution training should translate into noticeably improved skills of the trained employees or leaders at a moderate overall cost.

Tertiary conflict interventions

In this section, we summarize tertiary conflict intervention options. These interventions can help resolve specific conflict situations that have already escalated and are damaging the wellbeing and performance of involved organizational members. Often such escalated interpersonal work conflicts have negative ripple effects on the wellbeing and performance of even uninvolved members of the work unit and broader organization. Workplace mediation and workplace complaint programs are tertiary alternative dispute resolution interventions that can help resolve the issue without resorting to grievance, arbitration, or legal action.

Workplace mediation

The mediation of interpersonal conflict at work by a neutral third party has become very popular in governmental organizations (especially in North America), where discrimination cases about "protected characteristics" such as racial background, gender, disability, and so on, would otherwise fall to formal legal means (Nabatchi & Blomgren Bingham, 2010). The implementation of mediation programs varies widely (see recent review in Bollen & Euwema, 2013). Mediators may be amateur internal peers, professionals at a dispute resolution center run by the organization, or externally contracted professionals. Most programs that report high efficacy have specific selection criteria by which administrators determine the suitability of the case for mediation (McDermott & Obar, 2001; Nabatchi & Bingham, 2010; Wood & Leon, 2006). Another marker of successful programs is that the mediators focus on the relationship of the parties (more than obtaining "an agreement" or getting "a deal") and do not push for specific outcomes. Rather, they tend to focus on creating a fair process for all participants, pre-mediation preparation and caucusing (McDermott & Obar, 2001; Swaab & Brett, 2007), and issue and solution identification. To the extent that the mediator and program are successful in providing process and interpersonal fairness, they generate satisfaction among the participants (Bollen, Ittner, & Euwema, 2012).

Benefits?

Workplace mediation programs in governmental and military organizations in North America have documented success at reducing organizational costs, reducing the number of cases filed and litigated, and improving disputant settlement rates, satisfaction, and wellbeing, compared to the adversarial alternative processes (hearings, lawsuits, grievances. Positive satisfaction and case resolution statistics have been reported for the US Equal Employment Opportunity Commission (McDermott & Obar, 2001), and the US Postal Service REDRESS transformative mediation program (Nabatchi & Blomgren Bingham, 2010).

The second author of this chapter has recently completed a comprehensive evaluation of the workplace mediation program at the Canadian Armed Forces (Dolan, 2014). The Canadian Armed Forces workplace mediation program offers interest-based and transformative mediation of interpersonal work conflicts at external dispute resolution centers staffed by highly trained conflict resolution professionals. In 2014, Dolan completed a study of a sample of mediators and associated parties to a work conflict that revealed convergence among the stakeholders about the important features of the mediation process and what predicts resolution and satisfaction.

The study showed that 80% of the parties to mediation agreed to a formal settlement by the end of their mediation. Of the parties who had not reached signed minutes of settlement, 85% said they had made progress toward eventual agreement. When asked if the mediation helped their relationship with the other party, the majority of respondents either agreed or strongly agreed that it had helped. Approximately 93% of the parties would recommend the mediation program to someone else, and in the event they were involved in a future dispute more than 88% would use the mediation program again.

Parties to mediation were highly satisfied with the procedural aspects of how mediations were conducted, and reported similarly high levels of satisfaction with the fairness of how they were treated by the mediator. The parties indicated that mediators helped facilitate the development of realistic options, but avoided evaluating the case and did not press them to accept uncomfortable resolutions. The outcomes compare very favorably to comparable large-scale programs in other jurisdictions. They also appear to have a far-reaching effect not only on the relationships between individuals but also on the way in which members are likely to interact with and support the Canadian Forces as a larger organization.

Costs?

Workplace mediation requires investment on the part of the organization to train or hire mediators, to devise a fair, streamlined process, and to administer the process. A large part of workplace mediation's appeal, however, is that these costs are very modest compared to the costs of hearings and litigation. Early writings on workplace mediation gave many demonstrative examples of organizations reducing costs of discrimination and sexual harassment cases, as well as reducing the total number of litigations, by using workplace mediation (see for example, Costello, 1992; Carver & Vondra, 1994). Litigation easily costs organizations an average of $100,000 in direct costs (Cascio, 2000; Dana, 2012). More recently, Wood and Leon (2006) report an informal cost-benefit analysis of the New York City mediation program serving its 300,000 municipal employees. Mediation participants had 86% of cases resolved, in an average of 33.5 days, at an average cost of $200 per case, and with around 90% satisfaction with the process. In contrast, cases that proceeded to discrimination hearings had a 55% prehearing settlement rate. Those that proceeded to hearings were resolved in an average of 79 days, with an average cost of $1,200 per case. This comports with other authors' estimates that mediation is dramatically less costly than grievance, hearing, and litigation processes (Fox & Stallworth, 2009). Further, managers and human resources professionals report that the mediation agreements are upheld, there is improved employee camaraderie as a result of mediation, and that they observed "a 'ripple effect' extending to other employees" (Wood & Leon, 2006, p. 393).

Bottom line for workplace mediation

It is important to reiterate that the evidence for the success of workplace mediation programs comes from large, mostly governmental organizations that otherwise have only formal and adversarial alternatives (based on discrimination claims) for getting assistance with work conflict. In these formal and bureaucratic contexts, workplace mediation provides a welcome island of support focusing on underlying interests and repairing damaged relationships at the earliest point possible. In contrast, in the hospital and university study of conflict resolution services noted in the conflict-coaching section (Gilin Oore et al., 2016), the conflict resolution professionals involved report that only approximately 5%–10 % of the individuals they assist pursue formal mediation. We highlight this important context difference to aid interpretation of the statistics presented earlier: formal workplace mediation has shown incredible success but may only be an attractive alternative in the uniquely hierarchical, bureaucratic contexts in which it has thrived.

Complaint systems

A second tertiary workplace support for resolving escalated interpersonal conflicts is a complaint system. By "complaint system," we are referring to more formalized procedures for registering an objection to one's treatment at work that involves an outside party investigating and possibly rendering a decision about how to resolve the issue. We are specifically referring to remedial voice processes that are internal to the organization, nonunion, and nonlegal. Past research has called these types of systems variously "ombuds" processes (Hirschman, 1970), "non-union grievance procedures" (Feuille & Chachere, 1995), and "internal grievance procedures" (Olson-Buchanan & Boswell, 2008). Complaint systems are several steps closer to an adversarial, legal process than are alternative dispute resolution approaches such as conflict coaching or mediation. They are not consensual, and they typically focus on rights rather than interests; for this reason they are more common with conflicts that are over fairness, justice, the work contract, and perceived discrimination (Bendersky, 2010; Feuille & Chachere, 1995). Complaint systems typically involve written statements, investigations and/or hearings, and several steps of possible formal appeal. They are prevalent: approximately half of private large organizations have some sort of nonunion grievance process (Feuille & Chachere, 1995). In our experience working with organizations, complaint systems often exist in parallel with union grievance procedures, with the hope that they will help divert cases from the most expensive and lengthy processes (union grievances, legal cases).

Benefits?

Unlike the other workplace supports for conflict resolution that we have reviewed, complaint systems – while well-investigated – do not show generally positive impacts on employees. On the one hand, if they are administered in a manner that incorporates strong principles of procedural justice (Haraway, 2005), complaint systems may provide a path for employees to whistle blow, that is, to gain public exposure of a wrongdoing (Olson-Buchanan & Boswell, 2008). Similarly, in organizations with adversarial cultures, complaint systems may be a better "fit" for employees to voice concerns than more consensual, interest-based procedures like mediation (Olson-Buchanan & Boswell, 2008).

Costs?

On the other hand, research has raised significant red flags about the ability of complaint systems to enhance work wellbeing of employees. The first issue is whether the systems tend to be biased, because management often retains power over the complaint resolution mechanism (Carver & Vondra, 1994; Haraway, 2005). In an investigation of nonunion grievance procedures in 195 private firms, Feuille & Chachere (1995) found that in only 10% of complaint systems were the decision-makers independent from management. A second, even more disturbing trend, is the well-replicated finding of serious job-related retaliation (e.g., discharge, demotion, poor performance appraisal) and social retaliation (e.g., ostracism, bullying, threats) against employees who register complaints (Cortina & Magley, 2003; see also review in Harlos, 2010). What's worse, such retaliation is more common when the individual complained against has higher power in the organization, and when the complainant has lower status (Cortina & Magley, 2003). The resultant withdrawal and distress of the complaining employee (Boswell & Olson-Buchanan, 2004) may be extremely high, and this high distress is likely to lead to turnover (Lewin, 1987).

Bottom line for complaint systems

Internal complaint systems that do not demonstrate robust procedural fairness fail to provide substantial work wellbeing benefits and appear instead to be prone to significant weaknesses and abuse.

Recommendations for organizations: which conflict interventions?

Our foregoing review placed common workplace conflict resolution interventions along a continuum from the most preventive to the most reactive, and summarized the existing evidence for the benefits and costs of each intervention. We also noted any strategies for implementing the intervention that make it more likely to be beneficial to an organization. The final question we address in this section is: How should an organization choose which, if any, of these common conflict resolution supports to initiate to enhance the wellbeing of its employees? We make some recommendations based on the size, culture, values, and resources of the organization.

Small organizations

In small organizations (such as 50 employees and fewer), and those with a more family-like culture, the informal nature of the organization translates into low bureaucracy and low administrative resources. There may be only one individual who deals with human resources issues as part of their role as executive director, senior manager, or CEO. Such leaders are unlikely to have formal human resources training or the highly specialized skills of conflict resolution professionals. In such organizations, processes like conflict coaching, mediation, and complaint processes – which involve a heavy administrative load – are unlikely to make sense from a resource point of view (expertise, staff, time, money). We recommend instead that small organizations focus on primary prevention strategies for conflict management. The Canadian Armed Forces strategy of training a critical mass of the workforce in preventive conflict resolution skills, in order to infuse the collective with the capacity to avoid escalated conflict incidents (Dolan, 2014), is wise in this case. An external consultant with expertise in conflict styles, coaching conflict skills, and how to devise training initiatives, could be contracted on a periodic basis to provide effective skills development. Work-group civility interventions could also be a low-cost, intermittent, preventive strategy by which the small organization could set its own agenda and course for conflict prevention that matches its unique context and preferences.

Medium-sized organizations

In our experience, midsized organizations (50 to several hundred employees) have unique conflict resolution intervention needs. They are typically large enough to have a human resources function, but the human resources staff do not normally have adequate training in the unique repertoire of conflict resolution, training, and mediation skills required to effectively deal with disputes. Yet the handling of conflicts tends to fall in their hands. Further, the centralization of all employee relations administration (hiring, compensation, performance appraisal, and conflict management) in one small group of individuals means that the human resources staff often have difficulty creating sufficient distance between conflict resolution interventions and the power hierarchy of the workplace.

This is a challenging organizational context for conflict handling. We recommend that in midsized organizations, human resources staff be provided with professional training in conflict resolution interventions. Courses in conflict style assessment, conflict handling, and alternative dispute resolution or mediation may provide key skill development. Another key area is to allow sufficient support staff for conflict resolution processes so that this function can exist behind at least a modest firewall from the other functions of human resources. For example, a part-time, dedicated conflict administrative assistant or ombudsperson with physically private space might be a worthwhile investment of resources.

Large organizations

In larger organizations, strategies for designing and implementing conflict management systems are better developed. Ideally such organizations would implement an Integrated Conflict Management System (Lipsky, 2015), a thoughtfully orchestrated and comprehensive approach to conflict handling providing primary preventive, secondary, and tertiary conflict interventions. An Integrated Conflict Management System is possible, from a resource point of view, only at large organizations. It involves providing conflict handling options for all types of conflicts, creating a culture that values open and direct communication of dissenting views, providing multiple "access points" (supervisor, conflict professional, complaint process, union) for conflict assistance, and including preventive supports (Lipsky, 2015).

If larger organizations do not have the capacity for an integrated conflict management system, then the targeted conflict interventions they choose should be based on an assessment of the reason for intervention, the organizational needs, and the available resources. Primary and secondary interventions are likely to evidence a wide range of significant benefits in terms of both individual employee wellbeing and performance.

The tertiary interventions of workplace mediation and internal complaint systems are designed to capture and respond to individual cases. Mediation and complaint programs need to have a comprehensive set of policies and procedures to guide service delivery, as well as the oversight or management capacity to administer the program, respond to issues arising, and provide the necessary staff support. Those organizations that invest in the necessary level of skills and expertise, and develop and maintain the corresponding management and administration systems, are likely to appreciate significant benefits in terms of reduced organizational costs and improved individual and organizational wellbeing.

Conclusion

Workplace conflict resolution programs intended to achieve and maintain low levels of unresolved conflict have to be firmly grounded in the needs and interests of the individual and organizational clients they serve. Those interests will vary over time. A high degree of situational awareness is required to identify emerging needs and develop interventions that fit the culture, accurately address the objectives, and are able to demonstrate their ongoing value. Successful outcomes result from respectful dialogue where participants are fairly treated and able to take an active and meaningful role in the process. Enduring intervention successes will foster engagement and longer term commitment in support of organizational goals and objectives.

References

Andersson, L. M., & Pearson, C. M. (1999). Tit for tat? The spiraling effect of workplace incivility. *Academy of Management Review*, 24(3), 452–471.

Axelrod, L., & Johnson, R. (2005). *Turning Conflict into Profit: A Roadmap for Resolving Personal and Organizational Disputes*. Edmonton, Alberta: University of Alberta Press.

Ayoko, O. B., Callan, V. J., & Härtel, C. E. J. (2003). Workplace conflict, bullying, and counterproductive behaviors. *International Journal of Organizational Analysis*, 11(4), 283–301.

Bendersky, C. (2010). Organizational dispute resolution systems: A complementarities model. *Academy of Management Review*, 28(4), 643–656.

Bingham, L. B. (2004). Employment dispute resolution: The case for mediation. *Conflict Resolution Quarterly*, 22(1), 145–174.

Bollen, K., & Euwema, M. (July 2013). Workplace mediation: An underdeveloped research area. *Negotiation Journal*, 29, 329–353.

Bollen, K., Ittner, H., & Euwema, M. C. (2012). Mediating hierarchical labor conflicts: Procedural justice makes a difference-for subordinates. *Group Decision and Negotiation*, 21(5), 621–636.

Boswell, W. R., & Olson-Buchanan, J. B. (2004). Experiencing mistreatment at work: The role of grievance filing, nature of mistreatment, and employee withdrawal. *Academy of Management Journal*, 47(1), 129–139.

Brinkert, R. (2011). Conflict coaching training for nurse managers: A case study of a two-hospital health system. *Journal of Nursing Management*, 19, 80–91.

Brinkert, R. (2016). State of knowledge: Conflict coaching theory, application, and research. *Conflict Resolution Quarterly*, 33(4), 383–401.

Brubaker, D., Noble, C., Fincher, R., Park, S.K.Y, & Press, S. (2014). Conflict resolution in the workplace: What will the future bring? *Conflict Resolution Quarterly*, 31(4), 357–386.

Bush, R. A. B., & Folger, J. P. (2005). *The Promise of Mediation* (2nd ed.). San Francisco, CA: Jossey-Bass.

Carver, T. B., & Vondra, A. A. (1994). Alternative dispute resolution: Why it doesn't work and why it does. *Harvard Business Review*, 72(3), 120–130.

Cascio, W. F. (2000). *Costing Human Resources: The Financial Impact of Behavior in Organizations* (4th ed.). Cincinnati, OH: South Western.

Chiaburu, D. S., & Harrison, D. A. (2008). Do peers make the place? Conceptual synthesis and meta-analysis of coworker effects on perceptions, attitudes, OCBs, and performance. *Journal of Applied Psychology*, 93(5), 1082–1103.

Constantino, C. A., & Merchant, C. S. (1996). *Designing Conflict Management Systems*. San Franciso: Jossey-Bass.

Cooper, C. L., & Cartwright, S. (1997). An intervention strategy for workplace stress. *Journal of Psychosomatic Research*, 43(1), 7–16.

Cortina, L. M., & Magley, V. J. (2003). Raising voice, risking retaliation: Events following interpersonal mistreatment in the workplace. *Journal of Occupational Health Psychology*, 8(4), 247–265.

Costello, E. J. (1992). The mediation alternative in sex harassment cases. *Arbitration Journal*, 47(1), 16–23.

Dana, D. (2012). *The Dana Measure of Financial Cost of Organizational Conflict: A Tool for Demonstrating the Bottom-Line Impact of HRD and OD Interventions*. Available at: www.mediation-training-institute.com/CostCalculatorPublic_eng.php?Submit=Check+it+out

De Dreu, C. K. W., & Weingart, L. R. (2003). Task versus relationship conflict, team performance, and team member satisfaction: A meta-analysis. *Journal of Applied Psychology*, 88(4), 741–749.

de Wit, F. R. C., Greer, L. L., & Jehn, K. A. (2012). The paradox of intragroup conflict: A meta-analysis. *Journal of Applied Psychology*, 97(2), 360–390.

Dolan, N. (2014). *Settling Difference: New Approaches to Conflict Resolution in High-Security Organizations*. Unpublished doctoral dissertation.

Evers, W. J. G., Brouwers, A., & Tomic, W. (2006). A quasi-experimental study on management coaching effectiveness. *Consulting Psychology Journal: Practice and Research*, 58(3), 174–182.

Feuille, P., & Chachere, D. R. (1995). Looking fair or being fair: Remedial voice procedures in nonunion workplaces. *Journal of Management*, 21(1), 27–42.

Fox, S., & Stallworth, L. E. (2009). Building a framework for two internal organizational approaches to resolving and preventing workplace bullying: Alternative dispute resolution and training. *Consulting Psychology Journal: Practice and Research*, 61(3), 220–241.

Giebels, E., & Janssen, O. (2005). Conflict stress and reduced well-being at work: The buffering effect of third-party help. *European Journal of Work and Organizational Psychology*, 14(2), 137–155.

Gilin Oore, D., Holmvall, C., Harlos, K., Pope, K., LeBlanc, D., Solarz, B., Brownlow, B., Day, A., Leither, M., & Axelrod, L. (2016, June). *Comparison of Alternative Coflict Resolution with Formal Resolution Approaches for Employee Well-Being and Efficacy.* Paper presented at the International Association for Conflict Management, New York, New York.

Gilin Oore, D., Leiter, M. P., & LeBlanc, D. E. (2015). Individual and organizational factors promoting successful responses to workplace conflict. *Canadian Psychology*, 56(3), 301–310.

Halbesleben, J. R. B. (2006). Sources of social support and burnout: A meta-analytic test of the conservation of resources model. *Journal of Applied Psychology*, 91(5), 1134–1145.

Haraway, W. M. (2005). Employee grievance programs: Understanding the nexus between workplace justice, organizational legitimacy, and successful organizations. *Public Personnel Management*, 34(4), 329–343.

Harlos, K. (2010). If you build a remedial voice mechanism, will they come? Determinants of voicing interpersonal mistreatment at work. *Human Relations*, 63, 311–329.

Hirschman, A. O. (1970). *Exit, Voice, and Loyalty.* Cambridge, MA: Harvard University Press.

Jameson, J. K. (2001). Employee perceptions of the availability and use of interests-, rights-, and power-based conflict management strategies. *Conflict Resolution Quarterly*, 19(2), 163–196.

Jehn, K. A. (1995). A multimethod examination of the benefits and detriments of intragroup conflict. *Administrative Science Quarterly*, 40, 256–282.

Kals, E., & Jiranek, P. (2012). Organization justice. In: E. Kals & J. Maes (eds.), *Justice and Conflicts.* Berlin: Springer-Verlag, 219–235.

Kombarakaran, F. A., Yang, J. A., Baker, M. N., & Fernandes, P. B. (2008). Executive coaching: It works! *Consulting Psychology Journal: Practice and Research*, 60(1), 78–90.

LeBlanc, D., Gilin Oore, D., & Axelrod, L. (2014, July). *Workplace Conflict: Meaning and Measurement.* Paper presented at the annual meeting of the International Association for Conflict Management, Leiden, Netherlands.

LeBlanc, D., Gilin Oore, D., Calnan, K., & Solarz, B. (2012, July). *Perspective-Taking, Empathy, and Relational Conflict at Work: An Investigation among Participants in a Workplace Conflict Resolution Program.* Paper presented at the International Association for Conflict Management, Stellenbosch, South Africa.

Leiter, M. P., Day, A., Oore, D. G., & Laschinger, H.K.S. (2012). Getting better and staying better: Assessing civility, incivility, distress, and job attitudes one year after a civility intervention. *Journal of Occupational Health Psychology*, 17(4), 425–434.

Leiter, M. P., Laschinger, H.K.S., Day, A., & Oore, D. G. (2011). The impact of civility interventions on employee social behavior, distress, and attitudes. *The Journal of Applied Psychology*, 96(6), 1258–1274.

Lewin, D. (1987). Dispute resolution in the nonunion firm: A theoretical and empirical analysis. *Journal of Conflict Resolution*, 31(3), 465–502.

Lipsky, D. B. (2015). The future of conflict management systems. *Conflict Resolution Quarterly*, 33(Supplement 1), S27–S34.

Luthans, F., & Peterson, S. J. (2003). 360-Degree feedback with systematic coaching: Empirical analysis suggests a winning combination. *Human Resource Management*, 42(3), 243–256.

McDermott, E., & Obar, R. (2001). *The EEOC Mediation Program: Mediators' Perspective on the Parties, Processes, and Outcomes.* Available at: www.conflict-resolution.org/sitebody/acrobat/report2.pdf.

Nabatchi, T., & Blomgren Bingham, L. (2010). From postal to peaceful: Dispute systems design in the USPS REDRESS(R) program. *Review of Public Personnel Administration*, 30(2), 211–234.

Neilson, L. C. L., & English, P. (2001). The role of interest-based facilitation in designing accreditation standards: The Canadian experience. *Conflict Resolution Quarterly*, 18(3), 221–248.

Olson-Buchanan, J. B., & Boswell, W. R. (2008). An integrative model of experiencing and responding to mistreatment at work. *Academy of Management Review*, 33(1), 76–96.

Osatuke, K., Mohr, D., Ward, C., Moore, S. C., Dyrenforth, S., & Belton, L. (2009). Civility, respect, engagement in the workforce (CREW): Nationwide organization development intervention at veterans health administration. *Journal of Applied Behavioral Science*, 45(3), 384–410.

Phillips, B. (1999). Reformulating dispute narratives through active listening. *Mediation Quarterly*, 17(2), 161–180.

Roche, W. K., & Teague, P. (2012). The growing importance of workplace ADR. *International Journal of Human Resource Management*, 23(3), 447–458.

Skogstad, A., Einarsen, S., Torsheim, T., Aasland, M. S., & Hetland, H. (2007). The destructiveness of laissez-faire leadership behavior. *Journal of Occupational Health Psychology*, 12(1), 80–92.

Stevahn, L., Johnson, D. W., Johnson, R. T., & Real, D. (1996). The impact of a cooperative or individualistic context on the effectiveness of conflict resolution training. *American Educational Research Journal*, 33(4), 801–823.

Stevahn, L., Johnson, D. W., Johnson, R. T., & Schultz, R. (2002). Effects of conflict resolution training integrated into a high school social studies curriculum. *The Journal of Social Psychology*, 142(3), 305–331.

Swaab, R. I., & Brett, J. M. (2007, July). *Caucus with Care: The Impact of Pre-Mediation Caucuses on Conflict Resolution*. Paper presented at the annual meeting of the International Association for Conflict Management, Budapest, Hungary. Available at: https://papers.ssrn.com/sol3/papers.cfm?abstract_id=1080622.

Todorova, G., Bear, J. B., & Weingart, L. R. (2014). Can conflict be energizing? A study of task conflict, positive emotions, and job satisfaction. *Journal of Applied Psychology*, 99, 451–467.

Vianen, A. E. M., van & De Dreu, C. K. W. (2001). Personality in teams: Its relationship to social cohesion, task cohesion, and team performance. *European Journal of Work and Organizational Psychology*, 10(February 2015), 97–120.

Viswesvaran, C., Sanchez, J. I., & Fisher, J. (1999). The role of social support in the process of work stress: A meta-analysis. *Journal of Vocational Behavior*, 54, 314–334.

Wood, D. H., & Leon, D. M. (2006). Measuring value in mediation: A case study of workplace mediation in city government. *Ohio State Journal on Dispute Resolution*, 21(2), 383–408.

WHO (1948). Constitution of the World Health Organization. Geneva, World Health Organization.

Worthington, E. L., Berry, J. W., Hook, J. N., Davis, D. E., Scherer, M., Griffin, B. J., Wade, N. G., . . . Campana, K. L. (2015). Forgiveness-reconciliation and communication-conflict-resolution interventions versus retested controls in early married couples. *Journal of Counseling Psychology*, 62(1), 14–27.

Zweibel, E. B., Goldstein, R., Manwaring, J. A., & Marks, M. B. (2008). What sticks: How medical residents and academic health care faculty transfer conflict resolution training from workshop to the workplace. *Conflict Resolution Quarterly*, 25(3), 321–350.

Index